Grace

The BiG WORD

FOR KIDS

CEV

New Testament in Contemporary English
Revised Edition

Published by

The Bible Society in Australia Inc
30 York Road INGLEBURN NSW 2565
www.biblesociety.com.au

The Bible Society in New Zealand Inc
Private Bag 27901, WELLINGTON NEW ZEALAND
www.biblesociety.org.nz

Publication © The Bible Society in Australia Inc. 2000
CEV Text: © American Bible Society 1995

ISBN 978 0 647 50804 6
CET260BW 2008

Cover and Inside Art: Phil Watson

Permission to

What's it all about?

Welcome to the Big Word for Kids!

The Big Word for Kids is a book put together especially for you. In it you'll find lots of great things for you and your friends to know and think

about. Most importantly, you'll find out about a person named *Jesus*. The Big Word for Kids is part of the Bible (a *really* famous book) called the New Testament. It contains 27 little books, each with a very important message for kids and other people everywhere. Here are some things about the Bible and the New Testament you probably didn't know!

More people buy the Bible than any other book!

The New Testament has been translated into more than 800 languages!

Who is Jesus?

The Big Word for Kids is mostly about Jesus – the son of God. Most of it was written by his friends. The first part is called "Matthew". Matthew was one of Jesus' friends. He travelled around with Jesus, seeing what he did and learning from what he said. Other parts are more like an interview — "Luke" is written by a man named *Luke* who spoke to many people who knew Jesus.

Other books are letters written to people living in different places. "Romans" was written to people in Rome, Italy. A lot of what happened in the Big Word for Kids happened in a place called "Israel". The map on the next page shows Israel — have a good look for yourself.

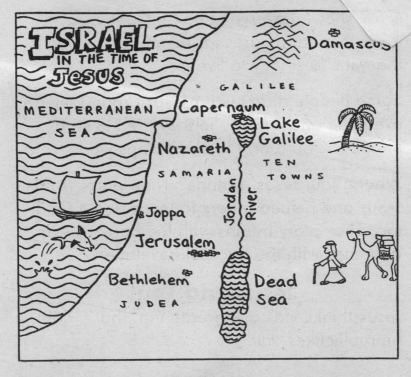

The Big Word for Kids is not just about Jesus, it is also about his friends. Jesus' friends liked what he did so much that they started to live life the way Jesus did. Through Jesus and his friends, God began to turn the world the *right* way up.

Jesus was able to do many things - he wanted people to see what God was like. Jesus wanted everyone to know that God loves them. Jesus made sick and sad people better and even brought a dead little girl back to life!

Jesus showed everyone he met that God loves them and cares for them. He showed them the best way to live.

Some people didn't want Jesus around telling everyone about God. So they tried to stop him, but God didn't let their plans work.

What about Jesus' friends? They learnt from Jesus and helped others to learn about God too. Their story begins with the book of Acts and ends with the book of Revelation.

Jesus and You!

Jesus thinks kids are great! Yep, that's right, he really likes *you*.

Some people thought Jesus would not hang around with kids, but they were WRONG. God sent Jesus to show how special you are to him. Jesus wants you to be the best you can be, and he wants you to be friends with him and his father, God.

Jesus knows that you are not perfect, but he is able to clear away the bad stuff in your life. You can trust God to forgive you for the bad things you have done, and change you from the inside into the best person that you can be — the person God wants you to be!

Jesus is alive today. You can talk to him if you want. You can't see him, but he can see and hear you!

Jesus and Prayer

Praying is just like talking. The difference is that you are talking to the person in control — Jesus! Don't only talk to Jesus when you are in trouble (but don't feel bad about calling for help!) Jesus is a friend you can talk to about anything. The more time you spend talking to Jesus and reading about him in the Bible the more you will get to know him and understand why Jesus can be the best friend you could ever have!

Using the Big Word

There are three steps to looking things up in the Big Word for Kids — finding the book, the chapter and the verse. Each little book has a title, for example, "Mark". Each book also has large bold numbers. These are the *chapter* numbers. Some of the sentences in each chapter have little numbers in front of some of the words. These are called the *verse* numbers.

Having little books, chapters and verses allows a single sentence or passage to be quickly looked up in any Bible. It's like a street map. Someone can give you a book name, chapter number and verse number and you can find it in the Bible. This is called a *reference*.

8 [1]One day another large crowd gathered around Jesus. They hadn't brought along anything to eat. So Jesus called his disciples together and said, [2]"I feel sorry for

For example, the reference of the Bible words on the last page looks like this:

Book name → **Mark 8.1-2** ← Verse numbers

↑ Chapter number

Its as easy as 1-2-3!

Guess What is in the Big Word

GUESS WHAT, on Big Word pages 10, 11 and 12, shows you what the Big Word for Kids says about a lot of different things. Have a read through them and see what you think

Great Escapes

- [ ] Mark 10.32-34 - Jesus is like one else

- [ ] Acts 16.22-39 — doors fly open

Battles

- [ ] Luke 4.1-15 — tempted by the devil

- [ ] Matthew 12.22-32 — Jesus and the demons

Eating

- [ ] Mark 8.1-10 — the big picnic

- [ ] Acts 10.9-16 — food served on a big sheet

Excuses

- [ ] Luke 9.57-62 — follow me

- [ ] Matthew 22.1-14 — a big party!

Miracles

☐ Matthew 8.5-13 — great faith!

☐ Mark 10.46-52 — he can see again

Heroes

☐ Mark 8.27-30 — God's chosen one

☐ Philippians 3.12-16 — running the race

Kids

☐ Mark 5.35-43 — the girl is only asleep

☐ Luke 18.15-27 — children and a rich guy

Doubters

☐ John 20.24-29 — wake up Thomas

☐ Acts 9.10-16 — I have chosen him

Villains

☐ Matthew 2.1-16 — a bad king

☐ Mark 15.6-15 — pleasing the crowd

Unusual Stories

☐ Mark 8.22-26 — a blind man sees

☐ Acts 20.1-12 — he is still alive

Animals

☐ Luke 5.4-10 — a big catch of fish

☐ Mark 5.1-20 — lots of pigs

Amazing Facts

☐ Luke 17.11-19 — ten healed in one hit

☐ Acts 28.1-6 — problem with a snake

Where things are in the Big Word

What does this word mean?

Here is a list of words you may not have seen before!

Baptised — *a way of being washed to show everyone that an old kind of life is ended and a new life with God is beginning.*

Commandments — *God's set of rules which show the best way for people to live.*

Disciple— *anyone who is a follower of Jesus and lives the way Jesus taught us.*

Eternal — *a word meaning for ever. Having eternal life with God means that life never ends!*

Holy Spirit — *the life of God who can live inside us and help us do things God's way.*

Satan — *another name for the Devil. The Devil tricks people into doing things that God doesn't want them to do.*

Son of Man — *a name Jesus used to describe himself. He used it so people knew that he was a real man who came from God.*

Soul — *your life on the inside. Other people can't get in touch with this part of your life in the same way you and God can.*

MATTHEW
ABOUT THIS BOOK

The Sermon on the Mount (chapter 5.1—7.28), the Lord's Prayer (6.9-13), and the Golden Rule (7.12: "Treat others as you want them to treat you") are all in this book. It is perhaps the best-known and the most-quoted of all the books that have ever been written about Jesus. That is one reason why Matthew was placed first among the four books about Jesus called Gospels.

One of the most important ideas found here is that God expects his people to obey him, and this is what is meant by the Greek word that appears in many translations as *righteousness*. It is used seven times by Matthew, but only once by Luke, and not at all by Mark. So it is an important clue to much of what Matthew wants his readers to understand about the teaching of Jesus.

Jesus first uses this word at his own baptism, when he tells John the Baptist, "We must do all that God wants us to do" (3.15). Then, during his Sermon on the Mount, he speaks five more times of what God's people must do to obey him (5.6, 10, 20; 6.1, 33). And finally, he reminds the chief priests and leaders of the people, "John the Baptist showed you how to do right" (21.32).

Matthew wanted to provide for the people of his time a record of Jesus' message and ministry. It is clear that the Old Testament Scriptures were very important to these people. And Matthew never fails to show when these texts point to the coming of Jesus as the Messiah sent from God. Matthew wrote this book to make sure Christians knew that their faith in Jesus as the Messiah was well-anchored in the Old Testament Scriptures, and to help them grow in faith.

Matthew ends his story with the words of Jesus to his followers, which tell what they are to do after he leaves them:

"I have been given all authority in heaven and on earth! Go to the people of all nations and make them my disciples. Baptise them in the name of the Father, the Son, and the Holy Spirit, and teach them to do

everything I have told you. I will be with you always, even until the end of the world." (Chapter 28.18b-20)

A QUICK LOOK AT THIS BOOK

- The Ancestors and Birth of Jesus (1.1—2.23)
- The Message of John the Baptist (3.1-12)
- The Baptism and Temptation of Jesus (3.13—4.11)
- Jesus in Galilee (4.12—18.35)
- Jesus Goes from Galilee to Jerusalem (19.1—20.34)
- Jesus' Last Week: His Trial and Death (21.1—27.66)
- Jesus Is Alive (28.1-20)

The Ancestors of Jesus
(Luke 3.23-38)

1 ¹Jesus Christ came from the family of King David and also from the family of Abraham. And this is a list of his ancestors. ²⁻⁶ᵃFrom Abraham to King David, his ancestors were:

Abraham, Isaac, Jacob, Judah and his brothers (Judah's sons were Perez and Zerah, and their mother was Tamar), Hezron;

Ram, Amminadab, Nahshon, Salmon, Boaz (his mother was Rahab), Obed (his mother was Ruth), Jesse, and King David.

⁶ᵇ⁻¹¹From David to the time of the exile in Babylonia, the ancestors of Jesus were:

David, Solomon (his mother had been Uriah's wife), Rehoboam, Abijah, Asa, Jehoshaphat, Jehoram;

Uzziah, Jotham, Ahaz, Hezekiah, Manasseh, Amon, Josiah, and Jehoiachin and his brothers.

¹²⁻¹⁶From the exile to the birth of Jesus, his ancestors were:

Jehoiachin, Shealtiel, Zerubbabel, Abiud, Eliakim, Azor, Zadok, Achim;

Eliud, Eleazer, Matthan, Jacob, and Joseph, the husband of Mary, the mother of Jesus, who is called the Messiah.

¹⁷There were 14 generations from Abraham to David. There were also 14 from David to the exile in Babylonia and 14 more to the birth of the Messiah.

The Birth of Jesus
(Luke 2.1-7)

18 This is how Jesus Christ was born. A young woman named Mary was engaged to Joseph from King David's family. But before they were married, she learnt that she was going to have a baby by God's Holy Spirit. 19 Joseph was a good man[a] and didn't want to embarrass Mary in front of everyone. So he decided to quietly call off the wedding.

20 While Joseph was thinking about this, an angel from the Lord came to him in a dream. The angel said, "Joseph, the baby that Mary will have is from the Holy Spirit. Go ahead and marry her. 21 Then after her baby is born, name him Jesus,[b] because he will save his people from their sins."

22 So the Lord's promise came true, just as the prophet had said, 23 "A virgin will have a baby boy, and he will be called Immanuel," which means "God is with us."

24 After Joseph woke up, he and Mary were soon married, just as the Lord's angel had told him to do. 25 But they didn't sleep together before her baby was born. Then Joseph named him Jesus.

The Wise Men

2 ¹When Jesus was born in the village of Bethlehem in Judea, Herod was king. During this time some wise men[c] from the east came to Jerusalem ²and said, "Where is the child born to be king of the Jews? We saw his star in the east[d] and have come to worship him."

³When King Herod heard about this, he was worried, and so was everyone else in Jerusalem. ⁴Herod brought together the chief priests and the teachers of the Law of Moses and asked them, "Where will the Messiah be born?"

⁵They told him, "He will be born in Bethlehem, just as the prophet wrote,

---

[a] *good man:* Or "kind man," or "man who always did the right thing." [b] *name him Jesus:* In Hebrew the name "Jesus" means "the Lord saves." [c] *wise men:* People famous for studying the stars. [d] *his star in the east:* Or "his star rise."

6   'Bethlehem in the land of Judea,
           you are very important
           among the towns of Judea.
       From your town will come a leader,
           who will be like a shepherd
           for my people Israel.' "

7Herod secretly called in the wise men and asked them when they had first seen the star. 8He told them, "Go to Bethlehem and search carefully for the child. As soon as you find him, let me know. I want to go and worship him too."

9The wise men listened to what the king said and then left. And the star they had seen in the east went on ahead of them until it stopped over the place where the child was. 10They were thrilled and excited to see the star.

11When the men went into the house and saw the child with Mary, his mother, they knelt down and worshipped him. They took out their gifts of gold, frankincense, and myrrhe and gave them to him. 12Later they were warned in a dream not to return to Herod, and they went back home by another road.

The Escape to Egypt

13After the wise men had gone, an angel from the Lord appeared to Joseph in a dream and said, "Get up! Hurry and take the child and his mother to Egypt! Stay there until I tell you to return, because Herod is looking for the child and wants to kill him."

14That night, Joseph got up and took his wife and the child to Egypt, 15where they stayed until Herod died. So the Lord's promise came true, just as the prophet had said, "I called my son out of Egypt."

The Killing of the Children

16When Herod found out that the wise men from the east had tricked him, he was very angry. He gave orders for his men to kill all the boys who lived in or near

---

efrankincense, and myrrh: Frankincense was a valuable powder that was burnt to make a sweet smell. Myrrh was a valuable sweet-smelling powder often used in perfume.

Bethlehem and were two years old and younger. This was based on what he had learnt from the wise men.

¹⁷So the Lord's promise came true, just as the prophet Jeremiah had said,

18 "In Ramah a voice was heard
　　crying and weeping loudly.
　Rachel was mourning for her children,
　and she refused to be comforted,
　　because they were dead."

The Return from Egypt

¹⁹After King Herod died, an angel from the Lord appeared in a dream to Joseph while he was still in Egypt. ²⁰The angel said, "Get up and take the child and his mother back to Israel. The people who wanted to kill him are now dead."

²¹Joseph got up and left with them for Israel. ²²But when he heard that Herod's son Archelaus was now ruler of Judea, he was afraid to go there. Then in a dream he was told to go to Galilee, ²³and they went to live there in the town of Nazareth. So the Lord's promise came true, just as the prophet had said, "He will be called a Nazarene."ᶠ

The Preaching of John the Baptist

(Mark 1.1-8; Luke 3.1-18; John 1.19-28)

3 ¹Years later, John the Baptist started preaching in the desert of Judea. ²He said, "Turn back to God! The kingdom of heavenᵍ will soon be here."ʰ

³John was the one the prophet Isaiah was talking about, when he said,

　　"In the desert someone is shouting,
　　'Get the road ready for the Lord!
　　　Make a straight path for him.' "

⁴John wore clothes made of camel's hair. He had a leather strap around his waist and ate grasshoppers and wild honey.

ᶠ*He will be called a Nazarene:* The prophet who said this is not known. ᵍ*kingdom of heaven:* In Matthew "kingdom of heaven" is used with the same meaning as "God's kingdom" in Mark and Luke. ʰ*will soon be here:* Or "is already here."

5From Jerusalem and all Judea and from the Jordan River Valley crowds of people went to John. 6They said how sorry they were for their sins, and he baptised them in the river.

7Many Pharisees and Sadducees also came to be baptised. But John said to them:

You snakes! Who warned you to run from the coming judgment? 8Do something to show that you have really given up your sins. 9And don't start telling yourselves that you belong to Abraham's family. I tell you that God can turn these stones into children for Abraham. 10An axe is ready to cut the trees down at their roots. Any tree that doesn't produce good fruit will be chopped down and thrown into a fire.

11I baptise you with water so that you'll give up your sins.*i* But someone more powerful is going to come, and I'm not good enough even to carry his sandals.*j* He'll baptise you with the Holy Spirit and with fire. 12His threshing fork is in his hand, and he is ready to separate the wheat from the husks.*k* He'll store the wheat in a barn and burn the husks in a fire that never goes out.

The Baptism of Jesus
(Mark 1.9-11; Luke 3.21, 22)

13Jesus left Galilee and went to the Jordan River to be baptised by John. 14But John kept objecting and said, "I ought to be baptised by you. Why have you come to me?"

15Jesus answered, "For now this is how it should be, because we must do all that God wants us to do." Then John agreed.

16So Jesus was baptised. And as soon as he came out of the water, the sky opened, and he saw the Spirit of God coming down on him like a dove. 17Then a voice from

---

iso that...sins: Or "because you have given up your sins." *jcarry his sandals:* This was one of the duties of a slave. *kHis threshing fork...husks:* After farmers had trampled out the grain, they used a large fork to toss the grain and the husks into the air. Wind would blow away the light husks, and the grain would fall back to the ground, where it could be gathered up.

heaven said, "This is my own dear Son, and I am pleased with him."

Jesus and the Devil
(Mark 1.12, 13; Luke 4.1-13)

4 ¹The Holy Spirit led Jesus into the desert, so that the devil could test him. ²After Jesus had gone without eating*ˡ* for 40 days and nights, he was very hungry. ³Then the devil came to him and said, "If you are God's Son, tell these stones to turn into bread."

⁴Jesus answered, "The Scriptures say:

'No-one can live only on food.

People need every word that God has spoken.' "

⁵Next, the devil took Jesus to the holy city and had him stand on the highest part of the temple. ⁶The devil said, "If you are God's Son, jump off. The Scriptures say:

'God will give his angels orders about you.

They will catch you in their arms,

and you won't hurt your feet on the stones.'"

⁷Jesus answered, "The Scriptures also say, 'Don't try to test the Lord your God!' "

⁸Finally, the devil took Jesus up onto a very high mountain and showed him all the kingdoms on earth and their power. ⁹The devil said to him, "I will give all this to you, if you will bow down and worship me."

¹⁰Jesus answered, "Go away Satan! The Scriptures say:

'Worship the Lord your God

and serve only him.' "

¹¹Then the devil left Jesus, and angels came to help him.

Jesus Begins His Work
(Mark 1.14, 15; Luke 4.14, 15)

¹²When Jesus heard that John had been put in prison, he went to Galilee. ¹³But instead of staying in Nazareth, Jesus moved to Capernaum. This town was beside Lake Galilee in the territory of Zebulun and Naphtali.*ᵐ* ¹⁴So

---

ˡwithout eating: The Jewish people sometimes went without eating (also called "fasting") to show their love for God or to show sorrow for their sins. *ᵐZebulun and Naphtali:* In Old Testament times these tribes were in northern Palestine, and in New Testament times many Gentiles lived where these tribes had once been.

God's promise came true, just as the prophet Isaiah had said,

> 15 "Listen, lands of Zebulun and Naphtali,
>   lands along the road to the sea
>   and east of the Jordan!
>   Listen Galilee, land of the Gentiles!
> 16   Although your people live in darkness,
>   they will see a bright light.
>   Although they live in the shadow of death,
>   a light will shine on them."

17Then Jesus started preaching, "Turn back to God! The kingdom of heaven will soon be here."[n]

Jesus Chooses Four Fishermen
(Mark 1.16-20; Luke 5.1-11)

18While Jesus was walking along the shore of Lake Galilee, he saw two brothers. One was Simon, also known as Peter, and the other was Andrew. They were fishermen, and they were casting their net into the lake. 19Jesus said to them, "Come with me! I will teach you how to bring in people instead of fish." 20At once the two brothers dropped their nets and went with him.

21Jesus walked on until he saw James and John, the sons of Zebedee. They were in a boat with their father, mending their nets. Jesus asked them to come with him too. 22Straight away they left the boat and their father, and went with Jesus.

Jesus Teaches, Preaches, and Heals
(Luke 6.17-19)

23Jesus went all over Galilee, teaching in the Jewish meeting places and preaching the good news about God's kingdom. He also healed every kind of disease and sickness. 24News about him spread all over Syria, and people with every kind of sickness or disease were brought to him. Some of them had a lot of demons in them, others were thought to be mad,[o] and still others couldn't walk. But Jesus healed them all.

---

[n]The kingdom of heaven will soon be here: See the two notes at 3.2.   [o]thought to be mad: In ancient times people with epilepsy were thought to be mad.

²⁵Large crowds followed Jesus from Galilee and the region around the ten cities known as Decapolis.ᵖ They also came from Jerusalem, Judea, and from across the Jordan River.

The Sermon on the Mount

5 ¹When Jesus saw the crowds, he went up on the side of a mountain and sat down.�q

Blessings

(Luke 6.20-23)

Jesus' disciples gathered around him, ²and he taught them:

3　God blesses those people who depend only on him.
　　They belong to the kingdom of heaven!ʳ

4　God blesses those people who grieve.
　　They will find comfort!

5　God blesses those people who are humble.
　　The earth will belong to them!

6　God blesses those people who want to obey himˢ
more than to eat or drink.
　　They will be given what they want!

7　God blesses those people who are merciful.
　　They will be treated with mercy!

8　God blesses those people whose hearts are pure.
　　They will see him!

9　God blesses those people who make peace.
　　They will be called his children!

10　God blesses those people
who are treated badly for doing right.
　　They belong to the kingdom of heaven.ᵗ

¹¹God will bless you when people insult you, mistreat you, and tell all kinds of evil lies about you because of me. ¹²Be happy and excited! You will have a great

---

ᵖ*Decapolis:* A group of ten cities east of Samaria and Galilee, where the people followed the Greek way of life.　q*sat down:* Teachers in the ancient world, including Jewish teachers, usually sat down when they taught.　ʳ*They belong to the kingdom of heaven:* Or "The kingdom of heaven belongs to them."　ˢ*who want to obey him:* Or "who want to do right" or "who want everyone to be treated right."　ᵗ*They belong to the kingdom of heaven:* See the note at 5.3.

reward in heaven. People did these same things to the prophets who lived long ago.

Salt and Light
(Mark 9.50; Luke 14.34, 35)

¹³You are like salt for everyone on earth. But if salt no longer tastes like salt, how can it make food salty? All it's good for is to be thrown out and walked on.

¹⁴You are like light for the whole world. A city built on top of a hill can't be hidden, ¹⁵and no-one would light a lamp and put it under a clay pot. A lamp is placed on a lamp stand, where it can give light to everyone in the house. ¹⁶Make your light shine, so that others will see the good that you do and will praise your Father in heaven.

The Law of Moses

¹⁷Don't suppose that I came to do away with the Law and the Prophets.ᵘ I didn't come to do away with them, but to give them their full meaning. ¹⁸Heaven and earth may disappear. But I promise you that not even a full stop or comma will ever disappear from the Law. Everything written in it must happen.

¹⁹If you reject even the least important command in the Law and teach others to do the same, you will be the least important person in the kingdom of heaven. But if you obey and teach others its commands, you will have an important place in the kingdom. ²⁰You must obey God's commands better than the Pharisees and the teachers of the Law obey them. If you don't, I promise you that you will never get into the kingdom of heaven.

Anger

²¹You know that our ancestors were told, "Do not murder" and "A murderer must be brought to trial." ²²But I promise you that if you are angry with

---

ᵘthe Law and the Prophets: The Jewish Scriptures, that is, the Old Testament.

someone,[v] you will have to stand trial. If you call someone a fool, you will be taken to court. And if you say that someone is worthless, you will be in danger of the fires of hell.

23So if you are about to place your gift on the altar and remember that someone is angry with you, 24leave your gift there in front of the altar. Make peace with that person, then come back and offer your gift to God.

25Before you are dragged into court, make friends with the person who has accused you of doing wrong. If you don't, you will be handed over to the judge and then to the officer who will put you in jail. 26I promise you that you won't get out until you have paid the last cent you owe.

Marriage

27You know the commandment which says, "Be faithful in marriage." 28But I tell you that if you look at another woman and want her, you are already unfaithful in your thoughts. 29If your right eye causes you to sin, poke it out and throw it away. It's better to lose one part of your body, than for your whole body to end up in hell. 30If your right hand causes you to sin, chop it off and throw it away! It's better to lose one part of your body, than for your whole body to be thrown into hell.

Divorce
(Matthew 19.9; Mark 10.11, 12; Luke 16.18)

31You have been taught that a man who divorces his wife must write out divorce papers for her.[w] 32But I tell you not to divorce your wife unless she has committed some terrible sexual sin.[x] If you divorce her, you will

[v]someone: In verses 22-24 the Greek text has "brother," which may mean people in general or other followers. [w]divorce papers: Jewish men could divorce their wives, but the women could not divorce their husbands. These papers were written to make it harder for a man to divorce his wife. Before this law was made, all a man had to do was to send his wife away and say that she was no longer his wife. [x]sexual sin: This probably refers to the laws about wrong kinds of marriages forbidden in Leviticus 18.6-18 or to some serious sexual sin.

cause her to be unfaithful, just as any man who marries her is guilty of taking another man's wife.

Promises

³³You know that our ancestors were told, "Don't use the Lord's name to make a promise unless you are going to keep it." ³⁴But I tell you not to swear by anything when you make a promise! Heaven is God's throne, so don't swear by heaven. ³⁵The earth is God's footstool, so don't swear by the earth. Jerusalem is the city of the great king, so don't swear by it. ³⁶Don't swear by your own head. You can't make one hair white or black. ³⁷When you make a promise, say only "Yes" or "No." Anything else comes from the devil.

Revenge

(Luke 6.29, 30)

³⁸You know that you've been taught, "An eye for an eye and a tooth for a tooth." ³⁹But I tell you not to try to get even with a person who has done something to you. When someone slaps your right cheek,^y turn and let that person slap your other cheek. ⁴⁰If someone sues you for your shirt, give up your coat as well. ⁴¹If a soldier forces you to carry his pack one kilometre, carry it two kilometres.^z ⁴²When people ask you for something, give it to them. When they want to borrow money, lend it to them.

Love

(Luke 6.27, 28, 32-36)

⁴³You have heard people say, "Love your neighbours and hate your enemies." ⁴⁴But I tell you to love your enemies and pray for anyone who mistreats you. ⁴⁵Then you will be acting like your Father in heaven. He makes the sun rise on both good and bad people. And he sends rain for the ones who do right and for the ones who do wrong. ⁴⁶If you love only those people

---

^yright cheek: A slap on the right cheek was a bad insult.　^ztwo kilometres: A Roman soldier had the right to force a person to carry his pack as far as one kilometre.

who love you, will God reward you for that? Even tax collectors[a] love their friends. [47]If you greet only your friends, what's so great about that? Don't even unbelievers do that? [48]But you must always act like your Father in heaven.

Giving

6 [1]When you do good deeds, don't try to show off. If you do, you won't get a reward from your Father in heaven.

[2]When you give to the poor, don't blow your own trumpet. That's what show-offs do in the meeting places and on the street corners, because they are always looking for praise. I can assure you that they already have their reward.

[3]When you give to the poor, don't let anyone know about it.[b] [4]Then your gift will be given in secret. Your Father knows what's done in secret, and he will reward you.

Prayer
(Luke 11.2-4)

[5]When you pray, don't be like those show-offs who love to stand up and pray in the meeting places and on the street corners. They do this just to look good. I can assure you that they already have their reward.

[6]When you pray, go into a room alone and close the door. Pray to your Father in private. He knows what's done in private, and he will reward you.

[7]When you pray, don't talk on and on as people do who don't know God. They think God likes to hear long prayers. [8]Don't be like them. Your Father knows what you need before you ask.

[9]You should pray like this:

Our Father in heaven,
help us to honour your name.

---

[a]*tax collectors:* These were usually Jewish people who paid the Romans for the right to collect taxes. They were hated by other Jews who thought of them as traitors to their country and to their religion.   [b]*don't let anyone know about it:* The Greek text has, "Don't let your left hand know what your right hand is doing."

10   Come and set up your kingdom,
        so that everyone on earth will obey you,
            as you are obeyed in heaven.
11   Give us our food for today.*c*
12   Forgive us for doing wrong,
        as we forgive others.
13   Keep us from being tempted
        and protect us from evil.*d*

14If you forgive others for the wrongs they do to you, your Father in heaven will forgive you. 15But if you don't forgive others, your Father won't forgive your sins.

Worshipping God by Going without Eating

16When you go without eating,*e* don't try to look gloomy as those show-offs do when they go without eating. I can assure you that they already have their reward. 17Instead, comb your hair and wash your face. 18Then others won't know that you are going without eating. But your Father sees what's done in private, and he will reward you.

Treasures in Heaven
(Luke 12.33, 34)

19Don't store up treasures on earth! Moths and rust can destroy them, and thieves can break in and steal them. 20Instead, store up your treasures in heaven, where moths and rust can't destroy them, and thieves can't break in and steal them. 21Your heart will always be where your treasure is.

Light
(Luke 11.34-36)

22Your eyes are like a window for your body. When they are good, you have all the light you need. 23But when your eyes are bad, everything is dark. If the light inside you is dark, you really are in the dark.

---

cour food for today: Or "the food that we need" or "our food for the coming day." *devil:* Or "the evil one," that is, the devil. Some manuscripts add, "The kingdom, the power, and the glory are yours for ever. Amen." *ewithout eating:* See the note at 4.2.

Money
(Luke 16.13)

²⁴You can't be the slave of two masters! You will like one more than the other or be more loyal to one than the other. You can't serve both God and money.

Worry
(Luke 12.22-31)

²⁵I tell you not to worry about your life. Don't worry about having something to eat, drink, or wear. Isn't life more than food or clothing? ²⁶Look at the birds in the sky! They don't plant or harvest. They don't even store grain in barns. Yet your Father in heaven takes care of them. Aren't you worth more than birds?

²⁷Can worry make you live longer?[f] ²⁸Why worry about clothes? Look how the wild flowers grow. They don't work hard to make their clothes. ²⁹But I tell you that Solomon with all his wealth[g] wasn't as well clothed as one of them. ³⁰God gives such beauty to everything that grows in the fields, even though it is here today and thrown into a fire tomorrow. He will surely do even more for you! Why do you have such little faith?

³¹Don't worry and ask yourselves, "Will we have anything to eat? Will we have anything to drink? Will we have any clothes to wear?" ³²Only people who don't know God are always worrying about such things. Your Father in heaven knows that you need all of these. ³³But more than anything else, put God's work first and do what he wants. Then the other things will be yours as well.

³⁴Don't worry about tomorrow. It will take care of itself. You have enough to worry about today.

Judging Others
(Luke 6.37, 38, 41, 42)

7 ¹Don't condemn others, and God won't condemn you. ²God will be as hard on you as you are on

---

[f]*live longer:* Or "grow taller."   [g]*Solomon with all his wealth:* The Jewish people thought that Solomon was the richest person who had ever lived.

others! He will treat you exactly as you treat them.

³You can see the speck in your friend's eye, but you don't notice the log in your own eye. ⁴How can you say, "My friend, let me take the speck out of your eye," when you don't see the log in your own eye? ⁵You're nothing but show-offs! First, take the log out of your own eye. Then you can see how to take the speck out of your friend's eye.

⁶Don't give to dogs what belongs to God. They will only turn and attack you. Don't throw pearls down in front of pigs. They will trample all over them.

Ask, Search, Knock
(Luke 11.9-13)

⁷Ask, and you will receive. Search, and you will find. Knock, and the door will be opened for you. ⁸Everyone who asks will receive. Everyone who searches will find. And the door will be opened for everyone who knocks. ⁹Would any of you give your hungry child a stone, if the child asked for some bread? ¹⁰Would you give your child a snake if the child asked for a fish? ¹¹As bad as you are, you still know how to give good gifts to your children. But your heavenly Father is even more ready to give good things to people who ask.

¹²Treat others as you want them to treat you. This is what the Law and the Prophets*ʰ* are all about.

The Narrow Gate
(Luke 13.24)

¹³Go in through the narrow gate. The gate to destruction is wide, and the road that leads there is easy to follow. A lot of people go through that gate. ¹⁴But the gate to life is very narrow. The road that leads there is so hard to follow that only a few people find it.

ʰ*the Law and the Prophets:* See the note at 5.17.

A Tree and Its Fruit
(Luke 6.43-45)

[15] Watch out for false prophets! They dress up like sheep, but inside they are wolves who have come to attack you. [16] You can tell what they are by what they do. No-one picks grapes or figs from thorn bushes. [17] A good tree produces good fruit, and a bad tree produces bad fruit. [18] A good tree can't produce bad fruit, and a bad tree can't produce good fruit. [19] Every tree that produces bad fruit will be chopped down and burnt. [20] You can tell who the false prophets are by their deeds.

A Warning
(Luke 13.26, 27)

[21] Not everyone who calls me their Lord will get into the kingdom of heaven. Only the ones who obey my Father in heaven will get in. [22] On the day of judgment many will call me their Lord. They will say, "We preached in your name, and in your name we forced out demons and worked many miracles." [23] But I will tell them, "I'll have nothing to do with you! Get out of my sight, you evil people!"

Two Builders
(Luke 6.47-49)

[24] Anyone who hears and obeys these teachings of mine is like a wise person who built a house on solid rock. [25] Rain poured down, rivers flooded, and winds beat against that house. But it didn't fall, because it was built on solid rock.

[26] Anyone who hears my teachings and doesn't obey them is like a foolish person who built a house on sand. [27] The rain poured down, the rivers flooded, and the winds blew and beat against that house. Finally, it fell with a crash.

[28] When Jesus finished speaking, the crowds were surprised at his teaching. [29] He taught them like someone with authority, and not like their teachers of the Law of Moses.

Jesus Heals a Man
(Mark 1.40-45; Luke 5.12-16)

8 ¹As Jesus came down the mountain, he was followed by large crowds. ²Suddenly a man with leprosy*i* came and knelt in front of Jesus. He said, "Lord, you have the power to make me well, if only you wanted to."

³Jesus put his hand on the man and said, "I want to! Now you are well." At once the man's leprosy disappeared. ⁴Jesus told him, "Don't tell anyone about this, but go and show the priest that you are well. Then take a gift to the temple just as Moses commanded, and everyone will know that you've been healed."*j*

Jesus Heals an Army Officer's Servant
(Luke 7.1-10; John 4.43-54)

⁵When Jesus was going into the town of Capernaum, an army officer came up to him and said, ⁶"Lord, my servant is at home in such terrible pain that he can't even move."

⁷"I will go and heal him," Jesus replied.

⁸But the officer said, "Lord, I'm not good enough for you to come into my house. Just give the order, and my servant will get well. ⁹I have officers who give orders to me, and I have soldiers who take orders from me. I can say to one of them, 'Go!' and he goes. I can say to another, 'Come!' and he comes. I can say to my servant, 'Do this!' and he'll do it."

¹⁰When Jesus heard this, he was so surprised that he turned and said to the crowd following him, "I tell you that in all of Israel I've never found anyone with this much faith! ¹¹Many people will come from everywhere to enjoy the feast in the kingdom of heaven with Abraham, Isaac, and Jacob. ¹²But the ones who should have been in the kingdom will be thrown out into the dark. They will cry and grit their teeth in pain."

*i*leprosy: In biblical times the word "leprosy" was used for many different kinds of skin diseases.   *j*everyone will know that you've been healed: People with leprosy had to be examined by a priest and told that they were well (that is "clean") before they could once again live a normal life in the Jewish community. The gift that Moses commanded was the sacrifice of some lambs together with flour mixed with olive oil.

¹³Then Jesus said to the officer, "You may go home now. Your faith has made it happen."

At once his servant was healed.

Jesus Heals Many People
(Mark 1.29-34; Luke 4.38-41)

¹⁴Jesus went to the home of Peter, where he found that Peter's mother-in-law was sick in bed with fever. ¹⁵He took her by the hand, and the fever left her. Then she got up and served Jesus a meal.

¹⁶That evening many people with demons in them were brought to Jesus. And with only a word he forced out the evil spirits and healed everyone who was sick. ¹⁷So God's promise came true, just as the prophet Isaiah had said,

"He healed our diseases
and made us well."

Some Who Wanted To Go with Jesus
(Luke 9.57-62)

¹⁸When Jesus saw the crowd,ᵏ he went across Lake Galilee. ¹⁹A teacher of the Law of Moses came up to him and said,"Teacher, I'll go anywhere with you!"

²⁰Jesus replied, "Foxes have dens, and birds have nests. But the Son of Man doesn't have a place to call his own."

²¹Another disciple said to Jesus, "Lord, let me wait till I bury my father."

²²Jesus answered, "Come with me, and let the dead bury their dead."ˡ

A Storm
(Mark 4.35-41; Luke 8.22-25)

²³After Jesus left in a boat with his disciples, ²⁴a terrible storm suddenly struck the lake, and waves started splashing into their boat.

Jesus was sound asleep, ²⁵so the disciples went over to

ᵏsaw the crowd: Some manuscripts have "large crowd." Others have "large crowds." ˡlet the dead bury their dead: For the Jewish people a proper burial of their dead was a very important duty. But Jesus teaches that following him is even more important.

him and woke him up. They said, "Lord, save us! We're going to drown!"

26But Jesus replied, "Why are you so afraid? You certainly don't have much faith." Then he got up and ordered the wind and the waves to calm down. And everything was calm.

27The men in the boat were amazed and said, "Who is this? Even the wind and the waves obey him."

Two Men with Demons in Them
(Mark 5.1-20; Luke 8.26-39)

28After Jesus had crossed the lake, he came to shore near the town of Gadara[m] and started down the road. Two men with demons in them came to him from the tombs.[n] They were so fierce that no-one could travel that way. 29Suddenly they shouted, "Jesus, Son of God, what do you want with us? Have you come to punish us before our time?"

30Not far from there a large herd of pigs was feeding. 31So the demons begged Jesus, "If you force us out, please send us into those pigs!" 32Jesus told them to go, and they went out of the men and into the pigs. All at once the pigs rushed down the steep bank into the lake and drowned.

33The people taking care of the pigs ran to the town and told everything, especially what had happened to the two men. 34Everyone in town came out to meet Jesus. When they saw him, they begged him to leave their part of the country.

Jesus Heals a Crippled Man
(Mark 2.1-12; Luke 5.17-26)

9 1Jesus got into a boat and crossed back over to the town where he lived.[o] 2Some people soon brought to him a crippled man lying on a mat. When Jesus saw how much faith they had, he said to the crippled man, "My friend, don't worry! Your sins are forgiven."

[m]Gadara: Some manuscripts have "Gergasa." Others have "Gerasa."   [n]tombs: It was thought that demons and evil spirits lived in tombs and in caves that were used for burying the dead.   [o]where he lived: Capernaum (see 4.13).

3Some teachers of the Law of Moses said to themselves, "Jesus must think he is God!"

4But Jesus knew what was in their minds, and he said, "Why are you thinking such evil things? 5Is it easier for me to tell this crippled man that his sins are forgiven or to tell him to get up and walk? 6But I will show you that the Son of Man has the right to forgive sins here on earth." So Jesus said to the man, "Get up! Pick up your mat and go home." 7The man got up and went home. 8When the crowds saw this, they were afraid*p* and praised God for giving such authority to people.

Jesus Chooses Matthew
(Mark 2.13-17; Luke 5.27-32)

9As Jesus was leaving, he saw a tax collector*q* named Matthew sitting at the place for paying taxes. Jesus said to him, "Come with me." Matthew got up and went with him.

10Later, Jesus and his disciples were having dinner at Matthew's house.*r* Many tax collectors and other sinners were also there. 11Some Pharisees asked Jesus' disciples, "Why does your teacher eat with tax collectors and other sinners?"

12Jesus heard them and answered, "Healthy people don't need a doctor, but sick people do. 13Go and learn what the Scriptures mean when they say, 'Instead of offering sacrifices to me, I want you to be merciful to others.' I didn't come to invite good people to be my followers. I came to invite sinners."

People Ask about Going without Eating
(Mark 2.18-22; Luke 5.33-39)

14One day some followers of John the Baptist came and asked Jesus, "Why do we and the Pharisees often go without eating,*s* while your disciples never do?"

15Jesus answered:

The friends of a bridegroom don't go without eating while he's still with them. But the time will come when he will be taken from them. Then they will go

---

*p*afraid: Some manuscripts have "amazed."   *q*tax collector: See the note at 5.46.
*r*Matthew's house: Or "Jesus' house."   *s*without eating: See the note at 4.2.

without eating.

¹⁶No-one uses a new piece of cloth to patch old clothes. The patch would shrink and tear a bigger hole.

¹⁷No-one pours new wine into old wineskins. The wine would swell and burst the old skins.ᵗ Then the wine would be lost, and the skins would be ruined. New wine must be put into new wineskins. Both the skins and the wine will then be safe.

A Dying Girl and a Sick Woman
(Mark 5.21-43; Luke 8.40-56)

¹⁸While Jesus was still speaking, a Jewish official came and knelt in front of him. The man said, "My daughter has just died! Please come and place your hand on her. Then she'll live again."

¹⁹Jesus and his disciples got up and went with the man.

²⁰A woman who had been bleeding for twelve years came up behind Jesus and barely touched his clothes. ²¹She had said to herself, "If I can just touch his clothes, I'll get well."

²²Jesus turned. He saw the woman and said, "Don't worry! You're now well because of your faith." At that moment she was healed.

²³When Jesus went into the home of the Jewish official and saw the musicians and the crowd of mourners,ᵘ ²⁴he said, "Get out of here! The little girl isn't dead. She's just asleep." Everyone started laughing at Jesus. ²⁵But after the crowd had been sent out of the house, Jesus went to the girl's bedside. He took her by the hand and helped her up.

²⁶News about this spread all over that part of the country.

Jesus Heals Two Blind Men

²⁷As Jesus was walking along, two blind men began following him and shouting, "Son of David,ᵛ have pity on us!"

²⁸After Jesus had gone indoors, the two blind men came

ᵗswell and burst the old skins: While the juice from grapes was becoming wine, it would swell and stretch the skins in which it had been stored. If the skins were old and stiff, they would burst. ᵘthe crowd of mourners: The Jewish people often hired mourners for funerals. ᵛSon of David: The Jewish people expected the Messiah to be from the family of King David, and for this reason the Messiah was often called the "Son of David."

up to him. He asked them, "Do you believe I can make you well?"

"Yes, Lord," they answered.

29Jesus touched their eyes and said, "Because of your faith, you will be healed." 30They were able to see, and Jesus strictly warned them not to tell anyone about him. 31But they left and talked about him to everyone in that part of the country.

Jesus Heals a Man Who Couldn't Talk

32As Jesus and his disciples were on their way, some people brought to him a man who couldn't talk because a demon was in him. 33After Jesus had forced the demon out, the man started talking. The crowds were so amazed that they began saying, "Nothing like this has ever happened in Israel!"

34But the Pharisees said, "The leader of the demons gives him the power to force out demons."

Jesus Has Pity on People

35Jesus went to every town and village. He taught in their meeting places and preached the good news about God's kingdom. Jesus also healed every kind of disease and sickness. 36When he saw the crowds, he felt sorry for them. They were confused and helpless, like sheep without a shepherd. 37He said to his disciples, "A large crop is in the fields, but there are only a few workers. 38Ask the Lord in charge of the harvest to send out workers to bring it in."

Jesus Chooses His Twelve Apostles
(Mark 3.13-19; Luke 6.12-16)

10 1Jesus called together his twelve disciples. He gave them the power to force out evil spirits and to heal every kind of disease and sickness. 2The first of the twelve apostles was Simon, better known as Peter. His brother Andrew was an apostle, and so were James and John, the two sons of Zebedee. 3Philip, Bartholomew, Thomas, Matthew the tax collector,w James the son of

wtax collector: See the note at 5.46.

Alphaeus, and Thaddaeus were also apostles. [4]The others were Simon, known as the Eager One,[x] and Judas Iscariot,[y] who later betrayed Jesus.

Instructions for the Twelve Apostles
(Mark 6.7-13; Luke 9.1-6)

[5]Jesus sent out the twelve apostles with these instructions:

Stay away from the Gentiles and don't go to any Samaritan town. [6]Go only to the people of Israel, because they are like a flock of lost sheep. [7]As you go, announce that the kingdom of heaven will soon be here.[z] [8]Heal the sick, raise the dead to life, heal people who have leprosy,[a] and force out demons. You received without paying, now give without being paid. [9]Don't take along any gold, silver, or copper coins. [10]And don't carry[b] a travelling bag or an extra shirt or sandals or a walking stick.

Workers deserve their food. [11]So when you go to a town or a village, find someone worthy enough to have you as their guest and stay with them until you leave. [12]When you go to a home, give it your blessing of peace. [13]If the home is deserving, let your blessing remain with them. But if the home isn't deserving, take back your blessing of peace. [14]If someone won't welcome you or listen to your message, leave their home or town. And shake the dust from your feet at them.[c] [15]I promise you that the day of judgment will be easier for the towns of Sodom and Gomorrah[d] than for that town.

---

[x]known as the Eager One: The Greek text has "Cananaean," which probably comes from a Hebrew word meaning "zealous" (see Luke 6.15). "Zealot" was the name later given to the members of a Jewish group that resisted and fought against the Romans. [y]Iscariot: This may mean "a man from Kerioth" (a place in Judea). But more probably it means "a man who was a liar" or "a man who was a betrayer." [z]will soon be here: Or "is already here." [a]leprosy: See the note at 8.2. [b]Don't take along...don't carry: Or "Don't accept...don't accept." [c]shake the dust from your feet at them: This was a way of showing rejection (see Acts 13.51). [d]Sodom and Gomorrah: During the time of Abraham the Lord destroyed these towns because the people there were so evil.

Warning about Trouble
(Mark 13.9-13; Luke 21.12-17)

¹⁶I am sending you like lambs into a pack of wolves. So be as wise as snakes and as innocent as doves. ¹⁷Watch out for people who will take you to court and have you beaten in their meeting places. ¹⁸Because of me, you will be dragged before rulers and kings to tell them and the Gentiles about your faith. ¹⁹But when someone arrests you, don't worry about what you will say or how you will say it. At that time you will be given the words to say. ²⁰But you will not really be the one speaking. The Spirit from your Father will tell you what to say.

²¹Brothers and sisters will betray one another and have each other put to death. Parents will betray their own children, and children will turn against their parents and have them killed. ²²Everyone will hate you because of me. But if you remain faithful until the end, you will be saved. ²³When people mistreat you in one town, hurry to another one. I promise you that before you have gone to all the towns of Israel, the Son of Man will come.

²⁴Disciples aren't better than their teacher, and slaves aren't better than their master. ²⁵It's enough for disciples to be like their teacher and for slaves to be like their master. If people call the head of the family Satan, what will they say about the rest of the family?

The One To Fear
(Luke 12.2-7)

²⁶Don't be afraid of anyone! Everything that is hidden will be found out, and every secret will be known. ²⁷Whatever I say to you in the dark, you must tell in the light. And you must announce from the housetops whatever I have whispered to you. ²⁸Don't be afraid of people. They can kill you, but they can't harm your soul. Instead, you should fear God who can destroy both your body and your soul in hell. ²⁹Aren't two sparrows sold for only a cent? But your Father knows when any one of them falls to the ground.

[30] Even the hairs on your head are counted. [31] So don't be afraid! You are worth much more than many sparrows.

Telling Others about Christ
(Luke 12.8, 9)

[32] If you tell others that you belong to me, I will tell my Father in heaven that you are my followers. [33] But if you reject me, I will tell my Father in heaven that you don't belong to me.

Not Peace, but Trouble
(Luke 12.51-53; 14.26, 27)

[34] Don't think that I came to bring peace to the earth! I came to bring trouble, not peace. [35] I came to turn sons against their fathers, daughters against their mothers, and daughters-in-law against their mothers-in-law. [36] Your worst enemies will be in your own family.

[37] If you love your father or mother or even your sons and daughters more than me, you aren't fit to be my disciples. [38] And unless you are willing to take up your cross and come with me, you aren't fit to be my disciples. [39] If you try to save your life, you will lose it. But if you give it up for me, you will surely find it.

Rewards
(Mark 9.41)

[40] Anyone who welcomes you welcomes me. And anyone who welcomes me also welcomes the one who sent me. [41] Anyone who welcomes a prophet, just because that person is a prophet, will be given the same reward as a prophet. Anyone who welcomes a good person, just because that person is good, will be given the same reward as a good person. [42] And anyone who gives one of my most humble followers a cup of cool water, just because that person is my follower, will surely be rewarded.

John the Baptist
(Luke 7.18-35)

11 ¹After Jesus had finished instructing his twelve disciples, he left and began teaching and preaching in the towns.ᵉ

²John was in prison when he heard what Christ was doing. So John sent some of his followers ³to ask Jesus, "Are you the one we should be looking for? Or must we wait for someone else?"

⁴Jesus answered, "Go and tell John what you've heard and seen. ⁵The blind are now able to see, and the lame can walk. People with leprosyᶠ are being healed, and the deaf can hear. The dead are raised to life, and the poor are hearing the good news. ⁶God will bless everyone who doesn't reject me because of what I do."

⁷As John's followers were going away, Jesus spoke to the crowds about John:

What sort of person did you go out into the desert to see? Was he like tall grass blown about by the wind? ⁸What kind of man did you go out to see? Was he someone dressed in fine clothes? People who dress like that live in the king's palace. ⁹What did you really go out to see? Was he a prophet? He certainly was. I tell you that he was more than a prophet. ¹⁰In the Scriptures God says about him, "I am sending my messenger ahead of you to get things ready for you." ¹¹I tell you that no-one ever born on this earth is greater than John the Baptist. But whoever is least in the kingdom of heaven is greater than John.

¹²From the time of John the Baptist until now, violent people have been trying to take over the kingdom of heaven by force. ¹³All the Books of the Prophets and the Law of Mosesᵍ told what was going to happen up to the time of John. ¹⁴And if you believe

---

ᵉ*the towns:* The Greek text has "their towns," which may refer to the towns of Galilee or to the towns where Jesus' disciples had lived.   ᶠ*leprosy:* See the note at 8.2.   ᵍ*the Books of the Prophets and the Law of Moses:* The Jewish Scriptures, that is, the Old Testament.

them, John is Elijah, the prophet you are waiting for.
[15]If you have ears, pay attention!

[16]You people are like children sitting in the market
and [17]shouting to each other,

"We played the flute, but you wouldn't dance!
We sang a funeral song,
but you wouldn't mourn!"

[18]John the Baptist did not go around eating and drinking,
and you said, "That man has a demon in him!" [19]But the
Son of Man goes around eating and drinking, and you say,
"That man eats and drinks too much! He is even a friend of
tax collectors[h] and sinners." Yet Wisdom is shown to be
right by what it does.

The Unbelieving Towns
(Luke 10.13-15)

[20]In the towns where Jesus had worked most of his
miracles, the people refused to turn to God. So Jesus was
upset with them and said:

[21]You people of Chorazin are in for trouble! You
people of Bethsaida are in for trouble too! If the
miracles that took place in your towns had happened
in Tyre and Sidon, the people there would have turned
to God long ago. They would have dressed in sackcloth
and put ashes on their heads.[i] [22]I tell you that on the
day of judgment the people of Tyre and Sidon will get
off easier than you will.

[23]People of Capernaum, do you think you will be
honoured in heaven? You will go down to hell! If the
miracles that took place in your town had happened
in Sodom, that town would still be standing. [24]So I tell
you that on the day of judgment the people of Sodom
will get off easier than you.

Come to Me and Rest
(Luke 10.21, 22)

[25]At that moment Jesus said:
My Father, Lord of heaven and earth, I am grateful

[h]tax collectors: See the note at 5.46.   [i]sackcloth...ashes on their heads:
This was one way that people showed how sorry they were for their sins.

that you hid all this from wise and educated people and showed it to ordinary people. [26] Yes, Father, that is what pleased you.

[27] My Father has given me everything, and he is the only one who knows the Son. The only one who truly knows the Father is the Son. But the Son wants to tell others about the Father, so that they can know him too.

[28] If you are tired from carrying heavy burdens, come to me and I will give you rest. [29] Take the yoke[j] I give you. Put it on your shoulders and learn from me. I am gentle and humble, and you will find rest. [30] This yoke is easy to bear, and this burden is light.

A Question about the Sabbath
(Mark 2.23-28; Luke 6.1-5)

12 [1] One Sabbath, Jesus and his disciples were walking through some wheat fields.[k] His disciples were hungry and began picking and eating grains of wheat. [2] Some Pharisees noticed this and said to Jesus, "Why are your disciples picking grain on the Sabbath? They're not supposed to do that!"

[3] Jesus answered:

You surely must have read what David did when he and his followers were hungry. [4] He went into the house of God, and then they ate the sacred loaves of bread that only priests are supposed to eat. [5] Haven't you read in the Law of Moses that the priests are allowed to work in the temple on the Sabbath? But no-one says that they are guilty of breaking the law of the Sabbath. [6] I tell you that there is something here greater than the temple. [7] Don't you know what the Scriptures mean when they say, "Instead of offering sacrifices to me, I want you to be merciful to others?" If you knew what this means, you wouldn't condemn these

---

[j] yoke: Yokes were put on the necks of animals, so that they could pull a plough or wagon. A yoke was a symbol of obedience and hard work. [k] walking through some wheat fields: It was the custom to let hungry travellers pick grains of wheat.

innocent disciples of mine. [8]So the Son of Man is Lord over the Sabbath.

A Man with a Crippled Hand
(Mark 3.1-6; Luke 6.6-11)

[9]Jesus left and went into one of the Jewish meeting places, [10]where there was a man whose hand was crippled. Some Pharisees wanted to accuse Jesus of doing something wrong, and they asked him, "Is it right to heal someone on the Sabbath?"

[11]Jesus answered, "If you had a sheep that fell into a ditch on the Sabbath, wouldn't you lift it out? [12]People are worth much more than sheep, and so it is right to do good on the Sabbath." [13]Then Jesus told the man, "Hold out your hand." The man did, and it became as healthy as the other one.

[14]The Pharisees left and started making plans to kill Jesus.

God's Chosen Servant

[15]When Jesus found out what was happening, he left there and large crowds followed him. He healed all of their sick people, [16]but warned them not to tell anyone about him. [17]So God's promise came true, just as Isaiah the prophet had said,

[18] "Here is my chosen servant!
I love him, and he pleases me.
I will give him my Spirit,
and he will bring justice to the nations.
[19] He won't shout or yell
or call out in the streets.
[20] He won't break off a bent reed
or put out a dying flame,
but he will make sure that justice is done.
[21] All nations will place their hope in him."

Jesus and the Ruler of the Demons
(Mark 3.20-30; Luke 11.14-23; 12.10)

[22]Some people brought to Jesus a man who was blind and couldn't talk because he had a demon in him. Jesus

cured the man, and then he was able to talk and see.
23The crowds were so amazed that they asked, "Could
Jesus be the Son of David?"[1]

24When the Pharisees heard this, they said, "He forces
out demons by the power of Beelzebul, the ruler of the
demons!"

25Jesus knew what they were thinking, and he said to
them:

Any kingdom where people fight each other will end
up ruined. And a town or family that fights will soon
destroy itself. 26So if Satan fights against himself, how
can his kingdom last? 27If I use the power of Beelzebul
to force out demons, whose power do your own
followers use to force them out? Your followers are
the ones who will judge you. 28But when I force out
demons by the power of God's Spirit, it proves that
God's kingdom has already come to you. 29How can
anyone break into a strong man's house and steal his
things, unless he first ties up the strong man? Then he
can take everything.

30If you are not on my side, you are against me. If
you don't gather in the harvest with me, you scatter
it. 31-32I tell you that any sinful thing you do or say can
be forgiven. Even if you speak against the Son of Man,
you can be forgiven. But if you speak against the Holy
Spirit, you can never be forgiven, either in this life or
in the life to come.

A Tree and Its Fruit
(Luke 6.43-45)

33A good tree produces only good fruit, and a bad tree
produces bad fruit. You can tell what a tree is like by
the fruit it produces. 34You are evil snakes, so how can
you say anything good? Your words show what is in
your hearts. 35Good people bring good things out of
their hearts, but evil people bring evil things out of
their hearts. 36I promise you that on the day of
judgment, everyone will have to account for every

---

[1]*Could Jesus be the Son of David:* Or "Does Jesus think he is the Son of
David?" See the note at 9.27.

careless word they have spoken. [37]On that day they will be told that they are either innocent or guilty because of the things they have said.

A Sign from Heaven
(Mark 8.11, 12; Luke 11.29-32)

[38]Some Pharisees and teachers of the Law of Moses said, "Teacher, we want you to show us a sign from heaven."

[39]But Jesus replied:

You want a sign because you are evil and won't believe! But the only sign you will get is the sign of the prophet Jonah. [40]He was in the stomach of a big fish for three days and nights, just as the Son of Man will be deep in the earth for three days and nights. [41]On the day of judgment the people of Nineveh[m] will stand there with you and condemn you. They turned to God when Jonah preached, and yet here is something far greater than Jonah. [42]The Queen of the South[n] will also stand there with you and condemn you. She travelled a long way to hear Solomon's wisdom, and yet here is something much greater than Solomon.

Return of an Evil Spirit
(Luke 11.24-26)

[43]When an evil spirit leaves a person, it travels through the desert, looking for a place to rest. But when the demon doesn't find a place, [44]it says, "I'll go back to the home I left." When it gets there and finds the place empty, clean, and fixed up, [45]it goes off and finds seven other evil spirits even worse than itself. They all come and make their home there, and the person ends up in a worse state than before. That's how it will be with you evil people of today.

---

[m]*Nineveh:* During the time of Jonah this city was the capital of the Assyrian Empire, which was Israel's worst enemy. But Jonah was sent there to preach, so that the people would turn to the Lord and be saved.   [n]*Queen of the South:* Sheba, probably a country in southern Arabia.

Jesus' Mother and Brothers
(Mark 3.31-35; Luke 8.19-21)

46While Jesus was still speaking to the crowds, his mother and brothers came and stood outside because they wanted to talk with him. 47Someone told Jesus, "Your mother and brothers are standing outside and want to talk with you."o

48Jesus answered, "Who is my mother and who are my brothers?" 49Then he pointed to his disciples and said, "These are my mother and my brothers! 50Anyone who obeys my Father in heaven is my brother or sister or mother."

A Story about a Farmer
(Mark 4.1-9; Luke 8.4-8)

13 1That same day Jesus left the house and went out beside Lake Galilee, where he sat down to teach.p 2Such large crowds gathered around him that he had to sit in a boat, while the people stood on the shore. 3Then he taught them many things by using stories. He said:

A farmer went out to scatter seed in a field. 4While the farmer was scattering the seed, some of it fell along the road and was eaten by birds. 5Other seeds fell on thin, rocky ground and quickly started growing because the soil wasn't very deep. 6But when the sun came up, the plants were scorched and dried up, because they didn't have enough roots. 7Some other seeds fell where thorn bushes grew up and choked the plants. 8But a few seeds did fall on good ground where the plants produced 100 or 60 or 30 times as much as was scattered. 9If you have ears, pay attention!

Why Jesus Used Stories
(Mark 4.10-12; Luke 8.9, 10)

10Jesus' disciples came to him and asked, "Why do you use nothing but stories when you speak to the people?"

---

oSomone...with you: Some manuscripts do not have verse 47.   psat down to teach: See the note at 5.1

[11]Jesus answered:

I have explained the secrets about the kingdom of heaven to you, but not to others. [12]Everyone who has something will be given more. But people who haven't got anything will lose even what little they have. [13]I use stories when I speak to them because when they look, they can't see, and when they listen, they can't hear or understand. [14]So God's promise came true, just as the prophet Isaiah had said,

"These people will listen and listen,
      but never understand.
They will look and look, but never see.
[15] All of them have stubborn minds!
Their ears are blocked up,
and their eyes are covered.
      They can't see or hear or understand.
If they could, they would turn to me,
and I would heal them."

[16]But God has blessed you, because your eyes can see and your ears can hear! [17]Many prophets and good people were eager to see what you see and to hear what you hear. But I tell you that they did not see or hear.

Jesus Explains the Story about the Farmer
(Mark 4.13-20; Luke 8.11-15)

[18]Now listen to the meaning of the story about the farmer:

[19]The seeds that fell along the road are the people who hear the message about the kingdom, but don't understand it. Then the evil one comes and snatches the message from their hearts. [20]The seeds that fell on rocky ground are the people who gladly hear the message and accept it straight away. [21]But they don't have deep roots, and they don't last very long. As soon as life gets hard or the message gets them into trouble, they give up.

[22]The seeds that fell among the thorn bushes are also people who hear the message. But they start worrying about the needs of this life and are fooled by the desire to get rich. So the message gets choked out, and they never produce anything. [23]The seeds that fell on good

ground are the people who hear and understand the message. They produce as much as 100 or 60 or 30 times what was planted.

Weeds among the Wheat

24Jesus then told them this story:

The kingdom of heaven is like what happened when a farmer scattered good seed in a field. 25But while everyone was sleeping, an enemy came and scattered weed seeds in the field and then left.

26When the plants came up and began to ripen, the farmer's servants could see the weeds. 27The servants came and asked, "Sir, didn't you scatter good seed in your field? Where did these weeds come from?"

28"An enemy did this," he replied.

His servants then asked, "Do you want us to go out and pull up the weeds?"

29"No!" he answered. "You might also pull up the wheat. 30Leave the weeds alone until harvest time. Then I'll tell my workers to gather the weeds and tie them up and burn them. But I'll have them store the wheat in my barn."

Stories about a Mustard Seed and Yeast
(Mark 4.30-32; Luke 13.18-21)

31Jesus told them another story:

The kingdom of heaven is like what happens when a farmer plants a mustard seed in a field. 32Although it's the smallest of all seeds, it grows larger than any garden plant and becomes a tree. Birds even come and nest on its branches.

33Jesus also said:

The kingdom of heaven is like what happens when a woman mixes a little yeast into three big batches of flour. Finally, all the dough rises.

The Reason for Teaching with Stories
(Mark 4.33, 34)

34Jesus used stories when he spoke to the people. In fact, he didn't tell them anything without using stories.

[35]So God's promise came true, just as the prophet[q] had said,

> "I will use stories to speak my message
> and to explain things that have been hidden
> since the creation of the world."

Jesus Explains the Story about the Weeds

[36]After Jesus left the crowd and went inside,[r] his disciples came to him and said, "Explain to us the story about the weeds in the wheat field."

[37]Jesus answered:

The one who scattered the good seed is the Son of Man. [38]The field is the world, and the good seeds are the people who belong to the kingdom. The weed seeds are those who belong to the evil one, [39]and the one who scattered them is the devil. The harvest is the end of time, and angels are the ones who bring in the harvest.

[40]Weeds are gathered and burnt. That's how it will be at the end of time. [41]The Son of Man will send out his angels, and they will gather from his kingdom everyone who does wrong or causes others to sin. [42]Then he will throw them into a flaming furnace, where people will cry and grit their teeth in pain. [43]But everyone who has done right will shine like the sun in their Father's kingdom. If you have ears, pay attention!

A Hidden Treasure

[44]The kingdom of heaven is like what happens when someone finds treasure hidden in a field and buries it again. A person like that is happy and goes and sells everything in order to buy that field.

A Valuable Pearl

[45]The kingdom of heaven is like what happens when a shop owner is looking for fine pearls. [46]After finding a very valuable one, the owner goes and sells everything in order to buy that pearl.

---

[q]the prophet: Some manuscripts have "the prophet Isaiah."   [r]went inside: Or "went home."

A Fish Net

47The kingdom of heaven is like what happens when a net is thrown into a lake and catches all kinds of fish. 48When the net is full, it's dragged to the shore, and the fishermen sit down to separate the fish. They keep the good ones, but throw the bad ones away. 49That's how it will be at the end of time. Angels will come and separate the evil people from the ones who have done right. 50Then those evil people will be thrown into a flaming furnace, where they will cry and grit their teeth in pain.

New and Old Treasures

51Jesus asked his disciples if they understood all these things. They said, "Yes, we do."

52So he told them, "Every student of the Scriptures who becomes a disciple in the kingdom of heaven is like someone who brings out new and old treasures from the storeroom."

The People of Nazareth Turn against Jesus
(Mark 6.1-6; Luke 4.16-30)

53When Jesus had finished telling these stories, he left 54and went to his home town. He taught in their meeting place, and the people were so amazed that they asked, "Where does he get all this wisdom and the power to work these miracles? 55Isn't he the son of the carpenter? Isn't Mary his mother, and aren't James, Joseph, Simon, and Judas his brothers? 56Don't his sisters still live here in our town? How can he do all this?" 57So the people were very unhappy because of what he was doing.

But Jesus said, "Prophets are honoured by everyone, except the people of their home town and their own family." 58And because the people didn't have any faith, Jesus didn't work many miracles there.

The Death of John the Baptist
(Mark 6.14-29; Luke 9.7-9)

14 1About this time Herod the ruler[s] heard the news about Jesus 2and told his officials, "This is John the

---

sHerod the ruler: Herod Antipas, the son of Herod the Great (see 2.1).

Baptist! He has come back from death, and that's why he has the power to work these miracles."

3-4Herod had earlier arrested John and had him chained and put in prison. He did this because John had told him, "It isn't right for you to take Herodias, the wife of your brother Philip." 5Herod wanted to kill John. But the people thought John was a prophet, and Herod was afraid of what they might do.

6When Herod's birthday came, the daughter of Herodias danced for the guests. She pleased Herod 7so much that he swore to give her whatever she wanted. 8But the girl's mother told her to say, "Here on a platter I want the head of John the Baptist!"

9The king was sorry for what he had said. But he didn't want to break the promise he had made in front of his guests. So he ordered a guard 10to go to the prison and cut off John's head. 11It was taken on a platter to the girl, and she gave it to her mother. 12John's followers took his body and buried it. Then they told Jesus what had happened.

Jesus Feeds 5000
(Mark 6.30-44; Luke 9.10-17; John 6.1-14)

13After Jesus heard about John, he crossed Lake Galilee^t to go to a place where he could be alone. But the crowds found out and followed him on foot from the towns. 14When Jesus got out of the boat, he saw the large crowd. He felt sorry for them and healed everyone who was sick.

15That evening the disciples came to Jesus and said, "This place is like a desert, and it's already late. Let the crowds leave, so they can go to the villages and buy some food."

16Jesus replied, "They don't have to leave. Why don't you give them something to eat?"

17But they said, "We've only got five small loaves of bread^u and two fish." 18Jesus asked his disciples to bring

---

^{t}crossed Lake Galilee: To the east side. ^{u}small loaves of bread: These would have been flat and round or in the shape of a bun.

the food to him, ¹⁹and he told the crowd to sit down on the grass. Jesus took the five loaves and the two fish. He looked up towards heaven and blessed the food. Then he broke the bread and handed it to his disciples, and they gave it to the people.

²⁰After everyone had eaten all they wanted, Jesus' disciples picked up 12 large baskets of leftovers.

²¹There were about 5000 men who ate, not counting the women and children.

Jesus Walks on the Water
(Mark 6.45-52; John 6.15-21)

²²Straight away, Jesus made his disciples get into a boat and start back across the lake.ᵛ But he stayed until he had sent the crowds away. ²³Then he went up on a mountain where he could be alone and pray. Later that evening, he was still there.

²⁴By this time the boat was a long way from the shore. It was going against the wind and was being tossed around by the waves. ²⁵A little while before morning, Jesus came walking on the water towards his disciples. ²⁶When they saw him, they thought he was a ghost. They were terrified and started screaming.

²⁷At once, Jesus said to them, "Don't worry! I am Jesus. Don't be afraid."

²⁸Peter replied, "Lord, if it's really you, tell me to come to you on the water."

²⁹"Come on!" Jesus said. Peter then got out of the boat and started walking on the water towards him.

³⁰But when Peter saw how strong the wind was, he was afraid and started sinking. "Save me, Lord!" he shouted.

³¹At once, Jesus reached out his hand. He helped Peter up and said, "You certainly don't have much faith. Why do you doubt?"

³²When Jesus and Peter got into the boat, the wind died down. ³³The men in the boat worshipped Jesus and said, "You really are the Son of God!"

ᵛback across the lake: To the west side.

Jesus Heals Sick People in Gennesaret
(Mark 6.53-56)

³⁴Jesus and his disciples crossed the lake and came to shore near the town of Gennesaret. ³⁵The people found out that he was there, and they sent word to everyone who lived in that part of the country. So they brought all the sick people to Jesus. ³⁶They begged him just to let them touch his clothes, and everyone who did was healed.

The Teaching of the Ancestors
(Mark 7.1-13)

15 ¹About this time some Pharisees and teachers of the Law of Moses came from Jerusalem. They asked Jesus, ²"Why don't your disciples obey what our ancestors taught us to do? They don't even wash their hands^w before they eat."

³Jesus answered:

Why do you disobey God and follow your own teaching? ⁴Didn't God command you to respect your father and mother? Didn't he tell you to put to death all who curse their parents? ⁵But you let people get away without helping their parents when they should. You let them say that what they have has been offered to God.^x ⁶Is this any way to show respect to your parents? You ignore God's commands in order to follow your own teaching. ⁷And you are nothing but show-offs! Isaiah the prophet was right when he wrote that God had said,

⁸   "All of you praise me with your words,
        but you never really think about me.
⁹   It is useless for you to worship me,
        when you teach rules made up by humans."

What Really Makes People Unclean
(Mark 7.14-23)

¹⁰Jesus called the crowd together and said, "Pay attention and try to understand what I mean. ¹¹The food

---

ʷ*wash their hands:* The Jewish people had strict laws about washing their hands before eating, especially if they had been out in public.   ˣ*has been offered to God:* According to Jewish custom, when people said something was offered to God, it belonged to him and couldn't be used for anyone else, not even for their own parents.

that you put into your mouth doesn't make you unclean and unfit to worship God. The bad words that come out of your mouth are what make you unclean."

12Then his disciples came over to him and asked, "Do you know that you insulted the Pharisees by what you said?"

13Jesus answered, "Every plant that my Father in heaven didn't plant will be pulled up by the roots. 14Stay away from those Pharisees! They are like blind people leading other blind people, and all of them will fall into a ditch."

15Peter replied, "What did you mean when you talked about the things that make people unclean?"

16Jesus then said:

Don't any of you know what I'm talking about by now? 17Don't you know that the food you put into your mouth goes into your stomach and then out of your body? 18But the words that come out of your mouth come from your heart. And they are what make you unfit to worship God. 19Out of your heart come evil thoughts, murder, unfaithfulness in marriage, vulgar deeds, stealing, telling lies, and insulting others. 20These are what make you unclean. Eating without washing your hands won't make you unfit to worship God.

A Woman's Faith
(Mark 7.24-30)

21Jesus left and went to the territory near the cities of Tyre and Sidon. 22Suddenly a Canaanite woman[y] from there came out shouting, "Lord and Son of David,[z] have pity on me! My daughter is full of demons." 23Jesus didn't say a word. But the woman kept following along and shouting, so his disciples came up and asked him to send her away.

24Jesus said, "I was sent only to the people of Israel! They are like a flock of lost sheep."

---

[y]Canaanite woman: This woman was not Jewish.   [z]Son of David: See the note at 9.27.

25The woman came closer. Then she knelt down and begged, "Please help me, Lord!"

26Jesus replied, "It isn't right to take food away from children and feed it to dogs."*a*

27"Lord, that's true," the woman said, "but even dogs get the crumbs that fall from their owner's table."

28Jesus answered, "Dear woman, you really do have a lot of faith, and you will be given what you want." At that moment her daughter was healed.

Jesus Heals Many People

29From there, Jesus went along Lake Galilee. Then he climbed a hill and sat down. 30Large crowds came and brought many people who were crippled or blind or lame or unable to talk. They placed them, and many others, in front of Jesus, and he healed them all. 31Everyone was amazed at what they saw and heard. People who had never spoken could now speak. The lame were healed, the crippled could walk, and the blind were able to see. Everyone was praising the God of Israel.

Jesus Feeds 4000
(Mark 8.1-10)

32Jesus called his disciples together and told them, "I feel sorry for these people. They have been with me for three days, and they haven't got anything to eat. I don't want to send them away hungry. They might faint on their way home."

33His disciples said, "This place is like a desert. Where can we find enough food to feed such a crowd?"

34Jesus asked them how much food they had. They replied, "Seven small loaves of bread*b* and a few little fish."

35After Jesus had told the people to sit down, 36he took the seven loaves of bread and the fish and gave thanks. He then broke them and handed them to his disciples, who passed them around to the crowds.

37Everyone ate all they wanted, and the leftovers filled

*a*feed it to dogs: The Jewish people sometimes referred to Gentiles as dogs.
*b*small loaves of bread: See the note at 14.17.

seven large baskets.

38There were 4000 men who ate, not counting the women and children.

39After Jesus had sent the crowds away, he got into a boat and sailed across the lake. He came to shore near the town of Magadan.c

A Demand for a Sign from Heaven
(Mark 8.11-13; Luke 12.54-56)

16 1The Pharisees and Sadducees came to Jesus and tried to test him by asking for a sign from heaven. 2He told them:

If the sky is red in the evening, you say the weather will be good. 3But if the sky is red and gloomy in the morning, you say it's going to rain. You can tell what the weather will be like by looking at the sky. But you don't understand what is happening now.d 4You want a sign because you are evil and won't believe! But the only sign you'll be given is what happened to Jonah.e Then Jesus left.

The Yeast of the Pharisees and Sadducees
(Mark 8.14-21)

5The disciples had forgotten to bring any bread when they crossed the lake.f 6Jesus then warned them, "Watch out! Guard against the yeast of the Pharisees and Sadducees."

7The disciples talked this over and said to each other, "He must be saying this because we didn't bring along any bread."

8Jesus knew what they were thinking and said:

You certainly don't have much faith! Why are you talking about not having any bread? 9Don't you understand? Have you forgotten about the 5000 people and all those baskets of leftovers from just five loaves of bread? 10And what about the 4000 people

---

cMagadan: The location is unknown. dIf the sky is red...what is happening now: The words of Jesus in verses 2 and 3 are not in some manuscripts. ewhat happened to Jonah: Jonah was in the stomach of a big fish for three days and nights (see 12.40). fcrossed the lake: To the east side.

and all those baskets of leftovers from only seven loaves of bread? [11]Don't you know by now that I'm not talking to you about bread? Watch out for the yeast of the Pharisees and Sadducees!

[12]Finally, the disciples understood that Jesus wasn't talking about the yeast used to make bread, but about the teaching of the Pharisees and Sadducees.

Who Is Jesus?
(Mark 8.27-30; Luke 9.18-21)

[13]When Jesus and his disciples were near the town of Caesarea Philippi, he asked them, "What do people say about the Son of Man?"

[14]The disciples answered, "Some people say you are John the Baptist or maybe Elijah[g] or Jeremiah or some other prophet."

[15]Then Jesus asked them, "But who do you say I am?"

[16]Simon Peter spoke up, "You are the Messiah, the Son of the living God."

[17]Jesus told him:

Simon, son of Jonah, you are blessed! You didn't discover this on your own. It was shown to you by my Father in heaven. [18]So I will call you Peter, which means "a rock." On this rock I will build my church, and death itself won't have any power over it. [19]I will give you the keys to the kingdom of heaven, and God in heaven will allow whatever you allow on earth. But he won't allow anything that you don't allow.

[20]Jesus told his disciples not to tell anyone that he was the Messiah.

Jesus Speaks about His Suffering and Death
(Mark 8.31—9.1; Luke 9.22-27)

[21]From then on, Jesus began telling his disciples what would happen to him. He said, "I must go to Jerusalem. There the nation's leaders, the chief priests, and the teachers of the Law of Moses will make me suffer terribly. I will be killed, but three days later I'll rise to life."

gElijah: Many of the Jewish people expected the prophet Elijah to come and prepare the way for the Messiah.

²²Peter took Jesus aside and told him to stop talking like that. He said, "God would never let this happen to you, Lord!"

²³Jesus turned to Peter and said, "Satan, get away from me! You're in my way because you think like everyone else and not like God."

²⁴Then Jesus said to his disciples:

If any of you want to be my followers, you must forget about yourself. You must take up your cross and follow me. ²⁵If you want to save your life,*ʰ* you'll destroy it. But if you give up your life for me, you'll find it. ²⁶What will you gain, if you own the whole world but destroy yourself? What would you give to get back your soul?

²⁷The Son of Man will soon come in the glory of his Father and with his angels to reward all people for what they have done. ²⁸I promise you that some of those standing here won't die before they see the Son of Man coming with his kingdom.

The True Glory of Jesus
(Mark 9.2-13; Luke 9.28-36)

17 ¹Six days later Jesus took Peter and the brothers James and John with him. They went up on a very high mountain where they could be alone. ²There in front of the disciples, Jesus was completely changed. His face was shining like the sun, and his clothes became as white as light.

³All at once Moses and Elijah were there talking with Jesus. ⁴So Peter said to him, "Lord, it's good for us to be here! Let's make three shelters, one for you, one for Moses, and one for Elijah."

⁵While Peter was still speaking, the shadow of a bright cloud passed over them. From the cloud a voice said, "This is my own dear Son, and I am pleased with him. Listen to what he says!" ⁶When the disciples heard the voice, they were so afraid that they fell flat on the ground. ⁷But Jesus came over and touched them. He said,

---

ʰlife: In verses 25 and 26 the same Greek word is translated "life," "yourself," and "soul."

"Get up and don't be afraid!" [8]When they opened their eyes, they saw only Jesus.

[9]On their way down from the mountain, Jesus warned his disciples not to tell anyone what they had seen until after the Son of Man had been raised from death.

[10]The disciples asked Jesus, "Don't the teachers of the Law of Moses say that Elijah must come before the Messiah does?"

[11]Jesus told them, "Elijah certainly will come and get everything ready. [12]In fact, he has already come. But the people didn't recognise him and treated him just as they wanted to. They will soon make the Son of Man suffer in the same way." [13]Then the disciples understood that Jesus was talking to them about John the Baptist.

Jesus Heals a Boy
(Mark 9.14-29; Luke 9.37-43a).

[14]Jesus and his disciples returned to the crowd. A man knelt in front of him [15]and said, "Lord, have pity on my son! He has a bad case of epilepsy and often falls into a fire or into water. [16]I brought him to your disciples, but none of them could heal him."

[17]Jesus said, "You people are too stubborn to have any faith! How much longer must I be with you? Why do I have to put up with you? Bring the boy here." [18]Then Jesus spoke sternly to the demon. It went out of the boy, and right then he was healed.

[19]Later the disciples went to Jesus in private and asked him, "Why couldn't we force out the demon?"

[20-21]Jesus replied:

It's because you haven't got enough faith! But I can promise you this. If you had faith no larger than a mustard seed, you could tell this mountain to move from here to there. And it would. Everything would be possible for you.[i]

---

[i]*for you:* Some manuscripts add, "But the only way to force out that kind of demon is by praying and going without eating."

Jesus Again Speaks about His Death
(Mark 9.30-32; Luke 9.43b-45)

22While Jesus and his disciples were going from place to place in Galilee, he told them, "The Son of Man will be handed over to people 23who will kill him. But three days later he will rise to life." All of this made the disciples very sad.

Paying the Temple Tax

24When Jesus and the others arrived in Capernaum, the collectors for the temple tax came to Peter and asked, "Does your teacher pay the temple tax?"

25"Yes, he does," Peter answered.

After they had returned home, Jesus went up to Peter and asked him, "Simon, what do you think? Do the kings of this earth collect taxes and fees from their own people or from foreigners?"[j]

26Peter answered, "From foreigners."

Jesus replied, "Then their own people[k] don't have to pay. 27But we don't want to cause trouble. So go and cast a line into the lake and pull out the first fish you hook. Open its mouth, and you'll find a coin. Use it to pay your taxes and mine."

Who Is the Greatest?
(Mark 9.33-37; Luke 9.46-48)

18 1About this time the disciples came to Jesus and asked him who would be the greatest in the kingdom of heaven. 2Jesus called a child over and had the child stand near him. 3Then he said:

I promise you this. If you don't change and become like a child, you will never get into the kingdom of heaven. 4But if you are as humble as this child, you are the greatest in the kingdom of heaven. 5And when you welcome one of these children because of me, you welcome me.

---

[j]*from their own people or from foreigners:* Or "from their children or from others." [k]*From foreigners...their own people:* Or "From other people...their children."

Temptations To Sin
(Mark 9.42-48; Luke 17.1, 2)

⁶It will be terrible for people who cause even one of my little followers to sin. Those people would be better off thrown into the deepest part of the ocean with a heavy stone tied around their necks! ⁷The world is in for trouble because of the way it causes people to sin. There will always be something to cause people to sin, but anyone who does this will be in for trouble.

⁸If your hand or foot causes you to sin, chop it off and throw it away! You would be better off going into life crippled or lame than to have two hands or two feet and be thrown into the fire that never goes out. ⁹If your eye causes you to sin, poke it out and get rid of it. You would be better off going into life with only one eye than to have two eyes and be thrown into the fires of hell.

The Lost Sheep
(Luke 15.3-7)

¹⁰⁻¹¹Don't be cruel to any of these little ones! I promise you that their angels are always with my Father in heaven.ˡ ¹²Let me ask you this. What would you do if you had 100 sheep and one of them wandered off? Wouldn't you leave the 99 on the hillside to go and look for the one that had wandered away? ¹³I am sure that finding it would make you happier than having the 99 that never wandered off. ¹⁴That's how it is with your Father in heaven. He doesn't want any of these little ones to be lost.

When Someone Sins
(Luke 17.3)

¹⁵If one of my followersᵐ sins against you, go and point out what was wrong. But do it in private, just between the two of you. If that person listens, you

---

ˡin heaven: Some manuscripts add, "The Son of Man came to save people who are lost." ᵐfollowers: The Greek text has "brother," which is used here and elsewhere in this chapter to refer to a follower of Christ.

have won back a follower. [16]But if that one refuses to listen, take along one or two others. The Scriptures teach that every complaint must be proven true by two or more witnesses. [17]If the follower refuses to listen to them, report the matter to the church. Anyone who refuses to listen to the church must be treated like an unbeliever or a tax collector.[n]

Allowing and Not Allowing

[18]I promise you that God in heaven will allow whatever you allow on earth, but he won't allow anything you don't allow. [19]I promise that when any two of you on earth agree about something you are praying for, my Father in heaven will do it for you. [20]Whenever two or three of you come together in my name,[o] I am there with you.

An Official Who Refused To Forgive

[21]Peter came up to the Lord and asked, "How many times should I forgive someone[p] who does something wrong to me? Is seven times enough?"
[22]Jesus answered:
Not just 7 times, but 77 times![q] [23]This story will show you what the kingdom of heaven is like:
One day a king decided to call in his officials and ask them to give an account of what they owed him. [24]As he was doing this, one official was brought in who owed him 50 million silver coins. [25]But he didn't have any money to pay what he owed. The king ordered him to be sold, along with his wife and children and all he owned, in order to pay the debt.
[26]The official got down on his knees and began begging, "Have pity on me, and I will pay you every cent I owe!" [27]The king felt sorry for him and let him go free. He even told the official that he didn't have to pay back the money.

[n]tax collector: See the note at 5.46. [o]in my name: Or "as my followers."
[p]someone: Or "a follower." See the note at 18.15. [q]77 times: Or "70 times 7."
The large number means that one follower should never stop forgiving another.

²⁸As the official was leaving, he happened to meet another official, who owed him 100 silver coins. So he grabbed the man by the throat. He started choking him and said, "Pay me what you owe!"

²⁹The man got down on his knees and began begging, "Have pity on me, and I will pay you back." ³⁰But the first official refused to have pity. Instead, he went and had the other official put in jail until he could pay what he owed.

³¹When some other officials found out what had happened, they felt sorry for the man who had been put in jail. Then they told the king what had happened. ³²The king called the first official back in and said, "You're an evil man! When you begged for mercy, I said you didn't have to pay back a cent. ³³Don't you think you should show pity to someone else, as I did to you?" ³⁴The king was so angry that he ordered the official to be tortured until he could pay back everything he owed. ³⁵That is how my Father in heaven will treat you, if you don't forgive each of my followers with all your heart.

Teaching about Divorce
(Mark 10.1-12)

19 ¹When Jesus finished teaching, he left Galilee and went to the part of Judea that is east of the Jordan River. ²Large crowds followed him, and he healed their sick people.

³Some Pharisees wanted to test Jesus. They came up to him and asked, "Is it right for a man to divorce his wife for just any reason?"

⁴Jesus answered, "Don't you know that in the beginning the Creator made a man and a woman? ⁵That's why a man leaves his father and mother and gets married. He becomes like one person with his wife. ⁶Then they are no longer two people, but one. And no-one should separate a couple that God has joined together."

⁷The Pharisees asked Jesus, "Why did Moses say that a man could write out divorce papers and send his wife away?"

⁸Jesus replied, "You are so heartless! That's why Moses

allowed you to divorce your wife. But from the beginning God didn't intend it to be that way. 9I say that if your wife has not committed some terrible sexual sin,ʳ you must not divorce her to marry someone else. If you do, you are unfaithful."

10The disciples said, "If that's how it is between a man and a woman, it's better not to get married."

11Jesus told them, "Only those people who have been given the gift of staying single can accept this teaching. 12Some people are unable to marry because of birth defects or because of what someone has done to their bodies. Others stay single for the sake of the kingdom of heaven. Anyone who can accept this teaching should do so."

Jesus Blesses Little Children
(Mark 10.13-16; Luke 18.15-17)

13Some people brought their children to Jesus, so that he could place his hands on them and pray for them. His disciples told the people to stop bothering him. 14But Jesus said, "Let the children come to me, and don't try to stop them! People who are like these children belong to God's kingdom."ˢ 15After Jesus had placed his hands on the children, he left.

A Rich Young Man
(Mark 10.17-31; Luke 18.18-30)

16A man came to Jesus and asked, "Teacher, what good thing must I do to have eternal life?"

17Jesus said to him, "Why do you ask me about what is good? Only God is good. If you want to have eternal life, you must obey his commandments."

18"Which ones?" the man asked.

Jesus answered, "Do not murder. Be faithful in marriage. Do not steal. Do not tell lies about others. 19Respect your father and mother. And love others as much as you love yourself." 20The young man said, "I've

---

ʳsome terrible sexual sin: See the note at 5.32.   ˢPeople who are like these children belong to God's kingdom: Or "God's kingdom belongs to people who are like these children."

obeyed all of these. What else must I do?"

²¹Jesus replied, "If you want to be perfect, go and sell everything you own! Give the money to the poor, and you will have riches in heaven. Then come and be my follower." ²²When the young man heard this, he was sad, because he was very rich.

²³Jesus said to his disciples, "It's terribly hard for rich people to get into the kingdom of heaven! ²⁴In fact, it's easier for a camel to go through the eye of a needle than for a rich person to get into God's kingdom."

²⁵When the disciples heard this, they were greatly surprised and asked, "How can anyone ever be saved?"

²⁶Jesus looked straight at them and said, "There are some things that people can't do, but God can do anything."

²⁷Peter replied, "Remember, we've left everything to be your followers! What will we get?"

²⁸Jesus answered:

Yes, all of you have become my followers. And so in the future world, when the Son of Man sits on his glorious throne, I promise that you will sit on 12 thrones to judge the 12 tribes of Israel. ²⁹All who have given up home or brothers and sisters or father and mother or children or land for me will be given 100 times as much. They will also have eternal life. ³⁰But many who are now first will be last, and many who are last will be first.

Workers in a Vineyard

20 ¹As Jesus was speaking about what the kingdom of heaven would be like, he said:

Early one morning a man went out to hire some workers for his vineyard. ²After he had agreed to pay them the usual amount for a day's work, he sent them off to his vineyard.

³About nine that morning, the man saw some other people standing in the market with nothing to do. ⁴He said he would pay them what was fair, if they would work in his vineyard. ⁵So they went.

At midday and again about three in the afternoon he returned to the market. And each time he made the same agreement with others who were loafing around with nothing to do.

⁶Finally, about five in the afternoon the man went back and found some others standing there. He asked them, "Why have you been standing here all day long doing nothing?"

⁷"Because no-one has hired us," they answered. Then he told them to go and work in his vineyard.

⁸That evening the owner of the vineyard told the man in charge of the workers to call them in and give them their money. He also told the man to begin with the ones who were hired last. ⁹When the workers arrived, the ones who had been hired at five in the afternoon were given a full day's pay.

¹⁰The workers who had been hired first thought they would be given more than the others. But when they were given the same, ¹¹they began complaining to the owner of the vineyard. ¹²They said, "The ones who were hired last worked for only one hour. But you paid them the same that you did us. And we worked in the hot sun all day long!"

¹³The owner answered one of them, "Friend, I didn't cheat you. I paid you exactly what we agreed on. ¹⁴Take your money now and go! What business is it of yours if I want to pay them the same that I paid you? ¹⁵Don't I have the right to do what I want with my own money? Why should you be jealous, if I want to be generous?"

¹⁶Jesus then said, "So it is. Everyone who is now first will be last, and everyone who is last will be first."

Jesus Again Tells about His Death
(Mark 10.32-34; Luke 18.31-34)

¹⁷As Jesus was on his way to Jerusalem, he took his twelve disciples aside and told them in private:˙

¹⁸We are now on our way to Jerusalem, where the Son of Man will be handed over to the chief priests and the teachers of the Law of Moses. They'll sentence him to death, ¹⁹and then they'll hand him over to foreigners˙ who will make fun of him. They'll beat him

---

ᵗforeigners: The Romans, who ruled Judea at this time.

and nail him to a cross. But on the third day he'll rise from death.

A Mother's Request
(Mark 10.35-45)

[20]The mother of James and John[u] came to Jesus with her two sons. She knelt down and started begging him to do something for her. [21]Jesus asked her what she wanted, and she said, "When you come into your kingdom, please let one of my sons sit at your right side and the other at your left."[v]

[22]Jesus answered, "Not one of you knows what you are asking. Are you able to drink from the cup[w] that I must soon drink from?"

James and John said, "Yes, we are!"

[23]Jesus replied, "You certainly will drink from my cup! But it isn't for me to say who will sit at my right side and at my left. That is for my Father to say."

[24]When the ten other disciples heard this, they were angry with the two brothers. [25]But Jesus called the disciples together and said:

You know that foreign rulers like to order their people around. And their great leaders have full power over everyone they rule. [26]But don't act like them. If you want to be great, you must be the servant of all the others. [27]And if you want to be first, you must be the slave of the rest. [28]The Son of Man did not come to be a slave master, but a slave who will give his life to rescue[x] many people.

Jesus Heals Two Blind Men
(Mark 10.46-52; Luke 18.35-43)

[29]Jesus was followed by a large crowd as he and his disciples were leaving Jericho. [30]Two blind men were sitting beside the road. And when they heard that Jesus

---

[u]mother of James and John: The Greek text has "mother of the sons of Zebedee" (see 26.37). [v]right side...left: The most powerful people in a kingdom sat at the right and left side of the king. [w]cup: In the Scriptures a cup is sometimes used as a symbol of suffering. To "drink from the cup" is to suffer. [x]rescue: The Greek word often means the payment of a price to free a slave or a prisoner.

was coming their way, they shouted, "Lord and Son of David,[y] have pity on us!"

31The crowd told them to be quiet, but they shouted even louder, "Lord and Son of David, have pity on us!"

32When Jesus heard them, he stopped and asked, "What do you want me to do for you?"

33They answered, "Lord, we want to see!"

34Jesus felt sorry for them and touched their eyes. Straight away they could see, and they became his followers.

Jesus Enters Jerusalem
(Mark 11.1-11; Luke 19.28-38; John 12.12-19)

21 1When Jesus and his disciples came near Jerusalem, he went to Bethphage on the Mount of Olives and sent two of them on ahead. 2He told them, "Go into the next village, where you will at once find a donkey and her colt. Untie the two donkeys and bring them to me. 3If anyone asks why you're doing that, just say, 'The Lord[z] needs them.' Straight away he'll let you have the donkeys."

4So God's promise came true, just as the prophet had said,

5   "Announce to the people of Jerusalem:
        'Your king is coming to you!
    He is humble and rides on a donkey.
        He comes on the colt of a donkey.' "

6The disciples left and did what Jesus had told them to do. 7They brought the donkey and its colt and laid some clothes on their backs. Then Jesus got on.

8Many people spread clothes in the road, while others put down branches[a] which they had cut from trees. 9Some people walked ahead of Jesus and others followed behind. They were all shouting,

    "Hooray[b] for the Son of David![c]

---

[y]Son of David: See the note at 9.27.   [z]The Lord: Or "The master of the donkeys."   [a]spread clothes...put down branches: This was one way that the Jewish people welcomed a famous person.   [b]Hooray: This translates a word that can mean "please save us." But it is most often used as a shout of praise to God.   [c]Son of David: See the note at 9.27.

God bless the one who comes
in the name of the Lord.
Hooray for God in heaven above!"

¹⁰When Jesus came to Jerusalem, everyone in the city was excited and asked, "Who can this be?"

¹¹The crowd answered, "This is Jesus, the prophet from Nazareth in Galilee."

Jesus in the Temple
(Mark 11.15-19; Luke 19.45-48; John 2.13-22)

¹²Jesus went into the temple and chased out everyone who was selling or buying. He turned over the tables of the money-changers and the benches of the ones who were selling doves. ¹³He told them, "The Scriptures say, 'My house should be called a place of worship.' But you've turned it into a place where robbers hide."

¹⁴Blind and lame people came to Jesus in the temple, and he healed them. ¹⁵But the chief priests and the teachers of the Law of Moses were angry when they saw his miracles and heard the children shouting praises to the Son of David. ¹⁶The men said to Jesus, "Don't you hear what those children are saying?"

"Yes, I do!" Jesus answered. "Don't you know that the Scriptures say, 'Children and infants will sing praises'?" ¹⁷Then Jesus left the city and went out to the village of Bethany, where he spent the night.

Jesus Puts a Curse on a Fig Tree
(Mark 11.12-14, 20-24)

¹⁸When Jesus got up the next morning, he was hungry. He started out for the city, ¹⁹and along the way he saw a fig tree. But when he came to it, he found only leaves and no figs. So he told the tree, "You will never again grow any fruit!" Just then the fig tree dried up.

²⁰The disciples were shocked when they saw how quickly the tree had dried up. ²¹But Jesus said to them, "If you have faith and don't doubt, I promise that you can do what I did to this tree. And you will be able to do even more. You can tell this mountain to get up and jump into the sea, and it will. ²²If you have faith when you pray, you will be given whatever you ask for."

A Question about Jesus' Authority
(Mark 11.27-33; Luke 20.1-8)

23Jesus had gone into the temple and was teaching when the chief priests and the leaders of the people came up to him. They asked, "What right do you have to do these things? Who gave you this authority?"

24Jesus answered, "I have just one question to ask you. If you answer it, I'll tell you where I got the right to do these things. 25Who gave John the right to baptise? Was it God in heaven or merely some human being?"

They thought it over and said to each other, "We can't say that God gave John this right. Jesus will ask us why we didn't believe John. 26On the other hand, these people think that John was a prophet, and we're afraid of what they might do to us. That's why we can't say that it was merely some human who gave John the right to baptise." 27So they told Jesus, "We don't know."

Jesus said, "Then I won't tell you who gave me the right to do what I do."

A Story about Two Sons

28Jesus said:

I'll tell you a story about a man who had two sons. Then you can tell me what you think. The father went to the older son and said, "Go and work in the vineyard today!" 29His son told him that he wouldn't do it, but later he changed his mind and went. 30The man then told his younger son to go and work in the vineyard. The boy said he would, but he didn't go. 31Which one of the sons obeyed his father?

"The older one," the chief priests and leaders answered. Then Jesus told them:

You can be sure that tax collectors[d] and prostitutes will get into the kingdom of God before you ever will! 32When John the Baptist showed you how to do right, you wouldn't believe him. But these evil people did believe. And even when you saw what they did, you still wouldn't change your minds and believe.

[d]tax collectors: See the note at 5.46.

Tenants of a Vineyard
(Mark 12.1-12; Luke 20.9-19)

33Jesus told the chief priests and leaders to listen to this story:

A land owner once planted a vineyard. He built a wall around it and dug a pit to crush the grapes in. He also built a lookout tower. Then he rented out his vineyard and left the country.

34When it was harvest time, the owner sent some servants to get his share of the grapes. 35But the tenants grabbed those servants. They beat one up, killed one, and stoned one of them to death. 36He then sent more servants than he did the first time. But the tenants treated them in the same way.

37Finally, the owner sent his own son to the tenants, because he thought they would respect him. 38But when they saw the man's son, they said, "Some day he will own the vineyard. Let's kill him! Then we can have it all for ourselves." 39So they grabbed him, threw him out of the vineyard, and killed him.

40Jesus asked, "When the owner of that vineyard comes, what do you suppose he'll do to those tenants?"

41The chief priests and leaders answered, "He'll kill them in some horrible way. Then he'll rent out his vineyard to people who will give him his share of grapes at harvest time."

42Jesus replied, "You surely know that the Scriptures say,
'The stone that the builders tossed aside
    is now the most important stone of all.
This is something the Lord has done,
    and it is amazing to us.'
43I tell you that God's kingdom will be taken from you and given to people who will do what he demands. 44Anyone who stumbles over this stone will be crushed, and anyone it falls on will be smashed to pieces."e

45When the chief priests and the Pharisees heard these stories, they knew that Jesus was talking about them. 46So they looked for a way to arrest Jesus. But they were afraid to, because the people thought he was a prophet.

epieces: Verse 44 is not in some manuscripts.

The Great Banquet
(Luke 14.15-24)

22 ¹Once again Jesus used stories to teach the people: ²The kingdom of heaven is like what happened when a king gave a wedding banquet for his son. ³The king sent some servants to tell the invited guests to come to the banquet, but the guests refused. ⁴He sent other servants to say to the guests, "The banquet is ready! My cattle and prize calves have all been prepared. Everything is ready. Come to the banquet!"

⁵But the guests didn't pay any attention. Some of them left for their farms, and some went to their places of business. ⁶Others grabbed the servants, then beat them up and killed them.

⁷This made the king so furious that he sent an army to kill those murderers and burn down their city. ⁸Then he said to the servants, "It's time for the wedding banquet, and the invited guests don't deserve to come. ⁹Go out to the street corners and tell everyone you meet to come to the banquet." ¹⁰They went out on the streets and brought in everyone they could find, good and bad alike. And the banquet room was filled with guests.

¹¹When the king went in to meet the guests, he found that one of them wasn't wearing the right kind of clothes for the wedding. ¹²The king asked, "Friend, why didn't you wear proper clothes for the wedding?" But the guest had no excuse. ¹³So the king gave orders for that person to be tied hand and foot and to be thrown outside into the dark. That's where people will cry and grit their teeth in pain. ¹⁴Many are invited, but only a few are chosen.

Paying Taxes
(Mark 12.13-17; Luke 20.20-26)

¹⁵The Pharisees got together and planned how they could trick Jesus into saying something wrong. ¹⁶They sent some of their followers and some of Herod's followers[f] to say to him, "Teacher, we know that you are

---

[f]*Herod's followers:* People who were political followers of the family of Herod the Great (see 2.1) and his son Herod Antipas (see 14.1), and who wanted Herod to be king in Jerusalem.

honest. You teach the truth about what God wants people to do. And you treat everyone with the same respect, no matter who they are. ¹⁷Tell us what you think! Should we pay taxes to the Emperor or not?"

¹⁸Jesus knew their evil thoughts and said, "Why are you trying to test me? You show-offs! ¹⁹Let me see one of the coins used for paying taxes." They brought him a silver coin, ²⁰and he asked, "Whose picture and name are on it?"

²¹"The Emperor's," they answered.

Then Jesus told them, "Give the Emperor what belongs to him and give God what belongs to God." ²²His answer surprised them so much that they walked away.

Life in the Future World
(Mark 12.18-27; Luke 20.27-40)

²³The Sadducees did not believe that people would rise to life after death. So that same day some of the Sadducees came to Jesus and said:

²⁴Teacher, Moses wrote that if a married man dies and has no children, his brother should marry the widow. Their first son would then be thought of as the son of the dead brother.

²⁵Once there were seven brothers who lived here. The first one married, but died without having any children. So his wife was left to his brother. ²⁶The same thing happened to the second and third brothers and finally to all seven of them. ²⁷At last the woman died. ²⁸When God raises people from death, whose wife will this woman be? She had been married to all seven brothers.

²⁹Jesus answered:

You are completely wrong! You don't know what the Scriptures teach. And you don't know anything about the power of God. ³⁰When God raises people to life, they won't marry. They will be like the angels in heaven. ³¹And as for people being raised to life, God was speaking to you when he said, ³²"I am the God worshipped by Abraham, Isaac, and Jacob."^g He isn't

---

^g*I am the God worshipped by Abraham, Isaac, and Jacob:* Jesus argues that if God is worshipped by these three, they must still be alive, because he is the God of the living.

the God of the dead, but of the living.
³³The crowds were surprised to hear what Jesus was teaching.

The Most Important Commandment
(Mark 12.28-34; Luke 10.25-28)

³⁴After Jesus had made the Sadducees look foolish, the Pharisees heard about it and got together. ³⁵One of them was an expert in the Jewish Law. So he tried to test Jesus by asking, ³⁶"Teacher, what is the most important commandment in the Law?"

³⁷Jesus answered:

Love the Lord your God with all your heart, soul, and mind. ³⁸This is the first and most important commandment. ³⁹The second most important commandment is like this one. And it is, "Love others as much as you love yourself." ⁴⁰All the Law of Moses and the Books of the Prophets[h] are based on these two commandments.

About David's Son
(Mark 12.35-37; Luke 20.41-44)

⁴¹While the Pharisees were still there, Jesus asked them, ⁴²"What do you think about the Messiah? Whose family will he come from?"

They answered, "He will be a son of King David."[i]

⁴³Jesus replied, "How then could the Spirit lead David to call the Messiah his Lord? David said,

⁴⁴   'The Lord said to my Lord:
    Sit at my right side[j]
        until I make your enemies
        into a footstool for you.'

⁴⁵If David called the Messiah his Lord, how can the Messiah be a son of King David?" ⁴⁶No one was able to give Jesus an answer, and from that day on, no-one dared ask him any more questions.

---

[h]the Law of Moses and the Books of the Prophets: The Jewish Scriptures, that is, the Old Testament. [i]son of King David: See the note at 9.27. [j]right side: The place of power and honour.

Jesus Condemns the Pharisees
and the Teachers of the Law of Moses
(Mark 12.38-40; Luke 11.37-52; 20.45-47)

23 ¹Jesus said to the crowds and to his disciples: ²The Pharisees and the teachers of the Law are experts in the Law of Moses. ³So obey everything they teach you, but don't do as they do. After all, they say one thing and do something else.

⁴They pile heavy burdens on people's shoulders and won't lift a finger to help. ⁵Everything they do is just to show off in front of others. They even make a big show of wearing Scripture verses on their foreheads and arms, and they wear big tassels*ᵏ* for everyone to see. ⁶They love the best seats at banquets and the front seats in the meeting places. ⁷And when they are in the market, they like to have people greet them as their teachers.

⁸But none of you should be called a teacher. You have only one teacher, and all of you are like brothers and sisters. ⁹Don't call anyone on earth your father. All of you have the same Father in heaven. ¹⁰None of you should be called the leader. The Messiah is your only leader. ¹¹Whoever is the greatest should be the servant of the others. ¹²If you put yourself above others, you will be put down. But if you humble yourself, you will be honoured.

¹³⁻¹⁴You Pharisees and teachers of the Law of Moses are in for trouble! You're nothing but show-offs. You lock people out of the kingdom of heaven. You won't go in yourselves, and you keep others from going in.*ˡ*

¹⁵You Pharisees and teachers of the Law of Moses are in for trouble! You're nothing but show-offs. You travel over land and sea to win one follower. And when

---

ᵏwearing Scripture verses...tassels: As a sign of their love for the Lord and his teachings, the Jewish people had started wearing Scripture verses in small leather boxes. But the Pharisees tried to show off by making the boxes bigger than necessary.   *ˡfrom going in:* Some manuscripts add, "You Pharisees and teachers are in for trouble! And you're nothing but show-offs! You cheat widows out of their homes and then pray long prayers just to show off. So you will be punished most of all."

you've done so, you make that person twice as fit for hell as you are.

¹⁶You're in for trouble! You are supposed to lead others, but you are blind. You teach that it doesn't matter if a person swears by the temple. But you say that it does matter if someone swears by the gold in the temple. ¹⁷You blind fools! Which is greater, the gold or the temple that makes the gold sacred?

¹⁸You also teach that it doesn't matter if a person swears by the altar. But you say that it does matter if someone swears by the gift on the altar. ¹⁹Are you blind? Which is more important, the gift or the altar that makes the gift sacred? ²⁰Anyone who swears by the altar also swears by everything on it. ²¹And anyone who swears by the temple also swears by God, who lives there. ²²To swear by heaven is the same as swearing by God's throne and by the one who sits on that throne.

²³You Pharisees and teachers are show-offs, and you're in for trouble! You give God a tenth of the spices from your garden, such as mint, dill, and cumin. Yet you neglect the more important matters of the Law, such as justice, mercy, and faithfulness. These are the important things you should have done, though you should not have left the others undone either. ²⁴You blind leaders! You strain out a small fly but swallow a camel.

²⁵You Pharisees and teachers are show-offs, and you're in for trouble! You wash the outside of your cups and dishes, while inside there is nothing but greed and selfishness. ²⁶You blind Pharisee! First clean the inside of a cup, and then the outside will also be clean.

²⁷You Pharisees and teachers are in for trouble! You're nothing but show-offs. You are like tombs that have been whitewashed.ᵐ On the outside they are beautiful, but inside they are full of bones and filth. ²⁸That's what you are like. Outside you look good, but

---

ᵐwhitewashed: Tombs were whitewashed to keep anyone from accidentally touching them. A person who touched a dead body or a tomb was considered unclean and could not worship with the rest of the Jewish people.

inside you are evil and only pretend to be good.

²⁹You Pharisees and teachers are nothing but show-offs, and you're in for trouble! You build monuments for the prophets and decorate the tombs of good people. ³⁰And you claim that you would not have taken part with your ancestors in killing the prophets. ³¹But you prove that you really are the relatives of the ones who killed the prophets. ³²So keep on doing everything they did. ³³You are nothing but snakes and the children of snakes! How can you escape going to hell?

³⁴I will send prophets and wise people and experts in the Law of Moses to you. But you will kill them or nail them to a cross or beat them in your meeting places or chase them from town to town. ³⁵That's why you will be held guilty for the murder of every good person, beginning with the good man Abel. This also includes Barachiah's son Zechariah,ⁿ the man you murdered between the temple and the altar. ³⁶I can promise that you people living today will be punished for all these things!

Jesus Loves Jerusalem
(Luke 13.34, 35)

³⁷Jerusalem, Jerusalem! Your people have killed the prophets and have stoned the messengers who were sent to you. I've often wanted to gather your people, as a hen gathers her chicks under her wings. But you wouldn't let me. ³⁸And now your temple will be deserted. ³⁹You won't see me again until you say,

"Blessed is the one who comes
      in the name of the Lord."

The Temple Will Be Destroyed
(Mark 13.1, 2; Luke 21.5, 6)

24 ¹After Jesus left the temple, his disciples came over and said, "Look at all these buildings!"

²Jesus replied, "Do you see these buildings? They will

ⁿ*Zechariah:* Genesis is the first book in the Jewish Scriptures, and it records that Abel was the first person to be murdered (see Genesis 4.8). Second Chronicles is the last book in the Jewish Scriptures, and the last murder that it tells about is that of Zechariah (see 2 Chronicles 24.20-21).

certainly be torn down! Not one stone will be left in place."

Warning about Trouble
(Mark 13.3-13; Luke 21.7-19)

³Later, as Jesus was sitting on the Mount of Olives, his disciples came to him in private and asked, "When will this happen? What will be the sign of your coming and of the end of the world?"

⁴Jesus answered:

Don't let anyone fool you. ⁵Many will come and claim to be me. They will say that they are the Messiah, and they will fool many people.

⁶You will soon hear about wars and threats of wars, but don't be afraid. These things will have to happen first, but that isn't the end. ⁷Nations and kingdoms will go to war against each other. People will starve to death, and in some places there will be earthquakes. ⁸But this is just the beginning of troubles.

⁹You will be arrested, punished, and even killed. Because of me, you will be hated by people of all nations. ¹⁰Many will give up and will betray and hate each other. ¹¹Many false prophets will come and fool a lot of people. ¹²Evil will spread and cause many people to stop loving others. ¹³But if you keep on being faithful right to the end, you will be saved. ¹⁴When the good news about the kingdom has been preached all over the world and told to all nations, the end will come.

The Horrible Thing
(Mark 13.14-23; Luke 21.20-24)

¹⁵Some day you will see that "Horrible Thing" in the holy place, just as the prophet Daniel said. Everyone who reads this must try to understand! ¹⁶If you are living in Judea at that time, run to the mountains. ¹⁷If you are on the roofº of your house,

---

ºroof: In Palestine the houses usually had a flat roof. Stairs on the outside led up to the roof, which was made of beams and boards covered with packed earth.

don't go inside to get anything. ¹⁸If you are out in the field, don't go back for your coat. ¹⁹It will be a terrible time for women who are expecting babies or nursing young children. ²⁰And pray that you won't have to escape in winter or on a Sabbath.ᵖ ²¹This will be the worst time of suffering since the beginning of the world, and nothing this terrible will ever happen again. ²²If God doesn't make the time shorter, no-one will be left alive. But because of God's chosen ones, he will make the time shorter.

²³Someone may say, "Here is the Messiah!" or "There he is!" But don't believe it. ²⁴False messiahs and false prophets will come and work great miracles and signs. They will even try to fool God's chosen ones. ²⁵But I have warned you ahead of time. ²⁶If you are told that the Messiah is out in the desert, don't go there! And if you are told that he is in some secret place, don't believe it! ²⁷The coming of the Son of Man will be like lightning that can be seen from east to west. ²⁸Where there is a corpse, there will always be vultures.�q

When the Son of Man Appears
(Mark 13.24-27; Luke 21.25-28)

²⁹Straight after those days of suffering,
"The sun will become dark,
    and the moon will no longer shine.
The stars will fall,
    and the powers in the skyʳ will be shaken."
³⁰Then a sign will appear in the sky. And there will be the Son of Man.ˢ All nations on earth will weep when they see the Son of Man coming on the clouds of heaven with power and great glory. ³¹At the sound

---

ᵖin winter or on a Sabbath: In Palestine the winters are cold and rainy and make travel difficult. The Jewish people were not allowed to travel for more than a kilometre on the Sabbath. For these reasons it was hard for them to escape from their enemies in the winter or on a Sabbath. qvultures: This may mean that when anything important happens, people soon know about it. Or it may mean that whenever something bad happens, curious people gather around and stare. But the word translated "vulture" also means "eagle" and may refer to the Roman army, which had an eagle as its symbol. ʳthe powers in the sky: In ancient times people thought that the stars were spiritual powers. ˢAnd there will be the Son of Man: Or "And it will be the Son of Man."

of a loud trumpet, he will send his angels to bring his chosen ones together from all over the earth.

A Lesson from a Fig Tree
(Mark 13.28-31; Luke 21.29-33)

³²Learn a lesson from a fig tree. When its branches sprout and start putting out leaves, you know that summer is near. ³³So when you see all these things happening, you will know that the time has almost come.ᵗ ³⁴I can promise you that some of the people of this generation will still be alive when all this happens. ³⁵The sky and the earth won't last for ever, but my words will.

No-one Knows the Day or Time
(Mark 13.32-37; Luke 17.26-30, 34-36)

³⁶No-one knows the day or hour. The angels in heaven don't know, and the Son himself doesn't know.ᵘ Only the Father knows. ³⁷When the Son of Man appears, things will be just as they were when Noah lived. ³⁸People were eating, drinking, and getting married right up to the day that the flood came and Noah went into the big boat. ³⁹They didn't know anything was happening until the flood came and swept them all away. That is how it will be when the Son of Man appears.

⁴⁰Two men will be in the same field, but only one will be taken. The other will be left. ⁴¹Two women will be together grinding grain, but only one will be taken. The other will be left. ⁴²So be on your guard! You don't know when your Lord will come. ⁴³Home owners never know when a thief is coming, and they are always on guard to keep one from breaking in. ⁴⁴Always be ready! You don't know when the Son of Man will come.

Faithful and Unfaithful Servants
(Luke 12.35-48)

⁴⁵Who are faithful and wise servants? Who are the ones the master will put in charge of giving the other

---

ᵗthe time has almost come: Or "he (that is, the Son of Man) will soon be here."
ᵘand the Son himself doesn't know: These words are not in some manuscripts.

servants their food supplies at the proper time? [46]Servants are fortunate if their master comes and finds them doing their job. [47]You may be sure that a servant who is always faithful will be put in charge of everything the master owns. [48]But suppose one of the servants thinks that the master won't return until late. [49]Suppose that evil servant starts beating the other servants and eats and drinks with people who are drunk. [50]If that happens, the master will surely come on a day and at a time when the servant least expects him. [51]That servant will then be punished and thrown out with the ones who only pretended to serve their master. There they will cry and grit their teeth in pain.

A Story about Ten Girls

25 [1]The kingdom of heaven is like what happened one night when ten girls took their oil lamps and went to a wedding to meet the groom.[v] [2]Five of the girls were foolish and five were wise. [3]The foolish ones took their lamps, but no extra oil. [4]The ones who were wise took along extra oil for their lamps.

[5]The groom was late arriving, and the girls became drowsy and fell asleep. [6]Then in the middle of the night someone shouted, "Here's the groom! Come and meet him!"

[7]When the girls got up and started getting their lamps ready, [8]the foolish ones said to the others, "Let us have some of your oil! Our lamps are going out."

[9]The girls who were wise answered, "There's not enough oil for all of us! Go and buy some for yourselves."

[10]While the foolish girls were on their way to get some oil, the groom arrived. The girls who were ready went into the wedding, and the doors were closed. [11]Later the other girls returned and shouted, "Sir, sir! Open the door for us!"

[12]But the groom replied, "I don't even know you!"

---

[v]*to meet the groom:* Some manuscripts add "and the bride." It was the custom for the groom to go to the home of the bride's parents to get his bride. Young girls and other guests would then go with them to the home of the groom's parents, where the wedding feast would take place.

¹³So, my disciples, always be ready! You don't know the day or the time when all this will happen.

A Story about Three Servants
(Luke 19.11-27)

¹⁴The kingdom is also like what happened when a man went away and put his three servants in charge of all he owned. ¹⁵The man knew what each servant could do. So he handed 5000 coins to the first servant, 2000 to the second, and 1000 to the third. Then he left the country.

¹⁶As soon as the man had gone, the servant with the 5000 coins used them to earn 5000 more. ¹⁷The servant who had 2000 coins did the same with his money and earned 2000 more. ¹⁸But the servant with 1000 coins dug a hole and hid his master's money in the ground.

¹⁹Some time later the master of those servants returned. He called them in and asked what they had done with his money. ²⁰The servant who had been given 5000 coins brought them in with the 5000 that he had earned. He said, "Sir, you gave me 5000 coins, and I've earned 5000 more."

²¹"Wonderful!" his master replied. "You're a good and faithful servant. I left you in charge of only a little, but now I'll put you in charge of much more. Come and share in my happiness!"

²²Next, the servant who had been given 2000 coins came in and said, "Sir, you gave me 2000 coins, and I've earned 2000 more."

²³"Wonderful!" his master replied. "You're a good and faithful servant. I left you in charge of only a little, but now I'll put you in charge of much more. Come and share in my happiness!"

²⁴The servant who had been given 1000 coins then came in and said, "Sir, I know that you are hard to get along with. You harvest what you don't plant and gather crops where you haven't scattered seed. ²⁵I was frightened and went out and hid your money in the ground. Here is every single coin!"

²⁶The master of the servant told him, "You're lazy

and good for nothing! You know that I harvest what I don't plant and gather crops where I haven't scattered seed. [27] You could have at least put my money in the bank, so that I could have earned interest on it."

[28] Then the master said, "Now your money will be taken away and given to the servant with 10 000 coins! [29] Everyone who has something will be given more, and they will have more than enough. But everything will be taken from those who haven't got anything. [30] You are a worthless servant, and you will be thrown out into the dark where people will cry and grit their teeth in pain."

The Final Judgment

[31] When the Son of Man comes in his glory with all of his angels, he will sit on his royal throne. [32] The people of all nations will be brought before him, and he will separate them, as shepherds separate their sheep from their goats.

[33] He will place the sheep on his right and the goats on his left. [34] Then the king will say to those on his right, "My father has blessed you! Come and receive the kingdom that was prepared for you before the world was created. [35] When I was hungry, you gave me something to eat, and when I was thirsty, you gave me something to drink. When I was a stranger, you welcomed me, [36] and when I was naked, you gave me clothes to wear. When I was sick, you took care of me, and when I was in jail, you visited me."

[37] Then the ones who pleased the Lord will ask, "When did we give you something to eat or drink? [38] When did we welcome you as a stranger or give you clothes to wear [39] or visit you while you were sick or in jail?"

[40] The king will answer, "Whenever you did it for any of my people, no matter how unimportant they seemed, you did it for me."

[41] Then the king will say to those on his left, "Get away from me! You are under God's curse. Go into the everlasting fire prepared for the devil and his angels! [42] I was hungry, but you didn't give me anything to

eat, and I was thirsty, but you didn't give me anything to drink. [43]I was a stranger, but you didn't welcome me, and I was naked, but you didn't give me any clothes to wear. I was sick and in jail, but you didn't take care of me."

[44]Then the people will ask, "Lord, when did we fail to help you when you were hungry or thirsty or a stranger or naked or sick or in jail?"

[45]The king will say to them, "Whenever you failed to help any of my people, no matter how unimportant they seemed, you failed to do it for me."

[46]Then Jesus said, "Those people will be punished for ever. But the ones who pleased God will have eternal life."

The Plot To Kill Jesus
(Mark 14.1, 2; Luke 22.1, 2; John 11.45-53)

26 [1]When Jesus had finished teaching, he told his disciples, [2]"You know that two days from now will be Passover. That is when the Son of Man will be handed over to his enemies and nailed to a cross."

[3]At that time the chief priests and the nation's leaders were meeting at the home of Caiaphas the high priest. [4]They planned how they could sneak around and have Jesus arrested and put to death. [5]But they said, "We mustn't do it during Passover, because the people will riot."

At Bethany
(Mark 14.3-9; John 12.1-8)

[6]Jesus was in the town of Bethany, eating at the home of Simon, who had leprosy.[w] [7]A woman came in with a bottle of expensive perfume and poured it on Jesus' head. [8]But when his disciples saw this, they became angry and complained, "Why such a waste? [9]We could have sold this perfume for a lot of money and given it to the poor."

[10]Jesus knew what they were thinking, and he said:

Why are you bothering this woman? She has done a

---

w/leprosy: See the note at 8.2.

beautiful thing for me. [11]You will always have the poor with you, but you won't always have me. [12]She has poured perfume on my body to prepare it for burial.[x] [13]You may be sure that wherever the good news is told all over the world, people will remember what she has done. And they will tell others.

Judas and the Chief Priests
(Mark 14.10, 11; Luke 22.3-6)

[14]Judas Iscariot[y] was one of the twelve disciples. He went to the chief priests [15]and asked, "How much will you give me if I help you arrest Jesus?" They paid Judas 30 silver coins, [16]and from then on he started looking for a good chance to betray Jesus.

Jesus Eats the Passover Meal with His Disciples
(Mark 14.12-21; Luke 22.7-13; John 13.21-30)

[17]On the first day of the Festival of Thin Bread, Jesus' disciples came to him and asked, "Where do you want us to prepare the Passover meal?"

[18]Jesus told them to go to a certain man in the city and tell him, "Our teacher says, 'My time has come! I want to eat the Passover meal with my disciples in your home.' " [19]They did as Jesus told them and prepared the meal.

[20-21]When Jesus was eating with his twelve disciples that evening, he said, "One of you will surely hand me over to my enemies."

[22]The disciples were very sad, and each one said to Jesus, "Lord, you can't mean me!"

[23]He answered, "One of you men who has eaten with me from this dish will betray me. [24]The Son of Man will die, as the Scriptures say. But it's going to be terrible for the one who betrays me! That man would be better off if he had never been born."

[25]Judas said, "Teacher, you surely don't mean me!"

---

[x]*poured perfume on my body to prepare it for burial:* The Jewish people taught that giving someone a proper burial was even more important than helping the poor. [y]*Iscariot:* See the note at 10.4.

"That's what you say!" Jesus replied. But later, Judas did betray him.

The Lord's Supper
(Mark 14.22-26; Luke 22.14-23; 1 Corinthians 11.23-25)

26During the meal Jesus took some bread in his hands. He blessed the bread and broke it. Then he gave it to his disciples and said, "Take this and eat it. This is my body."

27Jesus picked up a cup of wine and gave thanks to God. He then gave it to his disciples and said, "Take this and drink it. 28This is my blood, and with it God makes his agreement with you. It will be poured out, so that many people will have their sins forgiven. 29From now on I'm not going to drink any wine, until I drink new wine with you in my Father's kingdom." 30Then they sang a hymn and went out to the Mount of Olives.

Peter's Promise
(Mark 14.27-31; Luke 22.31-34; John 13.36-38)

31Jesus said to his disciples, "During this very night, all of you will reject me, as the Scriptures say,

'I will strike down the shepherd,
and the sheep will be scattered.'

32But after I'm raised to life, I'll go to Galilee ahead of you."

33Peter spoke up, "Even if all the others reject you, I never will!"

34Jesus replied, "I promise you that before a rooster crows tonight, you'll say three times that you don't know me." 35But Peter said, "Even if I have to die with you, I'll never say I don't know you."

All the others said the same thing.

Jesus Prays
(Mark 14.32-42; Luke 22.39-46)

36Jesus went with his disciples to a place called Gethsemane. When they got there, he told them, "Sit here while I go over there and pray."

37Jesus took along Peter and the two brothers, James

and John.[z] He was very sad and troubled, [38]and he said to them, "I'm so sad that I feel as if I'm dying. Stay here and keep awake with me."

[39]Jesus walked on a little way. Then he knelt with his face to the ground and prayed, "My Father, if it's possible, don't make me suffer by having me drink from this cup.[a] But do what you want, and not what I want."

[40]He came back and found his disciples sleeping. So he said to Peter, "Can't any of you stay awake with me for just one hour? [41]Stay awake and pray that you won't be tested. You want to do what is right, but you are weak."

[42]Again Jesus went to pray and said, "My Father, if there is no other way, and I must suffer, I will still do what you want."

[43]Jesus came back and found them sleeping again. They simply couldn't keep their eyes open. [44]He left them and prayed the same prayer once more.

[45]Finally, Jesus returned to his disciples and said, "Are you still sleeping and resting?[b] The time has come for the Son of Man to be handed over to sinners. [46]Get up! Let's go. The one who will betray me is already here."

Jesus Is Arrested
(Mark 14.43-50; Luke 22.47-53; John 18.3-12)

[47]Jesus was still speaking, when Judas the betrayer came up. He was one of the twelve disciples, and a large mob armed with swords and clubs was with him. They had been sent by the chief priests and the nation's leaders. [48]Judas had told them ahead of time, "Arrest the man I greet with a kiss."[c]

[49]Judas walked right up to Jesus and said, "Hello, teacher." Then Judas kissed him.

[50]Jesus replied, "My friend, why are you here?"[d]

The men grabbed Jesus and arrested him. [51]One of Jesus'

---

[z]*the two brothers, James and John:* The Greek text has "the two sons of Zebedee" (see 27.56). [a]*having me drink from this cup:* In the Scriptures "to drink from a cup" sometimes means to suffer (see the note at 20.22). [b]*Are you still sleeping and resting?:* Or "You may as well keep on sleeping and resting." [c]*the man I greet with a kiss:* It was the custom for people to greet each other with a kiss on the cheek. [d]*why are you here?:* Or "do what you came for."

followers pulled out a sword. He struck the servant of the high priest and cut off his ear.

⁵²But Jesus told him, "Put your sword away. Anyone who lives by fighting will die by fighting. ⁵³Don't you know that I could ask my Father, and straight away he would send me more than 12 armies of angels? ⁵⁴But then, how could the words of the Scriptures come true, which say that this must happen?"

⁵⁵Jesus said to the mob, "Why do you come with swords and clubs to arrest me like a criminal? Day after day I sat and taught in the temple, and you didn't arrest me. ⁵⁶But all this happened, so that what the prophets wrote would come true."

All of Jesus' disciples left him and ran away.

Jesus Is Questioned by the Council
(Mark 14.53-65; Luke 22.54, 55, 63-71; John 18.13, 14, 19-24)

⁵⁷After Jesus had been arrested, he was led off to the house of Caiaphas the high priest. The nation's leaders and the teachers of the Law of Moses were meeting there. ⁵⁸But Peter followed along at a distance and came to the courtyard of the high priest's palace. He went in and sat down with the guards to see what was going to happen.

⁵⁹The chief priests and the whole council wanted to put Jesus to death. So they tried to find some people who would tell lies about him in court.ᵉ ⁶⁰But they couldn't find any, even though many did come and tell lies. At last, two men came forward ⁶¹and said, "This man claimed that he would tear down God's temple and build it again in three days."

⁶²The high priest stood up and asked Jesus, "Why don't you say something in your own defence? Don't you hear the charges they are making against you?" ⁶³But Jesus didn't answer. So the high priest said, "With the living God looking on, you must tell the truth. Tell us, are you the Messiah, the Son of God?"ᶠ

⁶⁴"That's what you say!" Jesus answered. "But I tell all of you,

---

ᵉ*some people who would tell lies about him in court:* The Law of Moses taught that two witnesses were necessary before a person could be put to death (see verse 60). ᶠ*Son of God:* One of the titles used for the kings of Israel.

'Soon you will see the Son of Man
sitting at the right side[g] of God All-Powerful
and coming on the clouds of heaven.' "

65The high priest then tore his robe and said, "This man claims to be God! We don't need any more witnesses! You've heard what he said. 66What do you think?"

They answered, "He is guilty and deserves to die!" 67Then they spat in his face and hit him with their fists. Others slapped him 68and said, "You think you are the Messiah! So tell us who hit you!"

Peter Says He Doesn't Know Jesus
(Mark 14.66-72; Luke 22.56-62; John 18.15-18,25-27)

69While Peter was sitting out in the courtyard, a servant girl came up to him and said, "You were with Jesus from Galilee."

70But in front of everyone Peter said, "That isn't so! I don't know what you're talking about!"

71When Peter had gone out to the gate, another servant girl saw him and said to some people there, "This man was with Jesus from Nazareth."

72Again Peter denied it, and this time he swore, "I don't even know that man!"

73A little while later some people standing there walked over to Peter and said, "We know that you are one of them. We can tell it because you talk like someone from Galilee."

74Peter began to curse and swear, "I don't know that man!"

Just then a rooster crowed, 75and Peter remembered that Jesus had said, "Before a rooster crows, you'll say three times that you don't know me." Then Peter went out and cried hard.

Jesus Is Taken to Pilate
(Mark 15.1; Luke 23.1, 2; John 18.28-32)

27 1Early the next morning all the chief priests and the nation's leaders met and decided that Jesus

[g]right side: See the note at 22.44.

should be put to death. 2They tied him up and led him away to Pilate the governor.

The Death of Judas
(Acts 1.18, 19)

3Judas had betrayed Jesus, but when he learnt that Jesus had been sentenced to death, he was sorry for what he had done. He returned the 30 silver coins to the chief priests and leaders 4and said, "I have sinned by betraying a man who has never done anything wrong."

"So what? That's your problem," they replied. 5Judas threw the money into the temple and then went out and hanged himself.

6The chief priests picked up the money and said, "This money was paid to have a man killed. We can't put it in the temple treasury." 7Then they had a meeting and decided to buy a field that belonged to someone who made clay pots. They wanted to use it as a graveyard for foreigners. 8That's why people still call that place "Field of Blood." 9So the words of the prophet Jeremiah came true,

> "They took the 30 silver coins,
>   the price of a person
>   among the people of Israel.
> 10 They paid it for a potter's field,*h*
>   as the Lord had commanded me."

Pilate Questions Jesus
(Mark 15.2-5; Luke 23.3-5; John 18.33-38)

11Jesus was brought before Pilate the governor, who asked him, "Are you the king of the Jews?"

"Those are your words!" Jesus answered. 12And when the chief priests and leaders brought their charges against him, he didn't say a thing.

13Pilate asked him, "Don't you hear what crimes they say you've done?" 14But Jesus didn't say anything, and the governor was greatly amazed.

---

*h*a potter's field: Perhaps a field owned by someone who made clay pots. But it may have been a field where potters came to get clay or to make pots or to throw away their broken pieces of pottery.

The Death Sentence
(Mark 15.6-15; Luke 23.13-26; John 18.39—19.16)

15During Passover the governor always freed a prisoner chosen by the people. 16At that time a well-known terrorist named Jesus Barabbas[i] was in jail. 17So when the crowd came together, Pilate asked them, "Which prisoner do you want me to set free? Do you want Jesus Barabbas or Jesus who is called the Messiah?" 18Pilate knew that the leaders had brought Jesus to him because they were jealous.

19While Pilate was judging the case, his wife sent him a message. It said, "Don't have anything to do with that innocent man. I've had nightmares because of him."

20But the chief priests and the leaders convinced the crowds to ask for Barabbas to be set free and for Jesus to be killed. 21Pilate asked the crowd again, "Which of these two men do you want me to set free?"

"Barabbas!" they replied.

22Pilate asked them, "What am I to do with Jesus, who is called the Messiah?"

They all yelled, "Nail him to a cross!"

23Pilate answered, "But what crime has he done?"

"Nail him to a cross!" they yelled even louder.

24Pilate saw that there was nothing he could do and that the people were starting to riot. So he took some water and washed his hands[j] in front of them and said, "I won't have anything to do with killing this man. You are the ones doing it!"

25Everyone answered, "We and our own families will take the blame for his death!"

26Pilate set Barabbas free. Then he ordered his soldiers to beat Jesus with a whip and nail him to a cross.

Soldiers Make Fun of Jesus
(Mark 15.16-21; John 19.2, 3)

27The governor's soldiers led Jesus into the fortress[k] and brought together the rest of the troops. 28They

---

[i]Jesus Barabbas: Here and in verse 17 many manuscripts have "Barabbas."
[j]washed his hands: To show that he was innocent.   [k]fortress: The place where the Roman governor stayed. It was probably at Herod's palace west of Jerusalem, though it may have been Fortress Antonia north of the temple, where the Roman troops were stationed.

stripped off Jesus' clothes and put a scarlet robe[l] on him.
[29]They made a crown out of thorny branches and placed
it on his head, and they put a stick in his right hand. The
soldiers knelt down and pretended to worship him. They
made fun of him and shouted, "Hey, you king of the
Jews!" [30]Then they spat on him. They took the stick from
him and beat him on the head with it.

Jesus Is Nailed to a Cross
(Mark 15.22-32; Luke 23.27-43; John 19.17-27)

[31]When the soldiers had finished making fun of Jesus,
they took off the robe. They put his own clothes back on
him and led him off to be nailed to a cross. [32]On the way
they met a man from Cyrene named Simon, and they
forced him to carry Jesus' cross.

[33]They came to a place named Golgotha, which means
"Place of a Skull."[m] [34]There they gave Jesus some wine
mixed with a drug to ease the pain. But when Jesus tasted
what it was, he refused to drink it.

[35]The soldiers nailed Jesus to a cross and gambled to
see who would get his clothes. [36]Then they sat down to
guard him. [37]Above his head they put a sign that told
why he was nailed there. It read, "This is Jesus, the King
of the Jews." [38]The soldiers also nailed two criminals on
crosses, one to the right of Jesus and the other to his left.

[39]People who passed by said terrible things about Jesus.
They shook their heads and [40]shouted, "So you're the
one who claimed you could tear down the temple and
build it again in three days! If you are God's Son, save
yourself and come down from the cross!"

[41]The chief priests, the leaders, and the teachers of the
Law of Moses also made fun of Jesus. They said, [42]"He
saved others, but he can't save himself. If he is the king
of Israel, he should come down from the cross! Then we
will believe him. [43]He trusted God, so let God save him,
if he wants to. He even said he was God's Son." [44]The two
criminals also said cruel things to Jesus.

---

[l]scarlet robe: This was probably a Roman soldier's robe.   [m]Place of a Skull:
The place was probably given this name because it was near a large rock in
the shape of a human skull.

The Death of Jesus

(Mark 15.33-41; Luke 23.44-49; John 19.28-30)

[45]At midday the sky turned dark and stayed that way until three o'clock. [46]Then about that time Jesus shouted, "Eli, Eli, lema sabachthani?"[n] which means, "My God, my God, why have you deserted me?"

[47]Some of the people standing there heard Jesus and said, "He's calling for Elijah."[o] [48]One of them at once ran and grabbed a sponge. He soaked it in wine, then put it on a stick and held it up to Jesus.

[49]Others said, "Wait! Let's see if Elijah will come[p] and save him." [50]Once again Jesus shouted, and then he died.

[51]At once the curtain in the temple[q] was torn in two from top to bottom. The earth shook, and rocks split apart. [52]Graves opened, and many of God's people were raised to life. [53]Then after Jesus had risen to life, they came out of their graves and went into the holy city, where they were seen by many people.

[54]The officer and the soldiers guarding Jesus felt the earthquake and saw everything else that happened. They were frightened and said, "This man really was God's Son!"

[55]Many women had come with Jesus from Galilee to be of help to him, and they were there, looking on from a distance. [56]Mary Magdalene, Mary the mother of James and Joseph, and the mother of James and John[r] were some of these women.

Jesus Is Buried

(Mark 15.42-47; Luke 23.50-56; John 19.38-42)

[57]That evening a rich disciple named Joseph from the town of Arimathea [58]went and asked for Jesus' body. Pilate gave orders for it to be given to Joseph, [59]who took the body and wrapped it in a clean linen cloth. [60]Then

---

[n]*Eli...sabachthani:* These words are in Hebrew. [o]*Elijah:* In Aramaic the name "Elijah" sounds like "Eli," which means "my God." [p]*Elijah will come:* See the note at 16.14. [q]*curtain in the temple:* There were two curtains in the temple. One was at the entrance, and the other separated the holy place from the most holy place that the Jewish people thought of as God's home on earth. The second curtain is probably the one that is meant. [r]*of James and John:* The Greek text has "of Zebedee's sons" (see 26.37).

Joseph put the body in his own tomb that had been cut into solid rock[s] and had never been used. He rolled a big stone against the entrance to the tomb and went away.

⁶¹All this time Mary Magdalene and the other Mary were sitting across from the tomb.

⁶²On the next day, which was a Sabbath, the chief priests and the Pharisees went together to Pilate. ⁶³They said, "Sir, we remember what that liar said while he was still alive. He claimed that in three days he would come back from death. ⁶⁴So please order the tomb to be carefully guarded for three days. If you don't, his disciples may come and steal his body. They will tell the people that he's been raised to life, and this last lie will be worse than the first one."[t]

⁶⁵Pilate said to them, "All right, take some of your soldiers and guard the tomb as well as you know how." ⁶⁶So they sealed it tight and placed soldiers there to guard it.

Jesus Is Alive
(Mark 16.18; Luke 24.1-12; John 20.1-10)

28 ¹The Sabbath was over, and it was almost daybreak on Sunday when Mary Magdalene and the other Mary went to see the tomb. ²Suddenly a strong earthquake struck, and the Lord's angel came down from heaven. He rolled away the stone and sat on it. ³The angel looked as bright as lightning, and his clothes were white as snow. ⁴The guards shook from fear and fell down, as though they were dead.

⁵The angel said to the women, "Don't be afraid! I know you're looking for Jesus, who was nailed to a cross. ⁶He isn't here! God has raised him to life, just as Jesus said he would. Come, see the place where his body was lying. ⁷Now hurry! Tell his disciples that he has been raised to life and is on his way to Galilee. Go there, and you will see him. That is what I came to tell you."

⁸The women were frightened and yet very happy,

---

[s]*tomb...solid rock:* Some of the Jewish people buried their dead in rooms carved into solid rock. A heavy stone was rolled against the entrance.   [t]*the first one:* Probably the belief that Jesus is the Messiah.

as they hurried from the tomb and ran to tell his disciples. 9Suddenly Jesus met them and greeted them. They went near him, held on to his feet, and worshipped him. 10Then Jesus said, "Don't be afraid! Tell my followers to go to Galilee. They'll see me there."

Report of the Guard

11While the women were on their way, some soldiers who had been guarding the tomb went into the city. They told the chief priests everything that had happened. 12So the chief priests met with the leaders and decided to bribe the soldiers with a lot of money. 13They said to the soldiers, "Tell everyone that Jesus' disciples came during the night and stole his body while you were asleep. 14If the governor*u* hears about this, we'll talk to him. You won't have anything to worry about." 15The soldiers took the money and did what they were told. The Jewish people still tell each other this story.

What Jesus' Followers Must Do
(Mark 16.14-18; Luke 24.36-49; John 20.19-23; Acts 1.6-8)

16Jesus' eleven disciples went to a mountain in Galilee, where Jesus had told them to meet him. 17They saw him and worshipped him, but some of them doubted. 18Jesus came to them and said:

I have been given all authority in heaven and on earth! 19Go to the people of all nations and make them my disciples. Baptise them in the name of the Father, the Son, and the Holy Spirit, 20and teach them to do everything I have told you. I will be with you always, even until the end of the world.

ugovernor: Pontius Pilate.

MARK

ABOUT THIS BOOK

This is the shortest of the four New Testament books that tell about the life and teachings of Jesus, but it's also the most action-packed. From the very beginning of his ministry, Jesus worked mighty wonders. After choosing four followers (chapter 1.16-20), he immediately performed many miracles of healing. Among those healed were a man with an evil spirit in him (1.21-28), Simon's mother-in-law (1.30, 31), crowds of sick people (1.32-34), and a man with leprosy (1.40-45). Over and over again Mark tells how Jesus healed people, but always in such a way as to show that he did these miracles by the power of God.

The religious leaders refused to accept Jesus. This led to conflicts (2.2—3.6) that finally made them start looking for a way to kill him (11.18). But the demons saw the power of Jesus, and they knew that he was the Son of God, although Jesus wouldn't let them tell anyone.

This book is full of miracles that amazed the crowds and Jesus' followers. But, according to Mark, the most powerful miracle of Jesus is his suffering and death. The first person to understand this miracle was the Roman soldier who saw Jesus die on the cross and said, "This man really was the Son of God!" (15.39).

This Gospel is widely thought to be the first one written. The many explanations of Aramaic words and Jewish customs in Mark suggest that Mark wrote to Gentile or non-Jewish Christians. He wants to tell about Jesus and to encourage readers to believe in the power of Jesus to rescue them from sickness, demons, and death. He also wants to remind them that the new life of faith is not an easy life, and that they must follow Jesus by serving others and being ready to suffer as he did.

The first followers of Jesus to discover the empty tomb were three women, and the angel told them:

"Don't be alarmed! You are looking for Jesus from Nazareth, who was nailed to a cross. God has raised him to life, and he isn't here." (Chapter 16.6)

A QUICK LOOK AT THIS BOOK

The Preaching of John the Baptist
(Matthew 3.1-12; Luke 3.1-18; John 1.19-28)

1 ¹This is the good news about Jesus Christ, the Son of God.*ᵃ* ²It began just as God had said in the book written by Isaiah the prophet,

"I am sending my messenger
    to get the way ready for you.
3   In the desert someone is shouting,
    'Get the road ready for the Lord!
        Make a straight path for him.' "

⁴So John the Baptist showed up in the desert and told everyone, "Turn back to God and be baptised! Then your sins will be forgiven."

⁵From all Judea and Jerusalem crowds of people went to John. They said how sorry they were for their sins, and he baptised them in the Jordan River.

⁶John wore clothes made of camel's hair. He had a leather strap around his waist and ate grasshoppers and wild honey.

⁷John also told the people, "Someone more powerful is going to come. And I'm not good enough even to stoop down and untie his sandals.*ᵇ* ⁸I baptise you with water, but he'll baptise you with the Holy Spirit!"

The Baptism of Jesus
(Matthew 3.13-17; Luke 3.21, 22)

⁹About that time Jesus came from Nazareth in Galilee, and John baptised him in the Jordan River. ¹⁰As soon as

---

ᵃthe Son of God: These words are not in some manuscripts.   *ᵇuntie his sandals:* This was the duty of a slave.

Jesus came out of the water, he saw the sky open and the Holy Spirit coming down to him like a dove. [11]A voice from heaven said, "You are my own dear Son, and I am pleased with you."

Jesus and Satan
(Matthew 4.1-11; Luke 4.1-13)

[12]Straight away God's Spirit made Jesus go into the desert. [13]He stayed there for 40 days while Satan tested him. Jesus was with the wild animals, but angels took care of him.

Jesus Begins His Work
(Matthew 4.12-17; Luke 4.14, 15)

[14]After John was arrested, Jesus went to Galilee and spread the good news that comes from God.[c] [15]He said, "The time has come! God's kingdom will soon be here.[d] Turn back to God and believe the good news!"

Jesus Chooses Four Fishermen
(Matthew 4.18-22; Luke 5.1-11)

[16]As Jesus was walking along the shore of Lake Galilee, he saw Simon and his brother Andrew. They were fishermen and were casting their nets into the lake. [17]Jesus said to them, "Come with me! I'll teach you how to bring in people instead of fish." [18]At once the two brothers dropped their nets and went with him.

[19]Jesus walked on and soon saw James and John, the sons of Zebedee. They were in a boat, mending their nets. [20]At once Jesus asked them to come with him. They left their father in the boat with the hired workers and went with him.

A Man with an Evil Spirit
(Luke 4.31-37)

[21]Jesus and his disciples went to the town of Capernaum. Then on the next Sabbath he went into the

---

[c]that comes from God: Or "that is about God."   [d]will soon be here: Or "is already here."

Jewish meeting place and started teaching. 22Everyone
was amazed at his teaching. He taught with authority,
and not like the teachers of the Law of Moses. 23Suddenly
a man with an evil spirit*e* in him entered the meeting
place and yelled, 24"Jesus from Nazareth, what do you
want with us? Have you come to destroy us? I know who
you are! You are God's Holy One."

25Jesus told the evil spirit, "Be quiet and come out of
the man!" 26The spirit shook him. Then it gave a loud
shout and left.

27Everyone was completely surprised and kept saying
to each other, "What is this? It must be some new kind
of powerful teaching! Even the evil spirits obey him."
28News about Jesus quickly spread all over Galilee.

Jesus Heals Many People
(Matthew 8.14-17; Luke 4.38-41)

29As soon as Jesus left the meeting place with James and
John, they went home with Simon and Andrew. 30When
they got there, Jesus was told that Simon's mother-in-
law was sick in bed with fever. 31Jesus went to her. He
took hold of her hand and helped her up. The fever left
her, and she served them a meal.

32That evening after sunset,*f* all who were sick or had
demons in them were brought to Jesus. 33In fact, the
whole town gathered around the door of the house.
34Jesus healed all kinds of terrible diseases and forced out
a lot of demons. But the demons knew who he was, and
he didn't let them speak.

35Very early the next morning, Jesus got up and went
to a place where he could be alone and pray. 36Simon and
the others started looking for him. 37And when they
found him, they said, "Everyone is looking for you!"

38Jesus replied, "We must go to the nearby towns, so
that I can tell the good news to those people. This is why
I've come." 39Then Jesus went to Jewish meeting places
everywhere in Galilee, where he preached and forced out
demons.

---

eevil spirit: A Jewish person who had an evil spirit was considered "unclean"
and wasn't allowed to eat or worship with other Jewish people.   *fafter sunset:*
The Sabbath was over, and a new day began at sunset.

Jesus Heals a Man with Leprosy
(Matthew 8.1-4; Luke 5.12-16)

[40]A man with leprosy[g] came to Jesus and knelt down.[h] He begged, "You have the power to make me well, if only you wanted to."

[41]Jesus felt sorry for[i] the man. So he put his hand on him and said, "I want to! Now you are well." [42]At once the man's leprosy disappeared, and he was well.

[43]After Jesus strictly warned the man, he sent him on his way. [44]He said, "Don't tell anyone about this. Just go and show the priest that you are well. Then take a gift to the temple as Moses commanded, and everyone will know that you have been healed."[j]

[45]The man talked about it so much and told so many people, that Jesus could no longer go openly into a town. He had to stay away from the towns, but people still came to him from everywhere.

Jesus Heals a Crippled Man
(Matthew 9.1-8; Luke 5.17-26)

2 [1]Jesus went back to Capernaum, and a few days later people heard that he was at home.[k] [2]Then so many of them came to the house that there wasn't even standing room left in front of the door.

Jesus was still teaching [3]when four people came up, carrying a crippled man on a mat. [4]But because of the crowd, they couldn't get him to Jesus. So they made a hole in the roof[l] above him and let the man down in front of everyone.

[5]When Jesus saw how much faith they had, he said to the crippled man, "My friend, your sins are forgiven."

[6]Some of the teachers of the Law of Moses were sitting

---

[g]*leprosy:* In biblical times the word "leprosy" was used for many different kinds of skin diseases.   [h]*and knelt down:* These words are not in some manuscripts.   [i]*felt sorry for:* Some manuscripts have "was angry with."   [j]*everyone will know that you have been healed:* People with leprosy had to be examined by a priest and told that they were well (that is, "clean") before they could once again live a normal life in the Jewish community. The gift that Moses commanded was the sacrifice of some lambs together with flour mixed with olive oil.   [k]*at home:* Or "in the house" (perhaps Simon Peter's home).   [l]*roof:* In Palestine the houses usually had a flat roof. Stairs on the outside led up to the roof that was made of beams and boards covered with packed earth.

there. They started wondering, [7]"Why would he say such a thing? He must think he is God! Only God can forgive sins."

[8]Straight away, Jesus knew what they were thinking, and he said, "Why are you thinking such things? [9]Is it easier for me to tell this crippled man that his sins are forgiven or to tell him to get up and pick up his mat and go home? [10]I will show you that the Son of Man has the right to forgive sins here on earth." So Jesus said to the man, [11]"Get up! Pick up your mat and go home."

[12]The man got straight up. He picked up his mat and went out while everyone watched in amazement. They praised God and said, "We've never seen anything like this!"

Jesus Chooses Levi
(Matthew 9.9-13; Luke 5.27-32)

[13]Once again, Jesus went to the shore of Lake Galilee. A large crowd gathered around him, and he taught them. [14]As he walked along, he saw Levi, the son of Alphaeus. Levi was sitting at the place for paying taxes, and Jesus said to him, "Come with me!" So he got up and went with Jesus.

[15]Later, Jesus and his disciples were having dinner at Levi's house.[m] Many tax collectors[n] and other sinners had become followers of Jesus, and they were also guests at the dinner.

[16]Some of the teachers of the Law of Moses were Pharisees, and they saw that Jesus was eating with sinners and tax collectors. So they asked his disciples, "Why does he eat with tax collectors and sinners?"

[17]Jesus heard them and answered, "Healthy people don't need a doctor, but sick people do. I didn't come to invite good people to be my followers. I came to invite sinners."

People Ask about Going without Eating
(Matthew 9.14-17; Luke 5.33-39)

[18]The followers of John the Baptist and the Pharisees often went without eating.[o] Some people came and asked

---

[m]Levi's house: Or "Jesus' house." [n]tax collectors: These were usually Jewish people who paid the Romans for the right to collect taxes. They were hated by other Jews who thought of them as traitors to their country and to their religion. [o]without eating: The Jewish people sometimes went without eating (also called "fasting") to show their love for God or to show sorrow for their sins.

Jesus, "Why do the followers of John and those of the Pharisees often go without eating, while your disciples never do?"

¹⁹Jesus answered:

The friends of a bridegroom don't go without eating while he is still with them. ²⁰But the time will come when he'll be taken from them. Then they will go without eating.

²¹No-one patches old clothes by sewing on a piece of new cloth. The new piece would shrink and tear a bigger hole.

²²No-one pours new wine into old wineskins. The wine would swell and burst the old skins.^p Then the wine would be lost, and the skins would be ruined. New wine must be put into new wineskins.

A Question about the Sabbath
(Matthew 12.1-8; Luke 6.1-5)

²³One Sabbath Jesus and his disciples were walking through some wheat fields. His disciples were picking grains of wheat as they went along.^q ²⁴Some Pharisees asked Jesus, "Why are your disciples picking grain on the Sabbath? They aren't supposed to do that!"

²⁵Jesus answered, "Haven't you read what David did when he and his followers were hungry and in need? ²⁶It was during the time of Abiathar the high priest. David went into the house of God and ate the sacred loaves of bread that only priests are allowed to eat. He also gave some to his followers."

²⁷Jesus finished by saying, "People were not made for the good of the Sabbath. The Sabbath was made for the good of people. ²⁸So the Son of Man is Lord over the Sabbath."

A Man with a Crippled Hand
(Matthew 12.9-14; Luke 6.6-11)

3 ¹The next time that Jesus went into the meeting place, a man with a crippled hand was there. ²The

^p*swell and burst the old skins:* While the juice from grapes was becoming wine, it would swell and stretch the skins in which it had been stored. If the skins were old and stiff, they would burst.   ^q*went along:* It was the custom to let hungry travellers pick grains of wheat.

Pharisees[r] wanted to accuse Jesus of doing something wrong, and they kept watching to see if Jesus would heal him on the Sabbath.

[3]Jesus told the man to stand up where everyone could see him. [4]Then he asked, "On the Sabbath should we do good deeds or evil deeds? Should we save someone's life or destroy it?" But no-one said a word.

[5]Jesus was angry as he looked around at the people. Yet he felt sorry for them because they were so stubborn. Then he told the man, "Stretch out your hand." He did, and his bad hand was healed.

[6]The Pharisees left. And straight away they started making plans with Herod's followers[s] to kill Jesus.

Large Crowds Come to Jesus

[7]Jesus led his disciples down to the shore of the lake. Large crowds followed him from Galilee, Judea, [8]and Jerusalem. People came from Idumea, as well as other places east of the Jordan River. They also came from the region around the cities of Tyre and Sidon. All of these crowds came because they had heard what Jesus was doing. [9]He even had to tell his disciples to get a boat ready to keep him from being crushed by the crowds.

[10]After Jesus had healed many people, the other sick people begged him to let them touch him. [11]And whenever any evil spirits saw Jesus, they would fall to the ground and shout, "You are the Son of God!" [12]But Jesus warned the spirits not to say who he was.

Jesus Chooses His Twelve Apostles
(Matthew 10.1-4; Luke 6.12-16)

[13]Jesus decided to ask some of his disciples to go up onto a mountain with him, and they went. [14]Then he chose twelve of them to be his apostles,[t] so that they could be with him. He also wanted to send them out to preach [15]and to force out demons. [16]Simon was one of the twelve, and Jesus named him Peter. [17]There were also

---

[r]Pharisees: The Greek text has "they" (but see verse 6).   [s]Herod's followers: People who were political followers of the family of Herod the Great and his son Herod Antipas.   [t]to be his apostles: These words are not in some manuscripts.

James and John, the two sons of Zebedee. Jesus called them Boanerges, which means "Thunderbolts." [18]Andrew, Philip, Bartholomew, Matthew, Thomas, James son of Alphaeus, and Thaddaeus were also apostles. The others were Simon, known as the Eager One,[u] [19]and Judas Iscariot,[v] who later betrayed Jesus.

Jesus and the Ruler of Demons
(Matthew 12.22-32; Luke 11.14-23; 12.10)

[20]Jesus went back home,[w] and once again such a large crowd gathered that there was no chance even to eat. [21]When Jesus' family heard what he was doing, they thought he was crazy and went to get him under control.

[22]Some teachers of the Law of Moses came from Jerusalem and said, "This man is under the power of Beelzebul, the ruler of demons! He is even forcing out demons with the help of Beelzebul."

[23]Jesus told the people to gather around him. Then he spoke to them in riddles and said:

How can Satan force himself out? [24]A nation whose people fight each other won't last very long. [25]And a family that fights won't last long either. [26]So if Satan fights against himself, that will be the end of him.

[27]How can anyone break into the house of a strong man and steal his things, unless he first ties up the strong man? Then he can take everything.

[28]I promise you that any of the sinful things you say or do can be forgiven, no matter how terrible those things are. [29]But if you speak against the Holy Spirit, you can never be forgiven. That sin will be held against you for ever.

[30]Jesus said this because the people were saying that he had an evil spirit in him.

---

[u]known as the Eager One: The Greek text has "Cananaean," which probably comes from a Hebrew word meaning "zealous" (see Luke 6.15). "Zealot" was the name later given to the members of a Jewish group that resisted and fought against the Romans.   [v]Iscariot: This may mean "a man from Kerioth" (a place in Judea). But more probably it means "a man who was a liar" or "a man who was a betrayer."   [w]went back home: Or "entered a house" (perhaps the home of Simon Peter).

Jesus' Mother and Brothers
(Matthew 12.46-50; Luke 8.19-21)

31Jesus' mother and brothers came and stood outside. Then they sent someone with a message for him to come out to them. 32The crowd that was sitting around Jesus told him, "Your mother and your brothers and sisters*x* are outside and want to see you."

33Jesus asked, "Who is my mother and who are my brothers?" 34Then he looked at the people sitting around him and said, "Here are my mother and my brothers. 35Anyone who obeys God is my brother or sister or mother."

A Story about a Farmer
(Matthew 13.1-9; Luke 8.4-8)

4 1The next time Jesus taught beside Lake Galilee, a big crowd gathered. It was so large that he had to sit in a boat out on the lake, while the people stood on the shore. 2He used stories to teach them many things, and this is part of what he taught:

3Now listen! A farmer went out to scatter seed in a field. 4While the farmer was scattering the seed, some of it fell along the road and was eaten by birds. 5Other seeds fell on shallow, rocky ground and quickly started growing because the soil wasn't very deep. 6But when the sun came up, the plants were scorched and dried up, because they didn't have enough roots. 7Some other seeds fell where thorn bushes grew up and choked out the plants. So they didn't produce any grain. 8But a few seeds did fall on good ground where the plants grew and produced 30 or 60 or even 100 times as much as was scattered.

9Then Jesus said, "If you have ears, pay attention."

Why Jesus Used Stories
(Matthew 13.10-17; Luke 8.9, 10)

10When Jesus was alone with the twelve apostles and some others, they asked him about these stories. 11He answered:

---

xand sisters: These words are not in some manuscripts.

I've explained the secret about God's kingdom to you,
but for others I can use only stories. [12]The reason is,
"These people will look and look, but neversee.
They will listen and listen, but never understand.
If they did, they would turn to God,
and he would forgive them."

Jesus Explains the Story about the Farmer
(Matthew 13.18-23; Luke 8.11-15)

[13]Jesus told them:

If you don't understand this story, you won't
understand any others. [14]What the farmer is spreading
is really the message about the kingdom. [15]The seeds
that fell along the road are the people who hear the
message. But Satan soon comes and snatches it away
from them. [16]The seeds that fell on rocky ground are
the people who gladly hear the message and accept it
straight away. [17]But they haven't got any roots, and
they don't last very long. As soon as life gets hard or
the message gets them into trouble, they give up.

[18]The seeds that fell among the thorn bushes are also
people who hear the message. [19]But they start worrying
about the needs of this life. They are fooled by the
desire to get rich and to have all kinds of other things.
So the message gets choked out, and they never
produce anything. [20]The seeds that fell on good ground
are the people who hear and welcome the message.
They produce 30 or 60 or even 100 times as much as
was planted.

Light
(Luke 8.16-18)

[21]Jesus also said:

You don't light a lamp and put it under a clay pot or
under a bed. Don't you put a lamp on a lampstand?
[22]There is nothing hidden that will not be made public.
There is no secret that will not be well known.
[23]If you have ears, pay attention!

[24]Listen carefully to what you hear! The way you
treat others will be the way you will be treated—and
even worse. [25]Everyone who has something will be

given more. But people who don't have anything will lose what little they have.

Another Story about Seeds

26 Again Jesus said:

God's kingdom is like what happens when a farmer scatters seed in a field. 27 The farmer sleeps at night and is up and around during the day. Yet the seeds keep sprouting and growing, and he doesn't understand how. 28 It's the ground that makes the seeds sprout and grow into plants that produce grain. 29 Then when harvest season comes and the grain is ripe, the farmer cuts it with a sickle.y

A Mustard Seed
(Matthew 13.31, 32; Luke 13.18, 19)

30 Finally, Jesus said:

What is God's kingdom like? What story can I use to explain it? 31 It's like what happens when a mustard seed is planted in the ground. It's the smallest seed in all the world. 32 But once it's planted, it grows larger than any garden plant. It even puts out branches that are big enough for birds to nest in its shade.

The Reason for Teaching with Stories
(Matthew 13.34, 35)

33 Jesus used many other stories when he spoke to the people, and he taught them as much as they could understand. 34 He didn't tell them anything without using stories. But when he was alone with his disciples, he explained everything to them.

A Storm
(Matthew 8.23-27; Luke 8.22-25)

35 That evening, Jesus said to his disciples, "Let's cross to the east side." 36 So they left the crowd, and his disciples started across the lake with him in the boat. Some other boats followed along. 37 Suddenly a strong

---

ysickle: A knife with a long curved blade, used to cut grain and other crops.

wind struck the lake. Waves started splashing into the boat, and it was about to sink.

38Jesus was in the back of the boat with his head on a pillow, and he was asleep. His disciples woke him and said, "Teacher, don't you care that we're about to drown?"

39Jesus got up and ordered the wind and the waves to be quiet. The wind stopped, and everything was calm.

40Jesus asked his disciples, "Why were you afraid? Don't you have any faith?"

41Now they were more afraid than ever and said to each other, "Who is this? Even the wind and the waves obey him!"

A Man with Evil Spirits
(Matthew 8.28-34; Luke 8.26-39)

5 1Jesus and his disciples crossed Lake Galilee and came to shore near the town of Gerasa.z 2When he was getting out of the boat, a man with an evil spirit quickly ran to him 3from the graveyarda where he had been living. No-one was able to tie the man up any more, not even with a chain. 4He had often been put in chains and leg irons, but he broke the chains and smashed the leg irons. No-one could control him. 5Night and day he was in the graveyard or on the hills, yelling and cutting himself with stones.

6When the man saw Jesus in the distance, he ran up to him and knelt down. 7He shouted, "Jesus, Son of God in heaven, what do you want with me? Promise me in God's name that you won't torture me!" 8The man said this because Jesus had already told the evil spirit to come out of him.

9Jesus asked, "What is your name?"

The man answered, "My name is Lots, because I have 'lots' of evil spirits." 10He then begged Jesus not to send them away.

11Over on the hillside a large herd of pigs was feeding. 12So the evil spirits begged Jesus, "Send us into those pigs! Let us go into them." 13Jesus let them go, and they went out of the man and into the pigs. The whole herd of

zGerasa: Some manuscripts have "Gadara," and others have "Gergesa."
agraveyard: It was thought that demons and evil spirits lived in graveyards.

about 2000 pigs rushed down the steep bank into the lake and drowned.

¹⁴The men taking care of the pigs ran to the town and the farms to spread the news. Then the people came out to see what had happened. ¹⁵When they came to Jesus, they saw the man who had once been full of demons. He was sitting there with his clothes on and in his right mind, and they were terrified.

¹⁶Everyone who had seen what had happened talked about the man and the pigs. ¹⁷Then the people started begging Jesus to leave their part of the country.

¹⁸When Jesus was getting into the boat, the man begged to go with him. ¹⁹But Jesus wouldn't let him. Instead, he said, "Go home to your family and tell them how much the Lord has done for you and how good he's been to you."

²⁰The man went away into the region near the ten cities known as Decapolis*ᵇ* and began telling everyone how much Jesus had done for him. Everyone who heard what had happened was amazed.

A Dying Girl and a Sick Woman
(Matthew 9.18-26; Luke 8.40-56)

²¹Once again Jesus got into the boat and crossed Lake Galilee.ᶜ Then as he stood on the shore, a large crowd gathered around him. ²²The person in charge of the Jewish meeting place was also there. His name was Jairus, and when he saw Jesus, he went over to him. He knelt at Jesus' feet ²³and started begging him for help. He said, "My daughter is about to die! Please come and touch her, so she'll get well and live." ²⁴Jesus went with Jairus. Many people followed along and kept crowding around.

²⁵In the crowd was a woman who had been bleeding for 12 years. ²⁶She had gone to many doctors, and they hadn't done anything except cause her a lot of pain. She had paid them all the money she had. But instead of getting better, she only got worse.

ᵇ*the ten cities known as Decapolis:* A group of ten cities east of Samaria and Galilee, where the people followed the Greek way of life.   ᶜ*crossed Lake Galilee:* To the west side.

27The woman had heard about Jesus, so she came up behind him in the crowd and barely touched his clothes. 28She had said to herself, "If I can just touch his clothes, I'll get well." 29As soon as she touched them, her bleeding stopped, and she knew she was well.

30At that moment Jesus felt power go out from him. He turned to the crowd and asked, "Who touched my clothes?"

31His disciples said to him, "Look at all these people crowding around you! How can you ask who touched you?" 32But Jesus turned to see who had touched him.

33The woman knew what had happened to her. She came shaking with fear and knelt down in front of Jesus. Then she told him the whole story.

34Jesus said to the woman, "You're well now because of your faith. May God give you peace! You are healed, and you'll no longer be in pain."

35While Jesus was still speaking, some men came from Jairus' home and said, "Your daughter has died! Why bother the teacher any more?"

36Jesus heard*d* what they said, and he said to Jairus, "Don't worry. Just have faith!"

37Jesus didn't let anyone go with him except Peter and the two brothers, James and John. 38They went home with Jairus and saw the people crying and making a lot of noise.*e* 39Then Jesus went inside and said to them, "Why are you crying and carrying on like this? The child isn't dead. She's just asleep." 40But the people laughed at him.

After Jesus had sent them all out of the house, he took the girl's father and mother and his three disciples and went to where she was. 41-42He took the 12-year-old girl by the hand and said, "Talitha, koum!"*f* which means, "Little girl, get up!" The girl got straight up and started walking around.

Everyone was greatly surprised. 43But Jesus ordered them not to tell anyone what had happened. Then he said, "Give her something to eat."

*d*heard: Or "ignored." *e*crying and making a lot of noise: The Jewish people often hired mourners for funerals. *f*Talitha, koum: These words are in Aramaic, a language spoken in Palestine during the time of Jesus.

The People of Nazareth Turn against Jesus
(Matthew 13.53-58; Luke 4.16-30)

6 ¹Jesus left and returned to his home town*g* with his disciples. ²The next Sabbath he taught in the Jewish meeting place. Many of the people who heard him were amazed and asked, "How can he do all this? Where did he get such wisdom and the power to work these miracles? ³Isn't he the carpenter,*h* the son of Mary? Aren't James, Joseph, Judas, and Simon his brothers? Don't his sisters still live here in our town?" The people were very unhappy because of what he was doing.

⁴But Jesus said, "Prophets are honoured by everyone, except the people of their home town and their relatives and their own family." ⁵Jesus couldn't work any miracles there, except to heal a few sick people by placing his hands on them. ⁶He was surprised that the people didn't have any faith.

Instructions for the Twelve Apostles
(Matthew 10.5-15; Luke 9.1-6)

Jesus taught in all the neighbouring villages. ⁷Then he called together his twelve apostles and sent them out two by two with power over evil spirits. ⁸He told them, "You may take along a walking stick. But don't carry food or a travelling bag or any money. ⁹It's all right to wear sandals, but don't take along a change of clothes. ¹⁰When you are welcomed into a home, stay there until you leave that town. ¹¹If any place won't welcome you or listen to your message, leave and shake the dust from your feet*i* as a warning to them."

¹²The apostles left and started telling everyone to turn to God. ¹³They forced out many demons and healed a lot of sick people by putting olive oil*j* on them.

---

*g*home town: Nazareth.   *h*carpenter: The Greek word may also mean someone who builds or works with stone or brick.   *i*shake the dust from your feet: This was a way of showing rejection.   *j*olive oil: The Jewish people used olive oil as a way of healing people. Sometimes olive oil is a symbol for healing by means of a miracle (see James 5.14).

The Death of John the Baptist
(Matthew 14.1-12; Luke 9.7-9)

[14]Jesus became so well-known that Herod the ruler[k] heard about him. Some people thought he was John the Baptist, who had come back to life with the power to work miracles. [15]Others thought he was Elijah[l] or some other prophet who had lived long ago. [16]But when Herod heard about Jesus, he said, "This must be John! I had his head cut off, and now he's come back to life."

[17-18]Herod had earlier married Herodias, the wife of his brother Philip. But John had told him, "It isn't right for you to take your brother's wife!" So, in order to please Herodias, Herod arrested John and put him in prison.

[19]Herodias had a grudge against John and wanted to kill him. But she couldn't do it [20]because Herod was afraid of John and protected him. He knew that John was a good and holy man. Even though Herod was confused by what John said,[m] he was glad to listen to him. And he often did.

[21]Finally, Herodias got her chance when Herod gave a great birthday celebration for himself and invited his officials, his army officers, and the leaders of Galilee. [22]The daughter of Herodias[n] came in and danced for Herod and his guests. She pleased them so much that Herod said, "Ask for anything, and it's yours! [23]I swear that I'll give you as much as half of my kingdom, if you want it."

[24]The girl left and asked her mother, "What do you think I should ask for?"

Her mother answered, "The head of John the Baptist!"

[25]The girl hurried back and told Herod, "I want the head of John the Baptist on a platter, right now!"

[26]The king was very sorry for what he had said. But he didn't want to break the promise he had made in front of his guests. [27]At once he ordered a guard to cut off John's head there in prison. [28]The guard put the head on a platter and took it to the girl. Then she gave it to her mother.

[k]Herod the ruler: Herod Antipas, the son of Herod the Great.　[l]Elijah: Many of the Jewish people expected the prophet Elijah to come and prepare the way for the Messiah.　[m]was confused by what John said: Some manuscripts have "did many things because of what John said."　[n]Herodias: Some manuscripts have "Herod."

²⁹When John's followers learnt that he had been killed, they took his body and put it in a tomb.

Jesus Feeds 5000
(Matthew 14.13-21; Luke 9.10-17; John 6.1-14)

³⁰After the apostles returned to Jesus,ᵒ they told him everything they had done and taught. ³¹But so many people were coming and going that Jesus and the apostles didn't even have a chance to eat. Then Jesus said, "Let's go to a placeᵖ where we can be alone and get some rest." ³²They left in a boat for a place where they could be alone. ³³But many people saw them leave and worked out where they were going. So people from every town ran on ahead and got there first.

³⁴When Jesus got out of the boat, he saw the large crowds that were like sheep without a shepherd. He felt sorry for the people and started teaching them many things.

³⁵That evening the disciples came to Jesus and said, "This place is like a desert, and it's already late. ³⁶Let the crowds leave, so they can go to the farms and villages near here and buy something to eat."

³⁷Jesus replied, "You give them something to eat."

But they asked him, "Don't you know that it would take almost a year's wages�q to buy all of these people something to eat?"

³⁸Then Jesus said, "How much bread have you got? Go and see!"

They found out and answered, "We've got five small loaves of breadʳ and two fish." ³⁹Jesus told his disciples to get the people to sit down on the green grass. ⁴⁰They sat down in groups of 100 and groups of 50.

⁴¹Jesus took the five loaves and the two fish. He looked up towards heaven and blessed the food. Then he broke the bread and handed it to his disciples to give to

---

ᵒthe apostles returned to Jesus: From the mission on which he had sent them (see 6.7, 12, 13). ᵖa place: This was probably north-east of Lake Galilee (see verse 45). �q almost a year's wages: The Greek text has "200 silver coins." Each coin was the average day's wage for a worker. ʳsmall loaves of bread: These would have been flat and round or in the shape of a bun.

the people. He also divided the two fish, so that everyone could have some.

⁴²After everyone had eaten all they wanted, ⁴³Jesus' disciples picked up twelve large baskets of leftover bread and fish.

⁴⁴There were 5000 men who ate the food.

Jesus Walks on the Water
(Matthew 14.22-33; John 6.15-21)

⁴⁵Straight away, Jesus made his disciples get into the boat and start back across to Bethsaida. But he stayed until he had sent the crowds away. ⁴⁶Then he said goodbye to them and went up on the side of a mountain to pray.

⁴⁷Later that evening he was still there by himself, and the boat was somewhere in the middle of the lake. ⁴⁸He could see that the disciples were struggling hard, because they were rowing against the wind. Not long before morning, Jesus came towards them. He was walking on the water and was about to pass the boat.

⁴⁹When the disciples saw Jesus walking on the water, they thought he was a ghost, and they started screaming. ⁵⁰All of them saw him and were terrified. But at that same time he said, "Don't worry! I am Jesus. Don't be afraid." ⁵¹He then got into the boat with them, and the wind died down. The disciples were completely confused. ⁵²Their minds were closed, and they couldn't understand the true meaning of the loaves of bread.

Jesus Heals Sick People in Gennesaret
(Matthew 14.34-36)

⁵³Jesus and his disciples crossed the lake and brought the boat to shore near the town of Gennesaret. ⁵⁴As soon as they got out of the boat, the people recognised Jesus. ⁵⁵So they ran all over that part of the country to bring their sick people to him on mats. They brought them each time they heard where he was. ⁵⁶In every village or farm or market place where Jesus went, the people brought their sick to him. They begged him to let them just touch his clothes, and everyone who did was healed.

The Teaching of the Ancestors
(Matthew 15.1-9)

7 ¹Some Pharisees and several teachers of the Law of Moses from Jerusalem came and gathered around Jesus. ²They noticed that some of his disciples ate without first washing their hands.ˢ

³The Pharisees and all other Jewish people obey the teachings of their ancestors. They always wash their hands in the proper wayᵗ before eating. ⁴None of them will eat anything they buy in the market until it's washed. They also follow a lot of other teachings, such as washing cups, jugs, and bowls.ᵘ

⁵The Pharisees and teachers asked Jesus, "Why don't your disciples obey what our ancestors taught us to do? Why do they eat without washing their hands?"

⁶Jesus replied:

You are nothing but show-offs! The prophet Isaiah was right when he wrote that God had said,

"All of you praise me with your words,
> but you never really think about me.
⁷ It's useless for you to worship me,
> when you teach rules made up by humans."

⁸You disobey God's commands in order to obey what humans have taught. ⁹You are good at rejecting God's commands so that you can follow your own teachings! ¹⁰Didn't Moses command you to respect your father and mother? Didn't he tell you to put to death all who curse their parents? ¹¹But you let people get away without helping their parents when they should. You let them say that what they own has been offered to God.ᵛ ¹²You won't let those people help their parents. ¹³And you ignore God's commands in order to follow your own teaching. You do a lot of other things that are just as bad.

ˢ*washing their hands:* The Jewish people had strict laws about washing their hands before eating, especially if they had been out in public. ᵗ*in the proper way:* The Greek text has "with the fist," but the exact meaning is not clear. It could mean "to the wrist" or "to the elbow." ᵘ*bowls:* Some manuscripts add "and sleeping mats." ᵛ*offered to God:* According to Jewish custom, when anything was offered to God, it could not be used for anyone else, not even for a person's parents.

What Really Makes People Unclean
(Matthew 15.10-20)

14Jesus called the crowd together again and said, "Pay attention and try to understand what I mean. 15-16The food that you put into your mouth doesn't make you unclean and unfit to worship God. The bad words that come out of your mouth are what make you unclean."w

17After Jesus and his disciples had left the crowd and had gone into the house, they asked him what these sayings meant. 18He answered, "Don't you know what I'm talking about by now? You surely know that the food you put into your mouth can't make you unclean. 19It doesn't go into your heart, but into your stomach, and then out of your body." By saying this, Jesus meant that all foods were fit to eat.

20Then Jesus said:
What comes from your heart is what makes you unclean. 21Out of your heart come evil thoughts, vulgar deeds, stealing, murder, 22unfaithfulness in marriage, greed, meanness, deceit, indecency, envy, insults, pride, and foolishness. 23All of these come from your heart, and they are what make you unfit to worship God.

A Woman's Faith
(Matthew 15.21-28)

24Jesus left and went to the region near the city of Tyre, where he stayed in someone's home. He didn't want people to know he was there, but they found out anyway. 25A woman whose daughter had an evil spirit in her heard where Jesus was. And straight away she came and knelt down at his feet. 26The woman was Greek and had been born in the part of Syria known as Phoenicia. She begged Jesus to force the demon out of her daughter. 27But Jesus said, "The children must first be fed! It isn't right to take away their food and feed it to dogs."x

28The woman replied, "Lord, even dogs eat the crumbs that children drop from the table."

---

wunclean: Some manuscripts add, "If you have ears, pay attention."   xfeed it to dogs: The Jewish people often referred to Gentiles as dogs.

[29]Jesus answered, "That's true! You may go now. The demon has left your daughter." [30]When the woman got back home, she found her child lying on the bed. The demon had gone.

Jesus Heals a Man Who Was Deaf and Could Hardly Talk

[31]Jesus left the region around Tyre and went by way of Sidon towards Lake Galilee. He went through the land near the ten cities known as Decapolis.[y] [32]Some people brought to him a man who was deaf and could hardly talk. They begged Jesus just to touch him.

[33]After Jesus had taken him aside from the crowd, he stuck his fingers in the man's ears. Then he spat and put it on the man's tongue. [34]Jesus looked up towards heaven, and with a groan he said, "Effatha!"[z] which means "Open up!" [35]At once the man could hear, and he had no more trouble talking clearly.

[36]Jesus told the people not to say anything about what he had done. But the more he told them, the more they talked about it. [37]They were completely amazed and said, "Everything he does is good! He even heals people who can't hear or talk."

Jesus Feeds 4000
(Matthew 15.32-39)

8 [1]One day another large crowd gathered around Jesus. They hadn't brought along anything to eat. So Jesus called his disciples together and said, [2]"I feel sorry for these people. They've been with me for three days, and they haven't got anything to eat. [3]Some of them live a long way from here. If I send them away hungry, they might faint on their way home."

[4]The disciples said, "This place is like a desert. Where can we find enough food to feed such a crowd?"

[5]Jesus asked them how much food they had. They replied, "Seven small loaves of bread."[a]

---

[y]*the ten cities known as Decapolis:* See the note at 5.20.   [z]*Effatha:* This word is in Aramaic, a language spoken in Palestine during the time of Jesus. [a]*small loaves of bread:* See the note at 6.38.

6After Jesus told the crowd to sit down, he took the seven loaves and blessed them. He then broke the loaves and handed them to his disciples, who passed them out to the crowd. 7They also had a few little fish, and after Jesus had blessed these, he told the disciples to pass them around.

8-9The crowd of about 4000 people ate all they wanted, and the leftovers filled seven large baskets.

As soon as Jesus had sent the people away, 10he got into the boat with the disciples and crossed to the territory near Dalmanutha.b

A Sign from Heaven
(Matthew 16.1-4)

11The Pharisees came out and started an argument with Jesus. They wanted to test him by asking for a sign from heaven. 12Jesus groaned and said, "Why are you always looking for a sign? I can promise you that you won't be given one!" 13Then he left them. He again got into a boat and crossed over to the other side of the lake.

The Yeast of the Pharisees and of Herod
(Matthew 16.5-12)

14The disciples had forgotten to bring any bread, and they had only one loaf with them in the boat. 15Jesus warned them, "Watch out! Guard against the yeast of the Pharisees and of Herod."c

16The disciples talked this over and said to each other, "He must be saying this because we haven't got any bread."

17Jesus knew what they were thinking and asked, "Why are you talking about not having any bread? Don't you understand? Are your minds still closed? 18Are your eyes blind and your ears deaf? Don't you remember 19how many baskets of leftovers you picked up when I fed those 5000 people with only five small loaves of bread?"

"Yes," the disciples answered. "There were twelve baskets."

20Jesus then asked, "And how many baskets of leftovers

bDalmanutha: The place is unknown.   cHerod: Herod Antipas, the son of Herod the Great.

did you pick up when I broke seven small loaves of bread for those 4000 people?"

"Seven," they answered.

21"Don't you know what I am talking about by now?" Jesus asked.

Jesus Heals a Blind Man at Bethsaida

22As Jesus and his disciples were going into Bethsaida, some people brought a blind man to him and begged him to touch the man. 23Jesus took him by the hand and led him out of the village, where he spat into the man's eyes. He placed his hands on the blind man and asked him if he could see anything. 24The man looked up and said, "I see people, but they look like trees walking around."

25Once again Jesus placed his hands on the man's eyes, and this time the man stared. His eyes were healed, and he saw everything clearly. 26Jesus said to him, "You may return home now, but don't go into the village."

Who Is Jesus?
(Matthew 16.13-20; Luke 9.18-21)

27Jesus and his disciples went to the villages near the town of Caesarea Philippi. As they were walking along, he asked them, "What do people say about me?"

28The disciples answered, "Some say you are John the Baptist or maybe Elijah.d Others say you are one of the prophets."

29Then Jesus asked them, "But who do you say I am?"

"You are the Messiah!" Peter replied.

30Jesus warned the disciples not to tell anyone about him.

Jesus Speaks about His Suffering and Death
(Matthew 16.21-28; Luke 9.22-27)

31Jesus began telling his disciples what would happen to him. He said, "The nation's leaders, the chief priests, and the teachers of the Law of Moses will make the Son of Man suffer terribly. He'll be rejected and killed, but three days later he'll rise to life." 32Then Jesus explained clearly what he meant.

dElijah: See the note at 6.15.

Peter took Jesus aside and told him to stop talking like that. ³³But when Jesus turned and saw the disciples, he corrected Peter. He said to him, "Satan, get away from me! You are thinking like everyone else and not like God."

³⁴Jesus then told the crowd and the disciples to come closer, and he said:

If any of you want to be my followers, you must forget about yourself. You must take up your cross and follow me. ³⁵If you want to save your life,ᵉ you will destroy it. But if you give up your life for me and for the good news, you will save it. ³⁶What will you gain, if you own the whole world but destroy yourself? ³⁷What could you give to get back your soul?

³⁸Don't be ashamed of me and my message among these unfaithful and sinful people! If you are, the Son of Man will be ashamed of you when he comes in the glory of his Father with the holy angels.

9 ¹I can assure you that some of the people standing here won't die before they see God's kingdom come with power.

The True Glory of Jesus
(Matthew 17.1-13; Luke 9.28-36)

²Six days later Jesus took Peter, James, and John with him. They went up onto a high mountain, where they could be alone. There in front of the disciples, Jesus was completely changed. ³And his clothes became much whiter than any bleach on earth could make them. ⁴Then Moses and Elijah were there talking with Jesus.

⁵Peter said to Jesus, "Teacher, it's good for us to be here! Let's make three shelters, one for you, one for Moses, and one for Elijah." ⁶But Peter and the others were terribly frightened, and he didn't know what he was talking about.

⁷The shadow of a cloud passed over and covered them. From the cloud a voice said, "This is my Son, and I love him. Listen to what he says!" ⁸At once the disciples looked around, but they saw only Jesus.

⁹As Jesus and his disciples were coming down the

ᵉlife: In verses 35-37 the same Greek word is translated "life," "yourself," and "soul."

mountain, he told them not to say a word about what they had seen, until the Son of Man had been raised from death. ¹⁰So they kept it to themselves. But they wondered what he meant by the words "raised from death."

¹¹The disciples asked Jesus, "Don't the teachers of the Law of Moses say that Elijah must come before the Messiah does?"

¹²Jesus answered:

Elijah certainly will come[f] to get everything ready. But don't the Scriptures also say that the Son of Man must suffer terribly and be rejected? ¹³I can assure you that Elijah has already come. And people treated him just as they wanted to, as the Scriptures say they would.

Jesus Heals a Boy
(Matthew 17.14-20; Luke 9.37-43a)

¹⁴When Jesus and his three disciples came back down, they saw a large crowd around the other disciples. The teachers of the Law of Moses were arguing with them.

¹⁵The crowd was really surprised to see Jesus, and everyone hurried over to greet him.

¹⁶Jesus asked, "What are you arguing about?"

¹⁷Someone from the crowd answered, "Teacher, I brought my son to you. A demon keeps him from talking. ¹⁸Whenever the demon attacks my son, it throws him to the ground and makes him foam at the mouth and grit his teeth in pain. Then he becomes stiff. I asked your disciples to force out the demon, but they couldn't do it."

¹⁹Jesus said, "You people haven't got any faith! How much longer must I be with you? Why do I have to put up with you? Bring the boy to me."

²⁰They brought the boy, and as soon as the demon saw Jesus, it made the boy shake all over. He fell down and began rolling on the ground and foaming at the mouth.

²¹Jesus asked the boy's father, "How long has he been like this?"

The man answered, "Ever since he was a child. ²²The demon has often tried to kill him by throwing him into a fire or into water. Please have pity and help us if you can!"

---

[f]Elijah certainly will come: See the note at 6.15.

23Jesus replied, "Why do you say 'if you can'? Anything is possible for someone who has faith!"

24Straight away the boy's father shouted, "I do have faith! Please help me to have even more."

25When Jesus saw that a crowd was gathering fast, he spoke sternly to the evil spirit that had kept the boy from speaking or hearing. He said, "I order you to come out of the boy! Don't ever bother him again."

26The spirit screamed and made the boy shake all over. Then it went out of him. The boy looked dead, and almost everyone said he was. 27But Jesus took hold of his hand and helped him stand up.

28After Jesus and the disciples had gone back home and were alone, they asked him, "Why couldn't we force out that demon?"

29Jesus answered, "Only prayer can force out that kind of demon."

Jesus Again Speaks about His Death
(Matthew 17.22, 23; Luke 9.43b-45)

30Jesus left with his disciples and set off through Galilee. He didn't want anyone to know about it, 31because he was teaching the disciples that the Son of Man would be handed over to people who would kill him. But three days later he would rise to life. 32The disciples didn't understand what Jesus meant, and they were afraid to ask.

Who Is the Greatest?
(Matthew 18.1-5; Luke 9.46-48)

33Jesus and his disciples went to his home in Capernaum. After they were inside the house, Jesus asked them, "What were you arguing about along the way?" 34They had been arguing about which one of them was the greatest, and so they didn't answer.

35After Jesus sat down and told the twelve disciples to gather around him, he said, "If you want the place of honour, you must become a slave and serve others!"

36Then Jesus had a child stand near him. He put his arm around the child and said, 37"When you welcome even a child because of me, you welcome me. And when you welcome me, you welcome the one who sent me."

For or Against Jesus
(Luke 9.49, 50)

[38]John said, "Teacher, we saw a man using your name to force demons out of people. But he wasn't one of us, and we told him to stop."

[39]Jesus said to his disciples:

Don't stop him! No-one who works miracles in my name will soon turn and say something bad about me. [40]Anyone who isn't against us is for us. [41]And anyone who gives you a cup of water in my name, just because you belong to me, will surely be rewarded.

Temptations To Sin
(Matthew 18.6-9; Luke 17.1, 2)

[42]It will be terrible for people who cause even one of my little followers to sin. Those people would be better off thrown into the ocean with a heavy stone tied around their necks. [43-44]So if your hand causes you to sin, cut it off! You would be better off going into life crippled than to have two hands and be thrown into the fires of hell that never go out.[g] [45-46]If your foot causes you to sin, chop it off. You would be better off going into life lame than to have two feet and be thrown into hell.[h] [47]If your eye causes you to sin, get rid of it. You would be better off going into God's kingdom with only one eye than to have two eyes and be thrown into hell. [48]The worms there never die, and the fire never stops burning.

[49]Everyone must be salted with fire.[i]

[50]Salt is good. But if it no longer tastes like salt, how

---

[g]*never go out:* Some manuscripts add, "The worms there never die, and the fire never stops burning." [h]*thrown into hell:* Some manuscripts add, "The worms there never die, and the fire never stops burning." [i]*salted with fire:* Some manuscripts add "and every sacrifice will be seasoned with salt." The verse may mean that Christ's followers must suffer because of their faith.

can it be made salty again? Have salt among you and live at peace with each other.[j]

Teaching about Divorce
(Matthew 19.1-12; Luke 16.18)

10 [1]After Jesus left, he went to Judea and then on to the other side of the Jordan River. Once again large crowds came to him, and as usual, he taught them.

[2]Some Pharisees wanted to test Jesus. So they came up to him and asked if it was right for a man to divorce his wife. [3]Jesus asked them, "What does the Law of Moses say about that?"

[4]They answered, "Moses allows a man to write out divorce papers and send his wife away."

[5]Jesus replied, "Moses gave you this law because you are so heartless. [6]But in the beginning God made a man and a woman. [7]That's why a man leaves his father and mother and gets married. [8]He becomes like one person with his wife. Then they are no longer two people, but one. [9]And no-one should separate a couple that God has joined together."

[10]When Jesus and his disciples were back in the house, they asked him about what he had said. [11]He told them, "A man who divorces his wife and marries someone else is unfaithful to his wife. [12]A woman who divorces her husband[k] and marries again is also unfaithful."

Jesus Blesses Little Children
(Matthew 19.13-15; Luke 18.15-17)

[13]Some people brought their children to Jesus so that he could bless them by placing his hands on them. But his disciples told the people to stop bothering him.

[14]When Jesus saw this, he became angry and said, "Let the children come to me! Don't try to stop them. People who are like these little children belong to the kingdom

---

[j]*Have salt among you and live at peace with each other:* This may mean that when Christ's followers have to suffer because of their faith, they must still try to live at peace with each other.   [k]*A woman who divorces her husband:* Roman law let a woman divorce her husband, but Jewish law did not let a woman do this.

of God.¹ ¹⁵I promise you that you can't get into God's kingdom, unless you accept it the way a child does." ¹⁶Then Jesus took the children in his arms and blessed them by placing his hands on them.

A Rich Man
(Matthew 19.16-30; Luke 18.18-30)

¹⁷As Jesus was walking down a road, a man ran up to him. He knelt down, and asked, "Good teacher, what can I do to have eternal life?"

¹⁸Jesus replied, "Why do you call me good? Only God is good. ¹⁹You know the commandments. 'Do not murder. Be faithful in marriage. Do not steal. Do not tell lies about others. Do not cheat. Respect your father and mother.' "

²⁰The man answered, "Teacher, I've obeyed all these commandments since I was a young man."

²¹Jesus looked closely at the man. He liked him and said, "There's one thing you still need to do. Go and sell everything you own. Give the money to the poor, and you will have riches in heaven. Then come with me."

²²When the man heard Jesus say this, he went away gloomy and sad because he was very rich.

²³Jesus looked around and said to his disciples, "It's hard for rich people to get into God's kingdom!" ²⁴The disciples were shocked to hear this. So Jesus told them again, "It's terribly hard*m* to get into God's kingdom! ²⁵In fact, it's easier for a camel to go through the eye of a needle than for a rich person to get into God's kingdom."

²⁶Jesus' disciples were even more amazed. They asked each other, "How can anyone ever be saved?"

²⁷Jesus looked at them and said, "There are some things that people can't do, but God can do anything."

²⁸Peter replied, "Remember, we left everything to be your followers!"

²⁹Jesus told him:
        You can be sure that anyone who gives up home or

---

lPeople who are like these little children belong to the kingdom of God: Or "The kingdom of God belongs to people who are like these little children."
mhard: Some manuscripts add "for people who trust in their wealth." Others add "for the rich."

brothers or sisters or mother or father or children or land for me and for the good news [30]will be rewarded. In this world they will be given 100 times as many houses and brothers and sisters and mothers and children and pieces of land, though they will also be mistreated. And in the world to come, they will have eternal life. [31]But many who are now first will be last, and many who are now last will be first.

Jesus Again Tells about His Death
(Matthew 20.17-19; Luke 18.31-34)

[32]The disciples were confused as Jesus led them towards Jerusalem, and his other followers were afraid. Once again, Jesus took the twelve disciples aside and told them what was going to happen to him. He said:

[33]We are now on our way to Jerusalem where the Son of Man will be handed over to the chief priests and the teachers of the Law of Moses. They will sentence him to death and hand him over to foreigners,[n] [34]who will make fun of him and spit on him. They will beat him and kill him. But three days later he will rise to life.

The Request of James and John
(Matthew 20.20-28)

[35]James and John, the sons of Zebedee, came up to Jesus and asked, "Teacher, will you do us a favour?"

[36]Jesus asked them what they wanted, [37]and they answered, "When you come into your glory, please let one of us sit at your right side and the other at your left."[o]

[38]Jesus told them, "You don't really know what you're asking! Are you able to drink from the cup[p] that I must soon drink from, or be baptised as I must be baptised?"[q]

[39]"Yes, we are!" James and John answered.

Then Jesus replied, "You certainly will drink from the

---

[n]foreigners: The Romans who ruled Judea at this time.   [o]right side...left: The most powerful people in a kingdom sat at the right and left side of the king. [p]drink from the cup: In the Scriptures a "cup" is sometimes used as a symbol of suffering. To "drink from the cup" would be to suffer.   [q]as I must be baptised: Baptism is used with the same meaning that "cup" has in this verse.

cup from which I must drink. And you will be baptised just as I must! 40But it isn't for me to say who will sit at my right side and at my left. That is for God to decide."

41When the ten other disciples heard this, they were angry with James and John. 42But Jesus called the disciples together and said:

You know that those foreigners who call themselves kings like to order their people around. And their great leaders have full power over the people they rule. 43But don't act like them. If you want to be great, you must be the servant of all the others. 44And if you want to be first, you must be everyone's slave. 45The Son of Man did not come to be a slave master, but a slave who will give his life to rescue[r] many people.

Jesus Heals Blind Bartimaeus
(Matthew 20.29-34; Luke 18.35-43)

46Jesus and his disciples went to Jericho. And as they were leaving, they were followed by a large crowd. A blind beggar by the name of Bartimaeus son of Timaeus was sitting beside the road. 47When he heard that it was Jesus from Nazareth, he shouted, "Jesus, Son of David,[s] have pity on me!" 48Many people told the man to stop, but he shouted even louder, "Son of David, have pity on me!"

49Jesus stopped and said, "Call him over!"

They called out to the blind man and said, "Don't be afraid! Come on! He's calling for you." 50The man threw off his coat as he jumped up and ran to Jesus.

51Jesus asked, "What do you want me to do for you?"

The blind man answered, "Master,[t] I want to see!"

52Jesus told him, "You may go. Your eyes are healed because of your faith."

Straight away the man could see, and he went down the road with Jesus.

[r]rescue: The Greek word often, though not always, means the payment of money to free a slave or prisoner. [s]Son of David: The Jewish people expected the Messiah to be from the family of King David, so the Messiah was often called the "Son of David." [t]Master: A Hebrew word that may also mean "Teacher."

Jesus Enters Jerusalem
(Matthew 21.1-11; Luke 19.28-40; John 12.12-19)

11 ¹Jesus and his disciples reached Bethphage and Bethany near the Mount of Olives. When they were getting close to Jerusalem, Jesus sent two of them on ahead. ²He told them, "Go into the next village. As soon as you enter it, you'll find a young donkey that has never been ridden. Untie the donkey and bring it here. ³If anyone asks why you're doing that, say, 'The Lord*u* needs it and will soon bring it back.' "

⁴The disciples left and found the donkey tied near a door that faced the street. While they were untying it, ⁵some of the people standing there asked, "Why are you untying the donkey?" ⁶They told them what Jesus had said, and the people let them take it.

⁷The disciples led the donkey to Jesus. They put some of their clothes on its back, and Jesus got on. ⁸Many people spread clothes on the road, while others went to cut branches from the fields.*v*

⁹In front of Jesus and behind him, people went along shouting,

"Hooray!*w* God bless the one
who comes in the name of the Lord!
10   God bless the coming kingdom of our ancestor David.
Hooray for God in heaven above!"

¹¹After Jesus had gone to Jerusalem, he went into the temple and looked around at everything. But since it was already late in the day, he went back to Bethany with the twelve disciples.

Jesus Puts a Curse on a Fig Tree
(Matthew 21.18, 19)

¹²When Jesus and his disciples left Bethany the next morning, he was hungry. ¹³From a distance Jesus saw a fig tree covered with leaves, and he went to see if there were any figs on the tree. But there weren't any, because

---

uThe Lord: Or "The master of the donkey." *vspread...branches from the fields:* One way that the Jewish people welcomed a famous person. *wHooray:* This translates a word that can mean "please save us." But it is most often used as a shout of praise to God.

it wasn't the season for figs. ¹⁴So Jesus said to the tree, "Never again will anyone eat fruit from this tree!" The disciples heard him say this.

Jesus in the Temple
(Matthew 21.12-17; Luke 19.45-48; John 2.13-22)

¹⁵After Jesus and his disciples reached Jerusalem, he went into the temple and began chasing out everyone who was selling and buying. He turned over the tables of the money-changers and the benches of those who were selling doves. ¹⁶Jesus wouldn't let anyone carry things through the temple. ¹⁷Then he taught the people and said, "The Scriptures say, 'My house should be called a place of worship for all nations.' But you have made it a place where robbers hide!"

¹⁸The chief priests and the teachers of the Law of Moses heard what Jesus said, and they started looking for a way to kill him. They were afraid of him, because the crowds were completely amazed at his teaching.

¹⁹That evening, Jesus and the disciples went outside the city.

A Lesson from the Fig Tree
(Matthew 21.20-22)

²⁰As the disciples walked past the fig tree the next morning, they noticed that it was completely dried up, roots and all. ²¹Peter remembered what Jesus had said to the tree. Then Peter said, "Teacher, look! The tree you put a curse on has dried up."

²²Jesus told his disciples:

Have faith in God! ²³If you have faith in God and don't doubt, you can tell this mountain to get up and jump into the sea, and it will. ²⁴Everything you ask for in prayer will be yours, if you only have faith.

²⁵⁻²⁶Whenever you stand up to pray, you must forgive what others have done to you. Then your Father in heaven will forgive your sins.ˣ

ˣ*your sins:* Some manuscripts add, "But if you do not forgive others, God will not forgive you."

A Question about Jesus' Authority
(Matthew 21.23-27; Luke 20.1-8)

27 Jesus and his disciples returned to Jerusalem. And as he was walking through the temple, the chief priests, the nation's leaders, and the teachers of the Law of Moses came over to him. 28 They asked, "What right have you got to do these things? Who gave you this authority?"

29 Jesus answered, "I have just one question to ask you. If you answer it, I'll tell you where I got the right to do these things. 30 Who gave John the right to baptise? Was it God in heaven or merely some human being?"

31 They thought it over and said to each other, "We can't say that God gave John this right. Jesus will ask us why we didn't believe John. 32 On the other hand, these people think that John was a prophet. So we can't say that it was merely some human who gave John the right to baptise."

They were afraid of the crowd 33 and told Jesus, "We don't know."

Jesus replied, "Then I won't tell you who gave me the right to do what I do."

Tenants of a Vineyard
(Matthew 21.33-46; Luke 20.9-19)

12 1 Jesus then told them this story:

A farmer once planted a vineyard. He built a wall around it and dug a pit to crush the grapes in. He also built a lookout tower. Then he rented out his vineyard and left the country.

2 When it was harvest time, he sent a servant to get his share of the grapes. 3 The tenants grabbed the servant. They beat him up and sent him away without a thing.

4 The owner sent another servant, but the tenants beat him on the head and insulted him terribly. 5 Then the man sent another servant, and they killed him. He kept sending servant after servant. They beat some of them and killed others.

6 The owner had a son he loved very much. Finally, he sent his son to the tenants because he thought they

would respect him. ⁷But they said to themselves, "Some day he'll own this vineyard. Let's kill him! That way we can have it all for ourselves." ⁸So they grabbed the owner's son and killed him. Then they threw his body out of the vineyard.

⁹Jesus asked, "What do you think the owner of the vineyard will do? He'll come and kill those tenants and let someone else have his vineyard. ¹⁰You surely know that the Scriptures say,

'The stone that the builders tossed aside
        is now the most important stone of all.
¹¹ This is something the Lord has done,
        and it's amazing to us.' "

¹²The leaders knew that Jesus was really talking about them, and they wanted to arrest him. But because they were afraid of the crowd, they let him alone and left.

Paying Taxes
(Matthew 22.15-22; Luke 20.20-26)

¹³The Pharisees got together with Herod's followers.ʸ Then they sent some men to trick Jesus into saying something wrong. ¹⁴They went to him and said, "Teacher, we know that you are honest. You treat everyone with the same respect, no matter who they are. And you teach the truth about what God wants people to do. Tell us, should we pay taxes to the Emperor or not?"

¹⁵Jesus knew what they were up to, and he said, "Why are you trying to test me? Show me a coin!"

¹⁶They brought him a silver coin, and he asked, "Whose picture and name are on it?"

"The Emperor's," they answered.

¹⁷Then Jesus told them, "Give the Emperor what belongs to him and give God what belongs to God." The men were amazed at Jesus.

ʸ*Herod's followers:* People who were political followers of the family of Herod the Great and his son Herod Antipas.

Life in the Future World
(Matthew 22.23-33; Luke 20.27-40)

18 The Sadducees didn't believe that people would rise to life after death. So some of them came to Jesus and said:

19 Teacher, Moses wrote that if a married man dies and has no children, his brother should marry the widow. Their first son would then be thought of as the son of the dead brother. 20 There were once seven brothers. The first one married, but died without having any children. 21 The second brother married his brother's widow, and he also died without having children. The same thing happened to the third brother, 22 and finally to all seven brothers. At last the woman died. 23 When God raises people from death, whose wife will this woman be? After all, she had been married to all seven brothers.

24 Jesus answered:

You are completely wrong! You don't know what the Scriptures teach. And you don't know anything about the power of God. 25 When God raises people to life, they won't marry. They will be like the angels in heaven. 26 You surely know about people being raised to life. You know that in the story about Moses and the burning bush, God said, "I am the God worshipped by Abraham, Isaac, and Jacob."z 27 He isn't the God of the dead, but of the living. You Sadducees are all wrong.

The Most Important Commandment
(Matthew 22.34-40; Luke 10.25-28)

28 One of the teachers of the Law of Moses came up while Jesus and the Sadducees were arguing. When he heard Jesus give a good answer, he asked him, "What is the most important commandment?"

29 Jesus answered, "The most important one says: 'People of Israel, you have only one Lord and God. 30 You must love him with all your heart, soul, mind, and

---

z"I am the God worshipped by Abraham, Isaac, and Jacob": Jesus argues that if God is worshipped by these three, they must still be alive, because he is the God of the living.

strength.' ³¹The second most important commandment says: 'Love others as much as you love yourself.' No other commandment is more important than these."

³²The man replied, "Teacher, you are certainly right to say there is only one God. ³³It's also true that we must love God with all our heart, mind, and strength, and that we must love others as much as we love ourselves. These commandments are more important than all the sacrifices and offerings that we could possibly make."

³⁴When Jesus saw that the man had given a sensible answer, he told him, "You are not far from God's kingdom." After this, no-one dared ask Jesus any more questions.

About David's Son
(Matthew 22.41-46; Luke 20.41-44)

³⁵As Jesus was teaching in the temple, he said, "How can the teachers of the Law of Moses say that the Messiah will come from the family of King David? ³⁶The Holy Spirit led David to say,

> 'The Lord said to my Lord:
> Sit at my right side*a*
>   until I make your enemies into a footstool for you.'

³⁷If David called the Messiah his Lord, how can the Messiah be his son?"*b*

The large crowd enjoyed listening to Jesus teach.

Jesus Condemns the Pharisees
and the Teachers of the Law of Moses
(Matthew 23.1-36; Luke 20.45-47)

³⁸As Jesus was teaching, he said:

> Guard against the teachers of the Law of Moses! They love to walk around in long robes and be greeted in the market. ³⁹They like the front seats in the meeting places and the best seats at banquets. ⁴⁰But they cheat widows out of their homes and pray long prayers just to show off. They will be punished most of all.

---

*a**right side:* The place of power and honour.   *b**David...his son:* See the note at 10.47.

A Widow's Offering
(Luke 21.1-4)

[41]Jesus was sitting in the temple near the offering box and watching people put in their gifts. He noticed that many rich people were giving a lot of money. [42]Finally, a poor widow came up and put in two coins that were worth only a few cents. [43]Jesus told his disciples to gather around him. Then he said:

I tell you that this poor widow has put in more than all the others. [44]Everyone else gave what they didn't need. But she is very poor and gave everything she had. Now she doesn't have a cent to live on.

The Temple Will Be Destroyed
(Matthew 24.1, 2; Luke 21.5, 6)

13 [1]As Jesus was leaving the temple, one of his disciples said to him, "Teacher, look at these beautiful stones and wonderful buildings!"

[2]Jesus replied, "Do you see these huge buildings? They will certainly be torn down! Not one stone will be left in place."

Warning about Trouble
(Matthew 24.3-14; Luke 21.7-19)

[3]Later, as Jesus was sitting on the Mount of Olives across from the temple, Peter, James, John, and Andrew came to him in private. [4]They asked, "When will these things happen? What will be the sign that they are about to take place?"

[5]Jesus answered:

Watch out and don't let anyone fool you! [6]Many will come and claim to be me. They will use my name and fool many people.

[7]When you hear about wars and threats of wars, don't be afraid. These things will have to happen first, but that isn't the end. [8]Nations and kingdoms will go to war against each other. There will be earthquakes in many places, and people will starve to death. But this is just the beginning of troubles.

⁹Be on your guard! You will be taken to courts and beaten with whips in their meeting places. And because of me, you will have to stand before rulers and kings to tell about your faith. ¹⁰But before the end comes, the good news must be preached to all nations.

¹¹When you are arrested, don't worry about what you will say. You will be given the right words when the time comes. But you won't really be the ones speaking. Your words will come from the Holy Spirit.

¹²Brothers and sisters will betray each other and have each other put to death. Parents will betray their own children, and children will turn against their parents and have them killed. ¹³Everyone will hate you because of me. But if you keep on being faithful right to the end, you will be saved.

The Horrible Thing
(Matthew 24.15-21; Luke 21.20-24)

¹⁴Some day you will see that "Horrible Thing" where it should not be.ᶜ Everyone who reads this must try to understand! If you are living in Judea at that time, run to the mountains. ¹⁵If you are on the roofᵈ of your house, don't go inside to get anything. ¹⁶If you are out in the field, don't go back for your coat. ¹⁷It will be an awful time for women who are expecting babies or nursing young children. ¹⁸Pray that it won't happen in winter.ᵉ ¹⁹This will be the worst time of suffering since God created the world, and nothing this terrible will ever happen again. ²⁰If the Lord doesn't make the time shorter, no-one will be left alive. But because of his chosen and special ones, he will make the time shorter.

²¹If someone should say, "Here's the Messiah!" or "There he is!" don't believe it. ²²False messiahs and false prophets will come and work miracles and signs. They will even try to fool God's chosen ones. ²³But be on your guard! That's why I am telling you these things now.

ᶜ*where it should not be:* Probably the holy place in the temple.   ᵈ*roof:* See the note at 2.4.   ᵉ*in winter:* In Palestine the winters are cold and rainy and make travel difficult.

When the Son of Man Appears
(Matthew 24.29-31; Luke 21.25-28)

²⁴In those days, right after that time of suffering,
"The sun will become dark,
and the moon will no longer shine.
²⁵ The stars will fall,
and the powers in the sky^f will be
shaken."
²⁶Then the Son of Man will be seen coming in the clouds with great power and glory. ²⁷He will send his angels to gather his chosen ones from all over the earth.

A Lesson from a Fig Tree
(Matthew 24.32-35; Luke 21.29-33)

²⁸Learn a lesson from a fig tree. When its branches sprout and start putting out leaves, you know summer is near. ²⁹So when you see all these things happening, you will know that the time has almost come.^{g} ³⁰You can be sure that some of the people of this generation will still be alive when all this happens. ³¹The sky and the earth won't last for ever, but my words will.

No-one Knows the Day or Time
(Matthew 24.36-44)

³²No-one knows the day or the time. The angels in heaven don't know, and the Son himself doesn't know. Only the Father knows. ³³So watch out and be ready! You don't know when the time will come. ³⁴It's like what happens when a man goes away for a while and places his servants in charge of everything. He tells each of them what to do, and he orders the guard to keep alert. ³⁵So be alert! You don't know when the master of the house will come back. It could be in the evening or at midnight or before dawn or in the morning. ³⁶But if he comes suddenly, don't let him find you asleep. ³⁷I tell everyone just what I have told you. Be alert!

---

^{f}*the powers in the sky:* In ancient times people thought that the stars were spiritual powers. ^{g}*the time has almost come:* Or "he (that is, the Son of Man) will soon be here."

A Plot To Kill Jesus
(Matthew 26.1-5; Luke 22.1, 2; John 11.45-53)

14 ¹It was now two days before Passover and the Festival of Thin Bread. The chief priests and the teachers of the Law of Moses were planning how they could sneak around and have Jesus arrested and put to death. ²They were saying, "We mustn't do it during the festival, because the people will riot."

At Bethany
(Matthew 26.6-13; John 12.1-8)

³Jesus was eating in Bethany at the home of Simon, who once had leprosy,ʰ when a woman came in with a very expensive bottle of sweet-smelling perfume.ⁱ After breaking it open, she poured the perfume on Jesus' head. ⁴This made some of the guests angry, and they complained, "Why such a waste? ⁵We could have sold this perfume for more than 300 silver coins and given the money to the poor!" So they started saying cruel things to the woman.

⁶But Jesus said:

Leave her alone! Why are you bothering her? She's done a beautiful thing for me. ⁷You'll always have the poor with you. And whenever you want to, you can give to them. But you won't always have me here with you. ⁸She's done all she could by pouring perfume on my body to prepare it for burial. ⁹You can be sure that wherever the good news is told all over the world, people will remember what she's done. And they will tell others.

Judas and the Chief Priests
(Matthew 26.14-16; Luke 22.3-6)

¹⁰Judas Iscariotʲ was one of the twelve disciples. He went to the chief priests and offered to help them arrest Jesus. ¹¹They were glad to hear this, and they promised

---

ʰleprosy: In biblical times the word "leprosy" was used for many different skin diseases. ⁱsweet-smelling perfume: The Greek text has "perfume made of pure spikenard," a plant used to make perfume. ʲIscariot: See the note at 3.19.

to pay him. So Judas started looking for a good chance to betray Jesus.

Jesus Eats with His Disciples

(Matthew 26.17-25; Luke 22.7-14, 21-23; John 13.21-30)

¹²It was the first day of the Festival of Thin Bread, and the Passover lambs were being killed. Jesus' disciples asked him, "Where do you want us to prepare the Passover meal?"

¹³Jesus said to two of the disciples, "Go into the city, where you will meet a man carrying a jar of water.ᵏ Follow him, ¹⁴and when he goes into a house, say to the owner, 'Our teacher wants to know if you have a room where he can eat the Passover meal with his disciples.' ¹⁵The owner will take you upstairs and show you a large room furnished and ready for you to use. Prepare the meal there."

¹⁶The two disciples went into the city and found everything just as Jesus had told them. So they prepared the Passover meal.

¹⁷⁻¹⁸While Jesus and the twelve disciples were eating together that evening, he said, "The one who will betray me is now eating with me."

¹⁹This made the disciples sad, and one after another they said to Jesus, "Surely you don't mean me!"

²⁰He answered, "It is one of you twelve men who is eating from this dish with me. ²¹The Son of Man will die, just as the Scriptures say. But it's going to be terrible for the one who betrays me. That man would be better off if he'd never been born."

The Lord's Supper

(Matthew 26.26-30; Luke 22.14-23; 1 Corinthians 11.23-25)

²²During the meal Jesus took some bread in his hands. He blessed the bread and broke it. Then he gave it to his disciples and said, "Take this. It is my body."

²³Jesus picked up a cup of wine and gave thanks to God. He gave it to his disciples, and they all drank some.

ᵏ*a man carrying a jar of water:* A male slave carrying water could mean that the family was rich.

²⁴Then he said, "This is my blood, which is poured out for many people, and with it God makes his agreement. ²⁵From now on I won't drink any wine, until I drink new wine in God's kingdom." ²⁶Then they sang a hymn and went out to the Mount of Olives.

Peter's Promise
(Matthew 26.31-35; Luke 22.31-34; John 13.36-38)

²⁷Jesus said to his disciples, "All of you will reject me, as the Scriptures say,

'I will strike down the shepherd,
        and the sheep will be scattered.'

²⁸But after I'm raised to life, I'll go ahead of you to Galilee."

²⁹Peter spoke up, "Even if all the others reject you, I never will!"

³⁰Jesus replied, "This very night before a rooster crows twice, you will say three times that you don't know me."

³¹But Peter was so sure of himself that he said, "Even if I have to die with you, I'll never say that I don't know you!"

All the others said the same thing.

Jesus Prays
(Matthew 26.36-46; Luke 22.39-46)

³²Jesus went with his disciples to a place called Gethsemane, and he told them, "Sit here while I pray."

³³Jesus took along Peter, James, and John. He was sad and troubled and ³⁴told them, "I'm so sad that I feel as if I'm dying. Stay here and keep awake with me."

³⁵⁻³⁶Jesus walked on a little way. Then he knelt down on the ground and prayed, "Father,ˡ if it's possible, don't let this happen to me! Father, you can do anything. Don't make me suffer by getting me to drink from this cup.ᵐ But do what you want, and not what I want."

³⁷When Jesus came back and found the disciples sleeping, he said to Simon Peter, "Are you asleep? Can't you stay awake for just one hour? ³⁸Stay awake and pray that you won't be tested. You want to do what is right, but you are weak."

ˡFather: The Greek text has "Abba," which is an Aramaic word meaning "father."
ᵐby getting me to drink from this cup: See the note at 10.38.

³⁹Jesus went back and prayed the same prayer. ⁴⁰But when he returned to the disciples, he found them sleeping again. They simply couldn't keep their eyes open, and they didn't know what to say.

⁴¹When Jesus returned to the disciples the third time, he said, "Are you still sleeping and resting?ⁿ Enough of that! The time has come for the Son of Man to be handed over to sinners. ⁴²Get up! Let's go. The one who will betray me is already here."

Jesus Is Arrested
(Matthew 26.47-56; Luke 22.47-53; John 18.3-12)

⁴³Jesus was still speaking, when Judas the betrayer came up. He was one of the twelve disciples, and a mob of men armed with swords and clubs were with him. They had been sent by the chief priests, the nation's leaders, and the teachers of the Law of Moses. ⁴⁴Judas had told them ahead of time, "Arrest the man I greet with a kiss.º Tie him up tight and lead him away."

⁴⁵Judas walked right up to Jesus and said, "Teacher!" Then Judas kissed him, ⁴⁶and the men grabbed Jesus and arrested him.

⁴⁷Someone standing there pulled out a sword. He struck the servant of the high priest and cut off his ear.

⁴⁸Jesus said to the mob, "Why do you come with swords and clubs to arrest me like a criminal? ⁴⁹Day after day I was with you and taught in the temple, and you didn't arrest me. But what the Scriptures say must come true."

⁵⁰All of Jesus' disciples ran off and left him. ⁵¹One of them was a young man who was wearing only a linen cloth. And when the men grabbed him, ⁵²he left the cloth behind and ran away naked.

Jesus Is Questioned by the Council
(Matthew 26.57-68; Luke 22.54, 55, 63-71; John 18.13, 14, 19-24)

⁵³Jesus was led off to the high priest. Then the chief priests, the nation's leaders, and the teachers of the Law

ⁿ*Are you still sleeping and resting?:* Or "You may as well keep on sleeping and resting." º*greet with a kiss:* It was the custom for people to greet each other with a kiss on the cheek.

of Moses all met together. 54Peter had followed at a distance. And when he reached the courtyard of the high priest's house, he sat down with the guards to warm himself beside a fire.

55The chief priests and the whole council tried to find someone to accuse Jesus of a crime, so they could put him to death. But they couldn't find anyone to accuse him. 56Many people told lies against Jesus, but they didn't agree on what they said. 57Finally, some men stood up and lied about him. They said, 58"We heard him say he would tear down this temple that we built. He also claimed that in three days he would build another one without any help." 59But even then they didn't agree on what they said.

60The high priest stood up in the council and asked Jesus, "Why don't you say something in your own defence? Don't you hear the charges they are making against you?" 61But Jesus kept quiet and didn't say a word. The high priest asked him another question, "Are you the Messiah, the Son of the glorious God?"p

62"Yes, I am!" Jesus answered.

"Soon you will see the Son of Man
      sitting at the right sideq of God All-Powerful,
            and coming with the clouds of heaven."

63At once the high priest ripped his robe apart and shouted, "Why do we need more witnesses? 64You heard him claim to be God! What is your decision?" They all agreed that he should be put to death.

65Some of the people started spitting on Jesus. They blindfolded him, punched him with their fists, and said, "Tell us who hit you!" Then the guards took charge of Jesus and beat him.

Peter Says He Doesn't Know Jesus
(Matthew 26.69-75; Luke 22.56-62; John 18.15-18, 25-27)

66While Peter was still in the courtyard, a servant girl of the high priest came up 67and saw Peter warming himself by the fire. She stared at him and said, "You were

pSon of the glorious God: "Son of God" was one of the titles used for the kings of Israel.   qright side: See the note at 12.36.

with Jesus from Nazareth!"

⁶⁸Peter replied, "That isn't true! I don't know what you're talking about. I don't have any idea what you mean." He went out to the gate, and a rooster crowed.ʳ

⁶⁹The servant girl saw Peter again and said to the people standing there, "This man is one of them!"

⁷⁰"No, I'm not!" Peter replied.

A little while later some of the people said to Peter, "You certainly are one of them. You're a Galilean!"

⁷¹This time Peter began to curse and swear, "I don't even know the man you're talking about!"

⁷²Straight away the rooster crowed a second time. Then Peter remembered that Jesus had told him, "Before a rooster crows twice, you will say three times that you don't know me." So Peter started crying.

Pilate Questions Jesus
(Matthew 27.1, 2, 11-14; Luke 23.1-5; John 18.28-38)

15 ¹Early the next morning the chief priests, the nation's leaders, and the teachers of the Law of Moses met together with the whole Jewish council. They tied Jesus up and led him off to Pilate.

²He asked Jesus, "Are you the king of the Jews?"

"Those are your words," Jesus answered.

³The chief priests brought many charges against Jesus. ⁴Then Pilate questioned him again, "Haven't you got anything to say? Don't you hear what crimes they say you've done?" ⁵But Jesus didn't answer, and Pilate was amazed.

The Death Sentence
(Matthew 27.15-26; Luke 23.13-25; John 18.39—19.16)

⁶During Passover, Pilate always freed one prisoner chosen by the people. ⁷And at that time there was a prisoner named Barabbas. He and some others had been arrested for murder during a riot. ⁸The crowd now came and asked Pilate to set a prisoner free, just as he usually did.

⁹Pilate asked them, "Do you want me to free the king

ʳa rooster crowed: These words are not in some manuscripts.

of the Jews?" [10]Pilate knew that the chief priests had brought Jesus to him because they were jealous.

[11]But the chief priests told the crowd to ask Pilate to free Barabbas.

[12]Then Pilate asked the crowd, "What do you want me to do with this man you say is[s] the king of the Jews?"

[13]They yelled, "Nail him to a cross!"

[14]Pilate asked, "But what crime has he done?"

"Nail him to a cross!" they yelled even louder.

[15]Pilate wanted to please the crowd. So he set Barabbas free. Then he ordered his soldiers to beat Jesus with a whip and nail him to a cross.

Soldiers Make Fun of Jesus
(Matthew 27.27-30; John 19.2, 3)

[16]The soldiers led Jesus inside the courtyard of the fortress[t] and called together the rest of the troops. [17]They put a purple robe[u] on him, and on his head they placed a crown that they had made out of thorny branches. [18]They made fun of Jesus and shouted, "Hey, you king of the Jews!" [19]Then they beat him on the head with a stick. They spat on him and knelt down and pretended to worship him.

[20]When the soldiers had finished making fun of Jesus, they took off the purple robe. They put his own clothes back on him and led him off to be nailed to a cross. [21]Simon from Cyrene happened to be coming in from a farm, and they forced him to carry Jesus' cross. Simon was the father of Alexander and Rufus.

Jesus Is Nailed to a Cross
(Matthew 27.31-44; Luke 23.27-43; John 19.17-27)

[22]The soldiers took Jesus to Golgotha, which means "Place of a Skull."[v] [23]There they gave him some wine mixed with a drug to ease the pain, but he refused to drink it.

---

[s]*this man you say is:* These words are not in some manuscripts.   [t]*fortress:* The place where the Roman governor stayed, probably at Herod's palace west of Jerusalem, or possibly Fortress Antonia, north of the temple, where the Roman troops were stationed. [u]*purple robe:* This was probably a Roman soldier's robe. [v]*Place of a Skull:* The place was probably given this name because it was near a large rock in the shape of a human skull.

²⁴They nailed Jesus to a cross and gambled to see who would get his clothes. ²⁵It was about nine o'clock in the morning when they nailed him to the cross. ²⁶On it was a sign that said why he was nailed there. It read, "This is the King of the Jews." ²⁷⁻²⁸The soldiers also nailed two criminals on crosses, one to the right of Jesus and the other to his left.ʷ

²⁹People who passed by said terrible things about Jesus. They shook their heads and shouted, "Ha! So you're the one who claimed you could tear down the temple and build it again in three days. ³⁰Save yourself and come down from the cross!"

³¹The chief priests and the teachers of the Law of Moses also made fun of Jesus. They said to each other, "He saved others, but he can't save himself. ³²If he's the Messiah, the king of Israel, let him come down from the cross! Then we will see and believe." The two criminals also said cruel things to Jesus.

The Death of Jesus
(Matthew 27.45-56; Luke 23.44-49; John 19.28-30)

³³About midday the sky turned dark and stayed that way until around three o'clock. ³⁴Then about that time Jesus shouted, "Eloi, Eloi, lema sabachthani?"ˣ which means, "My God, my God, why have you deserted me?"

³⁵Some of the people standing there heard Jesus and said, "He's calling for Elijah."ʸ ³⁶One of them ran and grabbed a sponge. After he had soaked it in wine, he put it on a stick and held it up to Jesus. He said, "Let's wait and see if Elijah will comeᶻ and take him down!" ³⁷Jesus shouted and then died.

³⁸At once the curtain in the templeᵃ tore in two from top to bottom.

ʷleft: Some manuscripts add, "So the Scriptures came true which say, 'He was accused of being a criminal.' " ˣEloi...sabachthani: These words are in Aramaic, a language spoken in Palestine during the time of Jesus. ʸElijah: The name "Elijah" sounds something like "Eloi," which means "my God." ᶻsee if Elijah will come: See the note at 6.15. ᵃcurtain in the temple: There were two curtains in the temple. One was at the entrance, and the other separated the holy place from the most holy place that the Jewish people thought of as God's home on earth. The second curtain is probably the one which is meant.

[39]A Roman army officer was standing in front of Jesus. When the officer saw how Jesus died, he said, "This man really was the Son of God!"

[40-41]Some women were looking on from a distance. They had come with Jesus to Jerusalem. But even before this they had been his followers and had helped him while he was in Galilee. Mary Magdalene and Mary the mother of the younger James and of Joseph were two of these women. Salome was also one of them.

Jesus Is Buried
(Matthew 27.57-61; Luke 23.50-56; John 19.38-42)

[42]It was now the evening before the Sabbath, and the Jewish people were getting ready for that sacred day. [43]A man named Joseph from Arimathea was brave enough to ask Pilate for the body of Jesus. Joseph was a highly respected member of the Jewish council, and he was also waiting for God's kingdom to come.

[44]Pilate was surprised to hear that Jesus was already dead, and he called in the army officer to find out if Jesus had been dead very long. [45]After the officer told him, Pilate let Joseph have Jesus' body.

[46]Joseph bought a linen cloth and took the body down from the cross. He had it wrapped in the cloth, and he put it in a tomb that had been cut into solid rock. Then he rolled a big stone against the entrance to the tomb.

[47]Mary Magdalene and Mary the mother of Joseph were watching and saw where the body was placed.

Jesus Is Alive
(Matthew 28.1-8; Luke 24.1-12; John 20.1-10)

16 [1]After the Sabbath, Mary Magdalene, Salome, and Mary the mother of James bought some spices to put on Jesus' body. [2]Very early on Sunday morning, just as the sun was coming up, they went to the tomb. [3]On their way, they were asking one another, "Who will roll the stone away from the entrance for us?" [4]But when they looked, they saw that the stone had already been rolled away. And it was a huge stone!

[5]The women went into the tomb, and on the right side

they saw a young man in a white robe sitting there. They were alarmed.

⁶The man said, "Don't be alarmed! You are looking for Jesus from Nazareth, who was nailed to a cross. God has raised him to life, and he isn't here. You can see the place where they put his body. ⁷Now go and tell his disciples, and especially Peter, that he will go ahead of you to Galilee. You will see him there, just as he told you."

⁸When the women ran from the tomb, they were confused and shaking all over. They were too afraid to tell anyone what had happened.

ONE OLD ENDING TO MARK'S GOSPEL[b]

Jesus Appears to Mary Magdalene
(Matthew 28.9, 10; John 20.11-18)

⁹Very early on the first day of the week, after Jesus had risen to life, he appeared to Mary Magdalene. Earlier he had forced seven demons out of her. ¹⁰She left and told his friends, who were crying and mourning. ¹¹Even though they heard that Jesus was alive and that Mary had seen him, they wouldn't believe it.

Jesus Appears to Two Disciples
(Luke 24.13-35)

¹²Later, Jesus appeared in another form to two disciples, as they were on their way out of the city. ¹³But when these disciples told what had happened, the others wouldn't believe.

What Jesus' Followers Must Do
(Matthew 28.16-20; Luke 24.36-49; John 20.19-23; Acts 1.6-8)

¹⁴Afterwards, Jesus appeared to his eleven disciples as they were eating. He scolded them because they were too stubborn to believe the ones who had seen him after he had been raised to life. ¹⁵Then he told them:

Go and preach the good news to everyone in the world. ¹⁶Anyone who believes me and is baptised will

bOne Old Ending to Mark's Gospel: Verses 9-20 are not in some manuscripts.

be saved. But anyone who refuses to believe me will be condemned. [17]Everyone who believes me will be able to do wonderful things. By using my name they will force out demons, and they will speak new languages. [18]They will handle snakes and will drink poison and not be hurt. They will also heal sick people by placing their hands on them.

Jesus Returns to Heaven
(Luke 24.50-53; Acts 1.9-11)

[19]After the Lord Jesus had said these things to the disciples, he was taken back up to heaven where he sat down at the right side[c] of God. [20]Then the disciples left and preached everywhere. The Lord was with them, and the miracles they worked proved that their message was true.

ANOTHER OLD ENDING TO MARK'S GOSPEL[d]

[9-10]The women quickly told Peter and his friends what had happened. Later, Jesus sent the disciples to the east and to the west with his sacred and everlasting message of how people can be saved for ever.

---

[c]right side: See the note at 12.36.   [d]Another Old Ending to Mark's Gospel: Some manuscripts and early translations have both this shorter ending and the longer one (verses 9-20).

LUKE
ABOUT THIS BOOK

God's love is for everyone! Jesus came into the world to be the Saviour of all people! These are two of the main thoughts in this book. Several of the best-known stories that Jesus used for teaching about God's love are found only in Luke's Gospel: The Good Samaritan (chapter 10.25-37), A Lost Sheep (15.1-7), and A Lost Son (15.11-32). Only Luke tells us how Jesus visited in the home of a hated tax collector (19.1-10) and promised life in paradise to a dying criminal (23.39-43).

Luke mentions God's Spirit more than any of the other New Testament writers. For example, the power of the Spirit was with John the Baptist from the time he was born (1.15). And the angel promised Mary, "The Holy Spirit will come down to you....So your child will be called the holy Son of God" (1.35). Jesus followed the Spirit (4.1, 14, 18; 10.21) and taught that the Spirit is God's greatest gift (11.13).

Luke shows how important prayer was to Jesus. Jesus prayed often: after being baptised (3.21), before choosing the disciples (6.12), before asking his disciples who they thought he was (9.18), and before giving up his life on the cross (23.34, 46). From Luke we learn of three stories that Jesus told to teach about prayer (11.5-9; 18.1-8, 9-14).

An important part of Luke's story is the way in which he shows the concern of Jesus for the poor: the good news is preached to them (4.18; 7.22), they receive God's blessings (6.20), they are invited to the great feast (14.13, 21), the poor man Lazarus is taken to heaven by angels (16.20, 22), and Jesus commands his disciples to sell what they have and give the money to the poor (12.33).

To make sure that readers would understand that Jesus was raised physically from death, Luke reports that the risen Jesus ate a piece of fish (24.42, 43). There could be no mistake about the risen Jesus: he was not a ghost. His being raised from death was real and not someone's imagination. Luke also wrote another book—the Acts of the Apostles—to show what happened to Jesus' followers after he was raised from death and taken up to heaven. No other Gospel has a second volume that continues the story.

Luke closes this first book that he wrote by saying that Jesus returned to heaven. But just before Jesus leaves, he tells his disciples:

"The Scriptures say that the Messiah must suffer, then three days later he will rise from death. They also say that all people of every nation must be told in my name to turn to God, in order to be forgiven. So beginning in Jerusalem, you must tell everyone everything that has happened."   *(Chapter 24.46-48)*

A QUICK LOOK AT THIS BOOK

1 ¹Many people have tried to tell the story of what God has done among us. ²They wrote what we had been told by the ones who were there in the beginning and saw what happened. ³So I made a careful study*ᵃ* of everything and then decided to write and tell you exactly what took place. Honourable Theophilus, ⁴I have done this to let you know the truth about what you have heard.

An Angel Tells about the Birth of John

⁵When Herod was king of Judea, there was a priest by the name of Zechariah from the priestly group of Abijah. His wife Elizabeth was from the family of Aaron.*ᵇ* ⁶Both of them were good people and pleased the Lord God by

---

ᵃa careful study: Or "a study from the beginning."   *ᵇAaron:* The brother of Moses and the first priest.

obeying all that he had commanded. ⁷But they had no children. Elizabeth couldn't have any, and both Zechariah and Elizabeth were already old.

⁸One day Zechariah's group of priests were on duty, and he was serving God as a priest. ⁹According to the custom of the priests, he had been chosen to go into the Lord's temple that day and to burn incense,ᶜ ¹⁰while the people stood outside praying.

¹¹All at once an angel from the Lord appeared to Zechariah at the right side of the altar. ¹²Zechariah was confused and afraid when he saw the angel. ¹³But the angel told him:

Don't be afraid, Zechariah! God has heard your prayers. Your wife Elizabeth will have a son, and you must name him John. ¹⁴His birth will make you very happy, and many people will be glad. ¹⁵Your son will be a great servant of the Lord. He must never drink wine or beer, and the power of the Holy Spirit will be with him from the time he is born.

¹⁶John will lead many people in Israel to turn back to the Lord their God. ¹⁷He will go ahead of the Lord with the same power and spirit that Elijahᵈ had. And because of John, parents will be more thoughtful of their children. And people who now disobey God will begin to think as they ought to. That is how John will get people ready for the Lord.

¹⁸Zechariah said to the angel, "How will I know this is going to happen? My wife and I are both very old."

¹⁹The angel answered, "I am Gabriel, God's servant, and I was sent to tell you this good news. ²⁰You haven't believed what I've said. So you won't be able to say a thing until all this happens. But everything will take place when it is supposed to."

²¹The crowd was waiting for Zechariah and kept wondering why he was staying so long in the temple. ²²When he did come out, he couldn't speak, and they knew he had seen a vision. He motioned to them with his hands, but didn't say anything.

ᶜburn incense: This was done twice a day, once in the morning and again in the late afternoon.   ᵈElijah: The prophet Elijah was known for his power to work miracles.

23When Zechariah's time of service in the temple was over, he went home. 24Soon after that, his wife was expecting a baby, and for five months she didn't leave the house. She said to herself, 25"What the Lord has done for me will keep people from looking down on me."e

An Angel Tells about the Birth of Jesus

26One month later God sent the angel Gabriel to the town of Nazareth in Galilee 27with a message for a virgin named Mary. She was engaged to Joseph from the family of King David. 28The angel greeted Mary and said, "You are truly blessed! The Lord is with you."

29Mary was confused by the angel's words and wondered what they meant. 30Then the angel told Mary, "Don't be afraid! God is pleased with you, 31and you will have a son. His name will be Jesus. 32He will be great and will be called the Son of God Most High. The Lord God will make him king, as his ancestor David was. 33He will rule the people of Israel for ever, and his kingdom will never end."

34Mary asked the angel, "How can this happen? I'm not married!"

35The angel answered, "The Holy Spirit will come down to you, and God's power will come over you. So your child will be called the holy Son of God. 36Your relative Elizabeth is also going to have a son, even though she is old. No-one thought she could ever have a baby, but in three months she will have a son. 37Nothing is impossible for God!"

38Mary said, "I am the Lord's servant! Let it happen as you have said." And the angel left her.

Mary Visits Elizabeth

39A short time later Mary hurried to a town in the hill country of Judea. 40She went into Zechariah's home, where she greeted Elizabeth. 41When Elizabeth heard Mary's greeting, her baby moved inside her.

The Holy Spirit came upon Elizabeth. 42Then in a loud voice she said to Mary:

---

ekeep people from looking down on me: When a married woman could not have children, it was thought that the Lord was punishing her.

God has blessed you more than any other woman! He has also blessed the child you will have. ⁴³Why should the mother of my Lord come to me? ⁴⁴As soon as I heard your greeting, my baby became happy and moved inside me. ⁴⁵The Lord has blessed you because you believed that he will keep his promise.

Mary's Song of Praise

⁴⁶Mary said:

⁴⁷ With all my heart I praise the Lord,
    and I am glad because of God mySaviour.
⁴⁸ He cares for me, his humble servant.
    From now on, all people will say
      God has blessed me.
⁴⁹ God All-Powerful has done great things for me,
    and his name is holy.
⁵⁰ He always shows mercy
    to everyone who worships him.
⁵¹ The Lord has used his powerful arm
    to scatter those who are proud.
⁵² He drags strong rulers from their thrones
    and puts humble people in places of power.
⁵³ God gives the hungry good things to eat,
   and sends the rich away
    with nothing.
⁵⁴ He helps his servant Israel
    and is always merciful to his people.
⁵⁵ The Lord made this promise to our ancestors,
    to Abraham and his family for ever!

⁵⁶Mary stayed with Elizabeth for about three months. Then she went back home.

The Birth of John the Baptist

⁵⁷When Elizabeth's son was born, ⁵⁸her neighbours and relatives heard how kind the Lord had been to her, and they too were glad.

⁵⁹Eight days later they did for the child what the Law of Moses commands.ᶠ They were going to name him

---

ᶠwhat the Law of Moses commands: This refers to circumcision. It is the cutting off of skin from the private part of Jewish boys eight days after birth to show that they belong to the Lord.

Zechariah, after his father. ⁶⁰But Elizabeth said, "No! His name is John."

⁶¹The people argued, "No-one in your family has ever been named John." ⁶²So they motioned to Zechariah to find out what he wanted to name his son.

⁶³Zechariah asked for a writing tablet. Then he wrote, "His name is John." Everyone was amazed. ⁶⁴Straight away, Zechariah started speaking and praising God.

⁶⁵All the neighbours were frightened because of what had happened, and everywhere in the hill country people kept talking about these things. ⁶⁶Everyone who heard about this wondered what this child would grow up to be. They knew that the Lord was with him.

Zechariah Praises the Lord

⁶⁷The Holy Spirit came upon Zechariah, and he began to speak:

⁶⁸ Praise the Lord, the God of Israel!
    He has come to save his people.
⁶⁹ Our God has given us a mighty Saviour^g
    from the family of David his servant.
⁷⁰ Long ago the Lord promised
    by the words of his holy prophets
⁷¹ to save us from our enemies
    and from everyone who hates us.
⁷² God said he would be kind to our people
    and keep his sacred promise.
⁷³ He told our ancestor Abraham
⁷⁴ that he would rescue us from our enemies.
    Then we could serve him without fear,
⁷⁵ by being holy and good as long as we live.

⁷⁶ You, my son, will be called
    a prophet of God in heaven above.
    You will go ahead of the Lord
    to get everything ready for him.
⁷⁷ You will tell his people
    that they can be saved

---

^ga mighty Saviour: The Greek text has "a horn of salvation." In the Scriptures animal horns are often a symbol of great strength.

> when their sins are forgiven.
> 78 God's love and kindness will shine upon us
> like the sun that rises in the sky.[h]
> 79 On us who live in the dark shadow of death
> this light will shine
> to guide us into a life of peace.

80As John grew up, God's Spirit gave him great power. John lived in the desert until the time he was sent to the people of Israel.

The Birth of Jesus
(Matthew 1.18-25)

2 1About that time Emperor Augustus gave orders for the names of all the people to be listed in record books.[i] 2These first records were made when Quirinius was governor of Syria.[j]

3Everyone had to go to their own home town to be listed. 4So Joseph had to leave Nazareth in Galilee and go to Bethlehem in Judea. Long ago Bethlehem had been King David's home town, and Joseph went there because he was from David's family.

5Mary was engaged to Joseph and travelled with him to Bethlehem. She was soon going to have a baby, 6and while they were there, 7she gave birth to her firstborn[k] son. She dressed him in baby clothes[l] and laid him on a bed of hay, because there was no room for them in the inn.

The Shepherds

8That night in the fields near Bethlehem some shepherds were guarding their sheep. 9All at once an angel came down to them from the Lord, and the brightness of the Lord's glory flashed around them. The shepherds

---

[h]like the sun that rises in the sky: Or "like the Messiah coming from heaven." [i]names...listed in record books: This was done so that everyone could be made to pay taxes to the Emperor. [j]Quirinius was governor of Syria: It is known that Quirinius made a record of the people in AD 6 or 7. But the exact date of the record-taking that Luke mentions is not known. [k]firstborn: The Jewish people said that the firstborn son in each of their families belonged to the Lord. [l]dressed him in baby clothes: The Greek text has "wrapped him in wide strips of cloth," which was how young babies were dressed.

were frightened. [10]But the angel said, "Don't be afraid! I have good news for you, which will make everyone happy. [11]This very day in King David's home town a Saviour was born for you. He is Christ the Lord. [12]You will know who he is, because you will find him dressed in baby clothes and lying on a bed of hay."

[13]Suddenly many other angels came down from heaven and joined in praising God. They said:

[14]   "Praise God in heaven!

                    Peace on earth to everyone who pleases God."

[15]After the angels had left and gone back to heaven, the shepherds said to each other, "Let's go to Bethlehem and see what the Lord has told us about." [16]They hurried off and found Mary and Joseph, and they saw the baby lying on a bed of hay.

[17]When the shepherds saw Jesus, they told his parents what the angel had said about him. [18]Everyone listened and was surprised. [19]But Mary kept thinking about all this and wondering what it meant.

[20]As the shepherds returned to their sheep, they were praising God and saying wonderful things about him. Everything they had seen and heard was just as the angel had said.

[21]Eight days later Jesus' parents did for him what the Law of Moses commands.[m] And they named him Jesus, just as the angel had told Mary when he promised she would have a baby.

Simeon Praises the Lord

[22]The time came for Mary and Joseph to do what the Law of Moses says a mother is supposed to do after her baby is born.[n]

They took Jesus to the temple in Jerusalem and presented him to the Lord, [23]just as the Law of the Lord says, "Each firstborn[o] baby boy belongs to the Lord." [24]The Law of the Lord also says that parents have to offer

---

[m]what the Law of Moses commands: See the note at 1.59.   [n]after her baby is born: After a Jewish mother gave birth to a son, she was considered "unclean" and had to stay home for 33 days after the circumcision ceremony (see note at 1.59), and then offer a sacrifice to the Lord.   [o]firstborn: See the note at 2.7.

a sacrifice, giving at least a pair of doves or two young pigeons. So that is what Mary and Joseph did.

25At this time a man named Simeon was living in Jerusalem. Simeon was a good man. He loved God and was waiting for God to save the people of Israel. God's Spirit came to him 26and told him that he wouldn't die until he had seen Christ the Lord.

27When Mary and Joseph brought Jesus to the temple to do what the Law of Moses says should be done for a new baby, the Spirit told Simeon to go into the temple. 28Simeon took the baby Jesus in his arms and praised God,

29 "Lord, I am your servant,
and now I can die in peace,
because you have kept your promise to me.
30 With my own eyes I have seen
what you have done to save your people,
31 and foreign nations will also see this.
32 Your mighty power is a light for all nations,
and it will bring honour to your people Israel."

33Jesus' parents were surprised at what Simeon had said. 34Then he blessed them and told Mary, "This child of yours will cause many people in Israel to fall and others to stand. The child will be like a warning sign. Many people will reject him, 35and you, Mary, will suffer as though you had been stabbed by a dagger. But all this will show what people are really thinking."

Anna Speaks about the Child Jesus

36The prophet Anna was also there in the temple. She was the daughter of Phanuel from the tribe of Asher, and she was very old. In her youth she had been married for seven years, but her husband died. 37And now she was 84 years old.p Night and day she served God in the temple by praying and often going without eating.q

38At that time Anna came in and praised God. She spoke about the child Jesus to everyone who hoped for Jerusalem to be set free.

pAnd now she was 84 years old: Or "And now she had been a widow for 84 years." qwithout eating: The Jewish people sometimes went without eating (also called "fasting") to show their love for God or to show sorrow for their sins.

The Return to Nazareth

[39]After Joseph and Mary had done everything that the Law of the Lord commands, they returned home to Nazareth in Galilee. [40]The child Jesus grew. He became strong and wise, and God blessed him.

The Boy Jesus in the Temple

[41]Every year Jesus' parents went to Jerusalem for Passover. [42]And when Jesus was twelve years old, they all went there as usual for the celebration. [43]After Passover his parents left, but they didn't know that Jesus had stayed on in the city. [44]They thought he was travelling with some other people, and they went a whole day before they started looking for him. [45]When they couldn't find him with their relatives and friends, they went back to Jerusalem and started looking for him there.

[46]Three days later they found Jesus sitting in the temple, listening to the teachers and asking them questions. [47]Everyone who heard him was surprised at how much he knew and at the answers he gave.

[48]When his parents found him, they were amazed. His mother said, "Son, why have you done this to us? Your father and I have been very worried, and we've been searching for you!"

[49]Jesus answered, "Why did you have to look for me? Didn't you know that I would be in my Father's house?"[r] [50]But they didn't understand what he meant.

[51]Jesus went back to Nazareth with his parents and obeyed them. His mother kept on thinking about all that had happened.

[52]Jesus became wise, and he grew strong. God was pleased with him and so were the people.

The Preaching of John the Baptist
(Matthew 3.1-12; Mark 1.1-8; John 1.19-28)

3 [1]For 15 years[s] Emperor Tiberius had ruled that part of the world. Pontius Pilate was governor of Judea,

---

[r]in my Father's house: Or "doing my Father's work." [s]For 15 years: This was either AD 28 or 29, and Jesus was about 30 years old (see 3.23).

and Herod[t] was the ruler of Galilee. Herod's brother, Philip, was the ruler in the countries of Iturea and Trachonitis, and Lysanias was the ruler of Abilene. [2]Annas and Caiaphas were the Jewish high priests.[u]

At that time God spoke to Zechariah's son John, who was living in the desert. [3]So John went along the Jordan Valley, telling the people, "Turn back to God and be baptised! Then your sins will be forgiven." [4]Isaiah the prophet wrote about John when he said,

> "In the desert someone is shouting,
> 'Get the road ready for the Lord!
> Make a straight path for him.
> [5]   Fill up every valley
> and level every mountain and hill.
> Straighten the crooked paths
> and smooth out the rough roads.
> [6]   Then everyone will see the saving power of God.' "

[7]Crowds of people came out to be baptised, but John said to them, "You snakes! Who warned you to run from the coming judgment? [8]Do something to show that you really have given up your sins. Don't start saying that you belong to Abraham's family. God can turn these stones into children for Abraham.[v] [9]An axe is ready to cut the trees down at their roots. Any tree that doesn't produce good fruit will be cut down and thrown into a fire."

[10]The crowds asked John, "What should we do?"

[11]John told them, "If you have two coats, give one to someone who doesn't have any. If you have food, share it with someone else."

[12]When tax collectors[w] came to be baptised, they asked John, "Teacher, what should we do?"

[13]John told them, "Don't make people pay more than they owe."

---

[t]*Herod:* Herod Antipas, the son of Herod the Great.   [u]*Annas and Caiaphas...high priests:* Annas was high priest from AD 6 until 15. His son-in-law Caiaphas was high priest from AD 18 until 37.   [v]*children for Abraham:* The Jewish people thought they were God's chosen people because of God's promises to their ancestor Abraham.   [w]*tax collectors:* These were usually Jewish people who paid the Romans for the right to collect taxes. They were hated by other Jews who thought of them as traitors to their country and to their religion.

¹⁴Some soldiers asked him, "And what about us? What do we have to do?"

John told them, "Don't force people to pay money to make you leave them alone. Be satisfied with your pay."

¹⁵Everyone became excited and wondered, "Could John be the Messiah?"

¹⁶John said, "I'm just baptising with water. But someone more powerful is going to come, and I'm not good enough even to untie his sandals.[x] He will baptise you with the Holy Spirit and with fire. ¹⁷His threshing fork[y] is in his hand, and he is ready to separate the wheat from the husks. He will store the wheat in his barn and burn the husks with a fire that never goes out."

¹⁸In many different ways John preached the good news to the people. ¹⁹But to Herod the ruler, he said, "It was wrong for you to take Herodias, your brother's wife." John also said that Herod had done many other bad things. ²⁰Finally, Herod put John in jail, and this was the worst thing he ever did.

The Baptism of Jesus
(Matthew 3.13-17; Mark 1.9-11)

²¹While everyone else was being baptised, Jesus himself was baptised. Then as he prayed, the sky opened up, ²²and the Holy Spirit came down upon him in the form of a dove. A voice from heaven said, "You are my own dear Son, and I am pleased with you."

The Ancestors of Jesus
(Matthew 1.1-17)

²³When Jesus began to preach, he was about 30 years old. Everyone thought he was the son of Joseph. But his family went back through Heli, ²⁴Matthat, Levi, Melchi, Jannai, Joseph, ²⁵Mattathias, Amos, Nahum, Esli, Naggai, ²⁶Maath, Mattathias, Semein, Josech, Joda;

²⁷Joanan, Rhesa, Zerubbabel, Shealtiel, Neri, ²⁸Melchi, Addi, Cosam, Elmadam, Er, ²⁹Joshua, Eliezer, Jorim, Matthat, Levi;

---

[x]untie his sandals: This was the duty of a slave. [y]threshing fork: After Jewish farmers had trampled out the grain, they used a large fork to toss the grain and the husks into the air. Wind would blow away the light husks, and the grain would fall back to the ground, where it could be gathered up.

30Simeon, Judah, Joseph, Jonam, Eliakim, 31Melea, Menna, Mattatha, Nathan, David, 32Jesse, Obed, Boaz, Salmon, Nahshon;

33Amminadab, Admin, Arni, Hezron, Perez, Judah, 34Jacob, Isaac, Abraham, Terah, Nahor, 35Serug, Reu, Peleg, Eber, Shelah;

36Cainan, Arphaxad, Shem, Noah, Lamech, 37Methuselah, Enoch, Jared, Mahalaleel, Kenan, 38Enosh, and Seth.

The family of Jesus went all the way back to Adam and then to God.

Jesus and the Devil
(Matthew 4.1-11; Mark 1.12, 13)

4 1When Jesus returned from the Jordan River, the power of the Holy Spirit was with him, and the Spirit led him into the desert. 2For 40 days Jesus was tested by the devil, and during that time he went without eating.z When it was all over, he was hungry.

3The devil said to Jesus, "If you are God's Son, tell this stone to turn into bread."

4Jesus answered, "The Scriptures say, 'No-one can live only on food.' "

5Then the devil led Jesus up to a high place and quickly showed him all the nations on earth. 6The devil said, "I will give all this power and glory to you. It has been given to me, and I can give it to anyone I want to. 7Just worship me, and you can have it all."

8Jesus answered, "The Scriptures say:
'Worship the Lord your God and serve only him!' "

9Finally, the devil took Jesus to Jerusalem and got him to stand on top of the temple. The devil said, "If you are God's Son, jump off. 10-11The Scriptures say:
'God will tell his angels to take care of you.
They will catch you in their arms,
and you won't hurt your feet on the stones.' "

12Jesus answered, "The Scriptures also say, 'Don't try to test the Lord your God!' "

13After the devil had finished testing Jesus in every way possible, he left him for a while.

zwent without eating: See the note at 2.37.

Jesus Begins His Work
(Matthew 4.12-17; Mark 1.14, 15)

14Jesus returned to Galilee with the power of the Spirit. News about him spread everywhere. 15He taught in the Jewish meeting places, and everyone praised him.

The People of Nazareth Turn against Jesus
(Matthew 13.53-58; Mark 6.1-6)

16Jesus went back to Nazareth, where he had been brought up, and as usual he went to the meeting place on the Sabbath. When he stood up to read from the Scriptures, 17he was given the book of Isaiah the prophet. He opened it and read,

18 "The Lord's Spirit has come to me,
    because he has chosen me
        to tell the good news to the poor.
    The Lord has sent me
    to announce freedom for prisoners,
        to give sight to the blind, to free everyone who suffers,
19 and to say, 'This is the year the Lord has chosen.' "

20Jesus closed the book, then handed it back to the man in charge and sat down. Everyone in the meeting place looked straight at Jesus.

21Then Jesus said to them, "What you have just heard me read has come true today."

22All the people started talking about Jesus and were amazed at the wonderful things he said. They kept on asking, "Isn't he Joseph's son?"

23Jesus answered:

You will certainly want to tell me this saying, "Doctor, first make yourself well." You will tell me to do the same things here in my own home town that you heard I did in Capernaum. 24But you can be sure that no prophets are liked by the people of their own home town.

25Once during the time of Elijah there was no rain for three and a half years, and people everywhere were starving. There were many widows in Israel, 26but Elijah was sent only to a widow in the town of Zarephath near the city of Sidon. 27During the time of the prophet Elisha, many men in Israel had leprosy.[a] But no-one was healed, except Naaman who lived in Syria.

28When the people in the meeting place heard Jesus say this, they became so angry 29that they got up and threw him out of town. They dragged him to the edge of the cliff on which the town was built, because they wanted to throw him down from there. 30But Jesus slipped through the crowd and got away.

A Man with an Evil Spirit
(Mark 1.21-28)

31Jesus went to the town of Capernaum in Galilee and taught the people on the Sabbath. 32His teaching amazed them because he spoke with power. 33There in the Jewish meeting place was a man with an evil spirit. He yelled out, 34"Hey, Jesus of Nazareth, what do you want with us? Are you here to get rid of us? I know who you are! You are God's Holy One."

35Jesus ordered the evil spirit to be quiet and come out. The demon threw the man to the ground in front of everyone and left without harming him.

36They all were amazed and kept saying to each other, "What kind of teaching is this? He has power to order evil spirits out of people!" 37News about Jesus spread all over that part of the country.

Jesus Heals Many People
(Matthew 8.14-17; Mark 1.29-34)

38Jesus left the meeting place and went to Simon's home. When Jesus got there, he was told that Simon's mother-in-law was sick with a high fever. 39So Jesus went over to her and ordered the fever to go away. At once she was able to get up and serve them a meal.

40After the sun had set, people with all kinds of diseases were brought to Jesus. He put his hands on each one of them and healed them. 41Demons went out of many people and shouted, "You are the Son of God!" But Jesus

---

[a]leprosy: In biblical times the word "leprosy" was used for many different kinds of skin diseases.

ordered the demons not to speak because they knew he was the Messiah.

42 The next morning Jesus went out to a place where he could be alone, and crowds came looking for him. When they found him, they tried to stop him from leaving. 43 But Jesus said, "People in other towns must hear the good news about God's kingdom. That's why I was sent." 44 So he kept on preaching in the Jewish meeting places in Judea.*b*

Jesus Chooses His First Disciples
(Matthew 4.18-22; Mark 1.16-20)

5 1 Jesus was standing on the shore of Lake Gennesaret,*c* teaching the people as they crowded around him to hear God's message. 2 Near the shore he saw two boats left there by some fishermen who had gone to wash their nets. 3 Jesus got into the boat that belonged to Simon and asked him to row it out a little way from the shore. Then Jesus sat down*d* in the boat to teach the crowd.

4 When Jesus had finished speaking, he told Simon, "Row the boat out into the deep water and let your nets down to catch some fish."

5 "Master," Simon answered, "we've worked hard all night long and haven't caught a thing. But if you tell me to, I will let the nets down." 6 They did it and caught so many fish that their nets began ripping apart. 7 Then they signalled for their partners in the other boat to come and help them. The men came, and together they filled the two boats so full that they both began to sink.

8 When Simon Peter saw this happen, he knelt down in front of Jesus and said, "Lord, don't come near me! I'm a sinner." 9 Peter and everyone with him were completely surprised at all the fish they had caught. 10 His partners James and John, the sons of Zebedee, were surprised too.

Jesus told Simon, "Don't be afraid! From now on you

---

bJudea: Some manuscripts have "Galilee." *cLake Gennesaret:* Another name for Lake Galilee. *dsat down:* Teachers in the ancient world, including Jewish teachers, usually sat down when they taught.

will bring in people instead of fish." 11The men pulled their boats up on the shore. Then they left everything and went with Jesus.

Jesus Heals a Man with Leprosy
(Matthew 8.1-4; Mark 1.40-45)

12Jesus came to a town where there was a man who had leprosy.e When the man saw Jesus, he knelt down to the ground in front of Jesus and begged, "Lord, you have the power to make me well, if only you wanted to."

13Jesus put his hand on him and said, "I want to! Now you are well." At once the man's leprosy disappeared. 14Jesus told him, "Don't tell anyone about this, but go and show yourself to the priest. Offer a gift to the priest, just as Moses commanded, and everyone will know that you have been healed."f

15News about Jesus kept spreading. Large crowds came to listen to him teach and to be healed of their diseases. 16But Jesus would often go to a place where he could be alone and pray.

Jesus Heals a Crippled Man
(Matthew 9.1-8; Mark 2.1-12)

17One day some Pharisees and experts in the Law of Moses sat listening to Jesus teach. They had come from every village in Galilee and Judea and from Jerusalem.

God had given Jesus the power to heal the sick, 18and some people came carrying a crippled man on a mat. They tried to take him inside the house and put him in front of Jesus. 19But because of the crowd, they couldn't get him to Jesus. So they went up on the roof,g where they removed some tiles and let the mat down into the middle of the room.

eleprosy: See the note at 4.27.   feveryone will know that you have been healed: People with leprosy had to be examined by a priest and told that they were well (that is, "clean") before they could once again live a normal life in the Jewish community. The gift that Moses commanded was the sacrifice of some lambs together with flour mixed with olive oil.   groof: In Palestine the houses usually had a flat roof. Stairs on the outside led up to the roof, which was made of beams and boards covered with packed earth. Luke says that the roof was made of (clay) tiles, which were also used for making roofs in New Testament times.

²⁰When Jesus saw how much faith they had, he said to the crippled man, "My friend, your sins are forgiven."

²¹The Pharisees and the experts began arguing, "Jesus must think he is God! Only God can forgive sins."

²²Jesus knew what they were thinking, and he said, "Why are you thinking that? ²³Is it easier for me to tell this crippled man that his sins are forgiven or to tell him to get up and walk? ²⁴But now you will see that the Son of Man has the right to forgive sins here on earth." Jesus then said to the man, "Get up! Pick up your mat and walk home."

²⁵At once the man stood up in front of everyone. He picked up his mat and went home, giving thanks to God. ²⁶Everyone was amazed and praised God. What they saw surprised them, and they said, "We've seen a great miracle today!"

Jesus Chooses Levi
(Matthew 9.9-13; Mark 2.13-17)

²⁷Later, Jesus went out and saw a tax collector[h] named Levi sitting at the place for paying taxes. Jesus said to him, "Come with me." ²⁸Levi left everything and went with Jesus.

²⁹In his home Levi gave a big dinner for Jesus. Many tax collectors and other guests were also there.

³⁰The Pharisees and some of their teachers of the Law of Moses grumbled to Jesus' disciples, "Why do you eat and drink with those tax collectors and other sinners?"

³¹Jesus answered, "Healthy people don't need a doctor, but sick people do. ³²I didn't come to invite good people to turn to God. I came to invite sinners."

People Ask about Going without Eating
(Matthew 9.14-17; Mark 2.18-22)

³³Some people said to Jesus, "John's followers often pray and go without eating,[i] and so do the followers of the Pharisees. But your disciples never go without eating or drinking."

---

[h]tax collector: See the note at 3.12.   [i]without eating: See the note at 2.37.

34Jesus told them, "The friends of a bridegroom don't go without eating while he is still with them. 35But the time will come when he will be taken from them. Then they will go without eating."

36Jesus then told them these sayings:

No-one uses a new piece of cloth to patch old clothes. The patch would shrink and make the hole even bigger. 37No-one pours new wine into old wineskins. The new wine would swell and burst the old skins.[j] Then the wine would be lost, and the skins would be ruined. 38New wine must be put only into new wineskins.

39No-one wants new wine after drinking old wine. They say, "The old wine is better."

A Question about the Sabbath
(Matthew 12.1-8; Mark 2.23-28)

6 1One Sabbath when Jesus and his disciples were walking through some wheat fields,[k] the disciples picked some wheat. They rubbed the husks off with their hands and started eating the grain.

2Some Pharisees said, "Why are you picking grain on the Sabbath? You're not supposed to do that!"

3Jesus answered, "Haven't you read what David did when he and his followers were hungry? 4He went into the house of God and took the sacred loaves of bread that only priests were supposed to eat. He not only ate some himself, but even gave some to his followers."

5Jesus finished by saying, "The Son of Man is Lord over the Sabbath."

A Man with a Crippled Hand
(Matthew 12.9-14; Mark 3.1-6)

6On another Sabbath[l] Jesus was teaching in a Jewish meeting place, and a man with a crippled right hand was there. 7Some Pharisees and teachers of the Law of Moses

---

[j]swell and burst the old skins: While the juice from grapes was becoming wine, it would swell and stretch the skins in which it had been stored. If the skins were old and stiff, they would burst.   [k]walking through some wheat fields: It was the custom to let hungry travellers pick grains of wheat.   [l]On another Sabbath: Some manuscripts have a reading which may mean "the Sabbath after the next."

kept watching Jesus to see if he would heal the man. They did this because they wanted to accuse Jesus of doing something wrong.

8Jesus knew what they were thinking. So he told the man to stand up where everyone could see him. And the man stood up. 9Then Jesus asked, "On the Sabbath should we do good deeds or evil deeds? Should we save someone's life or destroy it?"

10After he had looked around at everyone, he told the man, "Stretch out your hand." He did, and his bad hand became completely well.

11The teachers and the Pharisees were furious and started saying to each other, "What can we do about Jesus?"

Jesus Chooses His Twelve Apostles
(Matthew 10.1-4; Mark 3.13-19)

12About that time Jesus went off to a mountain to pray, and he spent the whole night there. 13The next morning he called his disciples together and chose twelve of them to be his apostles. 14One was Simon, and Jesus named him Peter. Another was Andrew, Peter's brother. There were also James, John, Philip, Bartholomew, 15Matthew, Thomas, and James the son of Alphaeus. The rest of the apostles were Simon, known as the Eager One,*m* 16Jude, who was the son of James, and Judas Iscariot,*n* who later betrayed Jesus.

Jesus Teaches, Preaches, and Heals
(Matthew 4.23-25)

17Jesus and his apostles went down from the mountain and came to some flat, level ground. Many other disciples were there to meet him. Large crowds of people from all over Judea, Jerusalem, and the coastal cities of Tyre and Sidon were there too. 18These people had come to listen to Jesus and to be healed of their diseases. All who were

---

*m*known as the Eager One: The word "eager" translates the Greek word "zealot," which was a name later given to the members of a Jewish group that resisted and fought against the Romans. *n*Iscariot: This may mean "a man from Kerioth" (a place in Judea). But more probably it means "a man who was a liar" or "a man who was a betrayer."

troubled by evil spirits were also healed. [19]Everyone was trying to touch Jesus, because power was going out from him and healing them all.

Blessings and Troubles
(Matthew 5.1-12)

[20]Jesus looked at his disciples and said:

God will bless you people who are poor.
His kingdom belongs to you!
[21]   God will bless you hungry people.
You will have plenty to eat!
God will bless you people who are crying.
You will laugh!

[22]God will bless you when others hate you and won't have anything to do with you. God will bless you when people insult you and say cruel things about you, all because you are a follower of the Son of Man. [23]Long ago your own people did these same things to the prophets. So when this happens to you, be happy and jump for joy! You will have a great reward in heaven.

[24]   But you rich people are in for trouble.
You have already had an easy life!
[25]   You well-fed people are in for trouble.
You will go hungry!
You people who are laughing now are in for trouble.
· You are going to cry and weep!

[26]You are in for trouble when everyone says good things about you. That's what your own people said about those prophets who told lies.

Love for Enemies
(Matthew 5.38-48; 7.12a)

[27]This is what I say to all who will listen to me:

Love your enemies, and be good to everyone who hates you. [28]Ask God to bless anyone who curses you, and pray for everyone who is cruel to you. [29]If someone slaps you on one cheek, don't stop that person from slapping you on the other cheek. If someone wants to take your coat, don't try to keep back your shirt. [30]Give to everyone who asks and don't ask people to return what they have taken from you. ³¹Treat others just as you want to be treated.

³²If you love only someone who loves you, will God praise you for that? Even sinners love people who love them. ³³If you are kind only to someone who is kind to you, will God be pleased with you for that? Even sinners are kind to people who are kind to them. ³⁴If you lend money only to someone you think will pay you back, will God be pleased with you for that? Even sinners lend to sinners because they think they will get it all back.

³⁵But love your enemies and be good to them. Lend without expecting to be paid back.ᵒ Then you will get a great reward, and you will be the true children of God in heaven. He is good even to people who are unthankful and cruel. ³⁶Have pity on others, just as your Father has pity on you.

Judging Others
(Matthew 7.1-5)

³⁷Jesus said:

Don't judge others, and God won't judge you. Don't be hard on others, and God won't be hard on you. Forgive others, and God will forgive you. ³⁸If you give to others, you will be given a full amount in return. It will be packed down, shaken together, and spilling over into your lap. The way you treat others is the way you will be treated.

³⁹Jesus also used some sayings as he spoke to the people. He said:

Can one blind person lead another blind person? Won't they both fall into a ditch? ⁴⁰Are students better than their teacher? But when they are fully trained, they will be like their teacher.

⁴¹You can see the speck in your friend's eye. But you don't notice the log in your own eye. ⁴²How can you say, "My friend, let me take the speck out of your eye," when you don't see the log in your own eye? You

ᵒwithout expecting to be paid back: Some manuscripts have "without giving up on anyone."

show-offs! First, get the log out of your own eye. Then you can see how to take the speck out of your friend's eye.

A Tree and Its Fruit
(Matthew 7.17-20; 12.34b, 35)

⁴³A good tree can't produce bad fruit, and a bad tree can't produce good fruit. ⁴⁴You can tell what a tree is like by the fruit it produces. You can't pick figs or grapes from thorn bushes. ⁴⁵Good people do good things because of the good in their hearts. Bad people do bad things because of the evil in their hearts. Your words show what is in your heart.

Two Builders
(Matthew 7.24-27)

⁴⁶Why do you keep on saying that I am your Lord, when you refuse to do what I say? ⁴⁷Anyone who comes and listens to me and obeys me ⁴⁸is like someone who dug down deep and built a house on solid rock. When the flood came and the river rushed against the house, it was built so well that it didn't even shake. ⁴⁹But anyone who hears what I say and doesn't obey me is like someone whose house wasn't built on solid rock. As soon as the river rushed against that house, it was smashed to pieces!

Jesus Heals an Army Officer's Servant
(Matthew 8.5-13; John 4.43-54)

7 ¹After Jesus had finished teaching the people, he went to Capernaum. ²In that town an army officer's servant was sick and about to die. The officer liked this servant very much. ³And when he heard about Jesus, he sent some Jewish leaders to ask him to come and heal the servant.

⁴The leaders went to Jesus and begged him to do something. They said, "This man deserves your help! ⁵He loves our nation and even built us a meeting place." ⁶So Jesus went with them.

When Jesus wasn't far from the house, the officer sent

some friends to tell him, "Lord, don't go to any trouble for me! I'm not good enough for you to come into my house. 7And I'm certainly not worthy to come to you. Just say the word, and my servant will get well. 8I have officers who give orders to me, and I have soldiers who take orders from me. I can say to one of them, 'Go!' and he goes. I can say to another, 'Come!' and he comes. I can say to my servant, 'Do this!' and he'll do it."

9When Jesus heard this, he was so surprised that he turned and said to the crowd following him, "In all of Israel I've never found anyone with this much faith!"

10The officer's friends returned and found the servant well.

A Widow's Son

11Soon Jesus and his disciples were on their way to the town of Nain, and a big crowd was going along with them. 12As they came near the gate of the town, they saw people carrying out the body of a widow's only son. Many people from the town were walking along with her.

13When the Lord saw the woman, he felt sorry for her and said, "Don't cry!"

14Jesus went over and touched the stretcher on which the people were carrying the dead boy. They stopped, and Jesus said, "Young man, get up!" 15The boy sat up and began to speak. Jesus then gave him back to his mother.

16Everyone was frightened and praised God. They said, "A great prophet is here with us! God has come to his people."

17News about Jesus spread all over Judea and everywhere else in that part of the country.

John the Baptist
(Matthew 11.1-19)

18-19John's followers told John everything that was being said about Jesus. So he sent two of them to ask the Lord, "Are you the one we should be looking for? Or must we wait for someone else?"

20When these messengers came to Jesus, they said, "John the Baptist sent us to ask, 'Are you the one we should be looking for? Or are we supposed to wait for someone else?' "

²¹At that time Jesus was healing many people who were sick or in pain or were troubled by evil spirits, and he was giving sight to a lot of blind people. ²²Jesus said to the messengers sent by John, "Go and tell John what you have seen and heard. Blind people are now able to see, and the lame can walk. People who have leprosyᴾ are being healed, and the deaf can now hear. The dead are raised to life, and the poor are hearing the good news. ²³God will bless everyone who doesn't reject me because of what I do."

²⁴After John's messengers had gone, Jesus began speaking to the crowds about John:

What kind of person did you go out to the desert to see? Was he like tall grass blown about by the wind? ²⁵What kind of man did you really go out to see? Was he someone dressed in fine clothes? People who wear expensive clothes and live in luxury are in the king's palace. ²⁶What then did you go out to see? Was he a prophet? He certainly was! I tell you that he was more than a prophet. ²⁷In the Scriptures, God calls John his messenger and says, "I'm sending my messenger ahead of you to get things ready for you." ²⁸No-one ever born on this earth is greater than John. But whoever is least important in God's kingdom is greater than John.

²⁹Everyone had been listening to John. Even the tax collectors�q had obeyed God and had done what was right by letting John baptise them. ³⁰But the Pharisees and the experts in the Law of Moses refused to obey God and be baptised by John.

³¹Jesus went on to say:

What are you people like? What kind of people are you? ³²You are like children sitting in the market and shouting to each other,

"We played the flute, but you wouldn't dance!
We sang a funeral song, but you wouldn't cry!"

³³John the Baptist didn't go around eating and drinking, and you said, "John has a demon in him!" ³⁴But because the Son of Man goes around eating and drinking, you say,

ᴾleprosy: See the note at 4.27.   qtax collectors: See the note at 3.12.

"Jesus eats and drinks too much! He is even a friend of tax collectors and sinners." [35] Yet Wisdom is shown to be right by what its followers do.

Simon the Pharisee

[36] A Pharisee invited Jesus to have dinner with him. So Jesus went to the Pharisee's home and got ready to eat.[r]

[37] When a sinful woman in that town found out that Jesus was there, she bought an expensive bottle of perfume. [38] Then she came and stood behind Jesus. She cried and started washing his feet with her tears and drying them with her hair. The woman kissed his feet and poured the perfume on them.

[39] The Pharisee who had invited Jesus saw this and said to himself, "If this man really was a prophet, he would know what kind of woman is touching him! He would know that she is a sinner."

[40] Jesus said to the Pharisee, "Simon, I've got something to say to you."

"Teacher, what is it?" Simon replied.

[41] Jesus told him, "Two people were in debt to a moneylender. One of them owed him 500 silver coins, and the other owed him 50. [42] Since neither of them could pay him back, the moneylender said that they didn't have to pay him anything. Which one of them will like him more?"

[43] Simon answered, "I suppose it would be the one who had owed more and didn't have to pay it back."

"You are right," Jesus said.

[44] He turned towards the woman and said to Simon, "Have you noticed this woman? When I came into your home, you didn't give me any water so I could wash my feet. But she has washed my feet with her tears and dried them with her hair. [45] You didn't greet me with a kiss, but from the time I came in, she has not stopped kissing my

---

[r] *got ready to eat:* On special occasions the Jewish people often followed the Greek and Roman custom of lying down on their left side and leaning on their left elbow, while eating with their right hand. This is how the woman could come up behind Jesus and wash his feet (see verse 38).

feet. [46]You didn't even pour olive oil on my head,[s] but she has poured expensive perfume on my feet. [47]So I tell you that all her sins are forgiven, and that is why she has shown great love. But anyone who has been forgiven for only a little will show only a little love."

[48]Then Jesus said to the woman, "Your sins are forgiven."

[49]Some other guests started saying to one another, "Who is this who dares to forgive sins?"

[50]But Jesus told the woman, "Because of your faith, you are now saved.[t] May God give you peace!"

Women Who Helped Jesus

8 [1]Soon after this, Jesus was going through towns and villages, telling the good news about God's kingdom. His twelve apostles were with him; [2]and so were some women who had been healed of evil spirits and all sorts of diseases. One of the women was Mary Magdalene,[u] who once had seven demons in her. [3]Joanna, Susanna, and many others had also used what they owned to help Jesus[v] and his disciples. Joanna's husband Chuza was one of Herod's officials.[w]

A Story about a Farmer
(Matthew 13.1-9; Mark 4.1-9)

[4]When a large crowd from several towns had gathered around Jesus, he told them this story:

[5]A farmer went out to scatter seed in a field. While the farmer was doing it, some of the seeds fell along the road and were stepped on or eaten by birds. [6]Other seeds fell on rocky ground and started growing. But the plants didn't have enough water and soon dried

[s]washed my feet...greet me with a kiss...pour olive oil on my head: Guests in a home were usually offered water so they could wash their feet, because most people either went barefoot or wore sandals and would come into the house with very dusty feet. Guests were also greeted with a kiss on the cheek, and special ones often had sweet-smelling olive oil poured on their head. [t]saved: Or "healed." The Greek word may have either meaning. [u]Magdalene: Meaning "from Magdala," a small town on the western shore of Lake Galilee. There is no hint that she is the sinful woman in 7.36-50. [v]used what they owned to help Jesus: Women often helped Jewish teachers by giving them money. [w]Herod's officials: Herod Antipas, the son of Herod the Great.

up. ⁷Some other seeds fell where thorn bushes grew up and choked the plants. ⁸The rest of the seeds fell on good ground where they grew and produced 100 times as many seeds.

When Jesus had finished speaking, he said, "If you have ears, pay attention!"

Why Jesus Used Stories
(Matthew 13.10-17; Mark 4.10-12)

⁹Jesus' disciples asked him what the story meant. ¹⁰So he answered:

I have explained the secrets about God's kingdom to you, but for others I can only use stories. These people look, but they don't see, and they hear, but they don't understand.

Jesus Explains the Story about the Farmer
(Matthew 13.18-23; Mark 4.13-20)

¹¹This is what the story means: The seed is God's message, ¹²and the seeds that fell along the road are the people who hear the message. But the devil comes and snatches the message out of their hearts, so that they won't believe and be saved. ¹³The seeds that fell on rocky ground are the people who gladly hear the message and accept it. But they don't have deep roots, and they believe only for a little while. As soon as life gets hard, they give up.

¹⁴The seeds that fell among the thorn bushes are also people who hear the message. But they are so eager for riches and pleasures that they never produce anything. ¹⁵Those seeds that fell on good ground are the people who listen to the message and keep it in good and honest hearts. They last and produce a harvest.

Light
(Mark 4.21-25)

¹⁶No-one lights a lamp and puts it under a bowl or under a bed. A lamp is always put on a lampstand, so that people who come into a house will see the light. ¹⁷There is nothing hidden that won't be found. There

is no secret that won't be well known. [18]Pay attention to how you listen! Everyone who has something will be given more, but people who have nothing will lose what little they think they have.

Jesus' Mother and Brothers
(Matthew 12.46-50; Mark 3.31-35)

[19]Jesus' mother and brothers went to see him, but because of the crowd they couldn't get near him. [20]Someone told Jesus, "Your mother and brothers are standing outside and want to see you."

[21]Jesus answered, "My mother and my brothers are those people who hear and obey God's message."

A Storm
(Matthew 8.23-27; Mark 4.35-41)

[22]One day, Jesus and his disciples got into a boat, and he said, "Let's cross the lake."[x] They started out, [23]and while they were sailing across, he went to sleep.

Suddenly a strong wind struck the lake, and the boat started sinking. They were in danger. [24]So they went to Jesus and woke him up, "Master, Master! We're about to drown!"

Jesus got up and ordered the wind and waves to stop. They obeyed, and everything was calm. [25]Then Jesus asked the disciples, "Don't you have any faith?"

But they were frightened and amazed. They said to each other, "Who is this? He can give orders to the wind and the waves, and they obey him!"

A Man with Demons in Him
(Matthew 8.28-34; Mark 5.1-20)

[26]Jesus and his disciples sailed across Lake Galilee and came to shore near the town of Gerasa.[y] [27]As Jesus was getting out of the boat, he was met by a man from that town. The man had demons in him. He had gone naked for a long time and no longer lived in a house, but in the graveyard.[z]

---

[x]*cross the lake:* To the eastern shore of Lake Galilee, where most of the people were not Jewish.   [y]*Gerasa:* Some manuscripts have "Gergesa." [z]*graveyard:* It was thought that demons and evil spirits lived in graveyards.

²⁸The man saw Jesus and screamed. He knelt down in front of him and shouted, "Jesus, Son of God in heaven, what do you want with me? I beg you not to torture me!" ²⁹He said this because Jesus had already told the evil spirit to go out of him.

The man had often been attacked by the demon. And even though he had been bound with chains and leg irons and kept under guard, he smashed whatever bound him. Then the demon would force him out into lonely places.

³⁰Jesus asked the man, "What's your name?"

He answered, "My name is Lots." He said this because there were 'lots' of demons in him. ³¹They begged Jesus not to send them to the deep pit,ᵃ where they would be punished.

³²A large herd of pigs was feeding there on the hillside. So the demons begged Jesus to let them go into the pigs, and Jesus let them go. ³³Then the demons left the man and went into the pigs. The whole herd rushed down the steep bank into the lake and drowned.

³⁴When the men taking care of the pigs saw this, they ran to spread the news in the town and on the farms. ³⁵The people went out to see what had happened, and when they came to Jesus, they also found the man. The demons had gone out of him, and he was sitting there at the feet of Jesus. He had clothes on and was in his right mind. But the people were terrified.

³⁶Then all who had seen the man healed talked about it. ³⁷Everyone from around Gerasaᵇ begged Jesus to leave, because they were so frightened.

When Jesus got into the boat to start back, ³⁸the man who had been healed begged to go with him. But Jesus sent him off and said, ³⁹"Go back home and tell everyone how much God has done for you." The man then went all over town, telling people everything that Jesus had done for him.

A Dying Girl and a Sick Woman
(Matthew 9.18-26; Mark 5.21-43)

⁴⁰Everyone had been waiting for Jesus, and when he came back, a crowd was there to welcome him. ⁴¹Just

---

ᵃdeep pit: The place where evil spirits are kept and punished.   ᵇGerasa: See the note at 8.26.

then the man in charge of the Jewish meeting place came and knelt down in front of Jesus. His name was Jairus, and he begged Jesus to come to his home 42because his 12-year-old child was dying. She was his only daughter.

While Jesus was on his way, people were crowding all around him. 43In the crowd was a woman who had been bleeding for twelve years. She had spent everything she had on doctors,c but none of them could make her well.

44As soon as she came up behind Jesus and barely touched his clothes, her bleeding stopped.

45"Who touched me?" Jesus asked.

While everyone was denying it, Peter said, "Master, people are crowding all around and pushing you from every side."d

46But Jesus answered, "Someone touched me, because I felt power going out from me." 47The woman knew that she couldn't hide, so she came trembling and knelt down in front of Jesus. She told everyone why she had touched him and that she had been healed straight away.

48Jesus said to the woman, "You're well now because of your faith. May God give you peace!"

49While Jesus was speaking, someone came from Jairus' home and said, "Your daughter has died! Why bother the teacher any more?"

50When Jesus heard this, he told Jairus, "Don't worry! Have faith, and your daughter will get well."

51Jesus went into the house, but he didn't let anyone else go with him, except Peter, John, James, and the girl's father and mother. 52Everyone was crying and weeping for the girl. But Jesus said, "The child isn't dead. She's just asleep." 53The people laughed at him because they knew she was dead.

54Jesus took hold of the girl's hand and said, "Child, get up!" 55She came back to life and got straight up. Jesus told them to give her something to eat. 56Her parents were surprised, but Jesus ordered them not to tell anyone what had happened.

---

cShe had spent everything she had on doctors: Some manuscripts do not have these words. dfrom every side: Some manuscripts add "and you ask, 'Who touched me?'"

Instructions for the Twelve Apostles
(Matthew 10.5-15; Mark 6.7-13)

9 [1]Jesus called together his twelve apostles and gave them complete power over all demons and diseases. [2]Then he sent them to tell everyone about God's kingdom and to heal the sick. [3]He told them, "Don't take anything with you! Don't take a walking stick or a travelling bag or food or money or even a change of clothes. [4]When you are welcomed into a home, stay there until you leave that town. [5]If people won't welcome you, leave the town and shake the dust from your feet[e] as a warning to them."

[6]The apostles left and went from village to village, telling the good news and healing people everywhere.

Herod Is Worried
(Matthew 14.1-12; Mark 6.14-29)

[7]Herod[f] the ruler heard about all that was happening, and he was worried. Some people were saying that John the Baptist had come back to life. [8]Others were saying that Elijah had come[g] or that one of the prophets from long ago had come back to life. [9]But Herod said, "I had John's head cut off! Who is this I hear so much about?" Herod was eager to meet Jesus.

Jesus Feeds 5000
(Matthew 14.13-21; Mark 6.30-44; John 6.1-14)

[10]The apostles came back and told Jesus everything they had done. He then took them with him to the village of Bethsaida, where they could be alone. [11]But a lot of people found out about this and followed him. Jesus welcomed them. He spoke to them about God's kingdom and healed everyone who was sick.

[12]Late in the afternoon the twelve apostles came to Jesus and said, "Send the crowd to the villages and farms around here. They need to find a place to stay and something to

---

[e]shake the dust from your feet: This was a way of showing rejection. [f]Herod: Herod Antipas, the son of Herod the Great. [g]Elijah had come: Many of the Jewish people expected the prophet Elijah to come and prepare the way for the Messiah.

eat. There is nothing in this place. It's like a desert!"

13Jesus answered, "You give them something to eat."

But they replied, "We've only got five small loaves of bread[h] and two fish. If we are going to feed all these people, we will have to go and buy food." 14There were about 5000 men in the crowd.

Jesus said to his disciples, "Get the people to sit in groups of 50." 15They did this, and all the people sat down. 16Jesus took the five loaves and the two fish. He looked up towards heaven and blessed the food. Then he broke the bread and fish and handed them to his disciples to give to the people.

17Everyone ate all they wanted. What was left over filled twelve baskets.

Who Is Jesus?
(Matthew 16.13-19; Mark 8.27-29)

18When Jesus was alone praying, his disciples came to him, and he asked them, "What do people say about me?"

19They answered, "Some say that you are John the Baptist or Elijah[i] or a prophet from long ago who has come back to life."

20Jesus then asked them, "But who do you say I am?"

Peter answered, "You are the Messiah sent from God."

21Jesus strictly warned his disciples not to tell anyone about this.

Jesus Speaks about His Suffering and Death
(Matthew 16.20-28; Mark 8.30—9.1)

22Jesus told his disciples, "The nation's leaders, the chief priests, and the teachers of the Law of Moses will make the Son of Man suffer terribly. They will reject him and kill him, but three days later he will rise to life."

23Then Jesus said to all the people:

If any of you want to be my followers, you must forget about yourself. You must take up your cross each day and follow me. 24If you want to save your

---

[h]small loaves of bread: These would have been flat and round or in the shape of a bun.   [i]Elijah: See the note at 9.8.

life,[j] you will destroy it. But if you give up your life for me, you will save it. [25]What will you gain, if you own the whole world but destroy yourself or waste your life? [26]If you are ashamed of me and my message, the Son of Man will be ashamed of you when he comes in his glory and in the glory of his Father and the holy angels. [27]You can be sure that some of the people standing here won't die before they see God's kingdom.

The True Glory of Jesus
(Matthew 17.1-8; Mark 9.2-8)

[28]About eight days later Jesus took Peter, John, and James with him and went up on a mountain to pray. [29]While he was praying, his face changed, and his clothes became shining white. [30]Suddenly Moses and Elijah were there speaking with him. [31]They appeared in heavenly glory and talked about all that Jesus' death[k] in Jerusalem would mean.

[32]Peter and the other two disciples had been sound asleep. All at once they woke up and saw how glorious Jesus was. They also saw the two men who were with him.

[33]Moses and Elijah were about to leave, when Peter said to Jesus, "Master, it's good for us to be here! Let's make three shelters, one for you, one for Moses, and one for Elijah." But Peter didn't know what he was talking about.

[34]While Peter was still speaking, a shadow from a cloud passed over them, and they were frightened as the cloud covered them. [35]From the cloud a voice spoke, "This is my chosen Son. Listen to what he says!"

[36]After the voice had spoken, Peter, John, and James saw only Jesus. For some time they kept quiet and didn't say anything about what they had seen.

Jesus Heals a Boy
(Matthew 17.14-18; Mark 9.14-27)

[37]The next day Jesus and his three disciples came down from the mountain and were met by a large crowd. [38]Just

---

[j]life: In verses 24, 25 a Greek word which often means "soul" is translated "life" and "yourself." [k]Jesus' death: In Greek this is "his departure," which probably includes his rising to life and his return to heaven.

then someone in the crowd shouted, "Teacher, please do something for my son! He's my only child! 39A demon often attacks him and makes him scream. It shakes him until he foams at the mouth, and it won't leave him until it has completely worn the boy out. 40I begged your disciples to force out the demon, but they couldn't do it."

41Jesus said to them, "You people are stubborn and don't have any faith! How much longer must I be with you? Why do I have to put up with you?"

Then Jesus said to the man, "Bring your son to me." 42While the boy was being brought, the demon attacked him and made him shake all over. Jesus ordered the demon to stop. Then he healed the boy and gave him back to his father. 43Everyone was amazed at God's great power.

Jesus Again Speaks about His Death
(Matthew 17.22, 23; Mark 9.30-32)

While everyone was still amazed at what Jesus was doing, he said to his disciples, 44"Pay close attention to what I'm telling you! The Son of Man will be handed over to his enemies." 45But the disciples didn't know what he meant. The meaning was hidden from them. They couldn't understand it, and they were afraid to ask.

Who Is the Greatest?
(Matthew 18.1-5; Mark 9.33-37)

46Jesus' disciples were arguing about which one of them was the greatest. 47Jesus knew what they were thinking, and he had a child stand there beside him. 48Then he said to his disciples, "When you welcome even a child because of me, you welcome me. And when you welcome me, you welcome the one who sent me. Whichever one of you is the most humble is the greatest."

For or Against Jesus
(Mark 9.38-40)

49John said, "Master, we saw a man using your name to force demons out of people. But we told him to stop, because he isn't one of us."

[50]"Don't stop him!" Jesus said. "Anyone who isn't against you is for you."

A Samaritan Village Refuses To Receive Jesus

[51]Not long before it was time for Jesus to be taken up to heaven, he made up his mind to go to Jerusalem. [52]He sent some messengers on ahead to a Samaritan village to get things ready for him. [53]But he was on his way to Jerusalem, so the people there refused to welcome him. [54]When the disciples James and John saw what was happening, they asked, "Lord, do you want us to call down fire from heaven to destroy these people?"[l]

[55]But Jesus turned and corrected them for what they had said.[m] [56]Then they all went on to another village.

Three People Who Wanted To Be Followers
(Matthew 8.19-22)

[57]Along the way someone said to Jesus, "I'll go anywhere with you!"

[58]Jesus said, "Foxes have dens, and birds have nests, but the Son of Man doesn't have a place to call his own."

[59]Jesus told someone else to come with him. But the man said, "Lord, let me wait until I bury my father."[n]

[60]Jesus answered, "Let the dead take care of the dead, while you go and tell others about God's kingdom."

[61]Then someone said to Jesus, "I want to go with you, Lord, but first let me go back and take care of things at home."

[62]Jesus answered, "Anyone who starts ploughing and keeps looking back isn't worth anything to God's kingdom!"

---

[l]to destroy these people: Some manuscripts add "as Elijah did." [m]what they had said: Some manuscripts add, "and said, 'Don't you know what spirit you belong to? The Son of Man did not come to destroy people's lives, but to save them.' " [n]bury my father: The Jewish people taught that giving someone a proper burial was even more important than helping the poor.

The Work of the 72 Followers

10 [1]Later the Lord chose 72[o] other followers and sent them out two by two to every town and village where he was about to go. [2]He said to them:

A large crop is in the fields, but there are only a few workers. Ask the Lord in charge of the harvest to send out workers to bring it in. [3]Now go, but remember, I am sending you like lambs into a pack of wolves. [4]Don't take along a money bag or a travelling bag or sandals. And don't waste time greeting people on the road.[p] [5]As soon as you enter a home, say, "God bless this home with peace." [6]If the people living there are peace-loving, your prayer for peace will bless them. But if they are not peace-loving, your prayer will return to you. [7]Stay with the same family, eating and drinking whatever they give you, because workers are worth what they earn. Don't move around from house to house.

[8]If the people of a town welcome you, eat whatever they offer. [9]Heal their sick and say, "God's kingdom will soon be here!"[q]

[10]But if the people of a town refuse to welcome you, go out into the street and say, [11]"We are shaking the dust from our feet[r] as a warning to you. And you can be sure that God's kingdom will soon be here!"[s] [12]I tell you that on the day of judgment the people of Sodom will get off easier than the people of that town!

The Unbelieving Towns

(Matthew 11.20-24)

[13]You people of Chorazin are in for trouble! You people of Bethsaida are also in for trouble! If the miracles that took place in your towns had happened in Tyre and Sidon, the people there would have turned to God long ago. They would have dressed in sackcloth

---

[o]*72:* Some manuscripts have "70." According to Jewish tradition there were 70 nations on earth. But the ancient Greek translation of the Old Testament has "72" in place of "70." Jesus probably chose this number of followers to show that his message was for everyone in the world.   [p]*waste time greeting people on the road:* In those days a polite greeting could take a long time.   [q]*will soon be here:* Or "is already here."   [r]*shaking the dust from our feet:* This was a way of showing rejection.   [s]*will soon be here:* Or "is already here."

and put ashes on their heads.ᵗ ¹⁴On the day of judgment the people of Tyre and Sidon will get off easier than you will. ¹⁵People of Capernaum, do you think you will be honoured in heaven? Well, you will go down to hell!

¹⁶My followers, whoever listens to you is listening to me. Anyone who says "No" to you is saying "No" to me. And anyone who says "No" to me is really saying "No" to the one who sent me.

The Return of the 72

¹⁷When the 72ᵘ followers returned, they were excited and said, "Lord, even the demons obeyed when we spoke in your name!"

¹⁸Jesus told them:

I saw Satan fall from heaven like a flash of lightning. ¹⁹I have given you the power to trample on snakes and scorpions and to defeat the power of your enemy Satan. Nothing can harm you. ²⁰But don't be happy because evil spirits obey you. Be happy that your names are written in heaven!

Jesus Thanks His Father
(Matthew 11.25-27; 13.16, 17)

²¹At that same time, Jesus felt the joy that comes from the Holy Spirit,ᵛ and he said:

My Father, Lord of heaven and earth, I am grateful that you hid all this from wise and educated people and showed it to ordinary people. Yes, Father, that is what pleased you.

²²My Father has given me everything, and he is the only one who knows the Son. The only one who really knows the Father is the Son. But the Son wants to tell others about the Father, so that they can know him too.

²³Jesus then turned to his disciples and said to them in private, "You are really blessed to see what you see!

ᵗ*dressed in sackcloth...ashes on their heads:* This was one way that people showed how sorry they were for their sins. ᵘ*72:* See the note at 10.1. ᵛ*the Holy Spirit:* Some manuscripts have "his spirit."

24Many prophets and kings were eager to see what you see and to hear what you hear. But I tell you that they didn't see or hear."

The Good Samaritan

25An expert in the Law of Moses stood up and asked Jesus a question to see what he would say. "Teacher," he asked, "what must I do to have eternal life?"

26Jesus answered, "What is written in the Scriptures? How do you understand them?"

27The man replied, "The Scriptures say, 'Love the Lord your God with all your heart, soul, strength, and mind.' They also say, 'Love your neighbours as much as you love yourself.' "

28Jesus said, "You have given the right answer. If you do this, you will have eternal life."

29But the man wanted to show that he knew what he was talking about. So he asked Jesus, "Who are my neighbours?"

30Jesus replied:

As a man was going down from Jerusalem to Jericho, robbers attacked him and grabbed everything he had. They beat him up and ran off, leaving him half dead. 31A priest happened to be going down the same road. But when he saw the man, he walked by on the other side. 32Later a temple helper[w] came to the same place. But when he saw the man who had been beaten up, he also went by on the other side.

33A man from Samaria then came travelling along that road. When he saw the man, he felt sorry for him 34and went over to him. He treated his wounds with olive oil and wine[x] and bandaged them. Then he put him on his own donkey and took him to an inn, where he took care of him. 35The next morning he gave the innkeeper two silver coins and said, "Please take care of the man. If you spend more than this on him, I will pay you when I return."

---

[w]*temple helper:* A man from the tribe of Levi, whose job it was to work around the temple.   [x]*olive oil and wine:* In New Testament times these were used as medicine. Sometimes olive oil is a symbol for healing by means of a miracle (see James 5.14).

³⁶Then Jesus asked, "Which one of these three people was a real neighbour to the man who was beaten up by robbers?"

³⁷The teacher answered, "The one who showed pity." Jesus said, "Go and do the same!"

Martha and Mary

³⁸The Lord and his disciples were travelling along and came to a village. When they got there, a woman named Martha welcomed him into her home. ³⁹She had a sister named Mary, who sat down in front of the Lord and was listening to what he said. ⁴⁰Martha was worried about all that had to be done. Finally, she went to Jesus and said, "Lord, doesn't it bother you that my sister has left me to do all the work by myself? Tell her to come and help me!"

⁴¹The Lord answered, "Martha, Martha! You are worried and upset about so many things, ⁴²but only one thing is necessary. Mary has chosen what is best, and it won't be taken away from her."

Prayer
(Matthew 6.9-13; 7.7-11)

11 ¹When Jesus had finished praying, one of his disciples said to him, "Lord, teach us to pray, just as John taught his followers to pray."

²So Jesus told them, "Pray in this way:
'Father, help us to honour your name.
Come and set up your kingdom.
3   Give us each day the food we need.ʸ
4   Forgive our sins,
          as we forgive everyone who has done wrong to us.
And keep us from being tempted.' "
⁵Then Jesus went on to say:
Suppose one of you goes to a friend in the middle of the night and says, "Let me borrow three loaves of bread. ⁶A friend of mine has dropped in, and I haven't got anything for him to eat." ⁷And suppose your friend answers, "Don't bother me! The door is bolted,

---

ʸthe food we need: Or "food for today" or "food for the coming day."

and my children and I are in bed. I can't get up to give you anything."

⁸He may not get up and give you the bread, just because you are his friend. But he will get up and give you as much as you need, simply because you aren't ashamed to keep on asking.

⁹So I tell you to ask and you will receive, search and you will find, knock and the door will be opened for you. ¹⁰Everyone who asks will receive, everyone who searches will find, and the door will be opened for everyone who knocks. ¹¹Which one of you fathers would give your hungry child a snake if the child asked for a fish? ¹²Which one of you would give your child a scorpion if the child asked for an egg? ¹³As bad as you are, you still know how to give good gifts to your children. But your heavenly Father is even more ready to give the Holy Spirit to anyone who asks.

Jesus and the Ruler of Demons
(Matthew 12.22-30; Mark 3.20-27)

¹⁴Jesus forced a demon out of a man who couldn't talk. And after the demon had gone out, the man started speaking, and the crowds were amazed. ¹⁵But some people said, "He forces out demons by the power of Beelzebul, the ruler of the demons!"

¹⁶Others wanted to put Jesus to the test. So they asked him to show them a sign from God. ¹⁷Jesus knew what they were thinking, and he said:

A kingdom where people fight each other will end up in ruin. And a family that fights will break up. ¹⁸If Satan fights against himself, how can his kingdom last? Yet you say that I force out demons by the power of Beelzebul. ¹⁹If I use his power to force out demons, whose power do your own followers use to force them out? They are the ones who will judge you. ²⁰But if I use God's power to force out demons, it proves that God's kingdom has already come to you.

²¹When a strong man arms himself and guards his home, everything he owns is safe. ²²But if a stronger man comes and defeats him, he will carry off the weapons in which the strong man trusted. Then he

will divide with others what he has taken. [23]If you are not on my side, you are against me. If you don't gather in the crop with me, you scatter it.

Return of an Evil Spirit
(Matthew 12.43-45)

[24]When an evil spirit leaves a person, it travels through the desert, looking for a place to rest. But when it doesn't find a place, it says, "I'll go back to the home I left." [25]When it gets there and finds the place clean and tidied up, [26]it goes off and finds seven other evil spirits even worse than itself. They all come and make their home there, and that person ends up in worse shape than before.

Being Really Blessed

[27]While Jesus was still talking, a woman in the crowd spoke up, "The woman who gave birth to you and fed you is blessed!"

[28]Jesus replied, "That's true, but the people who are really blessed are the ones who hear and obey God's message!"[z]

A Sign from God
(Matthew 12.38-42; Mark 8.12)

[29]As crowds were gathering around Jesus, he said:

You people of today are evil! You keep looking for a sign from God. But what happened to Jonah[a] is the only sign you will be given. [30]Just as Jonah was a sign to the people of Nineveh, the Son of Man will be a sign to the people of today. [31]When the judgment comes, the Queen of the South[b] will stand there with you and condemn you. She travelled a long way to hear Solomon's wisdom, and yet here is something far greater than Solomon. [32]The people of Nineveh will

---

[z]"That's true, but the people who are really blessed...message": Or " 'That's not true, the people who are blessed...message.' " [a]what happened to Jonah: Jonah was in the stomach of a big fish for three days and nights (see Matthew 12.40). [b]Queen of the South: Sheba, probably a country in southern Arabia.

also stand there with you and condemn you. They turned to God when Jonah preached, and yet here is something far greater than Jonah.

Light
(Matthew 5.15; 6.22, 23)

33 No-one lights a lamp and then hides it or puts it under a clay pot. A lamp is put on a lampstand, so that everyone who comes into the house can see the light. 34 Your eyes are the lamp for your body. When your eyes are good, you have all the light you need. But when your eyes are bad, everything is dark. 35 So be sure that your light isn't darkness. 36 If you have light, and nothing is dark, then light will be everywhere, as when a lamp shines brightly on you.

Jesus Condemns the Pharisees and Teachers of the Law of Moses
(Matthew 23.1-36; Mark 12.38-40; Luke 20.45-47)

37 When Jesus finished speaking, a Pharisee invited him home for a meal. Jesus went and sat down to eat.c 38 The Pharisee was surprised that he didn't wash his handsd before eating. 39 So the Lord said to him:

You Pharisees clean the outside of cups and dishes, but on the inside you are greedy and evil. 40 You fools! Didn't God make both the outside and the inside?c 41 If you would only give what you have to the poor, everything you do would please God.

42 You Pharisees are in for trouble! You give God a tenth of the spices from your gardens, such as mint and rue. But you cheat people, and you don't love God. You should be fair and kind to others and still give a tenth to God.

43 You Pharisees are in for trouble! You love the front seats in the meeting places, and you like to be greeted

---

csat down to eat: See the note at 7.36.   ddidn't wash his hands: The Jewish people had strict laws about washing their hands before eating, especially if they had been out in public.   eDidn't God make both the outside and the inside?: Or "Doesn't the person who washes the outside always wash the inside too?"

with honour in the market. ⁴⁴But you are in for trouble! You are like unmarked graves*f* that people walk on without even knowing it.

⁴⁵A teacher of the Law of Moses spoke up, "Teacher, you said cruel things about us."

⁴⁶Jesus replied:

You teachers are also in for trouble! You load people down with heavy burdens, but you won't lift a finger to help them carry the loads. ⁴⁷Yes, you are really in for trouble. You build monuments to honour the prophets your own people murdered long ago. ⁴⁸You must think that was the right thing for your people to do, or else you wouldn't have built monuments for the prophets they murdered.

⁴⁹Because of your evil deeds, the Wisdom of God said, "I will send prophets and apostles to you. But you'll murder some and mistreat others." ⁵⁰You people living today will be punished for all the prophets who have been murdered since the beginning of the world. ⁵¹This includes every prophet from the time of Abel to the time of Zechariah,*g* who was murdered between the altar and the temple. You people will certainly be punished for all of this.

⁵²You teachers of the Law of Moses are really in for trouble! You carry the keys to the door of knowledge about God. But you never go in, and you keep others from going in.

⁵³Jesus was about to leave, but the teachers and the Pharisees wanted to get even with him. They tried to make him say what he thought about other things, ⁵⁴so that they could catch him saying something wrong.

Warnings

12 ¹As thousands of people crowded around Jesus and were stepping on each other, he told his disciples:

---

*f*unmarked graves: Tombs were whitewashed to keep anyone from accidentally touching them. A person who touched a dead body or a tomb was considered unclean and could not worship with other Jewish people.   *g*from the time of Abel...Zechariah: Genesis is the first book in the Jewish Scriptures, and it says that Abel was the first person to be murdered (see Genesis 4.8). Second Chronicles is the last book in the Jewish Scriptures, and the last murder that it tells about is that of Zechariah (see 2 Chronicles 24.20-21).

Be sure to guard against the dishonest teaching[h] of the Pharisees! It is their way of fooling people. [2]Everything that is hidden will be found out, and every secret will be known. [3]Whatever you say in the dark will be heard when it is day. Whatever you whisper in a closed room will be shouted from the housetops.

The One To Fear
(Matthew 10.28-31)

[4]My friends, don't be afraid of people. They can kill you, but after that, there is nothing else they can do. [5]God is the one you must fear. Not only can he take your life, but he can throw you into hell. God is certainly the one you should fear!

[6]Five sparrows are sold for just two small coins, but God doesn't forget one of them. [7]Even the hairs on your head are counted. So don't be afraid! You are worth much more than many sparrows.

Telling Others about Christ
(Matthew 10.32, 33; 12.32; 10.19, 20)

[8]If you tell others that you belong to me, the Son of Man will tell God's angels that you are my followers. [9]But if you reject me, you will be rejected in front of them. [10]If you speak against the Son of Man, you can be forgiven, but if you speak against the Holy Spirit, you can't be forgiven.

[11]When you are brought to trial in the Jewish meeting places or before rulers or officials, don't worry about how you will defend yourselves or what you will say. [12]At that time the Holy Spirit will tell you what to say.

A Rich Fool

[13]A man in a crowd said to Jesus, "Teacher, tell my brother to give me my share of what our father left us when he died."

[14]Jesus answered, "Who gave me the right to settle

[h]dishonest teaching: The Greek text has "yeast,"which is used here of a teaching that is not true (see Matthew 16.6, 12).

arguments between you and your brother?"

¹⁵Then he said to the crowd, "Don't be greedy! Owning a lot of things won't make your life safe."

¹⁶So Jesus told them this story:

A rich man's farm produced a big crop, ¹⁷and he said to himself, "What can I do? I haven't got a place large enough to store everything."

¹⁸Later, he said, "Now I know what I'll do. I'll tear down my barns and build bigger ones, where I can store all my grain and other goods. ¹⁹Then I'll say to myself, 'You've stored up enough good things to last for years to come. Live it up! Eat, drink, and enjoy yourself.' "

²⁰But God said to him, "You fool! Tonight you will die. Then who will get what you have stored up?"

²¹"This is what happens to people who store up everything for themselves, but are poor in the sight of God."

Worry
(Matthew 6.25-34)

²²Jesus said to his disciples:

I tell you not to worry about your life! Don't worry about having something to eat or wear. ²³Life is more than food or clothing. ²⁴Look at the crows! They don't plant or harvest, and they don't have storehouses or barns. But God takes care of them. You are much more important than any birds. ²⁵Can worry make you live longer?ⁱ ²⁶If you don't have power over small things, why worry about everything else?

²⁷Look how the wild flowers grow! They don't work hard to make their clothes. But I tell you that Solomon with all his wealthʲ wasn't as well clothed as one of these flowers. ²⁸God gives such beauty to everything that grows in the fields, even though it's here today and thrown into a fire tomorrow. Won't he do even more for you? You have such little faith!

²⁹Don't keep worrying about having something to

ⁱ*live longer:* Or "grow taller."   ʲ*Solomon with all his wealth:* The Jewish people thought that Solomon was the richest person who had ever lived.

eat or drink. [30]Only people who don't know God are always worrying about such things. Your Father knows what you need. [31]But put God's work first, and these things will be yours as well.

Treasures in Heaven
(Matthew 6.19-21)

[32]My little group of disciples, don't be afraid! Your Father wants to give you the kingdom. [33]Sell what you have and give the money to the poor. Make yourselves money bags that never wear out. Make sure your treasure is safe in heaven, where thieves can't steal it and moths can't destroy it. [34]Your heart will always be where your treasure is.

Faithful and Unfaithful Servants
(Matthew 24.45-51)

[35]Be ready and keep your lamps burning [36]just like those servants who wait up for their master to return from a wedding feast. As soon as he comes and knocks, they open the door for him. [37]Servants are fortunate if their master finds them awake and ready when he comes! I promise you that he will get ready and get his servants to sit down so he can serve them. [38]Those servants are really fortunate if their master finds them ready, even though he comes late at night or early in the morning. [39]You would surely not let a thief break into your home, if you knew when the thief was coming. [40]So always be ready! You don't know when the Son of Man will come.

[41]Peter asked Jesus, "Did you say this just for us or for everyone?"

[42]The Lord answered:

Who are faithful and wise servants? Who are the ones the master will put in charge of giving the other servants their food supplies at the proper time? [43]Servants are fortunate if their master comes and finds them doing their job. [44]A servant who is always faithful will surely be put in charge of everything the master owns.

[45]But suppose one of the servants thinks that the master won't return until late. Suppose that servant starts beating all the other servants and eats and drinks and gets drunk. [46]If that happens, the master will come on a day and at a time when the servant least expects him. That servant will then be punished and thrown out with the servants who can't be trusted.

[47]If servants are not ready or willing to do what their master wants them to do, they will be beaten hard. [48]But servants who don't know what their master wants them to do won't be beaten so hard for doing wrong. If God has been generous with you, he will expect you to serve him well. But if he has been more than generous, he will expect you to serve him even better.

Not Peace, but Trouble
(Matthew 10.34-36)

[49]I came to set fire to the earth, and I wish it was already on fire! [50]I am going to be put to a hard test. And I will have to suffer a lot of pain until it's over. [51]Do you think that I came to bring peace to earth? No indeed! I came to make people choose sides. [52]A family of five will be divided, with two of them against the other three. [53]Fathers and sons will turn against one another, and mothers and daughters will do the same. Mothers-in-law and daughters-in-law will also turn against each other.

Knowing What To Do
(Matthew 16.2, 3; 5.25, 26)

[54]Jesus said to all the people:

As soon as you see a cloud coming up in the west, you say, "It's going to rain," and it does. [55]When the south wind blows, you say, "It's going to get hot," and it does. [56]Are you trying to fool someone? You can predict the weather by looking at the earth and sky, but you don't really know what's going on right now. [57]Why don't you understand the right thing to do? [58]When someone accuses you of something, try to settle things before you are taken to court. If you don't, you will be dragged before the judge. Then the judge will hand you over to the jailer, and you will be locked up. 59You won't get out until you have paid the last cent you owe.

Turn Back to God

13 1About this same time Jesus was told that Pilate had given orders for some people from Galilee to be killed while they were offering sacrifices. 2Jesus replied:

Do you think that these people were worse sinners than everyone else in Galilee just because of what happened to them? 3Not at all! But you can be sure that if you don't turn back to God, every one of you will also be killed. 4What about those 18 people who died when the tower in Siloam fell on them? Do you think they were worse than everyone else in Jerusalem? 5Not at all! But you can be sure that if you don't turn back to God, every one of you will also die.

A Story about a Fig Tree

6Jesus then told them this story:

A man had a fig tree growing in his vineyard. One day he went out to pick some figs, but he didn't find any. 7So he said to the gardener, "For three years I have come looking for figs on this tree, and I haven't found any yet. Chop it down! Why should it take up space?"

8The gardener answered, "Master, leave it for another year. I'll dig around it and put some manure on it to make it grow. 9Maybe it will have figs on it next year. If it doesn't, you can have it cut down."

Healing a Woman on the Sabbath

10One Sabbath, Jesus was teaching in a Jewish meeting place, 11and a woman was there who had been crippled by an evil spirit for 18 years. She was completely bent over and couldn't straighten up. 12When Jesus saw the woman, he called her over and said, "You are now well."

¹³He placed his hands on her, and at once she stood up straight and praised God.

¹⁴The man in charge of the meeting place was angry because Jesus had healed someone on the Sabbath. So he said to the people, "Each week has six days when we can work. Come and be healed on one of those days, but not on the Sabbath."

¹⁵The Lord replied, "Are you trying to fool someone? Won't any one of you untie your bullock or donkey and lead it out to drink on a Sabbath? ¹⁶This woman belongs to the family of Abraham, but Satan has kept her bound for 18 years. Isn't it right to set her free on the Sabbath?" ¹⁷Jesus' words made his enemies ashamed. But everyone else in the crowd was happy about the wonderful things he was doing.

A Mustard Seed and Yeast
(Matthew 13.31-33; Mark 4.30-32)

¹⁸Jesus said, "What is God's kingdom like? What can I compare it with? ¹⁹It is like what happens when someone plants a mustard seed in a garden. The seed grows as big as a tree, and birds nest in its branches."

²⁰Then Jesus said, "What can I compare God's kingdom with? ²¹It is like what happens when a woman mixes yeast into three batches of flour. Finally, all the dough rises."

The Narrow Door
(Matthew 7.13, 14, 21-23)

²²As Jesus was on his way to Jerusalem, he taught the people in the towns and villages. ²³Someone asked him, "Lord, are only a few people going to be saved?"

Jesus answered:

²⁴Do all you can to go in by the narrow door! A lot of people will try to get in, but won't be able to. ²⁵Once the owner of the house gets up and locks the door, you will be left standing outside. You will knock on the door and say, "Sir, open the door for us!"

But the owner will answer, "I don't know a thing about you!"

26Then you will start saying, "We dined with you, and you taught in our streets."

27But he will say, "I really don't know who you are! Get away from me, you evil people!"

28Then when you have been thrown outside, you will weep and grit your teeth because you will see Abraham and Isaac and all the prophets in God's kingdom. 29People will come from all directions and sit down to feast in God's kingdom. 30There the ones who are now least important will be the most important, and those who are now most important will be least important.

Jesus and Herod

31At that time some Pharisees came to Jesus and said, "You had better get away from here! Herodk wants to kill you."

32Jesus said to them:

Go and tell that fox, "I am going to force out demons and heal people today and tomorrow, and three days later I'll be finished." 33But I am going on my way today and tomorrow and the next day. After all, Jerusalem is the place where prophets are killed.

Jesus Loves Jerusalem
(Matthew 23.37-39)

34Jerusalem, Jerusalem! Your people have killed the prophets and have stoned the messengers who were sent to you. I have often wanted to gather your people, as a hen gathers her chickens under her wings. But you wouldn't let me. 35Now your temple will be deserted. You won't see me again until the time when you say, "Blessed is the one who comes in the name of the Lord."

Jesus Heals a Sick Man

14 1One Sabbath, Jesus was having dinner in the home of an important Pharisee, and everyone was carefully watching Jesus. 2All of a sudden a man with

kHerod: Herod Antipas, the son of Herod the Great.

swollen legs stood up in front of him. [3]Jesus turned and asked the Pharisees and the teachers of the Law of Moses, "Is it right to heal on the Sabbath?" [4]But they didn't say a word.

Jesus took hold of the man. Then he healed him and sent him away. [5]Afterwards, Jesus asked the people, "If your son or your bullock falls into a well, wouldn't you pull him out straight away, even on the Sabbath?" [6]There was nothing they could say.

How To Be a Guest

[7]Jesus saw how the guests had tried to take the best seats. So he told them:

[8]When you are invited to a wedding feast, don't sit in the best place. Someone more important may have been invited. [9]Then the one who invited you will come and say, "Give your place to this other guest!" You will be embarrassed and will have to sit in the worst place.

[10]When you are invited to be a guest, go and sit in the worst place. Then the one who invited you may come and say, "My friend, take a better seat!" You will then be honoured in front of all the other guests. [11]If you put yourself above others, you will be put down. But if you humble yourself, you will be honoured.

[12]Then Jesus said to the man who had invited him:

When you give a dinner or a banquet, don't invite your friends and family and relatives and rich neighbours. If you do, they will invite you in return, and you will be paid back. [13]When you give a feast, invite the poor, the crippled, the lame, and the blind. [14]They can't pay you back. But God will bless you and reward you when his people rise from death.

The Great Banquet
(Matthew 22.1-10)

[15]After Jesus had finished speaking, one of the guests said, "The greatest blessing of all is to be at the banquet in God's kingdom!"

[16]Jesus told him:

A man once gave a great banquet and invited a lot of guests. ¹⁷When the banquet was ready, he sent a servant to tell the guests, "Everything is ready! Please come."

¹⁸One guest after another started making excuses. The first one said, "I bought some land, and I've got to look it over. Please excuse me."

¹⁹Another guest said, "I bought five teams of bullocks, and I need to try them out. Please excuse me."

²⁰Still another guest said, "I've just got married, and I can't be there."

²¹The servant told his master what happened, and the master became so angry that he said, "Go as fast as you can to every street and alley in town! Bring in everyone who is poor or crippled or blind or lame."

²²When the servant returned, he said, "Master, I've done what you told me, and there is still plenty of room for more people."

²³His master then told him, "Go out along the back roads and tracks and make people come in, so that my house will be full. ²⁴Not one of the guests I first invited will get even a bite of my food!"

Being a Disciple
(Matthew 10.37, 38)

²⁵Large crowds were walking along with Jesus, when he turned and said:

²⁶You can't be my disciple, unless you love me more than you love your father and mother, your wife and children, and your brothers and sisters. You can't come with me unless you love me more than you love your own life.

²⁷You can't be my disciple unless you carry your own cross and come with me.

²⁸Suppose one of you wants to build a tower. What is the first thing you will do? Won't you sit down and work out how much it will cost and if you have enough money to pay for it? ²⁹Otherwise, you will start building the tower, but not be able to finish. Then everyone who sees what is happening will laugh at you. ³⁰They will say, "You started building, but

couldn't finish the job."

³¹What will a king do if he has only 10 000 soldiers to defend himself against a king who is about to attack him with 20 000 soldiers? Before he goes out to battle, won't he first sit down and decide if he can win? ³²If he thinks he won't be able to defend himself, he will send messengers and ask for peace while the other king is still a long way off. ³³So then, you can't be my disciple unless you give away everything you own.

Salt and Light
(Matthew 5.13; Mark 9.50)

³⁴Salt is good, but if it no longer tastes like salt, how can it be made to taste salty again? ³⁵It is no longer good for the soil or even for the manure pile. People simply throw it out. If you have ears, pay attention!

One Sheep
(Matthew 18.12-14)

15 ¹Tax collectors¹ and sinners were all crowding around to listen to Jesus. ²So the Pharisees and the teachers of the Law of Moses started grumbling, "This man is friendly with sinners. He even eats with them."

³Then Jesus told them this story:

⁴If any of you has 100 sheep, and one of them gets lost, what will you do? Won't you leave the 99 in the field and go and look for the lost sheep until you find it? ⁵And when you find it, you will be so glad that you will put it on your shoulder ⁶and carry it home. Then you will call in your friends and neighbours and say, "Let's celebrate! I've found my lost sheep."

⁷Jesus said, "In the same way there is more happiness in heaven because of one sinner who turns to God than over 99 good people who don't need to."

One Coin

⁸Jesus told the people another story:

What will a woman do if she has ten silver coins and

---

¹Tax collectors: See the note at 3.12.

loses one of them? Won't she light a lamp, sweep the floor, and look carefully until she finds it? [9]Then she will call in her friends and neighbours and say, "Let's celebrate! I've found the coin I lost."

[10]Jesus said, "In the same way God's angels are happy when even one person turns to him."

Two Sons

[11]Jesus also told them another story:

Once a man had two sons. [12]The younger son said to his father, "Give me my share of the property." So the father divided his property between his two sons.

[13]Not long after that, the younger son packed up everything he owned and left for a foreign country, where he wasted all his money in wild living. [14]He had spent everything, when a bad famine spread through that whole land. Soon he had nothing to eat.

[15]He went to work for a man in that country, and the man sent him out to take care of his pigs.[m] [16]He would have been glad to eat what the pigs were eating,[n] but no-one gave him a thing.

[17]Finally, he came to his senses and said, "My father's workers have plenty to eat, and here I am, starving to death! [18]I will go to my father and say to him, 'Father, I've sinned against God in heaven and against you. [19]I'm no longer good enough to be called your son. Treat me like one of your workers.'"

[20]The younger son got up and started back to his father. But when he was still a long way away, his father saw him and felt sorry for him. He ran to his son and hugged and kissed him.

[21]The son said, "Father, I've sinned against God in heaven and against you. I'm no longer good enough to be called your son."

[22]But his father said to the servants, "Hurry and bring the best clothes and put them on him. Give him

---

[m]pigs: The Jewish religion taught that pigs weren't fit to eat or even touch. A Jewish man would be terribly insulted if he had to feed pigs, much less eat with them.   [n]what the pigs were eating: The Greek text has "(bean) pods," which were used to feed animals. Poor people sometimes ate them too.

a ring for his finger and sandals^o for his feet. [23]Get the best calf and prepare it, so we can eat and celebrate. [24]This son of mine was dead, but has now come back to life. He was lost and has now been found." And they began to celebrate.

[25]The older son had been out in the field. But when he came near the house, he heard the music and dancing. [26]So he called one of the servants over and asked, "What's going on here?"

[27]The servant answered, "Your brother has come home safe and sound, and your father ordered us to kill the best calf." [28]The older brother got so angry that he wouldn't even go into the house.

His father came out and begged him to go in. [29]But he said to his father, "For years I've worked for you like a slave and have always obeyed you. But you've never even given me a little goat, so that I could give a dinner for my friends. [30]This other son of yours wasted your money on prostitutes. And now that he has come home, you ordered the best calf to be killed for a feast."

[31]His father replied, "My son, you're always with me, and everything I have is yours. [32]But we should be glad and celebrate! Your brother was dead, but he's now alive. He was lost and has now been found."

A Dishonest Manager

16 [1]Jesus said to his disciples:

A rich man once had a manager to take care of his business. But he was told that his manager was wasting money. [2]So the rich man called him in and said, "What's this I hear about you? Tell me what you've done! You're no longer going to work for me."

[3]The manager said to himself, "What shall I do now that my master is going to fire me? I can't dig ditches, and I'm ashamed to beg. [4]I know what I'll do, so that people will welcome me into their homes after I've lost my job."

[5]Then one by one he called in the people who were

---

^{o}*ring...sandals:* These show that the young man's father fully accepted him as his son. A ring was a sign of high position in the family. Sandals showed that he was a son instead of a slave, since slaves did not usually wear sandals.

in debt to his master. He asked the first one, "How much do you owe my master?"

[6]"100 barrels of olive oil," the man answered.

So the manager said, "Take your bill and sit down and quickly write '50'."

[7]The manager asked someone else who was in debt to his master, "How much do you owe?"

"1000 bags[p] of wheat," the man replied.

The manager said, "Take your bill and write '800'."

[8]The master praised his dishonest manager for looking out for himself so well. That's how it is! The people of this world look out for themselves better than the people who belong to the light.

[9]My disciples, I tell you to use wicked wealth to make friends for yourselves. Then when it is gone, you will be welcomed into an eternal home. [10]Anyone who can be trusted in little matters can also be trusted in important matters. But anyone who is dishonest in little matters will be dishonest in important matters. [11]If you can't be trusted with this wicked wealth, who will trust you with true wealth? [12]And if you can't be trusted with what belongs to someone else, who will give you something that will be your own? [13]You can't be the slave of two masters. You will like one more than the other or be more loyal to one than to the other. You can't serve God and money.

Some Sayings of Jesus
(Matthew 11.12, 13; 5.31, 32; Mark 10.11, 12)

[14]The Pharisees really loved money. So when they heard what Jesus said, they made fun of him. [15]But Jesus told them:

You are always making yourselves look good, but God sees what is in your heart. The things that most people think are important are worthless as far as God is concerned.

[16]Until the time of John the Baptist, people had to obey the Law of Moses and the Books of the Prophets.[q]

---

[p]*1000 bags:* The Greek text has "100 measures," and each measure is about 350-400 litres.   [q]*the Law...Prophets:* The Jewish Scriptures, that is, the Old Testament.

But since God's kingdom has been preached, everyone is trying hard to get in. [17]Heaven and earth will disappear before the smallest letter of the Law does.

[18]It is a terrible sin[r] for a man to divorce his wife and marry another woman. It is also a terrible sin for a man to marry a divorced woman.

Lazarus and the Rich Man

[19]There was once a rich man who wore expensive clothes and every day ate the best food. [20]But a poor beggar named Lazarus was brought to the gate of the rich man's house. [21]He was happy just to eat the scraps that fell from the rich man's table. His body was covered with sores, and dogs kept coming up to lick them. [22]The poor man died, and angels took him to the place of honour next to Abraham.[s]

The rich man also died and was buried. [23]He went to hell[t] and was suffering terribly. When he looked up and saw Abraham far off and Lazarus at his side, [24]he said to Abraham, "Have pity on me! Send Lazarus to dip his finger in water and touch my tongue. I'm suffering terribly in this fire."

[25]Abraham answered, "My friend, remember that while you lived, you had everything good, and Lazarus had everything bad. Now he is happy, and you are in pain. [26]And besides, there is a deep valley between us, and no-one from either side can cross over."

[27]But the rich man said, "Abraham, then please send Lazarus to my father's home. [28]Let him warn my five brothers, so they won't come to this horrible place."

[29]Abraham answered, "Your brothers can read what Moses and the prophets[u] wrote. They should pay attention to that."

---

[r]a terrible sin: The Greek text uses a word that means the sin of being unfaithful in marriage.   [s]the place of honour next to Abraham: The Jewish people thought that heaven would be a banquet that God would give for them. Abraham would be the most important person there, and the guest of honour would sit next to him.   [t]hell: The Greek text has "hades," which the Jewish people often thought of as the place where the dead wait for the final judgment. [u]Moses and the prophets: see note at verse 16.

³⁰Then the rich man said, "No, that's not enough! If only someone from the dead would go to them, they would listen and turn to God."

³¹So Abraham said, "If they won't pay attention to Moses and the prophets, they won't listen even to someone who comes back from the dead."

Faith and Service
(Matthew 18.6, 7, 21, 22; Mark 9.42)

17 ¹Jesus said to his disciples:

There will always be something that causes people to sin. But anyone who causes them to sin is in for trouble. A person who causes even one of my little followers to sin ²would be better off thrown into the ocean with a heavy stone tied around their neck. ³So be careful what you do.

Correct any followersᵛ of mine who sin, and forgive the ones who say they are sorry. ⁴Even if one of them mistreats you seven times in one day and says, "I'm sorry," you should still forgive that person.

⁵The apostles said to the Lord, "Make our faith stronger!"

⁶Jesus replied:

If you had faith no bigger than a tiny mustard seed, you could tell this mulberry tree to pull itself up, roots and all, and to plant itself in the ocean. And it would!

⁷If your servant comes in from ploughing or from taking care of the sheep, would you say, "Welcome! Come on in and have something to eat"? ⁸No, you wouldn't say that. You would say, "Make me something to eat. Get ready to serve me, so I can have my meal. Then later on you can eat and drink." ⁹Servants don't deserve special thanks for doing what they are supposed to do. ¹⁰And that's how it should be with you. When you have done all you should, then say, "We are merely servants, and we've simply done our duty."

ᵛ*followers:* The Greek text has "brothers," which is often used in the New Testament for followers of Jesus.

Ten Men with Leprosy

[11]On his way to Jerusalem, Jesus went along the border between Samaria and Galilee. [12]As he was going into a village, ten men with leprosy[w] came towards him. They stood at a distance [13]and shouted, "Jesus, Master, have pity on us!"

[14]Jesus looked at them and said, "Go and show yourselves to the priests."[x]

On their way they were healed. [15]When one of them discovered that he was healed, he came back, shouting praises to God. [16]He bowed down at the feet of Jesus and thanked him. The man was from the country of Samaria.

[17]Jesus asked, "Weren't ten men healed? Where are the other nine? [18]Why was this foreigner the only one who came back to thank God?" [19]Then Jesus told the man, "You may get up and go. Your faith has made you well."

God's Kingdom
(Matthew 24.23-28, 37-41)

[20]Some Pharisees asked Jesus when God's kingdom would come. He answered, "God's kingdom isn't something you can see. [21]There is no use saying, 'Look! Here it is' or 'Look! There it is.' God's kingdom is here with you."[y]

[22]Jesus said to his disciples:

The time will come when you will long to see one of the days of the Son of Man, but you won't. [23]When people say to you, "Look there," or "Look here," don't go looking for him. [24]The day of the Son of Man will be like lightning flashing across the sky. [25]But first he must suffer terribly and be rejected by the people of today. [26]When the Son of Man comes, things will be just as they were when Noah lived. [27]People were eating, drinking, and getting married right up to the day when Noah went into the big boat. Then the flood came and drowned everyone on earth.

---

[w]*leprosy:* See note at 4.27.   [x]*show yourselves to the priests:* See note at 5.14.   [y]*here with you:* Or "in your hearts."

[28] When Lot[z] lived, people were also eating and drinking. They were buying, selling, planting, and building. [29] But on the very day Lot left Sodom, fiery flames poured down from the sky and killed everyone. [30] The same will happen on the day when the Son of Man appears.

[31] At that time no-one on a rooftop[a] should go down into the house to get anything. No-one in a field should go back to the house for anything. [32] Remember what happened to Lot's wife.[b]

[33] People who try to save their lives will lose them, and those who lose their lives will save them. [34] On that night two people will be sleeping in the same bed, but only one will be taken. The other will be left. [35-36] Two women will be together grinding wheat, but only one will be taken. The other will be left.[c]

[37] Then Jesus' disciples spoke up, "But where will this happen, Lord?"

Jesus said, "Where there is a corpse, there will always be vultures."[d]

A Widow and a Judge

18 [1] Jesus told his disciples a story about how they should keep on praying and never give up:

[2] In a town there was once a judge who didn't fear God or care about people. [3] In that same town there was a widow who kept going to the judge and saying, "Make sure that I get fair treatment in court."

[4] For a while the judge refused to do anything. Finally, he said to himself, "Even though I don't fear God or care about people, [5] I will help this widow

---

[z]Noah...Lot: When God destroyed the earth by a flood, he saved Noah and his family. When God destroyed the cities of Sodom and Gomorrah and the evil people who lived there, he rescued Lot and his family (see Genesis 19.1 29). [a]rooftop: See note at 5.19. [b]what happened to Lot's wife: She turned into a block of salt when she disobeyed God (see Genesis 19.26). [c]will be left: Some manuscripts add, "Two men will be in the same field, but only one will be taken. The other will be left." [d]Where...vultures: This saying may mean that when anything important happens, people soon know about it. Or the saying may mean that whenever something bad happens, curious people gather around and stare. But the word translated "vulture" also means "eagle" and may refer to the Roman army, which had an eagle as its symbol.

because she keeps on bothering me. If I don't help her, she'll wear me out."

⁶The Lord said:

Think about what that crooked judge said. ⁷Won't God protect his chosen ones who pray to him day and night? Won't he be concerned for them? ⁸He will surely hurry and help them. But when the Son of Man comes, will he find on this earth anyone with faith?

A Pharisee and a Tax Collector

⁹Jesus told a story to some people who thought they were better than others and who looked down on everyone else:

¹⁰Two men went into the temple to pray.ᵉ One was a Pharisee and the other a tax collector.ᶠ ¹¹The Pharisee stood by himself and prayed,ᵍ "God, I thank you that I am not greedy, dishonest, and unfaithful in marriage like other people. And I'm really glad that I'm not like that tax collector over there. ¹²I go without eatingʰ for two days a week, and I give you one tenth of all I earn."

¹³The tax collector stood off at a distance and didn't think he was good enough even to look up towards heaven. He was so sorry for what he had done that he pounded his chest and prayed, "God, have pity on me! I'm such a sinner."

¹⁴Then Jesus said, "When the two men went home, it was the tax collector and not the Pharisee who was pleasing to God. If you put yourself above others, you will be put down. But if you humble yourself, you will be honoured."

Jesus Blesses Little Children
(Matthew 19.13-15; Mark 10.13-16)

¹⁵Some people brought their little children for Jesus to bless. But when his disciples saw them doing this, they told the people to stop bothering him. ¹⁶So Jesus called

---

ᵉinto the temple to pray: Jewish people usually prayed there early in the morning and late in the afternoon. ᶠtax collector: See the note at 3.12. ᵍstood by himself and prayed: Some manuscripts have "stood up and prayed to himself." ʰwithout eating: See the note at 2.37.

the children over to him and said, "Let the children come
to me! Don't try to stop them. People who are like these
children belong to God's kingdom.[i] [17]You will never get
into God's kingdom unless you enter it like a child!"

A Rich and Important Man
(Matthew 19.16-30; Mark 10.17-31)

[18]An important man asked Jesus, "Good Teacher, what
must I do to have eternal life?"

[19]Jesus said, "Why do you call me good? Only God is
good. [20]You know the commandments: 'Be faithful in
marriage. Do not murder. Do not steal. Do not tell lies
about others. Respect your father and mother.' "

[21]He told Jesus, "I've obeyed all these commandments
since I was a young man."

[22]When Jesus heard this, he said, "There is one thing
you still need to do. Go and sell everything you own!
Give the money to the poor, and you will have riches in
heaven. Then come and be my follower." [23]When the
man heard this, he was sad, because he was very rich.

[24]Jesus saw how sad the man was. So he said, "It's
terribly hard for rich people to get into God's kingdom!
[25]In fact, it's easier for a camel to go through the eye of a
needle than for a rich person to get into God's kingdom."

[26]When the crowd heard this, they asked, "How can
anyone ever be saved?"

[27]Jesus replied, "There are some things that people
can't do, but God can do anything."

[28]Peter said, "Remember, we left everything to be your
followers!"

[29]Jesus answered, "You can be sure that anyone who
gives up home or wife or brothers or family or children
because of God's kingdom [30]will be given much more in
this life. And in the future world they will have eternal
life."

---

[i]*People who are like these children belong to God's kingdom:* Or "God's kingdom
belongs to people who are like these children."

Jesus Again Tells about His Death
(Matthew 20.17-19; Mark 10.32-34)

31Jesus took the twelve apostles aside and said:

We are now on our way to Jerusalem. Everything that the prophets wrote about the Son of Man will happen there. 32He will be handed over to foreigners,ʲ who will make fun of him, mistreat him, and spit on him. 33They will beat him and kill him, but three days later he will rise to life.

34The apostles didn't understand what Jesus was talking about. They couldn't understand, because the meaning of what he said was hidden from them.

Jesus Heals a Blind Beggar
(Matthew 20.29-34; Mark 10.46-52)

35When Jesus was coming close to Jericho, a blind man sat begging beside the road. 36The man heard the crowd walking by and asked what was happening. 37Some people told him that Jesus from Nazareth was passing by. 38So the blind man shouted, "Jesus, Son of David,ᵏ have pity on me!" 39The people who were going along with Jesus told the man to be quiet. But he shouted even louder, "Son of David, have pity on me!"

40Jesus stopped and told some people to bring the blind man over to him. When the blind man was getting near, Jesus asked, 41"What do you want me to do for you?"

"Lord, I want to see!" he answered.

42Jesus replied, "Look and you will see! Your eyes are healed because of your faith." 43Straight away the man could see, and he went with Jesus and started thanking God. When the crowds saw what happened, they praised God.

Zacchaeus

19 1Jesus was going through Jericho, 2where a man named Zacchaeus lived. He was in charge of

---

ʲforeigners: The Romans, who ruled Judea at this time.   ᵏSon of David: The Jewish people expected the Messiah to be from the family of King David, and for this reason the Messiah was often called the "Son of David."

collecting taxes[l] and was very rich. [3-4]Jesus was heading his way, and Zacchaeus wanted to see what he was like. But Zacchaeus was a short man and couldn't see over the crowd. So he ran ahead and climbed up into a sycamore tree.

[5]When Jesus got there, he looked up and said, "Zacchaeus, hurry down! I want to stay with you today." [6]Zacchaeus hurried down and gladly welcomed Jesus.

[7]Everyone who saw this started grumbling, "This man Zacchaeus is a sinner! And Jesus is going home to eat with him."

[8]Later that day Zacchaeus stood up and said to the Lord, "I'll give half of my property to the poor. And I'll now pay back four times as much[m] to everyone I've ever cheated."

[9]Jesus said to Zacchaeus, "Today you and your family have been saved,[n] because you are a true son of Abraham.[o] [10]The Son of Man came to look for and to save people who are lost."

A Story about Ten Servants
(Matthew 25.14-30)

[11]The crowd was still listening to Jesus as he was getting close to Jerusalem. Many of them thought that God's kingdom would soon appear, [12]and Jesus told them this story:

A prince once went to a foreign country to be crowned king and then to return. [13]But before leaving, he called in ten servants and gave each of them some money. He told them, "Use this to earn more money until I get back."

[14]But the people of his country hated him, and they sent messengers to the foreign country to say, "We don't want this man to be our king."

[15]After the prince had been made king, he returned

---

[l]*in charge of collecting taxes:* See the note at 3.12. [m]*pay back four times as much:* Both Jewish and Roman law said that a person must pay back four times the amount that was taken. [n]*saved:* Zacchaeus was Jewish, but it is only now that he is rescued from sin and placed under God's care. [o]*son of Abraham:* As used in this verse, the words mean that Zacchaeus is truly one of God's special people.

and called in his servants. He asked them how much they had earned with the money they had been given.

¹⁶The first servant came and said, "Sir, with the money you gave me I've earned ten times as much."

¹⁷"That's fine, my good servant!" the king said. "Since you've shown that you can be trusted with a small amount, you will be given ten cities to rule."

¹⁸The second one came and said, "Sir, with the money you gave me, I've earned five times as much."

¹⁹The king said, "You will be given five cities."

²⁰Another servant came and said, "Sir, here is your money. I kept it safe in a handkerchief. ²¹You are a hard man, and I was afraid of you. You take what isn't yours, and you harvest crops you didn't plant."

²²"You worthless servant!" the king told him. "You have condemned yourself by what you have just said. You knew that I'm a hard man, taking what isn't mine and harvesting what I haven't planted. ²³Why didn't you put my money in the bank? On my return, I could have had the money together with interest."

²⁴Then he said to some other servants standing there, "Take the money away from him and give it to the servant who earned ten times as much."

²⁵But they said, "Sir, he already has ten times as much!"

²⁶The king replied, "Those who have something will be given more. But everything will be taken away from those who haven't got anything. ²⁷Now bring me the enemies who didn't want me to be their king. Kill them while I watch!"

Jesus Enters Jerusalem

(Matthew 21.1-11; Mark 11.1-11; John 12.12-19)

²⁸When Jesus had finished saying all this, he went on towards Jerusalem. ²⁹As he was getting near Bethphage and Bethany on the Mount of Olives, he sent two of his disciples on ahead. ³⁰He told them, "Go into the next village, where you will find a young donkey that has never been ridden. Untie the donkey and bring it here. ³¹If anyone asks why you are doing that, just say, 'The Lord*ᵖ* needs it.' "

ᵖThe Lord: Or "The master of the donkey."

³²They went off and found everything just as Jesus had said. ³³While they were untying the donkey, its owners asked, "Why are you doing that?"

³⁴They answered, "The Lord needs it."

³⁵Then they led the donkey to Jesus. They put some of their clothes on its back and helped Jesus get on. ³⁶And as he rode along, the people spread clothes on the road[q] in front of him. ³⁷When Jesus was starting down the Mount of Olives, his large crowd of disciples were happy and praised God because of all the miracles they had seen. ³⁸They shouted,

"Blessed is the king who comes
in the name of the Lord!
Peace in heaven and glory to God."

³⁹Some Pharisees in the crowd said to Jesus, "Teacher, make your disciples stop shouting!"

⁴⁰But Jesus answered, "If they keep quiet, these stones will start shouting."

⁴¹When Jesus came closer and could see Jerusalem, he cried ⁴²and said:

It is too bad that today your people don't know what will bring them peace! Now it is hidden from them. ⁴³Jerusalem, the time will come when your enemies will build walls around you to attack you. Armies will surround you and close in on you from every side. ⁴⁴They will level you to the ground and kill your people. Not one stone in your buildings will be left on top of another. This will happen because you didn't see that God had come to save you.[r]

Jesus in the Temple
(Matthew 21.12-17; Mark 11.15-19; John 2.13-22)

⁴⁵When Jesus entered the temple, he started chasing out the people who were selling things. ⁴⁶He told them, "The Scriptures say, 'My house should be a place of worship.' But you have made it a place where robbers hide!"

---

[q]spread clothes on the road: This was one way that the Jewish people welcomed a famous person.   [r]that God had come to save you: The Jewish people looked for the time when God would come and rescue them from their enemies. But when Jesus came, many of them refused to obey him.

⁴⁷Each day, Jesus kept on teaching in the temple. So the chief priests, the teachers of the Law of Moses, and some other important people tried to have him killed. ⁴⁸But they couldn't find a way to do it, because everyone else was eager to listen to him.

A Question about Jesus' Authority
(Matthew 21.23-27; Mark 11.27-33)

20 ¹One day, Jesus was teaching in the temple and telling the good news. So the chief priests, the teachers, and the nation's leaders ²asked him, "What right have you got to do these things? Who gave you this authority?"

³Jesus replied, "I want to ask you a question. ⁴Who gave John the right to baptise? Was it God in heaven or merely some human being?"

⁵They talked this over and said to each other, ".We can't say that God gave John this right. Jesus will ask us why we didn't believe John. ⁶And we can't say that it was merely some human who gave John the right to baptise. The crowd will stone us to death, because they think John was a prophet."

⁷So they told Jesus, "We don't know who gave John the right to baptise."

⁸Jesus replied, "Then I won't tell you who gave me the right to do what I do."

Tenants of a Vineyard
(Matthew 21.33-46; Mark 12.1-12)

⁹Jesus told the people this story:

A man once planted a vineyard and rented it out. Then he left the country for a long time. ¹⁰When it was time to harvest the crop, he sent a servant to ask the tenants for his share of the grapes. But they beat up the servant and sent him away without anything. ¹¹So the owner sent another servant. The tenants also beat him up. They insulted him terribly and sent him away without a thing. ¹²The owner sent a third servant. He was also beaten terribly and thrown out of the vineyard.

¹³The owner then said to himself, "What am I going to do? I know what. I'll send my son, the one I love so much. They will surely respect him!"

¹⁴When the tenants saw the owner's son, they said to one another, "Some day he will own the vineyard. Let's kill him! Then we can have it all for ourselves." ¹⁵So they threw him out of the vineyard and killed him.

Jesus asked, "What do you think the owner of the vineyard will do? ¹⁶I'll tell you what. He will come and kill those tenants and let someone else have his vineyard."

When the people heard this, they said, "This must never happen!"

¹⁷But Jesus looked straight at them and said, "Then what do the Scriptures mean when they say, 'The stone that the builders tossed aside is now the most important stone of all'? ¹⁸Anyone who stumbles over this stone will get hurt, and anyone it falls on will be smashed to pieces."

¹⁹The chief priests and the teachers of the Law of Moses knew that Jesus was talking about them when he was telling this story. They wanted to arrest him straight away, but they were afraid of the people.

Paying Taxes
(Matthew 22.15-22; Mark 12.13-17)

²⁰Jesus' enemies kept watching him closely, because they wanted to hand him over to the Roman governor. So they sent some men who pretended to be good. But they were really spies trying to catch Jesus saying something wrong. ²¹The spies said to him, "Teacher, we know that you teach the truth about what God wants people to do. And you treat everyone with the same respect, no matter who they are. ²²Tell us, should we pay taxes to the Emperor or not?"

²³Jesus knew that they were trying to trick him. So he told them, ²⁴"Show me a coin." Then he asked, "Whose picture and name are on it?"

"The Emperor's," they answered.

²⁵Then he told them, "Give the Emperor what belongs

to him and give God what belongs to God." 26Jesus'
enemies could not catch him saying anything wrong
there in front of the people. They were amazed at his
answer and kept quiet.

Life in the Future World
(Matthew 22.23-33; Mark 12.18-27)

27The Sadducees didn't believe that people would rise
to life after death. So some of them came to Jesus 28and
said:

Teacher, Moses wrote that if a married man dies and
has no children, his brother should marry the widow.
Their first son would then be thought of as the son of
the dead brother.

29There were once seven brothers. The first one
married, but died without having any children. 30The
second one married his brother's widow, and he also
died without having any children. 31The same thing
happened to the third one. Finally, all seven brothers
married that woman and died without having any
children. 32At last the woman died. 33When God raises
people from death, whose wife will this woman be? All
seven brothers had married her.

34Jesus answered:

The people in this world get married. 35But in the
future world no-one who is worthy to rise from death
will either marry 36or die. They will be like the angels
and will be God's children, because they have been
raised to life.

37In the story about the burning bush, Moses clearly
shows that people will live again. He said, "The Lord is
the God worshipped by Abraham, Isaac, and Jacob."s
38So the Lord isn't the God of the dead, but of the
living. This means that everyone is alive as far as God
is concerned.

39Some of the teachers of the Law of Moses said,
"Teacher, you have given a good answer!" 40From then
on, no-one dared to ask Jesus any questions.

s"The Lord is the God worshipped by Abraham, Isaac, and Jacob": Jesus
argues that if God is worshipped by these three, they must be alive, because
he is the God of the living.

About David's Son
(Matthew 22.41-46; Mark 12.35-37)

⁴¹Jesus asked, "Why do people say that the Messiah will be the son of King David?ᵗ ⁴²In the book of Psalms, David himself says,

'The Lord said to my Lord,
43   Sit at my right sideᵘ
        until I make your enemies into a footstool for you.'
⁴⁴David spoke of the Messiah as his Lord, so how can the Messiah be his son?"

Jesus and the Teachers of the Law of Moses
(Matthew 23.1-36; Mark 12.38-40; Luke 11.37-54)

⁴⁵While everyone was listening to Jesus, he said to his disciples:
⁴⁶Guard against the teachers of the Law of Moses! They love to walk around in long robes, and they like to be greeted in the market. They want the front seats in the meeting places and the best seats at banquets. ⁴⁷But they cheat widows out of their homes and then pray long prayers just to show off. These teachers will be punished most of all.

A Widow's Offering
(Mark 12.41-44)

21 ¹Jesus looked up and saw some rich people tossing their gifts into the offering box. ²He also saw a poor widow putting in two small coins. ³And he said, "I tell you that this poor woman has put in more than all the others. ⁴Everyone else gave what they didn't need. But she is very poor and gave everything she had."

The Temple Will Be Destroyed
(Matthew 24.1,.2; Mark 13.1, 2)

⁵Some people were talking about the beautiful stones used to build the temple and about the gifts that had been placed in it. Jesus said, ⁶"Do you see these stones?

ᵗthe son of King David: See the note at 18.38.   ᵘright side: The place of power and honour.

The time is coming when not one of them will be left in place. They will all be knocked down."

Warning about Trouble
(Matthew 24.3-14; Mark 13.3-13)

7Some people asked, "Teacher, when will all this happen? How can we know when these things are about to take place?"

8Jesus replied:

Don't be fooled by those who will come and claim to be me. They will say, "I am Christ!" and "Now is the time!" But don't follow them. 9When you hear about wars and riots, don't be afraid. These things will have to happen first, but that isn't the end.

10Nations will go to war against one another, and kingdoms will attack each other. 11There will be great earthquakes, and in many places people will starve to death and suffer terrible diseases. All sorts of frightening things will be seen in the sky.

12Before all this happens, you will be arrested and punished. You will be tried in your meeting places and put in jail. Because of me you will be placed on trial before kings and governors. 13But this will be your chance to tell about your faith.

14Don't worry about what you will say to defend yourselves. 15I will give you the wisdom to know what to say. None of your enemies will be able to oppose you or to say that you are wrong. 16You will be betrayed by your own parents, brothers, family, and friends. Some of you will even be killed. 17Because of me, you will be hated by everyone. 18But don't worry!�v 19You will be saved by being faithful to me.

Jerusalem Will Be Destroyed
(Matthew 24.15-21; Mark 13.14-19)

20When you see Jerusalem surrounded by soldiers, you will know that it will soon be destroyed. 21If you are living in Judea at that time, run to the mountains.

---

vBut don't worry: The Greek text has "Not a hair of your head will be lost," which means, "There's no need to worry."

If you are in the city, leave it. And if you are out in the country, don't go back into the city. ²²This time of punishment is what is written about in the Scriptures. ²³It will be an awful time for women who are expecting babies or nursing young children! Everywhere in the land people will suffer horribly and be punished. ²⁴Some of them will be killed by swords. Others will be carried off to foreign countries. Jerusalem will be overrun by foreign nations until their time comes to an end.

When the Son of Man Appears
(Matthew 24.29-31; Mark 13.24-27)

²⁵Strange things will happen to the sun, moon, and stars. The nations on earth will be afraid of the roaring sea and tides, and they won't know what to do. ²⁶People will be so frightened that they will faint because of what is happening to the world. Every power in the sky will be shaken.ʷ ²⁷Then the Son of Man will be seen, coming in a cloud with great power and glory. ²⁸When all of this starts happening, stand up straight and be brave. You will soon be set free.

A Lesson from a Fig Tree
(Matthew 24.32-35; Mark 13.28-31)

²⁹Then Jesus told them a story:

When you see a fig tree or any other tree ³⁰putting out leaves, you know that summer will soon come. ³¹So, when you see these things happening, you know that God's kingdom will soon be here. ³²You can be sure that some of the people of this generation will still be alive when all of this takes place. ³³The sky and the earth won't last for ever, but my words will.

A Warning

³⁴Don't spend all of your time thinking about eating or drinking or worrying about life. If you do, the final

---

ʷEvery power in the sky will be shaken: In ancient times people thought that the stars were spiritual powers.

day will suddenly catch you [35]like a trap. That day will surprise everyone on earth. [36]Watch out and keep praying that you can escape all that is going to happen and that the Son of Man will be pleased with you.

[37]Jesus taught in the temple each day, and he spent each night on the Mount of Olives. [38]Everyone got up early and came to the temple to hear him teach.

A Plot To Kill Jesus

(Matthew 26.1-5, 14, 16; Mark 14.1, 2, 10, 11; John 11.45-53)

22 [1]The Festival of Thin Bread, also called Passover, was near. [2]The chief priests and the teachers of the Law of Moses were looking for a way to get rid of Jesus, because they were afraid of what the people might do. [3]Then Satan entered the heart of Judas Iscariot,[x] who was one of the twelve apostles.

[4]Judas went to talk with the chief priests and the officers of the temple police about how he could help them arrest Jesus. [5]They were very pleased and offered to pay Judas some money. [6]He agreed and started looking for a good chance to betray Jesus when the crowds were not around.

Jesus Eats with His Disciples

(Matthew 26.17-25; Mark 14.12-21; John 13.21-30)

[7]The day had come for the Festival of Thin Bread, and it was time to kill the Passover lambs. [8]So Jesus said to Peter and John, "Go and prepare the Passover meal for us to eat."

[9]But they asked, "Where do you want us to prepare it?"

[10]Jesus told them, "As you go into the city, you will meet a man carrying a jar of water.[y] Follow him into the house [11]and say to the owner, 'Our teacher wants to know where he can eat the Passover meal with his disciples.' [12]The owner will take you upstairs and show you a large room ready for you to use. Prepare the meal there."

---

[x]Iscariot: See the note at 6.16.　[y]a man carrying a jar of water: A male slave carrying water would probably mean that the family was rich.

13Peter and John left. They found everything just as Jesus had told them, and they prepared the Passover meal.

The Lord's Supper

(Matthew 26.26-30; Mark 14.22-26; 1 Corinthians 11.23-25)

14When the time came for Jesus and the apostles to eat, 15he said to them, "I have very much wanted to eat this Passover meal with you before I suffer. 16I tell you that I won't eat another Passover meal until it is finally eaten in God's kingdom."

17Jesus took a cup of wine in his hands and gave thanks to God. Then he told the apostles, "Take this wine and share it with each other. 18I tell you that I won't drink any more wine until God's kingdom comes."

19Jesus took some bread in his hands and gave thanks for it. He broke the bread and handed it to his apostles. Then he said, "This is my body, which is given for you. Eat this as a way of remembering me!"

20After the meal he took another cup of wine in his hands. Then he said, "This is my blood. It is poured out for you, and with it God makes his new agreement. 21The one who will betray me is here at the table with me! 22The Son of Man will die in the way that has been decided for him, but it will be terrible for the one who betrays him!"

23Then the apostles started arguing about who would ever do such a thing.

An Argument about Greatness

24The apostles got into an argument about which one of them was the greatest. 25So Jesus told them:

Foreign kings order their people around, and powerful rulers call themselves everyone's friends.ᶻ 26But don't be like them. The most important one of you should be like the least important, and your leader should be like a servant. 27Who do people think is the greatest, a person who is served or one who serves? Isn't it the

---

ᶻeveryone's friends: This translates a Greek word that rulers sometimes used as a title for themselves or for special friends.

one who is served? But I have been with you as a servant.

28You have stayed with me in all my troubles. 29So I will give you the right to rule as kings, just as my Father has given me the right to rule as a king. 30You will eat and drink with me in my kingdom, and you will each sit on a throne to judge the 12 tribes of Israel.

Jesus' Disciples Will Be Tested
(Matthew 26.31-35; Mark 14.27-31; John 13.36-38)

31Jesus said, "Simon, listen to me! Satan has demanded the right to test each one of you, as a farmer does when he separates wheat from the husks.ᵃ 32But Simon, I've prayed that your faith will be strong. And when you've come back to me, help the others."

33Peter said, "Lord, I'm ready to go with you to jail and even to die with you."

34Jesus replied, "Peter, I tell you that before a rooster crows tomorrow morning, you will say three times that you don't know me."

Money Bags, Travelling Bags, and Swords

35Jesus asked his disciples, "When I sent you out without a money bag or a travelling bag or sandals, did you need anything?"

"No!" they answered.

36Jesus told them, "But now, if you've got a money bag, take it with you. Also take a travelling bag, and if you haven't got a sword,ᵇ sell some of your clothes and buy one. 37Do this because the Scriptures say, 'He was considered a criminal.' This was written about me, and it will soon come true."

38The disciples said, "Lord, here are two swords!"

"Enough of that!" Jesus replied.

ᵃseparates wheat from the husks: See the note at 3.17.   ᵇmoney bag...travelling bag...sword: These were things that someone would take on a dangerous journey. Jesus was telling his disciples to be ready for anything that might happen. They seem to have understood what he meant (see 22.49-51).

Jesus Prays
(Matthew 26.36-46; Mark 14.32-42)

39Jesus went out to the Mount of Olives, as he often did, and his disciples went with him. 40When they got there, he told them, "Pray that you won't be tested."

41Jesus walked on a little way before he knelt down and prayed, 42"Father, if you will, please don't make me suffer by having to drink from this cup.c But do what you want, and not what I want."

43Then an angel from heaven came to help him. 44Jesus was in great pain and prayed so sincerely that his sweat fell to the ground like drops of blood.d

45Jesus got up from praying and went over to his disciples. They were asleep and worn out from being so sad. 46He said to them, "Why are you asleep? Wake up and pray that you won't be tested."

Jesus Is Arrested
(Matthew 26.47-56; Mark 14.43-50; John 18.3-11)

47While Jesus was still speaking, a crowd came up. It was led by Judas, one of the twelve apostles. He went over to Jesus and greeted him with a kiss.e

48Jesus asked Judas, "Are you betraying the Son of Man with a kiss?"

49When Jesus' disciples saw what was about to happen, they asked, "Lord, should we attack them with a sword?" 50One of the disciples even struck at the high priest's servant with his sword and cut off the servant's right ear.

51"Enough of that!" Jesus said. Then he touched the servant's ear and healed it.

52Jesus spoke to the chief priests, the temple police, and the leaders who had come to arrest him. He said, "Why do you come out with swords and clubs and treat me like a criminal? 53I was with you every day in the temple, and you didn't arrest me. But this is your time, and darknessf is in control."

---

cdrink from this cup: In the Scriptures "to drink from a cup" sometimes means to suffer. dThen an angel....like drops of blood: Verses 43, 44 are not in some manuscripts. egreeted him with a kiss: It was the custom for people to greet each other with a kiss on the cheek. fdarkness: Darkness stands for the power of the devil.

Peter Says He Doesn't Know Jesus
(Matthew 26.57, 58, 67-75; Mark 14.53, 54, 66-72; John 18.12-18, 25-27)

[54]Jesus was arrested and led away to the house of the high priest, while Peter followed at a distance. [55]Some people built a fire in the middle of the courtyard and were sitting around it. Peter sat there with them, [56]and a servant girl saw him. Then after she had looked at him carefully, she said, "This man was with Jesus!"

[57]Peter said, "Woman, I don't even know that man!"

[58]A little later someone else saw Peter and said, "You're one of them!"

"No, I'm not!" Peter replied.

[59]About an hour later another man insisted, "This man must have been with Jesus. They both come from Galilee."

[60]Peter replied, "I don't know what you're talking about!" At once, while Peter was still speaking, a rooster crowed.

[61]The Lord turned and looked at Peter. And Peter remembered that the Lord had said, "Before a rooster crows tomorrow morning, you will say three times that you don't know me." [62]Then Peter went out and cried hard.

[63]The men who were guarding Jesus made fun of him and beat him. [64]They put a blindfold on him and said, "Tell us who struck you!" [65]They kept on insulting Jesus in many other ways.

Jesus Is Questioned by the Council
(Matthew 26.59-66; Mark 14.55-64; John 18.19-24)

[66]At daybreak the nation's leaders, the chief priests, and the teachers of the Law of Moses got together and brought Jesus before their council. [67]They said, "Tell us! Are you the Messiah?"

Jesus replied, "If I said so, you wouldn't believe me. [68]And if I asked you a question, you wouldn't answer. [69]But from now on, the Son of Man will be seated at the right side of God All-Powerful."

[70]Then they asked, "Are you the Son of God?"[g]

[g]*Son of God:* This was one of the titles used for the kings of Israel.

Jesus answered, "You say I am!"[h]
71They replied, "Why do we need more witnesses? He said it himself!"

Pilate Questions Jesus

(Matthew 27.1, 2, 11-14; Mark 15.1-5; John 18.28-38)

23 1Everyone in the council got up and led Jesus off to Pilate. 2They started accusing him and said, "We caught this man trying to get our people to riot and to stop paying taxes to the Emperor. He also claims that he is the Messiah, our king."

3Pilate asked Jesus, "Are you the king of the Jews?"

"Those are your words," Jesus answered.

4Pilate told the chief priests and the crowd, "I don't find him guilty of anything."

5But they all kept on saying, "He's been teaching and causing trouble all over Judea. He started in Galilee and has now come all the way here."

Jesus Is Brought before Herod

6When Pilate heard this, he asked, "Is this man from Galilee?" 7After Pilate learned that Jesus came from the region ruled by Herod,[i] he sent him to Herod, who was in Jerusalem at that time.

8For a long time Herod had wanted to see Jesus and was very happy because he finally had this chance. He had heard many things about Jesus and hoped to see him work a miracle.

9Herod asked him a lot of questions, but Jesus didn't answer. 10Then the chief priests and the teachers of the Law of Moses stood up and accused him of all kinds of bad things.

11Herod and his soldiers made fun of Jesus and insulted him. They put a fine robe on him and sent him back to Pilate. 12That same day Herod and Pilate became friends, even though they had been enemies before this.

---

[h]You say I am: Or "That's what you say."   [i]Herod: Herod Antipas, the son of Herod the Great.

The Death Sentence
(Matthew 27.15-26; Mark 15.6-15; John 18.39—19.16)

13Pilate called together the chief priests, the leaders, and the people. 14He told them, "You brought Jesus to me and said he was a troublemaker. But I've questioned him here in front of you, and I haven't found him guilty of anything that you say he has done. 15Herod didn't find him guilty either and sent him back. This man doesn't deserve to be put to death! 16-17I'll just have him beaten with a whip and set free."*i*

18But the whole crowd shouted, "Kill Jesus! Give us Barabbas!" 19Now Barabbas was in jail because he had started a riot in the city and had murdered someone.

20Pilate wanted to set Jesus free, so he spoke again to the crowds. 21But they kept shouting, "Nail him to a cross! Nail him to a cross!"

22Pilate spoke to them a third time, "But what crime has he done? I haven't found him guilty of anything for which he should be put to death. I'll have him beaten with a whip and set free."

23The people kept on shouting as loud as they could for Jesus to be put to death. 24Finally, Pilate gave in. 25He freed the man who was in jail for rioting and murder, because he was the one the crowd wanted to be set free. Then Pilate handed Jesus over for them to do what they wanted with him.

Jesus Is Nailed to a Cross
(Matthew 27.31-44; Mark 15.21-32; John 19.17-27)

26As Jesus was being led away, some soldiers grabbed hold of a man from Cyrene named Simon. He was coming in from the fields, but they put the cross on him and made him carry it behind Jesus.

27A large crowd was following Jesus, and in the crowd a lot of women were crying and weeping for him. 28Jesus turned to the women and said:

---

i set free: Some manuscripts add, "Pilate said this, because at every Passover he was supposed to set one prisoner free for the Jewish people."

Women of Jerusalem, don't cry for me! Cry for yourselves and for your children. [29]Some day people will say, "Women who never had children are really fortunate!" [30]At that time everyone will say to the mountains, "Fall on us!" They will say to the hills, "Hide us!" [31]If this can happen when the wood is green, what do you think will happen when it is dry?[k]

[32]Two criminals were led out to be put to death with Jesus. [33]When the soldiers came to the place called "The Skull,"[l] they nailed Jesus to a cross. They also nailed the two criminals to crosses, one on each side of Jesus.

[34-35]Jesus said, "Father, forgive these people! They don't know what they're doing."[m]

While the crowd stood there watching Jesus, the soldiers gambled for his clothes. The leaders insulted him by saying, "He saved others. Now he should save himself, if he really is God's chosen Messiah!"

[36]The soldiers made fun of Jesus and brought him some wine. [37]They said, "If you're the king of the Jews, save yourself!"

[38]Above him was a sign that said, "This is the King of the Jews."

[39]One of the criminals hanging there also insulted Jesus by saying, "Aren't you the Messiah? Save yourself and save us!"

[40]But the other criminal told the first one off, "Don't you fear God? Aren't you getting the same punishment as this man? [41]We got what was coming to us, but he didn't do anything wrong." [42]Then he said to Jesus, "Remember me when you come into power!"

[43]Jesus replied, "I promise that today you will be with me in paradise."[n]

---

[k]If this can happen when the wood is green, what do you think will happen when it is dry?: This saying probably means, "If this can happen to an innocent person, what do you think will happen to one who is guilty?" [l]"The Skull": The place was probably given this name because it was near a large rock in the shape of a human skull. [m]Jesus said, "Father....doing": These words are not in some manuscripts. [n]paradise: In the Greek translation of the Old Testament, this word is used for the Garden of Eden. In New Testament times it was sometimes used for the place where God's people are happy and at rest, as they wait for the final judgment.

The Death of Jesus
(Matthew 27.45-56; Mark 15.33-41; John 19.28-30)

44Around midday the sky turned dark and stayed that way until the middle of the afternoon. 45The sun stopped shining, and the curtain in the templeo split down the middle. 46Jesus shouted, "Father, I put myself in your hands!" Then he died.

47When the Roman officer saw what had happened, he praised God and said, "Jesus must really have been a good man!"

48A crowd had gathered to see the terrible sight. Then after they had seen it, they felt broken-hearted and went home. 49All of Jesus' close friends and the women who had come with him from Galilee stood at a distance and watched.

Jesus Is Buried
(Matthew 27.57-61; Mark 15.42-47; John 19.38-42)

50-51There was a man named Joseph, who was from Arimathea in Judea. Joseph was a good and honest man, and he was eager for God's kingdom to come. He was also a member of the council, but he didn't agree with what they had decided.

52Joseph went to Pilate and asked for Jesus' body. 53He took the body down from the cross and wrapped it in fine cloth. Then he put it in a tomb that had been cut out of solid rock and had never been used. 54It was Friday, and the Sabbath was about to begin.p

55The women who had come with Jesus from Galilee followed Joseph and watched how Jesus' body was placed in the tomb. 56Then they went to prepare some sweet-smelling spices for his burial. But on the Sabbath they rested, as the Law of Moses commands.

ocurtain in the temple: There were two curtains in the temple. One was at the entrance, and the other separated the holy place from the most holy place that the Jewish people thought of as God's home on earth. The second curtain is probably the one which is meant. pthe Sabbath was about to begin: The Sabbath begins at sunset on Friday.

Jesus Is Alive
(Matthew 28.1-10; Mark 16.1-8; John 20.1-10)

24 ¹Very early on Sunday morning the women went to the tomb, carrying the spices that they had prepared. ²When they found the stone rolled away from the entrance, ³they went in. But they didn't find the body of the Lord𝑞 Jesus, ⁴and they didn't know what to think.

Suddenly two men in shining white clothes stood beside them. ⁵The women were afraid and bowed to the ground. But the men said, "Why are you looking in the place of the dead for someone who is alive? ⁶Jesus isn't here! He's been raised from death. Remember that while he was still in Galilee, he told you, ⁷'The Son of Man will be handed over to sinners who will nail him to a cross. But three days later he will rise to life.' " ⁸Then they remembered what Jesus had said.

⁹⁻¹⁰Mary Magdalene, Joanna, Mary the mother of James, and some other women were the ones who had gone to the tomb. When they returned, they told the eleven apostles and the others what had happened. ¹¹The apostles thought it was all nonsense, and they wouldn't believe.

¹²But Peter ran to the tomb. And when he stooped down and looked in, he saw only the burial clothes. Then he returned, wondering what had happened.𝑟

Jesus Appears to Two Disciples
(Mark 16.12, 13)

¹³That same day two of Jesus' disciples were going to the village of Emmaus, which was about 12 kilometres from Jerusalem. ¹⁴As they were talking and thinking about what had happened, ¹⁵Jesus came near and started walking along beside them. ¹⁶But they didn't know who he was.

¹⁷Jesus asked them, "What were you talking about as you walked along?"

𝑞*the Lord:* These words are not in some manuscripts.   𝑟*what had happened:* Verse 12 is not in some manuscripts.

The two of them stood there looking sad and gloomy. [18]Then the one named Cleopas asked Jesus, "Are you the only person from Jerusalem who doesn't know what was happening there these last few days?"

[19]"What do you mean?" Jesus asked.

They answered:

Those things that happened to Jesus from Nazareth. By what he did and said he showed that he was a powerful prophet, who pleased God and all the people. [20]Then the chief priests and our leaders had him arrested and sentenced to die on a cross. [21]We had hoped that he would be the one to set Israel free! But it has already been three days since all this happened.

[22]Some women in our group surprised us. They had gone to the tomb early in the morning, [23]but didn't find the body of Jesus. They came back, saying that they had seen a vision of angels who told them that he is alive. [24]Some men from our group went to the tomb and found it just as the women had said. But they didn't see Jesus either.

[25]Then Jesus asked the two disciples, "Why can't you understand? How can you be so slow to believe all that the prophets said? [26]Didn't you know that the Messiah would have to suffer before he was given his glory?" [27]Jesus then explained everything written about himself in the Scriptures, beginning with the Law of Moses and the Books of the Prophets.[s]

[28]When the two of them came near the village where they were going, Jesus seemed to be going further. [29]They begged him, "Stay with us! It's already late, and the sun is going down." So Jesus went into the house to stay with them.

[30]After Jesus sat down to eat, he took some bread. He blessed it and broke it. Then he gave it to them. [31]At once they knew who he was, but he disappeared. [32]They said to each other, "When he talked with us along the road and explained the Scriptures to us, didn't it warm our

---

[s]the Law...Prophets: See the note at 16.16.

hearts?" 33So they got straight up and returned to Jerusalem.

The two disciples found the eleven apostles and the others gathered together. 34And they learnt from the group that the Lord was really alive and had appeared to Peter. 35Then the disciples from Emmaus told them what happened on the road and how they knew he was the Lord when he broke the bread.

What Jesus' Followers Must Do

(Matthew 28.16-20; Mark 16.14-18; John 20.19-23; Acts 1.6-8)

36While Jesus' disciples were talking about what had happened, Jesus appeared and greeted them. 37They were frightened and terrified because they thought they were seeing a ghost.

38But Jesus said, "Why are you so frightened? Why do you doubt? 39Look at my hands and my feet and see who I am! Touch me and find out for yourselves. Ghosts don't have flesh and bones as you see I have."

40After Jesus said this, he showed them his hands and his feet. 41The disciples were so glad and amazed that they couldn't believe it. Jesus then asked them, "Have you got something to eat?" 42They gave him a piece of baked fish. 43He took it and ate it as they watched.

44Jesus said to them, "While I was still with you, I told you that everything written about me in the Law of Moses, the Books of the Prophets, and in the Psalms*t* had to happen."

45Then he helped them understand the Scriptures. 46He told them:

The Scriptures say that the Messiah must suffer, then three days later he will rise from death. 47They also say that all people of every nation must be told in my name to turn to God, in order to be forgiven. So beginning in Jerusalem, 48you must tell everyone everything that has happened. 49I will send you the

---

tPsalms: The Jewish Scriptures were made up of three parts: (1) the Law of Moses, (2) the Books of the Prophets, and (3) the Writings, which included the Psalms. Sometimes the Scriptures were just called the Law, or the Law (of Moses) and the Books of the Prophets.

one my Father has promised,ᵘ but you must stay in the city until you are given power from heaven.

Jesus Returns to Heaven
(Mark 16.19, 20; Acts 1.9-11)

⁵⁰Jesus led his disciples out to Bethany, where he raised his hands and blessed them. ⁵¹ As he was doing this, he left and was taken up to heaven.ᵛ ⁵²After his disciples had worshipped him,ʷ they returned to Jerusalem and were very happy. ⁵³They spent their time in the temple, praising God.

ᵘ*the one my Father has promised:* Jesus means the Holy Spirit.   ᵛ*and was taken up to heaven:* These words are not in some manuscripts.   ʷ*After his disciples had worshipped him:* These words are not in some manuscripts.

JOHN

ABOUT THIS BOOK

Who is Jesus Christ? John answers this question in the first chapter of his Gospel. Using the words of an early Christian hymn, he calls Jesus the "Word" by which God created everything and by which he gave life to everyone (chapter 1.3, 4). He shows how John the Baptist announced Jesus' coming, "Here is the Lamb of God who takes away the sin of the world" (1.29). When Philip met Jesus he knew Jesus was "the one that Moses and the Prophets wrote about" (1.45). And, in the words of Nathanael, Jesus is "the Son of God and the King of Israel" (1.49).

In John's Gospel we learn a lot about who Jesus is by observing what he said and did when he was with other people. These include a Samaritan woman who received Jesus' offer of life-giving water, a woman who had been caught in sin, his friend Lazarus who was brought back to life by Jesus, and his follower Thomas who doubted that Jesus was raised from death. Jesus also refers to himself as "I am", a phrase which translates the most holy name for God in the Hebrew Scriptures. He uses this name for himself when he makes his claim to be the life-giving bread, the light of the world, the good shepherd, and the true vine.

Jesus performs seven miracles that are more than miracles. Each of them is a "sign" that tells us something about Jesus as the Son of God. For example, by healing a lame man (5.1-8), Jesus shows that he is just like his Father, who never stops working (5.17). This sign also teaches that the Son does only what he sees his Father doing (5.19), and that like the Father "the Son gives life to anyone he wants to" (5.21).

The way John tells the story of Jesus is quite different from the other three gospels. Here, Jesus has long conversations with people about who he is and what God sent him to do. In these conversations he teaches many important things—for example, that he is the way, the truth and the life.

Why did John write? John himself tells us, "So that you will put your faith in Jesus as the Messiah and the Son of God" (20.31). How is this possible? Jesus answers that question in his words to Nicodemus:

"God loved the people of this world so much that he gave his only Son, so that everyone who has faith in him will have eternal life and never really die."

(Chapter 3.16)

A QUICK LOOK AT THIS BOOK

- A Hymn in Praise of the Word (1.1-18)
- The Message of John the Baptist (1.19-34)
- Jesus Chooses His First Disciples (1.35-51)
- Jesus' Seven Special Miracles (2.1—12.50)
- Jesus' Last Week: His Trial and Death (13.1—19.42)
- Jesus Is Alive (20.1-10)
- Jesus Appears to His Disciples (20.11—21.25)

The Word of Life

1 ¹ In the beginning was the one who is called the Word. The Word was with God and was truly God.
² From the very beginning the Word was with God.

³ And with this Word, God created all things.
Nothing was made without the Word.
Everything that was created
⁴ received its life from him,
and his life gave light to everyone.
⁵ The light keeps shining in the dark,
and darkness has never put it out.ᵃ
⁶ God sent a man named John,
⁷ who came to tell about the light
and to lead all people to have faith.
⁸ John wasn't that light.
He came only to tell about the light.

⁹ The true light that shines on everyone
was coming into the world.

ᵃput it out: Or "understood it."

10 The Word was in the world,
    but no-one knew him,
        though God had made the world with his Word.
11 He came into his own world,
    but his own nation did not welcome him.
12 Yet some people accepted him
    and put their faith in him.
        So he gave them the right to be
        the children of God.
13 They were not God's children by nature
        or because of any human desires.
    God himself was the one who made them his children.

14 The Word became a human being
    and lived here with us.
    We saw his true glory,
        the glory of the only Son of the Father.
    From him all the kindness and all the truth of God
        have come down to us.

15John spoke about him and shouted, "This is the one I told you would come! He is greater than I am, because he was alive before I was born."

16Because of all that the Son is, we have been given one blessing after another.*b* 17The Law was given by Moses, but Jesus Christ brought us undeserved kindness and truth. 18No-one has ever seen God. The only Son, who is truly God and is closest to the Father, has shown us what God is like.

John the Baptist Tells about Jesus
(Matthew 3.1-12; Mark 1.1-8; Luke 3.15-17)

19-20The Jewish leaders in Jerusalem sent priests and temple helpers to ask John who he was. He told them plainly, "I'm not the Messiah." 21Then when they asked him if he was Elijah, he said, "No, I'm not!" And when they asked if he was the Prophet,*c* he also said "No!"

22Finally, they said, "Who are you then? We have to give an answer to the ones who sent us. Tell us who you are!"

---

*b*one blessing after another: Or "one blessing in place of another." *c*the Prophet: Many of the Jewish people expected God to send them a prophet who would be like Moses, but with even greater power (see Deuteronomy 18.15, 18).

²³John answered in the words of the prophet Isaiah, "I'm only someone shouting in the desert, 'Get the road ready for the Lord!' "

²⁴Some Pharisees had also been sent to John. ²⁵They asked him, "Why are you baptising people, if you're not the Messiah or Elijah or the Prophet?"

²⁶John told them, "I use water to baptise people. But here with you is someone you don't know. ²⁷Even though I came first, I'm not good enough to untie his sandals." ²⁸John said this as he was baptising east of the Jordan River in Bethany.ᵈ

The Lamb of God

²⁹The next day, John saw Jesus coming towards him and said:

Here is the Lamb of God who takes away the sin of the world! ³⁰He is the one I told you about when I said, "Someone else will come. He is greater than I am, because he was alive before I was born." ³¹I didn't know who he was. But I came to baptise you with water, so that everyone in Israel would see him.

³²I was there and saw the Spirit come down on him like a dove from heaven. And the Spirit stayed on him. ³³Before this I didn't know who he was. But the one who sent me to baptise with water had told me, "You will see the Spirit come down and stay on someone. Then you will know that he is the one who will baptise with the Holy Spirit." ³⁴I saw this happen, and I tell you that he is the Son of God.

The First Disciples of Jesus

³⁵The next day, John was there again, and two of his followers were with him. ³⁶When he saw Jesus walking by, he said, "Here is the Lamb of God!" ³⁷John's two followers heard him, and they went with Jesus.

³⁸When Jesus turned and saw them, he asked, "What do you want?"

They answered, "Rabbi, where do you live?" The

ᵈBethany: An unknown village east of the Jordan with the same name as the village near Jerusalem.

Hebrew word "Rabbi" means "Teacher."

³⁹Jesus replied, "Come and see!" It was already about four o'clock in the afternoon when they went with him and saw where he lived. So they stayed on for the rest of the day.

⁴⁰One of the two men who had heard John and had gone with Jesus was Andrew, the brother of Simon Peter. ⁴¹The first thing Andrew did was to find his brother and tell him, "We've found the Messiah!" The Hebrew word "Messiah" means the same as the Greek word "Christ."

⁴²Andrew brought his brother to Jesus. And when Jesus saw him, he said, "Simon son of John, you will be called Cephas." This name can be translated as "Peter."ᵉ

Jesus Chooses Philip and Nathanael

⁴³⁻⁴⁴The next day Jesus decided to go to Galilee. There he met Philip, who was from Bethsaida, the home town of Andrew and Peter. Jesus said to Philip, "Come with me."

⁴⁵Philip then found Nathanael and said, "We have found the one that Moses and the Prophetsᶠ wrote about. He is Jesus, the son of Joseph from Nazareth."

⁴⁶Nathanael asked, "Can anything good come from Nazareth?"

Philip answered, "Come and see."

⁴⁷When Jesus saw Nathanael coming towards him, he said, "Here's a true descendant of our ancestor Israel. And he isn't deceitful."ᵍ

⁴⁸"How do you know me?" Nathanael asked.

Jesus answered, "Before Philip called you, I saw you under the fig tree."

⁴⁹Nathanael said, "Rabbi, you are the Son of God and the King of Israel!"

⁵⁰Jesus answered, "Did you believe me just because I said that I saw you under the fig tree? You will see

---

ᵉPeter: The Aramaic name "Cephas" and the Greek name "Peter" each mean "rock." ᶠMoses and the Prophets: The Jewish Scriptures, that is, the Old Testament. ᵍIsrael...not deceitful: Israel (meaning "a man who wrestled with God" or "a prince of God") was the name that the Lord gave to Jacob (meaning "cheater" or "deceiver"), the famous ancestor of the Jewish people.

something even greater. [51]I tell you for certain that you will see heaven open and God's angels going up and coming down on the Son of Man."[h]

Jesus at a Wedding in Cana

2 [1]Three days later Mary, the mother of Jesus, was at a wedding feast in the village of Cana in Galilee. [2]Jesus and his disciples had also been invited and were there.

[3]When the wine was all gone, Mary said to Jesus, "They haven't got any more wine."

[4]Jesus replied, "Mother, my time hasn't yet come![i] You mustn't tell me what to do."

[5]Mary then said to the servants, "Do whatever Jesus tells you to do."

[6]At the feast there were six stone water jars that were used by the people for washing themselves in the way that their religion said they must. Each jar held about 100 litres. [7]Jesus told the servants to fill them to the top with water. Then after the jars had been filled, [8]he said, "Now take some water and give it to the man in charge of the feast."

The servants did as Jesus told them, [9]and the man in charge drank some of the water that had now turned into wine. He didn't know where the wine had come from, but the servants did. He called the bridegroom over [10]and said, "The best wine is always served first. Then after the guests have had plenty, the other wine is served. But you have kept the best until last!"

[11]This was Jesus' first miracle,[j] and he did it in the village of Cana in Galilee. There Jesus showed his glory, and his disciples put their faith in him. [12]After this, he went with his mother, his brothers, and his disciples to the town of Capernaum, where they stayed for a few days.

---

[h]*going up and coming down on the Son of Man:* When Jacob (see the note at verse 47) was running from his brother Esau, he had a dream in which he saw angels going up and down on a ladder from earth to heaven (see Genesis 28.12). [i]*my time has not yet come!:* The time when the true glory of Jesus would be seen, and he would be recognised as God's Son (see 12.23). [j]*miracle:* The Greek text has "sign." In the Gospel of John the word "sign" is used for the miracle itself and as a way of pointing to Jesus as the Son of God.

Jesus in the Temple

(Matthew 21.12, 13; Mark 11.15-17; Luke 19.45, 46)

13Not long before the Jewish festival of Passover, Jesus went to Jerusalem. 14There he found people selling cattle, sheep, and doves in the temple. He also saw money-changers sitting at their tables. 15So he took some rope and made a whip. Then he chased everyone out of the temple, together with their sheep and cattle. He turned over the tables of the money-changers and scattered their coins.

16Jesus said to the people who had been selling doves, "Get those doves out of here! Don't make my Father's house a marketplace."

17The disciples then remembered that the Scriptures say, "My love for your house burns in me like a fire."

18The Jewish leaders asked Jesus, "What miracle will you work to show us why you've done this?"

19"Destroy this temple," Jesus answered, "and in three days I will build it again!"

20The leaders replied, "It took 46 years to build this temple. What makes you think you can rebuild it in three days?"

21But Jesus was talking about his body as a temple. 22And when he was raised from death, his disciples remembered what he had told them. Then they believed the Scriptures and the words of Jesus.

Jesus Knows What People Are Like

23In Jerusalem during Passover many people put their faith in Jesus, because they saw him work miracles. 24But Jesus knew what was in their hearts, and he wouldn't let them have power over him. 25No-one had to tell him what people were like. He already knew.

Jesus and Nicodemus

3 1There was a man named Nicodemus who was a Pharisee and a Jewish leader. 2One night he went to Jesus and said, "Sir, we know that God has sent you to teach us. You couldn't work these miracles, unless God was with you."

³Jesus replied, "I tell you for certain that you must be born from above*k* before you can see God's kingdom!"

⁴Nicodemus asked, "How can a grown man ever be born a second time?"

⁵Jesus answered:

I tell you for certain that before you can get into God's kingdom, you must be born not only by water, but by the Spirit. ⁶Humans give life to their children. Yet only God's Spirit can change you into a child of God. ⁷Don't be surprised when I say that you must be born from above. ⁸Only God's Spirit gives new life. The Spirit is like the wind that blows wherever it wants to. You can hear the wind, but you don't know where it comes from or where it is going.

⁹"How can this be?" Nicodemus asked.

¹⁰Jesus replied:

How can you be a teacher of Israel and not know these things? ¹¹I tell you for certain that we know what we are talking about because we have seen it ourselves. But none of you will accept what we say. ¹²If you don't believe when I talk to you about things on earth, how can you possibly believe if I talk to you about things in heaven?

¹³No-one has gone up to heaven except the Son of Man, who came down from there. ¹⁴And the Son of Man must be lifted up, just as that metal snake was lifted up by Moses in the desert.*l* ¹⁵Then everyone who has faith in the Son of Man will have eternal life.

¹⁶God loved the people of this world so much that he gave his only Son, so that everyone who has faith in him will have eternal life and never really die. ¹⁷God did not send his Son into the world to condemn its people. He sent him to save them! ¹⁸No-one who has faith in God's Son will be condemned. But everyone who doesn't have faith in him has already been condemned for not having faith in God's only Son.

---

k from above: Or "in a new way." The same Greek word is used in verses 7, 31.
l just as that metal snake was lifted up by Moses in the desert: When the Lord punished the people of Israel by sending snakes to bite them, he told Moses to hold a metal snake up on a pole. Everyone who looked at the snake was cured of the snake bites (see Numbers 21.4-9).

[19]The light has come into the world, and people who do evil things are judged guilty because they love the dark more than the light. [20]People who do evil hate the light and won't come to the light, because it clearly shows what they have done. [21]But everyone who lives by the truth will come to the light, because they want others to know that God is really the one doing what they do.

Jesus and John the Baptist

[22]Later, Jesus and his disciples went to Judea, where he stayed with them for a while and was baptising people.

[23-24]John had not yet been put in jail. He was at Aenon near Salim, where there was a lot of water, and people were coming there for John to baptise them.

[25]John's followers got into an argument with a Jewish man[m] about a ceremony of washing.[n] [26]They went to John and said, "Rabbi, you spoke about a man when you were with him east of the Jordan. He's now baptising people, and everyone is going to him."

[27]John replied:

No-one can do anything unless God in heaven allows it. [28]You surely remember how I told you that I'm not the Messiah. I'm only the one sent ahead of him.

[29]At a wedding the groom is the one who gets married. The best man is glad just to be there and to hear the groom's voice. That's why I'm so glad. [30]Jesus must become more important, while I become less important.

The One Who Comes from Heaven

[31]God's Son comes from heaven and is above all others. Everyone who comes from the earth belongs to the earth and speaks about earthly things. The one who comes from heaven is above all others. [32]He speaks about what he has seen and heard, and yet no one believes him. [33]But everyone who does believe him has shown that God is truthful. [34]The Son was sent to

[m]*a Jewish man:* Some manuscripts have "some Jewish men." [n]*about a ceremony of washing:* The Jewish people had many rules about washing themselves and their dishes, in order to make themselves fit to worship God.

speak God's message, and he has been given the full power of God's Spirit.

³⁵The Father loves the Son and has given him everything. ³⁶Everyone who has faith in the Son has eternal life. But no-one who rejects him will ever share in that life, and God will be angry with them for ever.

4 ¹Jesus knew that the Pharisees had heard that he was winning and baptising more followers than John was. ²But Jesus' disciples were really the ones doing the baptising, and not Jesus himself.

Jesus and the Samaritan Woman

³Jesus left Judea and set out for Galilee again. ⁴This time he had to go through Samaria, ⁵and on his way he came to the town of Sychar. It was near the field that Jacob had long ago given to his son Joseph. ⁶⁻⁸The well that Jacob had dug was still there, and Jesus sat down beside it because he was tired from travelling. It was midday, and after Jesus' disciples had gone into town to buy some food, a Samaritan woman came to draw water from the well.

Jesus asked her, "Would you please give me a drink of water?"

⁹"You are a Jew," she replied, "and I am a Samaritan woman. How can you ask me for a drink of water when Jews and Samaritans won't have anything to do with each other?"ᵒ

¹⁰Jesus answered, "You don't know what God wants to give you, and you don't know who is asking you for a drink. If you did, you would ask me for the water that gives life."

¹¹"Sir," the woman said, "you haven't even got a bucket, and the well is deep. Where are you going to get this life-giving water? ¹²Our ancestor Jacob dug this well for us, and his family and animals got water from it. Are you greater than Jacob?"

¹³Jesus answered, "Everyone who drinks this water will

ᵒwon't have anything to do with each other: Or "won't use the same cups." The Samaritans lived in the land between Judea and Galilee. They worshipped God differently from the Jews and did not get along with them.

get thirsty again. [14]But no-one who drinks the water I give will ever be thirsty again. The water I give is like a flowing fountain that gives eternal life."

[15]The woman replied, "Sir, please give me a drink of that water! Then I won't get thirsty and have to come to this well again."

[16]Jesus told her, "Go and bring your husband."

[17-18]The woman answered, "I haven't got a husband."

"That's right," Jesus replied, "you're telling the truth. You don't have a husband. You've already been married five times, and the man you're now living with isn't your husband."

[19]The woman said, "Sir, I can see that you are a prophet. [20]My ancestors worshipped on this mountain,[p] but you Jews say Jerusalem is the only place to worship."

[21]Jesus said to her:

Believe me, the time is coming when you won't worship the Father either on this mountain or in Jerusalem. [22]You Samaritans don't really know the one you worship. But we Jews do know the God we worship, and by using us, God will save the world. [23]But a time is coming, and it is already here! Even now the true worshippers are being led by the Spirit to worship the Father according to the truth. These are the ones the Father is seeking to worship him. [24]God is Spirit, and those who worship God must be led by the Spirit to worship him according to the truth.

[25]The woman said, "I know that the Messiah will come. He is the one we call Christ. When he comes, he'll explain everything to us."

[26]"I am that one," Jesus told her, "and I am speaking to you now."

[27]The disciples returned about this time and were surprised to find Jesus talking with a woman. But none of them asked him what he wanted or why he was talking with her.

[28]The woman left her water jar and ran back into town. She said to the people, [29]"Come and see a man who told me everything I've ever done! Could he be the Messiah?"

[p]*this mountain:* Mount Gerizim, near the city of Shechem.

³⁰Everyone in town went out to see Jesus.

³¹While this was happening, Jesus' disciples were saying to him, "Teacher, please eat something."

³²But Jesus told them, "I have food that you don't know anything about."

³³His disciples started asking each other, "Has someone brought him something to eat?"

³⁴Jesus said:

My food is to do what God wants! He is the one who sent me, and I must finish the work that he gave me to do. ³⁵You may say that there are still four months until harvest time. But I tell you to look, and you will see that the fields are ripe and ready to harvest.

³⁶Even now the harvest workers are receiving their reward by gathering a harvest that brings eternal life. Then everyone who planted the seed and everyone who harvests the crop will celebrate together. ³⁷So the saying proves to be true, "Some plant the seed, and others harvest the crop." ³⁸I'm sending you to harvest crops in fields where others have done all the hard work.

³⁹A lot of Samaritans in that town put their faith in Jesus because the woman had said, "This man told me everything I've ever done." ⁴⁰They came and asked him to stay in their town, and he stayed on for two days.

⁴¹Many more Samaritans put their faith in Jesus because of what they heard him say. ⁴²They told the woman, "We no longer have faith in Jesus just because of what you told us. We've heard him ourselves, and we're certain that he is the Saviour of the world!"

Jesus Heals an Official's Son
(Matthew 8.5-13; Luke 7.1-10)

⁴³⁻⁴⁴Jesus had said, "Prophets are honoured everywhere, except in their own country." Then two days later he left ⁴⁵and went to Galilee. The people there welcomed him, because they had gone to the festival in Jerusalem and had seen everything he had done.

⁴⁶While Jesus was in Galilee, he returned to the village of Cana, where he had turned the water into wine. There

was an official in Capernaum whose son was sick. ⁴⁷And
when the man heard that Jesus had come from Judea, he
went and begged him to keep his son from dying.

⁴⁸Jesus told the official, "You won't have faith unless
you see miracles and wonders!"

⁴⁹The man replied, "Lord, please come before my son
dies!"

⁵⁰Jesus then said, "Your son will live. Go back home to
him." The man believed Jesus and started back home.

⁵¹Some of the official's servants met him along the road
and told him, "Your son is better!" ⁵²He asked them when
the boy got better, and they answered, "The fever left
him yesterday at one o'clock."

⁵³The boy's father realised that at one o'clock the day
before, Jesus had told him, "Your son will live!" So the
man and everyone in his family put their faith in Jesus.

⁵⁴This was the second miracle^q that Jesus worked after
he left Judea and went to Galilee.

Jesus Heals a Sick Man

5 ¹Later, Jesus went to Jerusalem for another Jewish
festival.^r ²In the city near the sheep gate was a pool
with five porches, and its name in Hebrew was
Bethzatha.^s

³⁻⁴Many sick, blind, lame, and crippled people were
lying close to the pool.^t

⁵Beside the pool was a man who had been sick for 38
years. ⁶When Jesus saw the man and realised that he had
been crippled for a long time, he asked him, "Do you
want to be healed?"

⁷The man answered, "Lord, I don't have anyone to put
me in the pool when the water is stirred up. I try to get
in, but someone else always gets there first."

⁸Jesus told him, "Pick up your mat and walk!"
⁹Straight away the man was healed. He picked up his mat
and started walking around. The day on which this

---

^qmiracle: See the note at 2.11.   ^ranother Jewish festival: Either the Festival of
Shelters or Passover.   ^sBethzatha: Some manuscripts have "Bethesda" and
others have "Bethsaida."   ^tpool: Some manuscripts add, "They were waiting for
the water to be stirred, because an angel from the Lord would sometimes come
down and stir it. The first person to get into the pool after that would be healed."

happened was a Sabbath.

¹⁰When the Jewish leaders saw the man carrying his mat, they said to him, "This is the Sabbath! No-one is allowed to carry a mat on the Sabbath."

¹¹But he replied, "The man who healed me told me to pick up my mat and walk."

¹²They asked him, "Who is this man who told you to pick up your mat and walk?" ¹³But he didn't know who Jesus was, and Jesus had left because of the crowd.

¹⁴Later, Jesus met the man in the temple and told him, "You are now well. But don't sin any more or something worse might happen to you." ¹⁵The man left and told the leaders that Jesus was the one who had healed him. ¹⁶They started making a lot of trouble for Jesus because he did things like this on the Sabbath.

¹⁷But Jesus said, "My Father has never stopped working, and that's why I keep on working." ¹⁸Now the leaders wanted to kill Jesus for two reasons. First, he had broken the law of the Sabbath. But even worse, he had said that God was his Father, which made him equal with God.

The Son's Authority

¹⁹Jesus told the people:

I tell you for certain that the Son can't do anything on his own. He can do only what he sees the Father doing, and he does exactly what he sees the Father do. ²⁰The Father loves the Son and has shown him everything he does. The Father will show him even greater things, and you'll be amazed. ²¹Just as the Father raises the dead and gives life, so the Son gives life to anyone he wants to.

²²The Father doesn't judge anyone, but he has made his Son the judge of everyone. ²³The Father wants all people to honour the Son as much as they honour him. When anyone refuses to honour the Son, that is the same as refusing to honour the Father who sent him. ²⁴I tell you for certain that everyone who hears my message and has faith in the one who sent me has eternal life and will never be condemned. They have already gone from death to life.

²⁵I tell you for certain that the time will come, and

it is already here, when all of the dead will hear the voice of the Son of God. And those who listen to it will live! 26 The Father has the power to give life, and he has given that same power to the Son. 27 And he has given his Son the right to judge everyone, because he is the Son of Man.

28 Don't be surprised! The time will come when all of the dead will hear the voice of the Son of Man, 29 and they will come out of their graves. Everyone who has done good things will rise to life, but everyone who has done evil things will rise and be condemned.

30 I can't do anything on my own. The Father sent me, and he is the one who told me how to judge. I judge with fairness, because I obey him, and I don't just try to please myself.

Witnesses to Jesus

31 If I speak for myself, there is no way to prove I am telling the truth. 32 But there is someone else who speaks for me, and I know what he says is true. 33 You sent messengers to John, and he told them the truth. 34 I don't depend on what people say about me, but I tell you these things so that you can be saved. 35 John was a lamp that gave a lot of light, and you were glad to enjoy his light for a while.

36 But something more important than John speaks for me. I mean the things that the Father has given me to do! All of these speak for me and prove that the Father sent me.

37 The Father who sent me also speaks for me, but you have never heard his voice or seen him face to face. 38 You haven't believed his message, because you refused to have faith in the one he sent.

39 You search the Scriptures, because you think you'll find eternal life in them. The Scriptures tell you about me, 40 but you refuse to come to me for eternal life.

41 I don't care about human praise, 42 but I do know that none of you love God. 43 I have come with my Father's authority, and you haven't welcomed me. But you will welcome people who come on their own. 44 How could you possibly believe? You like to have

your friends praise you, and you don't care about praise that the only God can give!

⁴⁵Don't think that I will be the one to accuse you to the Father. You have put your hope in Moses, yet he is the very one who will accuse you. ⁴⁶Moses wrote about me, and if you had believed Moses, you would have believed me. ⁴⁷But if you don't believe what Moses wrote, how can you believe what I say?

Feeding Five Thousand
(Matthew 14.13-21; Mark 6.30-44; Luke 9.10-17)

6 ¹Jesus crossed Lake Galilee, which was also known as Lake Tiberias. ²A large crowd had seen him work miracles to heal the sick, and those people went with him. ³⁻⁴It was almost time for the Jewish festival of Passover, and Jesus went up a mountain with his disciples and sat down.ᵘ

⁵When Jesus saw the large crowd coming towards him, he asked Philip, "Where will we get enough food to feed all these people?" ⁶He said this to test Philip, since he already knew what he was going to do.

⁷Philip answered, "Don't you know that it would take almost a year's wagesᵛ just to buy only a little bread for each of these people?"

⁸Andrew, the brother of Simon Peter, was one of the disciples. He spoke up and said, ⁹"There's a boy here who has five small loavesʷ of barley bread and two fish. But what good is that with all these people?"

¹⁰The ground was covered with grass, and Jesus told his disciples to get everyone to sit down. About 5000 men were in the crowd. ¹¹Jesus took the bread in his hands and gave thanks to God. Then he passed the bread to the people, and he did the same with the fish, until everyone had plenty to eat.

¹²The people ate all they wanted, and Jesus told his disciples to gather up the leftovers, so that nothing

---

ᵘ*sat down:* Possibly to teach. Teachers in the ancient world, including Jewish teachers, usually sat down to teach.   ᵛ*almost a year's wages:* The Greek text has "200 silver coins." Each coin was worth the average day's wages for a worker.   ʷ*small loaves:* These would have been flat and round or in the shape of a bun.

would be wasted. [13]The disciples gathered them up and filled 12 large baskets with what was left over from the five barley loaves.

[14]After the people had seen Jesus work this miracle,[x] they began saying, "This must be the Prophet[y] who is to come into the world!" [15]Jesus realised that they would try to force him to be their king. So he went up a mountain, where he could be alone.

Jesus Walks on the Water
(Matthew 14.22-27; Mark 6.45-52)

[16]That evening, Jesus' disciples went down to the lake. [17]They got into a boat and set out for Capernaum. Later that evening Jesus had still not come to them, [18]and a strong wind was making the water rough.

[19]When the disciples had rowed for four or five kilometres, they saw Jesus walking on the water. He kept coming closer to the boat, and they were terrified. [20]But he said, "I am Jesus![z] Don't be afraid!" [21]The disciples wanted to take him into the boat, but suddenly the boat reached the shore where they were headed.

The Bread That Gives Life

[22]The people who had stayed on the east side of the lake knew that only one boat had been there. They also knew that Jesus had not left in it with his disciples. But the next day [23]some boats from Tiberias sailed near the place where the crowd had eaten the bread for which the Lord had given thanks. [24]They saw that Jesus and his disciples had left. Then they got into the boats and went to Capernaum to look for Jesus. [25]They found him on the west side of the lake and asked, "Rabbi, when did you get here?"

[26]Jesus answered, "I tell you for certain that you aren't looking for me because you saw the miracles,[a] but because you ate all the food you wanted. [27]Don't work

---

[x]*miracle:* See the note at 2.11.   [y]*the Prophet:* See the note at 1.21.   [z]*I am Jesus:* The Greek text has "I am" (see the note at 8.24).   [a]*miracles:* The Greek text has "signs" here and "sign" in verse 30 (see the note at 2.11).

for food that spoils. Work for food that gives eternal life.
The Son of Man will give you this food, because God the
Father has given him the right to do so."

28"What exactly does God want us to do?" the people
asked.

29Jesus answered, "God wants you to have faith in the
one he sent."

30They replied, "What miracle will you work, so that
we can have faith in you? What will you do? 31For
example, when our ancestors were in the desert, they
were given manna*b* to eat. It happened just as the
Scriptures say, 'God gave them bread from heaven to
eat.' "

32Jesus then told them, "I tell you for certain that
Moses wasn't the one who gave you bread from heaven.
My Father is the one who gives you the true bread from
heaven. 33And the bread that God gives is the one who
came down from heaven to give life to the world."

34The people said, "Lord, give us this bread and don't
ever stop!"

35Jesus replied:

I am the bread that gives life! No-one who comes to
me will ever be hungry. No-one who has faith in me
will ever be thirsty. 36I have told you already that you
have seen me and still don't have faith in me.
37Everything and everyone that the Father has given
me will come to me, and I won't turn any of them
away.

38I didn't come from heaven to do what I want! I
came to do what the Father wants me to do. He sent
me, 39and he wants to make certain that none of the
ones he has given me will be lost. Instead, he wants me
to raise them to life on the last day.*c* 40My Father wants
everyone who sees the Son to have faith in him and to
have eternal life. Then I will raise them to life on the
last day.

41The people started grumbling because Jesus had said

---

*b*manna: When the people of Israel were wandering through the desert, the Lord
gave them a special kind of food to eat. It tasted like a wafer and was called
"manna," which in Hebrew means, "What is this?"   *c*the last day: When God will
judge all people.

he was the bread that had come down from heaven.
⁴²They were asking each other, "Isn't he Jesus, the son of Joseph? Don't we know his father and mother? How can he say that he's come down from heaven?"

⁴³Jesus told them:

Stop grumbling! ⁴⁴No-one can come to me, unless the Father who sent me makes them want to come. But if they do come, I will raise them to life on the last day. ⁴⁵One of the prophets wrote, "God will teach all of them." And so everyone who listens to the Father and learns from him will come to me.

⁴⁶The only one who has seen the Father is the one who has come from him. No-one else has ever seen the Father. ⁴⁷I tell you for certain that everyone who has faith in me has eternal life.

⁴⁸I am the bread that gives life! ⁴⁹Your ancestors ate manna*d* in the desert, and later they died. ⁵⁰But the bread from heaven has come down, so that no-one who eats it will ever die.⁵¹I am that bread from heaven! Everyone who eats it will live for ever. My flesh is the life-giving bread that I give to the people of this world.

⁵²They started arguing with each other and asked, "How can he give us his flesh to eat?"

⁵³Jesus answered:

I tell you for certain that you won't live unless you eat the flesh and drink the blood of the Son of Man. ⁵⁴But if you do eat my flesh and drink my blood, you will have eternal life, and I will raise you to life on the last day. ⁵⁵My flesh is the true food, and my blood is the true drink. ⁵⁶If you eat my flesh and drink my blood, you are one with me, and I am one with you.

⁵⁷The living Father sent me, and I have life because of him. Now everyone who eats my flesh will live because of me. ⁵⁸The bread that comes down from heaven isn't like what your ancestors ate. They died, but whoever eats this bread will live for ever.

⁵⁹Jesus was teaching in a Jewish place of worship in Capernaum when he said these things.

---

*d*manna: See the note at 6.31.

The Words of Eternal Life

⁶⁰Many of Jesus' disciples heard him and said, "This is too hard for anyone to understand."

⁶¹Jesus knew that his disciples were grumbling. So he asked, "Does this bother you? ⁶²What if you should see the Son of Man go up to heaven where he came from? ⁶³The Spirit is the one who gives life! Human strength can do nothing. The words that I have spoken to you are from that life-giving Spirit. ⁶⁴But some of you refuse to have faith in me." Jesus said this, because from the beginning he knew who would have faith in him. He also knew which one would betray him.

⁶⁵Then Jesus said, "You can't come to me, unless the Father makes you want to come. That's why I've told these things to all of you."

⁶⁶Because of what Jesus said, many of his disciples turned their backs on him and stopped following him. ⁶⁷Jesus then asked his twelve disciples if they were going to leave him. ⁶⁸Simon Peter answered, "Lord, there's no-one else that we can go to! Your words give eternal life. ⁶⁹We have faith in you, and we're sure that you are God's Holy One."

⁷⁰Jesus told his disciples, "I chose all twelve of you, but one of you is a demon!" ⁷¹Jesus was talking about Judas, the son of Simon Iscariot.ᵉ He would later betray Jesus, even though he was one of the twelve disciples.

Jesus' Brothers Don't Have Faith in Him

7 ¹Jesus decided to leave Judea and to start going through Galilee because the Jewish leaders wanted to kill him. ²It was almost time for the Festival of Shelters, ³and Jesus' brothers said to him, "Why don't you go to Judea? Then your disciples can see what you are doing. ⁴No-one does anything in secret, if they want others to know about them. So let the world know what you are doing!" ⁵Even Jesus' own brothers hadn't yet become his followers.

⁶Jesus answered, "My time hasn't come yet,ᶠ but your time is always here. ⁷The people of this world can't hate

---

ᵉIscariot: See the note at 12.4.   ᶠMy time hasn't come yet: See the note at 2.4.

you. They hate me, because I tell them that they do evil things. ⁸Go on to the festival. My time hasn't come yet, and I'm not going." ⁹Jesus said this and stayed on in Galilee.

Jesus at the Festival of Shelters

¹⁰After Jesus' brothers had gone to the festival, he went secretly, without telling anyone.

¹¹During the festival the Jewish leaders looked for Jesus and asked, "Where is he?" ¹²The crowds even got into an argument about him. Some were saying, "Jesus is a good man," while others were saying, "He's lying to everyone." ¹³But the people were afraid of their leaders, and none of them talked in public about him.

¹⁴When the festival was about half over, Jesus went into the temple and started teaching. ¹⁵The leaders were surprised and said, "How does this man know so much? He has never been taught!"

¹⁶Jesus replied:

I'm not teaching something that I thought up. What I teach comes from the one who sent me. ¹⁷If you really want to obey God, you will know if what I teach comes from God or from me. ¹⁸If I wanted to bring honour to myself, I would speak for myself. But I want to honour the one who sent me. That is why I tell the truth and not a lie. ¹⁹Didn't Moses give you the Law? Yet none of you obey it! So why do you want to kill me?

²⁰The crowd replied, "You're crazy! What makes you think someone wants to kill you?"

²¹Jesus answered:

I worked one miracle,ᵍ and it amazed you. ²²Moses commanded you to circumcise your sons. But it wasn't really Moses who gave you this command. It was your ancestors, and even on the Sabbath you circumcise your sons ²³in order to obey the Law of Moses. Why are you angry with me for making someone completely well on the Sabbath? ²⁴Don't judge by appearances. Judge by what is right.

²⁵Some of the people from Jerusalem were saying,

ᵍone miracle: The healing of the lame man (5.1-18) (see also note at 2.11).

"Isn't this the man they want to kill? 26Yet here he is, speaking for everyone to hear. And no-one is arguing with him. Do you suppose the authorities know that he is the Messiah? 27But how could that be? No-one knows where the Messiah will come from, but we know where this man comes from."

28As Jesus was teaching in the temple, he shouted, "Do you really think you know me and where I came from? I didn't come on my own! The one who sent me is truthful, and you don't know him. 29But I know the one who sent me, because I came from him."

30Some of the people wanted to arrest Jesus right then. But no-one even laid a hand on him, because his time had not yet come.h 31A lot of people in the crowd put their faith in him and said, "When the Messiah comes, he surely won't perform more miraclesi than this man has done!"

Officers Sent To Arrest Jesus

32When the Pharisees heard the crowd arguing about Jesus, they got together with the chief priests and sent some temple police to arrest him. 33But Jesus told them, "I'll be with you a little while longer, and then I'll return to the one who sent me. 34You will look for me, but you won't find me. You can't go where I'm going."

35The Jewish leaders asked each other, "Where can he go to keep us from finding him? Is he going to some foreign country where our people live? Is he going there to teach the Greeks?j 36What did he mean by saying that we will look for him, but won't find him? Why can't we go where he's going?"

Streams of Life-Giving Water

37On the last and most important day of the festival, Jesus stood up and shouted, "If you are thirsty, come to me and drink! 38Have faith in me, and you will have life-giving water flowing from deep inside you, just as the Scriptures say." 39Jesus was talking about the Holy Spirit,

hhis time had not yet come: See the note at 2.4. imiracles: See note at 2.11.
jGreeks: Perhaps Gentiles or Jews who followed Greek customs.

who would be given to everyone that had faith in him. The Spirit hadn't yet been given to anyone, since Jesus hadn't yet been given his full glory.*k*

The People Take Sides

40When the crowd heard Jesus say this, some of them said, "He must be the Prophet!"*l* 41Others said, "He is the Messiah!" Others even said, "Can the Messiah come from Galilee? 42The Scriptures say that the Messiah will come from the family of King David. Doesn't this mean that he will be born in David's home town of Bethlehem?" 43The people started taking sides against each other because of Jesus. 44Some of them wanted to arrest him, but no-one laid a hand on him.

The Jewish Leaders Refuse To Have Faith in Jesus

45When the temple police returned to the chief priests and Pharisees, they were asked, "Why didn't you bring Jesus here?"

46They answered, "No-one has ever spoken like that man!"

47The Pharisees said to them, "Have you also been fooled? 48Not one of the chief priests or the Pharisees has faith in him. 49And these people who don't know the Law are under God's curse anyway."

50Nicodemus was there at the time. He was a member of the Jewish council, and was the same one who had earlier come to see Jesus.*m* He said, 51"Our Law doesn't let us condemn people before we hear what they have to say. We can't judge them before we know what they've done."

52Then they said, "Nicodemus, you must be from Galilee! Read the Scriptures, and you'll find that no prophet is to come from Galilee."

---

khadn't yet been given his full glory: In the Gospel of John, Jesus is given his full glory both when he is nailed to the cross and when he is raised from death to sit beside his Father in heaven.   *lthe Prophet:* See the note at 1.21.   *mwho had earlier come to see Jesus:* See 3.1-21.

A Woman Caught in Sin

8 [53]Everyone else went home, [1]but Jesus walked out to the Mount of Olives. [2]Then early the next morning he went to the temple. The people came to him, and he sat down[n] and started teaching them.

[3]The Pharisees and the teachers of the Law of Moses brought in a woman who had been caught in bed with a man who wasn't her husband. They made her stand in the middle of the crowd. [4]Then they said, "Teacher, this woman was caught sleeping with a man who isn't her husband. [5]The Law of Moses teaches that a woman like this should be stoned to death! What do you say?"

[6]They asked Jesus this question, because they wanted to test him and bring some charge against him. But Jesus simply bent over and started writing on the ground with his finger.

[7]They kept on asking Jesus about the woman. Finally, he stood up and said, "If any of you have never sinned, then go ahead and throw the first stone at her!" [8]Once again he bent over and began writing on the ground. [9]The people left one by one, beginning with the oldest. Finally, Jesus and the woman were there alone.

[10]Jesus stood up and asked her, "Where is everyone? Isn't there anyone left to accuse you?"

[11]"No sir," the woman answered.

Then Jesus told her, "I'm not going to accuse you either. You may go now, but don't sin any more."[o]

Jesus Is the Light for the World

[12]Once again Jesus spoke to the people. This time he said, "I am the light for the world! Follow me, and you won't be walking in the dark. You will have the light that gives life."

[13]The Pharisees objected, "You are the only one speaking for yourself, and what you say isn't true!"

[14]Jesus replied:

Even if I do speak for myself, what I say is true! I

---

[n]*sat down:* See the note at 6.3, 4.   [o]*don't sin any more:* Verses 1-11 are not in some manuscripts. In other manuscripts these verses are placed after 7.36 or after 21.25 or after Luke 21.38, with some differences in the text.

know where I came from and where I'm going. But you don't know where I'm from or where I'm going. [15]You judge in the same way that everyone else does, but I don't judge anyone. [16]If I did judge, I would judge fairly, because I wouldn't be doing it alone. The Father who sent me is here with me. [17]Your Law requires two witnesses to prove that something is true. [18]I am one of my witnesses, and the Father who sent me is the other one.

[19]"Where is your Father?" they asked.

"You don't know me or my Father!" Jesus answered. "If you knew me, you would know my Father."

[20]Jesus said this while he was still teaching in the place where the temple treasures were stored. But no-one arrested him, because his time had not yet come.[p]

You Can't Go Where I'm Going

[21]Jesus also told them, "I'm going away, and you will look for me. But you can't go where I'm going, and you will die with your sins unforgiven."

[22]The Jewish leaders asked, "Does he intend to kill himself? Is that what he means by saying we can't go where he is going?"

[23]Jesus answered, "You are from below, but I am from above. You belong to this world, but I don't. [24]That's why I said you will die with your sins unforgiven. If you don't have faith in me for who I am,[q] you will die, and your sins won't be forgiven."

[25]"Who are you?" they asked Jesus.

Jesus answered, "I'm exactly who I told you I was at the beginning. [26]There's a lot more I could say to condemn you. But the one who sent me is truthful, and I tell the people of this world only what I have heard from him."

[27]No-one understood that Jesus was talking to them about the Father.

[28]Jesus went on to say, "When you have lifted up the

---

[p]*his time had not yet come:* See the note at 2.4.   [q]*I am:* For the Jewish people the most holy name of God is "Yahweh," which may be translated "I am." In the Gospel of John "I am" is sometimes used by Jesus to show that he is that one.

Son of Man,ʳ you will know who I am. You will also know that I don't do anything on my own. I say only what my Father taught me. ²⁹The one who sent me is with me. I always do what pleases him, and he will never leave me."

³⁰After Jesus said this, many of the people put their faith in him.

The Truth Will Set You Free

³¹Jesus told the people who had faith in him, "If you keep on obeying what I have said, you truly are my disciples. ³²You will know the truth, and the truth will set you free."

³³They answered, "We are Abraham's children! We've never been anyone's slaves. How can you say we will be set free?"

³⁴Jesus replied:

I tell you for certain that anyone who sins is a slave of sin! ³⁵And slaves don't stay in the family for ever, though the Son will always remain in the family. ³⁶If the Son gives you freedom, you are free! ³⁷I know that you are from Abraham's family. Yet you want to kill me, because my message isn't really in your hearts. ³⁸I'm telling you what my Father has shown me, just as you are doing what your father has taught you.

Your Father Is the Devil

³⁹The people said to Jesus, "Abraham is our father!"

Jesus replied, "If you were Abraham's children, you would do what Abraham did. ⁴⁰Instead, you want to kill me for telling you the truth that God gave me. Abraham never did anything like that. ⁴¹But you are doing exactly what your father does."

"Don't accuse us of having someone else as our father!" they said. "We just have one father, and he is God."

⁴²Jesus answered:

If God was your Father, you would love me, because I came from God and only from him. He sent me. I didn't come on my own. ⁴³Why can't you understand

---

ʳ*lifted up the Son of Man:* See the note at 7.39.

what I am talking about? Can't you stand hearing what I am saying? 44Your father is the devil, and you do exactly what he wants. He has always been a murderer and a liar. There is nothing truthful about him. He speaks on his own, and everything he says is a lie. Not only is he a liar himself, but he is also the father of all lies.

45Everything I have told you is true, and you still refuse to have faith in me. 46Can any of you accuse me of sin? If you can't, why won't you have faith in me? After all, I'm telling you the truth. 47Anyone who belongs to God will listen to his message. But you refuse to listen, because you don't belong to God.

Jesus and Abraham

48The people told Jesus, "We were right to say that you are a Samaritan*s* and that you have a demon in you!"

49Jesus answered, "I don't have a demon in me. I honour my Father, and you refuse to honour me. 50I don't want honour for myself. But there is one who wants me to be honoured, and he is also the one who judges. 51I tell you for certain that if you obey my words, you will never die."

52Then the people said, "Now we're sure that you have a demon. Abraham is dead, and so are the prophets. How can you say that no-one who obeys your words will ever die? 53Are you greater than our father Abraham? He died, and so did the prophets. Who do you think you are?"

54Jesus replied, "If I honoured myself, it would mean nothing. My Father is the one who honours me. You claim that he is your God, 55even though you don't really know him. If I said I didn't know him, I would be a liar, just like all of you. But I know him, and I do what he says. 56Your father Abraham was really glad to see me."

57"You're not even 50 years old!" they said. "How could you have seen Abraham?"

58Jesus answered, "I tell you for certain that even before Abraham was, I was, and I am."*t* 59The people

---

sSamaritan: See 4.9 and the note there.   *I am:* See the note at 8.24.

picked up stones to kill Jesus, but he hid and left the temple.

Jesus Heals a Man Born Blind

9 [1]As Jesus walked along, he saw a man who had been blind since birth. [2]Jesus' disciples asked, "Teacher, why was this man born blind? Was it because he or his parents sinned?"

[3]"No, it wasn't!" Jesus answered. "But because of his blindness, you will see God work a miracle for him. [4]As long as it is day, we must do what the one who sent me wants me to do. When night comes, no-one can work. [5]While I am in the world, I am the light for the world."

[6]After Jesus said this, he spat on the ground. He made some mud and smeared it on the man's eyes. [7]Then he said, "Go and wash off the mud in Siloam Pool." The man went and washed in Siloam, which means "One Who Is Sent." When he had washed off the mud, he could see.

[8]The man's neighbours and the people who had seen him begging wondered if he really could be the same man. [9]Some of them said he was the same beggar, while others said he only looked like him. But he told them, "I am that man."

[10]"Then how can you see?" they asked.

[11]He answered, "Someone named Jesus made some mud and smeared it on my eyes. He told me to go and wash it off in Siloam Pool. When I did, I could see."

[12]"Where is he now?" they asked.

"I don't know," he answered.

The Pharisees Try To Find Out What Happened

[13-14]The day when Jesus made the mud and healed the man was a Sabbath. So the people took the man to the Pharisees. [15]They asked him how he was able to see, and he answered, "Jesus made some mud and smeared it on my eyes. Then after I washed it off, I could see."

[16]Some of the Pharisees said, "This man Jesus doesn't come from God. If he did, he wouldn't break the law of the Sabbath."

Others asked, "How could someone who is a sinner work such a miracle?"*u*

Since the Pharisees couldn't agree among themselves, [17]they asked the man, "What do you say about this one who healed your eyes?"

"He is a prophet!" the man told them.

[18]But the Jewish leaders wouldn't believe that the man had once been blind. They sent for his parents [19]and asked them, "Is this the son who you said was born blind? How can he now see?"

[20]The man's parents answered, "We are certain that he is our son, and we know that he was born blind. [21]But we don't know how he got his sight or who gave it to him. Ask him! He's old enough to speak for himself."

[22-23]The man's parents said this because they were afraid of the Jewish leaders. The leaders had already agreed that no-one was to have anything to do with anyone who said Jesus was the Messiah.

[24]The leaders called the man back and said, "Swear by God to tell the truth! We know that Jesus is a sinner."

[25]The man replied, "I don't know if he's a sinner or not. All I know is that I used to be blind, but now I can see!"

[26]"What did he do to you?" the Jewish leaders asked. "How did he heal your eyes?"

[27]The man answered, "I have already told you once, and you refused to listen. Why do you want me to tell you again? Do you also want to become his disciples?"

[28]The leaders insulted the man and said, "You are his follower! We are followers of Moses. [29]We are sure that God spoke to Moses, but we don't even know where Jesus comes from."

[30]"How strange!" the man replied. "He healed my eyes, and yet you don't know where he comes from. [31]We know that God listens only to people who love and obey him. God doesn't listen to sinners. [32]And this is the first time in history that anyone has ever given sight to someone born blind. [33]Jesus couldn't do anything unless he came from God."

[34]The leaders told the man, "You have been a sinner

umiracle: See the note at 2.11.

since the day you were born! Do you think you can teach us anything?" Then they said, "You can never come back into any of our meeting places!"

³⁵When Jesus heard what had happened, he went and found the man. Then Jesus asked, "Do you have faith in the Son of Man?"

³⁶He replied, "Sir, if you'll tell me who he is, I'll put my faith in him."

³⁷"You've already seen him," Jesus answered, "and right now he's talking with you."

³⁸The man said, "Lord, I put my faith in you!" Then he worshipped Jesus.

³⁹Jesus told him, "I came to judge the people of this world. I'm here to give sight to the blind and to make blind everyone who can see."

⁴⁰When the Pharisees heard Jesus say this, they asked, "Are we blind?"

⁴¹Jesus answered, "If you were blind, you wouldn't be guilty. But now that you claim to see, you'll keep on being guilty."

A Story about Sheep

10 ¹Jesus said:
I tell you for certain that only thieves and robbers climb over the fence instead of going in through the gate to the sheep pen. ²⁻³But the gatekeeper opens the gate for the shepherd, and he goes in through it. The sheep know their shepherd's voice. He calls each of them by name and leads them out.

⁴When he has led out all of his sheep, he walks in front of them, and they follow, because they know his voice. ⁵The sheep won't follow strangers. They don't recognise a stranger's voice, and they run away.

⁶Jesus told the people this story. But they didn't understand what he was talking about.

Jesus Is the Good Shepherd

⁷Jesus said:
I tell you for certain that I am the gate for the sheep. ⁸Everyone who came before me was a thief or a robber, and the sheep didn't listen to any of them. ⁹I am the

gate. All who come in through me will be saved. Through me they will come and go and find pasture.

¹⁰A thief comes only to rob, kill, and destroy. I came so that everyone would have life, and have it in its fullest. ¹¹I am the good shepherd, and the good shepherd gives up his life for his sheep. ¹²Hired workers aren't like the shepherd. They don't own the sheep, and when they see a wolf coming, they run off and leave the sheep. Then the wolf attacks and scatters the flock. ¹³Hired workers run away because they don't care about the sheep.

¹⁴I am the good shepherd. I know my sheep, and they know me. ¹⁵Just as the Father knows me, I know the Father, and I give up my life for my sheep. ¹⁶I have other sheep that aren't in this sheep pen. I must bring them together too, when they hear my voice. Then there will be one flock of sheep and one shepherd.

¹⁷The Father loves me, because I give up my life, so that I may receive it back again. ¹⁸No-one takes my life from me. I give it up willingly! I have the power to give it up and the power to receive it back again, just as my Father commanded me to do.

¹⁹The people took sides because of what Jesus had told them. ²⁰Many of them said, "He has a demon in him! He's crazy! Why listen to him?"

²¹But others said, "How could anyone with a demon in him say these things? No-one like that could give sight to a blind person!"

Jesus Is Rejected

²²That winter, Jesus was in Jerusalem for the Temple Festival. ²³One day he was walking in that part of the temple known as Solomon's Porch,ᵛ ²⁴and the people gathered all around him. They said, "How long are you going to keep us guessing? If you are the Messiah, tell us plainly!"

²⁵Jesus answered:

I have told you, and you refused to believe me. The things I do by my Father's authority show who I am.

ᵛSolomon's Porch: A public place with tall columns along the east side of the temple.

²⁶But since you aren't my sheep, you don't believe me. ²⁷My sheep know my voice, and I know them. They follow me, ²⁸and I give them eternal life, so that they will never be lost. No-one can snatch them out of my hand. ²⁹My Father gave them to me, and he is greater than all others.ʷ No-one can snatch them from his hands, ³⁰and I am one with the Father.

³¹Once again the Jewish leaders picked up stones in order to kill Jesus. ³²But he said, "I've shown you many good things that my Father sent me to do. Which one are you going to stone me for?"

³³They answered, "We're not stoning you because of any good thing you did. We are stoning you because you did a terrible thing. You are just a man, and here you are claiming to be God!"

³⁴Jesus replied:

In your Scriptures doesn't God say, "You are gods"? ³⁵You can't argue with the Scriptures, and God spoke to those people and called them gods. ³⁶So why do you accuse me of a terrible sin for saying that I am the Son of God? After all, it is the Father who prepared me for this work. He is also the one who sent me into the world. ³⁷If I don't do as my Father does, you should not believe me. ³⁸But if I do what my Father does, you should believe because of that, even if you don't have faith in me. Then you will know for certain that the Father is one with me, and I am one with the Father.

³⁹Again they wanted to arrest Jesus. But he escaped ⁴⁰and crossed the Jordan to the place where John had earlier been baptising. While Jesus was there, ⁴¹many people came to him. They were saying, "John didn't work any miracles, but everything he said about Jesus is true." ⁴²A lot of those people also put their faith in Jesus.

The Death of Lazarus

11 ¹⁻²A man by the name of Lazarus was sick in the village of Bethany. He had two sisters, Mary and Martha. This was the same Mary who later poured perfume on the Lord's head and wiped his feet with her

---

ʷ*he is greater than all others:* Some manuscripts have "they are greater than all others."

hair. ³The sisters sent a message to the Lord and told him that his good friend Lazarus was sick.

⁴When Jesus heard this, he said, "His sickness won't end in death. It will bring glory to God and his Son."

⁵Jesus loved Martha and her sister and brother. ⁶But he stayed where he was for two more days. ⁷Then he said to his disciples, "Now we'll go back to Judea."

⁸"Teacher," they said, "the people there want to stone you to death! Why do you want to go back?"

⁹Jesus answered, "Aren't there twelve hours in each day? If you walk during the day, you'll have light from the sun, and you won't stumble. ¹⁰But if you walk during the night, you'll stumble, because you haven't got any light." ¹¹Then he told them, "Our friend Lazarus is asleep, and I'm going there to wake him up."

¹²They replied, "Lord, if he's asleep, he'll get better." ¹³Jesus really meant that Lazarus was dead, but they thought he was talking only about sleep.

¹⁴Then Jesus told them plainly, "Lazarus is dead! ¹⁵I'm glad that I wasn't there, because now you'll have a chance to put your faith in me. Let's go to him."

¹⁶Thomas, whose nickname was "Twin," said to the other disciples, "Come on. Let's go, so we can die with him."

Jesus Brings Lazarus To Life

¹⁷When Jesus got to Bethany, he found that Lazarus had already been in the tomb for four days. ¹⁸Bethany was only about three kilometres from Jerusalem, ¹⁹and many people had come from the city to comfort Martha and Mary because their brother had died.

²⁰When Martha heard that Jesus had arrived, she went out to meet him, but Mary stayed in the house. ²¹Martha said to Jesus, "Lord, if you'd been here, my brother wouldn't have died. ²²Yet even now I know that God will do anything you ask."

²³Jesus told her, "Your brother will live again!"

²⁴Martha answered, "I know that he'll be raised to life on the last day,ˣ when all the dead are raised."

²⁵Jesus then said, "I am the one who raises the dead to life! Everyone who has faith in me will live, even if they

ˣthe last day: When God will judge all people.

die. ²⁶And everyone who lives because of faith in me will never really die. Do you believe this?"

²⁷"Yes, Lord!" she replied. "I believe that you are Christ, the Son of God. You are the one we hoped would come into the world."

²⁸After Martha said this, she went and privately said to her sister Mary, "The Teacher is here, and he wants to see you." ²⁹As soon as Mary heard this, she got up and went out to Jesus. ³⁰He was still outside the village where Martha had gone to meet him. ³¹Many people had come to comfort Mary, and when they saw her quickly leave the house, they thought she was going out to the tomb to cry. So they followed her.

³²Mary went to where Jesus was. Then as soon as she saw him, she knelt at his feet and said, "Lord, if you'd been here, my brother wouldn't have died."

³³When Jesus saw that Mary and the people with her were crying, he was terribly upset ³⁴and asked, "Where have you put his body?"

They replied, "Lord, come and you'll see."

³⁵Jesus started crying, ³⁶and the people said, "See how much he loved Lazarus."

³⁷Some of them said, "He gives sight to the blind. Why couldn't he have kept Lazarus from dying?"

³⁸Jesus was still terribly upset. So he went to the tomb, which was a cave with a stone rolled against the entrance. ³⁹Then he told the people to roll the stone away. But Martha said, "Lord, you know that Lazarus has been dead for four days, and there will be a bad smell."

⁴⁰Jesus replied, "Didn't I tell you that if you had faith, you would see the glory of God?"

⁴¹After the stone had been rolled aside, Jesus looked up towards heaven and prayed, "Father, I thank you for answering my prayer. ⁴²I know that you always answer my prayers. But I said this, so that the people here would believe that you sent me."

⁴³When Jesus had finished praying, he shouted, "Lazarus, come out!" ⁴⁴The man who had been dead came out. His hands and feet were wrapped with strips of burial cloth, and a cloth covered his face.

Jesus then told the people, "Untie him and let him go."

The Plot To Kill Jesus

(Matthew 26.1-5; Mark 14.1, 2; Luke 22.1, 2)

45Many of the people who had come to visit Mary saw the things that Jesus did, and they put their faith in him. 46Others went to the Pharisees and told them what Jesus had done. 47Then the chief priests and the Pharisees called the council together and said, "What should we do? This man is working a lot of miracles.y 48If we don't stop him now, everyone will put their faith in him. Then the Romans will come and destroy our temple and our nation."z

49One of the council members was Caiaphas, who was also high priest that year. He spoke up and said, "You people don't have any sense at all! 50Don't you know it's better for one person to die for the people than for the whole nation to be destroyed?" 51Caiaphas didn't say this on his own. As high priest that year, he was prophesying that Jesus would die for the nation. 52Yet Jesus would not die just for the Jewish nation. He would die to bring together all of God's scattered people. 53From that day on, the council started making plans to put Jesus to death.

54Because of this plot against him, Jesus stopped going around in public. He went to the town of Ephraim, which was near the desert, and he stayed there with his disciples.

55It was almost time for Passover. Many of the Jewish people who lived out in the country had come to Jerusalem to get themselves readya for the festival. 56They looked around for Jesus. Then when they were in the temple, they asked each other, "You don't think he will come here for Passover, do you?"

57The chief priests and the Pharisees told the people to let them know if any of them saw Jesus. That is how they hoped to arrest him.

ymiracles: See the note at 2.11. zdestroy our temple and our nation: The Jewish leaders were afraid that Jesus would lead his followers to rebel against Rome and that the Roman army would then destroy their nation. aget themselves ready: The Jewish people had to do certain things to prepare themselves to worship God.

At Bethany
(Matthew 26.6-13; Mark 14.3-9)

12 [1]Six days before Passover Jesus went back to Bethany, where he had raised Lazarus from death. [2]A meal had been prepared for Jesus. Martha was doing the serving, and Lazarus himself was there.

[3]Mary took a very expensive bottle of perfume[b] and poured it on Jesus' feet. She wiped them with her hair, and the sweet smell of the perfume filled the house.

[4]A disciple named Judas Iscariot[c] was there. He was the one who was going to betray Jesus, and he asked, [5]"Why wasn't this perfume sold for 300 silver coins and the money given to the poor?" [6]Judas didn't really care about the poor. He asked this because he carried the money bag and sometimes would steal from it.

[7]Jesus replied, "Leave her alone! She has kept this perfume for the day of my burial. [8]You will always have the poor with you, but you won't always have me."

A Plot To Kill Lazarus

[9]A lot of people came when they heard that Jesus was there. They also wanted to see Lazarus, because Jesus had raised him from death. [10]So the chief priests made plans to kill Lazarus. [11]He was the reason that many of the Jewish people were turning from them and putting their faith in Jesus.

Jesus Enters Jerusalem
(Matthew 21.1-11; Mark 11.1-11; Luke 19.28-40)

[12]The next day a large crowd was in Jerusalem for Passover. When they heard that Jesus was coming for the festival, [13]they took palm branches and went out to greet him.[d] They shouted,

"Hooray![e]

---

[b]*very expensive bottle of perfume:* The Greek text has "expensive perfume made of pure spikenard," a plant used to make perfume.　[c]*Iscariot:* This may mean "a man from Kerioth" (a place in Judea). But more probably it means "a man who was a liar" or "a man who was a betrayer."　[d]*took palm branches and went out to greet him:* This was one way that the Jewish people welcomed a famous person.　[e]*Hooray:* This translates a word that can mean "please save us." But it is most often used as a shout of praise to God.

God bless the one who comes in the name of the Lord!
God bless the King of Israel!"
[14]Jesus found a donkey and rode on it, just as the
Scriptures say,

[15] "People of Jerusalem, don't be afraid!
Your King is now coming,
and he is riding on a donkey."

[16]At first, Jesus' disciples didn't understand. But after
he had been given his glory,[f] they remembered all this.
Everything had happened exactly as the Scriptures said
it would.

[17-18]A crowd had come to meet Jesus because they had
seen him call Lazarus out of the tomb. They kept talking
about him and this miracle.[g] [19]But the Pharisees said to
each other, "There's nothing that can be done! Everyone
in the world is following Jesus."

Some Greeks Want To Meet Jesus

[20]Some Greeks[h] had gone to Jerusalem to worship
during Passover. [21]Philip from Bethsaida in Galilee was
there too. So they went to him and said, "Sir, we would
like to meet Jesus." [22]Philip told Andrew. Then the two
of them went to Jesus and told him.

The Son of Man Must Be Lifted Up

[23]Jesus said:
The time has come for the Son of Man to be given
his glory.[i] [24]I tell you for certain that a grain of wheat
that falls on the ground will never be more than one
grain unless it dies. But if it dies, it will produce lots of
wheat. [25]If you love your life, you will lose it. If you
give it up in this world, you will be given eternal life.
[26]If you serve me, you must go with me. My servants
will be with me wherever I am. If you serve me, my
Father will honour you.
[27]Now I'm deeply troubled, and I don't know what
to say. But I mustn't ask my Father to keep me from
this time of suffering. In fact, I came into the world to

[f]had been given his glory: See the note at 7.39.   [g]miracle: See the note at 2.11.
[h]Greeks: Perhaps Gentiles who worshipped with the Jews. See the note at 7.35.
[i]be given his glory: See the note at 7.39.

suffer. [28]So Father, bring glory to yourself.

A voice from heaven then said, "I have already brought glory to myself, and I will do it again!" [29]When the crowd heard the voice, some of them thought it was thunder. Others thought an angel had spoken to Jesus.

[30]Then Jesus told the crowd, "That voice spoke to help you, not me. [31]This world's people are now being judged, and the ruler of this world[j] is already being thrown out! [32]If I am lifted up above the earth, I'll make everyone want to come to me." [33]Jesus was talking about the way he would be put to death.

[34]The crowd said to Jesus, "The Scriptures teach that the Messiah will live for ever. How can you say that the Son of Man must be lifted up? Who is this Son of Man?"

[35]Jesus answered, "The light will be with you for only a little longer. Walk in the light while you can. Then you won't be caught walking blindly in the dark. [36]Have faith in the light while it's with you, and you will be children of the light."

The People Refuse To Have Faith in Jesus

After Jesus had said these things, he left and went into hiding. [37]He had worked a lot of miracles[k] among the people, but they were still not willing to have faith in him. [38]This happened so that what the prophet Isaiah had said would come true,

"Lord, who has believed our message?
And who has seen your mighty strength?"

[39]The people couldn't have faith in Jesus, because Isaiah had also said,

[40] "The Lord has blinded the eyes of the people,
and he has made the people stubborn.
He did this so that they could not see or understand,
and so that they would not turn to the Lord
and be healed."

[41]Isaiah said this, because he saw the glory of Jesus and spoke about him.[l] [42]Even then, many of the leaders put

---

[j]*world:* In the Gospel of John "world" sometimes refers to the people who live in this world and to the evil forces that control their lives.   [k]*miracles:* See the note at 2.11.   [l]*he saw the glory of Jesus and spoke about him:* Or "he saw the glory of God and spoke about Jesus."

their faith in Jesus, but they didn't tell anyone about it. The Pharisees had already given orders for the people not to have anything to do with anyone who had faith in Jesus. 43And besides, the leaders liked praise from others more than they liked praise from God.

Jesus Came To Save the World

44In a loud voice Jesus said:

Everyone who has faith in me also has faith in the one who sent me. 45And everyone who has seen me has seen the one who sent me. 46I am the light that has come into the world. No-one who has faith in me will stay in the dark.

47I am not the one who will judge those who refuse to obey my teachings. I came to save the people of this world, not to be their judge. 48But everyone who rejects me and my teachings will be judged on the last day[m] by what I have said. 49I don't speak on my own. I say only what the Father who sent me has told me to say. 50I know that his commands will bring eternal life. That's why I tell you exactly what the Father has told me.

Jesus Washes the Feet of His Disciples

13 1It was before Passover, and Jesus knew that the time had come for him to leave this world and to return to the Father. He had always loved his followers in this world, and he loved them to the very end.

2Even before the evening meal started, the devil had made Judas, the son of Simon Iscariot,[n] decide to betray Jesus.

3Jesus knew that he had come from God and would go back to God. He also knew that the Father had given him complete power. 4So during the meal Jesus got up, removed his outer garment, and wrapped a towel around his waist. 5He put some water into a large bowl. Then he began washing his disciples' feet and drying them with the towel he was wearing.

[m]the last day: See the note at 6.39.   [n]Iscariot: See the note at 12.4.

⁶But when he came to Simon Peter, that disciple asked, "Lord, are you going to wash my feet?"

⁷Jesus answered, "You don't really know what I'm doing, but later you will understand."

⁸"You'll never wash my feet!" Peter replied.

"If I don't wash you," Jesus told him, "you don't really belong to me."

⁹Peter said, "Lord, don't wash just my feet. Wash my hands and my head."

¹⁰Jesus answered, "People who have bathed and are clean all over need to wash just their feet. And you, my disciples, are clean, except for one of you." ¹¹Jesus knew who would betray him. That's why he said, "except for one of you."

¹²After Jesus had washed his disciples' feet and had put his outer garment back on, he sat down again.ᵒ Then he said:

Do you understand what I've done? ¹³You call me your teacher and Lord, and you should, because that is who I am. ¹⁴And if your Lord and teacher has washed your feet, you should do the same for each other. ¹⁵I have set the example, and you should do for each other exactly what I have done for you. ¹⁶I tell you for certain that servants aren't greater than their master, and messengers aren't greater than the one who sent them. ¹⁷You know these things, and God will bless you, if you do them.

¹⁸I am not talking about all of you. I know the ones I have chosen. But what the Scriptures say must come true. And they say, "The man who ate with me has turned against me!" ¹⁹I'm telling you this before it all happens. Then when it does happen, you will believe who I am.ᵖ ²⁰I tell you for certain that anyone who welcomes my messengers also welcomes me, and anyone who welcomes me welcomes the one who sent me.

ᵒsat down again: On special occasions the Jewish people followed the Greek and Roman custom of lying down on their left side and leaning on their left elbow, while eating with their right hand. ᵖI am: See note at 8.24.

Jesus Tells What Will Happen to Him
(Matthew 26.20-25; Mark 14.17-21; Luke 22.21-23)

21After Jesus had said these things, he was deeply troubled and told his disciples, "I tell you for certain that one of you will betray me." 22They were confused about what he meant. And they just stared at each other.

23Jesus' favourite disciple was sitting next to him at the meal, 24and Simon motioned for that disciple to find out which one Jesus meant. 25So the disciple leaned towards Jesus and asked, "Lord, which one of us are you talking about?"

26Jesus answered, "I will dip this piece of bread in the sauce and give it to the one I was talking about."

Then Jesus dipped the bread and gave it to Judas, the son of Simon Iscariot.q 27Right then Satan took control of Judas.

Jesus said, "Judas, go quickly and do what you have to do." 28No-one at the meal understood what Jesus meant. 29But because Judas was in charge of the money, some of them thought that Jesus had told him to buy something they needed for the festival. Others thought that Jesus had told him to give some money to the poor. 30Judas took the piece of bread and went out.

It was already night.

The New Command

31After Judas had gone, Jesus said:

Now the Son of Man will be given glory, and he will bring glory to God. 32Then, after God is given glory because of him, God will bring glory to him, and God will do it very soon.

33My children, I will be with you for a little while longer. Then you will look for me, but you won't find me. I tell you just as I told the people, "You can't go where I'm going." 34But I'm giving you a new command. You must love each other, just as I have loved you. 35If you love each other, everyone will know that you are my disciples.

qIscariot: See the note at 12.4.

Peter's Promise
(Matthew 26.31-35; Mark 14.27-31; Luke 22.31-34)

36Simon Peter asked, "Lord, where are you going?"

Jesus answered, "You can't go with me now, but later on you will."

37Peter asked, "Lord, why can't I go with you now? I would die for you!"

38"Would you really die for me?" Jesus asked. "I tell you for certain that before a rooster crows, you will say three times that you don't even know me."

Jesus Is the Way to the Father

14 1Jesus said to his disciples, "Don't be worried! Have faith in God and have faith in me.*r* 2There are many rooms in my Father's house. I wouldn't tell you this, unless it was true. I'm going there to prepare a place for each of you. 3After I've done this, I'll come back and take you with me. Then we'll be together. 4You know the way to where I'm going."

5Thomas said, "Lord, we don't even know where you are going! How can we know the way?"

6"I am the way, the truth, and the life!" Jesus answered. "Without me, no-one can go to the Father. 7If you had known me, you would have known the Father. But from now on, you do know him, and you have seen him."

8Philip said, "Lord, show us the Father. That's all we need."

9Jesus replied:

Philip, I have been with you for a long time. Don't you know who I am? If you have seen me, you have seen the Father. How can you ask me to show you the Father? 10Don't you believe that I am one with the Father and that the Father is one with me? What I say isn't said on my own. The Father who lives in me does these things.

11Have faith in me when I say that the Father is one with me and that I am one with the Father. Or else have faith in me simply because of the things I do.

rHave faith in God and have faith in me: Or "You have faith in God, so have faith in me."

¹²I tell you for certain that if you have faith in me, you will do the same things that I am doing. You will do even greater things, now that I am going back to the Father. ¹³Ask me, and I will do whatever you ask. This way the Son will bring honour to the Father. ¹⁴I will do whatever you ask me to do.

The Holy Spirit Is Promised

¹⁵Jesus said to his disciples:

If you love me, you will do as I command. ¹⁶Then I will ask the Father to send you the Holy Spirit who will help[s] you and always be with you. ¹⁷The Spirit will show you what is true. The people of this world can't accept the Spirit, because they don't see or know him. But you know the Spirit, who is with you and will keep on living in you.

¹⁸I won't leave you like orphans. I will come back to you. ¹⁹In a little while the people of this world won't be able to see me, but you will see me. And because I live, you will live. ²⁰Then you will know that I am one with the Father. You will know that you are one with me, and I am one with you. ²¹If you love me, you will do what I have said, and my Father will love you. I will also love you and show you what I'm like.

²²The other Judas, not Judas Iscariot,[t] then spoke up and asked, "Lord, what do you mean by saying that you'll show us what you are like, but you won't show the people of this world?"

²³Jesus replied:

If anyone loves me, they will obey me. Then my Father will love them, and we will come to them and live in them. ²⁴But anyone who doesn't love me won't obey me. What they have heard me say doesn't really come from me, but from the Father who sent me.

²⁵I have told you these things while I am still with you. ²⁶But the Holy Spirit will come and help[u] you, because the Father will send the Spirit to take my place. The Spirit will teach you everything and will remind

---

[s]help: The Greek word may mean "comfort," "encourage," or "defend."   [t]Iscariot: See the note at 12.4.   [u]help: See the note at 14.16.

you of what I said while I was with you.

²⁷I give you peace, the kind of peace that only I can give. It isn't like the peace that this world can give. So don't be worried or afraid.

²⁸You have already heard me say that I am going and that I will also come back to you. If you really love me, you should be glad that I am going back to the Father, because he is greater than I am.

²⁹I am telling you this before I leave, so that when it does happen, you will have faith in me. ³⁰I can't speak with you much longer, because the ruler of this world is coming. But he has no power over me. ³¹I obey my Father, so that everyone in the world might know that I love him.

It's time for us to go now.

Jesus Is the True Vine

15 ¹Jesus said to his disciples:
I am the true vine, and my Father is the gardener. ²He cuts away every branch of mine that doesn't produce fruit. But he trims clean every branch that does produce fruit, so that it will produce even more fruit. ³You are already clean because of what I have said to you.

⁴Stay joined to me, and I will stay joined to you. Just as a branch can't produce fruit unless it stays joined to the vine, you can't produce fruit unless you stay joined to me. ⁵I am the vine, and you are the branches. If you stay joined to me, and I stay joined to you, then you will produce lots of fruit. But you can't do anything without me. ⁶If you don't stay joined to me, you will be thrown away. You will be like dry branches that are gathered up and burnt in a fire.

⁷Stay joined to me and let my teachings become part of you. Then you can pray for whatever you want, and your prayer will be answered. ⁸When you become fruitful disciples of mine, my Father will be honoured. ⁹I have loved you, just as my Father has loved me. So make sure that I keep on loving you. ¹⁰If you obey me, I will keep loving you, just as my Father keeps loving me, because I have obeyed him.

[11]I have told you this to make you as completely happy as I am. [12]Now I tell you to love each other, as I have loved you. [13]The greatest way to show love for friends is to die for them. [14]And you are my friends, if you obey me. [15]Servants don't know what their master is doing, and so I don't speak to you as my servants. I speak to you as my friends, and I have told you everything that my Father has told me.

[16]You didn't choose me. I chose you and sent you out to produce fruit, the kind of fruit that will last. Then my Father will give you whatever you ask for in my name.[v] [17]So I command you to love each other.

The World's Hatred

[18]If the people of this world[w] hate you, just remember that they hated me first. [19]If you belonged to the world, its people would love you. But you don't belong to the world. I have chosen you to leave the world behind, and that's why its people hate you. [20]Remember how I told you that servants aren't greater than their master. So if people mistreat me, they will mistreat you. If they do what I say, they will do what you say.

[21]People will do to you exactly what they did to me. They will do it because you belong to me, and they don't know the one who sent me. [22]If I hadn't come and spoken to them, they wouldn't be guilty of sin. But now they have no excuse for their sin.

[23]Everyone who hates me also hates my Father. [24]I have done things that no-one else has ever done. If they hadn't seen me do these things, they wouldn't be guilty. But they did see me do these things, and they still hate me and my Father too. [25]That's why the Scriptures are true when they say, "People hated me for no reason."

[26]I will send you the Spirit who comes from the Father and shows what is true. The Spirit will help[x] you and will tell you about me. [27]Then you will also tell others about me, because you have been with me from the beginning.

---

[v]*in my name:* Or "because you are my followers." [w]*world:* See the note at 12.31. [x]*help:* See the note at 14.16.

16 ¹I am telling you this to keep you from being afraid. ²You will be chased out of the Jewish meeting places. And the time will come when people will kill you and think they are doing God a favour. ³They will do these things because they don't know either the Father or me. ⁴I am saying this to you now, so that when the time comes, you will remember what I have said.

The Work of the Holy Spirit

I was with you at the first, and so I didn't tell you these things. ⁵But now I am going back to the Father who sent me, and none of you asks me where I am going. ⁶You are very sad from hearing all of this. ⁷But I tell you that I am going to do what is best for you. That's why I am going away. The Holy Spirit can't come to help you until I leave. But after I have gone, I will send the Spirit to you.

⁸The Spirit will come and show the people of this world the truth about sin and God's justice and the judgment. ⁹The Spirit will show them that they are wrong about sin, because they didn't have faith in me. ¹⁰They are wrong about God's justice, because I'm going to the Father, and you won't see me again. ¹¹And they are wrong about the judgment, because God has already judged the ruler of this world.

¹²I have much more to say to you, but right now it would be more than you could understand. ¹³The Spirit shows what is true and will come and guide you into the full truth. The Spirit doesn't speak on his own. He will tell you only what he has heard from me, and he will let you know what is going to happen. ¹⁴The Spirit will bring glory to me by taking my message and telling it to you. ¹⁵Everything that the Father has is mine. That is why I have said that the Spirit takes my message and tells it to you.

Sorrow Will Turn into Joy

¹⁶Jesus told his disciples, "For a little while you won't see me, but after a while you will see me."

¹⁷They said to each other, "What does Jesus mean by

saying that for a little while we won't see him, but after a while we will see him? What does he mean by saying that he is going to the Father? [18]What is this 'little while' that he's talking about? We don't know what he means."

[19]Jesus knew that they had some questions, so he said:

You are wondering what I meant when I said that for a little while you won't see me, but after a while you will see me. [20]I tell you for certain that you will cry and be sad, but the world will be happy. You will be sad, but later you will be happy.

[21]When a woman is about to give birth, she is in great pain. But after it's all over, she forgets the pain and is happy, because she has brought a child into the world. [22]You are very sad now. But later I will see you, and you will be so happy that no-one will be able to change the way you feel. [23]When that time comes, you won't have to ask me about anything. I tell you for certain that the Father will give you whatever you ask for in my name. [24]You haven't asked for anything in this way before, but now you must ask in my name.[y] Then it will be given to you, so that you will be completely happy.

[25]I have used examples to explain to you what I've been talking about. But the time will come when I will speak to you plainly about the Father and will no longer use examples like these. [26]You will ask the Father in my name,[z] and I won't have to ask him for you. [27]God the Father loves you because you love me, and you believe that I have come from him. [28]I came from the Father into the world, but I'm leaving the world and returning to the Father.

[29]The disciples said, "Now you're speaking plainly to us! You're not using examples. [30]At last we know that you understand everything, and we don't have any more questions. Now we believe that you really have come from God."

[31]Jesus replied:

Do you really believe me? [32]The time will come and is already here when all of you will be scattered. Each of you will go back home and leave me by myself. But the Father will be with me, and I won't be alone. [33]I have told you this, so that you might have peace in your hearts because of me. While you are in the world, you will have to suffer. But cheer up! I have defeated the world.[a]

Jesus Prays

17 [1]After Jesus had finished speaking to his disciples, he looked up towards heaven and prayed:

Father, the time has come for you to bring glory to your Son, in order that he may bring glory to you. [2]And you gave him power over all people, so that he would give eternal life to everyone you give him. [3]Eternal life is to know you, the only true God, and to know Jesus Christ, the one you sent. [4]I have brought glory to you here on earth by doing everything you gave me to do. [5]Now, Father, give me back the glory that I had with you before the world was created.

[6]You have given me some followers from this world, and I have shown them what you are like. They were yours, but you gave them to me, and they have obeyed you. [7]They know that you gave me everything I have. [8]I told my followers what you told me, and they accepted it. They know that I came from you, and they believe that you are the one who sent me. [9]I'm praying for them, but not for those who belong to this world. My followers belong to you, and I'm praying for them. [10]All that I have is yours, and all that you have is mine, and they will bring glory to me.

[11]Holy Father, I am no longer in the world. I'm coming to you, but my followers are still in the world. So keep them safe by the power of the name that you have given me. Then they will be one with each other, just as you and I are one. [12]While I was with them, I kept them safe by the power you have given me. I guarded them, and not one of them was lost, except the one who had to be lost. This happened so that what the Scriptures say would come true.

[a]*world:* See the note at 12.31.

¹³I am on my way to you. But I say these things while I'm still in the world, so that my followers will have the same complete joy that I do. ¹⁴I have told them your message. But the people of this world hate them, because they don't belong to this world, just as I don't.

¹⁵Father, I don't ask you to take my followers out of the world, but keep them safe from the evil one. ¹⁶They don't belong to this world, and neither do I. ¹⁷Your word is the truth. So let this truth make them completely yours. ¹⁸I am sending them into the world, just as you sent me. ¹⁹I have given myself completely for their sake, so that they can belong completely to the truth.

²⁰I am not praying just for these followers. I am also praying for everyone else who will have faith because of what my followers will say about me. ²¹I want all of them to be one with each other, just as I am one with you and you are one with me. I also want them to be one with us. Then the people of this world will believe that you sent me.

²²I have honoured my followers in the same way that you honoured me, in order that they may be one with each other, just as we are one. ²³I am one with them, and you are one with me, so that they may become completely one. Then this world's people will know that you sent me. They will know that you love my followers as much as you love me.

²⁴Father, I want everyone you have given me to be with me, wherever I am. Then they will see the glory that you have given me, because you loved me before the world was created. ²⁵Good Father, the people of this world don't know you. But I know you, and my followers know that you sent me. ²⁶I told them what you are like, and I will tell them even more. Then the love that you have for me will become part of them, and I will be one with them.

Jesus Is Betrayed and Arrested
(Matthew 26.47-56; Mark 14.43-50; Luke 22.47-53)

18 ¹When Jesus had finished praying, he and his disciples crossed the Kidron Valley and went into a garden.*b* ²Jesus had often met there with his disciples, and Judas knew where the place was.

³⁻⁵Judas had promised to betray Jesus. So he went to the garden with some Roman soldiers and temple police, who had been sent by the chief priests and the Pharisees. They carried torches, lanterns, and weapons. Jesus already knew everything that was going to happen, but he asked, "Who are you looking for?"

They answered, "We're looking for Jesus from Nazareth!"

Jesus told them, "I am Jesus!"*c* ⁶At once they all backed away and fell to the ground.

⁷Jesus again asked, "Who are you looking for?"

"We're looking for Jesus from Nazareth," they answered.

⁸This time Jesus replied, "I have already told you that I am Jesus. If I'm the one you are looking for, let these others go. ⁹Then everything will happen, just as the Scriptures say, 'I didn't lose anyone you gave me.' "

¹⁰Simon Peter had brought along a sword. He now pulled it out and struck at the servant of the high priest. The servant's name was Malchus, and Peter cut off his right ear. ¹¹Jesus told Peter, "Put your sword away. I must drink from the cup*d* that the Father has given me."

Jesus Is Brought to Annas
(Matthew 26.57, 58; Mark 14.53, 54; Luke 22.54)

¹²The Roman officer and his men, together with the temple police, arrested Jesus and tied him up. ¹³They took him first to Annas, who was the father-in-law of Caiaphas, the high priest that year. ¹⁴This was the same Caiaphas who had told the Jewish leaders, "It's better if one person dies for the people."

Peter Says He Doesn't Know Jesus
(Matthew 26.69, 70; Mark 14.66-68; Luke 22.55-57)

¹⁵Simon Peter and another disciple followed Jesus. That disciple knew the high priest, and he followed Jesus into

---

b garden: The Greek word is usually translated "garden," but probably referred to an olive orchard.   *c I am Jesus:* The Greek text has "I am" (see the note at 8.24).   *d drink from the cup:* In the Scriptures a cup is sometimes used as a symbol of suffering. To "drink from the cup" is to suffer.

the courtyard of the high priest's house. [16]Peter stayed outside near the gate. But the other disciple came back out and spoke to the girl at the gate. She let Peter go in, [17]but asked him, "Aren't you one of that man's followers?"

"No, I'm not!" Peter answered.

[18]It was cold, and the servants and temple police had made a charcoal fire. They were warming themselves around it, when Peter went over and stood near the fire to warm himself.

Jesus Is Questioned by the High Priest
(Matthew 26.59-66; Mark 14.55-64; Luke 22.66-71)

[19]The high priest questioned Jesus about his followers and his teaching. [20]But Jesus told him, "I have spoken freely in front of everyone. And I have always taught in our meeting places and in the temple, where all of our people come together. I haven't said anything in secret. [21]Why are you questioning me? Why don't you ask the people who heard me? They know what I have said."

[22]As soon as Jesus said this, one of the temple police hit him and said, "That's no way to talk to the high priest!"

[23]Jesus answered, "If I have done something wrong, say so. But if not, why did you hit me?" [24]Jesus was still tied up, and Annas sent him to Caiaphas the high priest.

Peter Again Denies that He Knows Jesus
(Matthew 26.71-75; Mark 14.69-72; Luke 22.58-62)

[25]While Simon Peter was standing there warming himself, someone asked him, "Aren't you one of Jesus' followers?"

Again Peter denied it and said, "No, I'm not!"

[26]One of the high priest's servants was there. He was a relative of the servant whose ear Peter had cut off, and he asked, "Didn't I see you in the garden with that man?"

[27]Once more Peter denied it, and at that very moment a rooster crowed.

Jesus Is Tried by Pilate
(Matthew 27.1, 2, 11-14; Mark 15.1-5; Luke 23.1-5)

28It was early in the morning when Jesus was taken from Caiaphas to the building where the Roman governor stayed. But the crowd waited outside. Any of them who had gone inside would have become unclean and wouldn't be allowed to eat the Passover meal.[e]

29Pilate came out and asked, "What charges are you bringing against this man?"

30They answered, "He's a criminal! That's why we brought him to you."

31Pilate told them, "Take him and judge him by your own laws."

The crowd replied, "We're not allowed to put anyone to death." 32And so what Jesus said about his death[f] would soon come true.

33Pilate then went back inside. He called Jesus over and asked, "Are you the king of the Jews?"

34Jesus answered, "Are you asking this on your own or did someone tell you about me?"

35"You know I'm not a Jew!" Pilate said. "Your own people and the chief priests brought you to me. What have you done?"

36Jesus answered, "My kingdom doesn't belong to this world. If it did, my followers would have fought to keep me from being handed over to the Jewish leaders. No, my kingdom doesn't belong to this world."

37"So you are a king," Pilate replied.

"You are saying that I am a king," Jesus told him. "I was born into this world to tell about the truth. And everyone who belongs to the truth knows my voice."

38Pilate asked Jesus, "What is truth?"

---

[e]*would have become unclean and wouldn't be allowed to eat the Passover meal:* Jewish people who came in close contact with foreigners right before Passover weren't allowed to eat the Passover meal.   [f]*about his death:* Jesus had said that he would die by being "lifted up," which meant that he would die on a cross. The Romans killed criminals by nailing them on a cross, but they didn't let the Jews kill anyone in this way.

Jesus Is Sentenced to Death

(Matthew 27.15-31; Mark 15.6-20; Luke 23.13-25)

Pilate went back out and said, "I don't find this man guilty of anything! ³⁹And since I usually set a prisoner free for you at Passover, would you like me to set free the king of the Jews?"

⁴⁰They shouted, "No, not him! We want Barabbas." Now Barabbas was a terrorist.ᵍ

19 ¹Pilate gave orders for Jesus to be beaten with a whip. ²The soldiers made a crown out of thorny branches and put it on Jesus. Then they put a purple robe on him. ³They came up to him and said, "Hey, you king of the Jews!" They also hit him with their fists.

⁴Once again Pilate went out. This time he said, "I will have Jesus brought out to you again. Then you can see for yourselves that I have not found him guilty."

⁵Jesus came out, wearing the crown of thorns and the purple robe. Pilate said, "Here is the man!"ʰ

⁶When the chief priests and the temple police saw him, they yelled, "Nail him to a cross! Nail him to a cross!"

Pilate told them, "You take him and nail him to a cross! I don't find him guilty of anything."

⁷The crowd replied, "He claimed to be the Son of God! Our Jewish Law says that he must be put to death."

⁸When Pilate heard this, he was terrified. ⁹He went back inside and asked Jesus, "Where are you from?" But Jesus didn't answer.

¹⁰"Why won't you answer my question?" Pilate asked. "Don't you know that I have the power to let you go free or to nail you to a cross?"

¹¹Jesus replied, "If God hadn't given you the power, you couldn't do anything at all to me. But the one who handed me over to you did something even worse."

¹²Then Pilate wanted to set Jesus free. But the crowd again yelled, "If you set this man free, you are no friend of the Emperor! Anyone who claims to be a king is an enemy of the Emperor."

ᵍ*terrorist:* Someone who stirred up trouble against the Romans in the hope of gaining freedom for the Jewish people.   ʰ*"Here is the man!":* Or "Look at the man!"

13When Pilate heard this, he brought Jesus out. Then he sat down on the judge's bench at the place known as "The Stone Pavement." In Aramaic this pavement is called "Gabbatha." 14It was about midday on the day before Passover, and Pilate said to the crowd, "Look at your king!"

15"Kill him! Kill him!" they yelled. "Nail him to a cross!"

"So you want me to nail your king to a cross?" Pilate asked.

The chief priests replied, "The Emperor is our king!" 16Then Pilate handed Jesus over to be nailed to a cross.

Jesus Is Nailed to a Cross
(Matthew 27.32-44; Mark 15.21-32; Luke 23.26-43)

Jesus was taken away, 17and he carried his cross to a place known as "The Skull."[i] In Aramaic this place is called "Golgotha." 18There Jesus was nailed to the cross, and on each side of him a man was also nailed to a cross.

19Pilate ordered the charge against Jesus to be written on a board and put above the cross. It read, "Jesus of Nazareth, King of the Jews." 20The words were written in Hebrew, Latin, and Greek.

The place where Jesus was taken wasn't far from the city, and many of the Jewish people read the charge against him. 21So the chief priests went to Pilate and said, "Why did you write that he is King of the Jews? You should have written, 'He claimed to be King of the Jews.' "

22But Pilate told them, "What is written will not be changed!"

23After the soldiers had nailed Jesus to the cross, they divided up his clothes into four parts, one for each of them. But his outer garment was made from a single piece of cloth, and it didn't have any seams. 24The soldiers said to each other, "Let's not rip it apart. We'll gamble to see who gets it." This happened so that the Scriptures would come true, which say,

---

[i]The Skull: The place was probably given this name because it was near a large rock in the shape of a human skull.

"They divided up my clothes
and gambled for my garments."
The soldiers then did what they had decided.

25Jesus' mother stood beside his cross with her sister
and Mary the wife of Clopas. Mary Magdalene was
standing there too.ʲ 26When Jesus saw his mother and his
favourite disciple with her, he said to his mother, "This
man is now your son." 27Then he said to the disciple,
"She is now your mother." From then on, that disciple
took her into his own home.

The Death of Jesus
(Matthew 27.45-56; Mark 15.33-41; Luke 23.44-49)

28Jesus knew that he had now finished his work. And
in order to make the Scriptures come true, he said, "I'm
thirsty!" 29A jar of cheap wine was there. Someone then
soaked a sponge with the wine and held it up to Jesus'
mouth on the stem of a hyssop plant. 30After Jesus drank
the wine, he said, "Everything is done!" He bowed his
head and died.

A Spear Is Stuck in Jesus' Side

31The next day would be both a Sabbath and the
Passover. It was a special day for the Jewish people,ᵏ and
they did not want the bodies to stay on the crosses during
that day. So they asked Pilate to break the men's legsˡ and
take their bodies down. 32The soldiers first broke the legs
of the other two men who were nailed there. 33But when
they came to Jesus, they saw that he was already dead,
and they didn't break his legs.

34One of the soldiers stuck his spear into Jesus' side,

ʲJesus' mother stood beside his cross with her sister and Mary the wife of Clopas.
Mary Magdalene was standing there too: The Greek text may also be understood
to include only three women ("Jesus' mother stood beside the cross with her
sister, Mary the mother of Clopas. Mary Magdalene was standing there too.") or
merely two women ("Jesus' mother was standing there with her sister Mary of
Clopas, that is, Mary Magdalene."). "Of Clopas" may mean "daughter of" or
"mother of." ᵏa special day for the Jewish people: Passover could be any day
of the week. But according to the Gospel of John, Passover was on a Sabbath
in the year that Jesus was nailed to a cross. ˡbreak the men's legs: This was
the way that the Romans sometimes sped up the death of a person who had
been nailed to a cross.

and blood and water came out. 35We know this is true, because it was told by someone who saw it happen. Now you can have faith too. 36All this happened so that the Scriptures would come true, which say, "No bone of his body will be broken" 37and, "They will see the one in whose side they stuck a spear."

Jesus Is Buried
(Matthew 27.57-61; Mark 15.42-47; Luke 23.50-56)

38Joseph from Arimathea was one of Jesus' disciples. He had kept it secret though, because he was afraid of the Jewish leaders. But now he asked Pilate to let him have Jesus' body. Pilate gave him permission, and Joseph took it down from the cross.

39Nicodemus also came with about 30 kilograms of spices made from myrrh and aloes. This was the same Nicodemus who had visited Jesus one night.m 40The two men wrapped the body in a linen cloth, together with the spices, which was how the Jewish people buried their dead. 41In the place where Jesus had been nailed to a cross, there was a garden with a tomb that had never been used. 42The tomb was nearby, and since it was the time to prepare for the Sabbath, they were in a hurry to put Jesus' body there.

Jesus Is Alive
(Matthew 28.1-10; Mark 16.1-8; Luke 24.1-12)

20 1On Sunday morning while it was still dark, Mary Magdalene went to the tomb and saw that the stone had been rolled away from the entrance. 2She ran to Simon Peter and to Jesus' favourite disciple and said, "They have taken the Lord from the tomb! We don't know where they have put him."

3Peter and the other disciple started out for the tomb. 4They ran side by side, until the other disciple ran faster than Peter and got there first. 5He bent over and saw the strips of linen cloth lying inside the tomb, but he didn't go in.

mNicodemus who had visited Jesus one night: See the note at 3.1-21.

⁶When Simon Peter got there, he went into the tomb and saw the strips of cloth. ⁷He also saw the piece of cloth that had been used to cover Jesus' face. It was rolled up and in a place by itself. ⁸The disciple who got there first then went into the tomb, and when he saw it, he believed. ⁹At that time Peter and the other disciple didn't know that the Scriptures said Jesus would rise to life. ¹⁰So the two of them went back to the other disciples.

Jesus Appears to Mary Magdalene
(Mark 16.9-11)

¹¹Mary Magdalene stood crying outside the tomb. She was still weeping, when she stooped down ¹²and saw two angels inside. They were dressed in white and were sitting where Jesus' body had been. One was at the head and the other was at the foot. ¹³The angels asked Mary, "Why are you crying?"

She answered, "They've taken away my Lord's body! I don't know where they've put him."

¹⁴As soon as Mary said this, she turned around and saw Jesus standing there. But she didn't know who he was. ¹⁵Jesus asked her, "Why are you crying? Who are you looking for?"

She thought he was the gardener and said, "Sir, if you have taken his body away, please tell me, so I can go and get him."

¹⁶Then Jesus said to her, "Mary!"

She turned and said to him, "Rabboni." The Aramaic word "Rabboni" means "Teacher."

¹⁷Jesus told her, "Don't hold on to me! I have not yet gone to the Father. But tell my disciples that I'm going to the one who is my Father and my God, as well as your Father and your God." ¹⁸Mary Magdalene then went and told the disciples that she had seen the Lord. She also told them what he had said to her.

Jesus Appears to His Disciples
(Matthew 28.16-20; Mark 16.14-18; Luke 24.36-49)

¹⁹The disciples were afraid of the Jewish leaders, and on the evening of that same Sunday they locked themselves

in a room. Suddenly, Jesus appeared in the middle of the group. He greeted them [20]and showed them his hands and his side. When the disciples saw the Lord, they became very happy.

[21]After Jesus had greeted them again, he said, "I'm sending you, just as the Father has sent me." [22]Then he breathed on them and said, "Receive the Holy Spirit. [23]If you forgive anyone's sins, they will be forgiven. But if you don't forgive their sins, they won't be forgiven."

Jesus and Thomas

[24]Although Thomas the Twin was one of the twelve disciples, he wasn't with the others when Jesus appeared to them. [25]So they told him, "We have seen the Lord!"

But Thomas said, "First, I must see the nail scars in his hands and touch them with my finger. I must put my hand where the spear went into his side. I won't believe unless I do this!"

[26]A week later the disciples were together again. This time, Thomas was with them. Jesus came in while the doors were still locked and stood in the middle of the group. He greeted his disciples [27]and said to Thomas, "Put your finger here and look at my hands! Put your hand into my side. Stop doubting and have faith!"

[28]Thomas replied, "You are my Lord and my God!"

[29]Jesus said, "Thomas, do you have faith because you have seen me? The people who have faith in me without seeing me are the ones who are really blessed!"

Why John Wrote His Book

[30]Jesus worked many other miracles[n] for his disciples, and not all of them are written in this book. [31]But these are written so that you will put your faith in Jesus as the Messiah and the Son of God. If you have faith in[o] him, you will have true life.

Jesus Appears to Seven Disciples

21 [1]Jesus later appeared to his disciples along the shore of Lake Tiberias. [2]Simon Peter, Thomas the

---

[n]*miracles:* See the note at 2.11. [o]*put your faith in...have faith in:* Some manuscripts have "keep on having faith in...keep on having faith in."

Twin, Nathanael from Cana in Galilee, and the brothers
James and John,p were there, together with two other
disciples. 3Simon Peter said, "I'm going fishing!"

The others said, "We'll go with you." They went out
in their boat. But they didn't catch a thing that night.

4Early the next morning Jesus stood on the shore, but
the disciples didn't realise who he was. 5Jesus shouted,
"Friends, have you caught anything?"

"No!" they answered.

6So he told them, "Let your net down on the right side
of your boat, and you will catch some fish."

They did, and the net was so full of fish that they
couldn't drag it up into the boat.

7Jesus' favourite disciple told Peter, "It's the Lord!"
When Simon heard that it was the Lord, he put on the
clothes that he had taken off while he was working. Then
he jumped into the water. 8The boat was only about 100
metres from shore. So the other disciples stayed in the
boat and dragged in the net full of fish.

9When the disciples got out of the boat, they saw some
bread and a charcoal fire with fish on it. 10Jesus told his
disciples, "Bring some of the fish you just caught."
11Simon Peter got back into the boat and dragged the net
to shore. In it were 153 large fish, but still the net didn't
rip.

12Jesus said, "Come and eat!" But none of the disciples
dared ask who he was. They knew he was the Lord.
13Jesus took the bread in his hands and gave some of it to .
his disciples. He did the same with the fish. 14This was
the third time that Jesus appeared to his disciples after
he was raised from death.

Jesus and Peter

15When Jesus and his disciples had finished eating, he
asked, "Simon son of John, do you love me more than
the others do?"q

Simon Peter answered, "Yes, Lord, you know I do!"

"Then feed my lambs," Jesus said.

pthe brothers James and John: Greek "the two sons of Zebedee." qmore than
the others do?: Or "more than you love these things?"

¹⁶Jesus asked a second time, "Simon son of John, do you love me?"

Peter answered, "Yes, Lord, you know I love you!"

"Then take care of my sheep," Jesus told him.

¹⁷Jesus asked a third time, "Simon son of John, do you love me?"

Peter was hurt because Jesus had asked him three times if he loved him. So he told Jesus, "Lord, you know everything. You know I love you."

Jesus replied, "Feed my sheep. ¹⁸I tell you for certain that when you were a young man, you dressed yourself and went wherever you wanted to go. But when you are old, you will hold out your hands. Then others will wrap your belt around you and lead you where you don't want to go."

¹⁹Jesus said this to tell how Peter would die and bring honour to God. Then he said to Peter, "Follow me!"

Jesus and His Favourite Disciple

²⁰Peter turned and saw Jesus' favourite disciple following them. He was the same one who had sat next to Jesus at the meal and had asked, "Lord, who is going to betray you?" ²¹When Peter saw that disciple, he asked Jesus, "Lord, what about him?"

²²Jesus answered, "What is it to you, if I want him to live until I return? You must follow me." ²³So the rumour spread among the other disciples that this disciple wouldn't die. But Jesus didn't say he wouldn't die. He simply said, "What is it to you, if I want him to live until I return?"

²⁴This disciple is the one who told all of this. He wrote it down, and we know he is telling the truth.

²⁵Jesus did many other things. If they were all written in books, I don't suppose there would be room enough in the whole world for all the books.

ACTS
ABOUT THIS BOOK

This is the second book written by Luke. His first one is commonly known as the Gospel of Luke. In it he told "all that Jesus did and taught from the very first until he was taken up to heaven" (chapter 1.1, 2). In this book Luke continues the story by describing some of the struggles the disciples faced as they tried to obey the command of Jesus: "You will tell everyone about me in Jerusalem, in all Judea, in Samaria, and everywhere in the world" (1.8).

So many different countries are mentioned in Acts that the book may seem to have been written only to tell about the spread of the Christian message. But that is only part of the story. After Jesus was taken up to heaven, one of the big problems for his followers was deciding who could belong to God's people. And since Jesus and his first followers were Jews, it was only natural for many of them to think that his message was only for Jews. But in Acts the Spirit is always present to show that Jesus came to save both Jews and Gentiles, and that God wants followers from every nation and race to be part of his people.

The first conflict between Christians and Jews took place when some of the Jewish religious leaders rejected the message about Jesus (4.1-31; 7.1-59). But the most serious problems for the early church happened because the disciples at first failed to understand that anyone could become a follower of Jesus without first becoming a Jew. This began to change when Philip dared to take the message to the Samaritans (8.7-25), and when Peter went to the home of Cornelius, a captain in the Roman army (10.1-48).

Finally, Peter reported to the church in Jerusalem (11.1-18) and a meeting was held there (15.3-35) to discuss the question of who could become followers of Christ. Before the meeting was over, everyone agreed that the Spirit of God was leading them to reach out to Gentiles as well as Jews with the good news of Jesus.

The one who did the most for the spread of the faith was a man named Paul, and much of the book tells about his preaching among the Gentiles. Finally, he took the message to Rome, the world's most important city at that time (28.16-31). One of Luke's main reasons for writing was to show that nothing could keep the Christian message from spreading everywhere:

> For two years Paul stayed in a rented house and welcomed everyone who came to see him. He bravely preached about God's kingdom and taught about the Lord Jesus Christ, and no-one tried to stop him.
>
> (Chapter 28.30, 31)

A QUICK LOOK AT THIS BOOK

1 [1]Theophilus, I first wrote to you[a] about all that Jesus did and taught from the very first [2]until he was taken up to heaven. But before he was taken up, he gave orders to the apostles he had chosen with the help of the Holy Spirit.

[3]For 40 days after Jesus had suffered and died, he proved in many ways that he had been raised from death. He appeared to his apostles and spoke to them about God's kingdom. [4]While he was still with them, he said:

Don't leave Jerusalem yet. Wait here for the Father to give you the Holy Spirit, just as I told you he has

---

[a]I first wrote to you: The Gospel of Luke.

promised to do. ⁵John baptised with water, but in a few days you will be baptised with the Holy Spirit.

Jesus Is Taken to Heaven

⁶While the apostles were still with Jesus, they asked him, "Lord, are you now going to give Israel its own king again?"*b*

⁷Jesus said to them, "You don't need to know the time of those events that only the Father controls. ⁸But the Holy Spirit will come upon you and give you power. Then you will tell everyone about me in Jerusalem, in all Judea, in Samaria, and everywhere in the world." ⁹After Jesus had said this and while they were watching, he was taken up into a cloud. They couldn't see him, ¹⁰but as he went up, they kept looking up into the sky.

Suddenly two men dressed in white clothes were standing there beside them. ¹¹They said, "Why are you men from Galilee standing here and looking up into the sky? Jesus has been taken to heaven. But he will come back in the same way that you have seen him go."

Someone To Take the Place of Judas

¹²⁻¹³The Mount of Olives was about a kilometre from Jerusalem. The apostles who had gone there were Peter, John, James, Andrew, Philip, Thomas, Bartholomew, Matthew, James the son of Alphaeus, Simon, known as the Eager One,*c* and Judas the son of James.

After the apostles returned to the city, they went upstairs to the room where they had been staying.

¹⁴The apostles often met together and prayed with a single purpose in mind.*d* The women and Mary the mother of Jesus would meet with them, and so would his brothers. ¹⁵One day there were about 120 of the Lord's followers meeting together, and Peter stood up to speak to them. ¹⁶⁻¹⁷He said:

My friends, long ago by the power of the Holy Spirit,

---

*b*are you now going to give Israel its own king again?: Or "Are you now going to rule Israel as its king?"   *c*known as the Eager One: The Greek text has "Zealot", a name later given to the members of a Jewish group which resisted and fought against the Romans.   *d*met together and prayed with a single purpose in mind: Or "met together in a special place for prayer."

David said something about Judas, and what he said has now happened. Judas was one of us and had worked with us, but he brought the mob to arrest Jesus. [18]Then Judas bought some land with the money he was given for doing that evil thing. He fell head first into the field. His body burst open, and all his insides came out. [19]When the people of Jerusalem found out about this, they called the place Akeldama, which in the local language means "Field of Blood."

[20]In the book of Psalms it says,

"Leave his house empty,
   and don't let anyone live there."

It also says,

"Let someone else have his job."

[21-22]So we need someone else to help us tell others that Jesus has been raised from death. He must also be one of the men who was with us from the very beginning. He must have been with us from the time the Lord Jesus was baptised by John until the day he was taken to heaven.

[23]Two men were suggested: One of them was Joseph Barsabbas, known as Justus, and the other was Matthias. [24]Then they all prayed, "Lord, you know what everyone is like! Show us the one you have chosen [25]to be an apostle and to serve in place of Judas, who got what he deserved." [26]They drew names, and Matthias was chosen to join the group of the eleven apostles.

The Coming of the Holy Spirit

2 [1]On the day of Pentecost[e] all the Lord's followers were together in one place. [2]Suddenly there was a noise from heaven like the sound of a mighty wind! It filled the house where they were meeting. [3]Then they saw what looked like fiery tongues moving in all directions, and a tongue came and settled on each person there. [4]The Holy Spirit took control of everyone, and they began speaking whatever languages the Spirit let them speak.

---

[e]Pentecost: A Jewish festival that came 50 days after Passover and celebrated the wheat harvest. Jews later celebrated Pentecost as the time when they were given the Law of Moses.

⁵Many religious Jews from every country in the world were living in Jerusalem. ⁶And when they heard this noise, a crowd gathered. But they were surprised, because they were hearing everything in their own languages. ⁷They were excited and amazed, and said:

Don't all these who are speaking come from Galilee? ⁸Then why do we hear them speaking our very own languages? ⁹Some of us are from Parthia, Media, and Elam. Others are from Mesopotamia, Judea, Cappadocia, Pontus, Asia, ¹⁰Phrygia, Pamphylia, Egypt, parts of Libya near Cyrene, Rome, ¹¹⁻¹²Crete, and Arabia. Some of us were born Jews, and others of us have chosen to be Jews. Yet we all hear them using our own languages to tell the wonderful things God has done.

Everyone was excited and confused. Some of them even kept asking each other, "What does all this mean?" ¹³Others made fun of the Lord's followers and said, "They are drunk."

Peter Speaks to the Crowd

¹⁴Peter stood with the eleven apostles and spoke in a loud and clear voice to the crowd:

Friends and everyone else living in Jerusalem, listen carefully to what I have to say! ¹⁵You are wrong to think that these people are drunk. After all, it's only nine o'clock in the morning. ¹⁶But this is what God had the prophet Joel say,

¹⁷ "When the last days come,
    I will give my Spirit to everyone.
Your sons and daughters will prophesy.
Your young men will see visions,
        and your old men will have dreams.
¹⁸   In those days I will give my Spirit
    to my servants, both men and women,
        and they will prophesy.

¹⁹ I will work miracles in the sky above
    and wonders on the earth below.
        There will be blood and fire and clouds of smoke.
²⁰ The sun will turn dark,

and the moon will be as red as blood
before the great and wonderful day
of the Lord appears.
21   Then the Lord will save everyone
who asks for his help."
22Now, listen to what I have to say about Jesus from
Nazareth. God proved that he sent Jesus to you by
having him work miracles, wonders, and signs. All of
you know this. 23God had already planned and decided
that Jesus would be handed over to you. So you took
him and had evil men put him to death on a cross.
24But God set him free from death and raised him to
life. Death couldn't hold him in its power. 25What
David said are really the words of Jesus,
"I always see the Lord near me,
and I will not be afraid
with him at my right side.
26 Because of this, my heart will be glad,
my words will be joyful, and I will live in hope.
27 The Lord won't leave me in the grave.
I am his holy one,
and he won't let my body decay.
28 He has shown me the path to life,
and he makes me glad by being near me."
29My friends, it is right for me to speak to you about
our ancestor David. He died and was buried, and his
tomb is still here. 30But David was a prophet, and he
knew that God had made a promise he wouldn't break.
He had told David that someone from his own family
would some day be king.
31David knew this would happen, and so he told us
that Christ would be raised to life. He said that God
wouldn't leave him in the grave or let his body decay.
32All of us can tell you that God has raised Jesus to life!
33Jesus was taken up to sit at the right side[f] of God,
and he was given the Holy Spirit, just as the Father
had promised. Jesus is also the one who has given the
Spirit to us, and that's what you are now seeing and
hearing.

[f]right side: The place of honour and power.

34David didn't go up to heaven. So he wasn't talking about himself when he said, "The Lord told my Lord to sit at his right side, 35until he made my Lord's enemies into a footstool for him." 36Everyone in Israel should then know for certain that God has made Jesus both Lord and Christ, even though you put him to death on a cross.

37When the people heard this, they were very upset. They asked Peter and the other apostles, "Friends, what shall we do?"

38Peter said, "Turn back to God! Be baptised in the name of Jesus Christ, so that your sins will be forgiven. Then you will be given the Holy Spirit. 39This promise is for you and your children. It is for everyone our Lord God will choose, no matter where they live."

40Peter told them many other things as well. Then he said, "I beg you to save yourselves from what will happen to all these evil people." 41On that day about 3000 believed his message and were baptised. 42They spent their time learning from the apostles, and they were like family to each other. They also broke breadg and prayed together.

Life among the Lord's Followers

43Everyone was amazed by the many miracles and wonders that the apostles worked. 44All the Lord's followers often met together, and they shared everything they had. 45They would sell their property and possessions and give the money to whoever needed it. 46Day after day they met together in the temple. They broke bread together in different homes and shared their food happily and freely, 47while praising God. Everyone liked them, and each day the Lord added to their group others who were being saved.

Peter and John Heal a Lame Man

3 1The time of prayerh was about three o'clock in the afternoon, and Peter and John were going into the

---

gbroke bread: They ate together and celebrated the Lord's Supper. hThe time of prayer: Many of the Jewish people prayed in their homes at regular times each day (see Daniel 6.11), and on special occasions they prayed in the temple.

temple. [2]A man who had been born lame was being carried to the temple door. Each day he was placed beside this door, known as the Beautiful Gate. He sat there and begged from the people who were going in.

[3]The man saw Peter and John entering the temple, and he asked them for money. [4]But they looked straight at him and said, "Look up at us!"

[5]The man stared at them and thought he was going to get something. [6]But Peter said, "I haven't got any silver or gold! But I will give you what I do have. In the name of Jesus Christ from Nazareth, get up and start walking." [7]Peter then took him by the right hand and helped him up.

At once the man's feet and ankles became strong, [8]and he jumped up and started walking. He went with Peter and John into the temple, walking and jumping and praising God. [9]Everyone saw him walking around and praising God. [10]They knew that he was the beggar who had been lying beside the Beautiful Gate, and they were completely surprised. They couldn't imagine what had happened to the man.

Peter Speaks in the Temple

[11]While the man kept holding on to Peter and John, the whole crowd ran to them in amazement at the place known as Solomon's Porch.[i] [12]Peter saw that a crowd had gathered, and he said:

Friends, why are you surprised at what has happened? Why are you staring at us? Do you think we have some power of our own? Do you think we were able to make this man walk because we are so religious? [13]The God that Abraham, Isaac, Jacob, and our other ancestors worshipped has brought honour to his Servant[j] Jesus. He is the one you betrayed. You turned against him when he was being tried by Pilate, even though Pilate wanted to set him free.

[14]You rejected Jesus, who was holy and good. You asked for a murderer to be set free, [15]and you killed the

---

[i]Solomon's Porch: A public place with tall columns along the east side of the temple. [j]Servant: Or "Son."

one who leads people to life. But God raised him from death, and all of us can tell you what he has done. ¹⁶You see this man, and you know him. He put his faith in the name of Jesus and was made strong. Faith in Jesus made this man completely well while everyone was watching.

¹⁷My friends, I am sure that you and your leaders didn't know what you were doing. ¹⁸But God had his prophets say that his Messiah would suffer, and now he has kept that promise. ¹⁹So turn to God! Give up your sins, and you will be forgiven. ²⁰Then that time will come when the Lord will give you fresh strength. He will send you Jesus, his chosen Messiah. ²¹But Jesus must stay in heaven until God makes all things new, just as his holy prophets promised long ago.

²²Moses said, "The Lord your God will choose one of your own people to be a prophet, just as he chose me. Listen to everything he tells you. ²³No-one who disobeys that prophet will be one of God's people any longer."

²⁴Samuel and all the other prophets who came later also spoke about what is now happening. ²⁵You are really the ones God told his prophets to speak to. And you were given the promise that God made to your ancestors. He said to Abraham, "All nations on earth will be blessed because of someone from your family." ²⁶God sent his chosen Son[k] to you first, because God wanted to bless you and make each one of you turn away from your sins.

Peter and John Are Brought in Front of the Council

4 ¹The apostles were still talking to the people, when some priests, the captain of the temple guard, and some Sadducees arrived. ²These men were angry because the apostles were teaching the people that the dead would be raised from death, just as Jesus had been raised from death. ³It was already late in the afternoon, and they arrested Peter and John and put them in jail for the

---

[k]Son: Or "Servant."

night. ⁴But a lot of people who had heard the message believed it. So by now there were about 5000 followers of the Lord.

⁵The next morning the leaders, the elders, and the teachers of the Law of Moses met in Jerusalem. ⁶The high priest Annas was there, as well as Caiaphas, John, Alexander, and other members of the high priest's family. ⁷They brought in Peter and John and made them stand in the middle while they questioned them. They asked, "By what power and in whose name have you done this?"

⁸Peter was filled with the Holy Spirit and told the nation's leaders and the elders:

⁹You are questioning us today about a kind deed in which a crippled man was healed. ¹⁰But there is something we must tell you and everyone else in Israel. This man is standing here completely well because of the power of Jesus Christ from Nazareth. You put Jesus to death on a cross, but God raised him to life. ¹¹He is the stone that you builders thought was worthless, and now he is the most important stone of all. ¹²Only Jesus has the power to save! His name is the only one in all the world that can save anyone.

¹³The officials were amazed to see how brave Peter and John were, and they knew that these two apostles were only ordinary men and not well educated. The officials were certain that these men had been with Jesus. ¹⁴But they couldn't deny what had happened. The man who had been healed was standing there with the apostles.

¹⁵The officials commanded them to leave the council room. Then the officials said to each other, ¹⁶"What can we do with these men? Everyone in Jerusalem knows about this miracle, and we can't say it didn't happen. ¹⁷But to keep this thing from spreading, we'll warn them never again to speak to anyone about the name of Jesus." ¹⁸So they called the two apostles back in and told them that they must never, for any reason, teach anything about the name of Jesus.

¹⁹Peter and John answered, "Do you think God wants us to obey you or to obey him? ²⁰We can't keep quiet about what we've seen and heard."

21-22 The officials couldn't find any reason to punish Peter and John. So they threatened them and let them go. The man who was healed by this miracle was more than 40 years old, and everyone was praising God for what had happened.

Peter and Others Pray for Courage

23 As soon as Peter and John had been set free, they went back and told the others everything that the chief priests and the leaders had said to them. 24 When the rest of the Lord's followers heard this, they prayed together and said:

Master, you created heaven and earth, the sea, and everything in them. 25 And by the Holy Spirit you spoke to our ancestor David. He was your servant, and you told him to say:

"Why are all the Gentiles so furious?
Why do people make foolish plans?
26   The kings of earth prepare for war,
and the rulers join together
against the Lord and his Messiah."

27 Here in Jerusalem, Herod[l] and Pontius Pilate got together with the Gentiles and the people of Israel. Then they turned against your holy Servant[m] Jesus, your chosen Messiah. 28 They did what you in your power and wisdom had already decided would happen.

29 Lord, listen to their threats! We are your servants. So make us brave enough to speak your message. 30 Show your mighty power, as we heal people and work miracles and wonders in the name of your holy Servant Jesus.

31 After they had prayed, the meeting place shook. They were all filled with the Holy Spirit and bravely spoke God's message.

Sharing Possessions

32 The group of followers all felt the same way about everything. None of them claimed that their possessions

---

[l]Herod: Herod Antipas, the son of Herod the Great.   [m]Servant: Or "Son".

were their own, and they shared everything they had with each other. [33]In a powerful way the apostles told everyone that the Lord Jesus was now alive. God greatly blessed his followers,[n] [34]and no-one went in need of anything. Everyone who owned land or houses would sell them and bring the money [35]to the apostles. Then they would give the money to anyone who needed it.

[36-37]Joseph was one of the followers who had sold a piece of property and brought the money to the apostles. He was a Levite from Cyprus, and the apostles called him Barnabas, which means "one who encourages others."

Peter Condemns Ananias and Sapphira

5 [1]Ananias and his wife Sapphira also sold a piece of property. [2]But they agreed to cheat and keep some of the money for themselves.

So when Ananias took the rest of the money to the apostles, [3]Peter said, "Why has Satan made you keep back some of the money from the sale of the property? Why have you lied to the Holy Spirit? [4]The property was yours before you sold it, and even after you sold it, the money was still yours. What made you do such a thing? You didn't lie to people. You lied to God!"

[5]As soon as Ananias heard this, he dropped dead, and everyone who heard about it was frightened. [6]Some young men came in and wrapped up his body. Then they took it out and buried it.

[7]Three hours later Sapphira came in, but she didn't know what had happened to her husband. [8]Peter asked her, "Tell me, did you sell the property for this amount?"

"Yes," she answered, "that's the amount."

[9]Then Peter said, "Why did the two of you agree to test the Lord's Spirit? The men who buried Ananias are by the door, and they will carry you out!" [10]At once she fell at Peter's feet and died.

When the young men came back in, they found Sapphira lying there dead. So they carried her out and buried her beside her husband. [11]The church members

[n]God greatly blessed his followers: Or "Everyone highly respected his followers."

were afraid, and so was everyone else who heard what had happened.

Peter's Unusual Power

12 The apostles worked many miracles and wonders among the people. All of the Lord's followers often met in the part of the temple known as Solomon's Porch.º
13 No-one outside their group dared join them, even though everyone liked them very much.

14 Many men and women started having faith in the Lord. 15 Then sick people were brought out to the road and placed on beds and mats. It was hoped that Peter would walk past, and his shadow would fall on them and heal them. 16 A lot of people living in the towns near Jerusalem brought those who were sick or troubled by evil spirits, and they were all healed.

Trouble for the Apostles

17 The high priest and all the other Sadducees who were with him became jealous. 18 They arrested the apostles and put them in the city jail. 19 But that night an angel from the Lord opened the doors of the jail and led the apostles out. The angel said, 20 "Go to the temple and tell the people everything about this new life." 21 So they went into the temple before sunrise and started teaching.

The high priest and his men called together their council, which included all of Israel's leaders. Then they ordered the apostles to be brought to them from the jail. 22 The temple police who were sent to the jail didn't find the apostles. They returned and said, 23 "We found the jail locked tight and the guards standing at the doors. But when we opened the doors and went in, we didn't find anyone there." 24 The captain of the temple police and the chief priests listened to their report, but they didn't know what to think about it.

25 Just then someone came in and said, "Right now those men you put in jail are in the temple, teaching the people!" 26 The captain went with some of the temple police and brought the apostles back. But they didn't use

ºSolomon's Porch: See the note at 3.11.

force. They were afraid that the people might start throwing stones at them.

27 When the apostles were brought before the council, the high priest said to them, 28 "We told you plainly not to teach in the name of Jesus. But look what you've done! You've been teaching all over Jerusalem, and you're trying to blame us for his death."

29 Peter and the apostles replied:

We don't obey people. We obey God. 30 You killed Jesus by nailing him to a cross. But the God our ancestors worshipped raised him to life 31 and made him our Leader and Saviour. Then God gave him a place at his right side,*p* so that the people of Israel would turn back to him and be forgiven. 32 We are here to tell you about all this, and so is the Holy Spirit, who is God's gift to everyone who obeys God.

33 When the council members heard this, they became so angry that they wanted to kill the apostles. 34 But one of the members was the Pharisee Gamaliel, a highly respected teacher. He ordered the apostles to be taken out of the room for a little while. 35 Then he said to the council:

People of Israel, be careful what you do with these men. 36 Not long ago Theudas claimed to be someone important, and about 400 men joined him. But he was killed. All his followers were scattered, and that was the end of that.

37 Later, when the people of our nation were being counted, Judas from Galilee showed up. A lot of people followed him, but he was killed, and all his followers were scattered.

38 So I advise you to stay away from these men. Leave them alone. If what they are planning is something of their own doing, it will fail. 39 But if God is behind it, you can't stop it anyway, unless you want to fight against God.

The council members agreed with what he said, 40 and they called the apostles back in. They had them beaten with a whip and warned them not to speak in the name of Jesus. Then they let them go.

*p*right side: See the note at 2.33.

41The apostles left the council and were happy, because God had considered them worthy to suffer for the sake of Jesus. 42Every day they spent time in the temple and in one home after another. They never stopped teaching and telling the good news that Jesus is the Messiah.

Seven Leaders for the Church

6 1A lot of people were now becoming followers of the Lord. But some of the ones who spoke Greek started complaining about the ones who spoke Aramaic. They complained that the Greek-speaking widows were not given their share when the food supplies were handed out each day.

2The twelve apostles called the whole group of followers together and said, "We shouldn't give up preaching God's message in order to serve at tables.q 3My friends, choose seven men who are respected and wise and filled with God's Spirit. We will put them in charge of these things. 4We can spend our time praying and serving God by preaching."

5This suggestion pleased everyone, and they began by choosing Stephen. He had great faith and was filled with the Holy Spirit. Then they chose Philip, Prochorus, Nicanor, Timon, Parmenas, and also Nicolaus, who worshipped with the Jewish peopler in Antioch. 6These men were brought to the apostles. Then the apostles prayed and placed their hands on the men to show that they had been chosen to do this work. 7God's message spread, and many more people in Jerusalem became followers. Even a large number of priests put their faith in the Lord.

Stephen Is Arrested

8God gave Stephen the power to work great miracles and wonders among the people. 9But some Jews from Cyrene and Alexandria were members of a group who

---

qto serve at tables: This may mean either that they were in charge of handing out food to the widows or that they were in charge of the money, since the Greek word "table" may also mean "bank." rworshipped with the Jewish people: This translates the Greek word "proselyte" that means a Gentile who had accepted the Jewish religion.

called themselves "Free Men."[s] They started arguing with Stephen. Some others from Cilicia and Asia also argued with him. [10]But they were no match for Stephen, who spoke with the great wisdom that the Spirit gave him. [11]So they talked some men into saying, "We heard Stephen say terrible things against Moses and God!"

[12]They turned the people and their leaders and the teachers of the Law of Moses against Stephen. Then they all grabbed Stephen and dragged him in front of the council.

[13]Some men agreed to tell lies about Stephen, and they said, "This man keeps on saying terrible things about this holy temple and the Law of Moses. [14]We've heard him claim that Jesus from Nazareth will destroy this place and change the customs that Moses gave us." [15]Then all the council members stared at Stephen. They saw that his face looked like the face of an angel.

Stephen's Speech

7 [1]The high priest asked Stephen, "Are they telling the truth about you?"

[2]Stephen answered:

Friends, listen to me. Our glorious God appeared to our ancestor Abraham while he was still in Mesopotamia, before he had moved to Haran. [3]God told him, "Leave your country and your relatives and go to a land that I will show you." [4]Then Abraham left the land of the Chaldeans and settled in Haran.

After his father died, Abraham came and settled in this land where you now live. [5]God didn't give him any part of it, not even a square metre. But God did promise to give it to him and his family for ever, even though Abraham didn't have any children. [6]God said that Abraham's descendants would live for a while in a foreign land. There they would be slaves and would be mistreated for 400 years. [7]But he also said, "I will punish the nation that makes them slaves. Then later they will come and worship me in this place."

[s]*Free Men:* A group of Jewish men who had once been slaves, but had been freed.

⁸God said to Abraham, "Every son in each family must be circumcised to show that you have kept your agreement with me." So when Isaac was eight days old, Abraham circumcised him. Later, Isaac circumcised his son Jacob, and Jacob circumcised his twelve sons. ⁹These men were our ancestors.

Joseph was also one of our famous ancestors. His brothers were jealous of him and sold him as a slave to be taken to Egypt. But God was with him ¹⁰and rescued him from all his troubles. God made him so wise that the Egyptian king Pharaohᶦ thought highly of him. Pharaoh even made Joseph governor over Egypt and put him in charge of everything he owned.

¹¹Everywhere in Egypt and Canaan the grain crops failed. There was terrible suffering, and our ancestors couldn't find enough to eat. ¹²But when Jacob heard that there was grain in Egypt, he sent our ancestors there for the first time. ¹³It was on their second trip that Joseph told his brothers who he was, and Pharaoh learnt about Joseph's family.

¹⁴Joseph sent for his father and his relatives. In all, there were 75 of them. ¹⁵His father went to Egypt and died there, just as our ancestors did. ¹⁶Later their bodies were taken back to Shechem and placed in the tomb that Abraham had bought from the sons of Hamor.

¹⁷Finally, the time came for God to do what he had promised Abraham. By then the number of our people in Egypt had greatly increased. ¹⁸Another king was ruling Egypt, and he didn't know anything about Joseph. ¹⁹He tricked our ancestors and was cruel to them. He even made them leave their babies outside, so they would die.

²⁰During this time Moses was born. He was a very beautiful child, and for three months his parents took care of him in their home. ²¹Then when they were forced to leave him outside, the king's daughter found him and raised him as her own son. ²²Moses was given the best education in Egypt. He was a strong man and a powerful speaker.

ᶦPharaoh: A Hebrew word sometimes used for the title of the King of Egypt.

²³When Moses was 40 years old, he wanted to help the Israelites because they were his own people. ²⁴One day he saw an Egyptian mistreating one of them. So he rescued the man and killed the Egyptian. ²⁵Moses thought the rest of his people would realise that God was going to use him to set them free. But they didn't understand.

²⁶The next day Moses saw two of his own people fighting, and he tried to make them stop. He said, "Men, you are both Israelites. Why are you so cruel to each other?"

²⁷But the man who had started the fight pushed Moses aside and asked, "Who made you our ruler and judge? ²⁸Are you going to kill me, just as you killed that Egyptian yesterday?" ²⁹When Moses heard this, he ran away to live in the country of Midian. His two sons were born there.

³⁰Forty years later, an angel appeared to Moses from a burning bush in the desert near Mount Sinai. ³¹Moses was surprised by what he saw. He went closer to get a better look, and the Lord said, ³²"I am the God who was worshipped by your ancestors, Abraham, Isaac, and Jacob." Moses started shaking all over and didn't dare to look at the bush.

³³The Lord said to him, "Take off your sandals. The place where you are standing is holy. ³⁴With my own eyes I have seen the suffering of my people in Egypt. I have heard their groans and have come down to rescue them. Now I am sending you back to Egypt."

³⁵This was the same Moses that the people rejected by saying, "Who made you our leader and judge?" God's angel had spoken to Moses from the bush. And God had even sent the angel to help Moses rescue the people and be their leader.

³⁶In Egypt and at the Red Sea^u and in the desert, Moses rescued the people by working miracles and wonders for 40 years. ³⁷Moses is the one who told the

---

^uRed Sea: This name comes from the Bible of the early Christians, a translation made into Greek about 200 BC. It refers to the body of water that the Israelites crossed and was one of the marshes or fresh water lakes near the eastern part of the Nile Delta, where they lived and where the towns of Exodus 13.17—14.9 were located.

people of Israel, "God will choose one of your people to be a prophet, just as he chose me." [38]Moses brought our people together in the desert, and the angel spoke to him on Mount Sinai. There he was given these life-giving words to pass on to us. [39]But our ancestors refused to obey Moses. They rejected him and wanted to go back to Egypt.

[40]The people said to Aaron, "Make some gods to lead us! Moses led us out of Egypt, but we don't know what's happened to him now." [41]Then they made an idol in the shape of a calf. They offered sacrifices to the idol and were pleased with what they had done.

[42]God turned his back on his people and left them. Then they worshipped the stars in the sky, just as it says in the Book of the Prophets, "People of Israel, you didn't offer sacrifices and offerings to me during those 40 years in the desert. [43]Instead, you carried the tent where the god Molech is worshipped, and you took along the star of your god Rephan. You made those idols and worshipped them. So now I will have you carried off beyond Babylonia."

[44]The tent where our ancestors worshipped God was with them in the desert. This was the same tent that God had commanded Moses to make. And it was made like the model that Moses had seen. [45]Later it was given to our ancestors, and they took it with them when they went with Joshua. They carried the tent along as they took over the land from those people that God had chased out for them. Our ancestors used this tent until the time of King David. [46]He pleased God and asked him if he could build a house of worship for the people[v] of Israel. [47]And it was finally King Solomon who built a house for God.[w]

[48]But the Most High God doesn't live in houses made by humans. It is just as the prophet said, when he spoke for the Lord,

[49] "Heaven is my throne,
        and the earth is my footstool.
    What kind of house will you build for me?
    In what place will I rest?

---

[v]the people: Some manuscripts have "God."   [w]God: Or "the people."

⁵⁰   I have made everything."

⁵¹You stubborn and hard-headed people! You are always fighting against the Holy Spirit, just as your ancestors did. ⁵²Is there one prophet that your ancestors didn't mistreat? They killed the prophets who spoke about the coming of the One Who Obeys God.ˣ And now you have turned against him and killed him. ⁵³Angels gave you God's Law, but you still don't obey it.

Stephen Is Stoned To Death

⁵⁴When the council members heard Stephen's speech, they were angry and furious. ⁵⁵But Stephen was filled with the Holy Spirit. He looked towards heaven, where he saw our glorious God and Jesus standing at his right side.ʸ ⁵⁶Then Stephen said, "I see heaven open and the Son of Man standing at the right side of God!"

⁵⁷The council members shouted and covered their ears. At once they all attacked Stephen ⁵⁸and dragged him out of the city. Then they started throwing stones at him. The men who had brought charges against him put their coats at the feet of a young man named Saul.ᶻ

⁵⁹As Stephen was being stoned to death, he called out, "Lord Jesus, please welcome me!" ⁶⁰He knelt down and shouted, "Lord, don't blame them for what they have done." Then he died.

8 ¹⁻²Saul approved the stoning of Stephen. Some faithful followers of the Lord buried Stephen and mourned very much for him.

Saul Makes Trouble for the Church

At that time the church in Jerusalem suffered terribly. All of the Lord's followers, except the apostles, were scattered everywhere in Judea and Samaria. ³Saul started making a lot of trouble for the church. He went from house to house, arresting men and women and putting them in jail.

ˣOne Who Obeys God: That is, Jesus.   ʸstanding at his right side: The "right side" is the place of honour and power. "Standing" may mean that Jesus is welcoming Stephen (see verse 59). ᶻSaul: Better known as Paul, who became a famous follower of Jesus.

The Good News Is Preached in Samaria

⁴The Lord's followers who had been scattered went from place to place, telling the good news. ⁵Philip went to the city of Samaria and told the people about Christ. ⁶They crowded around Philip because they were eager to hear what he was saying and to see him work miracles. ⁷Many people with evil spirits were healed, and the spirits went out of them with a shout. A lot of crippled and lame people were also healed. ⁸Everyone in that city was very glad because of what was happening.

⁹For some time a man named Simon had lived in the city of Samaria and had amazed the people. He practised witchcraft and claimed to be somebody great. ¹⁰Everyone, rich and poor, crowded around him. They said, "This man is the power of God called 'The Great Power.' "

¹¹For a long time, Simon had used witchcraft to amaze the people, and they kept crowding around him. ¹²But when they believed what Philip was saying about God's kingdom and about the name of Jesus Christ, they were all baptised. ¹³Even Simon believed and was baptised. He stayed close to Philip, because he marvelled at all the miracles and wonders.

¹⁴The apostles in Jerusalem heard that some people in Samaria had accepted God's message, and they sent Peter and John. ¹⁵When the two apostles arrived, they prayed that the people would be given the Holy Spirit. ¹⁶Before this, the Holy Spirit had not been given to anyone in Samaria, though some of them had been baptised in the name of the Lord Jesus. ¹⁷Peter and John then placed their hands on everyone who had faith in the Lord, and they were given the Holy Spirit.

¹⁸Simon noticed that the Spirit was given only when the apostles placed their hands on the people. So he brought money ¹⁹and said to Peter and John, "Let me have this power too! Then anyone I place my hands on will also be given the Holy Spirit."

²⁰Peter said to him, "You and your money will both end up in hell if you think you can buy God's gift! ²¹You don't have any part in this, and God sees that your heart isn't right. ²²Get rid of these evil thoughts and ask God to forgive you. ²³I can see that you are jealous and bound

by your evil ways."

²⁴Simon said, "Please pray to the Lord, so that what you said won't happen to me."

²⁵After Peter and John had preached about the Lord, they returned to Jerusalem. On their way they told the good news in many villages of Samaria.

Philip and an Ethiopian Official

²⁶The Lord's angel said to Philip, "Go south*ᵃ* along the desert road that leads from Jerusalem to Gaza."*ᵇ* ²⁷So Philip left.

An important Ethiopian official happened to be going along that road in his chariot. He was the chief treasurer for Candace, the Queen of Ethiopia. The official had gone to Jerusalem to worship ²⁸and was now on his way home. He was sitting in his chariot, reading the book of the prophet Isaiah.

²⁹The Spirit told Philip to catch up with the chariot. ³⁰Philip ran up close and heard the man reading aloud from the book of Isaiah. Philip asked him, "Do you understand what you are reading?"

³¹The official answered, "How can I understand unless someone helps me?" He then invited Philip to come up and sit beside him.

³²The man was reading the passage that said,

"He was led like a sheep on its way to be killed.
He was silent as a lamb whose wool is being shorn,
      and he didn't say a word.
³³ He was treated like a nobody
      and didn't receive a fair trial.
How can he have children,
      if his life is snatched away?"

³⁴The official said to Philip, "Tell me, was the prophet talking about himself or about someone else?" ³⁵So Philip began at this place in the Scriptures and explained the good news about Jesus.

³⁶⁻³⁷As they were going along the road, they came to a

ᵃGo south: Or "About midday go." *ᵇthe desert road that leads from Jerusalem to Gaza:* Or "the road that leads from Jerusalem to Gaza in the desert."

place where there was some water. The official said,
"Look! Here's some water. Why can't I be baptised?"*c* 38He
ordered the chariot to stop. Then they both went down
into the water, and Philip baptised him.

39After they had come out of the water, the Lord's
Spirit took Philip away. The official never saw him again,
but he was very happy as he went on his way.

40Philip later appeared in Azotus. He went from town
to town, all the way to Caesarea, telling people about
Jesus.

Saul Becomes a Follower of the Lord
(Acts 22.6-16; 26.12-18)

9 1Saul kept on threatening to kill the Lord's followers.
He even went to the high priest 2and asked for letters
to the Jewish leaders in Damascus. He did this because
he wanted to arrest and take to Jerusalem any man or
woman who had accepted the Lord's Way.*d* 3When Saul
had almost reached Damascus, a bright light from heaven
suddenly flashed around him. 4He fell to the ground and
heard a voice that said, "Saul! Saul! Why are you so cruel
to me?"

5"Who are you?" Saul asked.

"I am Jesus," the Lord answered. "I am the one you are
so cruel to. 6Now get up and go into the city, where you
will be told what to do."

7The men with Saul stood there speechless. They had
heard the voice, but they hadn't seen anyone. 8Saul got
up from the ground, and when he opened his eyes, he
couldn't see a thing. Someone then led him by the hand
to Damascus, 9and for three days he was blind and didn't
eat or drink.

10A follower named Ananias lived in Damascus, and the
Lord spoke to him in a vision. Ananias answered, "Lord,
here I am."

11The Lord said to him, "Get up and go to the house of

---

cWhy can't I be baptised: Some manuscripts add, "Philip replied, 'You can, if
you believe with all your heart.' The official answered, 'I believe that Jesus
Christ is the Son of God.' " *daccepted the Lord's Way:* In the book of Acts,
this means to become a follower of the Lord Jesus.

Judas on Straight Street. When you get there, you will find a man named Saul from the city of Tarsus. Saul is praying, [12]and he has seen a vision. He saw a man named Ananias coming to him and putting his hands on him, so that he could see again."

[13]Ananias replied, "Lord, a lot of people have told me about the terrible things this man has done to your followers in Jerusalem. [14]Now the chief priests have given him the power to come here and arrest anyone who worships in your name."

[15]The Lord said to Ananias, "Go! I have chosen him to tell foreigners, kings, and the people of Israel about me. [16]I will show him how much he must suffer for worshipping in my name."

[17]Ananias left and went into the house where Saul was staying. Ananias placed his hands on him and said, "Saul, the Lord Jesus has sent me. He is the same one who appeared to you along the road. He wants you to be able to see and to be filled with the Holy Spirit."

[18]Suddenly something like fish scales fell from Saul's eyes, and he could see. He got up and was baptised. [19]Then he ate and felt much better.

Saul Preaches in Damascus

For several days Saul stayed with the Lord's followers in Damascus. [20]Soon he went to the Jewish meeting places and started telling people that Jesus is the Son of God. [21]Everyone who heard Saul was amazed and said, "Isn't this the man who caused so much trouble for those people in Jerusalem who worship in the name of Jesus? Didn't he come here to arrest them and take them to the chief priests?"

[22]Saul preached with such power that he completely confused the Jewish people in Damascus, as he tried to show them that Jesus is the Messiah.

[23]Later some of them made plans to kill Saul, [24]but he found out about it. He learnt that they were guarding the gates of the city day and night in order to kill him. [25]Then one night his followers let him down over the city wall in a large basket.

Saul in Jerusalem

26When Saul arrived in Jerusalem, he tried to join the followers. But they were all afraid of him, because they didn't believe he was a true follower. 27Then Barnabas helped him by taking him to the apostles. He explained how Saul had seen the Lord and how the Lord had spoken to him. Barnabas also said that when Saul was in Damascus, he had spoken bravely in the name of Jesus.

28Saul moved about freely with the followers in Jerusalem and told everyone about the Lord. 29He was always arguing with the Jews who spoke Greek, and so they tried to kill him. 30But the followers found out about this and took Saul to Caesarea. From there they sent him to the city of Tarsus.

31The church in Judea, Galilee, and Samaria now had a time of peace and kept on worshipping the Lord. The church became stronger, as the Holy Spirit encouraged it and helped it grow.

Peter Heals Aeneas

32While Peter was travelling from place to place, he visited the Lord's followers who lived in the town of Lydda. 33There he met a man named Aeneas, who for eight years had been sick in bed and couldn't move. 34Peter said to Aeneas, "Jesus Christ has healed you! Get up and make your bed."e Straight away he stood up.

35Many people in the towns of Lydda and Sharon saw Aeneas and became followers of the Lord.

Peter Brings Dorcas Back To Life

36In Joppa there was a follower named Tabitha. Her Greek name was Dorcas, which means "deer." She was always doing good things for people and had given much to the poor. 37But she got sick and died, and her body was washed and placed in an upstairs room. 38Joppa wasn't far from Lydda, and the followers heard that Peter was there. They sent two men to say to him, "Please come with us as quickly as you can!" 39Straight away, Peter went with them.

eand make up your bed: Or "and make something to eat."

The men took Peter upstairs into the room. Many
widows were there crying. They showed him the coats
and clothes that Dorcas had made while she was still
alive.

⁴⁰After Peter had sent everyone out of the room, he
knelt down and prayed. Then he turned to the body of
Dorcas and said, "Tabitha, get up!" The woman opened
her eyes, and when she saw Peter, she sat up. ⁴¹He took
her by the hand and helped her to her feet.

Peter called in the widows and the other followers and
showed them that Dorcas had been raised from death.
⁴²Everyone in Joppa heard what had happened, and many
of them put their faith in the Lord. ⁴³Peter stayed on for
a while in Joppa in the house of a man named Simon,
who made leather.

Peter and Cornelius

10 ¹In Caesarea there was a man named Cornelius,
who was the captain of a group of soldiers called
"The Italian Unit." ²Cornelius was a very religious man.
He worshipped God, and so did everyone else who lived
in his house. He had given a lot of money to the poor
and was always praying to God.

³One afternoon at about three o'clock,ᶠ Cornelius had
a vision. He saw an angel from God coming to him and
calling him by name. ⁴Cornelius was surprised and stared
at the angel. Then he asked, "What's this all about?"

The angel answered, "God has heard your prayers and
knows about your gifts to the poor. ⁵Now send some men
to Joppa for a man named Simon Peter. ⁶He is visiting
Simon the leather maker, who lives in a house near the
sea." ⁷After saying this, the angel left.

Cornelius called in two of his servants and one of his
soldiers who worshipped God. ⁸He explained everything
to them and sent them off to Joppa.

⁹The next day about midday these men were coming
near Joppa. Peter went up on the roofᵍ of the house to

ᶠat about three o'clock: Probably while he was praying (see 3.1 and the note
there).   ᵍroof: In Palestine the houses usually had a flat roof. Stairs on the
outside led up to the roof, which was made of beams and boards covered with
packed earth.

pray [10]and became very hungry. While the food was being prepared, he fell sound asleep and had a vision. [11]He saw heaven open, and something came down like a huge sheet held up by its four corners. [12]In it were all kinds of animals, snakes, and birds. [13]A voice said to him, "Peter, get up! Kill these and eat them."

[14]But Peter said, "Lord, I can't do that! I've never eaten anything that is unclean and not fit to eat."[h]

[15]The voice spoke to him again, "When God says that something can be used for food, don't say it isn't fit to eat."

[16]This happened three times before the sheet was suddenly taken back to heaven.

[17]Peter was still wondering what all of this meant, when the men sent by Cornelius came and stood at the gate. They had found their way to Simon's house [18]and were asking if Simon Peter was staying there.

[19]While Peter was still thinking about the vision, the Holy Spirit said to him, "Three[i] men are here looking for you. [20]Hurry down and go with them. Don't worry, I sent them."

[21]Peter went down and said to the men, "I'm the one you're looking for. Why have you come?"

[22]They answered, "Captain Cornelius sent us. He is a good man who worships God and is liked by the Jewish people. One of God's holy angels told Cornelius to send for you, so he could hear what you have to say." [23]Peter invited them to spend the night.

The next morning, Peter and some of the Lord's followers in Joppa left with the men who had come from Cornelius. [24]The next day they arrived in Caesarea where Cornelius was waiting for them. He had also invited his relatives and close friends.

[25]When Peter arrived, Cornelius greeted him. Then he knelt at Peter's feet and started worshipping him. [26]But Peter took hold of him and said, "Stand up! I am nothing more than a human."

[27]As Peter entered the house, he was still talking with

[h]*unclean and not fit to eat:* The Law of Moses taught that some foods were not fit to eat. [i]*Three:* One manuscript has "two"; some manuscripts have "some."

Cornelius. Many people were there, 28and Peter said to them, "You know that we Jews aren't allowed to have anything to do with other people. But God has shown me that he doesn't think anyone is unclean or unfit. 29I agreed to come here, but I want to know why you sent for me."

30Cornelius answered:

Four days ago at about three o'clock in the afternoon I was praying at home. Suddenly a man in bright clothes stood in front of me. 31He said, "Cornelius, God has heard your prayers, and he knows about your gifts to the poor. 32Now send to Joppa for Simon Peter. He is staying in the home of Simon the leather maker, who lives near the sea."

33I sent for you straight away, and you have been good enough to come. All of us are here in the presence of the Lord God, so that we can hear what he has to say.

34Peter then said:

Now I am certain that God treats all people alike. 35God is pleased with everyone who worships him and does right, no matter what nation they come from. 36This is the same message that God gave to the people of Israel, when he sent Jesus Christ, the Lord of all, to offer peace to them.

37You surely know what happenedʲ everywhere in Judea. It all began in Galilee after John had told everyone to be baptised. 38God gave the Holy Spirit and power to Jesus from Nazareth. He was with Jesus, as he went around doing good and healing everyone who was under the power of the devil. 39We all saw what Jesus did both in Israel and in the city of Jerusalem.

Jesus was put to death on a cross. 40But three days later, God raised him to life and let him be seen. 41Not everyone saw him. He was seen only by us, who ate and drank with him after he was raised from death. We were the ones God chose to tell others about him.

42God told us to announce clearly to the people that

ʲwhat happened: Or "the message that went."

Jesus is the one he has chosen to judge the living and the dead. ⁴³Every one of the prophets has said that all who have faith in Jesus will have their sins forgiven in his name.

⁴⁴While Peter was still speaking, the Holy Spirit took control of everyone who was listening. ⁴⁵Some Jewish followers of the Lord had come with Peter, and they were surprised that the Holy Spirit had been given to Gentiles. ⁴⁶Now they were hearing Gentiles speaking unknown languages and praising God.

Peter said, ⁴⁷"These Gentiles have been given the Holy Spirit, just as we have! I am certain that no-one would dare stop us from baptising them." ⁴⁸Peter ordered them to be baptised in the name of Jesus Christ, and they asked him to stay on for a few days.

Peter Reports to the Church in Jerusalem

11 ¹The apostles and the followers in Judea heard that Gentiles had accepted God's message. ²So when Peter came to Jerusalem, some of the Jewish followers started arguing with him. They wanted Gentile followers to be circumcised, and ³they said, "You stayed in the homes of Gentiles, and you even ate with them!"

⁴Then Peter told them exactly what had happened:

⁵I was in the town of Joppa and was praying when I fell sound asleep and had a vision. I saw heaven open, and something like a huge sheet held by its four corners came down to me. ⁶When I looked in it, I saw animals, wild beasts, snakes, and birds. ⁷I heard a voice saying to me, "Peter, get up! Kill these and eat them."

⁸But I said, "Lord, I can't do that! I've never taken a bite of anything that is unclean and not fit to eat."^k

⁹The voice from heaven spoke to me again, "When God says that something can be used for food, don't say it isn't fit to eat." ¹⁰This happened three times before it was all taken back into heaven.

¹¹Suddenly three men from Caesarea stood in front of the house where I was staying. ¹²The Holy Spirit told me to go with them and not to worry. Then six of

^kunclean and not fit to eat: See the note at 10.14.

the Lord's followers went with me to the home of a man [13]who told us that an angel had appeared to him. The angel had ordered him to send to Joppa for someone named Simon Peter. [14]Then Peter would tell him how he and everyone in his house could be saved.

[15]After I started speaking, the Holy Spirit was given to them, just as the Spirit had been given to us at the beginning. [16]I remembered that the Lord had said, "John baptised with water, but you will be baptised with the Holy Spirit." [17]God gave those Gentiles the same gift that he gave us when we put our faith in the Lord Jesus Christ. So how could I have gone against God?

[18]When they heard Peter say this, they stopped arguing and started praising God. They said, "God has now let Gentiles turn to him, and he has given life to them!"

The Church in Antioch

[19]Some of the Lord's followers had been scattered because of the terrible trouble that started when Stephen was killed. They went as far as Phoenicia, Cyprus, and Antioch, but they told the message only to the Jews.

[20]Some of the followers from Cyprus and Cyrene went to Antioch and started telling Gentiles[j] the good news about the Lord Jesus. [21]The Lord's power was with them, and many people turned to the Lord and put their faith in him. [22]News of what was happening reached the church in Jerusalem. Then they sent Barnabas to Antioch.

[23]When Barnabas got there and saw what God had been kind enough to do for them, he was very glad. So he begged them to remain faithful to the Lord with all their hearts. [24]Barnabas was a good man of great faith, and he was filled with the Holy Spirit. Many more people turned to the Lord.

[25]Barnabas went to Tarsus to look for Saul. [26]He found Saul and brought him to Antioch, where they met with

[j]*Gentiles:* This translates a Greek word that may mean "people who speak Greek" or "people who live as Greeks do." Here the word seems to mean "people who are not Jews." Some manuscripts have "Greeks," which also seems to mean "people who are not Jews."

the church for a whole year and taught many of its people. There in Antioch the Lord's followers were first called Christians.

[27]During this time some prophets from Jerusalem came to Antioch. [28]One of them was Agabus. Then with the help of the Spirit, he said that there would be a terrible famine everywhere in the world. And it happened when Claudius was Emperor.[m] [29]The followers in Antioch decided to send whatever help they could to the followers in Judea. [30]So they had Barnabas and Saul take their gifts to the church leaders in Jerusalem.

Herod Causes Trouble for the Church

12 [1]At that time King Herod[n] caused terrible suffering for some members of the church. [2]He ordered soldiers to cut off the head of James, the brother of John. [3]When Herod saw that this pleased the Jewish people, he had Peter arrested during the Festival of Thin Bread. [4]He put Peter in jail and ordered four squads of soldiers to guard him. Herod planned to put him on trial in public after the festival.

[5]While Peter was being kept in jail, the church never stopped praying to God for him.

Peter Is Rescued

[6]The night before Peter was to be put on trial, he was asleep and bound by two chains. A soldier was guarding him on each side, and two other soldiers were guarding the entrance to the jail. [7]Suddenly an angel from the Lord appeared, and light flashed around in the cell. The angel poked Peter in the side and woke him up. Then he said, "Quick! Get up!"

The chains fell off his hands, [8]and the angel said, "Get dressed and put on your sandals." Peter did what he was told. Then the angel said, "Now put on your coat and follow me." [9]Peter left with the angel, but he thought everything was only a dream. [10]They went past the two groups of soldiers, and when they came to the iron gate

[m]when Claudius was Emperor: AD 41-54.   [n]Herod: Herod Agrippa I, the grandson of Herod the Great.

to the city, it opened by itself. They went out and were going along the street, when all at once the angel disappeared.

¹¹Peter now realised what had happened, and he said, "I am certain that the Lord sent his angel to rescue me from Herod and from everything the Jewish leaders planned to do to me." ¹²Then Peter went to the house of Mary the mother of John whose other name was Mark. Many of the Lord's followers had come together there and were praying.

¹³Peter knocked on the gate, and a servant named Rhoda came to answer. ¹⁴When she heard Peter's voice, she was too excited to open the gate. She ran back into the house and said that Peter was standing there.

¹⁵"You are crazy!" everyone told her. But she kept saying that it was Peter. Then they said, "It must be his angel."ᵒ ¹⁶But Peter kept on knocking, until finally they opened the gate. They saw him and were completely amazed.

¹⁷Peter motioned for them to keep quiet. Then he told them how the Lord had led him out of jail. He also said, "Tell Jamesᵖ and the others what has happened." After that, he left and went somewhere else.

¹⁸The next morning the soldiers who had been on guard were terribly worried and wondered what had happened to Peter. ¹⁹Herod ordered his own soldiers to search for him, but they couldn't find him. Then he questioned the guards and had them put to death. After this, Herod left Judea to stay in Caesarea for a while.

Herod Dies

²⁰Herod and the people of Tyre and Sidon were very angry with each other. But their country got its food supply from the region that he ruled. So a group of them went to see Blastus, who was one of Herod's high officials. They convinced Blastus that they wanted to make peace between their cities and Herod, ²¹and a day was set for them to meet with him.

ᵒ*his angel:* Probably meaning "his guardian angel."   ᵖ*James:* The brother of the Lord.

Herod came dressed in his royal robes. He sat down on his throne and made a speech. 22 The people shouted, "You speak more like a god than a man!" 23 At once an angel from the Lord struck him down because he took the honour that belonged to God. Later, Herod was eaten by worms and died.

24 God's message kept spreading. 25 And after Barnabas and Saul had done the work they were sent to do, they went back to Jerusalem*q* with John, whose other name was Mark.

Barnabas and Saul Are Chosen and Sent

13 1 The church at Antioch had several prophets and teachers. They were Barnabas, Simeon, also called Niger, Lucius from Cyrene, Manaen, who was Herod's*r* close friend, and Saul. 2 While they were worshipping the Lord and going without eating,*s* the Holy Spirit told them, "Appoint Barnabas and Saul to do the work for which I have chosen them." 3 Everyone prayed and went without eating for a while longer. Next, they placed their hands on Barnabas and Saul to show that they had been appointed to do this work. Then everyone sent them on their way.

Barnabas and Saul in Cyprus

4 After Barnabas and Saul had been sent by the Holy Spirit, they went to Seleucia. From there they sailed to the island of Cyprus. 5 They arrived at Salamis and began to preach God's message in the Jewish meeting places. They also had John*t* as a helper.

6 Barnabas and Saul went all the way to the city of Paphos on the other end of the island, where they met a Jewish man named Bar-Jesus. He practised witchcraft and was a false prophet. 7 He also worked for Sergius Paulus, who was very smart and was the governor of the island. Sergius Paulus wanted to hear God's message, and he sent

q went back to Jerusalem: Some manuscripts have "left Jerusalem," and others have "went to Antioch."   *r Herod's:* Herod Antipas, the son of Herod the Great. *s going without eating:* The Jews often went without eating as a way of showing how much they loved God. This is also called "fasting."   *t John:* Whose other name was Mark (see 12.12, 25).

for Barnabas and Saul. 8But Bar-Jesus, whose other name was Elymas, was against them. He even tried to keep the governor from having faith in the Lord.

9Then Saul, better known as Paul, was filled with the Holy Spirit. He looked straight at Elymas 10and said, "You son of the devil! You are a liar, a crook, and an enemy of everything that is right. When will you stop speaking against the true ways of the Lord? 11The Lord is going to punish you by making you completely blind for a while."

Suddenly the man's eyes were covered by a dark mist, and he went around trying to get someone to lead him by the hand. 12When the governor saw what had happened, he was amazed at this teaching about the Lord. So he put his faith in the Lord.

Paul and Barnabas in Antioch of Pisidia

13Paul and the others left Paphos and sailed to Perga in Pamphylia. But John left them and went back to Jerusalem. 14The rest of them went on from Perga to Antioch in Pisidia. Then on the Sabbath they went to the Jewish meeting place and sat down.

15After the reading of the Law and the Prophets,u the leaders sent someone over to tell Paul and Barnabas, "Friends, if you have anything to say that will help the people, please say it."

16Paul got up. He motioned with his hand and said:
People of Israel, and everyone else who worships God, listen! 17The God of Israel chose our ancestors, and he let our people prosper while they were living in Egypt. Then with his mighty power he led them out, 18and for about 40 years he took care ofv them in the desert. 19He destroyed seven nations in the land of Canaan and gave their land to our people. 20All this happened in about 450 years.

Then God gave our people judges until the time of the prophet Samuel, 21but the people demanded a king. So for 40 years God gave them King Saul, the son of

---

uthe Law and the Prophets: The Jewish Scriptures, that is, the Old Testament.
vtook care of: Some manuscripts have "put up with."

Kish from the tribe of Benjamin. ²²Later, God removed Saul and let David rule in his place. God said about him, "David the son of Jesse is the kind of person who pleases me most! He does everything I want him to do."

²³God promised that someone from David's family would come to save the people of Israel, and that one is Jesus. ²⁴But before Jesus came, John was telling everyone in Israel to turn back to God and be baptised. ²⁵Then, when John's work was almost done, he said, "Who do you people think I am? Do you think I am the Promised One? He will come later, and I am not good enough to untie his sandals."

²⁶Now listen, you descendants of Abraham! Pay attention, all of you Gentiles who are here to worship God! Listen to this message about how to be saved, because it's for everyone. ²⁷The people of Jerusalem and their leaders didn't realise who Jesus was. And they didn't understand the words of the prophets that they read each Sabbath. So they condemned Jesus just as the prophets had said.

²⁸⁻²⁹They did exactly what the Scriptures said they would. Even though they couldn't find any reason to put Jesus to death, they still asked Pilate to have him killed.

After Jesus had been put to death, he was taken down from the cross^w and placed in a tomb. ³⁰But God raised him from death! ³¹Then for many days Jesus appeared to his followers who had gone with him from Galilee to Jerusalem. Now they are telling our people about him.

³²God made a promise to our ancestors. And we are here to tell you the good news ³³that he has kept this promise to us. It's just as the second Psalm says about Jesus,

> "You are my son because today
> I have become your Father."

³⁴God raised Jesus from death and will never let his body decay. It's just as God said,

---

^w*cross:* This translates a Greek word that means "wood," "pole," or "tree."

"I will make to you the same holy promise
that I made to David."

³⁵And in another psalm it says, "God will never let the
body of his Holy One decay."

³⁶When David was alive, he obeyed God. Then after
he died, he was buried in the family grave, and his
body decayed. ³⁷But God raised Jesus from death, and
his body did not decay.

³⁸My friends, the message is that Jesus can forgive
your sins! The Law of Moses couldn't set you free from
all your sins. ³⁹But everyone who has faith in Jesus is
set free. ⁴⁰Make sure that what the prophets have said
doesn't happen to you. They said,

⁴¹ "Look, you people who make fun of God!
Be amazed and disappear.
I will do something today that you won't believe,
even if someone tells you about it!"

⁴²As Paul and Barnabas were leaving the meeting, the
people begged them to say more about these same things
on the next Sabbath. ⁴³After the service, many Jews and
a lot of Gentiles who worshipped God went with them.
Paul and Barnabas begged them all to remain faithful to
God, who had been so kind to them.

⁴⁴The next Sabbath almost everyone in town came to
hear the message about the Lord.ˣ ⁴⁵When the Jewish
people saw the crowds, they were very jealous. They
insulted Paul and spoke against everything he said.

⁴⁶But Paul and Barnabas bravely said:
We had to tell God's message to you before we told it
to anyone else. But you rejected the message! This
proves that you don't deserve eternal life. Now we are
going to the Gentiles. ⁴⁷The Lord has given us this
command,

"I have placed you here as a light for the Gentiles.
You are to take the saving power of God
to people everywhere on earth."

⁴⁸This message made the Gentiles glad, and they
praised what they had heard about the Lord. Everyone
who had been chosen for eternal life then put their faith
in the Lord.

ˣthe Lord: Some manuscripts have "God."

⁴⁹The message about the Lord spread all over that region. ⁵⁰But the Jewish leaders went to some of the important men in the town and to some respected women who were religious. They turned them against Paul and Barnabas and started making trouble for them. They even chased them out of that part of the country.

⁵¹Paul and Barnabas shook the dust from that place off their feet*y* and went on to the city of Iconium.

⁵²But the Lord's followers in Antioch were very happy and were filled with the Holy Spirit.

Paul and Barnabas in Iconium

14 ¹Paul and Barnabas spoke in the Jewish meeting place in Iconium, just as they had done at Antioch, and many Jews and Gentiles*z* put their faith in the Lord. ²But the Jews who didn't have faith in him made the other Gentiles angry and turned them against the Lord's followers.

³Paul and Barnabas stayed there for a while, having faith in the Lord and bravely speaking his message. The Lord gave them the power to work miracles and wonders, and he showed that their message about his great kindness was true.

⁴The people of Iconium didn't know what to think. Some of them believed the Jewish group, and others believed the apostles. ⁵Finally, some Gentiles and Jews, together with their leaders, decided to make trouble for Paul and Barnabas and to stone them to death.

⁶⁻⁷But when the two apostles found out what was happening, they escaped to the region of Lycaonia. They preached the good news there in the towns of Lystra and Derbe and in the nearby countryside.

Paul and Barnabas in Lystra

⁸In Lystra there was a man who had been born with crippled feet and had never been able to walk. ⁹The man was listening to Paul speak, when Paul saw that he had

yshook the dust from that place off their feet: This was a way of showing rejection.   *zGentiles:* The Greek text has "Greeks," which probably means people who were not Jews. But it may mean Gentiles who worshipped with the Jews.

faith in Jesus and could be healed. So he looked straight at the man 10and shouted, "Stand up!" The man jumped up and started walking around.

11When the crowd saw what Paul had done, they yelled out in the language of Lycaonia, "The gods have turned into humans and have come down to us!" 12The people then gave Barnabas the name Zeus, and they gave Paul the name Hermes,ᵃ because he did the talking.

13The temple of Zeus was near the entrance to the city. Its priest and the crowds wanted to offer a sacrifice to Barnabas and Paul. So the priest brought some bulls and flowers to the city gates. 14When the two apostles found out about this, they tore their clothes in horror and ran to the crowd, shouting:

> 15Why are you doing this? We are humans just like you. Please give up all this foolishness. Turn to the living God, who made the sky, the earth, the sea, and everything in them. 16In times past, God let each nation go its own way. 17But he showed that he was there by the good things he did. God sends rain from heaven and makes your crops grow. He gives food to you and makes your hearts glad.

18Even after Paul and Barnabas had said all this, they could hardly keep the people from offering a sacrifice to them.

19Some Jewish leaders from Antioch and Iconium came and turned the crowds against Paul. They hit him with stones and dragged him out of the city, thinking he was dead. 20But when the Lord's followers gathered around Paul, he stood up and went back into the city. The next day he and Barnabas went to Derbe.

Paul and Barnabas Return to Antioch in Syria

21Paul and Barnabas preached the good news in Derbe and won some people to the Lord. Then they went back to Lystra, Iconium, and Antioch in Pisidia. 22They encouraged the followers and begged them to remain faithful. They told them, "We have to suffer a lot before

---

ᵃHermes: The Greeks thought of Hermes as the messenger of the other gods, especially of Zeus, their chief god.

we can get into God's kingdom." [23]Paul and Barnabas chose some leaders for each of the churches. Then they went without eating[b] and prayed that the Lord would take good care of these leaders.

[24]Paul and Barnabas went on through Pisidia to Pamphylia, [25]where they preached in the town of Perga. Then they went down to Attalia [26]and sailed to Antioch in Syria. It was there that they had been placed in God's care for the work they had now completed.[c]

[27]After arriving in Antioch, they called the church together. They told the people what God had helped them do and how he had made it possible for the Gentiles to believe. [28]Then they stayed there with the followers for a long time.

15 [1]Some people came from Judea and started teaching the Lord's followers that they couldn't be saved, unless they were circumcised as Moses had taught. [2]This caused trouble, and Paul and Barnabas argued with them about this teaching. So it was decided to send Paul and Barnabas and a few others to Jerusalem to discuss this problem with the apostles and the church leaders.

The Church Leaders Meet in Jerusalem

[3]The men who were sent by the church went through Phoenicia and Samaria, telling how the Gentiles had turned to God. This news made the Lord's followers very happy. [4]When the men arrived in Jerusalem, they were welcomed by the church, including the apostles and the leaders. They told them everything God had helped them do. [5]But some Pharisees had become followers of the Lord. They stood up and said, "Gentiles who have faith in the Lord must be circumcised and told to obey the Law of Moses."

[6]The apostles and church leaders met to discuss this problem about Gentiles. [7]They had talked it over for a long time, when Peter got up and said:

My friends, you know that God decided long ago to let me be the one from your group to preach the good

---

[b]*went without eating:* See the note at 13.2.   [c]*the work they had now completed:* See 13.1-3.

news to the Gentiles. God did this so that they would hear and obey him. [8]He knows what is in everyone's heart. And he showed that he had chosen the Gentiles, when he gave them the Holy Spirit, just as he had given his Spirit to us. [9]God treated them in the same way that he treated us. They put their faith in him, and he made their hearts pure.

[10]Now why are you trying to make God angry by placing a heavy burden on these followers? This burden was too heavy for us or our ancestors. [11]But our Lord Jesus was kind to us, and we are saved by faith in him, just as the Gentiles are.

[12]Everyone kept quiet and listened as Barnabas and Paul told how God had given them the power to work a lot of miracles and wonders for the Gentiles.

[13]After they had finished speaking, James[d] said:

My friends, listen to me! [14]Simon Peter[e] has told how God first came to the Gentiles and made some of them his own people. [15]This agrees with what the prophets wrote,

[16] "I, the Lord, will return
            and rebuild David's fallen house.
    I will build it from its ruins and set it up
  again.
[17]   Then other nations will turn to me
            and be my chosen ones.
    I, the Lord, say this. [18]I promised it long ago."

[19]And so, my friends, I don't think we should place burdens on the Gentiles who are turning to God. [20]We should simply write and tell them not to eat anything that has been offered to idols. They should be told not to eat the meat of any animal that has been strangled or that still has blood in it. They must also not commit any terrible sexual sins.[f]

[21]We must remember that the Law of Moses has been preached in city after city for many years, and every Sabbath it's read when we Jews meet.

---

[d]James: The Lord's brother.   [e]Simon Peter: The Greek text has "Simeon," which is another form of the name "Simon." The apostle Peter is meant.   [f]not commit any terrible sexual sins: This probably refers to the laws about the wrong kind of marriages that are forbidden in Leviticus 18.6-18 or to some serious sexual sin.

A Letter to Gentiles Who Had Faith in the Lord

22The apostles, the leaders, and all the church members decided to send some men to Antioch along with Paul and Barnabas. They chose Silas and Judas Barsabbas,g who were two leaders of the Lord's followers. 23They wrote a letter that said:

We apostles and leaders send friendly greetings to all of you Gentiles who are followers of the Lord in Antioch, Syria, and Cilicia.

24We have heard that some people from here have terribly upset you by what they said. But we didn't send them! 25So we met together and decided to choose some men and to send them to you along with our good friends Barnabas and Paul. 26These men have risked their lives for our Lord Jesus Christ. 27We are also sending Judas and Silas, who will tell you in person the same things that we are writing.

28The Holy Spirit has shown us that we should not place any extra burden on you. 29But you shouldn't eat anything offered to idols. You shouldn't eat any meat that still has the blood in it or any meat of any animal that has been strangled. You must also not commit any terrible sexual sins. If you follow these instructions, you will do well.

We send our best wishes.

30The four men left Jerusalem and went to Antioch. Then they called the church members together and gave them the letter. 31When the letter was read, everyone was pleased and greatly encouraged. 32Judas and Silas were prophets, and they spoke a long time, encouraging and helping the Lord's followers.

33The men from Jerusalem stayed on in Antioch for a while. And when they left to return to the ones who had sent them, the followers wished them well. 34-35But Paul and Barnabas stayed on in Antioch, where they and many others taught and preached about the Lord.h

gJudas Barsabbas: He may have been a brother of Joseph Barsabbas (see 1.23), but the name "Barsabbas" was often used by the Jewish people. hVerse 34, which says that Silas decided to stay on in Antioch, is not in some manuscripts.

Paul and Barnabas Go Their Separate Ways

³⁶Some time later Paul said to Barnabas, "Let's go back and visit the Lord's followers in the cities where we preached his message. Then we'll know how they are doing." ³⁷Barnabas wanted to take along John, whose other name was Mark. ³⁸But Paul didn't want to, because Mark had left them in Pamphylia and had stopped working with them.

³⁹Paul and Barnabas argued, then each of them went his own way. Barnabas took Mark and sailed to Cyprus, ⁴⁰but Paul took Silas and left after the followers had placed them in God's care. ⁴¹They travelled through Syria and Cilicia, encouraging the churches.

Timothy Works with Paul and Silas

16 ¹Paul and Silas went back to Derbe and Lystra, where there was a follower named Timothy. His mother was also a follower. She was Jewish, and his father was Greek. ²The Lord's followers in Lystra and Iconium said good things about Timothy, ³and Paul wanted him to go with them. But Paul first had him circumcised, because all the Jewish people around there knew that Timothy's father was Greek.ⁱ

⁴As Paul and the others went from city to city, they told the followers what the apostles and leaders in Jerusalem had decided, and they urged them to follow these instructions. ⁵The churches became stronger in their faith, and each day more people put their faith in the Lord.

Paul's Vision in Troas

⁶Paul and his friends went through Phrygia and Galatia, but the Holy Spirit wouldn't let them preach in Asia. ⁷After they arrived in Mysia, they tried to go into Bithynia, but the Spirit of Jesus wouldn't let them. ⁸So they went on throughʲ Mysia until they came to Troas. ⁹During the night, Paul had a vision of someone from

---

ⁱhad him circumcised...Timothy's father was Greek: Timothy would not have been acceptable to the Jews unless he had been circumcised, and Greeks did not circumcise their sons. ʲwent on through: or "passed by".

Macedonia who was standing there and begging him, "Come over to Macedonia and help us!" [10]After Paul had seen the vision, we began looking for a way to go to Macedonia. We were sure that God had called us to preach the good news there.

Lydia Becomes a Follower of the Lord

[11]We sailed straight from Troas to Samothrace, and the next day we arrived in Neapolis. [12]From there we went to Philippi, which is a Roman colony in the first district of Macedonia.[k]

We spent several days in Philippi. [13]Then on the Sabbath we went outside the city gate to a place by the river, where we thought there would be a Jewish meeting place for prayer. We sat down and talked with the women who came. [14]One of them was Lydia, who was from the city of Thyatira and sold expensive purple cloth. She was a worshipper of the Lord God, and he made her willing to accept what Paul was saying. [15]Then after she and her family were baptised, she kept on begging us, "If you think I really do have faith in the Lord, come and stay in my home." Finally, we accepted her invitation.

Paul and Silas Are Put in Jail

[16]One day on our way to the place of prayer, we were met by a slave girl. She had a spirit in her that gave her the power to tell the future. By doing this she made a lot of money for her owners. [17]The girl followed Paul and the rest of us and kept yelling, "These men are servants of the Most High God! They are telling you how to be saved."

[18]This went on for several days. Finally, Paul got so upset that he turned and said to the spirit, "In the name of Jesus Christ, I order you to leave this girl alone!" At once the evil spirit left her.

[19]When the girl's owners realised that they had lost all chances for making more money, they grabbed Paul and Silas and dragged them into court. [20]They told the officials, "These Jews are upsetting our city! [21]They are

---

[k]in the first district of Macedonia: Some manuscripts have "and the leading city of Macedonia."

telling us to do things we Romans are not allowed to do."

²²The crowd joined in the attack on Paul and Silas. Then the officials tore the clothes off the two men and ordered them to be beaten with a whip. ²³After they had been badly beaten, they were put in jail, and the jailer was told to guard them carefully. ²⁴The jailer did as he was told. He put them deep inside the jail and chained their feet to heavy blocks of wood.

²⁵About midnight Paul and Silas were praying and singing praises to God, while the other prisoners listened. ²⁶Suddenly a strong earthquake shook the jail to its foundations. The doors opened, and the chains fell from all the prisoners.

²⁷When the jailer woke up and saw that the doors were open, he thought that the prisoners had escaped. He pulled out his sword and was about to kill himself. ²⁸But Paul shouted, "Don't harm yourself! No-one has escaped."

²⁹The jailer asked for a torch and went into the jail. He was shaking all over as he knelt down in front of Paul and Silas. ³⁰After he had led them out of the jail, he asked, "What must I do to be saved?"

³¹They replied, "Have faith in the Lord Jesus and you will be saved! This is also true for everyone who lives in your home."

³²Then Paul and Silas told him and everyone else in his house about the Lord. ³³While it was still night, the jailer took them to a place where he could wash their cuts and bruises. Then he and everyone in his home were baptised. ³⁴They were very glad that they had put their faith in God. After this, the jailer took Paul and Silas to his home and gave them something to eat.

³⁵The next morning the officials sent some police with orders for the jailer to let Paul and Silas go. ³⁶The jailer told Paul, "The officials have ordered me to set you free. Now you can leave in peace."

³⁷But Paul told the police, "We are Roman citizens,ⁱ and the Roman officials had us beaten in public without giving us a trial. They threw us into jail. Now do they

---

ⁱRoman citizens: Only a small number of the people living in the Roman Empire were citizens, and they had special rights and privileges.

think they can secretly send us away? No, they can't! They will have to come here themselves and let us out."

³⁸When the police told the officials that Paul and Silas were Roman citizens, the officials were afraid. ³⁹So they came and apologised. They led them out of the jail and asked them to please leave town. ⁴⁰But Paul and Silas went straight to the home of Lydia, where they saw the Lord's followers and encouraged them. Then they left.

Trouble in Thessalonica

17 ¹After Paul and his friends had travelled through Amphipolis and Apollonia, they went on to Thessalonica. A Jewish meeting place was in that city. ²So as usual, Paul went there to worship, and on three Sabbaths he spoke to the people. He used the Scriptures ³to show them that the Messiah had to suffer, but that he would rise from death. Paul also told them that Jesus is the Messiah he was preaching about. ⁴Some of the Jews believed what Paul had said, and they became followers with Paul and Silas. Some Gentiles*ᵐ* and many important women also believed the message.

⁵The Jewish leaders were jealous and got some worthless loafers who hung around the marketplace to start a riot in the city. They wanted to drag Paul and Silas out to the mob, and so they went straight to Jason's home. ⁶But when they didn't find them there, they dragged out Jason and some of the Lord's followers. They took them to the city authorities and shouted, "Paul and Silas have been upsetting things everywhere. Now they have come here, ⁷and Jason has welcomed them into his home. All of them break the laws of the Roman Emperor by claiming that someone named Jesus is king."

⁸The officials and the people were upset when they heard this. ⁹So they made Jason and the other followers pay bail before letting them go.

People in Berea Welcome the Message

¹⁰That same night the Lord's followers sent Paul and Silas on to Berea, and after they arrived, they went to the

ᵐGentiles: See the note at 14.1.

Jewish meeting place. [11]The people in Berea were much nicer than those in Thessalonica, and they gladly accepted the message. Day after day they studied the Scriptures to see if these things were true. [12]Many of them put their faith in the Lord, including some important Greek women and several men.

[13]When the Jewish leaders in Thessalonica heard that Paul had been preaching God's message in Berea, they went there and caused trouble by turning the crowds against Paul.

[14]Straight away the followers sent Paul down to the coast, but Silas and Timothy stayed in Berea. [15]Some men went with Paul as far as Athens, and then returned with instructions for Silas and Timothy to join him as soon as possible.

Paul in Athens

[16]While Paul was waiting in Athens, he was upset to see all the idols in the city. [17]He went to the Jewish meeting place to speak to the Jews and to anyone who worshipped with them. Day after day he also spoke to everyone he met in the market. [18]Some of them were Epicureans[n] and some were Stoics,[o] and they started arguing with him.

People were asking, "What is this know-all trying to say?"

Some even said, "Paul must be preaching about foreign gods! That's what he means when he talks about Jesus and about people rising from death."[p]

[19]They brought Paul before a council called the Areopagus, and said, "Tell us what your new teaching is all about. [20]We've heard you say some strange things, and we want to know what you mean."

[21]More than anything else the people of Athens and the foreigners living there loved to hear and to talk about anything new. [22]So Paul stood up in front of the council and said:

[n]Epicureans: People who followed the teaching of a man named Epicurus, who taught that happiness should be the main goal in life. [o]Stoics: Followers of a man named Zeno, who taught that people should learn self-control and be guided by their consciences. [p]people rising from death: Or "a goddess named 'Rising from Death.'"

People of Athens, I see that you are very religious.
²³As I was going through your city and looking at the
things you worship, I found an altar with the words,
"To an Unknown God." You worship this God, but
you don't really know him. So I want to tell you about
him. ²⁴This God made the world and everything in it.
He is Lord of heaven and earth, and he doesn't live in
temples built by human hands. ²⁵He doesn't need help
from anyone. He gives life, breath, and everything else
to all people. ²⁶From one person God made all nations
who live on earth, and he decided when and where
every nation would be.

²⁷God has done all this, so that we will look for him
and reach out and find him. He isn't far from any of
us, ²⁸and he gives us the power to live, to move, and to
be who we are. "We are his children," just as some of
your poets have said.

²⁹Since we are God's children, we mustn't think that
he is like an idol made out of gold or silver or stone. He
isn't like anything that humans have thought up and
made. ³⁰In the past, God forgave all this because people
didn't know what they were doing. But now he says
that everyone everywhere must turn to him. ³¹He has
set a day when he will judge the world's people with
fairness. And he has chosen the man Jesus to do the
judging for him. God has given proof of this to all of us
by raising Jesus from death.

³²As soon as the people heard Paul say that a man had
been raised from death, some of them started laughing.
Others said, "We'll hear you talk about this some other
time." ³³When Paul left the council meeting, ³⁴some of
the men put their faith in the Lord and went with Paul.
One of them was a council member named Dionysius. A
woman named Damaris and several others also put their
faith in the Lord.

Paul in Corinth

18 ¹Paul left Athens and went to Corinth, ²where he
met Aquila, a Jewish man from Pontus. Not long
before this, Aquila had come from Italy with his wife
Priscilla, because Emperor Claudius had ordered the

Jewish people to leave Rome.*q* Paul went to see Aquila and Priscilla ³and found out that they were tent makers. Paul was a tent maker too. So he stayed with them, and they worked together.

⁴Every Sabbath, Paul went to the Jewish meeting place. He spoke to Jews and Gentiles*r* and tried to win them over. ⁵But after Silas and Timothy came from Macedonia, he spent all his time preaching to the Jews about Jesus the Messiah. ⁶Finally, they turned against him and insulted him. So he shook the dust from his clothes*s* and told them, "Whatever happens to you will be your own fault! I am not to blame. From now on I'm going to preach to the Gentiles."

⁷Paul then moved into the house of a man named Titius Justus, who worshipped God and lived next door to the Jewish meeting place. ⁸Crispus was the leader of the meeting place. He and everyone in his family put their faith in the Lord. Many others in Corinth also heard the message, and all the people who had faith in the Lord were baptised.

⁹One night, Paul had a vision, and in it the Lord said, "Don't be afraid to keep on preaching. Don't stop! ¹⁰I am with you, and you won't be harmed. Many people in this city belong to me." ¹¹Paul stayed on in Corinth for a year and a half, teaching God's message to the people.

¹²While Gallio was governor of Achaia, some of the Jewish leaders got together and grabbed Paul. They brought him into court ¹³and said, "This man is trying to make our people worship God in a way that is against our Law!"

¹⁴Even before Paul could speak, Gallio said, "If you were charging this man with a crime or some other wrong, I would have to listen to you. ¹⁵But since this concerns only words, names, and your own law, you will have to take care of it. I refuse to judge such matters." ¹⁶Then he sent them out of the court. ¹⁷The crowd grabbed Sosthenes, the Jewish leader, and beat him up in front of the court. But none of this mattered to Gallio.

---

qEmperor Claudius had ordered the Jewish people to leave Rome: Probably AD 49, though it may have been AD 41. *rGentiles:* Here the word is "Greeks." But see the note at 14.1. *sshook the dust from his clothes:* This means the same as shaking dust from the feet (see the note at 13.51).

Paul Returns to Antioch in Syria

18After Paul had stayed for a while with the Lord's followers in Corinth, he said goodbye to them and sailed on to Syria with Aquila and Priscilla. But before he left, he had his head shaved*t* at Cenchreae because he had made a promise to God.

19The three of them arrived in Ephesus, where Paul left Priscilla and Aquila. He then went into the Jewish meeting place to talk with the people there. 20They asked him to stay longer, but he refused. 21He said goodbye to them and said, "If God lets me, I'll come back."

22Paul sailed to Caesarea, where he greeted the church. Then he went on to Antioch. 23After staying there for a while, he left and visited several places in Galatia and Phrygia. He helped the followers there to become stronger in their faith.

Apollos in Ephesus

24A Jewish man named Apollos came to Ephesus. Apollos had been born in the city of Alexandria. He was a very good speaker and knew a lot about the Scriptures. 25He also knew much about the Lord's Way,*u* and he spoke about it with great excitement. What he taught about Jesus was right, but all he knew was John's message about baptism.

26Apollos started speaking bravely in the Jewish meeting place. But when Priscilla and Aquila heard him, they took him to their home and helped him understand God's Way even better.

27Apollos decided to travel through Achaia. So the Lord's followers wrote letters, encouraging the followers there to welcome him. After Apollos arrived in Achaia, he was a great help to everyone who had put their faith in the Lord Jesus because of God's kindness. 28He got into fierce arguments with the Jewish people, and in public he used the Scriptures to prove that Jesus is the Messiah.

---

*t*he had his head shaved: Paul had promised to be a "Nazirite" for a while. This meant that for the time of the promise, he could not cut his hair or drink wine. When the time was over, he would have to cut his hair and offer a sacrifice to God.   *u*the Lord's Way: See the note at 9.2.

Paul in Ephesus

19 ¹While Apollos was in Corinth, Paul travelled across the hill country to Ephesus, where he met some of the Lord's followers. ²He asked them, "When you put your faith in Jesus, were you given the Holy Spirit?"

"No!" they answered. "We've never even heard of the Holy Spirit."

³"Then why were you baptised?" Paul asked.

They answered, "Because of what John taught."ᵛ

⁴Paul replied, "John baptised people so that they would turn to God. But he also told them that someone else was coming, and that they should put their faith in him. Jesus is the one that John was talking about." ⁵After the people heard Paul say this, they were baptised in the name of the Lord Jesus. ⁶Then Paul placed his hands on them. The Holy Spirit was given to them, and they spoke unknown languages and prophesied. ⁷There were about twelve men in this group.

⁸For three months Paul went to the Jewish meeting place and talked bravely with the people about God's kingdom. He tried to win them over, ⁹but some of them were stubborn and refused to believe. In front of everyone they said terrible things about God's Way. Paul left and took the followers with him to the lecture hall of Tyrannus. He spoke there every day ¹⁰for two years, until every Jew and Gentileʷ in Asia had heard the Lord's message.

The Sons of Sceva

¹¹God gave Paul the power to work great miracles. ¹²People even took handkerchiefs and aprons that had touched Paul's body, and they carried them to everyone who was sick. All of the sick people were healed, and the evil spirits went out.

¹³Some Jewish men started going around trying to force out evil spirits by using the name of the Lord Jesus. They

---

ᵛThen why were you baptised?...Because of what John taught: Or "In whose name were you baptised?...We were baptised in John's name." ʷGentile: The text has "Greek(s)" (see the note at 14.1).

said to the spirits, "Come out in the name of that same Jesus that Paul preaches about!"

14Seven sons of a Jewish high priest named Sceva were doing this, 15when an evil spirit said to them, "I know Jesus! And I've heard about Paul. But who are you?" 16Then the man with the evil spirit jumped on them and beat them up. They ran out of the house, naked and bruised.

17When the Jews and Gentiles in Ephesus heard about this, they were so frightened that they praised the name of the Lord Jesus. 18Many who were followers now started telling everyone about the evil things they had been doing. 19Some who had been practising witchcraft even brought their books and burnt them in public. These books were worth about 50 000 silver coins. 20So the Lord's message spread and became even more powerful.

The Riot in Ephesus

21After all of this had happened, Paul decided*x* to visit Macedonia and Achaia on his way to Jerusalem. Paul had said, "From there I'll go on to Rome." 22So he sent his two helpers, Timothy and Erastus, to Macedonia. But he stayed on in Asia for a while.

23At that time there was serious trouble because of the Lord's Way.*y* 24A silversmith named Demetrius had a business that made silver models of the temple of the goddess Artemis. Those who worked for him earned a lot of money. 25Demetrius brought together everyone who was in the same business and said:

Friends, you know that we make a good living at this. 26But you have surely seen and heard how this man Paul is upsetting a lot of people, not only in Ephesus, but almost everywhere in Asia. He claims that the gods we humans make are not really gods at all. 27Everyone will start saying terrible things about our business. They will stop respecting the temple of the goddess Artemis, who is worshipped in Asia and all over the world. Our great goddess will be forgotten!

---

xPaul decided: Or "Paul was led by the Holy Spirit." *ythe Lord's Way:* See the note at 9.2.

²⁸When the workers heard this, they got angry and started shouting, "Great is Artemis, the goddess of the Ephesians!" ²⁹Soon the whole city was in a riot, and some men grabbed Gaius and Aristarchus, who had come from Macedonia with Paul. Then everyone in the crowd rushed to the place where the town meetings were held.

³⁰Paul wanted to go out and speak to the people, but the Lord's followers wouldn't let him. ³¹A few of the local officials were friendly to Paul, and they sent someone to warn him not to go.

³²Some of the people in the meeting were shouting one thing, and others were shouting something else. Everyone was completely confused, and most of them didn't even know why they were there.

³³Several of the Jewish leaders pushed a man named Alexander to the front of the crowd and started telling him what to say. He motioned with his hand and tried to explain what was going on. ³⁴But when the crowd saw that he was Jewish, they all shouted for two hours, "Great is Artemis, the goddess of the Ephesians!"

³⁵Finally, a town official made the crowd be quiet. Then he said:

People of Ephesus, who in the world doesn't know that our city is the centre for worshipping the great goddess Artemis? Who doesn't know that her image which fell from heaven is right here? ³⁶No-one can deny this, and so you should calm down and not do anything foolish. ³⁷You have brought men in here who haven't robbed temples or spoken against our goddess.

³⁸If Demetrius and his workers have a case against these men, we have courts and judges. Let them take their complaints there. ³⁹But if you want to do more than that, the matter will have to be brought before the city council. ⁴⁰We could easily be accused of starting a riot today. There is no excuse for it! We can't even give a reason for this uproar.

⁴¹After saying this, he told the people to leave.

Paul Goes through Macedonia and Greece

20 ¹When the riot was over, Paul sent for the followers and encouraged them. He then said

goodbye to them and left for Macedonia. 2As he travelled from place to place, he encouraged the followers with many messages. Finally, he went to Greece[z] 3and stayed there for three months.

Paul was about to sail to Syria. But some of the Jewish leaders plotted against him, so he decided to return by way of Macedonia. 4With him were Sopater, son of Pyrrhus from Berea, and Aristarchus and Secundus from Thessalonica. Gaius from Derbe was also with him, and so were Timothy and the two Asians, Tychicus and Trophimus. 5They went on ahead to Troas and waited for us there. 6After the Festival of Thin Bread, we sailed from Philippi. Five days later we met them in Troas and stayed there for a week.

Paul's Last Visit to Troas

7On the first day of the week[a] we met to break bread together.[b] Paul spoke to the people until midnight because he was leaving the next morning. 8In the upstairs room where we were meeting, there were a lot of lamps. 9A young man by the name of Eutychus was sitting on a window sill. While Paul was speaking, the young man got very sleepy. Finally, he went to sleep and fell three floors all the way down to the ground. When they picked him up, he was dead.

10Paul went down and bent over Eutychus. He took him in his arms and said, "Don't worry! He's alive." 11After Paul had gone back upstairs, he broke bread, and ate with us. He then spoke until dawn and left. 12Then the followers took the young man home alive and were very happy.

The Voyage from Troas to Miletus

13Paul decided to travel by land to Assos. The rest of us went on ahead by ship, and we were to take him aboard there. 14When he met us in Assos, he came aboard, and we sailed on to Mitylene. 15The next day we came to a

---

[z]*Greece:* Probably Corinth.   [a]*On the first day of the week:* Since the Jewish day began at sunset, the meeting would have begun in the evening.   [b]*break bread together:* See the note at 2.46.

place near Chios, and the following day we reached Samos. The day after that we sailed to Miletus. [16]Paul had decided to sail on past Ephesus, because he didn't want to spend too much time in Asia. He was in a hurry and wanted to be in Jerusalem in time for Pentecost.[c]

Paul Says Goodbye to the Church Leaders of Ephesus

[17]From Miletus, Paul sent a message for the church leaders at Ephesus to come and meet with him. [18]When they got there, he said:

You know everything I did during the time I was with you when I first came to Asia. [19]Some of the Jews plotted against me and caused me a lot of sorrow and trouble. But I served the Lord and was humble. [20]When I preached in public or taught in your homes, I didn't hold back from saying anything that would help you. [21]I told Jews and Gentiles to turn to God and have faith in our Lord Jesus.

[22]I don't know what will happen to me in Jerusalem, but I must obey God's Spirit and go there. [23]In every city I visit, I'm told by the Holy Spirit that I will be put in jail and will be in trouble in Jerusalem. [24]But I don't care what happens to me, as long as I finish the work that the Lord Jesus gave me to do. And that work is to tell the good news about God's great kindness.

[25]I have gone from place to place, preaching to you about God's kingdom, but now I know that none of you will ever see me again. [26]I tell you today that I am no longer responsible for any of you! [27]I have told you everything God wants you to know. [28]Look after yourselves and everyone the Holy Spirit has placed in your care. Be like shepherds to God's church. It is the flock that he bought with the blood of his own Son.[d]

[29]I know that after I am gone, others will come like fierce wolves to attack you. [30]Some of your own people will tell lies to win over the Lord's followers. [31]Be on your guard! Remember how day and night for three

years I kept warning you with tears in my eyes.

³²I now place you in God's care. Remember the message about his great kindness! This message can help you and give you what belongs to you as God's people. ³³I have never wanted anyone's money or clothes. ³⁴You know how I have worked with my own hands to make a living for myself and my friends. ³⁵By everything I did, I showed how you should work to help everyone who is weak. Remember that our Lord Jesus said, "More blessings come from giving than from receiving."

³⁶After Paul had finished speaking, he knelt down with all of them and prayed. ³⁷Everyone cried and hugged and kissed him. ³⁸They were especially sad because Paul had told them, "You will never see me again."

Then they went with him to the ship.

Paul Goes to Jerusalem

21 ¹After saying goodbye, we sailed straight to Cos. The next day we reached Rhodes and from there sailed on to Patara. ²We found a ship going to Phoenicia, so we got on board and sailed off.

³We came within sight of Cyprus and then sailed south of it on to the port of Tyre in Syria, where the ship was going to unload its cargo. ⁴We looked up the Lord's followers and stayed with them for a week. The Holy Spirit had told them to warn Paul not to go on to Jerusalem. ⁵But when the week was over, we started on our way again. All the men, together with their wives and children, walked with us from the town to the seashore. We knelt on the beach and prayed. ⁶Then after saying goodbye to each other, we got onto the ship, and they went back home.

⁷We sailed from Tyre to Ptolemaïs, where we greeted the followers and stayed with them for a day. ⁸The next day we went to Caesarea and stayed with Philip, the preacher. He was one of the seven men who helped the apostles, ⁹and he had four unmarriedᵉ daughters who prophesied.

ᵉunmarried: Or "virgin."

¹⁰We had been in Caesarea for several days, when the prophet Agabus came to us from Judea. ¹¹He took Paul's belt, and with it he tied up his own hands and feet. Then he told us, "The Holy Spirit says that some of the Jewish leaders in Jerusalem will tie up the man who owns this belt. They will also hand him over to the Gentiles." ¹²After Agabus said this, we and the followers living there begged Paul not to go to Jerusalem.

¹³But Paul answered, "Why are you crying and breaking my heart? I'm not only willing to be put in jail for the Lord Jesus, I'm even willing to die for him in Jerusalem!"

¹⁴Since we couldn't get Paul to change his mind, we gave up and prayed, "Lord, please make us willing to do what you want."

¹⁵Then we got ready to go to Jerusalem. ¹⁶Some of the followers from Caesarea went with us and took us to stay in the home of Mnason. He was from Cyprus and had been a follower from the beginning.

Paul Visits James

¹⁷When we arrived in Jerusalem, the Lord's followers gladly welcomed us. ¹⁸Paul went with us to see James[f] the next day, and all the church leaders were present. ¹⁹Paul greeted them and told how God had used him to help the Gentiles. ²⁰Everyone who heard this praised God and said to Paul:

My friend, you can see how many tens of thousands of the Jewish people have become followers! And all of them are eager to obey the Law of Moses. ²¹But they have been told that you are teaching those who live among the Gentiles to disobey this Law. They claim that you are telling them not to circumcise their sons or to follow Jewish customs.

²²What should we do now that our people have heard that you are here? ²³Please do what we ask, because four of our men have made special promises to God. ²⁴Join with them and prepare yourself for the ceremony that goes with the promises. Pay the cost

---

ᶠJames: The Lord's brother.

for their heads to be shaved. Then everyone will learn that the reports about you are not true. They will know that you do obey the Law of Moses.

25Some time ago we told the Gentile followers what we think they should do. We instructed them not to eat anything offered to idols. They were told not to eat any meat with blood still in it or the meat of an animal that has been strangled. They were also told not to commit any terrible sexual sins.g

26The next day Paul took the four men with him and got himself ready at the same time as they did. Then he went into the temple and said when the final ceremony would take place and when an offering would be made for each of them.

Paul Is Arrested

27When the period of seven days for the ceremony was almost over, some of the Jewish people from Asia saw Paul in the temple. They got a large crowd together and started attacking him. 28They were shouting, "Friends, help us! This man goes around everywhere, saying bad things about our nation and about the Law of Moses and about this temple. He has even brought shame to this holy temple by bringing in Gentiles." 29Some of them thought that Paul had brought Trophimus from Ephesus into the temple, because they had seen them together in the city.

30The whole city was in an uproar, and the people turned into a mob. They grabbed Paul and dragged him out of the temple. Then suddenly the doors were shut. 31The people were about to kill Paul when the Roman army commander heard that all Jerusalem was starting to riot. 32So he quickly took some soldiers and officers and ran to where the crowd had gathered.

As soon as the mob saw the commander and soldiers, they stopped beating Paul. 33The army commander went over and arrested him and had him bound with two chains. Then he tried to find out who Paul was and what he had done. 34Part of the crowd shouted one thing, and

gnot to commit any terrible sexual sins: See the note at 15.20.

part of them shouted something else. But they were making so much noise that the commander couldn't find out a thing. Then he ordered Paul to be taken into the fortress. ³⁵As they reached the steps, the crowd became so wild that the soldiers had to lift Paul up and carry him. ³⁶The crowd followed and kept shouting, "Kill him! Kill him!"

Paul Speaks to the Crowd

³⁷When Paul was about to be taken into the fortress, he asked the commander, "Can I say something to you?"

"How do you know Greek?" the commander asked. ³⁸"Aren't you that Egyptian who started a riot not long ago and led 4000 terrorists into the desert?"

³⁹"No!" Paul replied. "I am a Jew from Tarsus, an important city in Cilicia. Please let me speak to the crowd."

⁴⁰The commander told him he could speak, so Paul stood on the steps and motioned to the people. When they were quiet, he spoke to them in Aramaic:

22 ¹"My friends and leaders of our nation, listen as I explain what happened!" ²When the crowd heard Paul speak to them in Aramaic, they became even quieter. Then Paul said:

³I am a Jew, born and raised in the city of Tarsus in Cilicia. I was a student of Gamaliel and was taught to follow every single law of our ancestors. In fact, I was just as eager to obey God as any of you are today.

⁴I made trouble for everyone who followed the Lord's Way,ʰ and I even had some of them killed. I had others arrested and put in jail. I didn't care if they were men or women. ⁵The high priest and all the council members can tell you that this is true. They even gave me letters to the Jewish leaders in Damascus, so that I could arrest people there and bring them to Jerusalem to be punished.

⁶One day about midday I was getting close to Damascus, when a bright light from heaven suddenly

---

ʰ*followed the Lord's Way:* See the note at 9.2.

flashed around me. ⁷I fell to the ground and heard a voice asking, "Saul, Saul, why are you so cruel to me?"

⁸"Who are you?" I answered.

The Lord replied, "I am Jesus from Nazareth! I am the one you are so cruel to." ⁹The men who were travelling with me saw the light, but didn't hear the voice.

¹⁰I asked, "Lord, what do you want me to do?"

Then he told me, "Get up and go to Damascus. When you get there, you will be told what to do." ¹¹The light had been so bright that I couldn't see. And the other men had to lead me by the hand to Damascus.

¹²In that city there was a man named Ananias, who faithfully obeyed the Law of Moses and was well liked by all the Jewish people living there. ¹³He came to me and said, "Saul, my friend, you can now see again!"

At once I could see. ¹⁴Then Ananias told me, "The God that our ancestors worshipped has chosen you to know what he wants done. He has chosen you to see the One Who Obeys God*ⁱ* and to hear his voice. ¹⁵You must tell everyone what you have seen and heard. ¹⁶What are you waiting for? Get up! Be baptised, and wash away your sins by praying to the Lord."

¹⁷After this I returned to Jerusalem and went to the temple to pray. There I had a vision ¹⁸of the Lord who said to me, "Hurry and leave Jerusalem! The people won't listen to what you say about me."

¹⁹I replied, "Lord, they know that in many of our meeting places I arrested and beat people who had faith in you. ²⁰Stephen was killed because he spoke for you, and I stood there and cheered them on. I even guarded the clothes of the men who murdered him."

²¹But the Lord told me to go, and he promised to send me far away to the Gentiles.

²²The crowd listened until Paul said this. Then they started shouting, "Get rid of this man! He doesn't deserve to live." ²³They kept shouting. They waved their clothes around and threw dust into the air.

ⁱOne Who Obeys God: See the note at 7.52.

Paul and the Roman Army Commander

²⁴The Roman commander ordered Paul to be taken into the fortress and beaten with a whip. He did this to find out why the people were screaming at Paul.

²⁵While the soldiers were tying Paul up to be beaten, he asked the officer standing there, "Is it legal to beat a Roman citizen before he has been tried in court?"

²⁶When the officer heard this, he went to the commander and said, "What are you doing? This man is a Roman citizen!"

²⁷The commander went to Paul and asked, "Tell me, are you a Roman citizen?"

"Yes," Paul answered.

²⁸The commander then said, "I paid a lot of money to become a Roman citizen."ʲ

But Paul replied, "I was born a Roman citizen."

²⁹The men who were about to beat and question Paul quickly backed off. And the commander himself was frightened when he realised that he had put a Roman citizen in chains.

Paul Is Tried by the Council

³⁰The next day the commander wanted to know the real reason why the Jewish leaders had brought charges against Paul. So he had Paul's chains removed, and he ordered the chief priests and the whole council to meet. Then he had Paul led in and made him stand in front of them.

23 ¹Paul looked straight at the council members and said, "My friends, to this day I have served God with a clear conscience!"

²Then Ananias the high priest ordered the men standing beside Paul to hit him on the mouth. ³Paul turned to the high priest and said, "You whitewashed wall!ᵏ God will hit you. You sit there to judge me by the Law of Moses. But at the same time you order men to break the Law by hitting me."

⁴The men standing beside Paul asked, "Don't you

ʲ*Roman citizen:* See the note at 16.37.　ᵏ*whitewashed wall:* Someone who pretends to be good, but really isn't.

know you are insulting God's high priest?"

5Paul replied, "Oh! I didn't know he was the high priest. The Scriptures do tell us not to speak evil about a leader of our people."

6When Paul saw that some of the council members were Sadducees and others were Pharisees, he shouted, "My friends, I am a Pharisee and the son of a Pharisee. I am on trial simply because I believe that the dead will be raised to life."

7As soon as Paul said this, the Pharisees and the Sadducees got into a big argument, and the council members started taking sides. 8The Sadducees do not believe in angels or spirits or that the dead will rise to life. But the Pharisees believe in all of these, 9and so there was a lot of shouting. Some of the teachers of the Law of Moses were Pharisees. Finally, they became angry and said, "We don't find anything wrong with this man. Maybe a spirit or an angel really did speak to him."

10The argument became fierce, and the commander was afraid that Paul would be pulled apart. So he ordered the soldiers to go in and rescue Paul. Then they took him back into the fortress.

11That night the Lord stood beside Paul and said, "Don't worry! Just as you have told others about me in Jerusalem, you must also tell about me in Rome."

A Plot To Kill Paul

12-13The next morning more than 40 Jewish men got together and vowed that they wouldn't eat or drink anything until they had killed Paul. 14Then some of them went to the chief priests and the nation's leaders and said, "We have promised God that we wouldn't eat a thing until we have killed Paul. 15You and everyone in the council must go to the commander and pretend that you want to find out more about the charges against Paul. Ask for him to be brought before your court. Meanwhile, we'll be waiting to kill him before he gets there."

16When Paul's nephew heard about the plot, he went to the fortress and told Paul about it. 17So Paul said to one of the army officers, "Take this young man to the commander. He has something to tell him."

¹⁸The officer took him to the commander and said, "The prisoner named Paul asked me to bring this young man to you, because he has something to tell you."

¹⁹The commander took the young man aside and asked him in private, "What do you want to tell me?"

²⁰He answered, "Some men are planning to ask you to bring Paul down to the Jewish council tomorrow. They will claim that they want to find out more about him. ²¹But please don't do what they say. More than 40 men are going to attack Paul. They've made a vow not to eat or drink anything until they've killed him. Even now they are waiting to hear what you decide."

²²The commander sent the young man away after saying to him, "Don't let anyone know that you told me this."

Paul Is Sent to Felix the Governor

²³The commander called in two of his officers and told them, "By nine o'clock tonight have 200 soldiers ready to go to Caesarea. Take along 70 men on horseback and 200 foot soldiers with spears. ²⁴Get a horse ready for Paul and make sure that he gets safely through to Felix the governor."

²⁵The commander wrote a letter that said:

²⁶Greetings from Claudius Lysias to the Honourable Governor Felix:

²⁷Some Jews grabbed this man and were about to kill him. But when I found out that he was a Roman citizen, I took some soldiers and rescued him.

²⁸I wanted to find out what they had against him. So I brought him before their council ²⁹and learnt that the charges concern only their religious laws. This man isn't guilty of anything for which he should die or even be put in jail.

³⁰As soon as I learnt that there was a plot against him, I sent him to you and told their leaders to bring charges against him in your court.

³¹The soldiers obeyed the commander's orders, and that same night they took Paul to the city of Antipatris. ³²The next day the foot soldiers returned to the fortress and let

the soldiers on horseback take him the rest of the way. [33]When they came to Caesarea, they gave the letter to the governor and handed Paul over to him.

[34]The governor read the letter. Then he asked Paul and found out that he was from Cilicia. [35]The governor said, "I will listen to your case as soon as the people come to bring their charges against you." After saying this, he gave orders for Paul to be kept as a prisoner in Herod's palace.[l]

Paul Is Accused in the Court of Felix

24 [1]Five days later Ananias the high priest, together with some of their leaders and a lawyer named Tertullus, went to the governor to present their case against Paul. [2]So Paul was called in, and Tertullus stated the case against him:[m]

Honourable Felix, you have brought our people a long period of peace, and because of your concern our nation is much better off. [3]All of us are always grateful for what you have done. [4]I don't want to bother you, but please be patient with us and listen to me for just a few minutes.

[5]This man has been found to be a real pest and troublemaker for Jews all over the world. He is also a leader of a group called Nazarenes. [6-8]When he tried to disgrace the temple, we arrested him.[n] If you question him, you will find out for yourself that our charges are true.

[9]The Jewish crowd spoke up and agreed with what Tertullus had said.

Paul Defends Himself

[10]The governor motioned for Paul to speak, and he began:

I know that you have judged the people of our nation

---

[l]Herod's palace: The palace built by Herod the Great and used by the Roman governors of Palestine. [m]Paul was called in, and Tertullus stated the case against him: Or "Tertullus was called in and stated the case against Paul." [n]we arrested him: Some manuscripts add, "We wanted to judge him by our own laws. But Lysias the commander took him away from us by force. Then Lysias ordered us to bring our charges against this man in your court."

for many years, and I am glad to defend myself in your court.

[11] It was no more than twelve days ago that I went to worship in Jerusalem. You can find this out easily enough. [12] Never once did the Jews find me arguing with anyone in the temple. I didn't cause trouble in the Jewish meeting places or in the city itself. [13] There is no way that they can prove these charges that they are now bringing against me.

[14] I admit that their leaders think that the Lord's Way[o] which I follow is based on wrong beliefs. But I still worship the same God that my ancestors worshipped. And I believe everything written in the Law of Moses and in the Prophets.[p] [15] I am just as sure as these people are that God will raise from death everyone who is good or evil. [16] And because I am sure, I try my best to have a clear conscience in whatever I do for God or for people.

[17] After being away for several years, I returned here to bring gifts for the poor people of my nation and to offer sacrifices. [18] This is what I was doing when I was found going through a ceremony in the temple. I wasn't with a crowd, and there was no uproar. [19] Some Jews from Asia were there at that time, and if they have anything to say against me, they should be here now. [20] Or ask the ones who are here. They can tell you that they didn't find me guilty of anything when I was tried by their own council. [21] The only charge they can bring against me is what I shouted out in court, when I said, "I am on trial today because I believe that the dead will be raised to life!"

[22] Felix knew a lot about the Lord's Way.[q] But he brought the trial to an end and said, "I will make my decision after Lysias the commander arrives." [23] He then ordered the army officer to keep Paul under guard, but not to lock him up or to stop his friends from helping him.

---

[o]the Lord's Way: See the note at 9.2.   [p]Law of Moses...the Prophets: The Jewish Scriptures, that is, the Old Testament.   [q]the Lord's Way: See the note at 9.2.

Paul Is Kept Under Guard

24Several days later Felix and his wife Drusilla, who was Jewish, went to the place where Paul was kept under guard. They sent for Paul and listened while he spoke to them about having faith in Christ Jesus. 25But Felix was frightened when Paul started talking to them about doing right, about self-control, and about the coming judgment. So he said to Paul, "That's enough for now. You may go. But when I have time I will send for you." 26After this, Felix often sent for Paul and talked with him, because he hoped that Paul would offer him a bribe.

27Two years later Porcius Festus became governor in place of Felix. But since Felix wanted to do the Jewish leaders a favour, he kept Paul in jail.

Paul Asks To Be Tried by the Roman Emperor

25 1Three days after Festus had become governor, he went from Caesarea to Jerusalem. 2There the chief priests and some Jewish leaders told him about their charges against Paul. They also asked Festus 3if he would be willing to bring Paul to Jerusalem. They begged him to do this because they were planning to attack and kill Paul on the way. 4But Festus told them, "Paul will be kept in Caesarea, and I am soon going there myself. 5If he has done anything wrong, let your leaders go with me and bring charges against him there."

6Festus stayed in Jerusalem for eight or ten more days before going to Caesarea. Then the next day he took his placeas judge and had Paul brought into court. 7As soon as Paul came in, the Jewish leaders from Jerusalem crowded around him and said he was guilty of many serious crimes. But they couldn't prove anything. 8Then Paul spoke in his own defence, "I have not broken the Law of my people. And I haven't done anything against either the temple or the Emperor."

9Festus wanted to please the leaders. So he asked Paul, "Are you willing to go to Jerusalem and be tried by me on these charges?"

10Paul replied, "I am on trial in the Emperor's court, and that's where I should be tried. You know very well

that I haven't done anything to harm the Jewish nation.
[11]If I had done something deserving death, I wouldn't ask
to escape the death penalty. But I am not guilty of any
of these crimes, and no-one has the right to hand me
over to these people. I now ask to be tried by the Emperor
himself."

[12]After Festus had talked this over with members of his
council, he told Paul, "You have asked to be tried by the
Emperor, and to the Emperor you will go!"

Paul Speaks to Agrippa and Bernice

[13]A few days later King Agrippa and Bernice came to
Caesarea to visit Festus. [14]They had been there for several
days, when Festus told the king about the charges against
Paul. He said:

Felix left a man here in jail, [15]and when I went to
Jerusalem, the chief priests and the Jewish leaders
came and asked me to find him guilty. [16]I told them
that it isn't the Roman custom to hand a man over to
people who are bringing charges against him. He must
first have the chance to meet them face to face and to
defend himself against their charges.

[17]So when they came here with me, I wasted no time.
On the very next day I took my place on the judge's
bench and ordered him to be brought in. [18]But when
the men stood up to make their charges against him,
they didn't accuse him of any of the crimes that I
thought they would. [19]Instead, they argued with him
about some of their beliefs and about a dead man named
Jesus, who Paul said was alive.

[20]Since I didn't know how to find out the truth
about all this, I asked Paul if he would be willing to go
to Jerusalem and be put on trial there. [21]But Paul asked
to be kept in jail until the Emperor could decide his
case. So I ordered him to be kept here until I could
send him to the Emperor.

[22]Then Agrippa said to Festus, "I would also like to hear
what this man has to say."

Festus answered, "You can hear him tomorrow."

[23]The next day Agrippa and Bernice made a big show
as they came into the meeting room. High ranking army

officers and leading citizens of the town were also there. Festus then ordered Paul to be brought in ²⁴and said:

King Agrippa and other guests, look at this man! Every Jew from Jerusalem and Caesarea has come to me, demanding for him to be put to death. ²⁵I haven't found him guilty of any crime deserving death. But because he has asked to be judged by the Emperor, I have decided to send him to Rome.

²⁶I have to write some facts about this man to the Emperor. So I have brought him before all of you, but especially before you, King Agrippa. After we have talked about his case, I will then have something to write. ²⁷It makes no sense to send a prisoner to the Emperor without stating the charges against him.

Paul's Defence before Agrippa

26 ¹Agrippa told Paul, "You may now speak for yourself." Paul stretched out his hand and said:

²King Agrippa, I am glad for this chance to defend myself before you today on all these charges that my own people have brought against me. ³You know a lot about our religious customs and the beliefs that divide us. So I ask you to listen patiently to me.

⁴⁻⁵All the Jews have known me since I was a child. They know what kind of life I have lived in my own country and in Jerusalem. And if they were willing, they could tell you that I was a Pharisee, a member of a group that is stricter than any other. ⁶Now I am on trial because I believe the promise God made to our people long ago.

⁷Day and night our twelve tribes have earnestly served God, waiting for his promised blessings. King Agrippa, because of this hope, the Jewish leaders have brought charges against me. ⁸Why should any of you doubt that God raises the dead to life?

⁹I once thought that I should do everything I could to oppose Jesus from Nazareth. ¹⁰I did this first in Jerusalem, and with the authority of the chief priests I put many of God's people in jail. I even voted for them to be killed. ¹¹I often had them punished in our meeting places, and I tried to make them give up their

faith. In fact, I was so angry with them, that I went looking for them in foreign cities.

¹²King Agrippa, one day I was on my way to Damascus with the authority and permission of the chief priests. ¹³About midday I saw a light brighter than the sun. It flashed from heaven on me and on everyone travelling with me. ¹⁴We all fell to the ground. Then I heard a voice say to me in Aramaic, "Saul, Saul, why are you so cruel to me? It's foolish to fight against me!"

¹⁵"Who are you?" I asked.

Then the Lord answered, "I am Jesus! I am the one you are so cruel to. ¹⁶Now stand up. I have appeared to you, because I have chosen you to be my servant. You are to tell others what you have learnt about me and what I will show you later."

¹⁷The Lord also said, "I will protect you from the Jews and from the Gentiles that I am sending you to. ¹⁸I want you to open their eyes, so that they will turn from darkness to light and from the power of Satan to God. Then their sins will be forgiven, and by faith in me they will become part of God's holy people."

¹⁹King Agrippa, I obeyed this vision from heaven. ²⁰First I preached to the people in Damascus, and then I went to Jerusalem and all over Judea. Finally, I went to the Gentiles and said, "Stop sinning and turn to God! Then prove what you've done by the way you live."

²¹That's why some Jews grabbed me in the temple and tried to kill me. ²²But all this time God has helped me, and I have preached both to the rich and to the poor. I've told them only what the prophets and Moses said would happen. ²³I told them how the Messiah would suffer and be the first to be raised from death, so that he could bring light to his own people and to the Gentiles.

²⁴Before Paul finished defending himself, Festus shouted, "Paul, you're crazy! Too much learning has driven you out of your mind."

²⁵But Paul replied, "Honourable Festus, I am not crazy. What I'm saying is true, and it makes sense. ²⁶None of these things happened off in a corner somewhere. I am

sure that King Agrippa knows what I'm talking about. That's why I can speak so plainly to him."

27 Then Paul said to Agrippa, "Do you believe what the prophets said? I know you do."

28 Agrippa asked Paul, "In such a short time do you think you can talk me into being a Christian?"

29 Paul answered, "Whether it takes a short time or a long time, I wish you and everyone else who hears me today would become just like me! Except, of course, for these chains."

30 Then King Agrippa, Governor Festus, Bernice, and everyone who was with them got up. 31 But before they left, they said, "This man isn't guilty of anything. He doesn't deserve to die or to be put in jail."

32 Agrippa told Festus, "Paul could have been set free, if he hadn't asked to be tried by the Roman Emperor."

Paul Is Taken to Rome

27 1 When it was time for us to sail to Rome, Captain Julius from the Emperor's special troops was put in charge of Paul and the other prisoners. 2 We went aboard a ship from Adramyttium that was about to sail to some ports along the coast of Asia. Aristarchus from Thessalonica in Macedonia sailed on the ship with us.

3 The next day we came to shore at Sidon. Captain Julius was very kind to Paul. He even let him visit his friends, so they could give him whatever he needed. 4 When we left Sidon, the winds were blowing against us, and we sailed close to the island of Cyprus to be safe from the wind. 5 Then we sailed south of Cilicia and Pamphylia until we came to the port of Myra in Lycia. 6 There the army captain found a ship from Alexandria that was going to Italy. So he ordered us to board that ship.

7 We sailed along slowly for several days and had a hard time reaching Cnidus. The wind wouldn't let us go any further in that direction, so we sailed past Cape Salmone, where the island of Crete would protect us from the wind. 8 We went slowly along the coast and finally reached a place called Fair Havens, not far from the town of Lasea.

9 By now we had already lost a lot of time, and sailing

was no longer safe. In fact, even the Great Day of Forgiveness[r] was past. [10]Then Paul spoke to the crew of the ship, "Men, listen to me! If we sail now, our ship and its cargo will be badly damaged, and many lives will be lost." [11]But Julius listened to the captain of the ship and its owner, rather than to Paul.

[12]The harbour at Fair Havens wasn't a good place to spend the winter. Because of this, almost everyone agreed that we should at least try to sail along the coast of Crete as far as Phoenix. It had a harbour that opened towards the south-west and north-west,[s] and we could spend the winter there.

The Storm at Sea

[13]When a gentle wind from the south started blowing, the men thought it was a good time to do what they had planned. So they pulled up the anchor, and we sailed along the coast of Crete. [14]But soon a strong wind called "The North-easter" blew against us from the island. [15]The wind struck the ship, and we couldn't sail against it. So we let the wind carry the ship.

[16]We went along the island of Cauda on the side that was protected from the wind. We had a hard time holding the lifeboat in place, [17]but finally we got it where it belonged. Then the sailors wrapped ropes around the ship to hold it together. They lowered the sail and let the ship drift along, because they were afraid it might hit the sandbanks in the gulf of Syrtis.

[18]The storm was so fierce that the next day they threw some of the ship's cargo overboard. [19]Then on the third day, with their bare hands they threw overboard some of the ship's gear. [20]For several days we couldn't see either the sun or the stars. A strong wind kept blowing, and we finally gave up all hope of being saved.

[21]Since none of us had eaten anything for a long time, Paul stood up and told the men:

[r]*Great Day of Forgiveness:* This Jewish festival took place near the end of September. The sailing season was dangerous after the middle of September, and it was stopped completely between the middle of November and the middle of March.   [s]*south-west and north-west:* Or "north-east and south-east."

You should have listened to me! If you had stayed on in Crete, you wouldn't have had this damage and loss. 22But now I beg you to cheer up, because you will be safe. Only the ship will be lost.

23I belong to God, and I worship him. Last night he sent an angel 24to tell me, "Paul, don't be afraid! You will stand trial before the Emperor. And because of you, God will save the lives of everyone on the ship." 25Cheer up! I am sure that God will do exactly what he promised. 26But we will first be shipwrecked on some island.

27For 14 days and nights we had been blown around over the Mediterranean Sea. But about midnight the sailors realised that we were getting near land. 28They measured and found that the water was about 40 metres deep. A little later they measured again and found it was only about 30 metres. 29The sailors were afraid that we might hit some rocks, and they let down four anchors from the back of the ship. Then they prayed for daylight.

30The sailors wanted to escape from the ship. So they lowered the lifeboat into the water, pretending that they were letting down an anchor from the front of the ship. 31But Paul said to Captain Julius and the soldiers, "If the sailors don't stay on the ship, you won't have any chance to save your lives." 32The soldiers then cut the ropes that held the lifeboat and let it fall into the sea.

33Just before daylight Paul begged the people to eat something. He told them, "For 14 days you've been so worried that you haven't eaten a thing. 34I beg you to eat something. Your lives depend on it. Do this and not one of you will be hurt."

35After Paul had said this, he took a piece of bread and gave thanks to God. Then in front of everyone, he broke the bread and ate some. 36They all felt encouraged, and each of them ate something. 37There were 276 people on the ship, 38and after everyone had eaten, they threw the cargo of wheat into the sea to make the ship lighter.

The Shipwreck

39Morning came, and the ship's crew saw a coast that they didn't recognise. But they did see a cove with a beach. So they decided to try to run the ship aground on the beach. ⁴⁰They cut the anchors loose and let them sink into the sea. At the same time they untied the ropes that were holding the rudders. Next, they raised the sail at the front of the ship and let the wind carry the ship towards the beach. ⁴¹But it ran aground on a sandbank. The front of the ship stuck firmly in the sand, and the rear was being smashed by the force of the waves.

⁴²The soldiers decided to kill the prisoners to keep them from swimming away and escaping. ⁴³But Captain Julius wanted to save Paul's life, and he didn't let the soldiers do what they had planned. Instead, he ordered everyone who could swim to dive into the water and head for shore. ⁴⁴Then he told the others to hold on to planks of wood or parts of the ship. At last, everyone safely reached shore.

On the Island of Malta

28 ¹When we came ashore, we learnt that the island was called Malta. ²The local people were very friendly, and they welcomed us by building a fire, because it was rainy and cold.

³After Paul had gathered some wood and had put it on the fire, the heat caused a snake to crawl out, and it bit him on the hand. ⁴When the local people saw the snake hanging from Paul's hand, they said to each other, "This man must be a murderer! He didn't drown in the sea, but the goddess of justice will kill him anyway."

⁵Paul shook the snake off into the fire and wasn't harmed. ⁶The people kept thinking that Paul would either swell up or suddenly drop dead. They watched him for a long time, and when nothing happened to him, they changed their minds and said, "This man is a god."

⁷The governor of the island was named Publius, and he owned some of the land around there. Publius was very friendly and welcomed us into his home for three days. ⁸His father was in bed, sick with fever and stomach trouble, and Paul went to visit him. Paul healed the man by praying and placing his hands on him.

⁹After this happened, everyone on the island brought their sick people to Paul, and they were all healed. ¹⁰The

people were very respectful to us, and when we sailed, they gave us everything we needed.

From Malta to Rome

11Three months later we sailed in a ship that had been docked at Malta for the winter. The ship was from Alexandria in Egypt and was known as "The Twin Gods."*t* 12We arrived in Syracuse and stayed for three days. 13From there we sailed to Rhegium. The next day a south wind began to blow, and two days later we arrived in Puteoli. 14There we found some of the Lord's followers, who begged us to stay with them. A week later we left for the city of Rome.

15Some of the followers in Rome heard about us and came to meet us at the Market of Appius and at the Three Inns. When Paul saw them, he thanked God and was encouraged.

Paul in Rome

16We arrived in Rome, and Paul was allowed to live in a house by himself with a soldier to guard him.

17Three days after we got there, Paul called together some of the Jewish leaders and said:

My friends, I've never done anything to hurt our people, and I've never gone against the customs of our ancestors. But in Jerusalem I was handed over as a prisoner to the Romans. 18They looked into the charges against me and wanted to release me. They found that I hadn't done anything deserving death. 19The Jewish leaders disagreed, so I asked to be tried by the Emperor.

But I haven't got anything to say against my own nation. 20I am bound by these chains because of what we people of Israel hope for. That's why I have called you here to talk about this hope of ours.

21The leaders replied, "No-one from Judea has written us a letter about you. And not one of them has come here to report on you or to say anything against you. 22But

---

*t*known as "The Twin Gods": Or "carried on its bow a wooden carving of the Twin Gods." These gods were Castor and Pollux, two of the favourite gods among sailors.

we would like to hear what you have to say. We understand that people everywhere are against this new group."

²³They agreed on a time to meet with Paul, and many of them came to his house. From early morning until late in the afternoon, Paul talked to them about God's kingdom. He used the Law of Moses and the Books of the Prophets[u] to try to win them over to Jesus.

²⁴Some of the leaders agreed with what Paul said, but others did not. ²⁵Since they couldn't agree among themselves, they started leaving. But Paul said, "The Holy Spirit said the right thing when he sent Isaiah the prophet ²⁶to tell our ancestors,

> 'Go to these people and tell them:
> You will listen and listen,
>> but never understand.
> You will look and look, but never see.

²⁷
>> All of you have stubborn hearts.
> Your ears are stopped up, and your eyes are covered.
>> You can't see or hear or understand.
> If you could,
>> you would turn to me, and I would heal you.' "

²⁸⁻²⁹Paul said, "You can be sure that God wants to save the Gentiles! And they will listen."[v]

³⁰For two years Paul stayed in a rented house and welcomed everyone who came to see him. ³¹He bravely preached about God's kingdom and taught about the Lord Jesus Christ, and no-one tried to stop him.

---

[u]*Law of Moses and the Books of the Prophets:* The Jewish Bible, that is, the Old Testament.   [v]*And they will listen:* Some manuscripts add, "After Paul said this, the people left, but they got into a fierce argument among themselves."

ROMANS

ABOUT THIS LETTER

Paul wrote this letter to introduce himself and his message to the church at Rome. He had never been to this important city, although he knew the names of many Christians there and hoped to visit them soon (chapter 15.22—16.21). Paul tells them that he is an apostle, chosen to preach the good news (1.1). And the message he proclaims "is God's powerful way of saving all people who have faith, whether they are Jews or Gentiles" (1.16).

Paul reminds his readers, "All of us have sinned and fallen short of God's glory" (3.23). But how can we be made acceptable to God? This is the main question that Paul answers in this letter. He begins by showing how everyone has failed to do what God requires. The Jews have not obeyed the Law of Moses, and the Gentiles have refused even to think about God, although God has spoken to them in many different ways (1.18—3.20).

Now we see how God does make us acceptable to him (3.21):

God...accepts people only because they have faith in Jesus Christ....God treats us much better than we deserve, and because of Christ Jesus, he freely accepts us and sets us free from our sins. (Chapter 3.22b, 24)

God gave Jesus to die for our sins, and he raised him to life, so that we would be made acceptable to God. (Chapter 4.25)

A QUICK LOOK AT THIS LETTER

1 ¹From Paul, a servant of Christ Jesus.

God chose me to be an apostle, and he appointed me to preach the good news ²that he promised long ago by what his prophets said in the holy Scriptures. ³⁻⁴This good news is about his Son, our Lord Jesus Christ! As a human, he was from the family of David. But the Holy Spirit*a* proved that Jesus is the powerful Son of God,*b* because he was raised from death.

⁵Jesus was kind to me and chose me to be an apostle,*c* so that people of all nations would obey and have faith. ⁶You are some of those people chosen by Jesus Christ.

⁷This letter is to all of you in Rome. God loves you and has chosen you to be his very own people.

I pray that God our Father and our Lord Jesus Christ will be kind to you and will bless you with peace!

A Prayer of Thanks

⁸First, I thank God in the name of Jesus Christ for all of you. I do this because people everywhere in the world are talking about your faith. ⁹God has seen how I never stop praying for you, while I serve him with all my heart and tell the good news about his Son.

¹⁰In all my prayers, I ask God to make it possible for me to visit you. ¹¹I want to see you and share with you the same blessings that God's Spirit has given me. Then you will grow stronger in your faith. ¹²What I am saying is that we can encourage each other by the faith that is ours.

¹³My friends, I want you to know that I have often planned to come for a visit. But something has always kept me from doing it. I want to win followers to Christ in Rome, as I have done in many other places. ¹⁴⁻¹⁵It doesn't matter if people are civilised and educated, or if they are uncivilised and uneducated. I must tell the good news to everyone. That's why I am eager to visit all of you in Rome.

---

athe Holy Spirit: Or "his own spirit of holiness." *bproved that Jesus is the powerful Son of God:* Or "proved in a powerful way that Jesus is the Son of God." *cJesus was kind to me and chose me to be an apostle:* Or "Jesus was kind to us and chose us to be his apostles."

The Power of the Good News

[16]I am proud of the good news! It is God's powerful way of saving all people who have faith, whether they are Jews or Gentiles. [17]The good news tells how God accepts everyone who has faith, but only those who have faith.[d] It is just as the Scriptures say, "The people God accepts because of their faith will live."[e]

Everyone Is Guilty

[18]From heaven God shows how angry he is with all the wicked and evil things that sinful people do to crush the truth. [19]They know everything that can be known about God, because God has shown it all to them. [20]God's eternal power and character can't be seen. But from the beginning of creation, God has shown what these are like by all he has made. That's why those people don't have any excuse. [21]They know about God, but they don't honour him or even thank him. Their thoughts are useless, and their stupid minds are in the dark. [22]They claim to be wise, but they are fools. [23]They don't worship the glorious and eternal God. Instead, they worship idols that are made to look like humans who can't live for ever, and like birds, animals, and reptiles.

[24]So God let these people go their own way. They did what they wanted to do, and their filthy thoughts made them do shameful things with their bodies. [25]They gave up the truth about God for a lie, and they worshipped God's creation instead of God, who will be praised for ever. Amen.

[26]God let them follow their own evil desires. Women no longer wanted to have sex in a natural way, and they did things with each other that were not natural. [27]Men behaved in the same way. They stopped wanting to have sex with women and had strong desires for sex with other men. They did shameful things with each other, and what has happened to them is punishment for their foolish deeds.

[28]Since these people refused even to think about God,

---

[d]*but only those who have faith:* Or "and faith is all that matters." [e]*The people God accepts because of their faith will live:* Or "The people God accepts will live because of their faith."

he let their useless minds rule over them. That's why they do all sorts of indecent things. ²⁹They are evil, wicked, and greedy, as well as mean in every possible way. They want what others have, and they murder, argue, cheat, and are hard to get along with. They gossip, ³⁰say cruel things about others, and hate God. They are proud, conceited, and boastful, always thinking up new ways to do evil.

These people don't respect their parents. ³¹They are stupid, unreliable, and don't have any love or pity for others. ³²They know God has said that anyone who acts this way deserves to die. But they keep on doing evil things, and they even encourage others to do them.

God's Judgment Is Fair

2 ¹Some of you accuse others of doing wrong. But there is no excuse for what you do. When you judge others, you condemn yourselves, because you are guilty of doing the very same things. ²We know that God is right to judge everyone who behaves in this way. ³Do you really think God won't punish you, when you behave exactly like the people you accuse? ⁴You surely don't think much of God's wonderful goodness or of his patience and willingness to put up with you. Don't you know that the reason God is good to you is because he wants you to turn to him?

⁵But you are stubborn and refuse to turn to God. So you are making things even worse for yourselves on that day when he will show how angry he is and will judge the world with fairness. ⁶God will reward each of us for what we have done. ⁷He will give eternal life to everyone who has patiently done what is good in the hope of receiving glory, honour, and life that lasts for ever. ⁸But he will show how angry and furious he can be with every selfish person who rejects the truth and wants to do evil. ⁹All who are wicked will be punished with trouble and suffering. It doesn't matter if they are Jews or Gentiles. ¹⁰But all who do right will be rewarded with glory, honour, and peace, whether they are Jews or Gentiles. ¹¹God doesn't have any favourites!

¹²Those people who don't know about God's Law will

still be punished for what they do wrong. And the Law will be used to judge everyone who knows what it says. 13God accepts those who obey his Law, but not those who simply hear it.

14Some people naturally obey the Law's commands, even though they haven't got the Law. 15This proves that the conscience is like a law written in the human heart. And it will show whether we are forgiven or condemned, 16when God appoints Jesus Christ to judge everyone's secret thoughts, just as my message says.

The Jews and the Law

17Some of you call yourselves Jews. You trust in the Law and take pride in God. 18By reading the Scriptures you learn how God wants you to behave, and you discover what is right. 19You are sure that you are a guide for the blind and a light for all who are in the dark. 20And since there is knowledge and truth in God's Law, you think you can instruct fools and teach young people.

21But how can you teach others when you refuse to learn? You preach that it is wrong to steal. But do you steal? 22You say people should be faithful in marriage. But are you faithful? You hate idols, yet you rob their temples. 23You take pride in the Law, but you disobey the Law and bring shame to God. 24It is just as the Scriptures tell us, "You have made foreigners say insulting things about God."

25Being circumcised is worthwhile, if you obey the Law. But if you don't obey the Law, you are no better off than people who aren't circumcised. 26In fact, if they obey the Law, they are as good as anyone who is circumcised. 27So everyone who obeys the Law, but has never been circumcised, will condemn you. Even though you are circumcised and have the Law, you still don't obey its teachings.

28Just because you live like a Jew and are circumcised doesn't make you a real Jew. 29To be a real Jew you must obey the Law. True circumcision is something that happens deep in your heart, not something done to your body. And besides, you should want praise from God and not from humans.

3 ¹What good is it to be a Jew? What good is it to be circumcised? ²It is good in a lot of ways! First of all, God's messages were spoken to the Jews. ³It is true that some of them didn't believe the message. But does this mean that God can't be trusted, just because they didn't have faith? ⁴No, indeed! God tells the truth, even if everyone else is a liar. The Scriptures say about God,

> "Your words will be proven true,
> and in court you will win your case."

⁵If our evil deeds show how right God is, then what can we say? Is it wrong for God to become angry and punish us? What a foolish thing to ask. ⁶But the answer is, "No." Otherwise, how could God judge the world? ⁷Since your lies bring great honour to God by showing how truthful he is, you may ask why God still says you are a sinner. ⁸You might as well say, "Let's do something evil, so that something good will come of it!" Some people even claim that we are saying this. But God is fair and will judge them as well.

No-one Is Good

⁹What does all this mean? Does it mean that we Jews are better off[f] than the Gentiles? No, it doesn't! Jews, as well as Gentiles, are ruled by sin, just as I have said. ¹⁰The Scriptures tell us,

> "No-one is acceptable to God!
> ¹¹ Not one of them understands
> or even searches for God.
> ¹² They have all turned away and are worthless.
> There isn't one person who does right.
> ¹³ Their words are like an open pit,
> and their tongues are good only for telling lies.
> Each word is as deadly as the fangs of a snake,
> ¹⁴ and they say nothing but bitter curses.
> ¹⁵ These people quickly become violent.
> ¹⁶ Wherever they go, they leave ruin and destruction.
> ¹⁷ They don't know how to live in peace.
> ¹⁸ They don't even fear God."

¹⁹We know that everything in the Law was written for

---

[f]better off: Or "worse off."

those who are under its power. The Law says these things to stop anyone from making excuses and to let God show that the whole world is guilty. 20God doesn't accept people simply because they obey the Law. No, indeed! All the Law does is to point out our sin.

God's Way of Accepting People

21Now we see how God does make us acceptable to him. The Law and the Prophets*g* tell how we become acceptable, and it isn't by obeying the Law of Moses. 22God treats everyone alike. He accepts people only because they have faith in Jesus Christ. 23All of us have sinned and fallen short of God's glory. 24But God treats us much better than we deserve,*h* and because of Christ Jesus, he freely accepts us and sets us free from our sins. 25-26God sent Christ to be our sacrifice. Christ offered his life's blood, so that by faith in him we could come to God. And God did this to show that in the past he was right to be patient and forgive sinners. This also shows that God is right when he accepts people who have faith in Jesus.

27What is left for us to boast about? Not a thing! Is it because we obeyed some law? No! It is because of faith. 28We see that people are acceptable to God because they have faith, and not because they obey the Law. 29Does God belong only to the Jews? Isn't he also the God of the Gentiles? Yes, he is! 30There is only one God, and he accepts Gentiles as well as Jews, simply because of their faith. 31Do we destroy the Law by our faith? Not at all! We make it even more powerful.

The Example of Abraham

4 1Well then, what can we say about our ancestor Abraham? 2If he became acceptable to God because of what he did, then he would have something to boast about. But he would never be able to boast about it to

---

*g*The Law and the Prophets: The Jewish Scriptures, that is, the Old Testament. *h*treats us much better than we deserve: The Greek word *charis*, traditionally rendered "grace," is translated here and other places in the CEV to express the overwhelming kindness of God.

God. ³The Scriptures say, "God accepted Abraham because Abraham had faith in him."

⁴Money paid to workers isn't a gift. It is something they earn by working. ⁵But you can't make God accept you because of something you do. God accepts sinners only because they have faith in him. ⁶In the Scriptures David talks about the blessings that come to people who are acceptable to God, even though they don't do anything to deserve these blessings. David says,

7   "God blesses people whose sins are forgiven
         and whose evil deeds are forgotten.
8   The Lord blesses people
         whose sins are erased from his book."

⁹Are these blessings meant for circumcised people or for those who aren't circumcised? Well, the Scriptures say that God accepted Abraham because Abraham had faith in him. ¹⁰But when did this happen? Was it before or after Abraham was circumcised? Of course, it was before.

¹¹Abraham let himself be circumcised to show that he had been accepted because of his faith even before he was circumcised. This makes Abraham the father of all who are acceptable to God because of their faith, even though they are not circumcised. ¹²This also makes Abraham the father of everyone who is circumcised and has faith in God, as Abraham did before he was circumcised.

The Promise Is for All Who Have Faith

¹³God promised Abraham and his descendants that he would give them the world. This promise wasn't made because Abraham had obeyed a law, but because his faith in God made him acceptable. ¹⁴If Abraham and his descendants were given this promise because they had obeyed a law, then faith would mean nothing, and the promise would be worthless.

¹⁵God becomes angry when his law is broken. But where there isn't a law, it can't be broken. ¹⁶Everything depends on having faith in God, so that God's promise is assured by his great kindness. This promise isn't only for Abraham's descendants who have the Law. It is for all who are Abraham's descendants because they have faith,

just as he did. Abraham is the ancestor of us all. 17The Scriptures say that Abraham would become the ancestor of many nations. This promise was made to Abraham because he had faith in God, who raises the dead to life and creates new things.

18God promised Abraham a lot of descendants. And when it all seemed hopeless, Abraham still had faith in God and became the ancestor of many nations. 19Abraham's faith never became weak, not even when he was nearly 100 years old. He knew that he was almost dead and that his wife Sarah couldn't have children. 20But Abraham never doubted or questioned God's promise. His faith made him strong, and he gave all the credit to God.

21Abraham was certain that God could do what he had promised. 22So God accepted him, 23just as we read in the Scriptures. But these words were not written only for Abraham. 24They were written for us, since we will also be accepted because of our faith in God, who raised our Lord Jesus to life. 25God gave Jesus to die for our sins, and he raised him to life, so that we would be made acceptable to God.

What It Means To Be Acceptable to God

5 1By faith we have been made acceptable to God. And now, because of our Lord Jesus Christ, we live at peace*i* with God. 2Christ has also introduced us*j* to God's undeserved kindness on which we take our stand. So we are happy, as we look forward to sharing in the glory of God. 3But that's not all! We gladly suffer,*k* because we know that suffering helps us to endure. 4And endurance builds character, which gives us a hope 5that will never disappoint us. All of this happens because God has given us the Holy Spirit, who fills our hearts with his love.

6Christ died for us at a time when we were helpless and sinful. 7No-one is really willing to die for an honest person, though someone might be willing to die for a

---

*i*we live at peace: Some manuscripts have "let us live at peace." *j*introduced us: Some manuscripts add "by faith." *k*We gladly suffer: Or "Let us gladly suffer."

truly good person. ⁸But God showed how much he loved us by having Christ die for us, even though we were sinful.

⁹But there is more! Now that God has accepted us because Christ sacrificed his life's blood, we will also be kept safe from God's anger. ¹⁰Even when we were God's enemies, he made peace with us, because his Son died for us. Yet something even greater than friendship is ours. Now that we are at peace with God, we will be saved by his Son's life. ¹¹And in addition to everything else, we are happy because God sent our Lord Jesus Christ to make peace with us.

Adam and Christ

¹²Adam sinned, and that sin brought death into the world. Now everyone has sinned, and so everyone must die. ¹³Sin was in the world before the Law came. But no record of sin was kept, because there was no Law. ¹⁴Yet death still had power over all who lived from the time of Adam to the time of Moses. This happened, though not everyone disobeyed a direct command from God, as Adam did.

In some ways Adam is like Christ who came later. ¹⁵But the gift that God was kind enough to give was very different from Adam's sin. That one sin brought death to many others. Yet in an even greater way, Jesus Christ alone brought God's gift of kindness to many people.

¹⁶There is a lot of difference between Adam's sin and God's gift. That one sin led to punishment. But God's gift made it possible for us to be acceptable to him, even though we have sinned many times. ¹⁷Death ruled like a king because Adam had sinned. But that can't compare with what Jesus Christ has done. God has been so kind to us, and he has accepted us because of Jesus. And so we will live and rule like kings.

¹⁸Everyone was going to be punished because Adam sinned. But because of the good thing that Christ has done, God accepts us and gives us the gift of life. ¹⁹Adam disobeyed God and caused many others to be sinners. But Jesus obeyed him and will make many people acceptable to God.

²⁰The Law came, so that the full power of sin could be

seen. Yet where sin was powerful, God's kindness was even more powerful. 21Sin ruled by means of death. But God's kindness now rules, and God has accepted us because of Jesus Christ our Lord. This means that we will have eternal life.

Dead to Sin but Alive because of Christ

6 1What should we say? Should we keep on sinning, so that God's wonderful kindness will show up even better? 2No, we should not! If we are dead to sin, how can we go on sinning? 3Don't you know that all who share in Christ Jesus by being baptised also share in his death? 4When we were baptised, we died and were buried with Christ. We were baptised, so that we would live a new life, as Christ was raised to life by the glory of God the Father.

5If we shared in Jesus' death by being baptised, we will be raised to life with him. 6We know that the people we used to be were nailed to the cross with Jesus. This was done so that our sinful bodies would no longer be the slaves of sin. 7We know that sin doesn't have power over dead people.

8As surely as we died with Christ, we believe we will also live with him. 9We know that death no longer has any power over Christ. He died and was raised to life, never to die again. 10When Christ died, he died for sin once and for all. But now he is alive, and he lives only for God. 11In the same way, you must think of yourselves as dead to the power of sin. But Christ Jesus has given life to you, and you live for God.

12Don't let sin rule your body. After all, your body is bound to die, so don't obey its desires 13or let any part of it become a slave of evil. Give yourselves to God, as people who have been raised from death to life. Make every part of your body a slave that pleases God. 14Don't let sin keep ruling your lives. You are ruled by God's kindness and not by the Law.

Slaves Who Do What Pleases God

15What does all this mean? Does it mean we are free to sin, because we are ruled by God's wonderful kindness and not by the Law? Certainly not! [16]Don't you know that you are slaves of anyone you obey? You can be slaves of sin and die, or you can be obedient slaves of God and be acceptable to him. [17]You used to be slaves of sin. But I thank God that with all your heart you obeyed the teaching you received from me. [18]Now you are set free from sin and are slaves who please God.

[19]I am using these everyday examples, because in some ways you are still weak. You used to let the different parts of your body be slaves of your evil thoughts. But now you must make every part of your body serve God, so that you will belong completely to him.

[20]When you were slaves of sin, you didn't have to please God. [21]But what good did you receive from the things you did? All you have to show for them is your shame, and they lead to death. [22]Now you have been set free from sin, and you are God's slaves. This will make you holy and will lead you to eternal life. [23]Sin pays off with death. But God's gift is eternal life given by Jesus Christ our Lord.

An Example from Marriage

7 [1]My friends, you surely understand enough about law to know that laws only have power over people who are alive. [2]For example, the Law says that a man's wife must remain his wife as long as he lives. But once her husband is dead, she is free [3]to marry someone else. However, if she goes off with another man while her husband is still alive, she is said to be unfaithful.

[4]That is how it is with you, my friends. You are now part of the body of Christ and are dead to the power of the Law. You are free to belong to Christ, who was raised to life so that we could serve God. [5]When we thought only of ourselves, the Law made us have sinful desires. It made every part of our bodies into slaves who are doomed to die. [6]But the Law no longer rules over us. We are like dead people, and it can't have any power over us. Now we can serve God in a new way by obeying his Spirit, and not in the old way by obeying the written Law.

The Battle with Sin

[7]Does this mean that the Law is sinful? Certainly not! But if it hadn't been for the Law, I wouldn't have known what sin is really like. For example, I wouldn't have known what it means to want something that belongs to someone else, unless the Law had told me not to do that. [8]It was sin that used this command as a way of making me have all kinds of desires. But without the Law, sin is dead.

[9]Before I knew about the Law, I was alive. But as soon as I heard that command, sin came to life, [10]and I died. The very command that was supposed to bring life to me, instead brought death. [11]Sin used this command to trick me, and because of it I died. [12]Still, the Law and its commands are holy and correct and good.

[13]Am I saying that something good caused my death? Certainly not! It was sin that killed me by using something good. Now we can see how terrible and evil sin really is. [14]We know that the Law is spiritual. But I am merely a human, and I have been sold as a slave to sin. [15]In fact, I don't understand why I act the way I do. I don't do what I know is right. I do the things I hate. [16]Although I don't do what I know is right, I agree that the Law is good. [17]So I am not the one doing these evil things. The sin that lives in me is what does them.

[18]I know that my selfish desires won't let me do anything that is good. Even when I want to do right, I can't. [19]Instead of doing what I know is right, I do wrong. [20]And so, if I don't do what I know is right, I am no longer the one doing these evil things. The sin that lives in me is what does them.

[21]The Law has shown me that something in me keeps me from doing what I know is right. [22]With my whole heart I agree with the Law of God. [23]But in every part of me I discover something fighting against my mind, and it makes me a prisoner of sin that controls everything I do. [24]What a miserable person I am. Who will rescue me from this body that is doomed to die? [25]Thank God! Jesus Christ will rescue me.

So with my mind I serve the Law of God, although my selfish desires make me serve the law of sin.

Living by the Power of God's Spirit

8 ¹If you belong to Christ Jesus, you won't be punished. ²The Holy Spirit will give you life that comes from Christ Jesus and will set you*ʲ* free from sin and death. ³The Law of Moses can't do this, because our selfish desires make the Law weak. But God set you free when he sent his own Son to be like us sinners and to be a sacrifice for our sin. God used Christ's body to condemn sin. ⁴He did this, so that we would do what the Law commands by obeying the Spirit instead of our own desires.

⁵People who are ruled by their desires think only of themselves. Everyone who is ruled by the Holy Spirit thinks about spiritual things. ⁶If our minds are ruled by our desires, we will die. But if our minds are ruled by the Spirit, we will have life and peace. ⁷Our desires fight against God, because they do not and cannot obey God's laws. ⁸If we follow our desires, we can't please God.

⁹You are no longer ruled by your desires, but by God's Spirit, who lives in you. People who haven't got the Spirit of Christ in them don't belong to him. ¹⁰But Christ lives in you. So you are alive because God has accepted you, even though your bodies must die because of your sins. ¹¹Yet God raised Jesus to life! God's Spirit now lives in you, and he will raise you to life by his Spirit.

¹²My dear friends, we must not live to satisfy our desires. ¹³If you do, you will die. But you will live, if by the help of God's Spirit you say "No" to your desires. ¹⁴Only those people who are led by God's Spirit are his children. ¹⁵God's Spirit doesn't make us slaves who are afraid of him. Instead, we become his children and call him our Father.*ᵐ* ¹⁶God's Spirit makes us sure that we are his children. ¹⁷His Spirit lets us know that together with Christ we will be given what God has promised. We will also share in the glory of Christ, because we have suffered with him.

ʲyou: Some manuscripts have "me." *ᵐour Father:* The Greek text uses the Aramaic word "Abba" (meaning "father"), which shows the close relation between the children and their father.

A Wonderful Future for God's People

[18]I am sure that what we are suffering now can't compare with the glory that will be shown to us. [19]In fact, all creation is eagerly waiting for God to show who his children are. [20]Meanwhile, creation is confused, but not because it wants to be confused. God made it this way in the hope [21]that creation would be set free from decay and would share in the glorious freedom of his children. [22]We know that all creation is still groaning and is in pain, like a woman about to give birth.

[23]The Spirit makes us sure about what we will be in the future. But now we groan silently, while we wait for God to show that we are his children.[n] This means that our bodies will also be set free. [24]And this hope is what saves us. But if we already have what we hope for, there is no need to keep on hoping. [25]However, we hope for something we have not yet seen, and we patiently wait for it.

[26]In certain ways we are weak, but the Spirit is here to help us. For example, when we don't know what to pray for, the Spirit prays for us in ways that can't be put into words. [27]All of our thoughts are known to God. He can understand what is in the mind of the Spirit, as the Spirit prays for God's people. [28]We know that God is always at work for the good of everyone who loves him.[o] They are the ones God has chosen for his purpose, [29]and he has always known who his chosen ones would be. He had decided to let them become like his own Son, so that his Son would be the first of many children. [30]God then accepted the people he had already decided to choose, and he has shared his glory with them.

God's Love

[31]What can we say about all this? If God is on our side, can anyone be against us? [32]God did not keep back his

---

[n]*to show that we are his children:* These words are not in some manuscripts. The translation of the remainder of the verse would then read, "while we wait for God to set our bodies free."　[o]*God is always at work for the good of everyone who loves him:* Or "All things work for the good of everyone who loves God" or "God's Spirit always works for the good of everyone who loves God."

own Son, but he gave him for us. If God did this, won't he freely give us everything else? 33If God says his chosen ones are acceptable to him, can anyone bring charges against them? 34Or can anyone condemn them? No indeed! Christ died and was raised to life, and now he is at God's right side,*p* speaking to him for us. 35Can anything separate us from the love of Christ? Can trouble, suffering, and hard times, or hunger and nakedness, or danger and death? 36It is exactly as the Scriptures say,

"For you we face death all day long.
We are like sheep on their way to be butchered."

37In everything we have won more than a victory because of Christ who loves us. 38I am sure that nothing can separate us from God's love—not life or death, not angels or spirits, not the present or the future, 39and not powers above or powers below. Nothing in all creation can separate us from God's love for us in Christ Jesus our Lord!

God's Choice of Israel

9 1I am a follower of Christ, and the Holy Spirit is a witness to my conscience. So I tell the truth and I am not lying when I say 2my heart is broken and I am in great sorrow. 3I would gladly be placed under God's curse and be separated from Christ for the good of my own people. 4They are the descendants of Israel, and they are also God's chosen people. God showed them his glory. He made agreements with them and gave them his Law. The temple is theirs and so are the promises that God made to them. 5They have those famous ancestors, who were also the ancestors of Jesus Christ. I pray that God, who rules over all, will be praised for ever!*q* Amen.

6It can't be said that God broke his promise. After all, not all of the people of Israel are the true people of God. 7-8In fact, when God made the promise to Abraham, he meant only Abraham's descendants by his son Isaac. God was talking only about Isaac when he promised 9Sarah,

*p*right side: The place of power and honour. *q*Christ. I pray that God, who rules over all, will be praised forever: Or "Christ, who rules over all. I pray that God will be praised for ever" or "Christ. And I pray that Christ, who is God and rules over all, will be praised for ever."

"At this time next year I will return, and you will already have a son."

¹⁰Don't forget what happened to the twin sons of Isaac and Rebecca. ¹¹⁻¹²Even before they were born or had done anything good or bad, the Lord told Rebecca that her older son would serve the younger one. The Lord said this to show that he makes his own choices and that it wasn't because of anything either of them had done. ¹³That's why the Scriptures say that the Lord liked Jacob more than Esau.

¹⁴Are we saying that God is unfair? Certainly not! ¹⁵The Lord told Moses that he has pity and mercy on anyone he wants to. ¹⁶Everything then depends on God's mercy and not on what people want or do. ¹⁷In the Scriptures the Lord says to Pharaoh of Egypt, "I let you become king, so that I could show you my power and be praised by all people on earth." ¹⁸Everything depends on what God decides to do, and he can either have pity on people or make them stubborn.

God's Anger and Mercy

¹⁹Someone may ask, "How can God blame us, if he makes us behave in the way he wants us to?" ²⁰But, my friend, I ask, "Who do you think you are to question God? Does the clay have the right to ask the potter why he shaped it the way he did? ²¹Doesn't a potter have the right to make a fancy bowl and a plain bowl out of the same lump of clay?"

²²God wanted to show his anger and reveal his power against everyone who deserved to be destroyed. But instead, he patiently put up with them. ²³He did this by showing how glorious he is when he has pity on the people he has chosen to share in his glory. ²⁴Whether Jews or Gentiles, we are those chosen ones, ²⁵just as the Lord says in the book of Hosea,

"Although they are not my people,
    I will make them my people.
I will treat with love those nations
    that have never been loved.
²⁶ "Once they were told, 'You are not my people.'
But in that very place they will be called

children of the living God."
27And this is what the prophet Isaiah said about the
people of Israel,

"The people of Israel are as many
as the grains of sand along the beach.
But only a few who are left will be saved.
28   The Lord will be quick and sure to do on earth
what he has warned he will do."
29Isaiah also said,
"If the Lord All-Powerful
had not spared some of our descendants,
we would have been destroyed
like the cities of Sodom and Gomorrah."r

Israel and the Good News

30What does all of this mean? It means that the
Gentiles weren't trying to be acceptable to God, but they
found that he would accept them if they had faith. 31-32It
also means that the people of Israel were not acceptable
to God. And why not? It was because they were tryings
to be acceptable by obeying the Law instead of by
having faith in God. The people of Israel fell over the
stone that makes people stumble, 33just as God says in
the Scriptures,

"Look! I am placing in Zion
a stone to make people stumble and fall.
But those who have faith in that one
will never be disappointed."

10 1Dear friends, my greatest wish and my prayer to
God is for the people of Israel to be saved. 2I know
they love God, but they don't understand 3what makes
people acceptable to him. So they refuse to trust God, and
they try to be acceptable by obeying the Law. 4But Christ
makes the Law no longer necessaryt for those who
become acceptable to God by faith.

---

rSodom and Gomorrah: During the time of Abraham the Lord destroyed these
two cities because their people were so sinful.   sbecause they were trying:
Or "while they were trying" or "even though they were trying."   tBut Christ
makes the Law no longer necessary: Or "But Christ gives the full meaning to
the Law."

Anyone Can Be Saved

⁵Moses said that a person could become acceptable to God by obeying the Law. He did this when he wrote, "If you want to live, you must do all that the Law commands."

⁶But people whose faith makes them acceptable to God will never ask, "Who will go up to heaven to bring Christ down?" ⁷Neither will they ask, "Who will go down into the world of the dead to raise him to life?"

⁸All who are acceptable because of their faith simply say, "The message is as near as your mouth or your heart." And this is the same message we preach about faith. ⁹So you will be saved, if you honestly say, "Jesus is Lord," and if you believe with all your heart that God raised him from death. ¹⁰God will accept you and save you, if you truly believe this and tell it to others.

¹¹The Scriptures say that no-one who has faith will be disappointed, ¹²no matter if that person is a Jew or a Gentile. There is only one Lord, and he is generous to everyone who asks for his help. ¹³All who call out to the Lord will be saved.

¹⁴How can people have faith in the Lord and ask him to save them, if they have never heard about him? And how can they hear, unless someone tells them? ¹⁵And how can anyone tell them without being sent by the Lord? The Scriptures say it is a beautiful sight to see even the feet of someone coming to preach the good news. ¹⁶Yet not everyone has believed the message. For example, the prophet Isaiah asked, "Lord, has anyone believed what we said?"

¹⁷No-one can have faith without hearing the message about Christ. ¹⁸But am I saying that the people of Israel didn't hear? No, I am not! The Scriptures say,

"The message was told everywhere on earth.
It was announced all over the world."

¹⁹Did the people of Israel understand or not? Moses answered this question when he wrote that the Lord had said,

"I will make Israel jealous of people
who are a nation of nobodies.
I will make them angry at people
who don't understand a thing."

20Isaiah was fearless enough to say that the Lord had said,
    "I was found by people who were not looking for me.
    I appeared to the one
    who were not asking about me."
21And Isaiah said about the people of Israel,
    "All day long the Lord has reached out
        to people who are stubborn and refuse to obey."

God Has Not Rejected His People

11 1Am I saying that God has turned his back on his people? Certainly not! I am one of the people of Israel, and I myself am a descendant of Abraham from the tribe of Benjamin. 2God didn't turn his back on his chosen people. Don't you remember reading in the Scriptures how Elijah complained to God about the people of Israel? 3He said, "Lord, they killed your prophets and destroyed your altars. I am the only one left, and now they want to kill me."

4But the Lord told Elijah, "I still have 7000 followers who have not worshipped Baal." 5It is the same way now. God was kind to the people of Israel, and so a few of them are still his followers. 6This happened because of God's undeserved kindness and not because of anything they have done. It could not have happened except for God's kindness.

7This means that only a chosen few of the people of Israel found what all of them were searching for. And the rest of them were stubborn, 8just as the Scriptures say,
    "God made them so stupid that their eyes are blind,
        and their ears are still deaf."
9Then David said,
    "Turn their meals into bait for a trap,
    so that they will stumble
        and be given what they deserve.
10 Blindfold their eyes! Don't let them see.
    Bend their backs beneath a burden
        that will never be lifted."

Gentiles Will Be Saved

11Do I mean that the people of Israel fell, never to get up again? Certainly not! Their failure made it possible for the Gentiles to be saved, and this will make the people of Israel jealous. 12But if the rest of the world's people were helped so much by Israel's sin and loss, they will be helped even more by their full return.

13I am now speaking to you Gentiles, and as long as I am an apostle to you, I will take pride in my work. 14I hope in this way to make some of my own people jealous enough to be saved. 15When Israel rejected God,u the rest of the people in the world were able to turn to him. So when God makes friends with Israel, it will be like bringing the dead back to life. 16If part of a batch of dough is made holy by being offered to God, then all of the dough is holy. If the roots of a tree are holy, the rest of the tree is holy too.

17You Gentiles are like branches of a wild olive tree that were made to be part of a cultivated olive tree. You have taken the place of some branches that were cut away from it. And because of this, you enjoy the blessings that come from being part of that cultivated tree. 18But don't think you are better than the branches that were cut away. Just remember that you are not supporting the roots of that tree. Its roots are supporting you.

19Maybe you think those branches were cut away, so that you could be put in their place. 20That's true enough. But they were cut away because they did not have faith, and you are where you are because you do have faith. So don't be proud, but be afraid. 21If God cut away those natural branches, couldn't he do the same to you?

22Now you see both how kind and how hard God can be. He was hard on those who fell, but he was kind to you. And he will keep on being kind to you, if you keep on trusting in his kindness. Otherwise, you will be cut away too.

23If those other branches will start having faith, they will be made a part of that tree again. God has the power to put them back. 24After all, it wasn't natural for branches to be cut from a wild olive tree and to be made part of a cultivated olive tree. So it is much more likely

uWhen Israel rejected God: Or "when Israel was rejected."

that God will join the natural branches back to the cultivated olive tree.

The People of Israel Will Be Brought Back

²⁵My friends, I don't want you Gentiles to be too proud of yourselves. So I will explain the mystery of what has happened to the people of Israel. Some of them have become stubborn, and they will stay like that until the complete number of you Gentiles has come in. ²⁶In this way all of Israel will be saved, as the Scriptures say,

"From Zion someone will come to rescue us.
Then Jacob's descendants will stop being evil.
²⁷ This is what the Lord has promised to do
when he forgives their sins."

²⁸The people of Israel are treated as God's enemies, so that the good news can come to you Gentiles. But they are still the chosen ones, and God loves them because of their famous ancestors. ²⁹God doesn't take back the gifts he has given or forget about the people he has chosen.

³⁰At one time you Gentiles rejected God. But now Israel has rejected God, and you have been shown mercy. ³¹And because of the mercy shown to you, they will also be shown mercy. ³²All people have disobeyed God, and that's why he treats them as prisoners. But he does this, so that he can have mercy on all of them.

³³Who can measure the wealth and wisdom and knowledge of God? Who can understand his decisions or explain what he does?

³⁴ "Has anyone known the thoughts of the Lord
or given him advice?
³⁵ Has anyone lent something to the Lord
that must be repaid?"

³⁶Everything comes from the Lord. All things were made because of him and will return to him. Praise the Lord for ever! Amen.

Christ Brings New Life

12 ¹Dear friends, God is good. So I beg you to offer your bodies to him as a living sacrifice, pure and pleasing. That's the most sensible way to serve God. ²Don't be like the people of this world, but let God change the way you think. Then you will know how to do everything that is good and pleasing to him.

3I realise how kind God has been to me, and so I tell each of you not to think you are better than you really are. Use good sense and measure yourself by the amount of faith that God has given you. 4A body is made up of many parts, and each of them has its own use. 5That's how it is with us. There are many of us, but we each are part of the body of Christ, as well as part of one another.

6God has also given each of us different gifts to use. If we can prophesy, we should do it according to the amount of faith we have. 7If we can serve others, we should serve. If we can teach, we should teach. 8If we can encourage others, we should encourage them. If we can give, we should be generous. If we are leaders, we should do our best. If we are good to others, we should do it cheerfully.

Rules for Christian Living

9Be sincere in your love for others. Hate everything that is evil and hold tight to everything that is good. 10Love each other as brothers and sisters and honour others more than you do yourself. 11Never give up. Eagerly follow the Holy Spirit and serve the Lord. 12Let your hope make you glad. Be patient in time of trouble and never stop praying. 13Take care of God's needy people and welcome strangers into your home.

14Ask God to bless everyone who mistreats you. Ask him to bless them and not to curse them. 15When others are happy, be happy with them, and when they are sad, be sad. 16Be friendly with everyone. Don't be proud and feel that you are more clever than others. Make friends with ordinary people.v 17Don't mistreat someone who has mistreated you. But try to earn the respect of others, 18and do your best to live at peace with everyone.

19Dear friends, don't try to get even. Let God take revenge. In the Scriptures the Lord says,
    "I am the one to take revenge
        and pay them back."

---

vMake friends with ordinary people: Or "Do ordinary jobs."

20The Scriptures also say,
"If your enemies are hungry,
give them something to eat.
And if they are thirsty,
give them something to drink.
This will be the same as piling burning coals
on their heads."
21Don't let evil defeat you, but defeat evil with good.

Obey Rulers

13 1Obey the rulers who have authority over you. Only God can give authority to anyone, and he puts these rulers in their places of power. 2People who oppose the authorities are opposing what God has done, and they will be punished. 3Rulers are a threat to evil people, not to good people. There is no need to be afraid of the authorities. Just do right, and they will praise you for it. 4After all, they are God's servants, and it is their duty to help you.

If you do something wrong, you ought to be afraid, because these rulers have the right to punish you. They are God's servants who punish criminals to show how angry God is. 5But you should obey the rulers because you know it is the right thing to do, and not just because of God's anger.

6You must also pay your taxes. The authorities are God's servants, and it is their duty to take care of these matters. 7Pay all that you owe, whether it is taxes and fees or respect and honour.

Love

8Let love be your only debt! If you love others, you have done all that the Law demands. 9In the Law there are many commands, such as, "Be faithful in marriage. Do not murder. Do not steal. Do not want what belongs to others." But all of these are summed up in the command that says, "Love others as much as you love yourself." 10No-one who loves others will harm them. So love is all that the Law demands.

The Day When Christ Returns

[11]You know what sort of times we live in, and so you should live properly. It is time to wake up. You know that the day when we will be saved is nearer now than when we first put our faith in the Lord. [12]Night is almost over, and day will soon appear. We must stop behaving as people do in the dark and be ready to live in the light. [13]So behave properly, as people do in the day. Don't go to wild parties or get drunk or be vulgar or indecent. Don't quarrel or be jealous. [14]Let the Lord Jesus Christ be as near to you as the clothes you wear. Then you won't try to satisfy your selfish desires.

Don't Criticise Others

14 [1]Welcome all the Lord's followers, even those whose faith is weak. Don't criticise them for having beliefs that are different from yours. [2]Some think it is all right to eat anything, while those whose faith is weak will eat only vegetables. [3]But you shouldn't criticise others for eating or for not eating. After all, God welcomes everyone. [4]What right do you have to criticise someone else's servants? Only their Lord can decide if they are doing right, and the Lord will make sure that they do right.

[5]Some of the Lord's followers think one day is more important than another. Others think all days are the same. But each of you should make up your own mind. [6]Any followers who count one day more important than another day do it to honour their Lord. And any followers who eat meat give thanks to God, just like the ones who don't eat meat.

[7]Whether we live or die, it must be for God, rather than for ourselves. [8]Whether we live or die, it must be for the Lord. Alive or dead, we still belong to the Lord. [9]This is because Christ died and rose to life, so that he would be the Lord of the dead and of the living. [10]Why do you criticise other followers of the Lord? Why do you look down on them? The day is coming when God will judge all of us. [11]In the Scriptures God says,

> "I swear by my very life
> that everyone will kneel down
> and praise my name!"

[12]And so, each of us must give an account to God for what we do.

Don't Cause Problems for Others

[13]We must stop judging others. We must also make up our minds not to upset anyone's faith. [14]The Lord Jesus has made it clear to me that God considers all foods fit to eat. But if you think some foods are unfit to eat, then for you they are not fit.

[15]If you are hurting others by the foods you eat, you aren't guided by love. Don't let your appetite destroy someone Christ died for. [16]Don't let your right to eat bring shame to Christ. [17]God's kingdom isn't about eating and drinking. It's about pleasing God, about living in peace, and about true happiness. All this comes from the Holy Spirit. [18]If you serve Christ in this way, you will please God and be respected by people. [19]We should try[w] to live at peace and help each other have a strong faith.

[20]Don't let your appetite destroy what God has done. All foods are fit to eat, but it's wrong to cause problems for others by what you eat. [21]It's best not to eat meat or drink wine or do anything else that causes problems for other followers of the Lord. [22]What you believe about these things should be kept between you and God. You are fortunate, if your actions don't make you have doubts. [23]But if you do have doubts about what you eat, you are going against your beliefs. And you know that is wrong, because anything you do against your beliefs is sin.

Please Others and Not Yourself

15 [1]If our faith is strong, we should be patient with the Lord's followers whose faith is weak. We should try to please them instead of ourselves. [2]We should think of their good and try to help them by doing what pleases them. [3]Even Christ didn't try to please

[w]*We should try:* Some manuscripts have "We try."

himself. But as the Scriptures say, "The people who insulted you also insulted me." 4And the Scriptures were written to teach and encourage us by giving us hope. 5God is the one who makes us patient and cheerful. I pray that he will help you live at peace with each other, as you follow Christ. 6Then all of you together will praise God, the Father of our Lord Jesus Christ.

The Good News Is for Jews and Gentiles

7Honour God by accepting each other, as Christ has accepted you. 8I tell you that Christ came as a servant of the Jews to show that God has kept the promises he made to their famous ancestors. Christ also came, 9so that the Gentiles would praise God for being kind to them. It is just as the Scriptures say,
> "I will tell the nations about you,
> and I will sing praises to your name."

10The Scriptures also say to the Gentiles, "Come and celebrate with God's people."

11Again the Scriptures say,
> "Praise the Lord, all you Gentiles.
> All you nations, come and worship him."

12Isaiah says,
> "Someone from David's family will come to power.
> He will rule the nations,
> and they will put their hope in him."

13I pray that God, who gives hope, will bless you with complete happiness and peace because of your faith. And may the power of the Holy Spirit fill you with hope.

Paul's Work as a Missionary

14My friends, I am sure that you are very good and that you have all the knowledge you need to teach each other. 15But I have spoken to you plainly and have tried to remind you of some things. God was so kind to me! 16He chose me to be a servant of Christ Jesus for the Gentiles and to do the work of a priest in the service of his good news. God did this so that the Holy Spirit could make the Gentiles into a holy offering, pleasing to him.

17Because of Christ Jesus, I can take pride in my service for God. 18In fact, all I will talk about is how Christ let

me speak and work, so that the Gentiles would obey him.
¹⁹Indeed, I will tell how Christ worked miracles and
wonders by the power of the Holy Spirit. I have preached
the good news about him all the way from Jerusalem to
Illyricum. ²⁰But I have always tried to preach where
people have never heard about Christ. I am like a builder
who doesn't build on anyone else's foundation. ²¹It is
just as the Scriptures say,

> "All who haven't been told about him will see him,
>   and those who haven't heard about him
>   will understand."

Paul's Plan To Visit Rome

²²My work has always kept me from coming to see you.
²³Now there is nothing left for me to do in this part of
the world, and for years I have wanted to visit you. ²⁴So
I plan to stop off on my way to Spain. Then after a short,
but refreshing, visit with you, I hope you will quickly
send me on.

²⁵⁻²⁶I am now on my way to Jerusalem to deliver the
money that the Lord's followers in Macedonia and
Achaia collected for God's needy people. ²⁷This is
something they really wanted to do. But sharing their
money with the Jews was also like paying back a debt,
because the Jews had already shared their spiritual
blessings with the Gentiles. ²⁸After I have safely delivered
this money, I will visit you and then go on to Spain.
²⁹And when I do arrive in Rome, I know it will be with
the full blessings of Christ.

³⁰My friends, by the power of the Lord Jesus Christ
and by the love that comes from the Holy Spirit, I beg
you to pray sincerely with me and for me. ³¹Pray that
God will protect me from the unbelievers in Judea, and
that his people in Jerusalem will be pleased with what I
am doing. ³²Ask God to let me come to you and have a
pleasant and refreshing visit. ³³I pray that God, who gives
peace, will be with all of you. Amen.

Personal Greetings

16 ¹I have good things to say about Phoebe, who is a
leader in the church at Cenchreae. ²Welcome her

in a way that is proper for someone who has faith in the Lord and is one of God's own people. Help her in any way you can. After all, she has proved to be a respected leader for many others, including me.

³Give my greetings to Priscilla and Aquila. They have not only served Christ Jesus together with me, ⁴but they have even risked their lives for me. I am grateful for them and so are all the Gentile churches. ⁵Greet the church that meets in their home.

Greet my dear friend Epaenetus, who was the first person in Asia to have faith in Christ.

⁶Greet Mary, who has worked so hard for you.

⁷Greet my relatives^x Andronicus and Junias^y, who were in jail with me. They are highly respected by the apostles and were followers of Christ before I was.

⁸Greet Ampliatus, my dear friend whose faith is in the Lord.

⁹Greet Urbanus, who serves Christ along with us. Greet my dear friend Stachys.

¹⁰Greet Apelles, a faithful servant of Christ. Greet Aristobulus and his family.

¹¹Greet Herodion, who is a relative of mine.

Greet Narcissus and the others in his family, who have faith in the Lord.

¹²Greet Tryphaena and Tryphosa, who work hard for the Lord.

Greet my dear friend Persis. She also works hard for the Lord.

¹³Greet Rufus, that special servant of the Lord, and greet his mother, who has been like a mother to me.

¹⁴Greet Asyncritus, Phlegon, Hermes, Patrobas, and Hermas, as well as our friends who are with them.

¹⁵Greet Philologus, Julia, Nereus and his sister, and Olympas, and all of God's people who are with them.

¹⁶Be sure to give each other a warm greeting.

All of Christ's churches greet you.

¹⁷My friends, I beg you to watch out for anyone who causes trouble and divides the church by refusing to do what all of you were taught. Stay away from them!

---

^x*relatives:* Or "Jewish friends." ^y*Junias:* Or Junia. Some manuscripts have Julia.

[18]They want to serve themselves and not Christ the Lord. Their flattery and fancy talk fool people who don't know any better. [19]I am glad that everyone knows how well you obey the Lord. But still, I want you to understand what is good and not have anything to do with evil. [20]Then God, who gives peace, will soon crush Satan under your feet. I pray that our Lord Jesus will be kind to you.

[21]Timothy, who works with me, sends his greetings, and so do my relatives, Lucius, Jason, and Sosipater.

[22]I, Tertius, also send my greetings. I am a follower of the Lord, and I wrote this letter.[z]

[23-24]Gaius welcomes me and the whole church into his home, and he sends his greetings.

Erastus, the city treasurer, and our dear friend Quartus send their greetings too.[a]

Paul's Closing Prayer

[25]Praise God! He can make you strong by means of my good news, which is the message about[b] Jesus Christ. For ages and ages this message was kept secret, [26]but now at last it has been told. The eternal God commanded his prophets to write about the good news, so that all nations would obey and have faith. [27]And now, because of Jesus Christ, we can praise the only wise God for ever! Amen.[c]

---

[z]*I wrote this letter:* Paul probably dictated this letter to Tertius.   [a]*send their greetings too:* Some manuscripts add, "I pray that our Lord Jesus Christ will always be kind to you. Amen."   [b]*about:* Or "from."   [c]*Amen:* Some manuscripts have verses 25-27 after 14.23. Others have the verses here and after 14.23, and one manuscript has them after 15.33.

1 CORINTHIANS
ABOUT THIS LETTER

Although this letter is called the First Letter to the Corinthians, it is not really the first one that Paul wrote to this church. We know this because he mentions in this letter that he had written one before (chapter 5.9). The Christians in Corinth had also written to him (7.1), and part of First Corinthians contains Paul's answers to questions they had asked.

Corinth is a large port city in southern Greece. Paul began his work there in a Jewish meeting place, but he had to move next door to the home of a Gentile who had become a follower of Jesus (Acts 18.1-17). Most of the followers in Corinth were poor people (1 Corinthians 1.26-29), though some of them were wealthy (1 Corinthians 11.18-21), and one was even the city treasurer (Romans 16.23). While he was in Corinth, Paul worked as a tentmaker to earn a living (Acts 18.3; 1 Corinthians 4.12; 9.1-18).

Paul was especially concerned about the way the Corinthian Christians were always arguing and dividing themselves into groups (1.10—4.21) and about the way they treated one another (5.1—6.20). These are two of Paul's main concerns as he writes this letter. But he also wants to answer the questions they asked him about marriage (7.1-40) and food offered to idols (8.1-13). Paul encourages them to worship God the right way (10.1—14.40) and to be firm in their belief that God has given them victory over death (15.1-58).

Love, Paul tells them, is even more important than faith or hope. All of the problems in the church could be solved, if all the members would love one another, as Christians should:

> Love is kind and patient,
>   never jealous, boastful, proud, or rude....
> Love rejoices in the truth, but not in evil.
> Love is always supportive, loyal, hopeful, and trusting.
>   Love never fails!   (Chapter 13.4, 5a, 6-8a)

A QUICK LOOK AT THIS LETTER

* Paul's Greeting and Prayer (1.1-9)
* A Call for Unity (1.10—4.21)
* Problems in Relationships (5.1—7.40)
* Honouring God Instead of Idols (8.1—11.1)
* Guidance for Worship and Church Life (11.2—14.40)
* Christ's Victory Over Death (15.1-58)
* An Offering for the Poor (16.1-4)
* Paul's Travel Plans (16.5-12)
* Personal Concerns and Greetings (16.13-24)

1 ¹From Paul, chosen by God to be an apostle of Christ Jesus, and from Sosthenes, who is also a follower.

²To God's church in Corinth. Christ Jesus chose you to be his very own people, and you worship in his name, as we and all others do who call him Lord.

³My prayer is that God our Father and the Lord Jesus Christ will be kind to you and will bless you with peace!

⁴I never stop thanking my God for being kind enough to give you Christ Jesus, ⁵who helps you speak and understand so well. ⁶Now you are certain that everything we told you about our Lord Christ Jesus is true. ⁷You are not missing out on any blessings, as you wait for him to return. ⁸And until the day Christ does return, he will keep you completely innocent. ⁹God can be trusted, and he chose you to be partners with his Son, our Lord Jesus Christ.

Taking Sides

¹⁰My dear friends, as a follower of our Lord Jesus Christ, I beg you to get along with each other. Don't take sides. Always try to agree in what you think. ¹¹Several people from Chloe's family*a* have already reported to me that you keep arguing with each other. ¹²They have said that some of you claim to follow me, while others claim to follow Apollos or Peter*b* or Christ.

¹³Has Christ been divided up? Was I nailed to a cross

afamily: Family members and possibly slaves and others who may have lived in the house. *bPeter:* The Greek text has "Cephas," which is an Aramaic name meaning "rock." Peter is the Greek name with the same meaning.

for you? Were you baptised in my name? [14]I thank God[c] that I didn't baptise any of you except Crispus and Gaius. [15]Not one of you can say that you were baptised in my name. [16]I did baptise the family[d] of Stephanas, but I don't remember if I baptised anyone else. [17]Christ did not send me to baptise. He sent me to tell the good news without using big words that would make the cross of Christ lose its power.

Christ Is God's Power and Wisdom

[18]The message about the cross doesn't make any sense to lost people. But for those of us who are being saved, it is God's power at work. [19]As God says in the Scriptures,

"I will destroy the wisdom of all
who claim to be wise.
I will confuse those
who think they know so much."

[20]What happened to those wise people? What happened to those experts in the Scriptures? What happened to the ones who think they have all the answers? Didn't God show that the wisdom of this world is foolish? [21]God was wise and decided not to let the people of this world use their wisdom to learn about him.

Instead, God chose to save only those who believe the foolish message we preach. [22]Jews ask for miracles, and Greeks want something that sounds wise. [23]But we preach that Christ was nailed to a cross. Most Jews have problems with this, and most Gentiles think it's foolish. [24]Our message is God's power and wisdom for the Jews and the Greeks that he has chosen. [25]Even when God is foolish, he is wiser than everyone else, and even when God is weak, he is stronger than everyone else.

[26]My dear friends, remember what you were when God chose you. The people of this world didn't think that many of you were wise. Only a few of you were in places of power, and not many of you came from important families. [27]But God chose the foolish things of this world to put the wise to shame. He chose the weak things of

[c]*I thank God:* Some manuscripts have "I thank my God." [d]*family:* See the note at 1.11.

this world to put the powerful to shame.

28 What the world thinks is worthless, useless, and nothing at all, is what God has used to destroy what the world considers important. 29 God did all this to keep anyone from boasting to him. 30 You are God's children. He sent Christ Jesus to save us and to make us wise, acceptable, and holy. 31 So if you want to boast, do what the Scriptures say and boast about the Lord.

Speaking about Christ and the Cross

2 ¹Friends, when I came and told you the mystery[e] that God had shared with us, I didn't use big words or try to sound wise. ²In fact, while I was with you, I made up my mind to speak only about Jesus Christ, who had been nailed to a cross.

³At first, I was weak and trembling with fear. ⁴When I talked with you or preached, I didn't try to prove anything by sounding wise. I simply let God's Spirit show his power. ⁵That way you would have faith because of God's power and not because of human wisdom.

⁶We do use wisdom when speaking to people who are mature in their faith. But it isn't the wisdom of this world or of its rulers, who will soon disappear. ⁷We speak of God's hidden and mysterious wisdom that God decided to use for our glory long before the world began. ⁸The rulers of this world didn't know anything about this wisdom. If they had known about it, they would not have nailed the glorious Lord to a cross. ⁹But it's just as the Scriptures say,

> "What God has planned for people who love him
> is more than eyes have seen or ears have heard.
> It has never even entered our minds!"

¹⁰God's Spirit has shown you everything. His Spirit finds out everything, even what is deep in the mind of God. ¹¹You are the only one who knows what's in your own mind, and God's Spirit is the only one who knows what's in God's mind. ¹²But God has given us his Spirit. That's why we don't think the same way that the people of this world think. That's also why we can recognise the

---

emystery: Some manuscripts have "testimony."

blessings that God has given us.

[13]Every word we speak was taught to us by God's Spirit, not by human wisdom. And this same Spirit helps us teach spiritual things to spiritual people.[f] [14]That's why only someone who has God's Spirit can understand spiritual blessings. Anyone who doesn't have God's Spirit thinks these blessings are foolish. [15]People who are guided by the Spirit can make all kinds of judgments, but they can't be judged by others. [16]The Scriptures ask,

"Has anyone ever known the thoughts of the Lord
or given him advice?"

But we understand what Christ is thinking.[g]

Working Together for God

3 [1]My friends, you are acting like the people of this world. That's why I couldn't speak to you as spiritual people. You are like babies as far as your faith in Christ is concerned. [2]So I had to treat you like babies and feed you milk. You couldn't take solid food, and you still can't, [3]because you are not yet spiritual. You are jealous and argue with each other. This proves that you aren't spiritual and that you are acting like the people of this world.

[4]Some of you say that you follow me, and others claim to follow Apollos. Isn't that how ordinary people behave? [5]Apollos and I are merely servants who helped you to have faith. It was the Lord who made it all happen. [6]I planted the seeds, Apollos watered them, but God made them sprout and grow. [7]What matters isn't those who planted or watered, but God who made the plants grow. [8]The one who plants is just as important as the one who waters. And each one will be paid for what they do. [9]Apollos and I work together for God, and you are God's garden and God's building.

Only One Foundation

[10]God was kind and let me become an expert builder. I laid a foundation on which others have built. But we

---

[f]teach spiritual things to spiritual people: Or "compare spiritual things with spiritual things." [g]we understand what Christ is thinking: Or "we think as Christ does."

must each be careful how we build, [11]because Christ is the only foundation. [12-13]Whatever we build on that foundation will be tested by fire on the day of judgment. Then everyone will find out if we have used gold, silver, and precious stones, or wood, hay, and straw. [14]We will be rewarded if our building is left standing. [15]But if it's destroyed by the fire, we will lose everything. Yet we ourselves will be saved, like someone escaping from flames.

[16]All of you surely know that you are God's temple and that his Spirit lives in you. [17]Together you are God's holy temple, and God will destroy anyone who destroys his temple.

[18]Don't fool yourselves! If any of you think you are wise in the things of this world, you will have to become foolish before you can be truly wise. [19]This is because God considers the wisdom of this world to be foolish. It is just as the Scriptures say, "God catches the wise when they try to outsmart him." [20]The Scriptures also say, "The Lord knows that the plans made by wise people are useless." [21-22]So stop boasting about what anyone has done. Paul and Apollos and Peter[h] all belong to you. In fact, everything is yours, including the world, life, death, the present, and the future. Everything belongs to you, [23]and you belong to Christ, and Christ belongs to God.

The Work of the Apostles

4 [1]Think of us as servants of Christ who have been given the work of explaining God's mysterious ways. [2]And since our first duty is to be faithful to the one we work for, [3]it doesn't matter to me if I am judged by you or even by a court of law. In fact, I don't judge myself. [4]I don't know of anything against me, but that doesn't prove that I'm right. The Lord is my judge. [5]So don't judge anyone until the Lord returns. He will show what is hidden in the dark and what is in everyone's heart. Then God will be the one who praises each of us.

[6]Friends, I have used Apollos and myself as examples to teach you the meaning of the saying, "Follow the rules." I want you to stop saying that one of us is better than the other. [7]What is so special about you? What have

[h]Peter: See the note at 1.12.

you got that you weren't given? And if it was given to you, how can you boast? 8Are you already satisfied? Are you now rich? Have you become kings while we are still nobodies? I wish you were kings. Then we could have a share in your kingdom.

9It seems to me that God has put us apostles in the worst possible place. We are like prisoners on their way to death. Angels and the people of this world just laugh at us. 10Because of Christ we are thought of as fools, but Christ has made you wise. We are weak and hated, but you are powerful and respected. 11Even today we go hungry and thirsty and don't have anything to wear except rags. We are mistreated and don't have a place to live. 12We work hard with our own hands, and when people abuse us, we wish them well. When we suffer, we are patient. 13When someone curses us, we answer with kind words. Until now we are thought of as nothing more than the rubbish and garbage of this world.

14I am not writing to embarrass you. I want to help you, just as parents help their own dear children. 15Ten thousand people may teach you about Christ, but I am your only father. You became my children when I told you about Christ Jesus, 16and I want you to be like me. 17That's why I sent Timothy to you. I love him like a son, and he is a faithful servant of the Lord. Timothy will tell you what I do to follow Christ and how it agrees with what I always teach about Christ in every church.

18Some of you think I am not coming for a visit, and so you are boasting. 19But if the Lord lets me come, I will soon be there. Then I will find out if the ones who are doing all this boasting really have any power. 20God's kingdom isn't just a lot of words. It is power. 21What do you want me to do when I arrive? Do you want me to be hard on you or to be kind and gentle?

Immoral Followers

5 1I have heard terrible things about some of you. In fact, you are behaving worse than the Gentiles. A man is even sleeping with his own stepmother.*i* 2You are

iis even sleeping with his own stepmother: Or "has even married his own stepmother."

proud, when you ought to feel bad enough to chase away anyone who acts like that.

³⁻⁴I am with you only in my thoughts. But in the name of our Lord Jesus I have already judged this man, as though I were with you in person. So when you meet together and the power of the Lord Jesus is with you, I will be there too. ⁵You must then hand that man over to Satan. His body will be destroyed, but his spirit will be saved when the Lord Jesus returns.

⁶Stop being proud! Don't you know how a little yeast can spread through the whole batch of dough? ⁷Get rid of the old yeast! Then you will be like fresh bread made without yeast, and that is what you are. Our Passover lamb is Christ, who has already been sacrificed. ⁸So don't celebrate the festival by being evil and sinful, which is like serving bread made with yeast. Be pure and truthful and celebrate by using bread made without yeast.

⁹In my other letterʲ I told you not to have anything to do with immoral people. ¹⁰But I wasn't talking about the people of this world. You would have to leave this world to get away from everyone who is immoral or greedy or who cheats or worships idols. ¹¹I was talking about your own people who are immoral or greedy or worship idols or curse others or get drunk or cheat. Don't even eat with them! ¹²Why should I judge outsiders? Aren't we supposed to judge only church members? ¹³God judges everyone else. The Scriptures say, "Chase away any of your own people who are evil."

Taking Each Other to Court

6 ¹When one of you has a complaint against another, do you take your complaint to a court of sinners? Or do you take it to God's people? ²Don't you know that God's people will judge the world? And if you are going to judge the world, can't you settle small problems? ³Don't you know that we will judge angels? And if that is so, we can surely judge everyday matters. ⁴Why do you take everyday complaints to judges who are not

ʲother letter: An unknown letter that Paul wrote to the Christians at Corinth before he wrote this one.

respected by the church? [5]I say this to your shame. Aren't any of you wise enough to act as a judge between one follower and another? [6]Why should one of you take another to be tried by unbelievers?

[7]When one of you takes another to court, all of you lose. It would be better to let yourselves be cheated and robbed. [8]But instead, you cheat and rob other followers.

[9]Don't you know that evil people won't have a share in the blessings of God's kingdom? Don't fool yourselves! No-one who is immoral or worships idols, or is unfaithful in marriage or is a pervert, or behaves like a homosexual, [10]will share in God's kingdom. Neither will any thief or greedy person, or drunkard or anyone who curses and cheats others. [11]Some of you used to be like that. But now the name of our Lord Jesus Christ and the power of God's Spirit have washed you and made you holy and acceptable to God.

Honour God with Your Body

[12]Some of you say, "We can do anything we want to." But I tell you that not everything is good for us. So I refuse to let anything have power over me. [13]You also say, "Food is meant for our bodies, and our bodies are meant for food." But I tell you that God will destroy them both. We are not supposed to do indecent things with our bodies. We are to use them for the Lord who is in charge of our bodies. [14]God will raise us from death by the same power that he used when he raised our Lord to life.

[15]Don't you know that your bodies are part of the body of Christ? Is it right for me to join part of the body of Christ to a prostitute? No, it isn't! [16]Don't you know that a man who does that becomes part of her body? The Scriptures say, "The two of them will be like one person." [17]But anyone who is joined to the Lord is one in spirit with him.

[18]Don't be immoral in matters of sex. That is a sin against your own body in a way that no other sin is. [19]You surely know that your body is a temple where the Holy Spirit lives. The Spirit is in you and is a gift from God. You are no longer your own. [20]God paid a great price for you. So use your body to honour God.

Questions about Marriage

7 [1]Now I will answer the questions that you asked in your letter. You asked, "Is it best for people not to marry?"[k] [2]Well, having your own husband or wife should keep you from doing something immoral. [3]Husbands and wives should be fair with each other about having sex. [4]A wife belongs to her husband instead of to herself, and a husband belongs to his wife instead of to himself. [5]So don't refuse sex to each other, unless you agree not to have sex for a little while, in order to spend time in prayer. Then Satan won't be able to tempt you because of your lack of self-control. [6]In my opinion that is what should be done, though I don't know of anything the Lord said about this matter. [7]I wish that all of you were like me, but God has given different gifts to each of us.

[8]Here is my advice for people who have never been married and for widows. You should stay single, just as I am. [9]But if you don't have enough self-control, then go ahead and get married. After all, it is better to marry than to burn with desire.[l]

[10]I instruct married couples to stay together, and this is exactly what the Lord himself taught. A wife who leaves her husband [11]should either stay single or go back to her husband. And a husband should not leave his wife.

[12]I don't know of anything else the Lord said about marriage. All I can do is to give you my own advice. If your wife isn't a follower of the Lord, but is willing to stay with you, don't divorce her. [13]If your husband isn't a follower, but is willing to stay with you, don't divorce him. [14]Your husband or wife who isn't a follower is made holy by having you as a mate. This also makes your children holy and keeps them from being unclean in God's sight.

[15]If your husband or wife isn't a follower of the Lord and decides to divorce you, then you should agree to it. You are no longer bound to that person. After all, God chose you and wants you to live at peace. [16]And besides, how do you know if you will be able to save your husband or wife who isn't a follower?

---

[k]*people not to marry:* Or "married couples not to have sex." [l]*with desire:* Or "in the flames of hell."

Obeying the Lord at All Times

[17]In every church I tell the people to stay as they were when the Lord Jesus chose them and God called them to be his own. Now I say the same thing to you. [18]If you are already circumcised, don't try to change it. If you are not circumcised, don't get circumcised. [19]Being circumcised or uncircumcised isn't really what matters. The important thing is to obey God's commands. [20]So don't try to change what you were when God chose you. [21]Are you a slave? Don't let that bother you. But if you can win your freedom, you should. [22]When the Lord chooses slaves, they become his free people. And when he chooses free people, they become slaves of Christ. [23]God paid a great price for you. So don't become slaves of anyone else. [24]Stay what you were when God chose you.

Unmarried People

[25]I don't know of anything that the Lord said about people who have never been married.[m] But I will tell you what I think. And you can trust me, because the Lord has treated me with kindness. [26]We are now going through hard times, and I think it's best for you to stay as you are. [27]If you are married, stay married. If you aren't married, don't try to get married. [28]It isn't wrong to marry, even if you have never been married before. But those who marry will have a lot of trouble, and I want to protect you from that.

[29]My friends, what I mean is that the Lord will soon come,[n] and it won't matter if you are married or not. [30]It will be all the same if you are crying or laughing, or if you are buying or are completely broke. [31]It won't make any difference how much good you are getting from this world or how much you like it. This world as we know it is now passing away.

[32]I want all of you to be free from worry. An unmarried man worries about how to please the Lord. [33]But a married man has more worries. He must worry about the things of this world, because he wants to please his wife.

---

[m]people who have never been married: Or "virgins." [n]the Lord will soon come: Or "there's not much time left" or "the time for decision comes quickly."

³⁴So he is pulled in two directions. Unmarried women and women who have never been married⁰ worry only about pleasing the Lord, and they keep their bodies and minds pure. But a married woman worries about the things of this world, because she wants to please her husband. ³⁵What I am saying is for your own good—it isn't to limit your freedom. I want to help you to live right and to love the Lord above all else.

³⁶But suppose you are engaged to someone old enough to be married and you want her so much that all you can think about is getting married. Then go ahead and marry.ᵖ There is nothing wrong with that. ³⁷But it is better to have self-control and to make up your mind not to marry. ³⁸It is perfectly all right to marry, but it is better not to get married at all.

³⁹A wife should stay married to her husband until he dies. Then she is free to marry again, but only to a man who is a follower of the Lord. ⁴⁰However, I think I am obeying God's Spirit when I say she would be happier to stay single.

Food Offered to Idols

8 ¹In your letter you asked me about food offered to idols. All of us know something about this subject. But knowledge makes us proud of ourselves, while love makes us helpful to others. ²In fact, people who think they know so much don't know anything at all. ³But God has no doubts about who loves him.

⁴Even though food is offered to idols, we know that none of the idols in this world are alive. After all, there is only one God. ⁵Many things in heaven and on earth are called gods and lords, but none of them really are gods or lords. ⁶We have only one God, and he is the Father. He created everything, and we live for him. Jesus Christ is our only Lord. Everything was made by him, and by him

---

⁰*women who have never been married:* Or "virgins." ᵖ*But suppose you are engaged...go ahead and marry:* Verses 36-38 may also be translated: ³⁶"If you feel that you are not treating your grown daughter right by keeping her from getting married, then let her marry. You won't be doing anything wrong. ³⁷But it is better to have self-control and make up your mind not to let your daughter get married. ³⁸It is all right for you to let her marry. But it is better if you don't let her marry at all."

life was given to us.

7 Not everyone knows these things. In fact, many people have grown up with the belief that idols have life in them. So when they eat meat offered to idols, they are bothered by a weak conscience. 8 But food doesn't bring us any closer to God. We are no worse off if we don't eat, and we are no better off if we do.

9 Don't cause problems for someone with a weak conscience, just because you have the right to eat anything. 10 You know all this, and so it doesn't bother you to eat in the temple of an idol. But suppose a person with a weak conscience sees you and decides to eat food that's been offered to idols. 11 Then what you know has destroyed someone Christ died for. 12 When you sin by hurting a follower with a weak conscience, you sin against Christ. 13 So if I hurt one of the Lord's followers by what I eat, I will never eat meat as long as I live.

The Rights of an Apostle

9 1 I am free. I am an apostle. I have seen the Lord Jesus and have led you to have faith in him. 2 Others may think that I am not an apostle, but you are proof that I am an apostle to you.

3 When people question me, I tell them 4 that Barnabas and I have the right to our food and drink. 5 We each have the right to marry one of the Lord's followers and to take her along with us, just as the other apostles and the Lord's brothers and Peter^q do. 6 Are we the only ones who have to support ourselves by working at another job? 7 Do soldiers pay their own salaries? Don't people who raise grapes eat some of what they grow? Don't shepherds get milk from their own goats?

8-9 I am not saying this on my own authority. The Law of Moses tells us not to muzzle a bullock when it is grinding grain. But was God concerned only about a bullock? 10 No, he wasn't! He was talking about us. This was written in the Scriptures so that all who plough and all who grind the grain will look forward to sharing in the harvest.

^qPeter: See the note at 1.12.

11When we gave you the message, it was like planting spiritual seed. So we have the right to accept material things as our harvest from you. 12If others have the right to do this, we have an even greater right. But we haven't used this right of ours. We are willing to put up with anything to keep from causing trouble for the message about Christ.

13Don't you know that people who work in the temple make their living from what is brought to the temple? Don't you know that a person who serves at the altar is given part of what is offered? 14In the same way, the Lord wants everyone who preaches the good news to make a living from preaching this message.

15But I have never used these privileges of mine, and I am not writing this because I want to start now. I would rather die than have someone rob me of the right to take pride in this. 16I don't have any reason to boast about preaching the good news. Preaching is something God told me to do, and if I don't do it, I am doomed. 17If I preach because I want to, I will be paid. But even if I don't want to, it is still something God has sent me to do. 18What pay am I given? It's the chance to preach the good news free of charge and not to use the privileges that are mine because I am a preacher.

19I am not anyone's slave. But I have become a slave to everyone, so that I can win as many people as possible. 20When I am with the Jews, I live like a Jew to win Jews. They are ruled by the Law of Moses, and I am not. But I live by the Law to win them. 21And when I am with people who are not ruled by the Law, I forget about the Law to win them. Of course, I never really forget about the law of God. In fact, I am ruled by the law of Christ. 22When I am with people whose faith is weak, I live as they do to win them. I do everything I can to win everyone I possibly can. 23I do all this for the good news, because I want to share in its blessings.

A Race and a Fight

24You know that many runners enter a race, and only one of them wins the prize. So run to win! 25Athletes work hard to win a crown that can't last, but we do it for a crown that will last for ever. ²⁶I don't run without a goal. And I don't box by beating my fists in the air. ²⁷I keep my body under control and make it my slave, so I won't lose out after telling the good news to others.

Don't Worship Idols

10 ¹Friends, I want to remind you that all of our ancestors walked under the cloud and went through the sea. ²This was like being baptised and becoming followers of Moses. ³All of them also ate the same spiritual food ⁴and drank the same spiritual drink, which flowed from the spiritual rock that followed them. That rock was Christ. ⁵But most of them did not please God. So they died, and their bodies were scattered all over the desert.

⁶What happened to them is a warning to keep us from wanting to do the same evil things. ⁷They worshipped idols, just as the Scriptures say, "The people sat down to eat and drink. Then they got up to dance around." So don't worship idols. ⁸Some of those people did shameful things, and in a single day about 23 000 of them died. Don't do shameful things as they did. ⁹And don't try to test Christ,ʳ as some of them did and were later bitten by poisonous snakes. ¹⁰Don't even grumble, as some of them did and were killed by the destroying angel. ¹¹These things happened to them as a warning to us. All this was written in the Scriptures to teach us who live in these last days.

¹²Even if you think you can stand up to temptation, be careful not to fall. ¹³You are tempted in the same way that everyone else is tempted. But God can be trusted not to let you be tempted too much, and he will show you how to escape from your temptations.

¹⁴My friends, you must keep away from idols. ¹⁵I am speaking to you as people who have enough sense to know what I am talking about. ¹⁶When we drink from the cup that we ask God to bless, isn't that sharing in the blood of Christ? When we eat the bread that we break, isn't that sharing in the body of Christ? ¹⁷By sharing in

ʳ*Christ:* Some manuscripts have "the Lord."

the same loaf of bread, we become one body, even though there are many of us. [18]Aren't the people of Israel sharing in the worship when they gather around the altar and eat the sacrifices offered there? [19]Am I saying that either the idols or the food sacrificed to them is anything at all? [20]No, I am not! That food is really sacrificed to demons and not to God. I don't want you to have anything to do with demons. [21]You can't drink from the cup of demons and still drink from the Lord's cup. You can't eat at the table of demons and still eat at the Lord's table. [22]We would make the Lord jealous if we did that. And we aren't stronger than the Lord.

Always Honour God

[23]Some of you say, "We can do whatever we want to!" But I tell you that not everything may be good or helpful. [24]We should think about others and not about ourselves. [25]However, when you buy meat in the market, go ahead and eat it. Keep your conscience clear by not asking where the meat came from. [26]The Scriptures say, "The earth and everything in it belong to the Lord."

[27]If an unbeliever invites you to dinner, and you want to go, then go. Eat whatever you are served. Don't cause a problem for someone's conscience by asking where the food came from. [28-29]But if you are told that it has been sacrificed to idols, don't cause a problem by eating it. I don't mean a problem for yourself, but for the one who told you. Why should my freedom be limited by someone else's conscience? [30]If I give thanks for what I eat, why should anyone accuse me of doing wrong?

[31]When you eat or drink or do anything else, always do it to honour God. [32]Don't cause problems for Jews or Greeks or anyone else who belongs to God's church. [33]I always try to please others instead of myself, in the hope that many of them will be saved.

11 [1]You must follow my example, as I follow the example of Christ.

Rules for Worship

[2]I am proud of you, because you always remember me and obey the teachings I gave you. [3]Now I want you to

know that Christ is the head over all men, and a man is the head over a woman. But God is the head over Christ. 4This means that any man who prays or prophesies with something on his head brings shame to his head.

5But any woman who prays or prophesies without something on her head brings shame to her head. In fact, she may as well shave her head.*s* 6A woman should wear something on her head. It is a disgrace for a woman to shave her head or cut her hair. But if she refuses to wear something on her head, let her cut off her hair.

7Men were created to be like God and to bring honour to God. This means that a man should not wear anything on his head. Women were created to bring honour to men. 8It was the woman who was made from a man, and not the man who was made from a woman. 9He wasn't created for her. She was created for him. 10And so, because of this, and also because of the angels, a woman ought to wear something on her head, as a sign of her authority.*t*

11As far as the Lord is concerned, men and women need each other. 12It is true that the first woman came from a man, but all other men have been given birth by women. Yet God is the one who created everything. 13Ask yourselves if it is proper for a woman to pray without something on her head. 14Isn't it unnatural and disgraceful for men to have long hair? 15But long hair is a beautiful way for a woman to cover her head. 16This is how things are done in all of God's churches,*u* and that's why none of you should argue about what I have said.

Rules for the Lord's Supper

17Your worship services do you more harm than good. I am certainly not going to praise you for this. 18I am told that you can't get along with each other when you worship, and I am sure that some of what I have heard is true. 19You are bound to argue with each other, but it is easy to see which of you have God's approval.

---

sshe may as well shave her head: A woman's hair was a mark of beauty, and it was shameful for a woman to cut her hair short or to shave her head, so that she looked like a man. *tas a sign of her authority:* Or "as a sign that she is under someone's authority." *uThis is how things are done in all of God's churches:* Or "There is no set rule for this in any of God's churches."

²⁰When you meet together, you don't really celebrate the Lord's Supper. ²¹You even start eating before everyone gets to the meeting, and some of you go hungry, while others get drunk. ²²Don't you have homes where you can eat and drink? Do you hate God's church? Do you want to embarrass people who don't have anything? What can I say to you? I certainly can't praise you.

The Lord's Supper

(Matthew 26.26-29; Mark 14.22-25; Luke 22.14-20)

²³I have already told you what the Lord Jesus did on the night he was betrayed. And it came from the Lord himself.

He took some bread in his hands. ²⁴Then after he had given thanks, he broke it and said, "This is my body, which is given for you. Eat this and remember me."

²⁵After the meal, Jesus took a cup of wine in his hands and said, "This is my blood, and with it God makes his new agreement with you. Drink this and remember me."

²⁶The Lord meant that when you eat this bread and drink from this cup, you tell about his death until he comes.

²⁷But if you eat the bread and drink the wine in a way that isn't worthy of the Lord, you sin against his body and blood. ²⁸That's why you must examine the way you eat and drink. ²⁹If you fail to understand that you are the body of the Lord, you will condemn yourselves by the way you eat and drink. ³⁰That's why many of you are sick and weak and why a lot of others have died. ³¹If we carefully judge ourselves, we won't be punished. ³²But when the Lord judges and punishes us, he does it to keep us from being condemned with the rest of the world.

³³My dear friends, you should wait until everyone gets there before you start eating. ³⁴If you really are hungry, you can eat at home. Then you won't condemn yourselves when you meet together.

After I arrive, I will instruct you about the other matters.

Spiritual Gifts

12 ¹My friends, you asked me about spiritual gifts. ²I want you to remember that before you became followers of the Lord, you were led in all the wrong ways by idols that can't even talk. ³Now I want you to know that if you are led by God's Spirit, you will say that Jesus is Lord, and you will never curse Jesus.

⁴There are different kinds of spiritual gifts, but they all come from the same Spirit. ⁵There are different ways to serve the same Lord, ⁶and we can each do different things. Yet the same God works in all of us and helps us in everything we do.

⁷The Spirit has given each of us a special way of serving others. ⁸Some of us can speak with wisdom, while others can speak with knowledge, but these gifts come from the same Spirit. ⁹To others the Spirit has given great faith or the power to heal the sick ¹⁰or the power to work mighty miracles. Some of us are prophets, and some of us recognise when God's Spirit is present.ᵛ Others can speak different kinds of languages, and still others can tell what these languages mean. ¹¹But it is the Spirit who does all this and decides which gifts to give to each of us.

One Body with Many Parts

¹²The body of Christ has many different parts, just as any other body does. ¹³Some of us are Jews, and others are Gentiles. Some of us are slaves, and others are free. But God's Spirit baptised each of us and made us part of the body of Christ. Now we each drink from that same Spirit.ʷ

¹⁴Our bodies don't have just one part. They have many parts. ¹⁵Suppose a foot says, "I'm not a hand, and so I'm not part of the body." Wouldn't the foot still belong to the body? ¹⁶Or suppose an ear says, "I'm not an eye, and

---

ᵛrecognise...present: Or "and some of us recognise the difference between God's Spirit and other spirits." ʷSome of us are Jews...that same Spirit: Verse 13 may also be translated, "God's Spirit is inside each of us, and all around us as well. So it doesn't matter that some of us are Jews and others are Gentiles and that some are slaves and others are free. Together we are one body."

so I'm not part of the body." Wouldn't the ear still belong to the body? [17]If our bodies were only an eye, we couldn't hear a thing. And if they were only an ear, we couldn't smell a thing. [18]But God has put all parts of our body together in the way that he decided is best.

[19]A body isn't really a body, unless there is more than one part. [20]It takes many parts to make a single body. [21]That's why the eyes can't say they don't need the hands. That's also why the head can't say it doesn't need the feet. [22]In fact, we can't get along without the parts of the body that seem to be the weakest. [23]We take special care to dress up some parts of our bodies. We are modest about our personal parts, [24]but we don't have to be modest about other parts.

God put our bodies together in such a way that even the parts that seem the least important are valuable. [25]He did this to make all parts of the body work together smoothly, with each part caring about the others. [26]If one part of our body hurts, we hurt all over. If one part of our body is honoured, the whole body will be happy.

[27]Together you are the body of Christ. Each one of you is part of his body. [28]First, God chose some people to be apostles and prophets and teachers for the church. But he also chose some to work miracles or heal the sick or help others or be leaders or speak different kinds of languages. [29]Not everyone is an apostle. Not everyone is a prophet. Not everyone is a teacher. Not everyone can work miracles. [30]Not everyone can heal the sick. Not everyone can speak different kinds of languages. Not everyone can tell what these languages mean. [31]I want you to desire the best gifts.[x] So I will show you a much better way.

Love

13 [1]What if I could speak all languages
      of humans and of angels?
If I did not love others,
I would be nothing more than a noisy gong
      or a clanging cymbal.

---

[x]*I want you to desire the best gifts:* Or "You desire the best gifts."

2 What if I could prophesy
    and understand all secrets and all knowledge?
And what if I had faith that moved mountains?
    I would be nothing, unless I loved others.
3 What if I gave away all that I owned
and let myself be burnt alive?[y]
    I would gain nothing, unless I loved others.
4 Love is kind and patient,
    never jealous, boastful, proud, or [5]rude.
Love isn't selfish or quick tempered.
    It doesn't keep a record of wrongs that others do.
6 Love rejoices in the truth, but not in evil.
7 Love is always supportive, loyal,
hopeful, and trusting.
8   Love never fails!

Everyone who prophesies will stop,
    and unknown languages
    will no longer be spoken.
All that we know will be forgotten.
9 We don't know everything,
    and our prophecies are not complete.
10 But what is perfect will some day appear,
    and what isn't perfect will then disappear.

11 When we were children,
    we thought and reasoned as children do.
But when we grew up, we left our childish ways behind.
12 Now all we can see of God
    is like a cloudy picture in a mirror.
Later we will see him face to face.
We don't know everything, but then we will,
    just as God completely understands us.
13 For now there are faith, hope, and love.
    But of these three, the greatest is love.

Speaking Unknown Languages and Prophesying

14 [1]Love should be your guide. Be eager to have the gifts that come from the Holy Spirit, especially the

[y]and let myself be burnt alive: Some manuscripts have "so that I could boast."

gift of prophecy. [2]If you speak languages that others don't know, God will understand what you are saying, though no-one else will know what you mean. You will be talking about mysteries that only the Spirit understands. [3]But when you prophesy, you will be understood, and others will be helped. They will be encouraged and made to feel better.

[4]By speaking languages that others don't know, you help only yourself. But by prophesying you help everyone in the church. [5]I am glad for you to speak unknown languages, although I would rather you prophesy. In fact, prophesying does much more good than speaking unknown languages, unless someone can help the church by explaining what you mean.

[6]My friends, what good would it do, if I came and spoke unknown languages to you and didn't explain what I meant? How would I help you, unless I told you what God had shown me or gave you some knowledge or prophecy or teaching? [7]If all musical instruments sounded alike, how would you know the difference between a flute and a harp? [8]If a bugle call isn't clear, how would you know to get ready for battle?

[9]That's how it is when you speak unknown languages. If no-one can understand what you are talking about, you will only be talking to the wind. [10]There are many different languages in this world, and all of them make sense. [11]But if I don't understand the language that someone is using, we will be like foreigners to each other. [12]If you really want spiritual gifts, choose the ones that will be most helpful to the church.

[13]When we speak languages that others don't know, we should pray for the power to explain what we mean. [14]For example, if I use an unknown language in my prayers, my spirit prays but my mind is useless. [15]Then what should I do? There are times when I should pray with my spirit, and times when I should pray with my mind. Sometimes I should sing with my spirit, and at other times I should sing with my mind.

[16]Suppose some strangers are in your worship service, when you are praising God with your spirit. If they don't understand you, how will they know to say, "Amen"?

17You may be worshipping God in a wonderful way, but no-one else will be helped. 18I thank God that I speak unknown languages more than any of you. 19But words that make sense can help the church. That's why in church I would rather speak five words that make sense than speak 10 000 words in a language that others don't know.

20My friends, stop thinking like children. Think like mature people and be as innocent as tiny babies. 21In the Scriptures the Lord says,

> "I will use strangers who speak unknown languages
>   to talk to my people.
> They will speak to them in foreign languages,
>   but still my people won't listen to me."

22Languages that others don't know may mean something to unbelievers, but not to the Lord's followers. Prophecy, on the other hand, is for followers, not for unbelievers. 23Suppose everyone in your worship service started speaking unknown languages, and some outsiders or some unbelievers come in. Won't they think you are crazy? 24But suppose all of you are prophesying when those unbelievers and outsiders come in. They will realise that they are sinners, and they will want to change their ways because of what you are saying. 25They will say what is hidden in their hearts. Then they will kneel down and say to God, "We are certain that you are with these people."

Worship Must Be Orderly

26My friends, when you meet to worship, you must do everything for the good of everyone there. That's how it should be when someone sings or teaches or tells what God has said, or speaks an unknown language or explains what the language means. 27No more than two or three of you should speak unknown languages during the meeting. You must take turns, and someone should always be there to explain what you mean. 28If no-one can explain, you must keep silent in church and speak only to yourself and to God.

29Two or three people may prophesy, and everyone else must listen carefully. 30If someone sitting there receives a message from God, the speaker must stop and let the other person speak. 31Let only one person speak at a time, then all of you will learn something and be encouraged. 32A prophet should be willing to stop and let someone else speak. 33God wants everything to be done peacefully and in order.

When God's people meet in church, 34the women must not be allowed to speak. They must keep quiet and listen, as the Law of Moses teaches. 35If there is something they want to know, they can ask their husbands when they get home. It is disgraceful for women to speak in church. 36God's message did not start with you people, and you aren't the only ones it has reached.

37If you think of yourself as a prophet or a spiritual person, you will know that I am writing only what the Lord has commanded. 38So don't pay attention to anyone who ignores what I am writing. 39My friends, be eager to prophesy and don't stop anyone from speaking languages that others don't know. 40But do everything properly and in order.

Christ Was Raised to Life

15 1My friends, I want you to remember the message that I preached and that you believed and trusted. 2You will be saved by this message, if you hold firmly to it. But if you don't, your faith was all for nothing.

3I told you the most important part of the message exactly as it was told to me. That part is:

Christ died for our sins, as the Scriptures say.
4   He was buried, and three days later
          he was raised to life, as the Scriptures say.
5   Christ appeared to Peter,z then to the twelve.
6   After this, he appeared
          to more than 500 other followers.
     Most of them are still alive, but some have died.
7   He also appeared to James,
          and then to all of the apostles.

8Finally, he appeared to me, even though I am like someone who was born at the wrong time.a

---

zPeter: See the note at 1.12.   awho was born at the wrong time: The meaning of these words in Greek is not clear.

9I am the least important of all the apostles. In fact, I caused so much trouble for God's church that I don't even deserve to be called an apostle. 10But God was kind! He made me what I am, and his wonderful kindness wasn't wasted. I worked much harder than any of the other apostles, although it was really God's kindness at work and not me. 11But it doesn't matter if I preached or if they preached. All of you believed the message just the same.

God's People Will Be Raised to Life

12If we preach that Christ was raised from death, how can some of you say that the dead won't be raised to life? 13If they won't be raised to life, Christ himself wasn't raised to life. 14And if Christ wasn't raised to life, our message is worthless, and so is your faith. 15If the dead won't be raised to life, we have told lies about God by saying that he raised Christ to life, when he really did not.

16So if the dead won't be raised to life, Christ wasn't raised to life. 17Unless Christ was raised to life, your faith is useless, and you are still living in your sins. 18And those people who died after putting their faith in him are completely lost. 19If our hope in Christ is good only for this life, we are worse off than anyone else.

20But Christ has been raised to life! And he makes us certain that others will also be raised to life. 21Just as we will die because of Adam, we will be raised to life because of Christ. 22Adam brought death to all of us, and Christ will bring life to all of us. 23But we must each wait our turn. Christ was the first to be raised to life, and his people will be raised to life when he returns. 24Then after Christ has destroyed all powers and forces, the end will come, and he will give the kingdom to God the Father.

25Christ will rule until he puts all his enemies under his power, 26and the last enemy he destroys will be death. 27When the Scriptures say that he will put everything under his power, they don't include God. It was God who put everything under the power of Christ. 28After everything is under the power of God's Son, he will put himself under the power of God, who put everything under his Son's power. Then God will mean everything to everyone.

²⁹If the dead are not going to be raised to life, what will people do who are being baptised for them? Why are they being baptised for those dead people? ³⁰And why do we always risk our lives ³¹and face death every day? The pride that I have in you because of Christ Jesus our Lord is what makes me say this. ³²What do you think I gained by fighting wild animals in Ephesus? If the dead are not raised to life,

"Let's eat and drink.
Tomorrow we die."

³³Don't fool yourselves. Bad friends will destroy you. ³⁴Be sensible and stop sinning. You should be embarrassed that some people still don't know about God.

What Our Bodies Will Be Like

³⁵Some of you have asked, "How will the dead be raised to life? What kind of bodies will they have?" ³⁶Don't be foolish. A seed must die before it can sprout from the ground. ³⁷Wheat seeds and all other seeds look different from the shoots that come up. ³⁸This is because God gives everything the kind of body he wants it to have. ³⁹People, animals, birds, and fish are each made of flesh, but none of them are alike. ⁴⁰Everything in the heavens has a body, and so does everything on earth. But each one is very different from all the others. ⁴¹The sun isn't like the moon, the moon isn't like the stars, and each star is different.

⁴²That's how it will be when our bodies are raised to life. These bodies will die, but the bodies that are raised will live for ever. ⁴³These ugly and weak bodies will become beautiful and strong. ⁴⁴As surely as there are physical bodies, there are spiritual bodies. And our physical bodies will be changed into spiritual bodies.

⁴⁵The first man was named Adam, and the Scriptures tell us that he was a living person. But Jesus, who may be called the last Adam, is a life-giving spirit. ⁴⁶We see that the one with a spiritual body did not come first. He came after the one who had a physical body. ⁴⁷The first man was made from the dust of the earth, but the second

man came from heaven. 48Everyone on earth has a body like the body of the one who was made from the dust of the earth. And everyone in heaven has a body like the body of the one who came from heaven. 49Just as we are like the one who was made out of earth, we will be like the one who came from heaven.

50My friends, I want you to know that our bodies of flesh and blood will decay. This means that they can't share in God's kingdom, which lasts for ever. 51I will explain a mystery to you. Not every one of us will die, but we will all be changed. 52It will happen suddenly, quicker than the blink of an eye. At the sound of the last trumpet the dead will be raised. We will all be changed, so that we will never die again. 53Our dead and decaying bodies will be changed into bodies that won't die or decay. 54The bodies we now have are weak and can die. But they will be changed into bodies that are eternal. Then the Scriptures will come true,

"Death has lost the battle!
55   Where is its victory? Where is its sting?"
56Sin is what gives death its sting, and the Law is the power behind sin. 57But thank God for letting our Lord Jesus Christ give us the victory!

58My dear friends, stand firm and don't be shaken. Always keep busy working for the Lord. You know that everything you do for him is worthwhile.

A Collection for God's People

16 1When you collect money for God's people, I want you to do exactly what I told the churches in Galatia to do. 2That is, each Sunday each of you must put aside part of what you've earned. If you do this, you won't have to take up a collection when I come. 3Choose some followers to take the money to Jerusalem. I will send them on with the money and with letters which show that you approve of them. 4If you think I should go along, they can go with me.

Paul's Travel Plans

5After I've gone through Macedonia, I hope to see you 6and visit you for a while. I may even stay all winter, so that you can help me on my way to wherever I will be going next. [7]If the Lord lets me, I would rather come later for a longer visit than to stop off now for only a short visit. [8]I will stay in Ephesus until Pentecost, [9]because there's a wonderful opportunity for me to do some work here. But there are also many people who are against me.

[10]When Timothy arrives, give him a friendly welcome. He is doing the Lord's work, just as I am. [11]Don't let anyone mistreat him. I am looking for him to return to me together with the other followers. So when he leaves, send him off with your blessings.

[12]I have tried hard to get our friend Apollos to visit you with the other followers. He doesn't want to come just now, but he will come when he can.

Personal Concerns and Greetings

[13]Keep alert. Be firm in your faith. Stay brave and strong. [14]Show love in everything you do.

[15]You know that Stephanas and his family were the first in Achaia to have faith in the Lord. They have done all they can for God's people. My friends, I ask you [16]to obey leaders like them and to do the same for all others who work hard with you.

[17]I was glad to see Stephanas and Fortunatus and Achaicus. Having them here was like having you. [18]They made me feel much better, just as they made you feel better. You should appreciate people like them.

[19]Greetings from the churches in Asia.

Aquila and Priscilla, together with the church that meets in their house, send greetings in the name of the Lord.

[20]All of the Lord's followers send their greetings.

Give each other a warm greeting.

[21]I am signing this letter myself: PAUL.

[22]I pray that God will put a curse on everyone who doesn't love the Lord. And may the Lord come soon.

[23]I pray that the Lord Jesus will be kind to you.

[24]I love everyone who belongs to Christ Jesus.

2 CORINTHIANS

ABOUT THIS LETTER

In the beginning of this letter Paul answers the concerns of the Christians in Corinth who accused him of not living up to his promise to visit them. Paul had changed his mind for a good reason. He had stayed away from Corinth so that he would not seem to be too hard and demanding (chapter 1.23). He also wanted to see if they would follow his instructions about forgiving and comforting people who had sinned (2.5-11).

Paul reminds the Corinthians that God is generous and wants them to be just as generous in their giving to help God's people in Jerusalem and Judea (8.1—9.15).

Paul is a servant of God's new agreement (3.1-17). He is faithful in trying to bring people to God, even if it means terrible suffering for himself (4.1—6.13; 10.1—12.10). And what has God done to make it possible for us to come to him?

God has done it all! He sent Christ to make peace between himself and us, and he has given us the work of making peace between himself and others. What we mean is that God was in Christ, offering peace and forgiveness to the people of this world. And he has given us the work of sharing his message about peace.

(Chapter 5.18, 19)

A QUICK LOOK AT THIS LETTER

- Paul Gives Thanks to God (1.1-11)
- The Work of an Apostle for God's People (1.12—2.17)
- Guided by the Love of Christ (3.1—7.16)
- Gifts for the Poor (8.1—9.15)
- Paul Is a True Apostle (10.1—13.10)
- Final Greetings (13.11-13)

1 ¹From Paul, chosen by God to be an apostle of Jesus Christ, and from Timothy, who is also a follower.

To God's church in Corinth and to all of God's people in Achaia.

²I pray that God our Father and the Lord Jesus Christ will be kind to you and will bless you with peace!

Paul Gives Thanks

³Praise God, the Father of our Lord Jesus Christ! The Father is a merciful God, who always gives us comfort. ⁴He comforts us when we are in trouble, so that we can share that same comfort with others in trouble. ⁵We share in the terrible sufferings of Christ, but also in the wonderful comfort he gives. ⁶We suffer in the hope that you will be comforted and saved. And because we are comforted, you will also be comforted, as you patiently endure suffering like ours. ⁷You never disappoint us. You suffered as much as we did, and we know that you will be comforted as we were.

⁸My friends, I want you to know what a hard time we had in Asia. Our sufferings were so horrible and so unbearable that death seemed certain. ⁹In fact, we felt sure that we were going to die. But this made us stop trusting in ourselves and start trusting God, who raises the dead to life. ¹⁰God saved us from the threat of death,[a] and we are sure that he will do it again and again. ¹¹Please help us by praying for us. Then many people will give thanks for the blessings we receive in answer to all these prayers.

Paul's Change of Plans

¹²We can be proud of our clear conscience. We have always lived honestly and sincerely, especially when we were with you. And we were guided by God's wonderful kindness instead of by the wisdom of this world. ¹³I am not writing anything you can't read and understand. I hope you will understand it completely, ¹⁴just as you already partly understand us. Then when our Lord Jesus returns, you can be as proud of us as we are of you.

---

[a]*the threat of death:* Some manuscripts have "many threats of death."

15I was so sure of your pride in us that I had planned to visit you first of all. In this way you would have the blessing of two visits from me, 16once on my way to Macedonia and again on my return from there. Then you could send me on to Judea. 17Do you think I couldn't make up my mind about what to do? Or do I seem like someone who says "Yes" or "No" simply to please others? 18God can be trusted, and so can I, when I say that our answer to you has always been "Yes" and never "No." 19This is because Jesus Christ the Son of God is always "Yes" and never "No." And he is the one that Silas,b Timothy, and I told you about.

20Christ says "Yes" to all of God's promises. That's why we have Christ to say "Amen"c for us to the glory of God. 21And so God makes it possible for you and us to stand firmly together with Christ. God is also the one who chose us 22and put his Spirit in our hearts to show that we belong only to him.

23God is my witness that I stayed away from Corinth, just to keep from being hard on you. 24We are not bosses who tell you what to believe. We are working with you to make you glad, because your faith is strong.

2 1I have decided not to make my next visit with you so painful. 2If I make you feel bad, who would be left to cheer me up, except the people I had made to feel bad? 3The reason I want to be happy is to make you happy. I wrote as I did because I didn't want to visit you and be made to feel bad, when you should make me feel happy. 4At the time I wrote, I was suffering terribly. My eyes were full of tears, and my heart was broken. But I didn't want to make you feel bad. I only wanted to let you know how much I cared for you.

Forgiveness

5I don't want to be hard on you. But if one of you has made someone feel bad, I am not really the one who has been made to feel bad. Some of you are the ones. 6Most of you have already pointed out the wrong that person

---

bSilas: The Greek text has "Silvanus," which is another form of the name Silas.
cAmen: The word "amen" is used here with the meaning of "yes."

did, and that is punishment enough for what was done.

[7] When people sin, you should forgive and comfort them, so they won't give up in despair. [8] You should make them sure of your love for them.

[9] I also wrote because I wanted to test you and find out if you would follow my instructions. [10] I will forgive anyone you forgive. Yes, for your sake and with Christ as my witness, I have forgiven whatever needed to be forgiven. [11] I have done this to keep Satan from getting the better of us. We all know what goes on in his mind.

[12] When I went to Troas to preach the good news about Christ, I found that the Lord had already prepared the way. [13] But I was worried when I didn't find my friend Titus there. So I left the other followers and went on to Macedonia.

[14] I am grateful that God always makes it possible for Christ to lead us to victory. God also helps us spread the knowledge about Christ everywhere, and this knowledge is like the smell of perfume. [15-16] In fact, God thinks of us as a perfume that brings Christ to everyone. For people who are being saved, this perfume has a sweet smell and leads them to a better life. But for people who are lost, it has a bad smell and leads them to a horrible death.

No-one really has what it takes to do this work. [17] A lot of people try to get rich from preaching God's message. But we are God's sincere messengers, and by the power of Christ we speak our message with God as our witness.

God's New Agreement

3 [1] Are we once again boasting about ourselves? Do we need letters to you or from you to tell others about us? Some people do need letters that tell about them. [2] But you are our letter, and you are in our*d* hearts for everyone to read and understand. [3] You are like a letter written by Christ and delivered by us. But you aren't written with pen and ink or on tablets made of stone. You are written in our hearts by the Spirit of the living God.

[4] We are sure about all this. Christ makes us sure in the

*d*our: Some manuscripts have "your."

very presence of God. 5We don't have the right to claim that we have done anything on our own. God gives us what it takes to do all that we do. 6He makes us worthy to be the servants of his new agreement that comes from the Holy Spirit and not from a written Law. After all, the Law brings death, but the Spirit brings life.

7The Law of Moses brought only the promise of death, even though it was carved on stones and given in a wonderful way. Still the Law made Moses' face shine so brightly that the people of Israel couldn't look at it, even though it was a fading glory. 8So won't the agreement that the Spirit brings to us be even more wonderful? 9If something that brings the death sentence is glorious, won't something that makes us acceptable to God be even more glorious? 10In fact, the new agreement is so wonderful that the Law is no longer glorious at all. 11The Law was given with a glory that faded away. But the glory of the new agreement is much greater, because it will never fade away.

12This wonderful hope makes us feel like speaking freely. 13We are not like Moses. His face was shining, but he covered it to keep the people of Israel from seeing the brightness fade away. 14The people were stubborn, and something still keeps them from seeing the truth when the Law is read. Only Christ can take away the covering that keeps them from seeing.

15When the Law of Moses is read, they have their minds covered over 16with a covering that is removed only for those who turn to the Lord. 17The Lord and the Spirit are one and the same, and the Lord's Spirit sets us free. 18So our faces are not covered. They show the bright glory of the Lord, as the Lord's Spirit makes us more and more like our glorious Lord.

Treasure in Clay Jars

4 1God has been kind enough to trust us with this work. That's why we never give up. 2We don't do shameful things that must be kept secret. And we don't try to fool anyone or twist God's message around. God is our witness that we speak only the truth, so others will be sure that we can be trusted. 3If there is anything

hidden about our message, it is hidden only to someone who is lost.

⁴The god who rules this world has blinded the minds of unbelievers. They can't see the light, which is the good news about our glorious Christ, who shows what God is like. ⁵We are not preaching about ourselves. Our message is that Jesus Christ is Lord. He also sent us to be your servants. ⁶The Scriptures say, "God commanded light to shine in the dark." Now God is shining in our hearts to let you know that his glory is seen in Jesus Christ.

⁷We are like clay jars in which this treasure is stored. The real power comes from God and not from us. ⁸We often suffer, but we are never crushed. Even when we don't know what to do, we never give up. ⁹In times of trouble, God is with us, and when we are knocked down, we get up again. ¹⁰⁻¹¹We face death every day because of Jesus. Our bodies show what his death was like, so that his life can also be seen in us. ¹²This means that death is working in us, but life is working in you.

¹³In the Scriptures it says, "I spoke because I had faith." We have that same kind of faith. So we speak ¹⁴because we know that God raised the Lord Jesus to life. And just as God raised Jesus, he will also raise us to life. Then he will bring us into his presence together with you. ¹⁵All of this has been done for you, so that more and more people will know how kind God is and will praise and honour him.

Faith in the Lord

¹⁶We never give up. Our bodies are gradually dying, but we ourselves are being made stronger each day. ¹⁷These little troubles are getting us ready for an eternal glory that will make all our troubles seem like nothing. ¹⁸Things that are seen don't last for ever, but things that are not seen are eternal. That's why we keep our minds on the things that can't be seen.

5 ¹Our bodies are like tents that we live in here on earth. But when these tents are destroyed, we know that God will give each of us a place to live. These homes won't be buildings that someone has made, but they're in heaven and will last for ever. ²While we are here on earth, we sigh because we want to live in that heavenly home. ³We want to put it on like clothes and not be naked.

⁴These tents we now live in are like a heavy burden, and we groan. But we don't do this just because we want to leave these bodies that will die. It's because we want to change them for bodies that will never die. ⁵God is the one who makes all of this possible. He has given us his Spirit to make us certain that he will do it. ⁶So always be cheerful!

As long as we are in these bodies, we are away from the Lord. ⁷But we live by faith, not by what we see. ⁸We should be cheerful, because we would rather leave these bodies and be at home with the Lord. ⁹But whether we are at home with the Lord or away from him, we still try our best to please him. ¹⁰After all, Christ will judge each of us for the good or the bad that we do while living in these bodies.

Bringing People to God

¹¹We know what it means to respect the Lord, and we encourage everyone to turn to him. God himself knows what we are like, and I hope you also know what kind of people we are. ¹²We are not trying once more to boast about ourselves. But we want you to be proud of us, when you are with those who are not sincere and boast about what others think of them.

¹³If we seem out of our minds, it is between God and us. But if we are in our right minds, it is for your good. ¹⁴We are ruled by Christ's love for us. We are certain that if one person died for everyone else, then all of us have died. ¹⁵And Christ did die for all of us. He died so we would no longer live for ourselves, but for the one who died and was raised to life for us.

¹⁶We are careful not to judge people by what they seem to be, though we once judged Christ in that way. ¹⁷Anyone who belongs to Christ is a new person. The past is forgotten, and everything is new. ¹⁸God has done it all! He sent Christ to make peace between himself and us, and he has given us the work of making peace between himself and others.

¹⁹What we mean is that God was in Christ, offering peace and forgiveness to the people of this world. And he has given us the work of sharing his message about peace. ²⁰We were sent to speak for Christ, and God is begging you to listen to our message. We speak for Christ and sincerely ask you to make peace with God. ²¹Christ never sinned! But God treated him as a sinner, so that Christ could make us acceptable to God.

6 ¹We work together with God, and we beg you to make good use of God's kindness to you. ²In the Scriptures God says,

"When the time came, I listened to you,
    and when you needed help, I came to save you."
That time has come. This is the day for you to be saved.

³We don't want anyone to find fault with our work, and so we try hard not to cause problems. ⁴But in everything and in every way we show that we truly are God's servants. We have always been patient, though we have had a lot of trouble, suffering, and hard times. ⁵We have been beaten, put in jail, and hurt in riots. We have worked hard and have gone without sleep or food. ⁶But we have kept ourselves pure and have been understanding, patient, and kind. The Holy Spirit has been with us, and our love has been real. ⁷We have spoken the truth, and God's power has worked in us. In all our struggles we have said and done only what is right.

⁸Whether we were honoured or dishonoured or praised or cursed, we always told the truth about ourselves. But some people said we did not. ⁹We are unknown to others, but well known to you. We seem to be dying, and yet we are still alive. We have been punished, but never killed, ¹⁰and we are always happy, even in times of suffering. Although we are poor, we have made many people rich. And though we own nothing, everything is ours.

¹¹Friends in Corinth, we are telling the truth when we say that there is room in our hearts for you. ¹²We are not holding back on our love for you, but you are holding back on your love for us. ¹³I speak to you as I would speak to my own children. Please make room in your hearts for us.

The Temple of the Living God

14Stay away from people who are not followers of the Lord! Can someone who is good get along with someone who is evil? Are light and darkness the same? 15Is Christ a friend of Satan?e Can people who follow the Lord have anything in common with those who don't? 16Do idols belong in the temple of God? We are the temple of the living God, as God himself says,

"I will live with these people and walk among them.
I will be their God, and they will be my people."
17 The Lord also says,
"Leave them and stay away!
Don't touch anything that isn't clean.
Then I will welcome you 18and be your Father.
You will be my sons and my daughters,
as surely as I am God, the All-powerful."

7 1My friends, God has made us these promises. So we should stay away from everything that keeps our bodies and spirits from being clean. We should honour God and try to be completely like him.

The Church Makes Paul Happy

2Make a place for us in your hearts! We haven't mistreated or hurt anyone. We haven't cheated anyone. 3I am not saying this to be hard on you. But, as I've said before, you will always be in our thoughts, whether we live or die. 4I trust you completely.f I am always proud of you, and I am greatly encouraged. In all my trouble I am still very happy.

5After we came to Macedonia, we didn't have any chance to rest. We were faced with all kinds of problems. We were troubled by enemies and troubled by fears. 6But God cheers up people in need, and that is what he did when he sent Titus to us. 7Of course, we were glad to see Titus, but what really made us glad is the way you

---

eSatan: The Greek text has "Beliar," which is another form of the Hebrew word "Belial," meaning "wicked" or "useless." The Jewish people sometimes used this as a name for Satan.   fI trust you completely: Or "I have always spoken the truth to you" or "I can speak freely to you."

cheered him up. He told us how sorry you were and how concerned you were about me. And this made me even happier.

⁸I don't feel bad any more, even though my letter*g* hurt your feelings. I did feel bad at first, but I don't now. I know that the letter hurt you for a while. ⁹Now I am happy, but not because I hurt your feelings. It is because God used your hurt feelings to make you turn back to him, and none of you were harmed by us. ¹⁰When God makes you feel sorry enough to turn to him and be saved, you don't have anything to feel bad about. But when this world makes you feel sorry, it can cause your death.

¹¹Just look what God has done by making you feel sorry! You sincerely want to prove that you are innocent. You are angry. You are shocked. You are eager to see that justice is done. You have proved that you were completely right in this matter. ¹²When I wrote to you, it wasn't to accuse the one who was wrong or to support the one who was hurt. I wrote, so that God would show you how much you do care for us. ¹³And we were greatly encouraged.

Although we were encouraged, we felt even better when we saw how happy Titus was, because you had shown that he had nothing to worry about. ¹⁴We had told him how much we thought of you, and you did not disappoint us. Just as we have always told you the truth, so everything we told him about you has also proved to be true. ¹⁵Titus loves all of you very much, especially when he remembers how you obeyed him and how you trembled with fear when you welcomed him. ¹⁶It makes me really glad to know that I can depend on you.

Generous Giving

8 ¹My friends, we want you to know that the churches in Macedonia*h* have shown others how kind God is. ²Although they were going through hard times and were

---

gmy letter: There is no copy of this letter that Paul wrote to the church at Corinth.   *hchurches in Macedonia:* The churches that Paul had started in Philippi and Thessalonica. The church in Berea is probably also meant.

very poor, they were glad to give generously. ³They gave as much as they could afford and even more, simply because they wanted to. ⁴They even asked and begged us to let them have the joy of giving their money for God's people. ⁵And they did more than we had hoped. They gave themselves first to the Lord and then to us, just as God wanted them to do.

⁶Titus was the one who got you started doing this good thing, so we begged him to have you finish what you had begun. ⁷You do everything better than anyone else. You have stronger faith. You speak better and know more. You are eager to give, and you love us better.ⁱ Now you must give more generously than anyone else.

⁸I am not ordering you to do this. I am simply testing how real your love is by comparing it with the concern that others have shown. ⁹You know that our Lord Jesus Christ was kind enough to give up all his riches and become poor, so that you could become rich.

¹⁰A year ago you were the first ones to give, and you gave because you wanted to. So listen to my advice. ¹¹I think you should finish what you started. If you give according to what you have, you will prove that you are as eager to give as you were to think about giving. ¹²It doesn't matter how much you have. What matters is how much you are willing to give from what you have.

¹³I am not trying to make life easier for others by making life harder for you. But it's only fair ¹⁴for you to share with them when you have so much, and they have so little. Later, when they have more than enough, and you are in need, they can share with you. Then everyone will have a fair share, ¹⁵just as the Scriptures say,

> "Those who gathered too much had nothing left.
> Those who gathered only a little
> had all they needed."

Titus and His Friends

¹⁶I am grateful that God made Titus care as much about you as we do. ¹⁷When we begged Titus to visit you, he said he would. He wanted to because he cared so much

---

ⁱ*you love us better:* Some manuscripts have "we love you better."

for you. [18] With Titus we are also sending one of the Lord's followers who is well known in every church for spreading the good news. [19] The churches chose this follower to travel with us while we carry this gift that will bring praise to the Lord and show how much we hope to help. [20] We don't want anyone to find fault with the way we handle your generous gift. [21] But we want to do what pleases the Lord and what people think is right.

[22] We are also sending someone else with Titus and the other follower. We approve of this man. In fact, he has already shown us many times that he wants to help. And now he wants to help even more than ever, because he trusts you so much. [23] Titus is my partner, who works with me to serve you. The other two followers are sent by the churches, and they bring honour to Christ. [24] Treat them in such a way that the churches will see your love and will know why we boasted about you.

The Money for God's People

9 [1] I don't need to write to you about the money you plan to give for God's people. [2] I know how eager you are to give. And I have proudly told the Lord's followers in Macedonia that you people in Achaia have been ready for a whole year. Now your desire to give has made them want to give. [3] That's why I am sending Titus and the two others to you. I want you to be ready, just as I promised. This will prove that we weren't wrong to boast about you.

[4] Some followers from Macedonia may come with me, and I want them to find that you have the money ready. If you don't, I would be embarrassed for trusting you to do this. But you would be embarrassed even more. [5] So I have decided to ask Titus and the others to spend some time with you before I arrive. This way they can arrange to collect the money you have promised. Then you will have the chance to give because you want to, and not because you feel forced to.

[6] Remember this saying,
"A few seeds make a small harvest,
    but a lot of seeds make a big harvest."

7Each of you must make up your own mind about how much to give. But don't feel sorry that you must give, and don't feel that you are forced to give. God loves people who love to give. 8God can bless you with everything you need, and you'll always have more than enough to do all kinds of good things for others. 9The Scriptures say,

"God freely gives his gifts to the poor,
    and always does right."

10God gives seed to farmers and provides everyone with food. He will increase what you have, so that you can give even more to those in need. 11You will be blessed in every way, and you will be able to keep on being generous. Then many people will thank God when we deliver your gift.

12What you are doing is much more than a service that supplies God's people with what they need. It is something that will make many others thank God. 13The way in which you have proved yourselves by this service will bring honour and praise to God. You believed the message about Christ, and you obeyed it by sharing generously with God's people and with everyone else. 14Now they are praying for you and want to see you, because God used you to bless them so very much. 15Thank God for his gift that is too wonderful for words!

Paul Defends His Work for Christ

10 1Do you think I am a coward when I am with you and brave when I am far away? Well, I ask you to listen, because Christ himself was humble and gentle. 2Some people have said that we act like the people of this world. So when I arrive, I expect I will have to be firm and forceful in what I say to them. Please don't make me treat you that way. 3We live in this world, but we don't act like its people 4or fight our battles with the weapons of this world. Instead, we use God's power that can destroy fortresses. We destroy arguments 5and every bit of pride that keeps anyone from knowing God. We capture people's thoughts and make them obey Christ. 6And when you completely obey him, we will punish anyone who refuses to obey.

[7]You judge by appearances.[j] If any of you think you are the only ones who belong to Christ, then think again. We belong to Christ as much as you do. [8]Maybe I boast a little too much about the authority that the Lord gave me to help you and not to hurt you. Yet I'm not embarrassed to boast. [9]And I am not trying to scare you with my letters. [10]Some of you are saying, "Paul's letters are harsh and powerful. But in person, he is a weakling and has nothing worth saying." [11]Those people had better understand that when I am with you, I will do exactly what I say in my letters.

[12]We won't dare compare ourselves with those who think so much of themselves. But they are foolish to compare themselves with themselves. [13]We won't boast about something we don't have a right to boast about. We will only boast about the work that God has sent us to do, and you are part of that work. [14]We are not boasting more than we should. After all, we did bring the message about Christ to you.

[15]We don't boast about what others have done, as if we had done those things ourselves. But I hope that as you become stronger in your faith, we will be able to reach many more of the people around you.[k] That has always been our goal. [16]Then we will be able to preach the good news in other lands where we can't take credit for work someone else has already done. [17]The Scriptures say, "If you want to boast, then boast about the Lord." [18]You may boast about yourself, but the only approval that counts is the Lord's approval.

Paul and the False Apostles

11 [1]Please put up with a little of my foolishness. [2]I am as concerned about you as God is. You were like a virgin bride I had chosen only for Christ. [3]But now I fear that you will be tricked, just as Eve was tricked by that lying snake. I am afraid that you might stop thinking about Christ in an honest and sincere way. [4]We

[j]You judge by appearances: Or "Take a close look at yourselves." [k]we will be able to reach many more of the people around you: Or "you will praise us even more because of our work among you."

told you about Jesus, and you received the Holy Spirit and accepted our message. But you let some people tell you about another Jesus. Now you are ready to receive another spirit and accept a different message. 5I think I am as good as any of those super apostles. 6I may not speak as well as they do, but I know as much. And this has already been made perfectly clear to you.

7Was it wrong for me to lower myself and honour you by preaching God's message free of charge? 8I robbed other churches by taking money from them to serve you. 9Even when I was in need, I still didn't bother you. In fact, some of the Lord's followers from Macedonia brought me what I needed. I haven't been a burden to you in the past, and I will never be a burden. 10As surely as I speak the truth about Christ, no-one in Achaia can stop me from boasting about this. 11And it isn't because I don't love you. God himself knows how much I do love you.

12I plan to go on doing just what I have always done. Then those people won't be able to boast about doing the same things we are doing. 13Anyway, they are no more than false apostles and dishonest workers. They only pretend to be apostles of Christ. 14And it's no wonder. Even Satan tries to make himself look like an angel of light. 15So why does it seem strange for Satan's servants to pretend to do what is right? Some day they will get exactly what they deserve.

Paul's Sufferings for Christ

16I don't want any of you to think that I am a fool. But if you do, then let me be a fool and boast a little. 17When I do all this boasting, I do it as a fool and not for the Lord. 18Yet if others want to boast about what they have done, so will I. 19And since you are so clever, you will gladly put up with a fool. 20In fact, you let people make slaves of you and cheat you and steal from you. Why, you even let them strut around and slap you in the face. 21I am ashamed to say that we are too weak to behave in such a way.

If they can boast, so can I, but it is a foolish thing to do. 22Are they Hebrews? So am I. Are they Jews? So am I.

Are they from the family of Abraham? Well, so am I. ²³Are they servants of Christ? I am a fool to talk this way, but I serve him better than they do. I have worked harder and have been put in jail more times. I have been beaten with whips more and have been in danger of death more often.

²⁴Five times the Jews gave me 39 lashes with a whip. ²⁵Three times the Romans beat me with a big stick, and once my enemies stoned me. I have been shipwrecked three times, and I even had to spend a night and a day in the sea. ²⁶During my many travels, I have been in danger from rivers, robbers, Jews, and foreigners. My life has been in danger in cities, in deserts, at sea, and with people who only pretended to be the Lord's followers.

²⁷I have worked and struggled and spent many sleepless nights. I have gone hungry and thirsty and often had nothing to eat. I have been cold from not having enough clothes to keep me warm. ²⁸Besides everything else, each day I am burdened down, worrying about all the churches. ²⁹When others are weak, I am weak too. When others are tricked into sin, I get angry.[l]

³⁰If I have to boast, I will boast about how weak I am. ³¹God, the Father of our Lord Jesus, knows I am not lying. And God is to be praised for ever! ³²The governor of Damascus at the time of King Aretas had the city gates guarded, so that he could capture me. ³³But I escaped by being let down in a basket through a window in the city wall.

Visions from the Lord

12 ¹I have to boast. There is nothing to be gained by it, but I must boast about the visions and other things that the Lord has shown me. ²I know about one of Christ's followers who was taken up into the third heaven 14 years ago. I don't know if the man was still in his body when it happened, but God certainly knows.

³As I said, only God really knows if this man was in

---

[l]*When others are tricked into sin, I get angry:* Or "When others stumble into sin, I hurt for them."

his body at the time. [4]But he was taken up into paradise,[m] where he heard things that are too wonderful to tell. [5]I will boast about that man, but not about myself, except to say how weak I am.

[6]Yet even if I did boast, I would not be foolish. I would simply be speaking the truth. But I will try not to say too much. That way, none of you will think more highly of me than you should because of what you have seen me do and say. [7]Of course, I am now referring to the wonderful things I saw. One of Satan's angels was sent to make me suffer terribly, so that I wouldn't feel too proud.[n]

[8]Three times I begged the Lord to make this suffering go away. [9]But he replied, "My kindness is all you need. My power is strongest when you are weak." So if Christ keeps giving me his power, I will gladly boast about how weak I am. [10]Yes, I am glad to be weak or insulted or mistreated or to have troubles and sufferings, if it is for Christ. Because when I am weak, I am strong.

Paul's Concern for the Lord's Followers at Corinth

[11]I have been making a fool of myself. But you forced me to do it, when you should have been speaking up for me. I may be nothing at all, but I am as good as those super apostles. [12]When I was with you, I was patient and worked all the powerful miracles and signs and wonders of a true apostle. [13]You missed out on only one blessing that the other churches received. That is, you didn't have to support me. Forgive me for doing you wrong.

[14]I am planning to visit you for the third time. But I still won't make a burden of myself. What I really want is you, and not what you have. Children aren't supposed to save up for their parents, but parents are supposed to

---

[m]*paradise:* In the Greek translation of the Old Testament, this word is used for the Garden of Eden. In New Testament times it was sometimes used for the place where God's people are happy and at rest, as they wait for the final judgment. [n]*Of course...too proud:* Or "Because of the wonderful things that I saw, one of Satan's angels was sent to make me suffer terribly, so that I wouldn't feel too proud."

take care of their children. 15So I will gladly give all that I have and all that I am. Will you love me less for loving you too much? 16You agree that I wasn't a burden to you. Maybe that's because I was trying to catch you off guard and trick you. 17Were you cheated by any of those I sent to you? 18I urged Titus to visit you, and I sent another follower with him. But Titus didn't cheat you, and we felt and behaved the same way he did.

19Have you been thinking all along that we have been defending ourselves to you? Actually, we have been speaking to God as followers of Christ. But, my friends, we did it all for your good.

20I am afraid that when I come, we won't be pleased with each other. I fear that some of you may be arguing or jealous or angry or selfish or gossiping or insulting each other. I even fear that you may be proud and acting like a mob. 21I am afraid God will make me ashamed when I visit you again. I will feel like crying because many of you have never given up your old sins. You are still doing things that are immoral, indecent, and shameful.

Final Warnings and Greetings

13 1I am on my way to visit you for the third time. And as the Scriptures say, "Any charges must be proved true by at least two or three witnesses." 2During my second visit I warned you that I would punish you and anyone else who doesn't stop sinning. I am far away from you now, but I give you the same warning. 3This should prove to you that I am speaking for Christ. When he corrects you, he won't be weak. He will be powerful! 4Although he was weak when he was nailed to the cross, he now lives by the power of God. We are weak, just as Christ was. But you will see that we will live by the power of God, just as Christ does.

5Test yourselves and find out if you really are true to your faith. If you pass the test, you will discover that Christ is living in you. But if Christ isn't living in you, you have failed. 6I hope you will discover that we have not failed. 7We pray that you will stop doing evil things. We don't pray like this to make ourselves look good, but to get you to do right, even if we are failures.

8All we can do is to follow the truth and not fight against it. 9Even though we are weak, we are glad that you are strong, and we pray that you will do even better. 10I am writing these things to you before I arrive. This way I won't have to be hard on you when I use the authority that the Lord has given me. I was given this authority, so that I could help you and not destroy you.

11Goodbye, my friends. Do better and pay attention to what I have said. Try to get along and live peacefully with each other.

Now I pray that God, who gives love and peace, will be with you. 12Give each other a warm greeting. All of God's people send their greetings.

13I pray that the Lord Jesus Christ will bless you and be kind to you! May God bless you with his love, and may the Holy Spirit join all your hearts together.

GALATIANS
ABOUT THIS LETTER

From the very beginning of this letter to the churches in the region of Galatia (in central Asia Minor), Paul makes two things clear to his readers: he is a true apostle, and his message is the only true message (chapter 1.1-10). These statements were very important, because some people claimed that Paul was a false apostle with a false message.

Paul was indeed a true apostle, and his mission to the Gentiles was given to him by the Lord and approved by the apostles in Jerusalem (1.18—2.10). Paul had even corrected the apostle Peter, when he had stopped eating with Gentile followers who were not obeying the Law of Moses (2.1-18).

Faith is the only way to be saved. Paul insists that this was true already for Abraham, who had received God's promise by faith. And Paul leaves no doubt about what his own faith means to him:

I have been nailed to the cross with Christ. I have died, but Christ lives in me. And I now live by faith in the Son of God, who loved me and gave his life for me.
(Chapter 2.19b, 20)

A QUICK LOOK AT THIS LETTER

1 ¹⁻²From the apostle Paul and from all the Lord's followers with me.

I was chosen to be an apostle by Jesus Christ and by God the Father, who raised him from death. No mere human chose or appointed me to this work.

To the churches in Galatia.

³I pray that God the Father and our Lord Jesus Christ will be kind to you and will bless you with peace! ⁴Christ obeyed God our Father and gave himself as a sacrifice for our sins to rescue us from this evil world. ⁵God will be given glory for ever and ever. Amen.

The Only True Message

⁶I am shocked that you have so quickly turned from God, who chose you because of his wonderful kindness.ᵃ You have believed another message, ⁷when there is really only one true message. But some people are causing you trouble and want to make you turn away from the good news about Christ. ⁸I pray that God will punish anyone who preaches anything different from our message to you! It doesn't matter if that person is one of us or an angel from heaven. ⁹I have said it before, and I will say it again. I hope God will punish anyone who preaches anything different from what you have already believed.

¹⁰I am not trying to please people. I want to please God. Do you think I am trying to please people? If I were doing that, I would not be a servant of Christ.

How Paul Became an Apostle

¹¹My friends, I want you to know that no-one made up the message I preach. ¹²It wasn't given or taught to me by some mere human. My message came directly from Jesus Christ when he appeared to me.

¹³You know how I used to live as a Jew. I was cruel to God's church and even tried to destroy it. ¹⁴I was a much better Jew than anyone else my own age, and I obeyed every law that our ancestors had given us. ¹⁵But even before I was born, God had chosen me. He was kind and had decided ¹⁶to show me his Son, so that I would announce his message to the Gentiles. I didn't talk this over with anyone. ¹⁷I didn't say a word, not even to the men in Jerusalem who were apostles before I was. Instead, I went at once to Arabia, and afterwards I

ᵃhis wonderful kindness: Some manuscripts have "the wonderful kindness of Christ."

returned to Damascus.

[18]Three years later I went to visit Peter[b] in Jerusalem and stayed with him for 15 days. [19]The only other apostle I saw was James, the Lord's brother. [20]And in the presence of God I swear I am telling the truth.

[21]Later, I went to the regions of Syria and Cilicia. [22]But no-one who belonged to Christ's churches in Judea had ever seen me in person. [23]They had only heard that the one who had been cruel to them was now preaching the message that he had once tried to destroy. [24]And because of me, they praised God.

2 [1]Fourteen years later I went to Jerusalem with Barnabas. I also took along Titus. [2]But I went there because God had told me to go, and I explained the good news that I had been preaching to the Gentiles. Then I met privately with the ones who seemed to be the most important leaders. I wanted to make sure that my work in the past and my future work would not be for nothing.

[3]Titus went to Jerusalem with me. He was a Greek, but still he wasn't forced to be circumcised. [4]We went there because of those who pretended to be followers and had sneaked in among us as spies. They had come to take away the freedom that Christ Jesus had given us, and they were trying to make us their slaves. [5]But we wanted you to have the true message. That's why we didn't give in to them, not even for a second.

[6]Some of them were supposed to be important leaders, but I didn't care who they were. God doesn't have any favourites! None of these so-called special leaders added anything to my message. [7]They realised that God had sent me with the good news for Gentiles, and that he had sent Peter with the same message for Jews. [8]God, who had sent Peter on a mission to the Jews, was now using me to preach to the Gentiles.

[9]James, Peter, and John realised that God had given me the message about his undeserved kindness. And these men are supposed to be the backbone of the church. They even gave Barnabas and me a friendly handshake.

[b]Peter: The Greek text has "Cephas," which is an Aramaic name meaning "rock." Peter is the Greek name with the same meaning.

This was to show that we would work with Gentiles and that they would work with Jews. ¹⁰They only asked us to remember the poor, and that was something I had always been eager to do.

Paul Corrects Peter at Antioch

¹¹When Peter came to Antioch, I told him face to face that he was wrong. ¹²He used to eat with Gentile followers of the Lord, until James sent some Jewish followers. Peter was afraid of the Jews and soon stopped eating with Gentiles. ¹³He and the other Jews hid their true feelings so well that even Barnabas was fooled. ¹⁴But when I saw that they weren't really obeying the truth that is in the good news, I corrected Peter in front of everyone and said:

Peter, you are a Jew, but you live like a Gentile. So how can you force Gentiles to live like Jews?

¹⁵We are Jews by birth and aren't sinners like Gentiles. ¹⁶But we know that God accepts only those who have faith in Jesus Christ. No-one can please God by simply obeying the Law. So we put our faith in Christ Jesus, and God accepted us because of our faith.

¹⁷When we Jews started looking for a way to please God, we discovered that we are sinners too. Does this mean that Christ is the one who makes us sinners? No, it doesn't! ¹⁸But if I tear down something and then build it again, I prove that I was wrong at first. ¹⁹It was the Law itself that killed me and freed me from its power, so that I could live for God.

I have been nailed to the cross with Christ. ²⁰I have died, but Christ lives in me. And I now live by faith in the Son of God, who loved me and gave his life for me. ²¹I don't turn my back on God's undeserved kindness. If we can be acceptable to God by obeying the Law, it was useless for Christ to die.

Faith Is the Only Way

3 ¹You stupid Galatians! I told you exactly how Jesus Christ was nailed to a cross. Has someone now put an evil spell on you? ²I want to know only one thing. How were you given God's Spirit? Was it by obeying the

Law of Moses or by hearing about Christ and having faith in him? 3How can you be so stupid? Do you think that by yourself you can complete what God's Spirit started in you? 4Have you gone through all of this for nothing? Is it all really for nothing? 5God gives you his Spirit and works miracles in you. But does he do this because you obey the Law of Moses or because you have heard about Christ and have faith in him?

6The Scriptures say that God accepted Abraham because Abraham had faith. 7And so, you should understand that everyone who has faith is a child of Abraham.c 8Long ago the Scriptures said that God would accept the Gentiles because of their faith. That's why God told Abraham the good news that all nations would be blessed because of him. 9This means that everyone who has faith will share in the blessings that were given to Abraham because of his faith.

10Anyone who tries to please God by obeying the Law is under a curse. The Scriptures say, "Everyone who doesn't obey everything in the Law is under a curse." 11No-one can please God by obeying the Law. The Scriptures also say, "The people God accepts because of their faith will live."d

12The Law isn't based on faith. It promises life only to people who obey its commands. 13But Christ rescued us from the Law's curse, when he became a curse in our place. This is because the Scriptures say that anyone who is nailed to a tree is under a curse. 14And because of what Jesus Christ has done, the blessing that was promised to Abraham was taken to the Gentiles. This happened so that by faith we would be given the promised Holy Spirit.

The Law and the Promise

15My friends, I will use an everyday example to explain what I mean. Once someone agrees to something, no-one

---

ca child of Abraham: God chose Abraham, and so it was believed that anyone who was a child of Abraham was also a child of God (see the note at 3.29). dThe people God accepts because of their faith will live: Or "The people God accepts will live because of their faith."

else can change or cancel the agreement.[e] [16]That's how it is with the promises God made to Abraham and his descendant.[f] The promises were not made to many descendants, but only to one, and that one is Christ. [17]What I am saying is that the Law can't change or cancel God's promise that was made 430 years before the Law was given. [18]If we have to obey the Law in order to receive God's blessings, those blessings don't really come to us because of God's promise. But God was kind to Abraham and made him a promise.

[19]What is the use of the Law? It was given later to show that we sin. But it was only supposed to last until the coming of that descendant[g] who was given the promise. In fact, angels gave the Law to Moses, and he gave it to the people. [20]There is only one God, and the Law did not come directly from him.

Slaves and Children

[21]Does the Law disagree with God's promises? No, it doesn't! If any law could give life to us, we could become acceptable to God by obeying that law. [22]But the Scriptures say that sin controls everyone, so that God's promises will be for anyone who has faith in Jesus Christ.

[23]The Law controlled us and kept us under its power until the time came when we would have faith. [24]In fact, the Law was our teacher. It was supposed to teach us until we had faith and were acceptable to God. [25]But once a person has learnt to have faith, there is no more need to have the Law as a teacher.

[26]All of you are God's children because of your faith in Christ Jesus. [27]And when you were baptised, it was as though you had put on Christ in the same way you put on new clothes. [28]Faith in Christ Jesus is what makes each of you equal with each other, whether you are a Jew or a Greek, a slave or a free person, a man or a woman. [29]So if you belong to Christ, you are now part of

---

[e]*Once someone...cancel the agreement:* Or "Once a person makes out a will, no-one can change or cancel it." [f]*descendant:* The Greek text has "seed," which may mean one or many descendants. In this verse Paul says it means Christ. [g]*that descendant:* Jesus.

Abraham's family,[h] and you will be given what God has promised.

4 [1]Children who are under-age are no better off than slaves, even though everything their parents own will some day be theirs. [2]This is because children are placed in the care of guardians and teachers until the time their parents have set. [3]That is how it was with us. We were like children ruled by the powers of this world.

[4]But when the time was right, God sent his Son, and a woman gave birth to him. His Son obeyed the Law, [5]so he could set us free from the Law, and we could become God's children. [6]Now that we are his children, God has sent the Spirit of his Son into our hearts. And his Spirit tells us that God is our Father. [7]You are no longer slaves. You are God's children, and you will be given what he has promised.

Paul's Concern for the Galatians

[8]Before you knew God, you were slaves of gods that are not real. [9]But now you know God, or better still, God knows you. How can you turn back and become the slaves of those weak and pitiful powers?[i] [10]You even celebrate certain days, months, seasons, and years. [11]I'm afraid I have wasted my time working with you.

[12]My friends, I beg you to be like me, just as I once tried to be like you. Did you mistreat me [13]when I first preached to you? No you didn't, even though you knew I had come there because I was sick. [14]My illness must have caused you some trouble, but you didn't hate me or turn me away because of it. You welcomed me as though I was one of God's angels or even Christ Jesus himself. [15]Where is that good feeling now? I am sure that if it had been possible, you would have taken out your own eyes and given them to me. [16]Am I now your enemy, just because I told you the truth?

[17]Those people may be paying you a lot of attention, but it isn't for your good. They only want to keep you away from me, so you will pay them a lot of attention.

[h]*you are now part of Abraham's family:* Paul tells the Galatians that faith in Jesus Christ is what makes someone a true child of Abraham and of God (see the note at 3.7). [i]*powers:* Spirits were thought to control human lives and were believed to be connected with the movements of the stars.

18It's always good to give your attention to something worthwhile, even when I'm not with you. 19My children, I am in terrible pain until Christ may be seen living in you. 20I wish I was with you now. Then I would not have to talk this way. You really have me puzzled.

Hagar and Sarah

21Some of you would like to be under the rule of the Law of Moses. But do you know what the Law says? 22In the Scriptures we learn that Abraham had two sons. The mother of one of them was a slave, while the mother of the other one had always been free. 23The son of the slave woman was born in the usual way. But the son of the free woman was born because of God's promise.

24All of this has another meaning as well. Each of the two women stands for one of the agreements God made with his people. Hagar, the slave woman, stands for the agreement that was made at Mount Sinai. Everyone born into her family is a slave. 25Hagar also stands for Mount Sinai in Arabia*j* and for the present city of Jerusalem. She*k* and her children are slaves.

26But our mother is the city of Jerusalem in heaven above, and she isn't a slave. 27The Scriptures say about her,

"You have never had children,
but now you can be glad.
You have never given birth,
but now you can shout.
Once you had no children,
but now you will have more children
than a woman who has been married
for a long time."

28My friends, you were born because of this promise, just as Isaac was. 29But the child who was born in the natural way made trouble for the child who was born because of the Spirit. The same thing is happening today. 30The Scriptures say, "Get rid of the slave woman and her son! He won't be given anything. The son of the free

---

jHagar also stands for Mount Sinai in Arabia: Some manuscripts have "Sinai is a mountain in Arabia." This sentence would then be translated: "Sinai is a mountain in Arabia, and Hagar stands for the present city of Jerusalem."
kShe: "Hagar" or "Jerusalem."

woman will receive everything." 31My friends, we are children of the free woman and not of the slave.

Christ Gives Freedom

5 1Christ has set us free! This means we are really free. Now hold on to your freedom and don't ever become slaves of the Law again.

2I, Paul, promise you that Christ won't do you any good if you get circumcised. 3If you do, you must obey the whole Law. 4And if you try to please God by obeying the Law, you have cut yourself off from Christ and his wonderful kindness. 5But the Spirit makes us sure that God will accept us because of our faith in Christ. 6If you are a follower of Christ Jesus, it makes no difference whether you are circumcised or not. All that matters is your faith that makes you love others.

7You were doing so well until someone made you turn from the truth. 8And that person was certainly not sent by the one who chose you. 9A little yeast can change a whole batch of dough, 10but you belong to the Lord. That makes me certain that you will do what I say, instead of what someone else tells you to do. Whoever is causing trouble for you will be punished.

11My friends, if I still preach that people need to be circumcised, why am I in so much trouble? The message about the cross would no longer be a problem, if I told people to be circumcised. 12I wish that everyone who is upsetting you would not only get circumcised, but would cut off much more!

13My friends, you were chosen to be free. So don't use your freedom as an excuse to do anything you want. Use it as an opportunity to serve each other with love. 14All that the Law says can be summed up in the command to love others as much as you love yourself. 15But if you keep attacking each other like wild animals, you had better watch out or you will destroy yourselves.

God's Spirit and Our Own Desires

16If you are guided by the Spirit, you won't obey your selfish desires. 17The Spirit and your desires are enemies of each other. They are always fighting each other and keeping you from doing what you feel you should. [18]But if you obey the Spirit, the Law of Moses has no control over you.

[19]People's desires make them give in to immoral ways, filthy thoughts, and shameful deeds. [20]They worship idols, practise witchcraft, hate others, and are hard to get along with. People become jealous, angry, and selfish. They not only argue and cause trouble, but they are [21]envious. They get drunk, carry on at wild parties, and do other evil things as well. I told you before, and I am telling you again: No-one who does these things will share in the blessings of God's kingdom.

[22]God's Spirit makes us loving, happy, peaceful, patient, kind, good, faithful, [23]gentle, and self-controlled. There is no law against behaving in any of these ways. [24]And because we belong to Christ Jesus, we have killed our selfish feelings and desires. [25]God's Spirit has given us life, and so we should follow the Spirit. [26]But don't be conceited or make others jealous by claiming to be better than they are.

Help Each Other

6 [1]My friends, you are spiritual. So if someone is trapped in sin, you should gently lead that person back to the right path. But watch out, and don't be tempted yourself. [2]You obey the law of Christ when you offer each other a helping hand.

[3]If you think you are better than others, when you really aren't, you are wrong. [4]Do your own work well, and then you will have something to be proud of. But don't compare yourself with others. [5]We each must carry our own load.

[6]Share every good thing you have with anyone who teaches you what God has said.

[7]You can't fool God, so don't make a fool of yourself! You will harvest what you plant. [8]If you follow your selfish desires, you will harvest destruction, but if you follow the Spirit, you will harvest eternal life. [9]Don't get tired of helping others. You will be rewarded when the time is right, if you don't give up. [10]We should help

people whenever we can, especially if they are followers of the Lord.

Final Warnings

[11] You can see what big letters I make when I write with my own hand.

[12] Those people who are telling you to get circumcised are only trying to show how important they are. And they don't want to get into trouble for preaching about the cross of Christ. [13] They are circumcised, but they don't obey the Law of Moses. All they want is to boast about having you circumcised. [14] But I will never boast about anything except the cross of our Lord Jesus Christ. Because of his cross, the world is dead as far as I am concerned, and I am dead as far as the world is concerned.

[15] It doesn't matter if you are circumcised or not. All that matters is that you are a new person.

[16] If you follow this rule, you will belong to God's true people. God will treat you with undeserved kindness and will bless you with peace.

[17] On my own body are scars that prove I belong to Christ Jesus. So I don't want anyone to bother me any more.

[18] My friends, I pray that the Lord Jesus Christ will be kind to you! Amen.

EPHESIANS
ABOUT THIS LETTER

"Praise the God and Father of our Lord Jesus Christ for the spiritual blessings that Christ has brought us from heaven!" (chapter 1.3). Paul begins his letter to the Christians in Ephesus with a powerful reminder of the main theme of his message. Christ died on the cross to set us free (1.7, 8). But God raised Christ from death, and he now sits at God's right side in heaven, where he rules over this world. And he will rule over the future world as well (1.20, 21).

Christ brought Jews and Gentiles together by "breaking down the wall of hatred" that separated them (2.14) and he united them all as part of that holy temple where God's Spirit lives (2.22). This was according to God's eternal plan (3.11).

There is only one Lord, one Spirit of God, and one God, who is the Father of all people (4.4, 5). This means that Christians must let the Spirit keep their hearts united, so they can live at peace with each other (4.3). The idea of all Christians being one with Christ is so central to this letter that it occurs 20 times. There is one faith and one baptism by which believers become one body.

Ephesus was a port city on the western shore of Asia Minor (modern-day Turkey). In Paul's time this was the fourth largest city in the Roman Empire. It was also an ancient centre of nature religion where the goddess Artemis was widely worshipped (Acts 19).

Paul lets the Ephesians know that much is expected of people who are called to a new life (4.17—5.20). Followers of the Lord are God's dear children, and they must do as God does (5.1). They used to live in the dark, but they must now live in the light and make their light shine (5.8, 9).

Paul then teaches husbands and wives, children and parents, and slaves and masters how to live as Christians (5.21—6.9).

Paul never forgets how kind God is:

*But God was merciful! We were dead because of our sins,
but God loved us so much that he made us alive with
Christ, and God's wonderful kindness is what saves you.*
(Chapter 2.4, 5)

*You were saved by faith in God, who treats us much
better than we deserve. This is God's gift to you, and not
anything you have done on your own.   (Chapter 2.8)*

A QUICK LOOK AT THIS LETTER

* Greetings (1.1, 2)
* Christ Brings Spiritual Blessings (1.3—3.21)
* A New Life in Unity with Christ (4.1—6.20)
* Final Greetings (6.21-24)

1 ¹From Paul, chosen by God to be an apostle of
Christ Jesus.

To God's people who live in Ephesus and*ᵃ* are faithful
followers of Christ Jesus.

²I pray that God our Father and our Lord Jesus Christ
will be kind to you and will bless you with peace!

Christ Brings Spiritual Blessings

³Praise the God and Father of our Lord Jesus Christ for
the spiritual blessings that Christ has brought us from
heaven! ⁴Before the world was created, God had Christ
choose us to live with him and to be his holy and
innocent and loving people. ⁵God was kind*ᵇ* and decided
that Christ would choose us to be God's own adopted
children. ⁶God was very kind to us because of the Son he
dearly loves, and so we should praise God.

⁷⁻⁸Christ sacrificed his life's blood to set us free, which
means that our sins are now forgiven. Christ did this
because God was so kind to us. God has great wisdom and
understanding, ⁹and by what Christ has done, God has
shown us his own mysterious ways. ¹⁰Then when the

ᵃalive in Ephesus and: Some manuscripts do not have these words.   *ᵇholy*
and innocent and loving people. God was kind: Or "holy and innocent people.
God was loving and kind."

time is right, God will do all that he has planned, and Christ will bring together everything in heaven and on earth.

[11]God always does what he plans, and that's why he appointed Christ to choose us. [12]He did this so that we Jews would bring honour to him and be the first ones to have hope because of him. [13]Christ also brought you the truth, which is the good news about how you can be saved. You put your faith in Christ and were given the promised Holy Spirit to show that you belong to God. [14]The Spirit also makes us sure that we will be given what God has stored up for his people. Then we will be set free, and God will be honoured and praised.

Paul's Prayer

[15]I have heard about your faith in the Lord Jesus and your love for all of God's people. [16]So I never stop being grateful for you, as I mention you in my prayers. [17]I ask the glorious Father and God of our Lord Jesus Christ to give you his Spirit. The Spirit will make you wise and let you understand what it means to know God. [18]My prayer is that light will flood your hearts and that you will understand the hope that was given to you when God chose you. Then you will discover the glorious blessings that will be yours together with all of God's people.

[19]I want you to know about the great and mighty power that God has for us followers. It is the same wonderful power he used [20]when he raised Christ from death and let him sit at his right side[c] in heaven. [21]There Christ rules over all forces, authorities, powers, and rulers. He rules over all beings in this world and will rule in the future world as well. [22]God has put all things under the power of Christ, and for the good of the church he has made him the head of everything. [23]The church is Christ's body and is filled with Christ who completely fills everything.[d]

---

[c]right side: The place of power and honour.   [d]and is filled with Christ who completely fills everything: Or "which completely fills Christ and fully completes his work."

From Death to Life

2 ¹In the past you were dead because you sinned and fought against God. ²You followed the ways of this world and obeyed the devil. He rules the world, and his spirit has power over everyone who doesn't obey God. ³Once we were also ruled by the selfish desires of our bodies and minds. We had made God angry, and we were going to be punished like everyone else.

⁴⁻⁵But God was merciful! We were dead because of our sins, but God loved us so much that he made us alive with Christ, and God's wonderful kindness is what saves you. ⁶God raised us from death to life with Christ Jesus, and he has given us a place beside Christ in heaven. ⁷God did this so that in the future world he could show how truly good and kind he is to us because of what Christ Jesus has done. ⁸You were saved by faith in God, who treats us much better than we deserve.ᵉ This is God's gift to you, and not anything you have done on your own. ⁹It isn't something you have earned, so there is nothing you can boast about. ¹⁰God planned for us to do good things and to live as he has always wanted us to live. That's why he sent Christ to make us what we are.

United by Christ

¹¹Don't forget that you are Gentiles. In fact, you used to be called "uncircumcised" by those who take pride in being circumcised. ¹²At that time you didn't know about Christ. You were foreigners to the people of Israel, and you had no part in the promises that God had made to them. You were living in this world without hope and without God, ¹³and you were far from God. But Christ offered his life's blood as a sacrifice and brought you near to God.

¹⁴Christ has made peace between Jews and Gentiles, and he has united us by breaking down the wall of hatred that separated us. Christ gave his own body ¹⁵to destroy the Law of Moses with all its rules and commands. He

---

ᵉ*treats us much better than we deserve:* The Greek word *charis*, traditionally rendered "grace," is translated here and other places in the CEV to express the overwhelming kindness of God.

even brought Jews and Gentiles together as though we were only one person, when he united us in peace. [16]On the cross Christ did away with our hatred for each other. He also made peace[f] between us and God by uniting Jews and Gentiles in one body. [17]Christ came and preached peace to you Gentiles, who were far from God, and peace to us Jews, who were near God. [18]And because of Christ, all of us can come to the Father by the same Spirit.

[19]You Gentiles are no longer strangers and foreigners. You are citizens with everyone else who belongs to the family of God. [20]You are like a building with the apostles and prophets as the foundation and with Christ as the most important stone. [21]Christ is the one who holds the building together and makes it grow into a holy temple for the Lord. [22]And you are part of that building Christ has built as a place for God's own Spirit to live.

Paul's Mission to the Gentiles

3 [1]Christ Jesus made me his prisoner, so that I could help you Gentiles. [2]You have surely heard about God's kindness in choosing me to help you. [3]In fact, this letter tells you a little about how God has shown me his mysterious ways. [4]As you read the letter, you will also find out how well I really do understand the mystery about Christ. [5]No-one knew about this mystery until God's Spirit told it to his holy apostles and prophets. [6]And the mystery is this: Because of Christ Jesus, the good news has given the Gentiles a share in the promises that God gave to the Jews. God has also let the Gentiles be part of the same body.

[7]God treated me with kindness. His power worked in me, and it became my job to spread the good news. [8]I am the least important of all God's people. But God was kind and chose me to tell the Gentiles that because of Christ there are blessings that can't be measured. [9]God, who created everything, wanted me to help everyone understand the mysterious plan that had always been hidden in his mind. [10]Then God would use the church to show the powers and authorities in the spiritual world

[f]*He also made peace:* Or "The cross also made peace."

that he has many different kinds of wisdom.
¹¹God did this according to his eternal plan. And he was able to do what he had planned because of all that Christ Jesus our Lord had done. ¹²Christ now gives us courage and confidence, so that we can come to God by faith. ¹³That's why you shouldn't be discouraged when I suffer for you. After all, it will bring honour to you.

Christ's Love for Us

¹⁴I kneel in prayer to the Father. ¹⁵All beings in heaven and on earth receive their life from him.*ᵍ* ¹⁶God is wonderful and glorious. I pray that his Spirit will make you become strong followers ¹⁷and that Christ will live in your hearts because of your faith. Stand firm and be deeply rooted in his love. ¹⁸I pray that you and all of God's people will understand what is called wide or long or high or deep.*ʰ* ¹⁹I want you to know all about Christ's love, although it is too wonderful to be measured. Then your lives will be filled with all that God is.

²⁰⁻²¹I pray that Christ Jesus and the church will for ever bring praise to God. His power at work in us can do far more than we dare ask or imagine. Amen.

Unity with Christ

4 ¹As a prisoner of the Lord, I beg you to live in a way that is worthy of the people God has chosen to be his own. ²Always be humble and gentle. Patiently put up with each other and love each other. ³Try your best to let God's Spirit keep your hearts united. Do this by living at peace. ⁴All of you are part of the same body. There is only one Spirit of God, just as you were given one hope when you were chosen to be God's people. ⁵We have only one Lord, one faith, and one baptism. ⁶There is one God who is the Father of all people. Not only is God above all others, but he works by using all of us, and he lives in all of us.

⁷Christ has generously divided out his gifts to us. ⁸As the Scriptures say,

---

ᵍreceive their life from him: Or "know who they really are because of him."
ʰwhat is called wide or long or high or deep: This may refer to the heavenly Jerusalem or to God's love or wisdom or to the meaning of the cross.

"When he went up to the highest place,
　　he led away many prisoners
　　and gave gifts to people."
⁹When it says, "he went up," it means that Christ had been deep in the earth. ¹⁰This also means that the one who went deep into the earth is the same one who went into the highest heaven, so that he would fill the whole universe.

¹¹Christ chose some of us to be apostles, prophets, missionaries, pastors, and teachers, ¹²so that his people would learn to serve and his body would grow strong. ¹³This will continue until we are united by our faith and by our understanding of the Son of God. Then we will be mature, just as Christ is, and we will be completely like him.ʲ

¹⁴We must stop acting like children. We mustn't let deceitful people trick us by their false teachings, which are like winds that toss us around from place to place. ¹⁵Love should always make us tell the truth. Then we will grow in every way and be more like Christ, the head ¹⁶of the body. Christ holds it together and makes all of its parts work perfectly, as it grows and becomes strong because of love.

The Old Life and the New Life

¹⁷As a follower of the Lord, I order you to stop living like stupid, godless people. ¹⁸Their minds are in the dark, and they are stubborn and ignorant and have missed out on the life that comes from God. They no longer have any feelings about what is right, ¹⁹and they are so greedy that they do all kinds of indecent things.

²⁰⁻²¹But that isn't what you were taught about Jesus Christ. He is the truth, and you heard about him and learnt about him. ²²You were told that your foolish desires will destroy you and that you must give up your old way of life with all its bad habits. ²³Let the Spirit change your way of thinking ²⁴and make you into a new person. You were created to be like God, and so you must please him and be truly holy.

ʲand we will be completely like him: Or "and he is completely perfect."

Rules for the New Life

25We are part of the same body. Stop lying and start telling each other the truth. 26Don't get so angry that you sin. Don't go to bed angry 27and don't give the devil a chance.

28If you are a thief, stop stealing. Be honest and work hard, so you will have something to give to people in need.

29Stop all your dirty talk. Say the right thing at the right time and help others by what you say.

30Don't make God's Spirit sad. The Spirit makes you sure that some day you will be free from your sins.

31Stop being bitter and angry and mad at others. Don't yell at one another or curse each other or ever be rude. 32Instead, be kind and merciful, and forgive others, just as God forgave you because of Christ.

5 1Do as God does. After all, you are his dear children. 2Let love be your guide. Christ loved us*j* and offered his life for us as a sacrifice that pleases God.

3You are God's people, so don't let it be said that any of you are immoral or indecent or greedy. 4Don't use dirty or foolish or filthy words. Instead, say how thankful you are. 5Being greedy, indecent, or immoral is just another way of worshipping idols. You can be sure that people who behave in this way will never be part of the kingdom that belongs to Christ and to God.

Living as People of Light

6Don't let anyone trick you with foolish talk. God punishes everyone who disobeys him and says*k* foolish things. 7So don't have anything to do with anyone like that.

8You used to be like people living in the dark, but now you are people of the light because you belong to the Lord. So act like people of the light 9and make your light shine. Be good and honest and truthful, 10as you try to please the Lord. 11Don't take part in doing those worthless things that are done in the dark. Instead, show how wrong they are. 12It is disgusting even to talk about

jus: Some manuscripts have "you."   *ksays:* Or "does."

what is done in the dark. [13]But the light will show what these things are really like. [14]Light shows up everything,[l] just as the Scriptures say,

"Wake up from your sleep and rise from death.
Then Christ will shine on you."

[15]Act like people with good sense and not like fools. [16]These are evil times, so make every minute count. [17]Don't be stupid. Instead, find out what the Lord wants you to do. [18]Don't destroy yourself by getting drunk, but let the Spirit fill your life. [19]When you meet together, sing psalms, hymns, and spiritual songs, as you praise the Lord with all your heart. [20]Always use the name of our Lord Jesus Christ to thank God the Father for everything.

Wives and Husbands

[21]Honour Christ and put others first. [22]A wife should put her husband first, as she does the Lord. [23]A husband is the head of his wife, as Christ is the head and the Saviour of the church, which is his own body. [24]Wives should always put their husbands first, as the church puts Christ first.

[25]A husband should love his wife as much as Christ loved the church and gave his life for it. [26]He made the church holy by the power of his word, and he made it pure by washing it with water. [27]Christ did this, so that he would have a glorious and holy church, without faults or spots or wrinkles or any other flaws.

[28]In the same way, a husband should love his wife as much as he loves himself. A husband who loves his wife shows that he loves himself. [29]None of us hate our own bodies. We provide for them and take good care of them, just as Christ does for the church, [30]because we are each part of his body. [31]As the Scriptures say, "A man leaves his father and mother to get married, and he becomes like one person with his wife." [32]This is a great mystery, but I understand it to mean Christ and his church. [33]So each husband should love his wife as much as he loves himself, and each wife should respect her husband.

---

[l]*Light shows up everything:* Or "Everything that is seen in the light becomes light itself."

Children and Parents

6 [1]Children, you belong to the Lord, and you do the right thing when you obey your parents. The first commandment with a promise says, [2]"Obey your father and your mother, [3]and you will have a long and happy life."

[4]Parents, don't be hard on your children. Raise them properly. Teach them and instruct them about the Lord.

Slaves and Masters

[5]Slaves, you must obey your earthly masters. Show them great respect and be as loyal to them as you are to Christ. [6]Try to please them at all times, and not just when you think they are watching. You are slaves of Christ, so with your whole heart you must do what God wants you to do. [7]Gladly serve your masters, as though they were the Lord himself, and not simply people. [8]You know that you will be rewarded for any good things you do, whether you are slaves or free.

[9]Slave owners, you must treat your slaves with this same respect. Don't threaten them. They have the same Master in heaven that you do, and he doesn't have any favourites.

The Fight against Evil

[10]Finally, let the mighty strength of the Lord make you strong. [11]Put on all the armour that God gives, so you can defend yourself against the devil's tricks. [12]We are not fighting against humans. We are fighting against forces and authorities and against rulers of darkness and powers in the spiritual world. [13]So put on all the armour that God gives. Then when that evil day[m] comes, you will be able to defend yourself. And when the battle is over, you will still be standing firm.

[14]Be ready! Let the truth be like a belt around your waist, and let God's justice protect you like armour. [15]Your desire to tell the good news about peace should be

[m]*that evil day:* Either the present (see 5.16) or "the day of death" or "the day of judgment."

like shoes on your feet. [16]Let your faith be like a shield, and you will be able to stop all the flaming arrows of the evil one. [17]Let God's saving power be like a helmet, and for a sword use God's message that comes from the Spirit.

[18]Never stop praying, especially for others. Always pray by the power of the Spirit. Stay alert and keep praying for God's people. [19]Pray that I will be given the message to speak and that I may fearlessly explain the mystery about the good news. [20]I was sent to do this work, and that's the reason I am in jail. So pray that I will be brave and will speak as I should.

Final Greetings

[21-22]I want you to know how I am getting along and what I am doing. That's why I am sending Tychicus to you. He is a dear friend, as well as a faithful servant of the Lord. He will tell you how I am doing, and he will cheer you up.

[23]I pray that God the Father and the Lord Jesus Christ will give peace, love, and faith to every follower! [24]May God be kind to everyone who keeps on loving our Lord Jesus Christ.

PHILIPPIANS
ABOUT THIS LETTER

Paul wrote this letter from jail (chapter 1.7) to thank the Lord's followers at Philippi for helping him with their gifts and prayers (1.5; 4.10-19). He hopes to be set free, so that he can continue preaching the good news (3.17-19). But he knows that he might be put to death (1.21; 2.17; 3.10).

The city of Philippi is in the part of northern Greece which the Greeks call Macedonia. It was at Philippi that Paul had entered Europe for the first time, and there he preached the good news and began a church (Acts 16). He now warns the Christians at Philippi that they may have to suffer, just as Christ suffered and Paul is now suffering. If this happens, the Philippians should count it a blessing that comes from having faith in Christ (1.28-30).

There were problems in the church at Philippi, because some of the members claimed that people must obey the law of Moses, or they could not be saved. But Paul has no patience with such members and warns the church, "Watch out for those people who behave like dogs!" (3.2-11). This letter is also filled with joy. Even in jail, Paul is happy because he has discovered how to make the best of a bad situation and because he remembers all the kindness shown to him by the people in the church at Philippi.

Paul reminds them that God's people are to live in harmony (2.2; 4.2, 3) and to think the same way that Christ Jesus did:

> *Christ was truly God.*
> *But he did not try to remain equal with God.*
> *He gave up everything and became a slave,*
> *when he became like one of us.*

> *(Chapter 2.6, 7)*

A QUICK LOOK AT THIS LETTER

1 [1]From Paul and Timothy, servants of Christ Jesus.
To all of God's people who belong to Christ Jesus at Philippi and to all of your church officials and officers.[a]

[2]I pray that God our Father and the Lord Jesus Christ will be kind to you and will bless you with peace!

Paul's Prayer for the Church in Philippi

[3]Every time I think of you, I thank my God. [4]And whenever I mention you in my prayers, it makes me happy. [5]This is because you have taken part with me in spreading the good news from the first day you heard about it. [6]God is the one who began this good work in you, and I am certain that he won't stop before it is complete on the day that Christ Jesus returns.

[7]You have a special place in my heart. So it is only natural for me to feel the way I do. All of you have helped in the work that God has given me, as I defend the good news and tell about it here in jail. [8]God himself knows how much I want to see you. He knows that I care for you in the same way that Christ Jesus does.

[9]I pray that your love will keep on growing and that you will fully know and understand [10]how to make the right choices. Then you will still be pure and innocent when Christ returns. And until that day, [11]Jesus Christ will keep you busy doing good deeds that bring glory and praise to God.

What Life Means to Paul

[12]My dear friends, I want you to know that what has happened to me has helped to spread the good news. [13]The Roman guards and all the others know that I am here in jail because I serve Christ. [14]Now most of the Lord's followers have become brave and are fearlessly speaking

[a]*church officials and officers:* Or "bishops and deacons."

the message.*b*

15Some are preaching about Christ because they are jealous and envious of us. Others are preaching because they want to help. 16They love Christ and know that I am here to defend the good news about him. 17But the ones who are jealous of us are not sincere. They just want to cause trouble for me while I am in jail. 18But that doesn't matter. All that matters is that people are speaking about Christ, whether they are sincere or not. That is what makes me glad.

I will keep on being glad, 19because I know that your prayers and the help that comes from the Spirit of Christ Jesus will keep me safe. 20I honestly expect and hope that I will never do anything to be ashamed of. Whether I live or die, I always want to be as brave as I am now and bring honour to Christ.

21If I live, it will be for Christ, and if I die, I will gain even more. 22I don't know what to choose. I could keep on living and doing something useful. 23It is a hard choice to make. I want to die and be with Christ, because that would be much better. 24-25But I know that all of you still need me. That's why I am sure I will stay on to help you grow and be happy in your faith. 26Then, when I visit you again, you will have good reason to take great pride in Christ Jesus because of me.*c*

27Above all else, you must live in a way that brings honour to the good news about Christ. Then, whether I visit you or not, I will hear that all of you think alike. I will know that you are working together and that you are struggling side by side to get others to believe the good news.

28Be brave when you face your enemies. Your courage will show them that they are going to be destroyed, and it will show you that you will be saved. God will make all of this happen, 29and he has blessed you. Not only do you have faith in Christ, but you suffer for him. 30You saw me suffer, and you still hear about my troubles. Now you must suffer in the same way.

---

bthe message: Some manuscripts have "the Lord's message," and others have "God's message." *ctake great pride in Christ Jesus because of me:* Or "take great pride in me because of Christ Jesus."

True Humility

2 ¹Christ encourages you, and his love comforts you. God's Spirit unites you, and you are concerned for others. ²Now make me completely happy! Live in harmony by showing love for each other. Be united in what you think, as if you were only one person. ³Don't be jealous or proud, but be humble and consider others more important than yourselves. ⁴Care about them as much as you care about yourselves ⁵and think the same way that Christ Jesus thought:*d*

6   Christ was truly God.
       But he did not try to remain*e* equal with God.
7   Instead he gave up everything*f* and became a slave,
       when he became like one of us.

8   Christ was humble. He obeyed God
       and even died on a cross.
9   Then God gave Christ the highest place
       and honoured his name above all others.

10   So at the name of Jesus everyone will bow down,
         those in heaven, on earth, and under the earth.
11   And to the glory of God the Father
       everyone will openly agree,
         "Jesus Christ is Lord!"

Lights in the World

¹²My dear friends, you always obeyed when I was with you. Now that I am away, you should obey even more. So work with fear and trembling to discover what it really means to be saved. ¹³God is working in you to make you willing and able to obey him.

¹⁴Do everything without grumbling or arguing. ¹⁵Then you will be the pure and innocent children of God. You live among people who are crooked and evil, but you must not do anything that they can say is wrong. Try to shine as lights among the people of this world, ¹⁶as you

---

d think the same way that Christ Jesus thought: Or "think the way you should because you belong to Christ Jesus." *e remain:* Or "become." *f He gave up everything:* Greek, "He emptied himself."

hold firmly to*g* the message that gives life. Then on the day when Christ returns, I can take pride in you. I can also know that my work and efforts were not useless.

17Your faith in the Lord and your service are like a sacrifice offered to him. And my own blood may have to be poured out with the sacrifice.*h* If this happens, I will be glad and rejoice with you. 18In the same way, you should be glad and rejoice with me.

Timothy and Epaphroditus

19I want to be encouraged by news about you. So I hope the Lord Jesus will soon let me send Timothy to you. 20I haven't got anyone else who cares about you as much as he does. 21The others think only about what interests them and not about what concerns Christ Jesus. 22But you know what kind of person Timothy is. He has worked with me like a son in spreading the good news. 23I hope to send him to you, as soon as I find out what is going to happen to me. 24And I feel sure that the Lord will also let me come soon.

25I think I ought to send my dear friend Epaphroditus back to you. He is a follower and a worker and a soldier of the Lord, just as I am. You sent him to look after me, 26but now he is eager to see you. He is worried, because you heard he was sick. 27In fact, he was very sick and almost died. But God was kind to him, and also to me, and he kept me from being burdened down with sorrow.

28Now I am more eager than ever to send Epaphroditus back again. You will be glad to see him, and I won't have to worry any longer. 29Be sure to give him a cheerful welcome, just as people who serve the Lord deserve. 30He almost died working for Christ, and he risked his own life to do for me what you could not.

Being Acceptable to God

3 1Finally, my dear friends, be glad that you belong to the Lord. It doesn't bother me to write the same

---

*g*hold firmly to: Or "offer them." *h*my own blood may have to be poured out with the sacrifice: Offerings of water or wine were sometimes poured out when animals were sacrificed on the altar.

things to you that I have written before. In fact, it is for your own good.

2 Watch out for those people who behave like dogs! They are evil and want to do more than just circumcise you. 3 But we are the ones who are truly circumcised, because we worship by the power of God's Spirit[j] and take pride in Christ Jesus. We don't boast about what we have done, 4 although I could. Others may boast about themselves, but I have more reason to boast than anyone else. 5 I was circumcised when I was eight days old,[j] and I am from the nation of Israel and the tribe of Benjamin. I am a true Hebrew. As a Pharisee, I strictly obeyed the Law of Moses. 6 And I was so eager that I even made trouble for the church. I did everything the Law demands in order to please God.

7 But Christ has shown me that what I once thought was valuable is worthless. 8 Nothing is as wonderful as knowing Christ Jesus my Lord. I have given up everything else and count it all as rubbish. All I want is Christ 9 and to know that I belong to him. I could not make myself acceptable to God by obeying the Law of Moses. God accepted me simply because of my faith in Christ. 10 All I want is to know Christ and the power that raised him to life. I want to suffer and die as he did, 11 so that somehow I also may be raised to life.

Running Towards the Goal

12 I have not yet reached my goal, and I am not perfect. But Christ has taken hold of me. So I keep on running and struggling to take hold of the prize. 13 My friends, I don't feel that I have already arrived. But I forget what is behind, and I struggle for what is ahead. 14 I run towards the goal, so that I can win the prize of being called to heaven. This is the prize that God offers because of what Christ Jesus has done. 15 All of us who are mature should think in this same way. And if any of you think differently, God will make it clear to you. 16 But we must keep going in the direction that we are now headed.

[j] *by the power of God's Spirit:* Or "sincerely." [j] *when I was eight days old:* Jewish boys are circumcised eight days after birth.

¹⁷My friends, I want you to follow my example and learn from others who closely follow the example we set for you. ¹⁸I often warned you that many people are living as enemies of the cross of Christ. And now with tears in my eyes, I warn you again ¹⁹that they are headed for hell! They worship their stomachs and boast about the disgusting things they do. All they can think about are the things of this world.

²⁰But we are citizens of heaven and are eagerly waiting for our Saviour to come from there. Our Lord Jesus Christ ²¹has power over everything, and he will make these poor bodies of ours like his own glorious body.

4 ¹Dear friends, I love you and long to see you. Please keep on being faithful to the Lord. You are my pride and joy.

Paul Encourages the Lord's Followers

²Euodia and Syntyche, you belong to the Lord, so I beg you to stop arguing with each other. ³And, my true partner,*k* I ask you to help them. These women have worked together with me and with Clement and with the others in spreading the good news. Their names are now written in the book of life.*l*

⁴Always be glad because of the Lord! I will say it again: Be glad. ⁵Always be gentle with others. The Lord will soon be here. ⁶Don't worry about anything, but pray about everything. With thankful hearts offer up your prayers and requests to God. ⁷Then, because you belong to Christ Jesus, God will bless you with peace that no-one can completely understand. And this peace will control the way you think and feel.

⁸Finally, my friends, keep your minds on whatever is true, pure, right, holy, friendly, and proper. Don't ever stop thinking about what is truly worthwhile and worthy of praise. ⁹You know the teachings I gave you, and you know what you heard me say and saw me do. So follow my example. And God, who gives peace, will be with you.

---

*k*partner: Or "Syzygus," a person's name.   *l*the book of life: A book in which the names of God's people are written.

Paul Gives Thanks for the Gifts He Was Given

[10]The Lord has made me very grateful that at last you have thought about me once again. Actually, you were thinking about me all along, but you didn't have any chance to show it. [11]I am not complaining about having too little. I have learnt to be satisfied with[m] whatever I have. [12]I know what it is to be poor or to have plenty, and I have lived under all kinds of conditions. I know what it means to be full or to be hungry, to have too much or too little. [13]Christ gives me the strength to face anything.

[14]It was good of you to help me when I was having such a hard time. [15]My friends at Philippi, you remember what it was like when I started preaching the good news in Macedonia.[n] After I left there, you were the only church that became my partner by giving blessings and by receiving them in return. [16]Even when I was in Thessalonica, you helped me more than once. [17]I am not trying to get something from you, but I want you to receive the blessings that come from giving.

[18]I have been paid back everything, and with interest. I'm completely satisfied with the gifts that you had Epaphroditus bring me. They are like a sweet-smelling offering or like the right kind of sacrifice that pleases God. [19]I pray that God will take care of all your needs with the wonderful blessings that come from Christ Jesus! [20]May God our Father be praised for ever and ever. Amen.

Final Greetings

[21]Give my greetings to all who are God's people because of Christ Jesus.

The Lord's followers here with me send you their greetings.

[22]All of God's people send their greetings, especially those in the service of the Emperor.

[23]I pray that our Lord Jesus Christ will be kind to you and will bless your life!

---

[m]be satisfied with: Or "get by on." [n]when I started preaching the good news in Macedonia: Paul is talking about his first visit to Philippi (see Acts 16.12-40).

COLOSSIANS
ABOUT THIS LETTER

Colossae was an important city in western Asia Minor, about 160 kilometres east of the port city of Ephesus. Paul had never been to Colossae, but he was pleased to learn that the Christians there were strong in their faith (chapters 1.3-7; 2.6, 7). They had heard the good news from a man named Epaphras who had lived there (1.7; 4.12, 13), but was in jail with Paul (Philemon 23) at the time that Paul wrote this letter (1.14; 4.3, 10, 18).

Many of the church members in Colossae were Gentiles (1.27), and some of them were influenced by strange religious ideas and practices (2.16-23). They thought that to obey God fully they must give up certain physical desires and worship angels and other spiritual powers. But Paul wanted them to know that Christ was with God in heaven, ruling over all powers in the universe (3.1). And so, their worship should be directed to Christ.

Paul quotes a beautiful hymn that explains who Christ is:

Christ is exactly like God, who cannot be seen.
He is the firstborn Son, superior to all creation.

God himself was pleased to live fully in his Son.
And God was pleased for him to make peace
by sacrificing his blood on the cross.

(Chapter 1.15, 19, 20)

A QUICK LOOK AT THIS LETTER

+ Greetings (1.1, 2)
+ A Prayer of Thanks (1.3-8)
+ The Person and Work of Christ (1.9—2.19)
+ New Life with Christ (2.20—4.6)
+ Final Greetings (4.7-18)

1 ¹From Paul, chosen by God to be an apostle of Christ Jesus, and from Timothy, who is also a follower.
²To God's people who live in Colossae and are faithful followers of Christ.

I pray that God our Father will be kind to you and will bless you with peace!

A Prayer of Thanks

³Each time we pray for you, we thank God, the Father of our Lord Jesus Christ. ⁴We have heard of your faith in Christ and of your love for all of God's people, ⁵because what you hope for is kept safe for you in heaven. You first heard about this hope when you believed the true message, which is the good news.

⁶The good news is spreading all over the world with great success. It has spread in that same way among you, ever since the first day you learnt the truth about God's wonderful kindness ⁷from our good friend Epaphras. He works together with us for Christ and is a faithful worker for you.ᵃ ⁸He is also the one who told us about the love that God's Spirit has given you.

The Person and Work of Christ

⁹We have not stopped praying for you since the first day we heard about you. In fact, we always pray that God will show you everything he wants you to do and that you may have all the wisdom and understanding that his Spirit gives. ¹⁰Then you will live a life that honours the Lord, and you will always please him by doing good deeds. You will come to know God even better. ¹¹His glorious power will make you patient and strong enough to endure anything, and you will be truly happy.

¹²I pray that you will be grateful to God for letting you have a part in what he has promised his people in the kingdom of light. ¹³God rescued us from the dark power of Satan and brought us into the kingdom of his dear Son, ¹⁴who forgives our sins and sets us free.

¹⁵   Christ is exactly like God, who cannot be seen.
        He is the firstborn Son, superior to all creation.

ᵃyou: Some manuscripts have "us."

16   Everything was created by him,
      everything in heaven and on earth,
        everything seen and unseen,
    including all forces and powers,
      and all rulers and authorities.
  All things were created by God's Son,
      and everything was made for him.

17   God's Son was before all else,
      and by him everything is held together.
18   He is the head of his body, which is the church.
  He is the very beginning,
    the first to be raised from death,
      so that he would be above all others.

19   God himself was pleased to live fully in his Son.
20   And God was pleased for him to make peace
    by sacrificing his blood on the cross,
  so that all beings in heaven and on earth
    would be brought back to God.

21You used to be far from God. Your thoughts made you his enemies, and you did evil things. 22But his Son became a human and died. So God made peace with you, and now he lets you stand in his presence as people who are holy and faultless and innocent. 23But you must stay deeply rooted and firm in your faith. You must not give up the hope you received when you heard the good news. It was preached to everyone on earth, and I myself have become a servant of this message.

Paul's Service to the Church

24I am glad that I can suffer for you. I am pleased also that in my own body I can continue[b] the suffering of Christ for his body, the church. 25God's plan was to make me a servant of his church and to send me to preach his complete message to you. 26For ages and ages this message was kept secret from everyone, but now it has been explained to God's people. 27God did this because he wanted you Gentiles to understand his wonderful and glorious mystery. And the mystery is that Christ lives in

[b]continue: Or "complete."

you, and he is your hope of sharing in God's glory.

28 We announce the message about Christ, and we use all our wisdom to warn and teach everyone, so that all of Christ's followers will grow and become mature. 29 That's why I work so hard and use the mighty power he gives me.

2 1 I want you to know what a struggle I am going through for you, for God's people at Laodicea, and for all of those followers who have never met me. 2 I do it to encourage them. Then as their hearts are joined together in love, they will be wonderfully blessed with complete understanding. And they will truly know Christ. Not only is he the key to God's mystery, 3 but all wisdom and knowledge are hidden away in him. 4 I tell you these things to keep you from being fooled by fancy talk. 5 Even though I am not with you, I keep thinking about you. I am glad to know that you are living as you should and that your faith in Christ is strong.

Christ Brings Real Life

6 You have accepted Christ Jesus as your Lord. Now keep on following him. 7 Plant your roots in Christ and let him be the foundation for your life. Be strong in your faith, just as you were taught. And be grateful.

8 Don't let anyone fool you by using senseless arguments. These arguments may sound wise, but they are only human teachings. They come from the powers of this world c and not from Christ.

9 God lives fully in Christ. 10 And you are fully grown because you belong to Christ, who is over every power and authority. 11 Christ has also taken away your selfish desires, just as circumcision removes flesh from the body. 12 And when you were baptised, it was the same as being buried with Christ. Then you were raised to life because you had faith in the power of God, who raised Christ from death. 13 You were dead, because you were sinful and were not God's people. But God let Christ make you d alive, when he forgave all our sins.

c powers of this world: Spirits and unseen forces were thought to control human lives and were believed to be connected with the movements of the stars. d you: Some manuscripts have "us."

¹⁴God wiped out the charges that were against us for disobeying the Law of Moses. He took them away and nailed them to the cross. ¹⁵There Christ defeated all powers and forces. He let the whole world see them being led away as prisoners when he celebrated his victory.

¹⁶Don't let anyone tell you what you must eat or drink. Don't let them say that you must celebrate the New Moon festival, the Sabbath, or any other festival. ¹⁷These things are only a shadow of what was to come. But Christ is real!

¹⁸Don't be cheated by people who make a show of acting humbly and who worship angels.ᵉ They boast about seeing visions. But it is all nonsense, because their minds are filled with selfish desires. ¹⁹They are no longer part of Christ, who is the head of the whole body. Christ gives the body its strength, and he uses its joints and muscles to hold it together, as it grows by the power of God.

Christ Brings New Life

²⁰You died with Christ. Now the forces of the universeᶠ haven't got any power over you. Why do you live as if you had to obey such rules as, ²¹"Don't handle this. Don't taste that. Don't touch this."? ²²After these things are used, they are no longer good for anything. So why be bothered with the rules that humans have made up? ²³Obeying these rules may seem to be the smart thing to do. They appear to make you love God more and to be very humble and to have control over your body. But they don't really have any power over our desires.

3 ¹You have been raised to life with Christ. Now set your heart on what is in heaven, where Christ rules at God's right side.ᵍ ²Think about what is up there, not about what is here on earth. ³You died, which means that your life is hidden with Christ, who sits beside God. ⁴Christ gives meaning to yourʰ life, and when he appears, you will also appear with him in glory.

ᵉ*worship angels:* Or "worship with angels (in visions of heaven)." ᶠ*forces of the universe:* See the note at 2.8. ᵍ*right side:* The place of power and honour. ʰ*your:* Some manuscripts have "our."

5Don't be controlled by your body. Kill every desire for the wrong kind of sex. Don't be immoral or indecent or have evil thoughts. Don't be greedy, which is the same as worshipping idols. 6God is angry with people who disobey him by doing*i* these things. 7And that is exactly what you did, when you lived among people who behaved in this way. 8But now you must stop doing such things. You must stop being angry, hateful, and evil. You must no longer say insulting or cruel things about others. 9And stop lying to each other. You have given up your old way of life with its habits.

10Each of you is now a new person. You are becoming more and more like your Creator, and you will understand him better. 11It doesn't matter if you are a Greek or a Jew, or if you are circumcised or not. You may even be a barbarian or a Scythian,*j* and you may be a slave or a free person. Yet Christ is all that matters, and he lives in all of us.

12God loves you and has chosen you as his own special people. So be gentle, kind, humble, meek, and patient. 13Put up with each other, and forgive anyone who does you wrong, just as Christ has forgiven you. 14Love is more important than anything else. It is what ties everything completely together.

15Each one of you is part of the body of Christ, and you were chosen to live together in peace. So let the peace that comes from Christ control your thoughts. And be grateful. 16Let the message about Christ completely fill your lives, while you use all your wisdom to teach and instruct each other. With thankful hearts, sing psalms, hymns, and spiritual songs to God. 17Whatever you say or do should be done in the name of the Lord Jesus, as you give thanks to God the Father because of him.

Some Rules for Christian Living

18A wife must put her husband first. This is her duty as a follower of the Lord.

---

*i*people who disobey him by doing: Some manuscripts do not have these words.
*j*a barbarian or a Scythian: Barbarians were people who could not speak Greek and would be in the lower class of society. Scythians were people who were known for their cruelty.

¹⁹A husband must love his wife and not abuse her.

²⁰Children must always obey their parents. This pleases the Lord.

²¹Parents, don't be hard on your children. If you are, they might give up.

²²Slaves, you must always obey your earthly masters. Try to please them at all times, and not just when you think they are watching. Honour the Lord and serve your masters with your whole heart. ²³Do your work willingly, as though you were serving the Lord himself, and not just your earthly master. ²⁴In fact, the Lord Christ is the one you are really serving, and you know that he will reward you. ²⁵But Christ has no favourites! He will punish evil people, just as they deserve.

4 ¹Slave owners, be fair and honest with your slaves. Don't forget that you have a Master in heaven.

²Never give up praying. And when you pray, keep alert and be thankful. ³Be sure to pray that God will make a way for us to spread his message and explain the mystery about Christ, even though I am in jail for doing this. ⁴Please pray that I will make the message as clear as possible.

⁵When you are with unbelievers, always make good use of the time. ⁶Be pleasant and hold their interest when you speak the message. Choose your words carefully and be ready to give answers to anyone who asks questions.

Final Greetings

⁷Tychicus is the dear friend, who faithfully works and serves the Lord with us, and he will give you the news about me. ⁸I am sending him to cheer you up by telling you how we are getting along. ⁹Onesimus, that dear and faithful follower from your own group, is coming with him. The two of them will tell you everything that has happened here.

¹⁰Aristarchus is in jail with me. He sends greetings to you, and so does Mark, the cousin of Barnabas. You have already been told to welcome Mark, if he visits you. ¹¹Jesus, who is known as Justus, sends his greetings. These three men are the only Jewish followers who have

worked with me for the kingdom of God. They have given me much comfort.

12 Your own Epaphras, who serves Christ Jesus, sends his greetings. He always prays hard that you may fully know what the Lord wants you to do and that you may do it completely. 13 I have seen how much trouble he has gone through for you and for the followers in Laodicea and Hierapolis.

14 Our dear doctor Luke sends you his greetings, and so does Demas.

15 Give my greetings to the followers at Laodicea, especially to Nympha and the church that meets in her home.

16 After this letter has been read to your people, be sure to have it read in the church at Laodicea. And you should read the letter that I have sent to them.*k*

17 Remind Archippus to do the work that the Lord has given him to do.

18 I am signing this letter myself: PAUL.

Don't forget that I am in jail.

I pray that God will be kind to you.

---

kthe letter that I have sent to them: This is the only mention of the letter to the church at Laodicea.

1 THESSALONIANS
ABOUT THIS LETTER

Paul started the church in Thessalonica (chapter 2.13, 14), while working hard to support himself (2.9). In this important city of northern Greece, many of the followers had worshipped idols before becoming Christians (1.9). But they were faithful to the Lord, and because of them the Lord's message had spread everywhere in that region (1.8). This letter may have been the first one that Paul wrote, and maybe even the first of all the New Testament writings.

Some people in Thessalonica began to oppose Paul, and he had to escape to Athens. But he sent his young friend Timothy to find out how the Christians were doing (3.1-5). When Timothy returned, he gave Paul good reports of their faith and love (3.6-10).

The church itself had problems. Some of its members had stopped working, since they thought that the Lord would soon return (4.11, 12). Others were worried because relatives and friends had already died before Christ's return. So Paul tried to explain to them more clearly what would happen when the Lord returns (4.13-15), and then told them how they should live in the meantime (5.1-11).

Paul's final instructions are well worth remembering:

Always be joyful and never stop praying. Whatever happens, keep thanking God because of Jesus Christ. This is what God wants you to do. (Chapter 5.16-18)

A QUICK LOOK AT THIS LETTER

* Greetings (1.1-3)
* The Thessalonians' Faith and Example (1.4—3.13)
* A Life That Pleases God (4.1-12)
* What to Expect When the Lord Returns (4.13—5.11)
* Final Instructions and Greetings (5.12-28)

1

1From Paul, Silas,[a] and Timothy.

To the church in Thessalonica, the people of God the Father and of the Lord Jesus Christ.

I pray that God will be kind to you and will bless you with peace!

2We thank God for you and always mention you in our prayers. Each time we pray, 3we tell God our Father about your faith and loving work and about your firm hope in our Lord Jesus Christ.

The Thessalonians' Faith and Example

4My dear friends, God loves you, and we know he has chosen you to be his people. 5When we told you the good news, it was with the power and assurance that come from the Holy Spirit, and not simply with words. You knew what kind of people we were and how we helped you. 6So, when you accepted the message, you followed our example and the example of the Lord. You suffered, but the Holy Spirit made you glad.

7You became an example for all the Lord's followers in Macedonia and Achaia. 8And because of you, the Lord's message has spread everywhere in those regions. Now the news of your faith in God is known all over the world, and we don't have to say a thing about it. 9Everyone is talking about how you welcomed us and how you turned away from idols to serve the true and living God. 10They also tell how you are waiting for his Son Jesus to come from heaven. God raised him from death, and on the day of judgment Jesus will save us from God's anger.

Paul's Work in Thessalonica

2

1My friends, you know that our time with you wasn't wasted. 2As you remember, we had been mistreated and insulted at Philippi. But God gave us the courage to tell you the good news about him, even though many people caused us trouble. 3We didn't have any hidden motives when we won you over, and we didn't try to fool or trick anyone. 4God was pleased to trust us with his message. We didn't speak to please

aSilas: The Greek text has "Silvanus," another form of the name Silas.

people, but to please God who knows our motives.

⁵You also know that we didn't try to flatter anyone. God himself knows that what we did wasn't a cover-up for greed. ⁶We weren't trying to get you or anyone else to praise us. ⁷But as apostles, we could have demanded help from you. After all, Christ is the one who sent us. We chose to be like children or like a mother*b* nursing her baby. ⁸We cared so much for you, and you became so dear to us, that we were willing to give our lives for you when we gave you God's message.

⁹My dear friends, you surely haven't forgotten our hard work and hardships. You remember how night and day we struggled to make a living, so that we could tell you God's message without being a burden to anyone. ¹⁰Both you and God are witnesses that we were pure and honest and innocent in our dealings with you followers of the Lord. ¹¹You also know we did everything for you that parents would do for their own children. ¹²We begged, encouraged, and urged each of you to live in a way that would honour God. He is the one who chose you to share in his own kingdom and glory.

¹³We always thank God that you believed the message we preached. It came from him, and it isn't something made up by humans. You accepted it as God's message, and now he is working in you. ¹⁴My friends, you did the same as God's churches in Judea and the other followers of Christ Jesus there. And so, you were mistreated by your own people, in the same way they were mistreated by their people.

¹⁵Those Jews killed the Lord Jesus and the prophets, and they even chased us away. God doesn't like what they do and neither does anyone else. ¹⁶They keep us from speaking his message to the Gentiles and from leading them to be saved. The Jews have always gone too far with their sins. Now God has finally become angry and will punish them.

Paul Wants To Visit the Church Again

¹⁷My friends, we were kept from coming to you for a while, but we never stopped thinking about you. We were

---

b like children or like a mother: Some manuscripts have "as gentle as a mother."

eager to see you and tried our best to visit you in person. [18] We really wanted to come. I myself tried several times, but Satan always stopped us. [19] After all, when the Lord Jesus appears, who else but you will give us hope and joy and be like a glorious crown for us? [20] You alone are our glory and joy!

3 [1] Finally, we couldn't stand it any longer. We decided to stay in Athens by ourselves [2] and send our friend Timothy to you. He works with us as God's servant and preaches the good news about Christ. We wanted him to make you strong in your faith and to encourage you. [3] We didn't want any of you to be discouraged by all these troubles. You knew we would have to suffer, [4] because when we were with you, we told you this would happen. And we did suffer, as you well know. [5] At last, when I couldn't wait any longer, I sent Timothy to find out about your faith. I hoped that Satan had not tempted you and made all our work useless.

[6] Timothy has come back from his visit to you and has told us about your faith and love. He also said that you always have happy memories of us and that you want to see us as much as we want to see you.

[7] My friends, even though we have a lot of trouble and suffering, your faith makes us feel better about you. [8] Your strong faith in the Lord is like a breath of new life. [9] How can we possibly thank God enough for all the happiness you have brought us? [10] Day and night we sincerely pray that we will see you again and help you to have an even stronger faith.

[11] We pray that God our Father and our Lord Jesus will let us visit you. [12] May the Lord make your love for each other and for everyone else grow by leaps and bounds. That's how our love for you has grown. [13] And when our Lord comes with all of his people, I pray that he will make your hearts pure and innocent in the sight of God the Father.

A Life That Pleases God

4 [1] Finally, my dear friends, since you belong to the Lord Jesus, we beg and urge you to live as we taught you. Then you will please God. You are already living that way, but try even harder. [2]Remember the instructions we gave you as followers of the Lord Jesus. [3]God wants you to be holy, so don't be immoral in matters of sex. [4]Respect and honour your wife.[c] [5]Don't be a slave of your desires or live like people who don't know God. [6]You must not cheat any of the Lord's followers in matters of sex.[d] Remember, we warned you that he punishes everyone who does such things. [7]God didn't choose you to be filthy, but to be pure. [8]So if you don't obey these rules, you are not really disobeying us. You are disobeying God, who gives you his Holy Spirit.

[9]We don't have to write to you about the need to love each other. God has taught you to do this, [10]and you already have shown your love for all of his people in Macedonia. But, my dear friends, we ask you to do even more. [11]Try your best to live quietly, to mind your own business, and to work hard, just as we taught you to do. [12]Then you will be respected by people who are not followers of the Lord, and you won't have to depend on anyone.

The Lord's Coming

[13]My friends, we want you to understand how it will be for those followers who have already died. Then you won't grieve over them and be like people who haven't got any hope. [14]We believe that Jesus died and was raised to life. We also believe that when God brings Jesus back again, he will bring with him all who had faith in Jesus before they died. [15]Our Lord Jesus told us that when he comes, we won't go up to meet him ahead of his followers who have already died.

[16]With a loud command and with the shout of the chief angel and a blast of God's trumpet, the Lord will return from heaven. Then those who had faith in Christ before they died will be raised to life. [17]Next, all of us who are still alive will be taken up into the clouds together with them to meet the Lord in the sky. From that time on we will all be with the Lord for ever. [18]Encourage each other with these words.

[c]*your wife:* Or "your body." [d]*in matters of sex:* Or "in business."

5 ¹I don't need to write to you about the time or date when all this will happen. ²You surely know that the Lord's return[e] will be as a thief coming at night. ³People will think they are safe and secure. But destruction will suddenly strike them like the pains of a woman about to give birth. And they won't escape.

⁴My dear friends, you don't live in darkness, and so that day won't surprise you like a thief. ⁵You belong to the light and live in the day. We don't live in the night or belong to the dark. ⁶Others may sleep, but we should stay awake and be alert. ⁷People sleep during the night, and some even get drunk. ⁸But we belong to the day. So we must stay sober and let our faith and love be like a suit of armour. Our firm hope that we will be saved is our helmet.

⁹God doesn't intend to punish us, but wants us to be saved by our Lord Jesus Christ. ¹⁰Christ died for us, so that we could live with him, whether we are alive or dead when he comes. ¹¹That's why you must encourage and help each other, just as you are already doing.

Final Instructions and Greetings

¹²My friends, we ask you to be thoughtful of your leaders who work hard and tell you how to live for the Lord. ¹³Show them great respect and love because of their work. Try to get along with each other. ¹⁴My friends, we beg you to warn anyone who isn't living right. Encourage anyone who feels left out, help all who are weak, and be patient with everyone. ¹⁵Don't be hateful to people, just because they are hateful to you. Rather, be good to each other and to everyone else.

¹⁶Always be joyful ¹⁷and never stop praying. ¹⁸Whatever happens, keep thanking God because of Jesus Christ. This is what God wants you to do.

¹⁹Don't turn away God's Spirit ²⁰or ignore prophecies. ²¹Put everything to the test. Accept what is good ²²and don't have anything to do with evil.

²³I pray that God, who gives peace, will make you completely holy. And may your spirit, soul, and body be

---

[e]*the Lord's return:* The Greek text has "the day of the Lord."

kept healthy and faultless until our Lord Jesus Christ returns. 24The one who chose you can be trusted, and he will do this.

25Friends, please pray for us.

26Give the Lord's followers a warm greeting.

27In the name of the Lord I beg you to read this letter to all his followers.

28I pray that our Lord Jesus Christ will be kind to you!

2 THESSALONIANS
ABOUT THIS LETTER

In this letter to the believers in Thessalonica, Paul begins by thanking God that their faith and love keep growing all the time (chapter 1.3). They were going through a lot of troubles, but Paul insists that this is God's way of testing their faith, not a way of punishing them (1.4, 5).

Someone in Thessalonica claimed to have a letter from Paul, saying that the Lord had already returned (2.2). But Paul warns the church not to be fooled! The Lord will not return until after the "wicked one" has appeared (2.3).

Paul also warns against laziness (3.6-10), and he tells the church to guard against any followers who refuse to obey what he has written in this letter.

The letter closes with a prayer:

I pray that the Lord, who gives peace, will always bless you with peace. May the Lord be with all of you.
(Chapter 3.16)

A QUICK LOOK AT THIS LETTER

- Greetings (1.1, 2)
- The Lord's Return Will Bring Justice (1.3-12)
- The Lord Has Not Returned Yet (2.1-12)
- Be Faithful (2.13-17)
- Pray and Work (3.1-15)
- A Final Prayer (3.16-18)

1 ¹From Paul, Silas,[a] and Timothy.

To the church in Thessalonica, the people of God our Father and of the Lord Jesus Christ.

²I pray that God our Father and the Lord Jesus Christ will be kind to you and will bless you with peace!

---

[a]*Silas:* The Greek text has "Silvanus," which is another form of the name Silas.

When Christ Returns

³My dear friends, we always have good reason to thank God for you, because your faith in God and your love for each other keep growing all the time. ⁴That's why we boast about you to all of God's churches. We tell them how patient you are and how you keep on having faith, even though you are going through a lot of trouble and suffering.

⁵All of this shows that God judges fairly and that he is making you fit to share in his kingdom for which you are suffering. ⁶It is only right for God to punish everyone who is causing you trouble, ⁷but he will give you relief from your troubles. He will do the same for us, when the Lord Jesus comes from heaven with his powerful angels ⁸and with a flaming fire.

Our Lord Jesus will punish anyone who doesn't know God and won't obey his message. ⁹Their punishment will be eternal destruction, and they will be kept far from the presence of our Lord and his glorious strength. ¹⁰This will happen on that day when the Lord returns to be praised and honoured by all who have faith in him and belong to him. This includes you, because you believed what we said.

¹¹God chose you, and we keep praying that God will make you worthy of being his people. We pray for God's power to help you do all the good things that you hope to do and that your faith makes you want to do. ¹²Then, because God and our Lord Jesus Christ are so kind, you will bring honour to the name of our Lord Jesus, and he will bring honour to you.

The Lord's Return

2 ¹When our Lord Jesus returns, we will be gathered up to meet him. So I ask you, my friends, ²not to be easily upset or disturbed by people who claim that the Lord*b* has already come. They may say that they heard this directly from the Holy Spirit, or from someone else, or even that they read it in one of our letters. ³But don't be fooled! People will rebel against God. Then before the

---

bLord: The Greek text has "day of the Lord."

Lord returns, the wicked[c] one who is doomed to be destroyed will appear. [4]He will boast and oppose everything that is holy or sacred. He will even sit in God's temple and claim to be God. [5]Don't you remember that I told you this while I was still with you?

[6]You already know what is holding this wicked one back until it's time for him to come. [7]His mysterious power is already at work, but someone is holding him back. And the wicked one won't appear until that someone is out of the way. [8]Then he will appear, but the Lord Jesus will kill him simply by breathing on him. He will be completely destroyed by the Lord's glorious return.

[9]When the wicked one appears, Satan will pretend to work all kinds of miracles, wonders, and signs. [10]Lost people will be fooled by his evil deeds. They could be saved, but they will refuse to love the truth and accept it. [11]So God will make sure that they are fooled into believing a lie. [12]All of them will be punished, because they would rather do evil than believe the truth.

Be Faithful

[13]My friends, the Lord loves you, and it's only natural for us to thank God for you. God chose you to be the first ones to be saved.[d] His Spirit made you holy, and you put your faith in the truth. [14]God used our preaching as his way of inviting you to share in the glory of our Lord Jesus Christ. [15]My friends, that's why you must remain faithful and follow closely what we taught you in person and by our letters.

[16]God our Father loves us. He is kind and has given us eternal comfort and a wonderful hope. We pray that our Lord Jesus Christ and God our Father [17]will encourage you and help you always to do and say the right thing.

Pray for Us

3 [1]Finally, our friends, please pray for us. This will help the message about the Lord to spread quickly, and

---

[c]*wicked:* Some manuscripts have "sinful."   [d]*God chose you to be the first ones to be saved:* Some manuscripts have "From the beginning God chose you to be saved."

others will respect it, just as you do. ²Pray that we may be kept safe from worthless and evil people. After all, not everyone has faith. ³But the Lord can be trusted to make you strong and protect you from harm. ⁴He has made us sure that you are obeying what we taught you and that you will keep on obeying. ⁵I pray that the Lord will guide you to be as loving as God and as patient as Christ.

Warnings against Laziness

⁶My dear friends, in the name ofᵉ the Lord Jesus, I beg you not to have anything to do with any of your people who loaf around and refuse to obey the instructions we gave you. ⁷You surely know that you should follow our example. We didn't waste our time loafing, ⁸and we didn't accept food from anyone without paying for it. We didn't want to be a burden to any of you, so night and day we worked as hard as we could.

⁹We had the right not to work, but we wanted to set an example for you. ¹⁰We also gave you the rule that if you don't work, you don't eat. ¹¹Now we learn that some of you just loaf around and won't do any work, except the work of a busybody. ¹²So, for the sake of our Lord Jesus Christ, we ask and beg these people to settle down and start working for a living. ¹³Dear friends, you must never become tired of doing right.

¹⁴Be on your guard against any followers who refuse to obey what we have written in this letter. Put them to shame by not having anything to do with them. ¹⁵Don't consider them your enemies, but speak kindly to them as you would to any other follower.

Final Prayer

¹⁶I pray that the Lord, who gives peace, will always bless you with peace. May the Lord be with all of you.

¹⁷I always sign my letters as I am now doing: PAUL.

¹⁸I pray that our Lord Jesus Christ will be kind to all of you.

ᵉ*in the name of:* Or "as a follower of."

1 TIMOTHY

ABOUT THIS LETTER

Timothy travelled and worked with Paul (Romans 16.21; 1 Corinthians 16.10; Philippians 2.19), and because of their shared faith, Timothy was like a son to Paul (chapter 1.2). Timothy became one of Paul's most faithful co-workers, and Paul mentions Timothy in five of his letters.

Although this letter is addressed to Timothy personally, it actually addresses many of the concerns Paul had with the life of the entire church. Guidelines are given for choosing church officials (3.1-7), officers (3.8-13), and leaders (5.17-20).

Christians are to pray for everyone and to remember:

> *There is only one God,*
> *and Christ Jesus is the only one*
> *who can bring us to God.*   (Chapter 2.5a)

A QUICK LOOK AT THIS LETTER

- Greetings (1.1, 2)
- Instructions for Church Life (1.3—3.13)
- The Mystery of Our Religion (3.14—4.5)
- Paul's Advice to Timothy (4.6—6.21)

1 ¹From Paul.

God our Saviour and Christ Jesus commanded me to be an apostle of Christ Jesus, who gives us hope.

²Timothy, because of our faith, you are like a son to me. I pray that God our Father and our Lord Jesus Christ will be kind and merciful to you. May they bless you with peace!

Warning against False Teaching

³When I was leaving for Macedonia, I asked you to stay on in Ephesus and warn certain people there to stop spreading their false teachings. ⁴You needed to warn them to stop wasting their time on senseless stories and

endless lists of ancestors. Such things only cause arguments. They don't help anyone to do God's work that can only be done by faith.

⁵You must teach people to have genuine love, as well as a good conscience and true faith. ⁶There are some who have given up these for nothing but empty talk. ⁷They want to be teachers of the Law of Moses. But they don't know what they are talking about, even though they think they do.

⁸We know that the Law is good, if it is used in the right way. ⁹We also understand that it wasn't given to control people who please God, but to control lawbreakers, criminals, godless people, and sinners. It is for wicked and evil people, and for murderers, who would even kill their own parents. ¹⁰The Law was written for people who are sexual perverts or who live as homosexuals or are kidnappers or liars or won't tell the truth in court. It is for anything else that opposes the correct teaching ¹¹of the good news that the glorious and wonderful God has given me.

Being Thankful for God's Kindness

¹²I thank Christ Jesus our Lord. He has given me the strength for my work because he knew that he could trust me. ¹³I used to say terrible and insulting things about him, and I was cruel. But he had mercy on me because I didn't know what I was doing, and I had not yet put my faith in him. ¹⁴Christ Jesus our Lord was very kind to me. He has greatly blessed my life with faith and love just like his own.

¹⁵"Christ Jesus came into the world to save sinners." This saying is true, and it can be trusted. I was the worst sinner of all! ¹⁶But since I was worse than anyone else, God had mercy on me and let me be an example of the endless patience of Christ Jesus. He did this so that others would put their faith in Christ and have eternal life. ¹⁷I pray that honour and glory will always be given to the only God, who lives for ever and is the invisible and eternal King! Amen.

¹⁸Timothy, my son, the instructions I am giving you

are based on what some prophets[a] once said abo~~
you follow these instructions, you will fight like~~
soldier. ¹⁹You will be faithful and have a clear consc.~~
Some people have made a mess of their faith beca~~
they didn't listen to their consciences. ²⁰Two of them
are Hymenaeus and Alexander. I have given these men
over to the power of Satan, so they will learn not to
oppose God.

How To Pray

2 ¹First of all, I ask you to pray for everyone. Ask God
to help and bless them all, and tell God how thankful
you are for each of them. ²Pray for kings and others in
power, so that we may live quiet and peaceful lives as we
worship and honour God. ³This kind of prayer is good,
and it pleases God our Saviour. ⁴God wants everyone to
be saved and to know the whole truth, which is,

⁵   There is only one God,
      and Christ Jesus is the only one
        who can bring us to God.
    Jesus was truly human,
        and he gave himself to rescue all of us.
⁶   God showed us this at the right time.

⁷This is why God chose me to be a preacher and an apostle
of the good news. I am telling the truth. I am not lying.
God sent me to teach the Gentiles about faith and truth.

⁸I want everyone everywhere to lift innocent hands
towards heaven and pray, without being angry or arguing
with each other.

⁹I would like women to wear modest and sensible
clothes. They should not have fancy hair-dos, or wear
expensive clothes, or put on jewellery made of gold or
pearls. ¹⁰Women who claim to love God should do
helpful things for others, ¹¹and they should learn by
being quiet and paying attention. ¹²They should be silent
and not be allowed to teach or to tell men what to do.
¹³After all, Adam was created before Eve, ¹⁴and the man
Adam wasn't the one who was fooled. It was the woman

[a]prophets: Probably the Christian prophets referred to in 4.14.

Eve who was completely fooled and sinned. [15]But women will be saved by having children,[b] if they stay faithful, loving, holy, and modest.

Church Officials

3 [1]It is true that[c] anyone who desires to be a church official[d] wants to be something worthwhile. [2]That's why officials must have a good reputation and be faithful in marriage.[e] They must be self-controlled, sensible, well-behaved, friendly to strangers, and able to teach. [3]They must not be heavy drinkers or troublemakers. Instead, they must be kind and gentle and not love money.

[4]Church officials must be in control of their own families, and they must see that their children are obedient and always respectful. [5]If they don't know how to control their own families, how can they look after God's people?

[6]They must not be new followers of the Lord. If they are, they might become proud and be doomed along with the devil. [7]Finally, they must be well-respected by people who are not followers. Then they won't be trapped and disgraced by the devil.

Church Officers

[8]Church officers[f] should be serious. They must not be liars, heavy drinkers, or greedy for money. [9]And they must have a clear conscience and hold firmly to what God has shown us about our faith. [10]They must first prove themselves. Then if no-one has anything against them, they can serve as officers.

[11]Women[g] must also be serious. They must not gossip or be heavy drinkers, and they must be faithful in everything they do.

---

[b]*saved by having children:* Or "brought safely through childbirth" or "saved by the birth of a child" (that is, by the birth of Jesus) or "saved by being good mothers." [c]*It is true that:* These words may be taken with 2.15. If so, that verse would be translated: "It is true that women will be saved...holy, and modest." And 3.1 would be translated, "Anyone who desires...something worthwhile." [d]*church official:* Or "bishop." [e]*be faithful in marriage:* Or "be the husband of only one wife" or "have never been divorced." [f]*Church officers:* Or "Deacons." [g]*Women:* Either church officers or the wives of church officers.

¹²Church officers must be faithful in marriage.ʰ They must be in full control of their children and everyone else in their home. ¹³Those who serve well as officers will earn a good reputation and will be highly respected for their faith in Christ Jesus.

The Mystery of Our Religion

¹⁴I hope to visit you soon. But I am writing these instructions, ¹⁵so that if I am delayed, you will know how everyone who belongs to God's family ought to behave. After all, the church of the living God is the strong foundation of truth.

¹⁶Here is the great mystery of our religion:
Christʲ came as a human.
The Spirit proved that he pleased God,
    and he was seen by angels.

Christ was preached to the nations.
People in this world put their faith in him,
    and he was taken up to glory.

People Will Turn from Their Faith

4 ¹God's Spirit clearly says that in the last days many people will turn from their faith. They will be fooled by evil spirits and by teachings that come from demons. ²They will also be fooled by the false claims of liars whose consciences have lost all feeling. These liars ³will forbid people to marry or to eat certain foods. But God created these foods to be eaten with thankful hearts by his followers who know the truth. ⁴Everything God created is good. And if you give thanks, you may eat anything. ⁵What God has said and your prayer will make it fit to eat.

Paul's Advice to Timothy

⁶If you teach these things to other followers, you will be a good servant of Christ Jesus. You will show that you have grown up on the teachings about our faith and on

---

ʰbe faithful in marriage: See the note at 3.2. ʲChrist: The Greek text has "he," probably meaning "Christ." Some manuscripts have "God."

the good instructions you have obeyed. 7Don't have anything to do with worthless, senseless stories. Work hard to be truly religious. 8-9As the saying goes,

"Exercise is good for your body,
but religion helps you in every way.
It promises life now and for ever."

These words are worthwhile and should not be forgotten. 10We have put our hope in the living God, who is the Saviour of everyone, but especially of those who have faith. That's why we work and struggle so hard.ʲ

11Teach these things and tell everyone to do what you say. 12Don't let anyone make fun of you, just because you are young. Set an example for other followers by what you say and do, as well as by your love, faith, and purity.

13Until I arrive, be sure to keep on reading the Scriptures in worship, and don't stop preaching and teaching. 14Use the gift you were given when the prophets spoke and the group of church leadersᵏ blessed you by placing their hands on you. 15Remember these things and think about them, so everyone can see how well you are doing. 16Be careful about the way you live and about what you teach. Keep on doing this, and you will save not only yourself, but the people who hear you.

How To Act towards Others

5 1Don't correct an older man. Encourage him, as you would your own father. Treat younger men as you would your own brother, 2and treat older women as you would your own mother. Show the same respect to younger women that you would to your sister.

3Take care of any widow who is really in need. 4But if a widow has children or grandchildren, they should learn to serve God by taking care of her, as she once took care of them. This is what God wants them to do. 5A widow who is really in need is one who hasn't got any relatives.

ʲstruggle so hard: Some manuscripts have "are treated so badly." ᵏgroup of church leaders: Or "group of elders" or "group of presbyters" or "group of priests." This translates one Greek word, and it is related to the one used in 5.17, 19.

She has faith in God, and she keeps praying to him night and day, asking for his help.

⁶A widow who thinks only about having a good time is already dead, even though she is still alive.

⁷Tell all of this to everyone, so they will do the right thing. ⁸People who don't take care of their relatives, and especially their own families, have given up their faith. They are worse than someone who doesn't have faith in the Lord.

⁹For a widow to be put on the list of widows, she must be at least 60 years old, and she must have been faithful in marriage.ˡ ¹⁰She must also be well-known for doing all sorts of good things, such as raising children, giving food to strangers, welcoming God's people into her home,ᵐ helping people in need, and always making herself useful.

¹¹Don't put young widows on the list. They may later have a strong desire to get married. Then they will turn away from Christ ¹²and become guilty of breaking their promise to him. ¹³Besides, they will become lazy and get into the habit of going from house to house. Next, they will start gossiping and become busy-bodies, talking about things that are none of their business.

¹⁴I would prefer that young widows get married, have children, and look after their families. Then the enemy won't have any reason to say insulting things about us. ¹⁵Look what has already happened to some of the young widows! They have turned away to follow Satan.

¹⁶If a woman who is a follower has any widows in her family, sheⁿ should help them. This will keep the church from having that burden, and then the church can help widows who are really in need.

Church Leaders

¹⁷Church leadersᵒ who do their job well deserve to be paidᵖ twice as much, especially if they work hard at

---

preaching and teaching. [18]It is just as the Scriptures say, "Don't muzzle a bullock when you are using it to grind grain." You also know the saying, "Workers are worth their pay."

[19]Don't listen to any charge against a church leader, unless at least two or three people bring the same charges. [20]But if any of the leaders should keep on sinning, they must be corrected in front of the whole group, as a warning to everyone else.

[21]In the presence of God and Christ Jesus and their chosen angels, I order you to follow my instructions! Be fair with everyone, and don't have any favourites.

[22]Don't be too quick to accept people into the service of the Lord[q] by placing your hands on them.

Don't sin because others do, but stay close to God.

[23]Stop drinking only water. Take a little wine to help your stomach trouble and the other illnesses you always have.

[24]Some people get caught in their sins straight away, even before the time of judgment. But other people's sins don't show up until later. [25]It is the same with good deeds. Some are easily seen, but none of them can be hidden.

6 [1]If you are a slave, you should respect and honour your owner. This will keep people from saying bad things about God and about our teaching. [2]If any of you slaves have owners who are followers, you should show them respect. After all, they are also followers of Christ, and he loves them. So you should serve and help them the best you can.

False Teaching and True Wealth

These are the things you must teach and tell the people to do. [3]Anyone who teaches something different disagrees with the correct and godly teaching of our Lord Jesus Christ. [4]Those people who disagree are proud of themselves, but they don't really know a thing. Their minds are sick, and they like to argue over words. They cause jealousy, disagreements, unkind words, evil

[q]to accept...Lord: Or "to forgive people."

suspicions, 5and nasty quarrels. They have wicked minds and have missed out on the truth.

These people think religion is supposed to make you rich. 6And religion does make your life rich, by making you content with what you have. 7We didn't bring anything into this world, and we won't* take anything with us when we leave. 8So we should be satisfied just to have food and clothes. 9People who want to be rich fall into all sorts of temptations and traps. They are caught by foolish and harmful desires that drag them down and destroy them. 10The love of money causes all kinds of trouble. Some people want money so much that they have given up their faith and caused themselves a lot of pain.

Fighting a Good Fight for the Faith

11Timothy, you belong to God, so keep away from all these evil things. Try your best to please God and to be like him. Be faithful, loving, dependable, and gentle. 12Fight a good fight for the faith and claim eternal life. God offered it to you when you clearly told about your faith, while so many people listened. 13Now I ask you to make a promise. Make it in the presence of God, who gives life to all, and in the presence of Jesus Christ, who openly told Pontius Pilate about his faith. 14Promise to obey completely and fully all that you have been told until our Lord Jesus Christ returns.

15 The glorious God is the only Ruler,
   the King of kings and Lord of lords.
At the time that God has already decided,
   he will send Jesus Christ back again.

16 Only God lives for ever!
   And he lives in light that no-one can come near.
No human has ever seen God or ever can see him.
God will be honoured,
   and his power will last for ever. Amen.

17Warn the rich people of this world not to be proud or to trust in wealth that's easily lost. Tell them to have

---

we won't: Some manuscripts have "we certainly won't."

faith in God, who is rich and blesses us with everything we need to enjoy life. [18]Instruct them to do as many good deeds as they can and to help everyone. Remind the rich to be generous and share what they have. [19]This will lay a solid foundation for the future, so that they will know what true life is like.

[20]Timothy, guard what God has placed in your care! Don't pay any attention to that godless and stupid talk that sounds smart but really isn't. [21]Some people have even lost their faith by believing this talk.

I pray that the Lord will be kind to all of you!

2 TIMOTHY

ABOUT THIS LETTER

In his second letter to Timothy Paul is more personal than in his first one. Timothy is like a "dear child" to Paul, and Paul always mentions him in his prayers (chapter 1.2, 3) because he wants Timothy to be a "good soldier" of Christ Jesus and to learn to endure suffering (2.1, 3). Paul mentions Timothy's mother and grandmother by name in this letter and reminds Timothy how he had placed his hands on him as a special sign that the Spirit was guiding his work.

Some who claimed to be followers of the Lord had already been trapped by the devil, and Paul warns Timothy to run from those temptations that often catch young people (2.20-26; 3.1-9). He tells Timothy to keep preaching God's message, even if it's not the popular thing to do (4.2). He should also beware of false teachers.

Paul knows that he will soon die for his faith, but he will be rewarded for his faithfulness (4.6-8), and he reminds Timothy of the true message:

"If we died with Christ, we will live with him.
If we don't give up, we will rule with him."
(Chapter 2.11, 12a)

A QUICK LOOK AT THIS LETTER

- Greetings and Prayer for Timothy (1.1, 2)
- Don't Be Ashamed of the Lord (1.3-18)
- How To Be a Good Soldier of Christ (2.1-26)
- What People Will Be Like in the Last Days (3.1-9)
- Keep Being Faithful (3.10—4.8)
- Personal Instructions and Final Greetings (4.9-22)

1 ¹From Paul, an apostle of Christ Jesus.

God himself chose me to be an apostle, and he gave me the promised life that Jesus Christ makes possible.

²Timothy, you are like a dear child to me. I pray that God our Father and our Lord Christ Jesus will be kind and merciful to you and will bless you with peace!

Do Not Be Ashamed of the Lord

³Night and day I mention you in my prayers. I am always grateful for you, as I pray to the God my ancestors and I have served with a clear conscience. ⁴I remember how you cried, and I want to see you, because that will make me truly happy. ⁵I also remember the genuine faith of your mother Eunice. Your grandmother Lois had the same sort of faith, and I am sure that you have it as well. ⁶So I ask you to make full use of the gift that God gave you when I placed my hands on you.ᵃ Use it well. ⁷God's Spiritᵇ doesn't make cowards out of us. The Spirit gives us power, love, and self-control.

⁸Don't be ashamed to speak for our Lord. And don't be ashamed of me, just because I am in jail for serving him. Use the power that comes from God and join with me in suffering for telling the good news.

⁹ God saved us and chose us to be his holy people.
We did nothing to deserve this,
but God planned it because he is so kind.
Even before time began
God planned for Christ Jesus
to show kindness to us.

¹⁰ Now Christ Jesus has come
to show us the kindness of God.
Christ our Saviour defeated death
and brought us the good news.
It shines like a light and offers life that never ends.

¹¹My work is to be a preacher, an apostle, and a teacher.ᶜ ¹²That's why I am suffering now. But I am not ashamed! I know the one I have faith in, and I am sure that he can

---

ᵃwhen I placed my hands on you: Church leaders placed their hands on people who were being appointed to preach or teach (see 1 Timothy 4.14). ᵇGod's Spirit: Or "God." ᶜteacher: Some manuscripts add "of the Gentiles."

guard until the last day what he has trusted me with.*d*
13Now follow the example of the correct teaching I gave
you, and let the faith and love of Christ Jesus be your
model. 14You have been trusted with a wonderful
treasure. Guard it with the help of the Holy Spirit, who
lives within you.

15You know that everyone in Asia has turned against
me, especially Phygelus and Hermogenes.

16I pray that the Lord will be kind to the family of
Onesiphorus. He often cheered me up and wasn't
ashamed of me when I was put in jail. 17Then after he
arrived in Rome, he searched everywhere until he found
me. 18I pray that the Lord Jesus will ask God to show
mercy to Onesiphorus on the day of judgment. You
know how much he helped me in Ephesus.

A Good Soldier of Christ Jesus

2 1Timothy, my child, Christ Jesus is kind, and you
must let him make you strong. 2You have often heard
me teach. Now I want you to tell these same things to
followers who can be trusted to tell others.

3As a good soldier of Christ Jesus you must endure
your share of suffering. 4Soldiers on duty don't work at
outside jobs. They try only to please their commanding
officer. 5No-one wins an athletic contest without obeying
the rules. 6And farmers who work hard are the first to eat
what grows in their field. 7If you keep in mind what I
have told you, the Lord will help you understand
completely.

8Keep your mind on Jesus Christ! He was from the
family of David and was raised from death, just as my
good news says. 9And because of this message, I am locked
up in jail and treated like a criminal. But God's good
news isn't locked in jail, 10and so I am willing to put up
with anything. Then God's special people will be saved.
They will be given eternal glory because they belong to
Christ Jesus. 11Here is a true message:

"If we died with Christ, we will live with him.
12 If we don't give up, we will rule with him.

---

*d*what he has trusted me with: Or "what I have trusted him with."

If we deny that we know him,
    he will deny that he knows us.
13   If we are not faithful, he will still be faithful.
    Christ can't deny who he is."

An Approved Worker

14Don't let anyone forget these things. And with God^e
as your witness, you must warn them not to argue about
words. These arguments don't help anyone. In fact, they
ruin everyone who listens to them. 15Do your best to win
God's approval as a worker who doesn't need to be
ashamed and who teaches only the true message.

16Keep away from worthless and useless talk. It only
leads people further away from God. 17That sort of talk is
like a sore that won't heal. And Hymenaeus and Philetus
have been talking this way 18by teaching that the dead
have already been raised to life. This is far from the truth,
and it's destroying the faith of some people.

19But the foundation that God has laid is solid. On it is
written, "The Lord knows who his people are. So everyone
who worships the Lord must turn away from evil."

20In a large house some dishes are made of gold or
silver, while others are made of wood or clay. Some of
these are special, and others are not. 21That's also how it
is with people. The ones who stop doing evil and make
themselves pure will become special. Their lives will be
holy and pleasing to their Master, and they will be able
to do all kinds of good deeds.

22Run from temptations that capture young people.
Always do the right thing. Be faithful, loving, and easy
to get along with. Worship with people whose hearts are
pure. 23Stay away from stupid and senseless arguments.
These only lead to trouble, 24and God's servants must
not be troublemakers. They must be kind to everyone,
and they must be good teachers and very patient.

25Be humble when you correct people who oppose you.
Maybe God will lead them to turn to him and learn the
truth. 26They have been trapped by the devil, and he
makes them obey him, but God may help them escape.

---

^eGod: Some manuscripts have "the Lord," and others have "Christ."

What People Will Be Like in the Last Days

3 ¹You can be certain that in the last days there will be some very hard times. ²People will love only themselves and money. They will be proud, stuck-up, rude, and disobedient to their parents. They will also be ungrateful, godless, ³heartless, and hateful. Their words will be cruel, and they will have no self-control or pity. These people will hate everything that is good. ⁴They will be sneaky, reckless, and puffed up with pride. Instead of loving God, they will love pleasure. ⁵Even though they will make a show of being religious, their religion won't be real. Don't have anything to do with such people.

⁶Some men fool whole families, just to get power over those women who are slaves of sin and are controlled by all sorts of desires. ⁷These women always want to learn something new, but they never can discover the truth. ⁸Just as Jannes and Jambres[f] opposed Moses, these people are enemies of the truth. Their minds are sick, and their faith isn't real. ⁹But they won't get very far with their foolishness. Soon everyone will know the truth about them, just as Jannes and Jambres were found out.

Paul's Last Instructions to Timothy

¹⁰Timothy, you know what I teach and how I live. You know what I want to do and what I believe. You have seen how patient and loving I am, and how in the past I put up with ¹¹trouble and suffering in the cities of Antioch, Iconium, and Lystra. Yet the Lord rescued me from all those terrible troubles. ¹²Anyone who belongs to Christ Jesus and wants to live right will have trouble from others. ¹³But evil people who pretend to be what they aren't will become worse than ever, as they fool others and are fooled themselves.

¹⁴Keep on being faithful to what you were taught and to what you believed. After all, you know who taught you these things. ¹⁵Since childhood, you have known the

---

[f]Jannes and Jambres: These names are not found in the Old Testament. But many believe these were the names of the two Egyptian magicians who opposed Moses when he wanted to lead the people of Israel out of Egypt (see Exodus 7.11, 22).

Holy Scriptures that are able to make you wise enough to have faith in Christ Jesus and be saved. [16]Everything in the Scriptures is God's Word. All of it is useful for teaching and helping people and for correcting them and showing them how to live. [17]The Scriptures train God's servants to do all kinds of good deeds.

4 [1]When Christ Jesus comes as king, he will be the judge of everyone, whether they are living or dead. So with God and Christ as witnesses, I command you [2]to preach God's message. Do it willingly, even if it isn't the popular thing to do. You must correct people and point out their sins. But also cheer them up, and when you instruct them, always be patient. [3]The time is coming when people won't listen to good teaching. Instead, they will look for teachers who will please them by telling them only what they are itching to hear. [4]They will turn from the truth and eagerly listen to senseless stories. [5]But you must stay calm and be willing to suffer. You must work hard to tell the good news and to do your job well.

[6]Now the time has come for me to die. My life is like a drink offering[g] being poured out on the altar. [7]I have fought well. I have finished the race, and I have been faithful. [8]So a crown will be given to me for pleasing the Lord. He judges fairly, and on the day of judgment he will give a crown to me and to everyone else who wants him to appear with power.

Personal Instructions

[9]Come and see me as soon as you can. [10]Demas loves the things of this world so much that he left me and went to Thessalonica. Crescens has gone to Galatia, and Titus has gone to Dalmatia. [11]Only Luke has stayed with me.

Mark can be very helpful to me, so please find him and bring him with you. [12]I sent Tychicus to Ephesus.

[13]When you come, bring the coat I left at Troas with Carpus. Don't forget to bring the scrolls, especially the

---

[g]drink offering: Water or wine was sometimes poured out as an offering when an animal sacrifice was made.

ones made of leather.*h*

14Alexander, the metalworker, has hurt me in many ways. But the Lord will pay him back for what he has done. 15Alexander opposes what we preach. You had better watch out for him.

16When I was first put on trial, no-one helped me. In fact, everyone deserted me. I hope it won't be held against them. 17But the Lord stood beside me. He gave me the strength to tell his full message, so that all Gentiles would hear it. And I was kept safe from hungry lions. 18The Lord will always keep me from being harmed by evil, and he will bring me safely into his heavenly kingdom. Praise him for ever and ever! Amen.

Final Greetings

19Give my greetings to Priscilla and Aquila and to the family of Onesiphorus.

20Erastus stayed at Corinth.

Trophimus was sick when I left him at Miletus.

21Do your best to come before winter.

Eubulus, Pudens, Linus, and Claudia send you their greetings, and so do the rest of the Lord's followers.

22I pray that the Lord will bless your life and will be kind to you.

---

*h*the ones made of leather: A scroll was a kind of rolled-up book, and it could be made out of paper (called "papyrus") or leather (that is, animal skin) or even copper.

TITUS

ABOUT THIS LETTER

Paul mentions Titus several times in his letters as someone who worked with him in Asia Minor and Greece (2 Corinthians 2.13; 7.6, 13; 8.6, 16, 23; 12.18; Galatians 2.3). He is told by Paul to appoint church leaders and officials in Crete.

Paul instructs Titus to make sure that church leaders and officials have good reputations (chapter 1.5-9) and that all of the Lord's followers keep themselves pure and avoid arguments (1.10—2.9).

Paul includes special instructions for the different groups within the church in Crete. He reminds Titus that a new way of life is possible because of what God has done by sending Jesus Christ: God has saved them, washed them by the power of the Holy Spirit, and given them a fresh start and the hope of eternal life.

Paul also tells how we are saved:

> *God our Saviour showed us*
> *how good and kind he is.*
> *He saved us because of his mercy,*
> *and not because of any good things*
> *that we have done.* (Chapter 3.4, 5a)

A QUICK LOOK AT THIS LETTER

* Greetings and a Prayer for Titus (1.1-4)
* Instructions for Church Officials (1.5-16)
* Instructions for Church People (2.1—3.11)
* Personal Advice and Final Greetings (3.12-15)

1

¹From Paul, a servant of God and an apostle of Jesus Christ.

I encourage God's own people to have more faith and to understand the truth about religion. ²Then they will have the hope of eternal life that God promised long ago. And God never tells a lie! ³So, at the proper time, God our Saviour gave this message and told me to announce what he had said.

4 Titus, because of our faith, you are like a son to me. I pray that God our Father and Christ Jesus our Saviour will be kind to you and will bless you with peace!

What Titus Was To Do in Crete

5 I left you in Crete to do what had been left undone and to appoint leaders*a* for the churches in each town. As I told you, 6 they must have a good reputation and be faithful in marriage.*b* Their children must be followers of the Lord and not have a reputation for being wild and disobedient.

7 Church officials*c* are in charge of God's work, and so they must also have a good reputation. They must not be bossy, quick-tempered, heavy drinkers, bullies, or dishonest in business. 8 Instead, they must be friendly to strangers and enjoy doing good things. They must also be sensible, fair, pure, and self-controlled. 9 They must stick to the true message they were taught, so that their good teaching can help others and correct everyone who opposes it.

10 There are many who don't respect authority, and they fool others by talking nonsense. This is especially true of some Jewish followers. 11 But you must make them be quiet. They are after money, and they upset whole families by teaching what they shouldn't. 12 It's like one of their own prophets once said,

"The people of Crete always tell lies.

They are greedy and lazy like wild animals."

13 That surely is a true saying. And you should be hard on such people, so you can help them grow stronger in their faith. 14 Don't pay any attention to any of those senseless Jewish stories and human commands. These are made up by people who won't obey the truth.

15 Everything is pure for someone whose heart is pure. But nothing is pure for an unbeliever with a dirty mind. That person's mind and conscience are destroyed. 16 Such people claim to know God, but their actions prove that

---

a leaders: Or "elders" or "presbyters" or "priests."   *b be faithful in marriage:* Or "be the husband of only one wife" or "have never been divorced."   *c Church officials:* Or "Bishops."

they really don't. They are disgusting. They won't obey God, and they are too worthless to do anything good.

Instructions for Different Groups of People

2 ¹Titus, you must teach only what is correct. ²Tell the older men to have self-control and to be serious and sensible. Their faith, love, and patience must never fail.

³Tell the older women to behave as those who love the Lord should. They must not gossip about others or be slaves of wine. They must teach what is proper, ⁴so the younger women will be loving wives and mothers. ⁵Each of the younger women must be sensible and kind, as well as a good home-maker, who puts her own husband first. Then no-one can say insulting things about God's message.

⁶Tell the young men to have self-control in everything.

⁷Always set a good example for others. Be sincere and serious when you teach. ⁸Use clean language that no-one can criticise. Do this, and your enemies will be too ashamed to say anything against you.

⁹Tell slaves to always please their owners by obeying them in everything. Slaves must not talk back to their owners ¹⁰or steal from them. They must be completely honest and trustworthy. Then everyone will show great respect for what is taught about God our Saviour.

God's Kindness and the New Life

¹¹God has shown us how kind he is by coming to save all people. ¹²He taught us to give up our wicked ways and our worldly desires and to live decent and honest lives in this world. ¹³We are filled with hope, as we wait for the glorious return of our great God and Saviour Jesus Christ.ᵈ ¹⁴He gave himself to rescue us from everything that is evil and to make our hearts pure. He wanted us to be his own people and to be eager to do right.

¹⁵Teach these things, as you use your full authority to encourage and correct people. Make sure you earn everyone's respect.

ᵈ*the glorious return of our great God and Saviour Jesus Christ:* Or "the glorious return of our great God and our Saviour Jesus Christ" or "the return of Jesus Christ, who is the glory of our great God and Saviour."

Doing Helpful Things

3 ¹Remind your people to obey the rulers and authorities and not to be rebellious. They must always be ready to do something helpful ²and not say cruel things or argue. They should be gentle and kind to everyone. ³We used to be stupid, disobedient, and foolish, as well as slaves of all sorts of desires and pleasures. We were evil and jealous. Everyone hated us, and we hated everyone.

⁴　God our Saviour showed us
　　how good and kind he is.

⁵　He saved us because of his mercy,
　　and not because of any good things
　　　that we have done.

　　God washed us by the power of the Holy Spirit.
　　He gave us new birth and a fresh beginning.

⁶　　God sent Jesus Christ our Saviour
　　　to give us his Spirit.

⁷　Jesus treated us much better than we deserve.
　　He made us acceptable to God
　　　and gave us the hope of eternal life.

⁸This message is certainly true.

These teachings are useful and helpful for everyone. I want you to insist that the people follow them, so that all who have faith in God will be sure to do good deeds. ⁹But don't have anything to do with stupid arguments about ancestors. And stay away from disagreements and quarrels about the Jewish Law. Such arguments are useless and senseless.

¹⁰Warn troublemakers once or twice. Then don't have anything else to do with them. ¹¹You know that their minds are twisted, and their own sins show how guilty they are.

Personal Instructions and Greetings

¹²I plan to send Artemas or Tychicus to you. After he arrives, please try your best to meet me at Nicopolis. I have decided to spend the winter there.

¹³When Zenas the lawyer and Apollos get ready to

leave, help them as much as you can, so they won't have need of anything.

¹⁴Our people should learn to spend their time doing something useful and worthwhile.

¹⁵Greetings to you from everyone here. Greet all of our friends who share in our faith.

I pray that the Lord will be kind to all of you!

PHILEMON
ABOUT THIS LETTER

Philemon was a wealthy man who owned slaves and who used his large house for church meetings (verse 2). He probably lived in Colossae, since Paul's letter to the Colossians mentions Onesimus, a slave of Philemon, and Archippus (Colossians 4.9, 17).

Paul is writing from jail on behalf of Onesimus, a runaway slave owned by Philemon. Onesimus had become a follower of the Lord and a valuable friend to Paul, and Paul is writing to encourage Philemon to accept Onesimus also as a friend and follower of the Lord.

This letter is an excellent example of the art of letter-writing in the Roman world, and it is the most personal of all Paul's letters. The way the letter is written suggests that Paul and Philemon were close friends.

A QUICK LOOK AT THIS LETTER

- Greetings to Philemon (1-3)
- Paul Speaks to Philemon about Onesimus (4-22)
- Final Greetings and a Prayer (23-25)

1From Paul, who is in jail for serving Christ Jesus, and from Timothy, who is like a brother because of our faith.

Philemon, you work with us and are very dear to us. This letter is to you 2and to the church that meets in your home. It is also to our dear friend Apphia and to Archippus, who serves the Lord as we do.

3I pray that God our Father and our Lord Jesus Christ will be kind to you and will bless you with peace!

Philemon's Love and Faith

4Philemon, each time I mention you in my prayers, I thank God. 5I hear about your faith in our Lord Jesus and about your love for all of God's people. 6As you share your faith with others, I pray that they may come to know all the blessings Christ has given us. 7My friend, your love has made me happy and has greatly encouraged me. It has also cheered the hearts of God's people.

Paul Speaks to Philemon about Onesimus

[8]Christ gives me the courage to tell you what to do. [9]But I would rather ask you to do it simply because of love. Yes, as someone[a] in jail for Christ, [10]I beg you to help Onesimus![b] He is like a son to me because I led him to Christ here in jail. [11]Before this, he was useless to you, but now he is useful both to you and to me.

[12]Sending Onesimus back to you makes me very sad. [13]I would like to keep him here with me, where he could take your place in helping me while I am here in prison for preaching the good news. [14]But I won't do anything unless you agree to it first. I want your act of kindness to come from your heart, and not be something you feel forced to do.

[15]Perhaps Onesimus was taken from you for a little while so that you could have him back for good, [16]but not as a slave. Onesimus is much more than a slave. To me he is a dear friend, but to you he is even more, both as a person and as a follower of the Lord.

[17]If you consider me a friend because of Christ, then welcome Onesimus as you would welcome me. [18]If he has cheated you or owes you anything, charge it to my account. [19]With my own hand I write: I, PAUL, WILL PAY YOU BACK. But don't forget that you owe me your life. [20]My dear friend and follower of Christ our Lord, please cheer me up by doing this for me.

[21]I am sure you will do all I have asked, and even more. [22]Please get a room ready for me. I hope your prayers will be answered, and I can visit you.

[23]Epaphras is also here in jail for being a follower of Christ Jesus. He sends his greetings, [24]and so do Mark, Aristarchus, Demas, and Luke, who work together with me.

[25]I pray that the Lord Jesus Christ will be kind to you!

---

[a]*someone:* Greek "a messenger" or "an old man."   [b]*Onesimus:* In Greek this name means "useful."

HEBREWS

ABOUT THIS LETTER

Many religious people in the first century after Jesus' birth, both Jews and Gentiles, had questions about the religion of the early Christians. They were looking for evidence that this new faith was genuine. Jews had the miracle of crossing the Red Sea and the agreement made with God at Mount Sinai to support their faith. But what miracles did Christians have? Jews had beautiful worship ceremonies and a high priest who offered sacrifices in the temple so that the people would be forgiven. But what did Christians have? How could this new Christian faith, centred in Jesus, offer forgiveness of sins and friendship with God?

The letter to the Hebrews was written to answer exactly these kinds of questions. In it the author tells the readers how important Jesus really is. He is greater than any of God's angels (chapter 1.5-14), greater than any prophet, and greater even than Moses and Joshua (2.1—4.14). Jesus is the perfect high priest because he never sinned, and by offering his own life he has made the perfect sacrifice for sin once and for all time (9.23—10.18). By his death and return from death he has opened the way for all people to come to God (4.14—5.10; 7.1—8.13).

This letter has much to say about the importance of faith. The writer points out that what Jesus offers comes only by faith. And this faith makes his followers sure of what they hope for and gives them proof of things that can't be seen. The writer praises God's faithful people of the past (11.1-40) and encourages those who follow Jesus now to keep their eyes on him as they run the race (12.1-3).

What does it mean to have a high priest like Jesus?

Jesus understands every weakness of ours, because he was tempted in every way that we are. But he did not sin! So whenever we are in need, we should come bravely before the throne of our merciful God. There we will be treated with undeserved kindness, and we will find help.
(Chapter 4.15, 16)

A QUICK LOOK AT THIS LETTER

1 ¹Long ago in many ways and at many times God's prophets spoke his message to our ancestors. ²But now at last, God sent his Son to bring his message to us. God created the universe by his Son, and everything will some day belong to the Son. ³God's Son has all the brightness of God's own glory and is like him in every way. By his own mighty word, he holds the universe together.

After the Son had washed away our sins, he sat down at the right side*a* of the glorious God in heaven. ⁴He had become much greater than the angels, and the name he was given is far greater than any of theirs.

God's Son Is Greater than Angels

⁵God has never said to any of the angels,
"You are my Son, because today
I have become your Father!"
Neither has God said to any of them,
"I will be his Father, and he will be my Son!"
⁶When God brings his firstborn Son*b* into the world, he commands all of his angels to worship him.
⁷And when God speaks about the angels, he says,
"I change my angels into wind
and my servants into flaming fire."

---

*a*right side: The place of honour and power. *b*firstborn Son: The first son born into a family had certain privileges that the other children did not have. In 12.23 "firstborn" refers to God's special people.

8But God says about his Son,
>"You are God, and you will rule as King for ever!
>Your*c* royal power brings about justice.
9   You loved justice and hated evil,
>and so I, your God, have chosen you.
>I appointed you and made you happier
>than any of your friends."

10The Scriptures also say, "In the beginning, Lord,
>you were the one
>who laid the foundation of the earth
>and created the heavens.
11   They will all disappear and wear out like clothes,
>but you will last for ever.
12   You will roll them up like a robe
>and change them like a garment.
>But you are always the same, and you will live for ever."

13God never said to any of the angels, "Sit at my right side
>until I make your enemies
>into a footstool for you!"
14Angels are merely spirits sent to serve people who are going to be saved.

This Great Way of Being Saved

2 1We must give our full attention to what we were told, so that we won't drift away. 2The message spoken by angels proved to be true, and all who disobeyed or rejected it were punished as they deserved. 3So if we refuse this great way of being saved, how can we hope to escape? The Lord himself was the first to tell about it, and people who heard the message proved to us that it was true. 4God himself showed that his message was true by working all kinds of powerful miracles and wonders. He also gave his Holy Spirit to anyone he chose to.

The One Who Leads Us To Be Saved

5We know that God did not put the future world under

---

cYour: Some manuscripts have "His."

the power of angels. 6Somewhere in the Scriptures someone says to God,

"What makes you care about us humans?
Why are you concerned for weaklings such as we?
7 You made us lower than the angels for a while.
Yet you have crowned us with glory and honour.*d*
8 And you have put everything under our power!"

God has put everything under our power and hasn't left anything out of our power. But we still don't see it all under our power. 9What we do see is Jesus, who for a little while was made lower than the angels. Because of God's wonderful kindness, Jesus died for everyone. And now that Jesus has suffered and died, he is crowned with glory and honour!

10Everything belongs to God, and all things were created by his power. So God did the right thing when he made Jesus perfect by suffering, as Jesus led many of God's children to be saved and to share in his glory. 11Jesus and the people he makes holy all belong to the same family. That is why he isn't ashamed to call them his brothers and sisters. 12He even said to God,

"I will tell them your name and sing your praises
when they come together to worship."

13He also said,

"I will trust God."

Then he said,

"Here I am with the children God has given me."

14We are people of flesh and blood. That is why Jesus became one of us. He died to destroy the devil, who had power over death. 15But he also died to rescue all of us who live each day in fear of dying. 16Jesus clearly did not come to help angels, but he did come to help Abraham's descendants. 17He had to be one of us, so that he could serve God as our merciful and faithful high priest and sacrifice himself for the forgiveness of our sins. 18And now that Jesus has suffered and was tempted, he can help anyone else who is tempted.

---

d and honour: Some manuscripts add "and you have placed us in charge of all you created."

Jesus Is Greater than Moses

3 ¹My friends, God has chosen you to be his holy people. So think about Jesus, the one we call our apostle and high priest! ²Jesus was faithful to God, who appointed him, just as Moses was faithful in serving all of^e God's people. ³But Jesus deserves more honour than Moses, just as the builder of a house deserves more honour than the house. ⁴Of course, every house is built by someone, and God is really the one who built everything.

⁵Moses was a faithful servant and told God's people what would be said in the future. ⁶But Christ is the Son in charge of God's people. And we are those people, if we keep on being brave and don't lose hope.

A Rest for God's People

⁷It is just as the Holy Spirit says,
    "If you hear God's voice today,
⁸   don't be stubborn!
    Don't rebel like those people
        who were tested in the desert.
⁹⁻¹⁰   For 40 years your ancestors tested God
        and saw the things he did.

    "Then God got tired of them and said,
    'You people never show good sense,
        and you don't understand
        what I want you to do.'
¹¹   God became angry and told the people,
        'You will never enter my place of rest!' "

¹²My friends, watch out! Don't let evil thoughts or doubts make any of you turn from the living God. ¹³You must encourage one another each day. And you must keep on while there is still a time that can be called "today." If you don't, then sin may fool some of you and make you stubborn. ¹⁴We were sure about Christ when we first became his people. So let's hold tightly to our faith until the end. ¹⁵The Scriptures say,
    "If you hear his voice today,
        don't be stubborn like those who rebelled."

^e*all of:* Some manuscripts do not have these words.

¹⁶Who were those people who heard God's voice and rebelled? Weren't they the same ones who came out of Egypt with Moses? ¹⁷Who were the people who made God angry for 40 years? Weren't they the ones who sinned and died in the desert? ¹⁸And who did God say would never enter his place of rest? Weren't they the ones who disobeyed him? ¹⁹We see that those people didn't enter the place of rest because they didn't have faith.

4 ¹The promise to enter the place of rest is still good, and we must take care that none of you miss out. ²We have heard the message, just as they did. But they failed to believe what they heard, and the message didn't do them any good. ³Only people who have faith will enter the place of rest. It is just as the Scriptures say,

"God became angry and told the people,
'You will never enter my place of rest!' "

God said this, even though everything has been ready from the time of creation. ⁴In fact, somewhere the Scriptures say that by the seventh day, God had finished his work, and so he rested. ⁵We also read that he later said, "You people will never enter my place of rest!" ⁶This means that the promise to enter is still good, because those who first heard about it disobeyed and did not enter. ⁷Much later God told David to make the promise again, just as I have already said,

"If you hear his voice today,
don't be stubborn!"

⁸If Joshua had really given the people rest, there wouldn't be any need for God to talk about another day of rest. ⁹But God has promised us a Sabbath when we will rest, even though it hasn't yet come. ¹⁰On that day God's people will rest from their work, just as God rested from his work.

¹¹We should do our best to enter that place of rest, so that none of us will disobey and miss going there, as they did. ¹²What God has said isn't only alive and active! It is sharper than any double-edged sword. His word can cut through our spirits and souls and through our joints and marrow, until it discovers the desires and thoughts of our hearts. ¹³Nothing is hidden from God! He sees through everything, and we will have to tell him the truth.

Jesus Is the Great High Priest

14 We have a great high priest, who has gone into heaven, and he is Jesus the Son of God. That is why we must hold on to what we have said about him. 15 Jesus understands every weakness of ours, because he was tempted in every way that we are. But he did not sin! 16 So whenever we are in need, we should come bravely before the throne of our merciful God. There we will be treated with undeserved kindness, and we will find help.

5 1 Every high priest is appointed to help others by offering gifts and sacrifices to God beçause of their sins. 2 A high priest has weaknesses of his own, and he feels sorry for foolish and sinful people. 3 That is why he must offer sacrifices for his own sins and for the sins of others. 4 But no-one can have the honour of being a high priest simply by wanting to be one. Only God can choose a priest, and God is the one who chose Aaron.

5 That is how it was with Christ. He became a high priest, but not just because he wanted the honour of being one. It was God who told him,

"You are my Son, because today
I have become your Father!"

6 In another place, God says,

"You are a priest for ever
just like Melchizedek."*f*

7 God had the power to save Jesus from death. And while Jesus was on earth, he begged God with loud crying and tears to save him. He truly worshipped God, and God listened to his prayers. 8 Jesus is God's own Son, but still he had to suffer before he could learn what it really means to obey God. 9 Suffering made Jesus perfect, and now he can save for ever all who obey him. 10 This is because God chose him to be a high priest like Melchizedek.

Warning against Turning Away

11 Much more could be said about this subject. But it is hard to explain, and all of you are slow to understand.

f Melchizedek: When Melchizedek is mentioned in the Old Testament, he is described as a priest who lived before Aaron. Nothing is said about his ancestors or his death (see 7.3 and Genesis 14.17-20).

¹²By now you should have been teachers, but once again you need to be taught the simplest things about what God has said. You need milk instead of solid food. ¹³People who live on milk are like babies who don't really know what is right. ¹⁴Solid food is for mature people who have been trained to know right from wrong.

6 ¹We must try to become mature and start thinking about more than just the basic things we were taught about Christ. We shouldn't need to keep talking about why we ought to turn from deeds that bring death and why we ought to have faith in God. ²And we shouldn't need to keep teaching about baptisms*g* or about the laying on of hands*h* or about people being raised from death and the future judgment. ³Let's grow up, if God is willing.

⁴⁻⁶But what about people who turn away after they have already seen the light and have received the gift from heaven and have shared in the Holy Spirit? What about those who turn away after they have received the good message of God and the powers of the future world? There is no way to bring them back. What they are doing is the same as nailing the Son of God to a cross and insulting him in public!

⁷A field is useful to farmers, if there is enough rain to make good crops grow. In fact, God will bless that field. ⁸But land that produces only thorn bushes is worthless. It is likely to fall under God's curse, and in the end it will be set on fire.

⁹My friends, we are talking this way. But we are sure that you are doing those really good things that people do when they are being saved. ¹⁰God is always fair. He will remember how you helped his people in the past and how you are still helping them. You belong to God, and he won't forget the love you have shown his people. ¹¹We wish that each of you would always be eager to show how strong and lasting your hope really is. ¹²Then you would never be lazy. You would be following the example

---

*g*baptisms: Or "ceremonies of washing."   *h*laying on of hands: This was a ceremony in which church leaders and others put their hands on people to show that those people were chosen to do some special kind of work.

of those who had faith and were patient until God kept his promise to them.

God's Promise Is Sure

¹³No-one is greater than God. So he made a promise in his own name when he said to Abraham, ¹⁴"I, the Lord, will bless you with many descendants!" ¹⁵Then after Abraham had been very patient, he was given what God had promised. ¹⁶When anyone wants to settle an argument, they make a vow by using the name of someone or something greater than themselves. ¹⁷So when God wanted to prove for certain that his promise to his people couldn't be broken, he made a vow. ¹⁸God can't tell lies! And so his promises and vows are two things that can never be changed.

We have run to God for safety. Now his promises should greatly encourage us to take hold of the hope that is right in front of us. ¹⁹This hope is like a firm and steady anchor for our souls. In fact, hope reaches behind the curtain^j and into the most holy place. ²⁰Jesus has gone there ahead of us, and he is our high priest for ever, just like Melchizedek.^j

The Priestly Family of Melchizedek

7 ¹Melchizedek was both king of Salem and priest of God Most High. He was the one who went out and gave Abraham his blessing, when Abraham returned from killing the kings. ²Then Abraham gave him a tenth of everything he had.

The meaning of the name Melchizedek is "King of Justice." But since Salem means "peace," he is also "King of Peace." ³We are not told that he had a father or mother or ancestors or beginning or end. He is like the Son of God and will be a priest for ever.^k

⁴Notice how great Melchizedek is! Our famous ancestor Abraham gave him a tenth of what he had taken from

---

^jbehind the curtain: In the tent that was used for worship, a curtain separated the "holy place" from the "most holy place," which only the high priest could enter.   ^jMelchizedek: See the note at 5.6.   ^kwill be a priest for ever: See the note at 5.6.

his enemies. ⁵The Law teaches that even Abraham's descendants must give a tenth of what they possess. And they are to give this to their own relatives, who are the descendants of Levi and are priests. ⁶Although Melchizedek wasn't a descendant of Levi, Abraham gave him a tenth of what he had. Then Melchizedek blessed Abraham, who had been given God's promise. ⁷Everyone agrees that a person who gives a blessing is greater than the one who receives the blessing.

⁸Priests are given a tenth of what people earn. But all priests die, except Melchizedek, and the Scriptures teach that he is alive. ⁹Levi's descendants are now the ones who receive a tenth from people. We could even say that when Abraham gave Melchizedek a tenth, Levi also gave him a tenth. ¹⁰This is because Levi was born later into the family of Abraham, who gave a tenth to Melchizedek.

¹¹Even though the Law of Moses says that the priests must be descendants of Levi, those priests can't make anyone perfect. So there needs to be a priest like Melchizedek, rather than one from the priestly family of Aaron.¹ ¹²And when the rules for selecting a priest are changed, the Law must also be changed.

¹³The person we are talking about is our Lord, who came from a tribe that had never had anyone to serve as a priest at the altar. ¹⁴Everyone knows he came from the tribe of Judah, and Moses never said that priests would come from that tribe.

¹⁵All of this becomes clearer, when someone who is like Melchizedek is appointed to be a priest. ¹⁶That person wasn't appointed because of his ancestors, but because his life can never end. ¹⁷The Scriptures say about him,

> "You are a priest for ever,
> just like Melchizedek."

¹⁸In this way a weak and useless command was put aside, ¹⁹because the Law can't make anything perfect. At the same time, we are given a much better hope, and it can bring us close to God.

---

¹descendants of Levi...from the priestly family of Aaron: Levi was the ancestor of the tribe from which priests and their helpers (called "Levites") were chosen. Aaron was the first high priest.

[20-21]God himself made a promise when this priest was appointed. But he didn't make a promise like this when the other priests were appointed. The promise he made is,

> "I, the Lord, promise that you will be a priest for ever! And I will never change my mind!"

[22]This means that Jesus guarantees us a better agreement with God. [23]There have been a lot of other priests, and all of them have died. [24]But Jesus will never die, and so he will be a priest for ever! [25]He is for ever able to save[m] the people he leads to God, because he always lives to speak to God for them.

[26]Jesus is the high priest we need. He is holy and innocent and faultless, and not at all like us sinners. Jesus is honoured above all beings in heaven, [27]and he is better than any other high priest. Jesus doesn't need to offer sacrifices each day for his own sins and then for the sins of the people. He offered a sacrifice once and for all, when he gave himself. [28]The Law appoints priests who have weaknesses. But God's promise, which came later than the Law, appoints his Son. And he is the perfect high priest for ever.

A Better Promise

8 [1]What I mean is that we have a high priest who sits at the right side[n] of God's great throne in heaven. [2]He also serves as the priest in the most holy place[o] inside the real tent there in heaven. This tent of worship was set up by the Lord, not by humans.

[3]Since all priests must offer gifts and sacrifices, Christ also needed to have something to offer. [4]If he were here on earth, he would not be a priest at all, because here the Law appoints other priests to offer sacrifices. [5]But the tent where they serve is just a copy and a shadow of the real one in heaven. Before Moses made the tent, he was told, "Be sure to make it exactly like the pattern you were shown on the mountain!" [6]Now Christ has been appointed to serve as a priest in a much better way, and

---

[m]*for ever able to save:* Or "able to save for ever."   [n]*right side:* See the note at 1.3.   [o]*most holy place:* See the note at 6.19.

he has given us much assurance of a better agreement.

⁷If the first agreement with God had been all right, there would not have been any need for another one. ⁸But the Lord found fault with it and said,

> "I tell you the time will come,
>   when I will make a new agreement
>   with the people of Israel and the people of Judah.
>
> ⁹ It won't be like the agreement
>   that I made with their ancestors,
>   when I took them by the hand
>   and led them out of Egypt.
>   They broke their agreement with me,
>   and I stopped caring about them!
>
> ¹⁰ "But now I tell the people of Israel
>   this is my new agreement:
>   'The time will come when I, the Lord,
>   will write my laws on their minds and hearts.
>   I will be their God, and they will be my people.
> ¹¹ Not one of them will have to teach another
>   to know me, their Lord.'
>
> "All of them will know me,
>   no matter who they are.
> ¹² I will treat them with kindness,
>   even though they are wicked.
>   I will forget their sins."

¹³When the Lord talks about a new agreement, he means that the first one is out of date. And anything that is old and useless will soon disappear.

The Tent in Heaven

9 ¹The first promise that was made included rules for worship and a tent for worship here on earth. ²The first part of the tent was called the holy place, and a lampstand, a table, and the sacred loaves of bread were kept there.

³Behind the curtain was the most holy place. ⁴The gold altar that was used for burning incense was in this holy place. The gold-covered sacred chest was also there, and inside it were three things. First, there was a gold jar filled

with manna.p Then there was Aaron's walking stick that
sprouted.q Finally, there were the flat stones with the Ten
Commandments written on them. 5On top of the chest
were the glorious creatures with wingsr opened out above
the place of mercy.s

Now isn't the time to go into detail about these things.
6But this is how everything was when the priests went
each day into the first part of the tent to do their duties.
7However, only the high priest could go into the second
part of the tent, and he went in only once a year. Each
time he carried blood to offer for his sins and for any sins
that the people had committed without meaning to.

8All of this is the Holy Spirit's way of saying that
no-one could enter the most holy place while the tent
was still the place of worship. 9This also has a meaning
for today. It shows that we can't make our consciences
clear by offering gifts and sacrifices. 10These rules are
merely about such things as eating and drinking and
ceremonies for washing ourselves. And rules about
physical things will last only until the time comes to
change them for something better.

Christ Freed Us from Sin For Ever

11Christ came as the high priest of the good things that
are now here.t He also went into a much better tent that
wasn't made by humans and that doesn't belong to this
world. 12Then Christ went once and for all into the most
holy place and freed us from sin for ever. He did this
by offering his own blood instead of the blood of goats
and bulls.

13According to the Jewish religion, those people who
become unclean are not fit to worship God. Yet they will

---

pmanna: When the people of Israel were wandering through the desert, the
Lord provided them with food that could be made into thin wafers. This food
was called manna, which in Hebrew means "What is it?"   qAaron's walking
stick that sprouted: According to Numbers 17.1-11, Aaron's walking stick
sprouted and produced almonds to show that the Lord was pleased with him
and Moses.   rglorious creatures with wings: Two of these creatures (called
"cherubim" in Hebrew and Greek) with outspread wings were on top of the
sacred chest and were symbols of God's throne.   splace of mercy: The lid of
the sacred chest, which was thought to be God's throne on earth.   tthat are
now here: Some manuscripts have "that were coming."

be considered clean, if they are sprinkled with the blood of goats and bulls and with the ashes of a sacrificed calf. [14]But Christ was sinless, and he offered himself as an eternal and spiritual sacrifice to God. That's why his blood is much more powerful and makes our[u] consciences clear. Now we can serve the living God and no longer do things that lead to death.

[15]Christ died to rescue those who had sinned and broken the old agreement. Now he brings his chosen ones a new agreement with its guarantee of God's eternal blessings! [16]In fact, making an agreement of this kind is like writing a will. This is because the one who makes the will must die before it is of any use. [17]In other words, a will doesn't go into effect as long as the one who made it is still alive.

[18]Blood was also used[v] to put the first agreement into effect. [19]Moses told the people all that the Law said they must do. Then he used red wool and a hyssop plant to sprinkle the people and the book of the Law with the blood of bulls and goats[w] and with water. [20]He told the people, "With this blood God makes his agreement with you." [21]Moses also sprinkled blood on the tent and on everything else that was used in worship. [22]The Law says that almost everything must be sprinkled with blood, and no sins can be forgiven unless blood is offered.

Christ's Great Sacrifice

[23]These things are only copies of what is in heaven, and so they had to be made holy by these ceremonies. But the real things in heaven must be made holy by something better. [24]This is why Christ didn't go into a tent that had been made by humans and was only a copy of the real one. Instead, he went into heaven and is now there with God to help us.

[25]Christ didn't have to offer himself many times. He wasn't like a high priest who goes into the most holy place each year to offer the blood of an animal. [26]If he

---

[u]our: Some manuscripts have "your," and others have "their." [v]Blood was also used: Or "There also had to be a death." [w]blood of bulls and goats: Some manuscripts do not have "and goats."

had offered himself every year, he would have suffered many times since the creation of the world. But instead, near the end of time he offered himself once and for all, so that he could be a sacrifice that does away with sin.

27 We die only once, and then we are judged. 28 So Christ died only once to take away the sins of many people. But when he comes again, it will not be to take away sin. He will come to save everyone who is waiting for him.

10 1 The Law of Moses is like a shadow of the good things to come. This shadow isn't the good things themselves, because it can't free people from sin by the sacrifices that are offered year after year. 2 If there were worshippers who already have their sins washed away and their consciences made clear, there wouldn't be any need to go on offering sacrifices. 3-4 But the blood of bulls and goats can't take away sins. It only reminds people of their sins from one year to the next.

5 When Christ came into the world, he said to God,

> "Sacrifices and offerings are not what you want,
>   but you have given me my body.
> 6   No, you are not pleased with animal sacrifices
>   and offerings for sin."

7 Then Christ said,

> "And so, my God, I have come
> to do what you want,
>   as the Scriptures say."

8 The Law teaches that offerings and sacrifices must be made because of sin. But why did Christ mention these things and say that God didn't want them? 9 Well, it was to do away with offerings and sacrifices and to replace them. That is what he meant by saying to God, "I have come to do what you want." 10 So we are made holy because Christ obeyed God and offered himself once for all.

11 The priests do their work each day, and they keep on offering sacrifices that can never take away sins. 12 But Christ offered himself as a sacrifice that is good for ever. Now he is sitting at God's right side,x 13 and he will stay there until his enemies are put under his power. 14 By his

xright side: See the note at 1.3.

one sacrifice he has for ever set free from sin the people he brings to God.

¹⁵The Holy Spirit also speaks of this by telling us that the Lord said,

¹⁶ "When the time comes,
    I will make an agreement with them.
I will write my laws on their minds and hearts.
¹⁷ Then I will forget about their sins
    and no longer remember their evil deeds."

¹⁸When sins are forgiven, there is no more need to offer sacrifices.

Encouragement and Warning

¹⁹My friends, the blood of Jesus gives us courage to enter the most holy place ²⁰by a new way that leads to life! And this way takes us through the curtain that is Christ himself.

²¹We have a great high priest who is in charge of God's house. ²²So let's come near to God with pure hearts and a confidence that comes from having faith. Let's keep our hearts pure, our consciences free from evil, and our bodies washed with clean water. ²³We must hold tightly to the hope that we say is ours. After all, we can trust the one who made the agreement with us. ²⁴We should keep on encouraging each other to be thoughtful and to do helpful things. ²⁵Some people have got out of the habit of meeting for worship, but we mustn't do that. We should keep on encouraging each other, especially since you know that the day of the Lord's coming is getting closer.

²⁶No sacrifices can be made for people who decide to sin after they find out about the truth. ²⁷They are God's enemies, and all they can look forward to is a terrible judgment and a furious fire. ²⁸If two or more witnesses accused someone of breaking the Law of Moses, that person could be put to death. ²⁹But it is much worse to dishonour God's Son and to disgrace the blood of the promise that made us holy. And it's just as bad to insult the Holy Spirit, who shows us mercy. ³⁰We know that God has said he will punish and take revenge. We also know that the Scriptures say the Lord will judge his

people. 31It is a terrible thing to fall into the hands of the living God!

32Don't forget all the hard times you went through when you first received the light. 33Sometimes you were abused and mistreated in public, and at other times you shared in the sufferings of others. 34You were kind to people in jail. And you gladly let your possessions be taken away, because you knew you had something better, something that would last for ever.

35Keep on being brave! It will bring you great rewards. 36Learn to be patient, so that you will please God and be given what he has promised. 37As the Scriptures say,

"God is coming soon! It won't be very long.
38   The people God accepts will live
             because of their faith.ʸ
       But he isn't pleased with anyone who turns back."
39We are not like those people who turn back and get destroyed. We will keep on having faith until we are saved.

The Great Faith of God's People

11 1Faith makes us sure of what we hope for and gives us proof of what we can't see. 2It was their faith that made our ancestors pleasing to God.

3Because of our faith, we know that the world was made at God's command. We also know that what can be seen was made out of what can't be seen.

4Because Abel had faith, he offered God a better sacrifice than Cain did. God was pleased with him and his gift, and even though Abel is now dead, his faith still speaks for him.

5Enoch had faith and didn't die. He pleased God, and God took him up to heaven. That's why his body was never found. 6But without faith no-one can please God. We must believe that God is real and that he rewards everyone who searches for him.

7Because Noah had faith, he was warned about something that had not yet happened. He obeyed and built a boat that saved him and his family. In this way

---

ʸThe people God accepts will live because of their faith: Or "The people God accepts because of their faith will live."

the people of the world were judged, and Noah was given the blessings that come to everyone who pleases God.

⁸Abraham had faith and obeyed God. He was told to go to the land that God had said would be his, and he left for a country he had never seen. ⁹Because Abraham had faith, he lived as a stranger in the promised land. He lived there in a tent, and so did Isaac and Jacob, who were later given the same promise. ¹⁰Abraham did this, because he was waiting for the eternal city that God had planned and built.

¹¹Even when Sarah was too old to have children, she had faith that God would do what he had promised, and she had a son. ¹²Her husband Abraham was almost dead, but he became the ancestor of many people. In fact, there are as many of them as there are stars in the sky or grains of sand along the beach.

¹³Every one of those people died. But they still had faith, even though they hadn't received what they had been promised. They were glad just to see these things from far away, and they agreed that they were only strangers and foreigners on this earth. ¹⁴When people talk this way, it is clear that they are looking for a place to call their own. ¹⁵If they had been talking about the land where they had once lived, they could have gone back at any time. ¹⁶But they were looking forward to a better home in heaven. That's why God wasn't ashamed for them to call him their God. He even built a city for them.

¹⁷⁻¹⁸Abraham had been promised that Isaac, his only son,ᶻ would continue his family. But when Abraham was tested, he had faith and was willing to sacrifice Isaac, ¹⁹because he was sure that God could raise people to life. This was just like getting Isaac back from death.

²⁰Isaac had faith, and he promised blessings to Jacob and Esau. ²¹Later, when Jacob was about to die, he leaned on his walking stick and worshipped. Then because of his faith he blessed each of Joseph's sons. ²²And just before Joseph died, he had faith that God would lead the people

---

ᶻ*his only son:* Although Abraham had a son by a slave woman, his son Isaac was considered his only son, because he was born as a result of God's promise to Abraham.

of Israel out of Egypt. So he told them to take his bones with them.

²³Because Moses' parents had faith, they kept him hidden until he was three months old. They saw that he was a beautiful child, and they were not afraid to disobey the king's orders.^a ²⁴Then after Moses grew up, his faith made him refuse to be called Pharaoh's grandson. ²⁵He chose to be mistreated with God's people instead of having the good time that sin could bring for a little while. ²⁶Moses knew that the treasures of Egypt were not as wonderful as what he would receive from suffering for the Messiah,^b and he looked forward to his reward.

²⁷Because of his faith, Moses left Egypt. Moses had seen the invisible God and wasn't afraid of the king's anger. ²⁸His faith also made him celebrate Passover. He sprinkled the blood of animals on the doorposts, so that the firstborn sons of the people of Israel wouldn't be killed by the destroying angel.

²⁹Because of their faith, the people walked through the Red Sea^c on dry land. But when the Egyptians tried to do it, they were drowned.

³⁰God's people had faith, and when they had walked around the city of Jericho for seven days, its walls fell down.

³¹Rahab had been a prostitute, but she had faith and welcomed the spies. So she wasn't killed with the people who disobeyed.

³²What else can I say? There isn't enough time to tell about Gideon, Barak, Samson, Jephthah, David, Samuel, and the prophets. ³³Their faith helped them conquer kingdoms, and because they did right, God made promises to them. They closed the jaws of lions ³⁴and put out raging fires and escaped from the swords of their enemies. Although they were weak, they were given the strength and power to chase foreign armies away.

---

^athe king's orders: The king of Egypt ordered all Israelite baby boys to be left outside their homes, so they would die or be killed. ^bthe Messiah: Or "Christ." ^cRed Sea: This name comes from the Bible of the early Christians, a translation made into Greek about 200BC. It refers to the body of water that the Israelites crossed and was one of the marshes or fresh water lakes near the eastern part of the Nile Delta, where they lived and where the towns of Exodus 13.17—14.9 were located.

[35]Some women received their loved ones back from
death. Many of these people were tortured, but they
refused to be released. They were sure that they would
get a better reward when the dead are raised to life.
[36]Others were made fun of and beaten with whips, and
some were chained in jail. [37]Still others were stoned to
death or sawn in two[d] or killed with swords. Some had
nothing but sheep skins or goat skins to wear. They were
poor, mistreated, and tortured. [38]The world didn't
deserve these good people, who had to wander in deserts
and on mountains and had to live in caves and holes in
the ground.

[39]All of them pleased God because of their faith! But
still they died without being given what had been
promised. [40]This was because God had something better
in store for us. And he didn't want them to reach the goal
of their faith without us.

A Large Crowd of Witnesses

12 [1]Such a large crowd of witnesses is all around us!
So we must get rid of everything that slows us
down, especially the sin that just won't let go. And we
must be determined to run the race that is ahead of us.
[2]We must keep our eyes on Jesus, who leads us and
makes our faith complete. He endured the shame of being
nailed to a cross, because he knew that later on he would
be glad he did. Now he is seated at the right side[e] of God's
throne! [3]So keep your mind on Jesus, who put up with
many insults from sinners. Then you won't get
discouraged and give up.

[4]None of you have yet been hurt[f] in your battle
against sin. [5]But you have forgotten that the Scriptures
say to God's children,

> "When the Lord punishes you,
>   don't make light of it,
>   and when he corrects you, don't be discouraged.
> [6]   The Lord corrects the people he loves
>   and disciplines those he calls his own."

---

[d]*sawn in two:* Some manuscripts have "tested" or "tempted."   [e]*right side:* See
the note at 1.3.   [f]*hurt:* Or "killed."

7Be patient when you are being corrected! This is how God treats his children. Don't all parents correct their children? 8God corrects all of his children, and if he doesn't correct you, then you don't really belong to him. 9Our earthly fathers correct us, and we still respect them. Isn't it even better to be given true life by letting our spiritual Father correct us?

10Our human fathers correct us for a short time, and they do it as they think best. But God corrects us for our own good, because he wants us to be holy, as he is. 11It is never fun to be corrected. In fact, at the time it is always painful. But if we learn to obey by being corrected, we will do right and live at peace.

12Now stand up straight! Stop your knees from shaking 13and walk a straight path. Then lame people will be healed, instead of getting worse.

Warning against Turning from God

14Try to live at peace with everyone! Live a clean life. If you don't, you will never see the Lord. 15Make sure that no-one misses out on God's wonderful kindness. Don't let anyone become bitter and cause trouble for the rest of you. 16Watch out for immoral and ungodly people like Esau, who sold his future blessing*g* for only one meal. 17You know how he later wanted it back. But there was nothing he could do to change things, even though he begged his father and cried.

18You haven't come to a place like Mount Sinai*h* that can be seen and touched. There is no flaming fire or dark cloud or storm 19or trumpet sound. The people of Israel heard a voice speak. But they begged it to stop, 20because they couldn't obey its commands. They were even told to kill any animal that touched the mountain. 21The sight was so frightening that Moses said he shook with fear.

22You have now come to Mount Zion and to the heavenly Jerusalem. This is the city of the living God,

gsold his future blessing: As the firstborn son, Esau had certain privileges that were known as a "birthright." *ha place like Mount Sinai:* The Greek text has "a place," but the writer is referring to the time when the Lord spoke to the people of Israel from Mount Sinai (see Exodus 19.16-25).

where thousands and thousands of angels have come to celebrate. [23]Here you will find all of God's dearest children,[i] whose names are written in heaven. And you will find God himself, who judges everyone. Here also are the spirits of those good people who have been made perfect. [24]And Jesus is here! He is the one who makes God's new agreement with us, and his sprinkled blood says much better things than the blood of Abel.[j]

[25]Make sure that you obey the one who speaks to you. The people of Israel didn't escape, when they refused to obey the one who spoke to them at Mount Sinai. Do you think you can possibly escape, if you refuse to obey the one who speaks to you from heaven? [26]When God spoke the first time, his voice shook only the earth. This time he has promised to shake the earth once again, and heaven too.

[27]The words "once again" mean that these created things will some day be shaken and removed. Then what can't be shaken will last. [28]We should be grateful that we were given a kingdom that can't be shaken. And in this kingdom we please God by worshipping him and by showing him great honour and respect. [29]Our God is like a destructive fire!

Service That Pleases God

13 [1]Keep being concerned about each other as the Lord's followers should.

[2]Be sure to welcome strangers into your home. By doing this, some people have welcomed angels as guests, without even knowing it.

[3]Remember the Lord's people who are in jail and be concerned for them. Don't forget those who are suffering, but imagine that you are there with them.

[4]Have respect for marriage. Always be faithful to your partner, because God will punish anyone who is immoral or unfaithful in marriage.

[5]Don't fall in love with money. Be satisfied with what

[i]all of God's dearest children: The Greek text has "the gathering of the first-born children" (see the note at 1.6).   [j]blood of Abel: Cain and Abel were the two sons of Adam and Eve. Cain murdered Abel (see Genesis 4.1-16).

you have. The Lord has promised that he will not leave us or desert us. ⁶That should make you feel like saying,
"The Lord helps me! Why should I be afraid
of what people can do to me?"

⁷Don't forget about your leaders who taught you God's message. Remember what kind of lives they lived and try to have faith like theirs.

⁸Jesus Christ never changes! He is the same yesterday, today, and for ever. ⁹Don't be fooled by any kind of strange teachings. It is better to receive strength from God's undeserved kindness than to depend on certain foods. After all, these foods don't really help the people who eat them. ¹⁰But we have an altar where even the priests who serve in the place of worship have no right to eat.

¹¹After the high priest offers the blood of animals as a sin offering, the bodies of those animals are burnt outside the camp. ¹²Jesus himself suffered outside the city gate, so that his blood would make people holy. ¹³That's why we should go outside the camp to Jesus and share in his disgrace. ¹⁴On this earth we haven't got a city that lasts for ever, but we are waiting for such a city.

¹⁵Our sacrifice is to keep offering praise to God in the name of Jesus. ¹⁶But don't forget to help others and to share your possessions with them. This too is like offering a sacrifice that pleases God.

¹⁷Obey your leaders and do what they say. They are watching over you, and they must answer to God. So don't make them sad as they do their work. Make them happy. Otherwise, they won't be able to help you at all.

¹⁸Pray for us. Our consciences are clear, and we always try to live right. ¹⁹I especially want you to pray that I can visit you again soon.

Final Prayers and Greetings

²⁰God gives peace, and he raised our Lord Jesus Christ from death. Now Jesus is like a Great Shepherd whose blood was used to make God's eternal agreement with his flock.ᵏ ²¹I pray that God will make you ready to obey him

ᵏwhose blood was used to make God's eternal agreement with his flock: See 9.18-22.

and that you will always be eager to do right. May Jesus help you do what pleases God. To Jesus Christ be glory for ever and ever! Amen.

22My friends, I have written only a short letter to encourage you, and I beg you to pay close attention to what I have said.

23By now you surely must know that our friend Timothy is out of jail. If he gets here in time, I will bring him with me when I come to visit you.

24Please give my greetings to your leaders and to the rest of the Lord's people.

His followers from Italy send you their greetings.

25I pray that God will be kind to all of you!*l*

---

lto all of you!: Some manuscripts add "Amen."

JAMES
ABOUT THIS LETTER

This is a good example of a general letter, because it is addressed to Christians scattered throughout the Roman Empire. Though written as a letter, it is more like a short book of instructions for daily living.

For James faith means action! In fact, the entire book is a series of examples that show faith in action in wise and practical ways.

His advice was clear and to the point: If you are poor, don't despair! Don't give up when your faith is being tested. Don't get angry quickly. Don't favour the rich over the poor. Do good things for others. Control your tongue and desires. Surrender to God and rely on his wisdom. Resist the devil. Don't boast about what you are going to do. If you are rich, use your money to help the poor. Be patient and kind, and pray for those who need God's help.

A QUICK LOOK AT THIS LETTER

- Greetings (1.1)
- A Life of Faith and Wisdom (1.2-18)
- Hearing and Obeying God's Message (1.19-27)
- Don't Favour the Rich and Powerful (2.1-13)
- Faith and Works (2.14-26)
- Wisdom and Words (3.1-18)
- Warning against Friendship with the World (4.1-5.6)
- Patience, Kindness, and Prayer (5.7-20)

1 ¹From James, a servant of God and of our Lord Jesus Christ.

Greetings to the twelve tribes scattered all over the world.ᵃ

Faith and Wisdom

²My friends, be glad, even if you have a lot of trouble. ³You know that you learn to endure by having your faith

---

ᵃtwelve tribes scattered all over the world: James is saying that the Lord's followers are like the tribes of Israel that were scattered everywhere by their enemies.

tested. 4But you must learn to endure everything, so that you will be completely mature and not lacking in anything.

5If any of you need wisdom, you should ask God, and it will be given to you. God is generous and won't correct you for asking. 6But when you ask for something, you must have faith and not doubt. Anyone who doubts is like an ocean wave tossed around in a storm. 7-8If you are that kind of person, you can't make up your mind, and you surely can't be trusted. So don't expect the Lord to give you anything at all.

Poor People and Rich People

9Any of God's people who are poor should be glad that he thinks so highly of them. 10But any who are rich should be glad when God makes them humble. Rich people will disappear like wild flowers 11scorched by the burning heat of the sun. The flowers lose their blossoms, and their beauty is destroyed. That is how the rich will disappear, as they go about their business.

Trials and Temptations

12God will bless you, if you don't give up when your faith is being tested. He will reward you with a glorious life,b just as he rewards everyone who loves him.

13Don't blame God when you are tempted! God can't be tempted by evil, and he doesn't use evil to tempt others. 14We are tempted by our own desires that drag us off and trap us. 15Our desires make us sin, and when sin is finished with us, it leaves us dead.

16Don't be fooled, my dear friends. 17Every good and perfect gift comes down from the Father who created all the lights in the heavens. He is always the same and never makes dark shadows by changing. 18He wanted us to be his own special people,c and so he sent the true message to give us new birth.

---

ba glorious life: The Greek text has "the crown of life." In ancient times an athlete who had won a contest was rewarded with a crown of flowers as a sign of victory. chis own special people: The Greek text has "the first of his creatures." The Law of Moses taught that the firstborn of all animals and the first part of the harvest were special and belonged to the Lord.

Hearing and Obeying

19My dear friends, you should be quick to listen and slow to speak or to get angry. 20If you are angry, you can't do any of the good things that God wants done. 21You must stop doing anything immoral or evil. Instead be humble and accept the message that is planted in you to save you.

22Obey God's message! Don't fool yourselves by just listening to it. 23If you hear the message and don't obey it, you are like people who stare at themselves in a mirror 24and forget what they look like as soon as they leave. 25But you must never stop looking at the perfect law that sets you free. God will bless you in everything you do, if you listen and obey, and don't just hear and forget.

26If you think you are being religious, but can't control your tongue, you are fooling yourself, and everything you do is useless. 27Religion that pleases God the Father must be pure and spotless. You must help needy orphans and widows and not let this world make you evil.

Warning against Having Favourites

2 1My friends, if you have faith in our glorious Lord Jesus Christ, you won't treat some people better than others. 2Suppose a rich person wearing fancy clothes and a gold ring comes to one of your meetings. And suppose a poor person dressed in worn-out clothes also comes. 3You mustn't give the best seat to the one in fancy clothes and tell the one who is poor to stand at the side or sit on the floor. 4That is the same as saying that some people are better than others, and you would be acting like a crooked judge.

5My dear friends, pay attention. God has given a lot of faith to the poor people in this world. He has also promised them a share in his kingdom that he will give to everyone who loves him. 6You mistreat the poor. But isn't it the rich who boss you around and drag you off to court? 7Aren't they the ones who make fun of your Lord?

8You will do all right, if you obey the most important

law[d] in the Scriptures. It is the law that commands us to love others as much as we love ourselves. [9]But if you treat some people better than others, you have done wrong, and the Scriptures teach that you have sinned.

[10]If you obey every law except one, you are still guilty of breaking them all. [11]The same God who told us to be faithful in marriage also told us not to murder. So even if you are faithful in marriage, but murder someone, you still have broken God's Law.

[12]Speak and act like people who will be judged by the law that sets us free. [13]Do this, because on the day of judgment there will be no pity for those who have not had pity on others. But even in judgment, God is merciful![e]

Faith and Works

[14]My friends, what good is it to say you have faith, when you don't do anything to show that you really do have faith? Can that kind of faith save you? [15]If you know someone who hasn't got any clothes or food, [16]you shouldn't just say, "I hope all goes well for you. I hope you will be warm and have plenty to eat." What good is it to say this, unless you do something to help? [17]Faith that doesn't lead us to do good deeds is all alone and dead!

[18]Suppose someone disagrees and says, "It is possible to have faith without doing kind deeds."

I would answer, "Prove that you have faith without doing kind deeds, and I will prove that I have faith by doing them." [19]You surely believe there is only one God. That's fine. Even demons believe this, and it makes them shake with fear.

[20]Does some stupid person want proof that faith without deeds is useless? [21]Well, our ancestor Abraham pleased God by putting his son Isaac on the altar to sacrifice him. [22]Now you see how Abraham's faith and deeds worked together. He proved that his faith was real by what he did. [23]This is what the Scriptures mean by

[d]most important law: The Greek text has "royal law," meaning the one given by the king (that is, God).　[e]But even in judgment, God is merciful!: Or "So be merciful, and you will be shown mercy on the day of judgment."

saying, "Abraham had faith in God, and God was pleased with him." That's how Abraham became God's friend.

24You can now see that we please God by what we do and not only by what we believe. 25For example, Rahab had been a prostitute. But she pleased God when she welcomed the spies and sent them home by another way.

26Anyone who doesn't breathe is dead, and faith that doesn't do anything is just as dead!

The Tongue

3 1My friends, we shouldn't all try to become teachers. In fact, teachers will be judged more strictly than others. 2All of us do many wrong things. But if you can control your tongue, you are mature and able to control your whole body.

3By putting a bit into the mouth of a horse, we can turn the horse in different directions. 4It takes strong winds to move a large sailing ship, but the captain uses only a small rudder to make it go in any direction. 5Our tongues are small too, and yet they boast about big things.

It takes only a spark to start a forest fire! 6The tongue is like a spark. It is an evil power that dirties the rest of the body and sets a person's entire life on fire with flames that come from hell itself. 7All kinds of animals, birds, reptiles, and sea creatures can be tamed and have been tamed. 8But our tongues get out of control. They are restless and evil, and always spreading deadly poison.

9-10My dear friends, with our tongues we speak both praises and curses. We praise our Lord and Father, and we curse people who were created to be like God, and this isn't right. 11Can clean water and dirty water both flow from the same spring? 12Can a fig tree produce olives or a grapevine produce figs? Does fresh water come from a well full of salt water?

Wisdom from Above

13Are any of you wise or sensible? Then show it by living right and by being humble and wise in everything you do. 14But if your heart is full of bitter jealousy and selfishness, don't boast or lie to cover up the truth.

15That kind of wisdom doesn't come from above. It is earthly and selfish and comes from the devil himself. 16Whenever people are jealous or selfish, they cause trouble and do all sorts of cruel things. 17But the wisdom that comes from above leads us to be pure, friendly, gentle, sensible, kind, helpful, genuine, and sincere. 18When peacemakers plant seeds of peace, they will harvest justice.

Friendship with the World

4 1Why do you fight and argue with each other? Isn't it because you are full of selfish desires that fight to control your body? 2You want something you haven't got, and you will do anything to get it. You will even kill! But you still can't get what you want, and you won't get it by fighting and arguing. You should pray for it. 3Yet even when you do pray, your prayers aren't answered, because you pray just for selfish reasons.

4You people aren't faithful to God! Don't you know that if you love the world, you are God's enemies? And if you decide to be a friend of the world, you make yourself an enemy of God. 5Do you doubt the Scriptures that say, "God truly cares about the Spirit he has put in us"?f 6In fact, God treats us with even greater kindness, just as the Scriptures say,

"God opposes everyone who is proud,
     but he is kind to everyone who is humble."

7Surrender to God! Resist the devil, and he will run from you. 8Come near to God, and he will come near to you. Clean up your lives, you sinners. Purify your hearts, you people who can't make up your mind. 9Be sad and sorry and weep. Stop laughing and start crying. Be gloomy instead of glad. 10Be humble in the Lord's presence, and he will honour you.

Saying Cruel Things about Others

11My friends, don't say cruel things about others! If you do, or if you condemn others, you are condemning God's

---

fGod truly cares about the Spirit he has put in us: One possible meaning for the Greek text; other translations are possible, such as, "the Spirit that God put in us truly cares."

Law. And if you condemn the Law, you put yourself above the Law and refuse to obey either it ¹²or God who gave it. God is our judge, and he can save or destroy us. What right do you have to condemn anyone?

Warning against Boasting

¹³You should know better than to say, "Today or tomorrow we will go to the city. We'll do business there for a year and make a lot of money!" ¹⁴What do you know about tomorrow? How can you be so sure about your life? It is nothing more than mist that appears for only a little while before it disappears. ¹⁵You should say, "If the Lord lets us live, we will do these things." ¹⁶Yet you are stupid enough to boast, and it is wrong to be so proud. ¹⁷If you don't do what you know is right, you have sinned.

Warning to the Rich

5 ¹You rich people should cry and weep! Terrible things are going to happen to you. ²Your treasures have already rotted, and moths have eaten your clothes. ³Your money has rusted, and the rust will be evidence against you, as it burns your body like fire. Yet you keep on storing up wealth in these last days. ⁴You refused to pay the people who worked in your fields, and now their unpaid wages are shouting out against you. The Lord All-Powerful has surely heard the cries of the workers who harvested your crops.

⁵While here on earth, you have thought only of filling your own stomachs and having a good time. But now you are like fat cattle on their way to be butchered. ⁶You have condemned and murdered innocent people, who couldn't even fight back.

Be Patient and Kind

⁷My friends, be patient until the Lord returns. Think of farmers who wait patiently for the spring and summer rains to make their valuable crops grow. ⁸Be patient like those farmers and don't give up. The Lord will soon be here! ⁹Don't grumble about each other or you will be judged, and the judge is right outside the door.

¹⁰My friends, follow the example of the prophets who spoke for the Lord. They were patient, even when they had to suffer. ¹¹In fact, we praise the ones who endured the most. You remember how patient Job was and how the Lord finally helped him. The Lord did this because he is so merciful and kind.

¹²My friends, above all else, don't take an oath. You mustn't swear by heaven or by earth or by anything else. "Yes" or "No" is all you need to say. If you say anything more, you will be condemned.

¹³If you are having trouble, you should pray. And if you are feeling good, you should sing praises. ¹⁴If you are sick, ask the church leaders*g* to come and pray for you. Ask them to put olive oil*h* on you in the name of the Lord. ¹⁵If you have faith when you pray for sick people, they will get well. The Lord will heal them, and if they have sinned, he will forgive them.

¹⁶If you have sinned, you should tell each other what you have done. Then you can pray for one another and be healed. The prayer of an innocent person is powerful, and it can help a lot. ¹⁷Elijah was just as human as we are, and for three and a half years his prayers kept the rain from falling. ¹⁸But when he did pray for rain, it fell from the skies and made the crops grow.

¹⁹My friends, if any followers have wandered away from the truth, you should try to lead them back. ²⁰If you turn sinners from the wrong way, you will save them from death, and many of their sins will be forgiven.

---

*g*church leaders: Or "elders" or "presbyters" or "priests." *h*olive oil: The Jewish people used olive oil for healing.

1 PETER
ABOUT THIS LETTER

In this letter Peter has much to say about suffering. He shows how it can be a way of serving the Lord, of sharing the faith, and of being tested. The letter was written to Christians scattered all over the northern part of Asia Minor. In this part of the Roman Empire many Christians had already suffered unfair treatment from people who didn't believe in Jesus. And they could expect to suffer even more.

Peter was quick to offer encouragement. His letter reminds the readers that some of the Lord's followers may have to go through times of hard testing. But this should make them glad, Peter declares, because it will strengthen their faith and bring them honour on the day when Jesus Christ returns (chapter 1.6, 7).

Peter reminds them that Christ suffered here on earth, and when his followers suffer for doing right they are sharing his sufferings (2.18-25; 4.12-17). In fact, Christians should expect to suffer for their faith (3.8—4.19).

But because of who God is and because of what God has done by raising Jesus Christ from death, Christians can have hope in the future. Just as Christ suffered before he received honour from God, so will Christians be tested by suffering before they receive honour when the Lord returns. Peter uses poetic language to remind his readers of what Christ has done:

> *Christ died once for our sins.*
> *An innocent person died for those who are guilty.*
> *Christ did this to bring you to God,*
> *when his body was put to death*
> *and his spirit was made alive.* (Chapter 3.18)

A QUICK LOOK AT THIS LETTER

1 ¹From Peter, an apostle of Jesus Christ.
To God's people who are scattered like foreigners in Pontus, Galatia, Cappadocia, Asia, and Bithynia.
²God the Father decided to choose you as his people, and his Spirit has made you holy. You have obeyed Jesus Christ and are sprinkled with his blood.*a*

I pray that God will be kind to you and will keep on giving you peace!

A Real Reason for Hope

³Praise God, the Father of our Lord Jesus Christ. God is so good, and by raising Jesus from death, he has given us new life and a hope that lives on. ⁴God has something stored up for you in heaven, where it will never decay or be ruined or disappear.

⁵You have faith in God, whose power will protect you until the last day.*b* Then he will save you, just as he has always planned to do. ⁶On that day you will be glad, even if you have to go through many hard trials for a while. ⁷Your faith will be like gold that has been tested in a fire. And these trials will prove that your faith is worth much more than gold that can be destroyed. They will show that you will be given praise and honour and glory when Jesus Christ returns.

⁸You have never seen Jesus, and you don't see him now. But still you love him and have faith in him, and no words can tell how glad and happy ⁹you are to be saved. That's why you have faith.

¹⁰Some prophets spoke about how kind God would be to you, and they searched hard to find out more about

---

asprinkled with his blood: According to Exodus 24.3-8 the people of Israel were sprinkled with the blood of bulls to show they would keep their agreement with God. Peter says that it is the blood of Jesus that seals the agreement between God and his people (see Hebrews 9.18-21).   *bthe last day:* When God will judge all people.

the way you would be saved. ¹¹The Spirit of Christ was in them and was telling them how Christ would suffer and would then be given great honour. So they searched to find out exactly who Christ would be and when this would happen. ¹²But they were told that they were serving you and not themselves. They preached to you by the power of the Holy Spirit, who was sent from heaven. And their message was only for you, even though angels would like to know more about it.

Chosen To Live a Holy Life

¹³Be alert and think straight. Put all your hope in how kind God will be to you when Jesus Christ appears. ¹⁴Behave like obedient children. Don't let your lives be controlled by your desires, as they used to be. ¹⁵Always live as God's holy people should, because God is the one who chose you, and he is holy. ¹⁶That's why the Scriptures say, "I am the holy God, and you must be holy too."

¹⁷You say that God is your Father, but God doesn't have favourites! He judges all people by what they do. So you must honour God while you live as strangers here on earth. ¹⁸You were rescued[c] from the useless way of life that you learnt from your ancestors. But you know that you were not rescued by such things as silver or gold that don't last for ever. ¹⁹You were rescued by the precious blood of Christ, that spotless and innocent lamb. ²⁰Christ was chosen even before the world was created, but because of you, he didn't come until these last days. ²¹And when he did come, it was to lead you to have faith in God, who raised him from death and honoured him in a glorious way. That's why you have put your faith and hope in God.

²²You obeyed the truth,[d] and your souls were made pure. Now you sincerely love each other. But you must keep on loving with all your heart. ²³Do this because God has given you new birth by his message that lives on for

---

[c]*rescued:* The Greek word often, though not always, means payment of a price to free a slave or prisoner.   [d]*You obeyed the truth:* Some manuscripts add "by the power of the Spirit."

ever. ²⁴The Scriptures say,

"Humans wither like grass,
    and their glory fades like wild flowers.
Grass dries up, and flowers fall to the ground.
²⁵   But what the Lord has said will stand for ever."

Our good news to you is what the Lord has said.

A Living Stone and a Holy Nation

2 ¹Stop being hateful! Stop trying to fool people, and start being sincere. Don't be jealous or say cruel things about others. ²Be like newborn babies who are thirsty for the pure spiritual milk that will help you grow and be saved. ³You have already found out how good the Lord really is.

⁴Come to Jesus Christ. He is the living stone that people have rejected, but which God has chosen and highly honoured. ⁵And now you are living stones that are being used to build a spiritual house. You are also a group of holy priests, and with the help of Jesus Christ you will offer sacrifices that please God. ⁶It is just as God says in the Scriptures,

"Look! I am placing in Zion
    a choice and precious cornerstone.
        No-one who has faith in that one
        will be disappointed."

⁷You are followers of the Lord, and that stone is precious to you. But it isn't precious to those who refuse to follow him. They are the builders who tossed aside the stone that turned out to be the most important one of all. ⁸They disobeyed the message and stumbled and fell over that stone, because they were doomed.

⁹But you are God's chosen and special people. You are a group of royal priests and a holy nation. God has brought you out of darkness into his marvellous light. Now you must tell about all the wonderful things that he has done. The Scriptures say,

¹⁰ "Once you were nobody.
    Now you are God's people.
    At one time no-one had pity on you.
        Now God has treated you with kindness.

Live as God's Servants Should

11Dear friends, you are foreigners and strangers on this earth. So I beg you not to surrender to those desires that fight against you. 12Always let others see you behaving properly, even though they may still accuse you of doing wrong. Then on the day of judgment, they will honour God by telling the good things they saw you do.

13The Lord wants you to obey all human authorities, especially the Emperor, who rules over everyone. 14You must also obey governors, because they are sent by the Emperor to punish criminals and to praise good citizens. 15God wants you to silence stupid and ignorant people by doing right. 16You are free, but still you are God's servants, and you mustn't use your freedom as an excuse for doing wrong. 17Respect everyone and show special love for God's people. Honour God and respect the Emperor.

The Example of Christ's Suffering

18Servants, you must obey your masters and always show respect to them. Do this, not only to those who are kind and thoughtful, but also to those who are cruel. 19God will bless you, even if others treat you unfairly for being loyal to him. 20You don't gain anything by being punished for some wrong you have done. But God will bless you, if you have to suffer for doing something good. 21After all, God chose you to suffer as you follow in the footsteps of Christ, who set an example by suffering for you.

22 Christ did not sin or ever tell a lie.
23 Although he was abused,
he never tried to get even.
And when he suffered, he made no threats.
Instead, he had faith in God,
who judges fairly.
24 Christ carried the burden of our sins.
He was nailed to the cross,
so that we would stop sinning
and start living right.
By his cuts and bruises you are healed.

25 You had wandered away like sheep.
Now you have returned
to the one who is your shepherd
and protector.

Wives and Husbands

3 ¹If you are a wife, you must put your husband first. Even if he opposes our message, you will win him over by what you do. No-one else will have to say anything to him, ²because he will see how you honour God and live a pure life. ³Don't depend on things like fancy hairdos or gold jewellery or expensive clothes to make you look beautiful. ⁴Be beautiful in your heart by being gentle and quiet. This kind of beauty will last, and God considers it very special.

⁵Long ago those women who worshipped God and put their hope in him made themselves beautiful by putting their husbands first. ⁶For example, Sarah obeyed Abraham and called him her master. You are her true children, if you do right and don't let anything frighten you.

⁷If you are a husband, you should be thoughtful of your wife. Treat her with honour, because she isn't as strong as you are, and she shares with you in the gift of life. Then nothing will stand in the way of your prayers.

Suffering for Doing Right

⁸Finally, all of you should agree and have concern and love for each other. You should also be kind and humble. ⁹Don't be hateful and insult people just because they are hateful and insult you. Instead, treat everyone with kindness. You are God's chosen ones, and he will bless you. The Scriptures say,

10 "Do you really love life? Do you want to be happy?
Then stop saying cruel things
and stop telling lies.
11 Give up your evil ways and do right,
as you find and follow the road
that leads to peace.
12 The Lord watches over everyone who obeys him,
and he listens to their prayers.

But he opposes everyone who does evil."

¹³Can anyone really harm you for being eager to do good deeds? ¹⁴Even if you have to suffer for doing good things, God will bless you. So stop being afraid and don't worry about what people might do. ¹⁵Honour Christ and let him be the Lord of your life.

Always be ready to give an answer when someone asks you about your hope. ¹⁶Give a kind and respectful answer and keep your conscience clear. This way you will make people ashamed for saying bad things about your good conduct as a follower of Christ. ¹⁷You are better off to obey God and suffer for doing right than to suffer for doing wrong.

¹⁸   Christ died once for our sins.
An innocent person died
for those who are guilty.
Christ did this to bring you to God,
when his body was put to death
and his spirit was made alive.

¹⁹Christ then preached to the spirits that were being kept in prison. ²⁰They had disobeyed God while Noah was building the boat, but God had been patient with them. Eight people went into that boat and were brought safely through the flood.

²¹Those flood waters were like baptism that now saves you. But baptism is more than just washing your body. It means turning to God with a clear conscience, because Jesus Christ was raised from death. ²²Christ is now in heaven, where he sits at the right side*e* of God. All angels, authorities, and powers are under his control.

Being Faithful to God

4 ¹Christ suffered here on earth. Now you must be ready to suffer as he did, because suffering shows that you have stopped sinning. ²It means you have turned from your own desires and want to obey God for the rest of your life. ³You have already lived long enough like people who don't know God. You were immoral and followed your evil desires. You went around drinking and

e right side: The place of honour and power.

partying and carrying on. In fact, you even worshipped disgusting idols. 4Now your former friends wonder why you have stopped running around with them, and they curse you for it. 5But they will have to answer to God, who judges the living and the dead. 6The good news has even been preached to the dead,f so that after they have been judged for what they have done in this life, their spirits will live with God.

7Everything will soon come to an end. So be serious and be sensible enough to pray.

8Most important of all, you must sincerely love each other, because love wipes away many sins.

9Welcome people into your home and don't grumble about it.

10Each of you has been blessed with one of God's many wonderful gifts to be used in the service of others. So use your gift well. 11If you have the gift of speaking, preach God's message. If you have the gift of helping others, do it with the strength that God supplies. Everything should be done in a way that will bring honour to God because of Jesus Christ, who is glorious and powerful for ever. Amen.

Suffering for Being a Christian

12Dear friends, don't be surprised or shocked that you are going through testing that is like walking through fire. 13Be glad for the chance to suffer as Christ suffered. It will prepare you for even greater happiness when he makes his glorious return.

14Count it a blessing when you suffer for being a Christian. This shows that God's glorious Spirit is with you. 15But you deserve to suffer if you are a murderer, a thief, a crook, or a busybody. 16Don't be ashamed to suffer for being a Christian. Praise God that you belong to him. 17God has already begun judging his own people. And if his judgment begins with us, imagine how terrible it will be for those who refuse to obey his message. The Scriptures say,

---

fthe dead: Either people who died after becoming followers of Christ or the people of Noah's day (see 3.19).

18 "If good people barely escape,
   what will happen to sinners
      and to others who don't respect God?"

19If you suffer for obeying God, you must have complete faith in your faithful Creator and keep on doing right.

Helping Christian Leaders

5 ¹Church leaders,ᵍ I am writing to encourage you. I too am a leader, as well as a witness to Christ's suffering, and I will share in his glory when it is shown to us.

²Just as shepherds watch over their sheep, you must watch over everyone God has placed in your care. Do it willingly in order to please God, and not simply because you think you must. Let it be something you want to do, instead of something you do merely to make money. ³Don't be bossy to those people who are in your care, but set an example for them. ⁴Then when Christ the Chief Shepherd returns, you will be given a crown that will never lose its glory.

⁵All of you young people should obey your elders. In fact, everyone should be humble towards everyone else. The Scriptures say,
      "God opposes proud people,
         but he helps everyone who is humble."

⁶Be humble in the presence of God's mighty power, and he will honour you when the time comes. ⁷God cares for you, so turn all your worries over to him.

⁸Be on your guard and stay awake. Your enemy, the devil, is like a roaring lion, sneaking around to find someone to attack. ⁹But you must resist the devil and stay strong in your faith. You know that all over the world the Lord's followers are suffering just as you are. ¹⁰But God shows undeserved kindness to everyone. That's why he appointed Christ Jesus to choose you to share in his eternal glory. You will suffer for a while, but God will make you complete, steady, strong, and firm. ¹¹God will be in control for ever! Amen.

---

gChurch leaders: Or "Elders" or "Presbyters" or "Priests."

Final Greetings

[12]Silvanus helped me write this short letter, and I consider him a faithful follower of the Lord. I wanted to encourage you and tell you how kind God really is, so that you will keep on having faith in him.

[13]Greetings from the Lord's followers in Babylon.[h] They are God's chosen ones.

Mark, who is like a son to me, sends his greetings too.

[14]Give each other a warm greeting. I pray that God will give peace to everyone who belongs to Christ.[i]

---

[h]*Babylon:* This may be a secret name for the city of Rome.   [i]*Christ:* Some manuscripts add "Amen."

2 PETER

ABOUT THIS LETTER

The writer of this letter wants the readers to know that Christians must live in a way that pleases God (chapter 1.3) and hold firmly to the truth they were given (1.12).

He warns them that false prophets and teachers had entered the Christian community and were trying to lead the Lord's followers away from the truth. But they will be punished for their evil deeds (2.1-22). When false teachers are at work, Christians must stick to their faith and be examples for others of right living. They must have understanding, self-control and patience, and they should show love for God and all people.

The readers must never forget that the Lord's return is certain, no matter what others may say (3.1-18):

Don't forget that for the Lord one day is the same as a thousand years, and a thousand years is the same as one day. The Lord isn't slow about keeping his promises, as some people think he is. In fact, God is patient, because he wants everyone to turn from sin and no-one to be lost. (Chapter 3.8, 9)

A QUICK LOOK AT THIS LETTER

- Greetings and Prayer (1.1, 2)
- How the Lord's Followers Should Live (1.3-15)
- The Glory of Christ (1.16-21)
- False Prophets and Teachers (2.1-22)
- The Lord's Return Is Certain (3.1-18)

1 ¹From Simon Peter, a servant and an apostle of Jesus Christ.

To everyone who shares with us in the privilege of believing that our God and Saviour Jesus Christ will do what is just and fair.*a*

---

aTo everyone who...just and fair: Or "To everyone whose faith in the justice and fairness of our God and Saviour Jesus Christ is as precious as our own faith."

²I pray that God will be kind to you and will let you live in perfect peace! May you keep learning more and more about God and our Lord Jesus.

Living as the Lord's Followers Should

³We have everything we need to live a life that pleases God. It was all given to us by God's own power, when we learnt that he had invited us to share in his wonderful goodness. ⁴God made great and marvellous promises, so that his nature would become part of us. Then we could escape our evil desires and the corrupt influences of this world.

⁵Do your best to improve your faith. You can do this by adding goodness, understanding, ⁶self-control, patience, devotion to God, ⁷concern for others, and love. ⁸If you keep growing in this way, it will show that what you know about our Lord Jesus Christ has made your lives useful and meaningful. ⁹But if you don't grow, you are like someone who is near-sighted or blind, and you've forgotten that your past sins are forgiven.

¹⁰My friends, you must do all you can to show that God has really chosen and selected you. If you keep on doing this, you won't stumble and fall. ¹¹Then our Lord and Saviour Jesus Christ will give you a glorious welcome into his kingdom that will last for ever.

¹²You are holding firmly to the truth that you were given. But I am still going to remind you of these things. ¹³In fact, I think I should keep on reminding you until I leave this body. ¹⁴And our Lord Jesus Christ has already told me that I will soon leave it behind. ¹⁵That is why I am doing my best to make sure that each of you remembers all of this after I am gone.

The Message about the Glory of Christ

¹⁶When we told you about the power and the return of our Lord Jesus Christ, we weren't telling clever stories that someone had made up. But with our own eyes we saw his true greatness. ¹⁷God, our great and wonderful Father, truly honoured him by saying, "This is my own dear Son, and I am pleased with him." ¹⁸We were there with Jesus on the holy mountain and heard this voice

speak from heaven.

¹⁹All of this makes us even more certain that what the prophets said is true. So you should pay close attention to their message, as you would to a lamp shining in some dark place. You must keep on paying attention until daylight comes and the morning star rises in your hearts. ²⁰But you need to realise that no-one alone can understand any of the prophecies in the Scriptures. ²¹The prophets didn't think these things up on their own, but they were guided by the Spirit of God.

False Prophets and Teachers

2 ¹Sometimes false prophets spoke to the people of Israel. False teachers will also sneak in and speak harmful lies to you. But these teachers don't really belong to the Master who paid a great price for them, and they will quickly destroy themselves. ²Many people will follow their evil ways and cause others to tell lies about the true way. ³They will be greedy and cheat you with smooth talk. But long ago God decided to punish them, and God doesn't sleep.

⁴God didn't have pity on the angels that sinned. He had them tied up and thrown into the dark pits of hell until the time of judgment. ⁵And during Noah's time, God didn't have pity on the ungodly people of the world. He destroyed them with a flood, though he did save eight people, including Noah, who preached the truth.

⁶God punished the cities of Sodom and Gomorrah*b* by burning them to ashes, and this is a warning to anyone else who wants to sin.

⁷⁻⁸Lot lived right and was greatly troubled by the terrible way those wicked people were living. He was a good man, and day after day he suffered because of the evil things he saw and heard. So the Lord rescued him. ⁹This shows that the Lord knows how to rescue godly people from their sufferings and to punish evil people while they wait for the day of judgment.

¹⁰The Lord is especially hard on people who disobey

bSodom and Gomorrah: During the time of Abraham the Lord destroyed these cities because the people there were so evil (see Genesis 19.24).

him and don't think of anything except their own filthy desires. They are reckless and proud and aren't afraid of cursing the glorious beings in heaven. ¹¹Although angels are more powerful than these evil beings,ᶜ even the angels don't dare to accuse them to the Lord.

¹²These people are no better than senseless animals that live by their feelings and are born to be caught and killed. They speak evil of things they don't know anything about. But their own corrupt deeds will destroy them. ¹³They have done evil, and they will be rewarded with evil.

They think it is fun to have wild parties during the day. They are immoral, and the meals they eat with you are spoilt by the shameful and selfish way they carry on.ᵈ ¹⁴All they think about is having sex with someone else's husband or wife. There is no end to their wicked deeds. They trick people who are easily fooled, and their minds are filled with greedy thoughts. But they are headed for trouble!

¹⁵They have left the true road and have gone down the wrong path by following the example of the prophet Balaam. He was the son of Beor and loved what he got from being a crook. ¹⁶But a donkey corrected him for this evil deed. It spoke to him with a human voice and made him stop his foolishness.

¹⁷These people are like dried up water holes and clouds blown by a windstorm. The darkest part of hell is waiting for them. ¹⁸They boast out loud about their stupid nonsense. And by being vulgar and crude, they trap people who have barely escaped from living the wrong kind of life. ¹⁹They promise freedom to everyone. But they are merely slaves of filthy living, because people are slaves of whatever controls them.

²⁰When they learnt about our Lord and Saviour Jesus Christ, they escaped from the filthy things of this world. But they are again caught up and controlled by these filthy things, and now they are in a worse state than

---

ᶜevil beings: or "evil teachers." ᵈand the meals they eat with you are spoilt by the shameful and selfish way they carry on: Some manuscripts have "and the meals they eat with you are spoilt by the shameful way they carry on during your feasts of Christian love."

they were at first. 21They would have been better off if they had never known about the right way. Even after they knew what was right, they turned their backs on the holy commandments that they were given. 22What happened to them is just like the true saying,

"A dog will come back to lick up its own vomit.
A pig that's been washed will roll in the mud."

The Lord Will Return

3 1My dear friends, this is the second letter I have written to encourage you to do some honest thinking. I don't want you to forget 2what God's prophets said would happen. You must never forget what the holy prophets taught in the past. And you must remember what the apostles told you our Lord and Saviour has commanded us to do.

3But first you must realise that in the last days some people won't think about anything except their own selfish desires. They will make fun of you 4and say, "Didn't your Lord promise to come back? Yet the first leaders have already died, and the world hasn't changed a bit."

5They will say this because they want to forget that long ago the heavens and the earth were made at God's command. The earth came out of water and was made from water. 6Later it was destroyed by the waters of a mighty flood. 7But God has commanded the present heavens and earth to remain until the day of judgment. Then they will be set on fire, and ungodly people will be destroyed.

8Dear friends, don't forget that for the Lord one day is the same as a thousand years, and a thousand years is the same as one day. 9The Lord isn't slow about keeping his promises, as some people think he is. In fact, God is patient, because he wants everyone to turn from sin and no-one to be lost.

10The day of the Lord's return will surprise us like a thief. The heavens will disappear with a loud noise, and the heat will melt the whole universe.e Then the earth

ethe whole universe: Probably the sun, moon, and stars, or the elements that everything in the universe is made of.

and everything on it will be seen for what they are.*f*

¹¹Everything will be destroyed. So you should serve and honour God by the way you live. ¹²You should look forward to the day when God judges everyone, and you should try to make it come soon.*g* On that day the heavens will be destroyed by fire, and everything else will melt in the heat. ¹³But God has promised us a new heaven and a new earth, where justice will rule. We are really looking forward to that!

¹⁴My friends, while you are waiting, you should make certain that the Lord finds you pure, spotless, and living at peace. ¹⁵Don't forget that the Lord is patient because he wants people to be saved. This is also what our dear friend Paul said when he wrote to you with the wisdom that God had given him. ¹⁶Paul talks about these same things in all his letters, but part of what he says is hard to understand. Some ignorant and unsteady people even destroy themselves by twisting what he said. They do the same thing with other Scriptures too.

¹⁷My dear friends, you have been warned ahead of time! So don't let the errors of evil people lead you down the wrong path and make you lose your balance. ¹⁸Let the wonderful kindness and the understanding that come from our Lord and Saviour Jesus Christ help you to keep on growing. Praise Jesus now and for ever! Amen.*h*

---

f will be seen for what they are: Some manuscripts have "will go up in flames."
g and you should try to make it come soon: Or "and you should eagerly desire that day to come."   *h Amen:* Some manuscripts do not have "Amen."

1 JOHN

ABOUT THIS LETTER

John wants Christian believers to know that when we tell God about our sins, God will forgive us and take them away (chapter 1.9).

The true test of faith is love for each other (3.11-24). Because God is love, his people must be like him (4.1-21). For a complete victory over sin, we must not only love others, but we must believe that Jesus, the Son of God, is truly Christ, and that his death for us was real (5.1-12).

Remember:

The Word that gives life was from the beginning,
and this is the one our message is about.

(Chapter 1.1)

A QUICK LOOK AT THIS LETTER

1 ¹The Word that gives life was from the beginning, and this is the one our message is about.

Our ears have heard, our own eyes have seen, and our hands touched this Word.

²The one who gives life appeared! We saw it happen, and we are witnesses to what we have seen. Now we are telling you about this eternal life that was with the Father and appeared to us. ³We are telling you what we have seen and heard, so that you may share in this life with us. And we share in it with the Father and with his Son Jesus Christ. ⁴We are writing to tell you these things, because this makes us*ᵃ* truly happy.

ᵃus: Some manuscripts have "you."

God Is Light

⁵Jesus told us that God is light and doesn't have any darkness in him. Now we are telling you.

⁶If we say that we share in life with God and keep on living in the dark, we are lying and aren't living by the truth. ⁷But if we live in the light, as God does, we share in life with each other. And the blood of his Son Jesus washes all our sins away. ⁸If we say that we haven't sinned, we are fooling ourselves, and the truth isn't in our hearts. ⁹But if we confess our sins to God, he can always be trusted to forgive us and take our sins away.

¹⁰If we say that we have not sinned, we make God a liar, and his message isn't in our hearts.ᵇ

Christ Helps Us

2 ¹My children, I am writing this so that you won't sin. But if you do sin, Jesus Christ always does the right thing, and he will speak to the Father for us. ²Christ is the sacrifice that takes away our sins and the sins of all the world's people.

³When we obey God, we are sure that we know him. ⁴But if we claim to know him and don't obey him, we are lying and the truth isn't in our hearts. ⁵We truly love God only when we obey him as we should, and then we know that we belong to him. ⁶If we say we are his, we must follow the example of Christ.

The New Commandment

⁷My dear friends, I am not writing to give you a new commandment. It is the same one that you were first given, and it is the message you heard. ⁸But it really is a new commandment, and you know its true meaning, just as Christ does. You can see the darkness fading away and the true light already shining.

⁹If we claim to be in the light and hate someone, we are still in the dark. ¹⁰But if we love others, we are in the

ᵇ*and his message isn't in our hearts:* Or "because we have not accepted his message."

light, and we don't cause problems for them.c 11If we
hate others, we are living and walking in the dark.
We don't know where we are going, because we can't see
in the dark.

12   Children, I am writing to you,
        because your sins have been forgiven
            in the name of Christ.
13   Parents, I am writing to you, because you have known
            the one who was there from the beginning.
    Young people, I am writing to you,
        because you have defeated the evil one.
14   Children, I am writing to you,
        because you have known the Father.
    Parents, I am writing to you, because you have known
        the one who was there from the beginning.
    Young people, I am writing to you,
    because you are strong.
    God's message is firm in your hearts,
        and you have defeated the evil one.

15Don't love the world or anything that belongs to the
world. If you love the world, you can't love the Father.
16Our foolish pride comes from this world, and so do our
selfish desires and our desire to have everything we see.
None of this comes from the Father. 17The world and the
desires it causes are disappearing. But if we obey God, we
will live for ever.

The Enemy of Christ

18Children, this is the last hour. You heard that the
enemy of Christ would appear at this time, and many of
Christ's enemies have already appeared. So we know that
the last hour is here. 19These people came from our own
group, yet they were not part of us. If they had been part
of us, they would have stayed with us. But they left,
which proves that they did not belong to our group.

cand we don't cause problems for them: Or "and we can see anything that
might make us fall."

²⁰Christ, the Holy One,ᵈ has blessedᵉ you, and now all of you understand.ᶠ ²¹I didn't need to write to you about the truth, since you already know it. You also know that liars don't belong to the truth. ²²And a liar is anyone who says that Jesus isn't truly Christ. Anyone who says this is an enemy of Christ and rejects both the Father and the Son. ²³If we reject the Son, we reject the Father. But if we say that we accept the Son, we have the Father. ²⁴Keep thinking about the message you first heard, and you will always be one in your heart with the Son and with the Father. ²⁵The Sonᵍ has promised usʰ eternal life.

²⁶I am writing to warn you about those people who are misleading you. ²⁷But Christ has blessed you with the Holy Spirit.ⁱ Now the Spirit stays in you, and you don't need any teachers. The Spirit is truthful and teaches you everything. So stay one in your heart with Christ, just as the Spirit has taught you to do.

Children of God

²⁸Children, stay one in your hearts with Christ. Then when he returns, we will have confidence and won't have to hide in shame. ²⁹You know that Christ always does right and that everyone who does right is a child of God.

3 ¹Think how much the Father loves us. He loves us so much that he lets us be called his children, as we truly are. But since the people of this world didn't know who Christʲ is, they don't know who we are. ²My dear friends, we are already God's children, though what we will be hasn't yet been seen. But we do know that when

---

ᵈ*Christ, the Holy One:* The Greek text has "the Holy One" which may refer either to Christ or to God the Father.   ᵉ*blessed:* This translates a word which means "to pour olive oil on (someone's head)." In Old Testament times it was the custom to pour olive oil on a person's head when that person was chosen to be a priest or a king. Here the meaning is not clear. It may refer to the ceremony of pouring olive oil on the followers of the Lord right before they were baptised or it may refer to the gift of the Holy Spirit which they were given at baptism (see verse 27).   ᶠ*now all of you understand:* Some manuscripts have "you understand all things."   ᵍ*The Son:* The Greek text has "he" and may refer to God the Father.   ʰ*us:* Some manuscripts have "you."   ⁱ*Christ has blessed you with the Holy Spirit:* The Greek text has "You received a pouring on of olive oil from him" (see verse 20). The "pouring on of olive oil" is here taken to refer to the gift of the Holy Spirit, and "he" may refer either to Christ or to the Father.   ʲ*Christ:* The Greek text has "he" and may refer to God.

Christ returns, we will be like him, because we will see him as he truly is. ³This hope makes us keep ourselves holy, just as Christ*k* is holy.

⁴Everyone who sins breaks God's law, because sin is the same as breaking God's law. ⁵You know that Christ came to take away sins. He isn't sinful, ⁶and people who stay one in their hearts with him won't keep on sinning. If they do keep on sinning, they don't know Christ, and they have never seen him.

⁷Children, don't be fooled. Anyone who does right is good, just like Christ himself. ⁸Anyone who keeps on sinning belongs to the devil. He has sinned from the beginning, but the Son of God came to destroy all that he has done. ⁹God's children cannot keep on being sinful. His life-giving power*l* lives in them and makes them his children, so that they cannot keep on sinning. ¹⁰You can tell God's children from the devil's children, because those who belong to the devil refuse to do right or to love each other.

Love Each Other

¹¹From the beginning you were told that we must love each other. ¹²Don't be like Cain, who belonged to the devil and murdered his own brother. Why did he murder him? He did it because his brother was good, and he was evil. ¹³My friends, don't be surprised if the people of this world hate you. ¹⁴Our love for each other proves that we have gone from death to life. But if you don't love each other, you are still under the power of death.

¹⁵If you hate each other, you are murderers, and we know that murderers don't have eternal life. ¹⁶We know what love is because Jesus gave his life for us. That's why we must give our lives for each other. ¹⁷If we have all we need and see one of our own people in need, we must have pity on that person, or else we cannot say we love God. ¹⁸Children, you show love for others by truly helping them, and not merely by talking about it.

¹⁹When we love others, we know that we belong to the

---

kChrist: The Greek text has "that one" and may refer to God. *lHis life-giving power*: The Greek text has "his seed."

truth, and we feel at ease in the presence of God. 20But even if we don't feel at ease, God is greater than our feelings, and he knows everything. 21Dear friends, if we feel at ease in the presence of God, we will have the courage to come near him. 22He will give us whatever we ask, because we obey him and do what pleases him. 23God wants us to have faith in his Son Jesus Christ and to love each other. This is also what Jesus taught us to do. 24If we obey God's commandments, we will stay one in our hearts with him, and he will stay one with us. The Spirit that he has given us is proof that we are one with him.

God Is Love

4 1Dear friends, don't believe everyone who claims to have the Spirit of God. Test them all to find out if they really do come from God. Many false prophets have already gone out into the world, 2and you can know which ones come from God. His Spirit says that Jesus Christ had a truly human body. 3But when someone doesn't say this about Jesus, you know that person has a spirit that doesn't come from God and is the enemy of Christ. You knew that this enemy was coming into the world and is already here now.

4Children, you belong to God, and you have defeated these enemies. God's Spiritm is in you and is more powerful than the one that is in the world. 5These enemies belong to this world, and the world listens to them, because they speak its language. 6We belong to God, and everyone who knows God will listen to us. But the people who don't know God won't listen to us. That is how we can tell the Spirit that speaks the truth from the one that tells lies.

7My dear friends, we must love each other. Love comes from God, and when we love each other, it shows that we have been given new life. We are now God's children, and we know him. 8God is love, and anyone who doesn't love others has never known him. 9God showed his love

---

mGod's Spirit: The Greek text has "he" and may refer to the Spirit or to God or to Jesus.

for us when he sent his only Son into the world to give us life. [10]Real love isn't our love for God, but his love for us. God sent his Son to be the sacrifice by which our sins are forgiven. [11]Dear friends, since God loved us this much, we must love each other.

[12]No-one has ever seen God. But if we love each other, God lives in us, and his love is truly in our hearts.

[13]God has given us his Spirit. That is how we know that we are one with him, just as he is one with us. [14]God sent his Son to be the Saviour of the world. We saw his Son and are now telling others about him. [15]God stays one with everyone who openly says that Jesus is the Son of God. That's how we stay one with God [16]and are sure that God loves us.

God is love. If we keep on loving others, we will stay one in our hearts with God, and he will stay one with us. [17]If we truly love others and live as Christ did in this world, we won't be worried about the day of judgment. [18]A real love for others will chase those worries away. The thought of being punished is what makes us afraid. It shows that we haven't really learnt to love.

[19]We love because God loved us first. [20]But if we say we love God and don't love each other, we are liars. We can't see God. So how can we love God, if we don't love the people we can see? [21]The commandment that God has given us is: "Love God and love each other!"

Victory over the World

5 [1]If we believe that Jesus is truly Christ, we are God's children. Everyone who loves the Father will also love his children. [2]If we love and obey God, we know that we will love his children. [3]We show our love for God by obeying his commandments, and they are not hard to follow.

[4]Every child of God can defeat the world, and our faith is what gives us this victory. [5]No-one can defeat the world without having faith in Jesus as the Son of God.

Who Jesus Is

[6]Water and blood came out from the side of Jesus Christ. It wasn't just water, but water and

blood.[n] The Spirit tells about this, because the Spirit is truthful. [7]In fact, there are three who tell about it. [8]They are the Spirit, the water, and the blood, and they all agree.

[9]We believe what people tell us. But we can trust what God says even more, and God is the one who has spoken about his Son. [10]If we have faith in God's Son, we have believed what God has said. But if we don't believe what God has said about his Son, it's the same as calling God a liar. [11]God has also said that he gave us eternal life and that this life comes to us from his Son. [12]And so, if we have God's Son, we have this life. But if we don't have the Son, we don't have this life.

Knowing about Eternal Life

[13]All of you have faith in the Son of God, and I have written to let you know that you have eternal life. [14]We are certain that God will hear our prayers when we ask for what pleases him. [15]And if we know that God listens when we pray, we are sure that our prayers have already been answered.

[16]Suppose you see one of our people commit a sin that isn't a deadly sin. You can pray, and that person will be given eternal life. But the sin mustn't be one that is deadly. [17]Everything that is wrong is sin, but not all sins are deadly.

[18]We are sure that God's children don't keep on sinning. God's own Son protects them, and the devil can't harm them.

[19]We are certain that we come from God and that the rest of the world is under the power of the devil.

[20]We know that Jesus Christ the Son of God has come and has shown us the true God. And because of Jesus, we now belong to the true God who gives eternal life.

[21]Children, you must stay away from idols.

---

[n]*Water and blood came out from the side of Jesus Christ. It wasn't just water, but water and blood:* See John 19.34. It is also possible to translate, "Jesus Christ came by the water of baptism and by the blood of his death! He wasn't only baptised, but he bled and died." The purpose of the verse is to explain that Jesus was truly human and that he really died.

2 JOHN
ABOUT THIS LETTER

John writes again about the importance of love in a Christian's life. He points out that truth and love must go together. We must also believe that Christ was truly human, and we must love each other.

A QUICK LOOK AT THIS LETTER

◆ Greetings and Prayer (1-3)
◆ Truth and Love (4-11)
◆ Final Greetings (12, 13)

¹From the church leader.ᵃ

To a very special woman and her children.ᵇ I truly love all of you, and so does everyone else who knows the truth. ²We love you because the truth is now in our hearts, and it will be there for ever.

³I pray that God the Father and Jesus Christ his Son will be kind and merciful to us! May they give us peace and truth and love.

Truth and Love

⁴I was very glad to learn that some of your children are obeying the truth, as the Father told us to do. ⁵Dear friend, I am not writing to tell you and your children to do something you haven't done before. I am writing to tell you to love each other, which is the first thing you were told to do. ⁶Love means that we do what God tells us. And from the beginning, he told you to love him.

⁷Many liars have gone out into the world. These deceitful liars are saying that Jesus Christ did not have a truly human body. But they are liars and the enemies of Christ. ⁸So be sure not to lose what weᶜ have worked for.

ᵃchurch leader: Or "elder" or "presbyter" or "priest." ᵇvery special woman and her children: A group of the Lord's followers who met together for worship. "The children of your...sister" (see verse 13) is another group of followers. "Very special" (here and verse 13) probably means "chosen (by the Lord)." ᶜwe: Some manuscripts have "you."

If you do, you won't be given your full reward. [9]Don't keep changing what you were taught about Christ, or else God will no longer be with you. But if you hold firmly to what you were taught, both the Father and the Son will be with you. [10]If people won't agree to this teaching, don't welcome them into your home or even greet them. [11]Greeting them is the same as taking part in their evil deeds.

Final Greetings

[12]I have much more to tell you, but I don't want to write it with pen and ink. I want to come and talk to you in person, because that will make us[d] really happy.

[13]Greetings from the children of your very special sister.[e]

---

[d]us: Some manuscripts have "you."   [e]sister: See the note at verse 1.

3 JOHN
ABOUT THIS LETTER

In this letter the writer reminds Christian readers that they should help support those who go to other parts of the world to tell others about the Lord. The letter is written to an important church member named Gaius, who had been very helpful to Christians who travelled around and preached the good news.

A QUICK LOOK AT THIS LETTER

* Greetings to Gaius (1-4)
* The Importance of Working Together (5-12)
* Final Greetings (13-15)

Greetings

¹From the church leader.*a*
To my dear friend Gaius.

I love you because we follow the truth, ²dear friend, and I pray that all goes well for you. I hope that you are as strong in body as I know you are in spirit. ³It makes me very happy when the Lord's followers come by and speak openly of how you obey the truth. ⁴Nothing brings me greater happiness than to hear that my children*b* are obeying the truth.

Working Together

⁵Dear friend, you have always been faithful in helping other followers of the Lord, even the ones you didn't know before. ⁶They have told the church about your love. They say you were good enough to welcome them and to send them on their mission in a way that God's servants deserve. ⁷When they left to tell others about the Lord, they decided not to accept help from anyone who wasn't a follower. ⁸We must support people like them, so

---

a church leader: Or "elder" or "presbyter" or "priest."   *b children:* Probably persons that the leader had led to be followers of the Lord.

that we can take part in what they are doing to spread the truth.

⁹I wrote to the church. But Diotrephes likes to be the most important leader, and he won't pay any attention to us. ¹⁰So if I come, I will remind him of how he has been attacking us with gossip. Not only has he been doing this, but he refuses to welcome any of the Lord's followers who come by. And when other church members want to welcome them, he puts them out of the church.

¹¹Dear friend, don't copy the evil deeds of others! Follow the example of people who do kind deeds. They are God's children, but those who are always doing evil have never seen God.

¹²Everyone speaks well of Demetrius, and so does the true message that he teaches. I also speak well of him, and you know what I say is true.

Final Greetings

¹³I have much more to say to you, but I don't want to write it with pen and ink. ¹⁴I hope to see you soon, and then we can talk in person.

¹⁵I pray that God will bless you with peace!

Your friends send their greetings. Please give a personal greeting to each of our friends.

JUDE

ABOUT THIS LETTER

Jude has much to say about false teachers. They are evil! God will punish them, and Christians should not follow their teaching or imitate the way they live.

Jude ends with a beautiful prayer-like blessing:

Offer praise to God our Saviour because of our Lord Jesus Christ! Only God can keep you from falling and make you pure and joyful in his glorious presence. Before time began and now and for ever more, God is worthy of glory, honour, power, and authority. Amen.

(24, 25)

A QUICK LOOK AT THIS LETTER

* Greetings (1, 2)
* Defending the Faith against False Teachers (3-23)
* Final Prayer (24, 25)

Greetings

¹From Jude, a servant of Jesus Christ and the brother of James.

To all who are chosen and loved by God the Father and are kept safe by Jesus Christ.

²I pray that God will greatly bless you with kindness, peace, and love!

False Teachers

³My dear friends, I really wanted to write to you about God's saving power at work in our lives. But instead, I must write and ask you to defend the faith that God has once and for all given to his people. ⁴Some godless people have sneaked in among us and are saying, "God treats us much better than we deserve, and so it's all right to be immoral." They even deny that we must obey Jesus Christ as our only Master and Lord. But long ago the Scriptures warned that these godless people were doomed.

⁵Don't forget what happened to those people that the

Lord rescued from Egypt. Some of them didn't have faith, and he later destroyed them. 6You also know about the angels*a* who didn't do their work and left their proper places. God chained them with everlasting chains and is now keeping them in dark pits until the great day of judgment. 7We should also be warned by what happened to the cities of Sodom and Gomorrah*b* and the nearby towns. Their people became immoral and did all sorts of sexual sins. Then God made an example of them and punished them with eternal fire.

8The people I am talking about are behaving just like those dreamers who destroyed their own bodies. They reject all authority and insult angels. 9Even Michael, the chief angel, didn't dare to insult the devil, when the two of them were arguing about the body of Moses.*c* All Michael said was, "The Lord will punish you!"

10But these people insult powers they don't know anything about. They are like senseless animals that end up getting destroyed, because they live only by their feelings. 11Now they are in for real trouble. They have followed Cain's example*d* and have made the same mistake that Balaam*e* did by caring only for money. They have also rebelled against God, just as Korah did.*f* Because of all this, they will be destroyed.

12These people are filthy minded, and by their shameful and selfish actions they spoil the meals you eat together. They are like clouds blown along by the wind, but never bringing any rain. They are like leafless trees, uprooted and dead, and unable to produce fruit. 13Their shameful deeds show up like foam on wild ocean waves.

---

aangels: This may refer to the angels who liked the women on earth so much that they came down and married them (see Genesis 6.2). *bSodom and Gomorrah:* During the time of Abraham the Lord destroyed these cities because the people there were so evil (see Genesis 19.23-29). *cMichael...the body of Moses:* This refers to what was said in an ancient Jewish book about Moses. *dCain's example:* Cain murdered his brother Abel. *eBalaam:* Balaam refused to curse the people of Israel for profit (see Numbers 22.18; 24.13), though he led them to be unfaithful to the Lord (see Numbers 25.1-3; 31.16). But by New Testament times, some Jewish teachers taught that Balaam was greedy and did accept money to curse them. *fjust as Korah did:* Together with Dathan and Abiram, Korah led a rebellion against Moses and Aaron (see Numbers 16.1-35; 26.9, 10).

They are like wandering stars for ever doomed to the darkest pits of hell.

[14]Enoch was the seventh person after Adam, and he was talking about these people when he said:

> Look! The Lord is coming with thousands and thousands of holy angels [15]to judge everyone. He will punish all those ungodly people for all the evil things they have done. The Lord will surely punish those ungodly sinners for every evil thing they have ever said about him.

[16]These people grumble and complain and live by their own selfish desires. They boast about themselves and flatter others to get what they want.

More Warnings

[17]My dear friends, remember the warning you were given by the apostles of our Lord Jesus Christ. [18]They told you that near the end of time, selfish and godless people would start making fun of God. [19]And now these people are already making you turn against each other. They think only about this life, and they don't have God's Spirit.

[20]Dear friends, keep building on the foundation of your most holy faith, as the Holy Spirit helps you to pray. [21]And keep in step with God's love, as you wait for our Lord Jesus Christ to show how kind he is by giving you eternal life. [22]Be helpful to[g] all who may have doubts. [23]Rescue any who need to be saved, as you would rescue someone from a fire. Then with fear in your own hearts, have mercy on everyone who needs it. But hate even the clothes of those who have been made dirty by their filthy deeds.

Final Prayer

[24-25]Offer praise to God our Saviour because of our Lord Jesus Christ! Only God can keep you from falling and make you pure and joyful in his glorious presence. Before time began and now and for ever more, God is worthy of glory, honour, power, and authority. Amen.

[g]*Be helpful to:* Some manuscripts have "Correct."

REVELATION
ABOUT THIS BOOK

This book tells what John had seen in a vision about God's message and about what Jesus Christ had said and done (chapter 1.2). The message has three main parts: 1) There are evil forces at work in the world, and Christians may have to suffer and die; 2) Jesus is Lord, and he will conquer all people and powers who oppose God; and 3) God has wonderful rewards in store for his faithful people, who remain faithful to him, especially for those who lose their lives in his service.

This was a powerful message of hope for those early Christians who had to suffer or die for their faith. In this book they learnt that, in spite of the cruel power of the Roman Empire, the Lamb of God would win the final victory. And this gave them the courage to be faithful.

Because this book is so full of visions that use ideas and word pictures from the Old Testament, it was like a book with secret messages for the early Christians. The book could be passed around and be understood by Christians, but an official of the Roman empire wouldn't be able to understand it. For example, when the fall of Babylon is described (chapter 18), the early Christians knew that this pointed to the fall of the Roman empire. This knowledge gave them hope.

At the beginning of this book there are seven letters to seven churches. These letters show what different groups of the Lord's followers will do in times of persecution (2.1—3.22).

The author uses many powerful images to describe God's power and judgment. The vision of God's throne (4.1-11) and of the scroll and the Lamb (5.1-14) show that God and Christ are in control of all human and supernatural events. Opening the seven seals (6.1—8.5), blowing the seven trumpets (8.6—11.19), and emptying the seven bowls (16.1-21) are among the visions that show God's fierce judgment on the world.

After the suffering has ended, God's faithful people will receive the greatest blessing of all:

God's home is now with his people. He will live with them, and they will be his own. Yes, God will make his home among his people. He will wipe all tears from their eyes, and there will be no more death, suffering, crying, or pain. These things of the past are gone for ever.

(Chapter 21.3, 4)

A QUICK LOOK AT THIS BOOK

1 ¹This is what God showed to Jesus Christ, so that he could tell his servants what must happen soon. Christ then sent his angel with the message to his servant John. ²And John told everything that he had seen about God's message and about what Jesus Christ had said and done.

³God will bless everyone who reads this prophecy to others,ᵃ and he will bless everyone who hears and obeys it. The time is almost here.

⁴From John to the seven churches in Asia.ᵇ

I pray that you will be blessed
with kindness and peace
        from God, who is and was and is coming.
May you receive kindness and peace

ᵃ*who reads this prophecy to others:* A public reading, in a worship service.
ᵇ*Asia:* The section 1.4—3.22 is in the form of a letter. Asia was in the eastern part of the Roman Empire and is present-day Turkey.

from the seven spirits before the throne of God.
5 May kindness and peace be yours
from Jesus Christ, the faithful witness.

Jesus was the first to conquer death,
and he is the ruler of all earthly kings.
Christ loves us, and by his blood
he set us free from our sins.
6 He lets us rule as kings
and serve God his Father as priests.
To him be glory and power for ever and ever!
Amen.
7 Look! He is coming with the clouds.
Everyone will see him,
even the ones who stuck a sword through him.
All people on earth will weep because of him.
Yes, it will happen! Amen.

8The Lord God says, "I am Alpha and Omega,c the one who is and was and is coming. I am God All-Powerful!"

A Vision of the Risen Lord

9I am John, a follower together with all of you. We suffer because Jesus is our king, but he gives us the strength to endure. I was sent to Patmos Island,d because I had preached God's message and had talked about Jesus. 10On the Lord's day the Spirit took control of me, and behind me I heard a loud voice that sounded like a trumpet. 11The voice said, "Write in a book what you see. Then send it to the seven churches in Ephesus, Smyrna, Pergamum, Thyatira, Sardis, Philadelphia, and Laodicea."e

12When I turned to see who was speaking to me, I saw seven gold lampstands. 13There with the lampstands was someone who seemed to be the Son of Man.f He was wearing a robe that reached down to his feet, and a gold cloth was wrapped around his chest. 14His head and his

cAlpha and Omega: The first and last letters of the Greek alphabet, which sometimes mean "first" and "last." dPatmos Island: A small island where prisoners were sometimes kept by the Romans. eEphesus...Laodicea: Ephesus was in the centre with the six other cities forming a semi-circle around it. fSon of Man: That is, Jesus.

hair were as white as wool or snow, and his eyes looked like flames of fire. [15]His feet were glowing like bronze being heated in a furnace, and his voice sounded like the roar of a waterfall. [16]He held seven stars in his right hand, and a sharp double-edged sword was coming from his mouth. His face was shining as bright as the sun at midday.

[17]When I saw him, I fell at his feet like a dead person. But he put his right hand on me and said:

Don't be afraid! I am the first, the last, [18]and the living one. I died, but now I am alive for ever more, and I have the keys to death and the world of the dead.[g] [19]Write what you have seen and what is, and what will happen after these things. [20]I will explain the mystery of the seven stars that you saw at my right side and the seven gold lampstands. The seven stars are the angels[h] of the seven churches, and the lampstands are the seven churches.

The Letter to Ephesus

2 [1]This is what you must write to the angel of the church in Ephesus:

I am the one who holds the seven stars in my right hand, and I walk among the seven gold lampstands. Listen to what I say.

[2]I know everything you have done, including your hard work and how you have endured. I know you won't put up with anyone who is evil. When some people pretended to be apostles, you tested them and found out that they were liars. [3]You have endured and gone through hard times because of me, and you have not given up.

[4]But I do have something against you! And it's this: You don't have as much love as you used to. [5]Think about where you have fallen from, and then turn back and do as you did at first. If you don't turn back, I will come and take away your lampstand. [6]But there is one thing you are doing right. You hate what the

---

[g]*keys to death and the world of the dead:* That is, power over death and the world of the dead.   [h]*angels:* Perhaps guardian angels that represent the churches, or they may be church leaders or messengers sent to the churches.

Nicolaitans[i] are doing, and so do I.

[7]If you have ears, listen to what the Spirit says to the churches. I will let everyone who wins the victory eat from the life-giving tree in God's wonderful garden.

The Letter to Smyrna

[8]This is what you must write to the angel of the church in Smyrna:

I am the first and the last. I died, but now I am alive! Listen to what I say.

[9]I know how much you suffer and how poor you are, but you are rich. I also know the cruel things being said about you by people who claim to be Jews. But they are not really Jews. They are a group that belongs to Satan.

[10]Don't worry about what you will suffer. The devil will throw some of you into jail, and you will be tested and made to suffer for ten days. But if you are faithful until you die, I will reward you with a glorious life.[j]

[11]If you have ears, listen to what the Spirit says to the churches. Whoever wins the victory will not be hurt by the second death.[k]

The Letter to Pergamum

[12]This is what you must write to the angel of the church in Pergamum:

I am the one who has the sharp double-edged sword! Listen to what I say.

[13]I know that you live where Satan has his throne.[l] But you have kept true to my name. Right there where Satan lives, my faithful witness Antipas[m] was taken from you and put to death. Even then you didn't give up your faith in me.

[i]Nicolaitans: Nothing else is known about these people, though it is possible that they claimed to be followers of Nicolaus from Antioch (see Acts 6.5). [j]a glorious life: The Greek text has "a crown of life." In ancient times an athlete who had won a contest was rewarded with a crown of flowers as a sign of victory. [k]second death: The first death is physical, and the "second death" is eternal. [l]where...his throne: The meaning is uncertain, but it may refer to the city as a centre of pagan worship or of Emperor worship. [m]Antipas: Nothing else is known about this man.

[14]I do have a few things against you. Some of you are following the teaching of Balaam.[n] Long ago he told Balak to teach the people of Israel to eat food that had been offered to idols and to be immoral. [15]Now some of you are following the teaching of the Nicolaitans.[o] [16]Turn back! If you don't, I will come quickly and fight against these people. And my words will cut like a sword.

[17]If you have ears, listen to what the Spirit says to the churches. To everyone who wins the victory, I will give some of the hidden food.[p] I will also give each one a white stone[q] with a new name[r] written on it. No-one will know that name except the one who is given the stone.

The Letter to Thyatira

[18]This is what you must write to the angel of the church in Thyatira:

I am the Son of God! My eyes are like flames of fire, and my feet are like bronze. Listen to what I say.

[19]I know everything about you, including your love, your faith, your service, and how you have endured. I know that you are doing more now than you have ever done before. [20]But I still have something against you because of that woman Jezebel.[s] She calls herself a prophet, and you let her teach and mislead my servants to do immoral things and to eat food offered to idols. [21]I gave her a chance to turn from her sins, but she

---

[n]Balaam: According to Numbers 22—24, Balaam refused to disobey the Lord. But in other books of the Old Testament, he is spoken of as evil (see Deuteronomy 23.4, 5; Joshua 13.22; 24.9, 10; Nehemiah 13.2). [o]Nicolaitans: See note at 2.6. [p]hidden food: When the people of Israel were going through the desert, the Lord provided a special food for them. Some of this was placed in a jar and stored in the sacred chest (Exodus 16). According to later Jewish teaching, the prophet Jeremiah rescued the sacred chest when the temple was destroyed by the Babylonians. He hid the chest in a cave, where it would stay until God came to save his people. [q]white stone: The meaning is uncertain. It may be the same as a ticket that lets a person into God's banquet where the "hidden food" is eaten. Or it may be a symbol of victory. [r]a new name: Either the name of Christ or God or the name of the follower who is given the stone. [s]Jezebel: Nothing else is known about her. This may have been her real name or a name that was given to her because she was like Queen Jezebel (see 1 Kings 19.1, 2; 21.1-26).

didn't want to stop doing these immoral things.

²²I am going to strike down Jezebel. Everyone who does these immoral things with her will also be punished, if they don't stop. ²³I will even kill her followers.ᵗ Then all the churches will see that I know everyone's thoughts and feelings. I will treat each of you as you deserve.

²⁴Some of you in Thyatira don't follow Jezebel's teaching. You don't know anything about what her followers call the "deep secrets of Satan." So I won't burden you down with any other commands. ²⁵But until I come, you must hold firmly to the teaching you have.

²⁶I will give power over the nations to everyone who wins the victory and keeps on obeying me until the end. ²⁷⁻²⁸I will give each of them the same power that my Father has given me. They will rule the nations with an iron rod and smash those nations to pieces like clay pots. I will also give them the morning star.ᵘ

²⁹If you have ears, listen to what the Spirit says to the churches.

The Letter to Sardis

3 ¹This is what you must write to the angel of the church in Sardis:

I have the seven spirits of God and the seven stars. Listen to what I say.

I know what you are doing. Everyone may think you are alive, but you are dead. ²Wake up! You have only a little strength left, and it's almost gone. So try to become stronger. I have found that you aren't completely obeying God. ³Remember the teaching that you were given and that you heard. Hold firmly to it and turn from your sins. If you don't wake up, I will come when you least expect it, just as a thief does.

⁴A few of you in Sardis have not dirtied your clothes with sin. You will walk with me in white clothes,

---

ᵗ*her followers:* Or "her children." ᵘ*the morning star:* Probably the star that signals the end of night and the beginning of day. In 22.16 Christ is called the "morning star."

because you are worthy. [5]Everyone who wins the victory will wear white clothes. Their names won't be erased from the book of life,[v] and I will tell my Father and his angels that they are my followers.

[6]If you have ears, listen to what the Spirit says to the churches.

The Letter to Philadelphia

[7]This is what you must write to the angel of the church in Philadelphia:

I am the one who is holy and true, and I have the keys that belonged to David.[w] When I open a door, no-one can close it. And when I close a door, no-one can open it. Listen to what I say.

[8]I know everything you have done. And I have placed before you an open door that no-one can close. You weren't very strong, but you obeyed my message and didn't deny that you are my followers.[x] [9]Now you will see what I will do with those people who belong to Satan's group. They claim to be Jews, but they are liars. I will make them come and kneel down at your feet. Then they will know that I love you.

[10]You obeyed my message and endured. So I will protect you from the time of testing that everyone in all the world must go through. [11]I am coming soon. So hold firmly to what you have, and no-one will take away the crown that you will be given as your reward.

[12]Everyone who wins the victory will be made into a pillar in the temple of my God, and they will stay there for ever. I will write on each of them the name of my God and the name of his city. It is the new Jerusalem that my God will send down from heaven. I will also write on them my own new name.

[13]If you have ears, listen to what the Spirit says to the churches.

---

[v]*book of life:* The book in which the names of God's people are written. [w]*the keys that belonged to David:* The keys stand for authority over David's kingdom. [x]*didn't deny that you are my followers:* Or "didn't say evil things about me."

The Letter to Laodicea

[14] This is what you must write to the angel of the church in Laodicea:

I am the one called Amen![y] I am the faithful and true witness and the source[z] of God's creation. Listen to what I say.

[15] I know everything you have done, and you are not cold or hot. I wish you were either one or the other. [16] But since you are lukewarm and neither cold nor hot, I will spit you out of my mouth. [17] You claim to be rich and successful and to have everything you need. But you don't know how badly off you are. You are pitiful, poor, blind, and naked.

[18] Buy your gold from me. It has been refined in a fire, and it will make you rich. Buy white clothes from me. Wear them and you can cover up your shameful nakedness. Buy medicine for your eyes, so that you will be able to see.

[19] I correct and punish everyone I love. So make up your minds to turn away from your sins. [20] Listen! I am standing and knocking at your door. If you hear my voice and open the door, I will come in and we will eat together. [21] Everyone who wins the victory will sit with me on my throne, just as I won the victory and sat with my Father on his throne.

[22] If you have ears, listen to what the Spirit says to the churches.

Worship in Heaven

4 [1] After this, I looked and saw a door that opened into heaven. Then the voice that had spoken to me at first and that sounded like a trumpet said, "Come up here! I will show you what must happen next." [2] Just then the Spirit took control of me, and there in heaven I saw a throne and someone sitting on it. [3] The one who was sitting there sparkled like precious stones of jasper[a] and carnelian.[b] A rainbow that looked like an emerald[c] surrounded the throne.

---

[y] *Amen:* Meaning "Trustworthy."   [z] *source:* Or "beginning."   [a] *jasper:* Usually green or clear.   [b] *carnelian:* Usually deep-red or reddish-white.   [c] *emerald:* A precious stone, usually green.

⁴Twenty-four other thrones were in a circle around that throne. And on each of these thrones there was an elder dressed in white clothes and wearing a gold crown. ⁵Flashes of lightning and roars of thunder came out from the throne in the centre of the circle. Seven torches, which are the seven spirits of God, were burning in front of the throne. ⁶Also in front of the throne was something that looked like a glass sea, clear as crystal.

Around the throne in the centre were four living creatures covered front and back with eyes. ⁷The first creature was like a lion, the second one was like a bull, the third one had the face of a human, and the fourth was like a flying eagle. ⁸Each of the four living creatures had six wings, and their bodies were covered with eyes. Day and night they never stopped singing,

"Holy, holy, holy is the Lord, the all-powerful God,
    who was and is and is coming!"

⁹The living creatures kept praising, honouring, and thanking the one who sits on the throne and who lives for ever and ever. ¹⁰At the same time the 24 elders knelt down before the one sitting on the throne. And as they worshipped the one who lives for ever, they placed their crowns in front of the throne and said,

¹¹ "Our Lord and God, you are worthy
        to receive glory, honour, and power.
    You created all things,
        and by your decision they are
        and were created."

The Scroll and the Lamb

5 ¹In the right hand of the one sitting on the throne I saw a scroll*ᵈ* that had writing on the inside and on the outside. And it was sealed in seven places. ²I saw a mighty angel ask with a loud voice, "Who is worthy to open the scroll and break its seals?" ³No-one in heaven or on earth or under the earth was able to open the scroll or see inside it.

⁴I cried hard because no-one was found worthy to open

ᵈscroll: A roll of paper or special leather used for writing on. Sometimes a scroll would be sealed on the outside with one or more pieces of wax.

the scroll or see inside it. 5Then one of the elders said to me, "Stop crying and look! The one who is called both the 'Lion from the Tribe of Judah'e and 'King David's Great Descendant'f has won the victory. He will open the book and its seven seals."

6Then I looked and saw a Lamb standing in the centre of the throne that was surrounded by the four living creatures and the elders. The Lamb looked as if it had once been killed. It had seven horns and seven eyes, which are the seven spiritsg of God, sent out to all the earth.

7The Lamb went over and took the scroll from the right hand of the one who sat on the throne. 8After he had taken it, the four living creatures and the 24 elders knelt down before him. Each of them had a harp and a gold bowl full of incense,h which are the prayers of God's people. 9Then they sang a new song,

> "You are worthy to receive the scroll
> and open its seals,
> > because you were killed.
> And with your own blood you bought for God
> > people from every tribe, language
> > nation, and race.
> 10   You let them become kings and serve God as priests,
> > and they will rule on earth."

11As I looked, I heard the voices of a lot of angels around the throne and the voices of the living creatures and of the elders. There were millions and millions of them, 12and they were saying in a loud voice,

> "The Lamb who was killed
> is worthy to receive power,
> > riches, wisdom, strength, honour,
> > glory, and praise."

13Then I heard all beings in heaven and on the earth and under the earth and in the sea offer praise. Together, all of them were saying,

---

e'Lion from the Tribe of Judah': In Genesis 49.9 the tribe of Judah is called a young lion, and King David was from Judah.   f'King David's Great Descendant': The Greek text has "the root of David" which is a title for the Messiah based on Isaiah 11.1, 10.   gthe seven spirits: Some manuscripts have "the spirits."   hincense: A material that produces a sweet smell when burnt. Sometimes it is a symbol for the prayers of God's people.

"Praise, honour, glory, and strength
for ever and ever
to the one who sits on the throne
and to the Lamb!"

¹⁴The four living creatures said "Amen," while the elders knelt down and worshipped.

Opening the Seven Seals

6 ¹At the same time that I saw the Lamb open the first of the seven seals, I heard one of the four living creatures shout with a voice like thunder. It said, "Come out!" ²Then I saw a white horse. Its rider carried a bow and was given a crown. He had already won some victories, and he went out to win more.

³When the Lamb opened the second seal, I heard the second living creature say, "Come out!" ⁴Then another horse came out. It was fiery red. And its rider was given the power to take away all peace from the earth, so that people would slaughter one another. He was also given a big sword.

⁵When the Lamb opened the third seal, I heard the third living creature say, "Come out!" Then I saw a black horse, and its rider had a balance scale in one hand. ⁶I heard what sounded like a voice from somewhere among the four living creatures. It said, "A kilogram of wheat will cost you a whole day's wages! Three kilograms of barley will cost you a day's wages too. But don't ruin the olive oil or the wine."

⁷When the Lamb opened the fourth seal, I heard the voice of the fourth living creature say, "Come out!" ⁸Then I saw a pale green horse. Its rider was named Death, and Death's Kingdom followed behind. They were given power over a quarter of the earth, and they could kill its people with swords, famines, diseases, and wild animals.

⁹When the Lamb opened the fifth seal, I saw under the altar the souls of everyone who had been killed for speaking God's message and talking about their faith. ¹⁰They shouted, "Master, you are holy and faithful! How long will it be before you judge and punish the people of this earth who killed us?"

¹¹Then each of those who had been killed was given a

white robe and told to rest for a little while. They had to wait until the complete number of the Lord's other servants and followers would be killed.

12When I saw the Lamb open the sixth seal, I looked and saw a great earthquake. The sun turned as dark as sackcloth,ʲ and the moon became as red as blood. 13The stars in the sky fell to earth, just like figs shaken loose by a windstorm. 14Then the sky was rolled up like a scroll,ʲ and all mountains and islands were moved from their places.

15The kings of the earth, its famous people, and its military leaders hid in caves or behind rocks on the mountains. They hid there together with the rich and the powerful and with all the slaves and free people. 16Then they shouted to the mountains and the rocks, "Fall on us! Hide us from the one who sits on the throne and from the anger of the Lamb. 17That terrible day has come! God and the Lamb will show their anger, and who can face it?"

The 144 000 Are Marked for God

7 1-2After this I saw four angels. Each one was standing on one of the earth's four corners. The angels held back the four winds, so that no wind would blow on the earth or on the sea or on any tree. These angels had also been given the power to harm the earth and the sea. Then I saw another angel come up from where the sun rises in the east, and he was ready to put the mark of the living God on people. He shouted to the four angels, 3"Don't harm the earth or the sea or any tree! Wait until I've marked the foreheads of the servants of our God."

4Then I heard how many people had been marked on the forehead. There were 144 000, and they came from every tribe of Israel:

5   12 000 from Judah,
     12 000 from Reuben,
     12 000 from Gad,

ʲsackcloth: A rough, dark-coloured cloth made from goat or camel hair and used to make grain sacks. It was worn in times of trouble or sorrow.   ʲscroll: See the note at 5.1.

6 12 000 from Asher,
12 000 from Naphtali,
12 000 from Manasseh,
7 12 000 from Simeon,
12 000 from Levi,
12 000 from Issachar,
8 12 000 from Zebulun,
12 000 from Joseph, and
12 000 from Benjamin.

People from Every Nation

9After this, I saw a large crowd with more people than could be counted. They were from every race, tribe, nation, and language, and they stood before the throne and before the Lamb. They wore white robes and held palm branches in their hands, 10as they shouted,
"Our God, who sits upon the throne,
has the power to save his people,
and so does the Lamb."
11The angels who stood around the throne knelt in front of it with their faces to the ground. The elders and the four living creatures knelt there with them. Then they all worshipped God 12and said,
"Amen! Praise, glory, wisdom,
thanks, honour, power,
and strength belong to our God
for ever and ever! Amen!"
13One of the elders asked me, "Do you know who these people are that are dressed in white robes? Do you know where they come from?"
14"Sir," I answered, "you must know."
Then he told me:
"These are the ones
who have gone through the great suffering.
They have washed their robes
in the blood of the Lamb
and have made them white.
15 And so they stand before the throne of God
and worship him in his temple day and night.
The one who sits on the throne
will spread his tent over them.

16   They will never hunger or thirst again,
        and they won't be troubled
            by the sun or any scorching heat.
17   The Lamb in the centre of the throne
        will be their shepherd.
        He will lead them to streams of life-giving water,
            and God will wipe all tears from their eyes."

The Seventh Seal Is Opened

8 ¹When the Lamb opened the seventh seal, there was silence in heaven for about half an hour. ²I noticed that the seven angels who stood before God were each given a trumpet.

³Another angel, who had a gold container for incense,^k came and stood at the altar. This one was given a lot of incense to offer with the prayers of God's people on the gold altar in front of the throne. ⁴Then the smoke of the incense, together with the prayers of God's people, went up to God from the hand of the angel.

⁵After this, the angel filled the incense container with fire from the altar and threw it on the earth. Thunder roared, lightning flashed, and the earth shook.

The Trumpets

⁶The seven angels now got ready to blow their trumpets.

⁷When the first angel blew his trumpet, hail and fire mixed with blood were thrown down on the earth. A third of the earth, a third of the trees, and a third of all green plants were burnt.

⁸When the second angel blew his trumpet, something like a great fiery mountain was thrown into the sea. A third of the sea turned to blood, ⁹a third of the living creatures in the sea died, and a third of the ships was destroyed.

¹⁰When the third angel blew his trumpet, a great star fell from heaven. It was burning like a torch, and it fell on a third of the rivers and on a third of the springs of water. ¹¹The name of the star was Bitter, and a third of

---

^kincense: See the note at 5.8.

the water turned bitter. Many people died because the water was so bitter.

12 When the fourth angel blew his trumpet, a third of the sun, a third of the moon, and a third of the stars were struck. They each lost a third of their light. So during a third of the day there was no light, and a third of the night was also without light.

13 Then I looked and saw a lone eagle flying across the sky. It was shouting, "Trouble, trouble, trouble to everyone who lives on earth! The other three angels are now going to blow their trumpets."

9 ¹ When the fifth angel blew his trumpet, I saw a star*l* fall from the sky to earth. It was given the key to the tunnel that leads down to the deep pit. ² As it opened the tunnel, smoke poured out like the smoke of a great furnace. The sun and the air turned dark because of the smoke. ³ Locusts*m* came out of the smoke and covered the earth. They were given the same power that scorpions have.

⁴ The locusts were told not to harm the grass on the earth or any plant or any tree. They were to punish only those people who didn't have God's mark on their foreheads. ⁵ The locusts were allowed to make them suffer for five months, but not to kill them. The suffering they caused was like the sting of a scorpion. ⁶ In those days people will want to die, but they won't be able to. They will hope for death, but it will escape from them.

⁷ These locusts looked like horses ready for battle. On their heads they wore something like gold crowns, and they had human faces. ⁸ Their hair was like a woman's long hair, and their teeth were like those of a lion. ⁹ On their chests they wore armour made of iron. Their wings roared like an army of horse-drawn chariots rushing into battle. ¹⁰ Their tails were like a scorpion's tail with a sting that had the power to hurt someone for five months. ¹¹ Their king was the angel in charge of the deep pit. In Hebrew his name was Abaddon, and in Greek it was Apollyon.*n*

---

l star: In the ancient world, stars were often thought of as living beings, such as angels.   *m Locusts:* a type of grasshopper that comes in swarms and causes great damage to crops.   *n Abaddon...Apollyon:* The Hebrew word "Abaddon" and the Greek word "Apollyon" each mean "destruction."

¹²The first horrible thing has now happened! But wait. Two more horrible things will happen soon.

¹³Then the sixth angel blew his trumpet. I heard a voice speak from the four corners of the gold altar that stands in the presence of God. ¹⁴The voice spoke to this angel and said, "Release the four angels who are tied up beside the great Euphrates River." ¹⁵The four angels had been prepared for this very hour and day and month and year. Now they were set free to kill a third of all people.

¹⁶By listening, I could tell there were more than 200 million of these war horses. ¹⁷In my vision their riders wore fiery-red, dark-blue, and yellow armour on their chests. The heads of the horses looked like lions, with fire and smoke and sulphur coming out of their mouths. ¹⁸One third of all people were killed by the three terrible troubles caused by the fire, the smoke, and the sulphur. ¹⁹The horses had powerful mouths, and their tails were like poisonous snakes that bite and hurt.

²⁰The people who lived through these terrible troubles didn't turn away from the idols they had made, and they didn't stop worshipping demons. They kept on worshipping idols that were made of gold, silver, bronze, stone, and wood. Not one of these idols could see, hear, or walk. ²¹No-one stopped murdering or practising witchcraft or being immoral or stealing.

The Angel and the Little Scroll

10 ¹I saw another powerful angel come down from heaven. This one was covered with a cloud, and a rainbow was over his head. His face was like the sun, his legs were like columns of fire, ²and with his hand he held a little scroll° that had been unrolled. He stood there with his right foot on the sea and his left foot on the land. ³Then he shouted with a voice that sounded like a growling lion. Thunder roared seven times.

⁴After the thunder stopped, I was about to write what it had said. But a voice from heaven shouted, "Keep it secret! Don't write these things."

⁵The angel I had seen standing on the sea and the land

°scroll: See the note at 5.1.

then held his right hand up towards heaven. ⁶He made a promise in the name of God who lives for ever and who created heaven, earth, the sea, and every living creature. The angel said, "You won't have to wait any longer. ⁷God told his secret plans to his servants the prophets, and it will all happen by the time the seventh angel sounds his trumpet."

⁸Once again the voice from heaven spoke to me. It said, "Go and take the open scroll from the hand of the angel standing on the sea and the land."

⁹When I went over to ask the angel for the little scroll, the angel said, "Take the scroll and eat it! Your stomach will turn sour, but the taste in your mouth will be as sweet as honey." ¹⁰I took the little scroll from the hand of the angel and ate it. The taste was as sweet as honey, but my stomach turned sour.

¹¹Then some voices said, "Keep on telling what will happen to the people of many nations, races, and languages, and also to kings."

The Two Witnesses

11 ¹An angel gave me a measuring stick and said: Measure around God's temple. Be sure to include the altar and everyone worshipping there. ²But don't measure the courtyard outside the temple building. Leave it out. It has been given to those people who don't know God, and they will trample all over the holy city for 42 months. ³My two witnesses will wear sackcloth,ᵖ while I let them preach for 1260 days.

⁴These two witnesses are the two olive trees and the two lampstands that stand in the presence of the Lord who rules the earth. ⁵Any enemy who tries to harm them will be destroyed by the fire that comes out of their mouths. ⁶They have the power to lock up the sky and to keep rain from falling while they are prophesying. And whenever they want to, they can turn water to blood and cause all kinds of terrible troubles on earth.

⁷After the two witnesses have finished preaching God's message, the beast that lives in the deep pit will come up

ᵖsackcloth: See the note at 6.12.

and fight against them. It will win the battle and kill them. [8]Their bodies will be left lying in the streets of the same great city where their Lord was nailed to a cross. And that city is spiritually like the city of Sodom or the country of Egypt.

[9]For three and a half days the people of every nation, tribe, language, and race will stare at the bodies of these two witnesses and refuse to let them be buried. [10]Everyone on earth will celebrate and be happy. They will give gifts to each other, because of what happened to the two prophets who caused them so much trouble. [11]But three and a half days later, God will breathe life into their bodies. They will stand up, and everyone who sees them will be terrified.

[12]The witnesses then heard a loud voice from heaven, saying, "Come up here." And while their enemies were watching, they were taken up to heaven in a cloud. [13]At that same moment there was a terrible earthquake that destroyed a tenth of the city. Seven thousand people were killed, and the rest were frightened and praised the God who rules in heaven.

[14]The second horrible thing has now happened! But the third one will be here soon.

The Seventh Trumpet

[15]At the sound of the seventh trumpet, loud voices were heard in heaven. They said,

"Now the kingdom of this world
    belongs to our Lord and to his Chosen One!
And he will rule for ever and ever!"

[16]Then the 24 elders, who were seated on thrones in God's presence, knelt down and worshipped him. [17]They said,

"Lord God All-Powerful, you are and you were,
    and we thank you.
You used your great power and started ruling.
[18]   When the nations got angry,
        you became angry too!
Now the time has come for the dead to be judged.
It's time for you to reward
your servants the prophets

and all of your people who honour your name,
no matter who they are.
It's time to destroy everyone
who has destroyed the earth."

19 The door to God's temple in heaven was then opened, and the sacred chest q could be seen inside the temple. I saw lightning and heard roars of thunder. The earth trembled and huge hailstones fell to the ground.

The Woman and the Dragon

12 1 Something important appeared in the sky. It was a woman whose clothes were the sun. The moon was under her feet, and a crown made of 12 stars was on her head. 2 She was about to give birth, and she was crying because of the great pain.

3 Something else appeared in the sky. It was a huge red dragon with seven heads and ten horns, and a crown on each of its seven heads. 4 With its tail, it dragged a third of the stars from the sky and threw them down to the earth. Then the dragon turned towards the woman, because it wanted to eat her child as soon as it was born.

5 The woman gave birth to a son, who would rule all nations with an iron rod. The boy was snatched away. He was taken to God and placed on his throne. 6 The woman ran into the desert to a place that God had prepared for her. There she would be taken care of for 1260 days.

Michael Fights the Dragon

7 A war broke out in heaven. Michael and his angels were fighting against the dragon and its angels. 8 But the dragon lost the battle. It and its angels were forced out of their places in heaven 9 and were thrown down to the earth. Yes, that old snake and his angels were thrown out of heaven! That snake, who fools everyone on earth, is known as the devil and Satan. 10 Then I heard a voice from heaven shout,

"Our God has shown his saving power,

q*sacred chest:* In Old Testament times the sacred chest was kept in the tent used for worship. It was the symbol of God's presence with his people and also of his agreement with them.

and his kingdom has come!
God's own Chosen One has shown his authority.
Satan accused our people
in the presence of God day and night.
Now he has been thrown out!

11   Our people defeated Satan
because of the blood[r] of the Lamb
and the message of God.
They were willing to give up their lives.

12   The heavens should rejoice,
together with everyone who lives there.
But pity the earth and the sea,
because the devil was thrown down
to the earth.
He knows his time is short, and he is very angry."

13 When the dragon realised that it had been thrown down to the earth, it tried to make trouble for the woman who had given birth to a son. 14 But the woman was given two wings like those of a huge eagle, so that she could fly into the desert. There she would escape from the snake and be taken care of for a time, two times, and half a time.

15 The snake then spewed out water like a river to sweep the woman away. 16 But the earth helped her and swallowed the water that had come from the dragon's mouth. 17 This made the dragon terribly angry with the woman. So it started a war against the rest of her children. They are the people who obey God and are faithful to what Jesus did and taught. 18 The dragon[s] stood on the beach beside the sea.

The Two Beasts

13 1 I looked and saw a beast coming up from the sea. This one had ten horns and seven heads, and a crown was on each of its ten horns. On each of its heads were names that were an insult to God. 2 The beast that I saw had the body of a leopard, the feet of a bear, and the

---

[r]blood: Or "death."   [s]The dragon: The text has "he," and some manuscripts have "I."

mouth of a lion. The dragon handed over its own power and throne and great authority to this beast. ³One of its heads seemed to have been fatally wounded, but now it was well. Everyone on earth marvelled at this beast, ⁴and they worshipped the dragon who had given its authority to the beast. They also worshipped the beast and said, "No-one is like this beast! No-one can fight against it."

⁵The beast was allowed to boast and claim to be God, and for 42 months it was allowed to rule. ⁶The beast cursed God, and it cursed the name of God. It even cursed the place where God lives, as well as everyone who lives in heaven with God. ⁷It was allowed to fight against God's people and defeat them. It was also given authority over the people of every tribe, nation, language, and race. ⁸The beast was worshipped by everyone whose name wasn't written before the time of creation in the book of the Lamb who was killed.ᶠ

9   If you have ears, then listen!
10   If you are doomed to be captured,
          you will be captured.
     If you are doomed to be killed by a sword,
          you will be killed by a sword.

This means that God's people must learn to endure and be faithful!

¹¹I now saw another beast. This one came out of the ground. It had two horns like a lamb, but spoke like a dragon. ¹²It worked for the beast whose fatal wound had been healed. And it used all its authority to force the earth and its people to worship that beast. ¹³It worked mighty miracles, and while people watched, it even made fire come down from the sky.

¹⁴This second beast fooled people on earth by working miracles for the first one. Then it talked them into making an idol in the form of the beast that didn't die after being wounded by a sword. ¹⁵It was allowed to put breath into the idol, so that it could speak. Everyone who refused to worship the idol of the beast was put to death. ¹⁶All people were forced to put a mark on their right hand

---

ᶠnot written...was killed: Or "not written in the book of the Lamb who was killed before the time of creation."

or forehead. Whether they were powerful or weak, rich or poor, free people or slaves, [17]they all had to have this mark, or else they couldn't buy or sell anything. This mark stood for the name of the beast and for the number of its name.

[18]You need wisdom to understand the number of the beast! But if you are smart enough, you can figure this out. Its number is 666, and it stands for a person.

The Lamb and His 144 000 Followers

14 [1]I looked and saw the Lamb standing on Mount Zion![u] With him were 144 000, who had his name and his Father's name written on their foreheads. [2]Then I heard a sound from heaven that was like a roaring flood or loud thunder or even like the music of harps. [3]And a new song was being sung in front of God's throne and in front of the four living creatures and the elders. No-one could learn that song, except the 144 000 who had been rescued from the earth. [4]All of these are pure virgins, and they follow the Lamb wherever he leads. They have been rescued to be presented to God and the Lamb as the most precious people[v] on earth. [5]They never tell lies, and they are innocent.

The Messages of the Three Angels

[6]I saw another angel. This one was flying across the sky and had the eternal good news to announce to the people of every race, tribe, language, and nation on earth. [7]The angel shouted, "Worship and honour God! The time has come for him to judge everyone. Kneel down before the one who created heaven and earth, the oceans, and every stream."

[8]A second angel followed and said, "The great city of Babylon has fallen! This is the city that made all nations drunk and immoral. Now God is angry, and Babylon has fallen."

[9]Finally, a third angel came and shouted:

[u]*Mount Zion:* Another name for Jerusalem.   [v]*the most precious people:* The Greek text has "the first people." The Law of Moses taught that the firstborn of all animals and the first part of the harvest were special and belonged to the Lord.

Here is what will happen if you worship the beast and the idol and have the mark of the beast on your hand or forehead. [10] You will have to drink the wine that God gives to everyone who makes him angry. You will feel his mighty anger, and you will be tortured with fire and burning sulphur, while the holy angels and the Lamb look on.

[11] If you worship the beast and the idol and accept the mark of its name, you will be tortured day and night. The smoke from your torture will go up for ever and ever, and you will never be able to rest.

[12] God's people must learn to endure. They must also obey his commands and have faith in Jesus.

[13] Then I heard a voice from heaven say, "Put this in writing. From now on, the Lord will bless everyone who has faith in him when they die."

The Spirit answered, "Yes, they will rest from their hard work, and they will be rewarded for what they have done."

The Earth Is Harvested

[14] I looked and saw a bright cloud, and someone who seemed to be the Son of Man[w] was sitting on the cloud. He wore a gold crown on his head and held a sharp sickle[x] in his hand. [15] An angel came out of the temple and shouted, "Start cutting with your sickle! Harvest season is here, and all crops on earth are ripe." [16] The one on the cloud swung his sickle and harvested the crops.

[17] Another angel with a sharp sickle then came out of the temple in heaven. [18] After this, an angel with power over fire came from the altar and shouted to the angel who had the sickle. He said, "All grapes on earth are ripe! Harvest them with your sharp sickle." [19] The angel swung his sickle on earth and cut off its grapes. He threw them into a pit[y] where they were trampled on as a sign of God's anger. [20] The pit was outside the city, and when the grapes were mashed, blood flowed out. The blood turned into a

[w]Son of Man: That is, Jesus.   [x]sickle: A knife with a long curved blade, used to cut grain and other crops.   [y]pit: It was the custom to put grapes in a pit (called a wine press) and trample on them to make juice that would later turn to wine.

river that was over 300 kilometres long and almost deep enough to cover a horse.

The Last of the Terrible Troubles

15 ¹After this, I looked at the sky and saw something else that was strange and important. Seven angels were bringing the last seven terrible troubles. When these are ended, God will no longer be angry.

²Then I saw something that looked like a glass sea mixed with fire, and people were standing on it. They were the ones who had defeated the beast and the idol and the number that tells the name of the beast. God had given them harps, ³and they were singing the song that his servant Moses and the Lamb had sung. They were singing,

> "Lord God All-Powerful,
> you have done great and marvellous things.
> You are the ruler of all nations,
> and you do what is right and fair.
> ⁴ Lord, who doesn't honour and praise your name?
> You alone are holy,
> and all nations will come and worship you,
> because you have shown
> that you judge with fairness."

⁵After this, I noticed something else in heaven. The sacred tent used for a temple was open. ⁶And the seven angels who were bringing the terrible troubles were coming out of it. They were dressed in robes of pure white linen and wore belts made of pure gold. ⁷One of the four living creatures gave each of the seven angels a bowl made of gold. These bowls were filled with the anger of God who lives for ever and ever. ⁸The temple quickly filled with smoke from the glory and power of God. No-one could enter it until the seven angels had finished pouring out the seven last troubles.

The Bowls of God's Anger

16 ¹From the temple I heard a voice shout to the seven angels, "Go and empty the seven bowls of God's anger on the earth."

²The first angel emptied his bowl on the earth. At once

ugly and painful sores broke out on everyone who had the mark of the beast and worshipped the idol.

³The second angel emptied his bowl on the sea. Straight away the sea turned into blood like that of a dead person, and every living thing in the sea died.

⁴The third angel emptied his bowl into the rivers and streams. At once they turned to blood. ⁵Then I heard the angel, who has power over water, say,

"You have always been,
    and you always will be the holy God.
You had the right to judge in this way.
6 They poured out the bloodᶻ of your people
    and your prophets.
So you gave them blood to drink,
    as they deserve!"

⁷After this, I heard the altar shout,
"Yes, Lord God All-Powerful,
    your judgments are honest and fair."

⁸The fourth angel emptied his bowl on the sun, and it began to scorch people like fire. ⁹Everyone was scorched by its great heat, and all of them cursed the name of God who had power over these terrible troubles. But no-one turned to God and praised him.

¹⁰The fifth angel emptied his bowl on the throne of the beast. At once darkness covered its kingdom, and its people began biting their tongues in pain. ¹¹And because of their painful sores, they cursed the God who rules in heaven. But still they didn't stop doing evil things.

¹²The sixth angel emptied his bowl on the great Euphrates River, and it completely dried up to make a road for the kings from the east. ¹³An evil spirit that looked like a frog came out of the mouth of the dragon. One also came out of the mouth of the beast, and another out of the mouth of the false prophet. ¹⁴These evil spirits had the power to work miracles. They went to every king on earth, to bring them together for a war against God All-Powerful. But that will be the day of God's great victory.

¹⁵Remember that Christ says, "When I come, it will

ᶻ*They poured out the blood:* A way of saying, "They murdered."

surprise you like a thief! But God will bless you, if you are awake and ready. Then you won't have to walk around naked and be ashamed."

[16]Those armies came together in a place that in Hebrew is called Armagedon.[a]

[17]As soon as the seventh angel emptied his bowl in the air, a loud voice from the throne in the temple shouted, "It's done!" [18]There were flashes of lightning, roars of thunder, and the worst earthquake in all history. [19]The great city of Babylon split into three parts, and the cities of other nations fell. So God made Babylon drink from the wine cup that was filled with his anger. [20]Every island ran away, and the mountains disappeared. [21]Hailstones, weighing over 40 kilograms each, fell from the sky on people. Finally, the people cursed God, because the hail was so terrible.

The Prostitute and the Beast

17 [1]One of the seven angels who had emptied the bowls came over and said to me, "Come on! I will show you how God will punish that shameless prostitute who sits on many oceans. [2]Every king on earth has slept with her, and her shameless ways are like wine that has made everyone on earth drunk."

[3]With the help of the Spirit, the angel took me into the desert, where I saw a woman sitting on a red beast. The beast was covered with names that were an insult to God, and it had seven heads and ten horns. [4]The woman was dressed in purple and scarlet robes, and she wore jewellery made of gold, precious stones, and pearls. In her hand she held a gold cup filled with the filthy and nasty things she had done. [5]On her forehead a mysterious name was written:

I AM THE GREAT CITY OF BABYLON,
THE MOTHER OF EVERY IMMORAL
AND FILTHY THING ON EARTH.

[6]I could tell that the woman was drunk on the blood of God's people who had given their lives for Jesus. This

---

[a]Armagedon: The Hebrew form of the name would be "Har Megeddo," meaning "Hill of Megeddo," where many battles were fought in ancient times (see Judges 5.19; 2 Kings 23.29, 30).

surprising sight amazed me, [7]and the angel said:

Why are you so amazed? I will explain the mystery about this woman and about the beast she is sitting on, with its seven heads and ten horns. [8]The beast you saw is one that used to be and no longer is. It will come back from the deep pit, but only to be destroyed. Everyone on earth whose names were not written in the book of life[b] before the time of creation will be amazed. They will see this beast that used to be and no longer is, but will be once more.

[9]Anyone with wisdom can figure this out. The seven heads that the woman is sitting on stand for seven hills. These heads are also seven kings. [10]Five of the kings are dead. One is ruling now, and the other one has not yet come. But when he does, he will rule for only a little while.

[11]You also saw a beast that used to be and no longer is. That beast is one of the seven kings who will return as the eighth king, but only to be destroyed.

[12]The ten horns that you saw are ten more kings, who have not yet come into power, and they will rule with the beast for only a short time. [13]They all think alike and will give their power and authority to the beast. [14]These kings will go to war against the Lamb. But he will defeat them, because he is Lord over all lords and King over all kings. His followers are chosen and special and faithful.

[15]The oceans that you saw the prostitute sitting on are crowds of people from all races and languages. [16]The ten horns and the beast will start hating the shameless woman. They will strip off her clothes and leave her naked. Then they will eat her flesh and throw the rest of her body into a fire. [17]God is the one who made these kings all think alike and decide to give their power to the beast. And they will do this until what God has said comes true.

[18]The woman you saw is the great city that rules over all kings on earth.

[b]book of life: The book in which the names of God's people are written.

The Fall of Babylon

18 ¹I saw another angel come from heaven. This one had great power, and the earth was bright because of his glory.² The angel shouted,

"Fallen! Powerful Babylon has fallen
    and is now the home of demons.
It is the den of every filthy spirit
and of all unclean birds,
    and every dirty and hated animal.
³ Babylon's evil and immoral wine
    has made all nations drunk.
Every king on earth has slept with her,
and every merchant on earth is rich
    because of her evil desires."

⁴ Then I heard another voice from heaven shout,
"My people, you must escape from Babylon.
    Don't take part in her sins
    and share her punishment.
⁵ Her sins are piled as high as heaven.
    God has remembered the evil she has done.
⁶ Treat her as she has treated others.
    Make her pay double for what she has done.
Make her drink twice as much
    of what she mixed for others.
⁷ That woman honoured herself
with a life of luxury.
    Reward her now with suffering and pain.

"Deep in her heart Babylon said, 'I am the queen!
Never will I be a widow
    or know what it means to be sad.'
⁸ And so, in a single day she will suffer the pain
    of sorrow, hunger, and death.
Fire will destroy her dead body,
    because her judge is the powerful Lord God."

⁹Every king on earth who slept with her and shared in her luxury will mourn. They will weep, when they see the smoke from that fire. ¹⁰Her sufferings will frighten them, and they will stand at a distance and say,

"Pity that great and powerful city! Pity Babylon!
    In a single hour her judgment has come."

¹¹Every merchant on earth will mourn, because there is no-one to buy their goods. ¹²There won't be anyone to buy their gold, silver, jewels, pearls, fine linen, purple cloth, silk, scarlet cloth, sweet-smelling wood, fancy carvings of ivory and wood, as well as things made of bronze, iron, or marble. ¹³No-one will buy their cinnamon, spices, incense, myrrh, frankincense,ᶜ wine, olive oil, fine flour, wheat, cattle, sheep, horses, chariots, slaves, and other humans.

¹⁴　Babylon, the things your heart desired
　　　have all escaped from you.
　　Every luxury and all your glory
　　　will be lost for ever.
　　You will never get them back.

¹⁵The merchants had become rich because of her. But when they saw her sufferings, they were terrified. They stood at a distance, crying and mourning. ¹⁶Then they shouted,

　　　"Pity the great city of Babylon!
　　She dressed in fine linen
　　　and wore purple and scarlet cloth.
　　She had jewellery made of gold
　　　and precious stones and pearls.

¹⁷　Yet in a single hour her riches disappeared."

Every ship's captain and passenger and sailor stood at a distance, together with everyone who does business by travelling on the sea. ¹⁸When they saw the smoke from her fire, they shouted, "This was the greatest city ever!"

¹⁹They cried loudly, and in their sorrow they threw dust on their heads, as they said,

　　　"Pity the great city of Babylon!
　　Everyone who sailed the seas
　　　became rich from her treasures.
　　But in a single hour the city was destroyed.

²⁰　The heavens should be happy
　　　with God's people and apostles and prophets.
　　God has punished her for them."

²¹A powerful angel then picked up a huge stone and

ᶜ*myrrh, frankincense:* Myrrh was a valuable sweet-smelling powder often used in perfume. Frankincense was a valuable powder that was burnt to make a sweet smell.

threw it into the sea. The angel said,
> "This is how the great city of Babylon
>> will be thrown down, never to rise again.
22   The music of harps and singers
and of flutes and trumpets
> will no longer be heard.
No workers will ever set up shop in that city,
> and the sound of grinding grain
>> will be silenced for ever.
23   Lamps will no longer shine anywhere in Babylon,
and couples will never again
> say wedding vows there.
Her merchants ruled the earth,
> and by her witchcraft she fooled all nations.
24   On the streets of Babylon is found the blood
of God's people and of his prophets,
> and everyone else."

19 ¹After this, I heard what sounded like a lot of voices in heaven, and they were shouting,
> "Praise the Lord!
To our God belongs the glorious power to save,
2   because his judgments are honest and fair.
That filthy prostitute
> ruined the earth with shameful deeds.
But God has judged her and made her pay the price
> for murdering his servants."

³Then the crowd shouted, "Praise the Lord!
> Smoke will never stop rising
>> from her burning body."

⁴After this, the 24 elders and the four living creatures all knelt before the throne of God and worshipped him. They said, "Amen! Praise the Lord!"

The Marriage Supper of the Lamb

⁵From the throne a voice said,
> "If you worship and fear our God,
>> give praise to him, no matter who you are."

⁶Then I heard what seemed to be a large crowd that sounded like a roaring flood and loud thunder all mixed together. They were saying,

"Praise the Lord!
Our Lord God All-Powerful now rules as king.
7   So we will be glad and happy
         and give him praise.
The wedding day of the Lamb is here,
         and his bride is ready.
8   She will be given a wedding dress
         made of pure and shining linen.
This linen stands for the good things
         God's people have done."

9Then the angel told me, "Put this in writing. God will bless everyone who is invited to the wedding feast of the Lamb." The angel also said, "These things that God has said are true."

10I knelt at the feet of the angel and began to worship him. But the angel said, "Don't do that! I am a servant, just like you and everyone else who tells about Jesus. Don't worship anyone but God. Everyone who tells about Jesus does it by the power of the Spirit."

The Rider on the White Horse

11I looked and saw that heaven was open, and a white horse was there. Its rider was called Faithful and True, and he is always fair when he judges or goes to war. 12He had eyes like flames of fire, and he was wearing a lot of crowns. His name was written on him, but he was the only one who knew what the name meant.

13The rider wore a robe that was covered with[d] blood, and he was known as "The Word of God." 14He was followed by armies from heaven that rode on horses and were dressed in pure white linen. 15From his mouth a sharp sword went out to attack the nations. He will rule them with an iron rod and will show the fierce anger of God All-Powerful by trampling the grapes in the pit where wine is made. 16On the part of the robe that covered his thigh was written, "KING OF KINGS AND LORD OF LORDS."

17I then saw an angel standing on the sun, and he

---

[d]covered with: Some manuscripts have "sprinkled with."

shouted to all the birds flying in the sky, "Come and join in God's great feast! [18]You can eat the flesh of kings, rulers, leaders, horses, riders, free people, slaves, important people, and everyone else."

[19]I also saw the beast and all kings of the earth come together. They fought against the rider on the white horse and against his army. [20]But the beast was captured and so was the false prophet. This is the same prophet who had worked miracles for the beast, so that he could fool everyone who had the mark of the beast and worshipped the idol. The beast and the false prophet were thrown alive into a lake of burning sulphur. [21]But the rest of their army was killed by the sword that came from the mouth of the rider on the horse. Then birds stuffed themselves on the dead bodies.

The Thousand Years

20[1]I saw an angel come down from heaven, carrying the key to the deep pit and a big chain. [2]He chained the dragon for 1000 years. It is that old snake, who is also known as the devil and Satan. [3]Then the angel threw the dragon into the pit. He locked and sealed it, so that 1000 years would go by before the dragon could fool the nations again. But after that, it would have to be set free for a little while.

[4]I saw thrones, and sitting on those thrones were the ones who had been given the right to judge. I also saw the souls of the people who had their heads cut off because they had told about Jesus and preached God's message. They were the same ones who hadn't worshipped the beast or the idol, and they had refused to let its mark be put on their hands or foreheads. They will come to life and rule with Christ for 1000 years.

[5-6]These people are the first to be raised to life, and they are especially blessed and holy. The second death[e] has no power over them. They will be priests for God and Christ and will rule with them for 1000 years.

No other dead people were raised to life until 1000 years later.

---

[e]*second death:* The first death is physical, and the "second death" is eternal.

Satan Is Defeated

⁷At the end of the 1000 years, Satan will be set free. ⁸He will fool the countries of Gog and Magog, which are at the far ends of the earth, and their people will follow him into battle. They will have as many followers as there are grains of sand along the beach, ⁹and they will march all the way across the earth. They will surround the camp of God's people and the city that his people love. But fire will come down from heaven and destroy the whole army. ¹⁰Then the devil who fooled them will be thrown into the lake of fire and burning sulphur. He will be there with the beast and the false prophet, and they will be in pain day and night for ever and ever.

The Judgment at the Great White Throne

¹¹I saw a great white throne with someone sitting on it. Earth and heaven tried to run away, but there was no place for them to go. ¹²I also saw all the dead people standing in front of that throne. Every one of them was there, no matter who they had once been. Several books were opened, and then the book of life*f* was opened. The dead were judged by what those books said they had done.

¹³The sea gave up the dead people who were in it, and death and its kingdom also gave up their dead. Then everyone was judged by what they had done. ¹⁴Afterwards, death and its kingdom were thrown into the lake of fire. This is the second death.*g* ¹⁵Anyone whose name wasn't written in the book of life was thrown into the lake of fire.

The New Heaven and the New Earth

21 ¹I saw a new heaven and a new earth. The first heaven and the first earth had disappeared, and so had the sea. ²Then I saw New Jerusalem, that holy city, coming down from God in heaven. It was like a bride dressed in her wedding gown and ready to meet her husband.

---

*f*book of life: See the note at 3.5.   *g*second death: See the note at 20.5-6.

³I heard a loud voice shout from the throne:

God's home is now with his people. He will live with them, and they will be his own. Yes, God will make his home among his people. ⁴He will wipe all tears from their eyes, and there will be no more death, suffering, crying, or pain. These things of the past are gone for ever.

⁵Then the one sitting on the throne said:

I am making everything new. Write down what I have said. My words are true and can be trusted. ⁶Everything is finished! I am Alpha and Omega,ʰ the beginning and the end. I will freely give water from the life-giving fountain to everyone who is thirsty. ⁷All who win the victory will be given these blessings. I will be their God, and they will be my people.

⁸But I will tell you what will happen to cowards and to everyone who is unfaithful or dirty-minded or who murders or is sexually immoral or uses witchcraft or worships idols or tells lies. They will be thrown into that lake of fire and burning sulphur. This is the second death.ⁱ

The New Jerusalem

⁹I saw one of the seven angels who had the bowls filled with the seven last terrible troubles. The angel came to me and said, "Come on! I will show you the one who will be the bride and wife of the Lamb." ¹⁰Then with the help of the Spirit, he took me to the top of a very high mountain. There he showed me the holy city of Jerusalem coming down from God in heaven.

¹¹The glory of God made the city bright. It was dazzling and crystal clear like a precious jasper stone. ¹²The city had a high and thick wall with 12 gates, and each one of them was guarded by an angel. On each of the gates was written the name of one of the 12 tribes of Israel. ¹³Three of these gates were on the east, three were on the north, three more were on the south, and the other three were on the west. ¹⁴The city was built on 12 foundation stones. On each of the stones was written the

ʰAlpha and Omega: See the note at 1.8. ⁱsecond death: See the note at 20.5-6.

name of one of the Lamb's twelve apostles.

15The angel who spoke to me had a gold measuring stick to measure the city and its gates and its walls. 16The city was shaped like a cube, because it was just as high as it was wide. When the angel measured the city, it was about 2500 kilometres high and 2500 kilometres wide. 17Then the angel measured the wall, and by our measurements it was about 65 metres high.

18The wall was built of jasper, and the city was made of pure gold, clear as crystal. 19Each of the 12 foundations was a precious stone. The first was jasper,*j* the second was sapphire, the third was agate, the fourth was emerald, 20the fifth was onyx, the sixth was carnelian, the seventh was chrysolite, the eighth was beryl, the ninth was topaz, the tenth was chrysoprase, the eleventh was jacinth, and the twelfth was amethyst. 21Each of the 12 gates was a solid pearl. The streets of the city were made of pure gold, clear as crystal.

22I didn't see a temple there. The Lord God All-Powerful and the Lamb were its temple. 23And the city didn't need the sun or the moon. The glory of God was shining on it, and the Lamb was its light.

24Nations will walk by the light of that city, and kings will bring their riches there. 25Its gates are always open during the day, and night never comes. 26The glorious treasures of nations will be brought into the city. 27But nothing unworthy will be allowed to enter. No-one who is dirty-minded or who tells lies will be there. Only those whose names are written in the Lamb's book of life*k* will be in the city.

22 1The angel showed me a river that was crystal clear, and its waters gave life. The river came from the throne where God and the Lamb were seated. 2Then it flowed down the middle of the city's main street. On

---

*j*jasper: The precious and semi-precious stones mentioned in verses 19 and 20 are of different colours. *Jasper* is usually green or clear; *sapphire* is blue; *agate* has circles of brown and white; *emerald* is green; *onyx* has different bands of colour; *carnelian* is deep-red or reddish-white; *chrysolite* is olive-green; *beryl* is green or bluish-green; *topaz* is yellow; *chrysoprase* is apple-green; *jacinth* is reddish-orange; and *amethyst* is deep purple.   *k*book of life: see note at 3.5.

each side of the river are trees^j that grow a different kind of fruit each month of the year. The fruit gives life, and the leaves are used as medicine to heal the nations.

³God's curse will no longer be on the people of that city. He and the Lamb will be seated there on their thrones, and its people will worship God ⁴and will see him face to face. God's name will be written on the foreheads of the people. ⁵Never again will night appear, and no-one who lives there will ever need a lamp or the sun. The Lord God will be their light, and they will rule for ever.

The Coming of Christ

⁶Then I was told:

These words are true and can be trusted. The Lord God controls the spirits of his prophets, and he is the one who sent his angel to show his servants what must happen straight away. ⁷Remember, I am coming soon! God will bless everyone who pays attention to the message of this book.

⁸My name is John, and I am the one who heard and saw these things. Then after I had heard and seen all this, I knelt down and began to worship at the feet of the angel who had shown it to me.

⁹But the angel said,

Don't do that! I am a servant, just like you. I am the same as a follower or a prophet or anyone else who obeys what is written in this book. God is the one you should worship.

¹⁰Don't keep the prophecies in this book a secret. These things will happen soon.

¹¹Evil people will keep on being evil, and everyone who is dirty-minded will still be dirty-minded. But good people will keep on doing right, and God's people will always be holy.

¹²Then I was told:

I am coming soon! And when I come, I will reward everyone for what they have done. ¹³I am Alpha and

---

^j*trees:* The Greek has "tree," which is used in a collective sense of trees on both sides of the heavenly river.

Omega,[m] the first and the last, the beginning and the end.

¹⁴God will bless all who have washed their robes. They will each have the right to eat fruit from the tree that gives life, and they can enter the gates of the city. ¹⁵But outside the city will be dogs, witches, immoral people, murderers, idol worshippers, and everyone who loves to tell lies and do wrong.

¹⁶I am Jesus! And I am the one who sent my angel to tell all of you these things for the churches. I am David's Great Descendant,[n] and I am also the bright morning star.[o]

¹⁷The Spirit and the bride say, "Come!"

Everyone who hears this[p] should say, "Come!"

If you are thirsty, come! If you want life-giving water, come and take it. It's free!

¹⁸Here is my warning for everyone who hears the prophecies in this book:

If you add anything to them, God will make you suffer all the terrible troubles written in this book. ¹⁹If you take anything away from these prophecies, God will not let you have part in the life-giving tree and in the holy city described in this book.

²⁰The one who has spoken these things says, "I am coming soon!"

So, Lord Jesus, please come soon!

²¹I pray that the Lord Jesus will be kind to all of you.

---

m Alpha and Omega: See the note at 1.8.   *n David's Great Descendant:* See the note at 5.5.   *o the bright morning star:* Probably thought of as the brightest star (see 2.27, 28).   *p who hears this:* The reading of the book of Revelation in a service of worship.